ONE WEEK LOAN

OLDER PEOPLE IN LAW AND SOCIETY

Older People in Law and Society

JONATHAN HERRING

OXFORD
UNIVERSITY PRESS

OXFORD

UNIVERSITY PRESS

Great Clarendon Street, Oxford OX2 6DP

Oxford University Press is a department of the University of Oxford.
It furthers the University's objective of excellence in research, scholarship,
and education by publishing worldwide in

Oxford New York

Auckland Cape Town Dar es Salaam Hong Kong Karachi
Kuala Lumpur Madrid Melbourne Mexico City Nairobi
New Delhi Shanghai Taipei Toronto

With offices in

Argentina Austria Brazil Chile Czech Republic France Greece
Guatemala Hungary Italy Japan Poland Portugal Singapore
South Korea Switzerland Thailand Turkey Ukraine Vietnam

Oxford is a registered trade mark of Oxford University Press
in the UK and in certain other countries

Published in the United States
by Oxford University Press Inc., New York

© J. Herring, 2009

British Library Cataloguing in Publication Data

Data available

Library of Congress Cataloging in Publication Data

Data available

Typeset by Newgen Imaging Systems (P) Ltd., Chennai, India
Printed by CPI Antony Rowe, Chippenham, Wiltshire

ISBN 978-0-19-922902-4

1 3 5 7 9 10 8 6 4 2

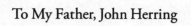

To My Father, John Herring

Preface

It is remarkable how little has been written on the English law and older people. While elder law is a well-established field of study in the United States, I do not know of any English law degree which offers it as an option. This book was born of a belief that the interaction of law and ageing is enormously important and raises a host of fascinating issues. One of the themes of this book is that the issues raised show how ageist assumptions underpin much of the law. The problems of 'older people' are often the problems with legal notions, rather than particular problems with old age. In other words, the study of elder law has as much to teach us about the law generally as it does about the law and old age in particular.

Inevitably in a book of this nature, it has not been possible to provide a comprehensive analysis of every legal issue raised by old age. Furthermore, to keep the book to a reasonable length it has not been possible to give issues the depth of analysis they deserve. A thorough study of the issues surrounding pension provision would require several volumes. References to further reading appear in the footnotes.

I have greatly benefited from the support of many friends and colleagues while writing this book. Professor George P Smith II had been a fount of encouragement and friendship, not to mention wisdom. Shazia Choudhry, Michelle Madden Dempsey, John Eekelaar, Sandra Fredman, Elaine Palser, Rachel Taylor, and many others have been great colleagues to work with and friends to be with in many different ways. My wife, Kirsten Johnson, and daughters, Laurel, Joanna, and Darcy, kept laughing and telling me 'go and write a book' when they had had enough of me!

Table of Contents

Table of Cases   xv
Table of Statutory Instruments   xxiii
Table of Statutes   xxv
Table of Treaties, Conventions etc   xxix

1. **Introduction**   1
   What is old age?   2
   Law and older people   4
      The case against elder law   6
      The justification for elder law   6
   Structure of the book   9

2. **Ageism and Age Discrimination**   12
   Introduction   12
   Ageism   13
      Social disadvantage among older people   15
      The glorification of youth   18
      Language   18
      Media representation of old age   19
      Overt discrimination in public services   20
      Social separation and older people   20
      The intersection of age, race, and sex   21
      Thinking further about ageism   22
      Analogies between ageism and sexism or racism   24
   Age discrimination   26
      Defining discrimination   26
      Direct and indirect discrimination   29
   Discrimination on the basis of age   30
   The Employment Equality (Age) Regulations 2006   33
      Extent of law   35
      The definition of discrimination   36
      Harassment on the grounds of age   39
      Discrimination by victimization   39
      Exemptions   40
      Remedies   40
   Controversial issues   40
      Justification for discrimination   40
      Occupational requirement   44

Retirement   45

Positive action   47

The impact of the regulations   48

The new equality law   49

Conclusion   50

3. **Capacity, Incapacity, and Old Age**   52

Introduction   52

Basic legal principles   53
   The competent   53
   Defining capacity   54
   Treatment of a person lacking capacity   57

Difficult issues in treating those lacking capacity   59
   Use of force and best interests   59
   To what extent are the values, character, and views while competent
   relevant to assessing best interests?   59
   Relevance of current views   61
   To what extent are the views or interests of those caring
   for the incapacitated individual relevant?   65
   End-of-life issues   66
   Critics of the best interests principle   67

Advance decisions   69
   Law   69
   Philosophical debates over advance directives   74

Lasting power of attorney   82

Deputies and the court of protection   83

Those deemed just competent   84
   The importance of autonomy   84
   Autonomy and harmful decisions   85
   Autonomy and decisions contrary to the individual's previous values   87
   Conclusion on the just competent   89

Mental Health Act 1983   89

Conclusion   90

4. **Carers**   94

Introduction   94

Statistics on carers   97

State support for carers   100
   Benefits for carers   100
   Availability of care services   101
   Direct payments   105

Government reforms   107

Housing issues   108

Carers and the Mental Capacity Act 2005   109
    Interpreting the Mental Capacity Act   110
    Ethical arguments   113
Carers and autonomy   115
Healthcare rationing and carers   118
Carers and other areas of the law   121
A human rights response   121
Ethic of care   124
    Critics of an ethic of care   128
    Putting an ethic of care into practice   129
Conclusion   130

5. Elder Abuse   **132**

Introduction   132
The difficulties in defining elder abuse   134
    Elder abuse or abuse of vulnerable people   135
    At what age does abuse become elder abuse?   137
    Who perpetuates elder abuse?   137
    Limiting abuse to physical abuse?   138
    Must the abuse be age-related?   139
    Legitimacy   139
    Must the abuse be intentional?   139
    How serious must the abuse be?   140
    Societal elder abuse   140
A consideration of some popular definitions   141
The forms of elder abuse   143
    Financial abuse   144
    Sexual abuse   145
    The misuse of medication   146
    Elder abuse and gender   147
Statistics   147
    Who is abusing?   149
    Who is abused?   150
    What kinds of abuse take place?   150
The causes of elder abuse   150
    Micro causes   151
    Macro causes   157
    Ageism and elder abuse   159
Institutional abuse   162
    The voices of those in care homes   166
    Good care homes   167
    Restraint   169
Regulation   170

The Health and Social Care Act 2008   172
The Protection of Vulnerable Adults list   173
Multi-agency work   175
Criminal law   176
Causing or allowing the death of a child or vulnerable adult   176
Ill-treatment or neglect of a person lacking capacity   177
Failings of the current criminal law   178
Prosecutions without the victim's consent   179
Civil law   180
Civil remedies by public agencies   181
Need for court order   185
Changing attitudes and responses to elder abuse   187
Dependency and care   187
Social context   189
Statutory regime for elder abuse   189
Commissioner for older people   194
Mandatory reporting   195
Conclusion   195

6. **Older People and Financial Issues**   197
Introduction   197
The 'demographic time bomb'   197
Poverty in old age   199
Benefit payments for older people   201
Basic state pension   201
State second pension or state earnings-related pension
scheme (SERPS)   202
Pension credit and guarantee credit   202
Other benefits, discounted charges, and concessions   202
Benefits and funds for special needs   202
Assistance with care   203
Means-testing benefits   203
Low take-up rates   204
Pensions   206
The objectives of pension systems   207
Balancing state and private funding   207
Paying now or paying later   208
Pensions as savings or a form of insurance   209
Regulation of pension markets   209
Forms of pension   210
Economic issues   211
What retirement age should be used?   212
The current state of pensions   213
The current system   214

Gender and pensions 215

Reform of pensions 216
The need for reform: 'the pensions crisis' 216

The reforms 218
Consideration of the reforms 220

Funding care 223
Solutions 226
Messages from Scotland 228

Family financial obligations and older people 228
Financial liabilities of parents towards adult children 230
Should we enforce filial responsibility? 231

Conclusion 234

7. Grandparenthood 235

Introduction 235

Sociological issues 236
The changing nature of families and the role of grandparents 237
What do grandparents do with grandchildren? 240
Grandparent-headed homes 242
Differences between grandparents 242

The law of grandparents 243
ECHR and grandparents 244
Disputes over residence 244
Disputes over contact 245
Debate over the law 249

Public law 257
Grandparents when the local authority removes the child 257
Adoption of children and privacy 257
Involving grandparents in decision-making 260
Orders where the grandparent is to be the carer 261
Grandparental care 266

Conclusion 268

8. Older People and Healthcare 270

Introduction 270

The social care and healthcare distinction 271

Ageing and health 274
Medicalization and old age 277

Rationing and older people 279
General issues 279
Quality adjusted life years (QALY) 282

Ageism and QALY 283
Fair innings 286

Rawls/Daniels   288
Harris   289
Public opinion and age discrimination   290
NICE and age   291

Legal challenges to rationing decisions   293
Treatment overseas   297

Examples of age discrimination in the health setting   298
Mental health   301
Breast and cervical cancer screening   301
Malnourishment   302

Palliative care   302
Conclusion   305

9. Inheritance   307

Introduction   307
People's expectations surrounding inheritance   309
Making a will   312
The contents of a will   314
Wills and ownership   315
The law and wills   316
The law and succession: testamentary freedom?   316
Testamentary capacity   321
Intestacy   323
The law on intestacy   324

Inheritance (Provision for Family and Dependants) Act 1975   328
The justifications for the Act   328
Who can apply under the Act?   330
What can be claimed?   331
Attempts to avoid the Act   333
Comments on the Act   333

Proprietary estoppel   334
Inheritance tax   337
Conclusion   341

10. Conclusion   342

Index   349

Table of Cases

A (A Minor) (Contact Application: Grandparent), Re; Sub Nom: A (Section 8
    Order: Grandparent Application), Re; A (A Minor) (Grandparent: Contact),
    Re [1995] 2 F.L.R. 153; [1996] 1 F.C.R. 467; [1995] Fam. Law 540; (1995)
    159 J.P.N. 812, CA (Civ Div) 246, 247, 248
A (A Minor) (Contact: Leave to Apply), Re [1995] 3 F.C.R. 543; (1995)
    159 J.P.N. 722, Fam Div 247, 250
A (Mental Patient: Sterilisation), Re; Sub Nom: A (Medical Treatment: Male
    Sterilisation), Re; R-B (A Patient) v Official Solicitor; RB (Male Patient:
    Sterilisation), Re [2000] 1 F.L.R. 549; [2000] 1 F.C.R. 193; [2000] Lloyd's
    Rep. Med. 87; (2000) 53 B.M.L.R. 66; [2000] Fam. Law 242; (2000)
    97(2) L.S.G. 30, CA (Civ Div) 58, 182
A and W (Minors) (Residence Order: Leave to Apply), Re; Sub Nom: A (Minors)
    (Residence Order), Re [1992] Fam. 182; [1992] 3 W.L.R. 422; [1992] 3 All E.R. 872;
    [1992] 2 F.L.R. 154; 91 L.G.R. 401; [1992] Fam. Law 439, CA (Civ Div) 246
A Local Authority v BS; Sub Nom: S (Adult's Lack of Capacity: Carer and Residence),
    Re [2003] EWHC 1909 (Fam); [2003] 2 F.L.R. 1235; (2004) 7 C.C.L. Rep. 132;
    (2004) 75 B.M.L.R. 185; [2003] Fam. Law 870, Fam Div 113, 181, 182
A Local Authority v E [2007] EWHC 2396 (Fam); [2008] 1 F.L.R. 978; [2008]
    1 F.C.R. 389; [2008] Fam. Law 24, Fam Div 55, 184
A v United Kingdom [1998] 2 F.L.R. 959; [1998] 3 F.C.R. 597; (1999) 27
    E.H.R.R. 611; 5 B.H.R.C. 137; [1998] Crim. L.R. 892; [1998]
    H.R.C.D. 870; [1998] Fam. Law 733, ECHR 192
A Primary Care Trust v AH [2008] EWHC 1403 (Fam), CP. 62
AJ (A Child) (Adoption Order or Special Guardianship Order), Re; Sub Nom:
    JJ v AT [2007] EWCA Civ 55; [2007] 1 F.L.R. 507; [2007] 1 F.C.R. 308;
    [2007] Fam. Law 387; (2007) 104(8) L.S.G. 38, CA (Civ Div) 262, 263
Abbott v Richardson [2006] EWHC 1291 (Ch); [2006] W.T.L.R. 1567, Ch D 321, 323
Abrams v United States (1919) 250 US 616. 63
Ahsan v University Hospitals Leicester NHS Trust [2006] EWHC 2624 (QB);
    [2007] P.I.Q.R. P19, QBD. 60, 80, 111, 112
Airedale NHS Trust v Bland [1993] A.C. 789; [1993] 2 W.L.R. 316; [1993]
    1 All E.R. 821; [1993] 1 F.L.R. 1026; [1994] 1 F.C.R. 485; [1993] 4 Med. L.R. 39;
    (1993) 12 B.M.L.R. 64; [1993] Fam. Law 473; (1993) 143 N.L.J. 199, HL. 67

B (Consent to Treatment: Capacity), Re; Sub Nom: B v NHS Hospital Trust; B
    (Adult: Refusal of Medical Treatment), Re [2002] EWHC 429 (Fam); [2002]
    2 All E.R. 449; [2002] 1 F.L.R. 1090; [2002] 2 F.C.R. 1; [2002] Lloyd's Rep.
    Med. 265; (2002) 65 B.M.L.R. 149; [2002] Fam. Law 423; (2002) 99(17)
    L.S.G. 37; (2002) 152 N.L.J. 470; (2002) 146 S.J.L.B. 83, Fam Div 56, 126
B v B (Adult Student: Liability to Support); Sub Nom: B v B (Financial Provision for
    Child) [1998] 1 F.L.R. 373; [1998] 1 F.C.R. 49; [1998] Fam. Law 131, CA (Civ Div). 230
B Borough Council v S [2006] EWHC 2584 (Fam); [2007] 1 F.L.R. 1600;
    [2007] 1 F.C.R. 574; (2006) 9 C.C.L. Rep. 596; (2007) 93 B.M.L.R. 1;
    [2007] Fam. Law 119, Fam Div 113, 183

B City Council v S [2006] EWHC 3065 (Fam); [2007] 1 F.L.R. 1223; [2007]
    U.K.H.R.R. 588; [2007] Fam. Law 300, Fam Div. 258, 259
Baker v Thomas [2008] EWHC 937, Ch 330
Banks v Goodfellow (1869–70) L.R. 5 Q.B. 549, QB 321
Baynes v Hedger [2008] EWHC 1587 (Ch), Ch D. 331
Belgian Linguistic Case (A/6) (1979–80) 1 E.H.R.R. 252, ECHR 30
Bicknell v HM Coroner for Birmingham and Solihull [2007] EWHC 2547 (Admin);
    (2008) 99 B.M.L.R. 1, QBD (Admin). 169
Bilka-Kaufhaus GmbH v Weber von Hartz (170/84) [1986] E.C.R. 1607;
    [1986] 2 C.M.L.R. 701; [1987] I.C.R. 110; [1986] I.R.L.R. 317, ECJ 41
Bloxham v Bruckhaus, 2205086/2006 44
Bolton Hospitals NHS Trust v O [2002] EWHC 2871; [2003] 1 F.L.R. 824;
    [2003] Fam. Law 319, Fam Div 55
Bouette v Rose [2000] 1 F.C.R.185 229
Boyle v United Kingdom (A/282-B) [1994] 2 F.C.R. 822; (1995) 19 E.H.R.R. 179, ECHR . . . 244
Brooklyn House Ltd v Commission for Social Care Inspection [2006] EWHC 1165;
    (2006) 9 C.C.L. Rep. 394; (2006) 91 B.M.L.R. 22, QBD (Admin) 177
Burden v United Kingdom (13378/05) [2008] S.T.C. 1305; [2008] 2 F.C.R. 244;
    10 I.T.L. Rep. 772; [2008] Fam. Law 628; [2008] 18 E.G. 126 (C.S.); (2008)
    158 N.L.J. 672, ECHR (Grand Chamber) 339

C (A Child) v XYZ County Council; Sub Nom: C (A Child), Re [2007] EWCA
    Civ 1206; [2008] 3 W.L.R. 445; [2008] 1 F.L.R. 1294; [2007] 3 F.C.R. 659;
    [2008] H.R.L.R. 9; [2008] Fam. Law 301, CA (Civ Div) 258, 259
C (Children), Re [2005] EWCA Civ 705, CA (Civ Div) 245
C (Responsible Authority), Re; Sub Nom: C v M; AC v RM [2005] EWHC 2939 (Fam);
    [2006] 1 F.L.R. 919; [2006] Fam. Law 270, Fam Div 267
Campbell v Mirror Group Newspapers Ltd; Sub Nom: Campbell v MGN Ltd [2004]
    UKHL 22; [2004] 2 A.C. 457; [2004] 2 W.L.R. 1232; [2004] 2 All E.R. 995;
    [2004] E.M.L.R. 15; [2004] H.R.L.R. 24; [2004] U.K.H.R.R. 648;
    16 B.H.R.C. 500; (2004) 101(21) L.S.G. 36; (2004) 154 N.L.J. 733;
    (2004) 148 S.J.L.B. 572, HL 253
Carr v Isard [2006] EWHC 2095, Ch 315
Chalmers v Johns [1999] 1 F.L.R. 392; [1999] 2 F.C.R. 110; [1999] Fam. Law 16,
    CA (Civ Div) 180
Chester v Afshar [2004] UKHL 41; [2005] 1 A.C. 134; [2004] 3 W.L.R. 927;
    [2004] 4 All E.R. 587; [2005] P.I.Q.R. P12; [2005] Lloyd's Rep. Med. 109;
    (2005) 81 B.M.L.R. 1; [2005] P.N.L.R. 14; (2004) 101(43) L.S.G. 34;
    (2004) 154 N.L.J. 1589; (2004) 148 S.J.L.B. 1215, HL 53
Ciba v Davies [2006] EWHC 3745 (Ch), Ch D 321
Ciebrant (Deceased), Re [2008] EWHC 1268 (Ch), Ch D 336
Coleman v Attridge Law (C-303/06) [2008] I.R.L.R. 722, ECJ (Grand Chamber) 121
Collins v Wilcock [1984] 1 W.L.R. 1172; [1984] 3 All E.R. 374; (1984)
    79 Cr. App. R. 229; (1984) 148 J.P. 692; [1984] Crim. L.R. 481; (1984)
    81 L.S.G. 2140; (1984) 128 S.J. 660, DC 53
Cooke v Turner (1846) 15 M & W 727 333
Corrigan v Attridge Law [2008] ICR 1128. 37
Coventry (Deceased), Re; Sub Nom: Coventry v Coventry [1980] Ch. 461;
    [1979] 3 W.L.R. 802; [1979] 3 All E.R. 815; (1979) 123 S.J. 606, CA (Civ Div) 332
Cunliffe v Fielden; Sub Nom: Fielden v Cunliffe [2005] EWCA Civ 1508;
    [2006] Ch. 361; [2006] 2 W.L.R. 481; [2006] 2 All E.R. 115; [2006]

1 F.L.R. 745; [2005] 3 F.C.R. 593; [2006] W.T.L.R. 29; (2005–06) 8 I.T.E.L.R. 855;
   [2006] Fam. Law 263; (2006) 103(3) L.S.G. 26, CA (Civ Div) 333, 334
Cyprus v Turkey (1976) 4 E.H.R.R. 282 122

D (Care: Natural Parent Presumption), Re; Sub Nom: D (Minors) (Natural Parent
   Presumption), Re; D (A Minor) (Residence: Natural Parent), Re [1999] 1 F.L.R. 134;
   [1999] 2 F.C.R. 118; [1999] Fam. Law 12; (2000) 164 J.P.N. 45, CA (Civ Div) 245

E v United Kingdom (33218/96) [2003] 1 F.L.R. 348; [2002] 3 F.C.R. 700;
   (2003) 36 E.H.R.R. 31; [2003] Fam. Law 157, ECHR. 123, 192, 193
Ealing LBC v KS [2008] EWHC 636 (Fam); [2008] Fam. Law 633, Fam Div 182, 184
Edwards (Deceased), Re; Sub Nom: Edwards v Edwards [2007] EWHC 1119 (Ch);
   [2007] W.T.L.R. 1387, Ch D (Cardiff) 323
Espinosa v Bourke; Espinosa v Isaacs; Espinosa v Wilson [1999] 1 F.L.R. 747;
   [1999] 3 F.C.R. 76; [1999] Fam. Law 210, CA (Civ Div) 332
Evans v Knight and Moore [1822] 1 Add 299. 322
Evanturel v Evanturel (1874–75) L.R. 6 P.C. 1, PC (Can) 333

F (Adult: Court's Jurisdiction), Re; Sub Nom: F (Adult Patient), Re [2001] Fam. 38;
   [2000] 3 W.L.R. 1740; [2000] 2 F.L.R. 512; [2000] 3 F.C.R. 30; [2000]
   U.K.H.R.R. 712; (2000) 3 C.C.L. Rep. 210; [2000] Lloyd's Rep. Med. 381;
   (2000) 55 B.M.L.R. 81; [2000] M.H.L.R. 120; [2000] Fam. Law 709;
   (2000) 97(35) L.S.G. 37; (2000) 97(36) L.S.G. 41, CA (Civ Div) 181, 182
F and R (Section 8 Order: Grandparents' Application), Re [1995] 1 F.L.R. 524;
   [1995] Fam. Law 235, Fam Div 248, 250
Fuller v Fuller, February 8, 2005 . . . . .321, 323

Garland (Deceased), Re; Sub Nom: Garland v Morris [2007] EWHC 2 (Ch);
   [2007] 2 F.L.R. 528; [2007] W.T.L.R. 797; [2007] Fam. Law 585, Ch D. 329
Golder v United Kingdom (A/18) (1979–80) 1 E.H.R.R. 524, ECHR 247
Graham v Murphy [1997] 1 F.L.R. 860; [1997] 2 F.C.R. 441; [1997] Fam. Law 393, Ch D . . . 333
Gully v Dix; Sub Nom: Dix (Deceased), Re [2004] EWCA Civ 139;
   [2004] 1 W.L.R. 1399; [2004] 1 F.L.R. 918; [2004] 1 F.C.R. 453;
   [2004] W.T.L.R. 331; [2004] Fam. Law 334; (2004) 101(6) L.S.G. 32;
   (2004) 148 S.J.L.B. 116, CA (Civ Div). 330
Guzzardi v Italy (A/39) (1981) 3 E.H.R.R. 333, ECHR. 186

H v United Kingdom (11559/85) (1986) 45 D. & R. 281, Eur Comm HR 247
H (Children) (Care Proceedings), Re [2003] EWCA Civ 369, CA (Civ Div) 260
H (Residence: Grandparent), Re [2000] Fam. Law 715, Fam Div 245
HE v A Hospital NHS Trust [2003] EWHC 1017 (Fam); [2003] 2 F.L.R. 408;
   [2003] Fam. Law 733, Fam Div 71, 72
HL v United Kingdom (2004) 40 E.H.R.R. 761 . . . . 186, 187
HL v United Kingdom (45508/99); Sub Nom: L v United Kingdom (45508/99)
   (2005) 40 E.H.R.R. 32; 17 B.H.R.C. 418; (2004) 7 C.C.L. Rep. 498; [2005]
   Lloyd's Rep. Med. 169; (2005) 81 B.M.L.R. 131; [2004] M.H.L.R. 236, ECHR 59, 65
HM v Switzerland (2002) 38 E.H.R.R. 314. 186
Hampton v Lord Chancellor ET/2300835/2007 . . . . 26, 43
Hancock (Deceased), Re; Sub Nom: Snapes v Aram [1998] 2 F.L.R. 346; [1999]
   1 F.C.R. 500; [1998] Fam. Law 520; (1998) 95(20) L.S.G. 35; (1998) 142 S.J.L.B.
   167, CA (Civ Div) 330, 332

Hansen v Barker-Benfield; Sub Nom: Barker-Benfield (Deceased), Re [2006] EWHC
    1119 (Ch); [2006] W.T.L.R. 1141; (2006) 150 S.J.L.B. 708, Ch D 321, 322, 323
Hoff v Atherton [2004] EWCA Civ 1554; [2005] W.T.L.R. 99, CA (Civ Div) 322

Ireland v United Kingdom (A/25) (1979–80) 2 E.H.R.R. 25, ECHR 191

J (A Child) (Adoption Order), Re [2003] EWCA Civ 1097, CA (Civ Div) 262
J (A Child) (Leave to Issue Application for Residence Order), Re [2002] EWCA
    Civ 1346; [2003] 1 F.L.R. 114; [2003] Fam. Law 27, CA (Civ Div) 246, 247, 250
J (A Minor) (Wardship: Medical Treatment), Re [1991] Fam. 33; [1991]
    2 W.L.R. 140; [1990] 3 All E.R. 930; [1991] 1 F.L.R. 366; [1991]
    F.C.R. 370; [1990] 2 Med. L.R. 67; (1990) 140 N.L.J. 1533, CA (Civ Div) 296
JE v DE; Sub Nom: DE, Re [2006] EWHC 3459 (Fam); [2007] 2 F.L.R. 1150;
    (2007) 10 C.C.L. Rep. 149; [2007] M.H.L.R. 39; [2008] Fam. Law 118, Fam Div 185
Jennings v Rice [2002] EWCA Civ 159; [2003] 1 F.C.R. 501; [2003]
    1 P. & C.R. 8; [2002] W.T.L.R. 367; [2002] N.P.C. 28; [2002]
    2 P. & C.R. DG2, CA (Civ Div) 307, 334
Jones v Jones, unreported, October 9, 2006, Ch D 321

Karner v Austria (40016/98) [2003] 2 F.L.R. 623; [2004] 2 F.C.R. 563; (2004)
    38 E.H.R.R. 24; 14 B.H.R.C. 674; [2003] Fam. Law 724, ECHR. 340
Knowles (Deceased), Re; Sub Nom: Knowles v Knowles [2008] UKPC 30, PC (Ant) 334
Kostic v Chaplin [2007] EWHC 2298 (Ch); (2007–08) 10 I.T.E.L.R. 364, Ch D 322, 323

L (A Child), Re; Sub Nom: L (A Child) (Special Guardianship: Surname), Re;
    E (A Child), Re [2007] EWCA Civ 196; [2007] 2 F.L.R. 50; [2007] 1 F.C.R. 804;
    [2007] Fam. Law 498, CA (Civ Div) 264
L v Birmingham City Council; Sub Nom: R. (on the application of Johnson) v
    Havering LBC; Johnson v Havering LBC; YL v Birmingham City Council
    [2007] UKHL 27; [2008] 1 A.C. 95; [2007] 3 W.L.R. 112; [2007] 3 All E.R. 957;
    [2007] H.R.L.R. 32; [2008] U.K.H.R.R. 346; [2007] H.L.R. 44; [2008]
    B.L.G.R. 273; (2007) 10 C.C.L. Rep. 505; [2007] LS Law Medical 472;
    (2007) 96 B.M.L.R. 1; (2007) 104(27) L.S.G. 29; (2007) 157 N.L.J. 938;
    (2007) 151 S.J.L.B. 860; [2007] N.P.C. 75, HL 173
L v Finland [2000] 2 F.L.R. 118; [2000] 3 F.C.R. 219; (2001) 31 E.H.R.R. 30;
    [2000] Fam. Law 536, ECHR 252
Ledger v Wootton [2007] EWHC 2599 (Ch); [2008] W.T.L.R. 235, Ch D (Birmingham) . . . 322
LLBC v TG [2007] EWHC 2640 (Fam); (2008) 11 C.C.L. Rep. 161, Fam Div. 183
Loxley v BAE Systems Land Systems (Munitions & Ordnance) Ltd,
    UKEAT/0156/08/RN, EAT 41

M (Care Proceedings: Judicial Review), Re [2003] EWHC 850 (Admin); [2003]
    2 F.L.R. 171; [2004] 1 F.C.R. 302; [2003] Fam. Law 479, QBD (Admin) 183
M (Minors in Care) (Contact: Grandmother's Application),
    Re [1995] 2 F.L.R. 86; [1995] 3 F.C.R. 551; [1995] Fam. Law 540;
    (1995) 159 J.P.N. 757, CA (Civ Div). 246, 247, 261
M (Minors) (Sexual Abuse: Evidence), Re [1993] 1 F.L.R. 822; [1993] 1 F.C.R. 253;
    [1993] Fam. Law 456, CA (Civ Div). 247, 260
MB (Caesarean Section), Re; Sub Nom: MB (Medical Treatment), Re [1997]
    2 F.L.R. 426; [1997] 2 F.C.R. 541; [1997] 8 Med. L.R. 217; (1997) 38 B.M.L.R.
    175; [1997] Fam. Law 542; (1997) 147 N.L.J. 600, CA (Civ Div). 111, 112
MC v Bulgaria (39272/98) (2005) 40 E.H.R.R. 20; 15 B.H.R.C. 627, ECHR 192

MJ (A Child) (Adoption Order or Special Guardianship Order), Re; Sub Nom:
  J v Newport City Council [2007] EWCA Civ 56; [2007] 1 F.L.R. 691;
  [2007] 1 F.C.R. 329; [2007] Fam. Law 389; (2007) 104(8) L.S.G. 38, CA (Civ Div)...... 262
MM (An Adult), Re [2007] EWHC 2003 .... 54, 55, 63, 146, 182, 183
McCoy v James McGregor & Sons, 00237/07IT..................................... 36
Marckx v Belgium (6833/74), 13 June 1979.. 244
Massachusetts Board of Retirement v Murgia 427 US 307 (1976) 25

N (A Child) (Residence Order: Procedural Mismanagement), Re; Sub Nom:
  N (A Child) (Residence: Appointment of Solicitor: Placement with Extended
  Family), Re [2001] 1 F.L.R. 1028; [2001] Fam. Law 423, CA (Civ Div)................ 245
Nathan v Leonard [2002] EWHC 1701 (Ch); [2003] 1 W.L.R. 827; [2003]
  4 All E.R. 198; [2002] W.T.L.R. 1061; (2001–02) 4 I.T.E.L.R. 909;
  (2002) 99(28) L.S.G. 32; (2002) 146 S.J.L.B. 160; [2002] N.P.C. 79, Ch D 333
Negus v Bahouse [2007] EWHC 2628 (Ch); [2008] 1 F.L.R. 381; [2008] 1 F.C.R.
  768; [2008] W.T.L.R. 97; [2008] Fam. Law 208, Ch D 331
Nielsen v Denmark (A/144); Sub Nom: Nielsen v Denmark (10929/84) (1989)
  11 E.H.R.R. 175, ECHR.. 186, 252
Norfolk and Norwich Healthcare NHS Trust v W [1996] 2 F.L.R. 613;
  [1997] 1 F.C.R. 269; (1997) 34 B.M.L.R. 16; [1997] Fam. Law 17, Fam Div 181

Olmstead v United States, 277 US 438,478 (1928) 116

P (A Minor) (Residence Order: Child's Welfare), Re; Sub Nom: P (Section 91(14)
  Guidelines: Residence and Religious Heritage), Re [2000] Fam. 15; [1999]
  3 W.L.R. 1164; [1999] 3 All E.R. 734; [1999] 2 F.L.R. 573; [1999] 2 F.C.R. 289;
  [1999] Fam. Law 531; (1999) 163 J.P.N. 712; (1999) 96(21) L.S.G. 38; (1999)
  149 N.L.J. 719; (1999) 143 S.J.L.B. 141, CA (Civ Div)........................... 247
P v G (Family Provision: Relevance of Divorce Provision); Sub Nom: P v E [2004]
  EWHC 2944 (Fam); [2006] 1 F.L.R. 431; [2007] W.T.L.R. 691; [2006] Fam.
  Law 178, Fam Div 317
Palacios de la Villa v Cortefiel Servicios SA (C-411/05) [2008] All E.R. (EC) 249;
  [2008] 1 C.M.L.R. 16; [2007] I.R.L.R. 989; [2007] Pens. L.R. 411, ECJ
  (Grand Chamber) 41
Powell v Benney [2007] EWCA Civ 1283; (2007) 151 S.J.L.B. 1598; [2008]
  1 P. & C.R. DG12, CA (Civ Div)...................................... 335, 336
Pretty v United Kingdom (2346/02); Sub Nom: R. (on the application of Pretty) v
  DPP (2346/02) [2002] 2 F.L.R. 45; [2002] 2 F.C.R. 97; (2002) 35 E.H.R.R. 1;
  12 B.H.R.C. 149; (2002) 66 B.M.L.R. 147; [2002] Fam. Law 588;
  (2002) 152 N.L.J. 707, ECHR 122
Price v United Kingdom (1988) 55 DR 224 244
Price v United Kingdom (33394/96) (2002) 34 E.H.R.R. 53; 11 B.H.R.C. 401;
  (2002) 5 C.C.L. Rep. 306; [2001] Po. L.R. 245; [2001] Prison L.R. 359;
  [2001] Crim. L.R. 916, ECHR. 191

R (A Child) (Adoption: Duty to Investigate), Re; Sub Nom: Z CC v R; R (A Child)
  (Adoption: Disclosure), Re [2001] 1 F.L.R. 365; [2001] 1 F.C.R. 238; [2001]
  Fam. Law 8, Fam Div. 257, 258
R (A Child) (Special Guardianship Order), Re; Sub Nom: Birmingham City
  Council v R [2006] EWCA Civ 1748; [2007] Fam. 41; [2007] 2 W.L.R. 1130;
  [2007] 1 F.L.R. 564; [2007] 1 F.C.R. 121, CA (Civ Div) 261, 264

R (Children) (Care Proceedings: Maternal Grandmother's Applications), Re;
 Sub Nom: G v A Local Authority [2007] EWCA Civ 139; [2007] 1 F.C.R. 439;
 (2007) 151 S.J.L.B. 334, CA (Civ Div) 262
R. v Cambridge DHA Ex p. B (No.1) [1995] 1 W.L.R. 898; [1995] 2 All E.R. 129;
 [1995] 1 F.L.R. 1056; [1995] 2 F.C.R. 485; [1995] 6 Med. L.R. 250; [1995]
 C.O.D. 407; [1995] Fam. Law 480; (1995) 145 N.L.J. 415, CA (Civ Div) 294, 296
R. v Ethical Committee of St Mary's Hospital Ex p. Harriott; Sub Nom:
 R. v St Mary's Hospital Ex p. Harriott [1988] 1 F.L.R. 512; [1988]
 Fam. Law 165; (1987) 137 N.L.J. 1038, DC. 294
R. v Hinks [2000] UKHL 53 145
R. v Newington (1990) 91 Cr. App. R. 247; [1990] Crim. L.R. 593; (1990)
 87(12) L.S.G. 40; (1990) 134 S.J. 785, CA (Crim Div) 178
R. v North and East Devon HA Ex p. Coughlan [2001] Q.B. 213; [2000] 2 W.L.R.
 622; [2000] 3 All E.R. 850; (2000) 2 L.G.L.R. 1; [1999] B.L.G.R. 703;
 (1999) 2 C.C.L. Rep. 285; [1999] Lloyd's Rep. Med. 306; (2000) 51
 B.M.L.R. 1; [1999] C.O.D. 340; (1999) 96(31) L.S.G. 39; (1999)
 143 S.J.L.B. 213, CA (Civ Div) 272, 293
R. v North Derbyshire HA Ex p. Fisher (1998) 10 Admin. L.R. 27; (1997–98)
 1 C.C.L. Rep. 150; [1997] 8 Med. L.R. 327; (1997) 38 B.M.L.R. 76, QBD 294
R. v North West Lancashire HA Ex p. A; R. v North West Lancashire
 HA Ex p. D; R. v North West Lancashire HA Ex p. G [2000] 1 W.L.R. 977;
 [2000] 2 F.C.R. 525; (1999) 2 C.C.L. Rep. 419; [1999] Lloyd's Rep. Med. 399;
 (2000) 53 B.M.L.R. 148, CA (Civ Div) 297
R. v North West Lancashire HA Ex p. A; R. v North West Lancashire HA Ex p. D;
 R. v North West Lancashire HA Ex p. G [2000] 1 W.L.R. 977; [2000]
 2 F.C.R. 525; (1999) 2 C.C.L. Rep. 419; [1999] Lloyd's Rep. Med. 399;
 (2000) 53 B.M.L.R. 148, CA (Civ Div) 294
R. v Secretary of State for Social Services Ex p. Hincks (1980) 1 B.M.L.R. 93 . . . . 293, 295
R. v Secretary of State for Social Services, Ex p. Walker (1987) 3 B.M.L.R. 32 295
R. v Sheffield HA, Ex.p Seale (1994) 25 B.M.L.R. 1 . . . . 294, 295
R. (on the application of B) v Lewisham LBC; Sub Nom: B v Lewisham LBC
 [2008] EWHC 738 (Admin); (2008) 11 C.C.L. Rep. 369; [2008] A.C.D. 59;
 [2008] Fam. Law 640, QBD (Admin) 265
R. (on the application of Burke) v General Medical Council [2005] EWCA Civ 1003;
 [2006] Q.B. 273; [2005] 3 W.L.R. 1132; [2005] 2 F.L.R. 1223; [2005] 3 F.C.R.
 169; [2005] H.R.L.R. 35; [2006] U.K.H.R.R. 509; (2005) 8 C.C.L. Rep. 463;
 [2005] Lloyd's Rep. Med. 403; (2005) 85 B.M.L.R. 1; [2006] A.C.D. 27;
 [2005] Fam. Law 776; (2005) 155 N.L.J. 1457, CA (Civ Div). 53, 70
R. (on the application of Cavanagh) v Health Service Commissioner; R. (on the
 application of Bhatt) v Health Service Commissioner; R. (on the application
 of Redmond) v Health Service Commissioner [2005] EWCA Civ 1578; [2006]
 1 W.L.R. 1229; [2006] 3 All E.R. 543; [2006] 1 F.C.R. 7;
 (2006) 91 B.M.L.R. 40, CA (Civ Div) 293
R. (on the application of Gordon) v Bromley NHS Primary Care Trust [2006]
 EWHC 2462 (Admin), QBD (Admin) 295
R. (on the application of Rogers) v Swindon NHS Primary Care Trust; Sub Nom:
 Rogers v Swindon NHS Primary Care Trust [2006] EWCA Civ 392; [2006]
 1 W.L.R. 2649; (2006) 9 C.C.L. Rep. 451; [2006] Lloyd's Rep. Med. 364;
 (2006) 89 B.M.L.R. 211; (2006) 103(17) L.S.G. 23; (2006) 156 N.L.J. 720;
 (2006) 150 S.J.L.B. 575, CA (Civ Div). 119, 120, 294, 295

R. (on the application of Stephenson) v Stockton on Tees BC [2005] EWCA Civ 960;
  [2005] 3 F.C.R. 248; [2006] B.L.G.R. 135; (2005) 8 C.C.L. Rep. 517, CA (Civ Div) 103
R. (on the application of Thomas) v Havering LBC, Unreported, September 4, 2008,
  QBD (Admin) 173
R. (on the application of Watts) v Bedford Primary Care Trust; Sub Nom: R.
  (on the application of Watts) v Secretary of State for Health [2004] EWCA
  Civ 166; [2004] 2 C.M.L.R. 55; [2004] Eu. L.R. 595; (2004) 77 B.M.L.R.
  26, CA (Civ Div); [2003] EWHC 2228 (Admin); [2003] 3 C.M.L.R. 23;
  [2004] Eu. L.R. 25; (2003) 6 C.C.L. Rep. 566; [2004] Lloyd's Rep. Med. 113;
  (2003) 100(39) L.S.G. 38, QBD (Admin) 297
Raven, Re; Sub Nom: Spencer v national Association for the Prevention of Consumption
  and Other Forms of Tuberculosis [1915] 1 Ch. 673, Ch D 333
Rees v Newbery; Sub Nom: Lankesheer (Deceased), Re [1998] 1 F.L.R. 1041;
  [1998] Fam. Law 320, Ch D. 331
Rieme v Sweden (A/226B) (1993) 16 E.H.R.R. 155, ECHR 122
Rutherford v Secretary of State for Trade and Industry; Sub Nom: Rutherford v
  Harvest Towncircle Ltd (In Liquidation); Secretary of State for Trade and
  Industry v Rutherford; Bentley v Secretary of State for Trade and Industry
  [2006] UKHL 19; [2006] 4 All E.R. 577; [2006] I.C.R. 785; [2006]
  I.R.L.R. 551; (2006) 103(20) L.S.G. 24; (2006) 150 S.J.L.B. 604, HL 34, 38, 41

S (A Child) (Adoption Order or Special Guardianship Order), Re; Sub Nom:
  DO v LP [2007] EWCA Civ 54; [2007] 1 F.L.R. 819; [2007] 1 F.C.R. 271;
  [2007] Fam. Law 390, CA (Civ Div) 262, 263
S (A Child) (Identification: Restrictions on Publication), Re; Sub Nom: S (A Child)
  (Identification: Restriction on Publication), Re [2004] UKHL 47; [2005]
  1 A.C. 593; [2004] 3 W.L.R. 1129; [2004] 4 All E.R. 683; [2005] E.M.L.R. 2;
  [2005] 1 F.L.R. 591; [2004] 3 F.C.R. 407; [2005] H.R.L.R. 5; [2005] U.K.H.R.R.
  129; 17 B.H.R.C. 646; [2005] Crim. L.R. 310; (2004) 154 N.L.J. 1654; (2004)
  148 S.J.L.B. 1285, HL 193, 253
S (A Minor) (Contact: Grandparents), Re [1996] 1 F.L.R. 158; [1996] 3 F.C.R. 30;
  [1996] Fam. Law 76, CA (Civ Div) 248
S (Adult Patient) (Inherent Jurisdiction: Family Life), Re; Sub Nom: Sheffield
  CC v S [2002] EWHC 2278 (Fam); [2003] 1 F.L.R. 292; [2003] Fam.
  Law 91, Fam Div 112, 113, 184, 185
S and S v United Kingdom (10375/83) 40 DR 196. 244
SA (Vulnerable Adult with Capacity: Marriage), Re; Sub Nom: A Local Authority v
  MA [2005] EWHC 2942 (Fam); [2006] 1 F.L.R. 867; [2007] 2 F.C.R. 563;
  (2007) 10 C.C.L. Rep. 193; [2006] Fam. Law 268, Fam Div. 182
Salgueiro da Silva Mouta v Portugal (33290/96) [2001] 1 F.C.R. 653;
  (2001) 31 E.H.R.R. 47; 2001 Fam. L.R. 2, ECHR 121
Saulle v Nouvet [2007] EWHC 2902 (QB); [2008] LS Law Medical 201;
  [2008] W.T.L.R. 729, QBD 54
Scammell v Farmer [2008] EWHC 1100 (Ch); (2008) 152(23) S.J.L.B. 31, Ch D 321, 322
Schloendorff v Society of N.Y. Hosp., 105 NE 92, 93 (NY1914) 115
Seldon v Clarkson, Wright & Jakes, ET/1100275/2007. 44
Stevenson v Abington (1863) 9 LT 74. 333
Storck v Germany (2005) 43 E.H.R.R. 96. . . . . .185, 186
Sunderland City Council v P; Sub Nom: Sunderland City Council v PS; PS
  (Incapacitated or Vulnerable Adult), Re [2007] EWHC 623 (Fam); [2007]

2 F.L.R. 1083; (2007) 10 C.C.L. Rep. 295; [2007] LS Law Medical 507;
    [2007] Fam. Law 695, Fam Div 181, 185

T (Adult: Refusal of Treatment), Re; Sub Nom: T (Consent to Medical Treatment)
    (Adult Patient), Re [1993] Fam. 95; [1992] 3 W.L.R. 782; [1992] 4 All E.R. 649;
    [1992] 2 F.L.R. 458; [1992] 2 F.C.R. 861; [1992] 3 Med. L.R. 306; [1993]
    Fam. Law 27; (1992) 142 N.L.J. 1125, CA (Civ Div) 88
T v S (Financial Provision for Children) [1994] 2 F.L.R. 883; [1994] 1 F.C.R. 743;
    [1995] Fam. Law 11, Fam Div 230
T v W (Contact: Reasons for Refusing Leave) [1996] 2 F.L.R. 473; [1997]
    1 F.C.R. 118; [1996] Fam. Law 666; (1996) 160 J.P.N. 1102, Fam Div 246
Thorner v Curtis; Sub Nom: Thorner v Major [2008] EWCA Civ 732; [2008]
    2 F.C.R. 435; (2008) 152(27) S.J.L.B. 32, CA (Civ Div) 335
Troxel v Granville 530 US 57 (2000) 254, 255

Uglow v Uglow [2004] EWCA Civ 987; [2004] W.T.L.R. 1183, CA (Civ Div) 335

Valasinas v Lithuania (44558/98) 12 B.H.R.C. 266; [2001] Prison L.R. 365, ECHR 191

W (A Child) (Contact Application: Procedure), Re; Sub Nom: W (A Child)
    (Contact: Leave to Apply), Re [2000] 1 F.L.R. 263; [2000] 1 F.C.R. 185;
    [2000] Fam. Law 82, Fam Div 250, 254
W (A Minor) (Contact: Application by Grandparent), Re [1997] 1 F.L.R. 793;
    [1997] 2 F.C.R. 643; [1997] Fam. Law 390; (1997) 161 J.P.N. 770, Fam Div 248
W Healthcare NHS Trust v H [2004] EWCA Civ 1324; [2005] 1 W.L.R. 834, CA (Civ Div) . . . 69
W v Vale of Glamorgan CC; Sub Nom: G (Protocol for Judicial Case Management),
    Re [2004] EWHC 116 (Fam); [2004] 1 F.L.R. 1119; [2004] Fam. Law 327, Fam Div 260
Watson (Deceased), Re [1999] 1 F.L.R. 878; [1999] 3 F.C.R. 595; [1999] Fam. Law 211;
    (1999) 96(2) L.S.G. 28; (1999) 143 S.J.L.B. 51, Ch D 330
Wayling v Jones [1995] 2 F.L.R. 1029; [1996] 2 F.C.R. 41; (1995) 69 P. & C.R. 170;
    [1996] Fam. Law 88; [1993] E.G. 153 (C.S.), CA (Civ Div) 334
Westendorp v Warwick [2006] EWHC 915; (2006) 150 S.J.L.B. 608, Ch D 321
Wilkinson v Springwell Engineering, ET/25074/07 36

X v Switzerland (8924/80) 24 DR 183 244
X, Y and Z v United Kingdom (21830/93) [1997] 2 F.L.R. 892; [1997]
    3 F.C.R. 341; (1997) 24 E.H.R.R. 143; (1998) 39 B.M.L.R. 128;
    [1997] Fam. Law 605; (1997) 94(17) L.S.G. 25, ECHR 244

Y (Children) (Occupation Order), Re; Sub Nom: Y (Children) (Matrimonial Home:
    Vacation), Re [2000] 2 F.C.R. 470, CA (Civ Div) 180
Y (Mental Patient: Bone Marrow Donation), Re; Sub Nom: Y (Mental Incapacity:
    Bone Marrow Transplant), Re; Y (Adult Patient) (Transplant: Bone Marrow),
    Re [1997] Fam. 110; [1997] 2 W.L.R. 556; [1996] 2 F.L.R. 787; [1997]
    2 F.C.R. 172; (1997) 35 B.M.L.R. 111; [1997] Fam. Law 91, Fam Div 110

Z v United Kingdom (29392/95) [2001] 2 F.L.R. 612; [2001] 2 F.C.R. 246;
    (2002) 34 E.H.R.R. 3; 10 B.H.R.C. 384; (2001) 3 L.G.L.R. 51; (2001)
    4 C.C.L. Rep. 310; [2001] Fam. Law 583, ECHR 192

Table of Statutory Instruments

Care Homes Regulations SI 2001/3965 171
Employment Equality (Age) Regulations SI 2006/1031 . . . . 4, 20, 33, 35, 50
   reg.1(1)(b) 38
   reg.3 40
      (1) 36
         (b) 40
      (2) 36
      (3) 36
         (b) 36
   reg.4(1) 39
      (2) 39
   reg.6(1) 39
      (2) 39
   reg.7 35
      (4) 35
   reg.8(2) 44
   reg.9 35
   reg.12 35
   reg.15 35
   reg.17 35
   reg.18 35
   reg.19 35
   reg.20 35
   reg.27 40
   reg.28 40
   reg.29 47
      (1) 47
      (2) 47
      (3) 47
   reg.30 . . . . 35, 40
   reg.31 40
   reg.32 41
   reg.38(1) 40
        (b) 40
      (2) 40
   Sch.6 45
Equality Act (Sexual Orientation) Regulations SI 2007/1263 . . . . 29, 49
Mental Capacity (Deprivation of Liberty: Standard Authorisations, Assessments and
   Ordinary Residence) Regulations 2008 59
Sex Discrimination (Gender Re-assignment) Regulations SI 1999/1102 34
Special Guardianship Regulations SI 2005/1109 263

Table of Statutes

Administration of Estates Act 1925 324
Adoption and Children Act 2002. ....257, 258
  s.1 259
    (4)(f) 259
  s.67 330
  s.115. 262
Care Standards Act 2000. .... 162, 170, 174, 177
  s.23 170
Carers and Disabled Children Act 2000 101
Carers (Equal Opportunities) Act 2004. 102
  s.1 102
  s.2 102
Carers (Recognition and Services) Act 1995. 101
Child Support Act 1991 230
Children Act 1989 .... 230, 243, 250
  Pt.IV 190
  s.1 .... 244, 246
    (1) 247
  s.8 244
  s.10(9) 246
  s.14B 265
  s.14C(3) 264
  s.17. 267
  s.31 ....190, 191
  s.91(14) 263
  s.105 243
  Sch.1, para.2 230
Civil Partnership Act 2004
  Sch.4, para.15(5) 330
Commissioner for Older People (Wales) Act 2006. 194
Crime and Disorder Act 1998
  ss 28–32. 179
Disability Discrimination Act 1995. 294
Domestic Violence, Crime and Victims Act 2004
  s.5 176
    (1)(d) 177
    (6) 176
Employment Rights Act 1996
  s.57A(1) 102
Equality Act 2006 49
Family Law Act 1996. 180
  s.42A 180
Finance Act 2006
  Pt.IV 337
Health and Social Care Act 2001

s.49 272
  (1) 272
  (2) 272
Health and Social Care Act 2008. . . . . 170, 171, 172, 173
s.1 172
ss 26–32. 171
s.31 172
s.35 172
s.145. 173
  (1) 173
Health and Social Services and Social Security Adjudications Act 1983
s.17. . . . . 103, 272
Human Rights Act 1998 . . . . 112, 173, 196, 253, 254, 259, 262
s.6 . . . . 173, 296
  (3)(b) 173
s.7 . . . . 173, 296
s.8 173
Human Tissue Act 2004 121
Inheritance (Provision for Family and Dependants) Act 1975 . . . . .317, 318, 320, 326, 328,
                                                  329, 331, 333, 334
s.1(1) 330
s.3(2) 332
Intestates Estates Act 1952. 324
Law Reform (Succession) Act 1995
s.2 330
Married Women's Property Act 1893. 317
Matrimonial Causes Act 1973 230
s.29 230
Mental Capacity Act 2005. . . . . 10, 52, 54, 55, 56, 57, 59, 62, 68, 69, 74, 83,
                                 89, 90, 109, 110, 112, 113, 145, 169, 181, 322, 345
s.1(2)–(6) 53
  (2) 54
  (4) 56
  (6) 59
s.2(2) 55
  (3) 56
s.3(1) 54, 55
s.4 109
  (5) 61, 66, 67
  (6) 60, 61, 62, 70, 111
   (c). 111
  (7) 65, 109
  (10) 66
s.5 . . . . .57, 63
s.6 169
  (2) 59
  (3)(a)–(b) 59
s.8 57
s.15. 83
  (1)(c). 62
s.16. 57

s.17 83
s.20 83
s.24 . . . . 69, 72
s.25(2) 71, 72
(c) 72
(4) 71
(c) 72
(6) 69
s.26(2) 72
(3) 72
s.44(1) 177
(2) 177
s.47 181
s.48 181
Mental Health Act 1983 . . . . 54, 89, 90, 121
s.1(2) 90
s.2 90
s.3(2) 89
s.4 90
s.127 177
s.135 190
Mental Health Act 2007 89
National Health Service Act 1977 272
National Health Service and Community Care Act 1990
s.47 190
Pensions Act 2004 . . . . 209, 214
Pensions Act 2007
Pt.3 219
ss 1–2 219
s.5 219
s.13 219
Protection from Harassment Act 1997 180
Race Relations Act 1976 34
Registered Homes Act 1984 . . . . 162, 170
Sex Discrimination Act 1975 34
Sexual Offences Act 2003 145
Work and Families Act 2006 102

Table of Treaties, Conventions etc

TREATIES

EC Treaty 34

CONVENTIONS

European Convention on Human Rights 121, 173
   Art.1, Protocol 1 300
   Art.2 . . . . 173, 296, 300
   Art.3 . . . . 123, 191, 192, 193, 194, 296
   Art.5 . . . . 64, 185
     (1) 185
   Art.6 246
   Art.8 . . . . .112, 123, 185, 193, 244, 246, 252, 255, 297, 300
     (1) 193, 252, 259
     (2) 112, 123, 252, 259
   Art.9 300
   Art.14 . . . . .30, 34, 121, 294, 297, 300

CHARTER

European Social Charter
   Art.23 342

DIRECTIVES

Treatment Framework Directive 2000/78 . . . . .34, 45, 121
   Recital 11. 34
   Art.6(1) 41

1

Introduction

Wonderful news! People in the UK are living longer. We have more people older now than we have ever had. Life expectancy is on a relentless increase.

Yet this is rarely seen as wonderful news in the media. Instead, the headlines we read are: 'How Bad is the UK's Pension Crisis?';[1] 'Lib-Dem Leader "too old"';[2] or 'Older Care a Stain on Country'.[3] The European Commission has produced mountains of paperwork seeking to meet the 'challenges' of an ageing population.[4] The changing age demographic is one of those great 'dilemmas' politicians love to talk about, but seem to prefer not to do anything about until after the next election. The repercussions of having an ageing society are complex and only the brave will predict with confidence the economic, political, and social ramifications.[5]

Age Concern has declared that 'Britain is going through an extraordinary demographic transition'.[6] In 2008 for the first time there were more people over 60 than children under the age of 18.[7] In 2008 a quarter more people will turn 60 than did so just four years previously.[8] In 2005 there were 20.3 million people over the age of 50. That is an increase of 2.5 per cent since 2002. Over a third of the population is now aged over 50.[9] In 2008 there were 2.7 million people over the age of 80, some 4.5 per cent of the population.[10] And all the signs are that the growth in the numbers of older people will continue, with it being predicted that there will be a quarter more people aged over 80 in 10 years time than there are currently. The number of people aged over 65 is expected to rise by over

---

[1] BBC News Online, 'How Bad is the UK's Pensions Crisis?', 23 September 2006.

[2] BBC News Online, 'Lib-Dem Leader Too Old, says Owen', 6 February 2007.

[3] BBC News Online, 'Elderly Care Stain on Country', 29 April 2008.

[4] eg European Commission, *European Social Models: The Challenge of an Ageing Population* (European Commission, 2006).

[5] eg Her Majesty's Government, *Opportunity Age* (Stationery Office, 2005); Department of Health, *A New Ambition For Old Age: Next Steps In Implementing the National Service Framework for Older People* (Department of Health, 2006); and Department of Health, *Independence, Wellbeing and Choice* (Department of Health, 2005).

[6] Age Concern, *The Age Agenda* (Age Concern, 2008), at 1.

[7] National Statistics, *Ageing* (National Statistics, 2008).

[8] Age Concern, *The Age Agenda* (Age Concern, 2008), at 1.

[9] Age Concern, *Older People in the UK* (Age Concern, 2008), at 1.

[10] Age Concern, *The Age Agenda* (Age Concern, 2008), at 1.

60 per cent in the next 25 years.[11] Life expectancy will grow by at least one year for every decade. Many philosophers, but fewer doctors, are discussing the possibility of immortality.[12] That may be a bit premature, but the discussions on how to 'age well' and enjoy an 'active retirement' are not. And they are concepts which not many decades ago would have been the privilege of only a few.[13]

These demographic changes will impact on society in profound ways. We now have a significant number of healthy older people and yet their place in society is marginalized. Society's social, economic, and community structures reflect the now old-fashioned model of a life of work, followed by a short retirement characterized by ill health and then death.[14] The result is that older people are often isolated from society and in poverty, in particular our older women: 1.8 million pensioners are in poverty and two-thirds of these are women.[15] Women from ethnic minority groups are particularly badly hit. Forty-two per cent of pensioners from the Pakistani/Bangladeshi communities live in poverty.[16] We see here how the disadvantages of old age intersect with patriarchy and racial discrimination to create extensive disadvantage. The disadvantages faced by old people are not just financial, but extend to a variety of forms of social exclusion, as will be discussed in chapter 2.[17]

What is old age?

There is much dispute over how to define old age. One way of doing so is to state that all those over a particular age are 'older people'. The World Health Organization uses the age of 60.[18] Opponents of such an approach object that setting a particular age at which a person becomes old would be arbitrary. Among people of any given age there will be a huge variation in health, lifestyle, appearance, etc. It would be difficult to say anything that would be true for all those of a particular age, except something about their birthdays. Furthermore, use of a particular age as the boundary of old age would lead to people asking why, on a particular moment in time, they suddenly become 'old' when the day before they were not. There is, perhaps, a more important objection. As Helen Small notes: 'The age we feel is not necessarily the same as our calendrical age, nor is it the same as how we are perceived, or how we register ourselves being perceived by

---

[11] Age Concern, *Older People in the UK* (Age Concern, 2008), at 1.
[12] J Harris, 'Imitations of Immortality' (2000) 288 *Science* 59.
[13] Successful ageing is addressed in J Hendricks and L Russell Hatch, 'Lifestyle Aging' in R Binstock and L George (eds), *Handbook of Aging and the Social Sciences* (Academic Press, 2006).
[14] K Land and Y Yang, 'Morbidity, Disability and Mortality' in R Binstock and L George (eds), *Handbook of Aging and the Social Sciences* (Academic Press, 2006).
[15] Age Concern, *The Age Agenda* (Age Concern, 2008), at 15.   [16] Ibid.
[17] Social Exclusion Unit, *A Sure Start to Later Life* (SEU, 2006).
[18] B Brandl and T Meuer, 'Domestic Abuse In Later Life' (2001) 8 *Elder Law Journal* 298.

others'.[19] So our chronological age is only one aspect of what it is to experience age personally and in our society.

Supporters of an age-based definition of old age might reply that inevitably the law has to use generalizations, even if that means that some people are unfairly categorized. We do this with children for example. Children under the age of 17 are not allowed to drive, even though there may well be some under-17s who can.[20] But this raises the issue of why it is that we want to use the category of older people in the law. Is it to mark out a category of people who are particularly vulnerable, or upon whom it is justifiable to place certain obligations? While generally speaking those under the age of 16 are not able to make complex competent decisions, it is not clear whether we could make any generalization of any kind about older people.[21] But returning to the issue of why 'older people' should be a category of interest might lead us to a different way of defining old age.[22]

One alternative would be to define 'older people' as those who have reached the age when a state pension becomes payable. This would be the age at which the state would have indicated that they could be expected to stop work and undertake retirement. The benefits of this approach would be that there would be a clear definition of the category. Furthermore, it would link the definition of old age to being a pensioner, which itself is linked with the problems of poverty, vulnerability, and social exclusion. These are the very reasons why the category of older people might be of interest to politicians, lawyers, and academics. The difficulty with this definition is that it is increasingly outdated. As we shall see in chapter 6 the notion of retirement is undergoing a major rethink. Indeed, it is becoming increasingly rare for there to be a particular point in time when a person stops full-time work and starts retirement. The chapter also discusses the changes in employment law which are starting to protect an employee's right to choose their own date of retirement.

A third approach, and one I would advocate, is that an older person is one who is treated as an 'older person' by society. Research suggests that people rarely define themselves as 'old'. However, others start to refer to a person as 'old' and there are certain things that are recognized by the person themselves as characteristics of 'being old'.[23] The benefit of this approach is that it acknowledges that there are no particular disadvantages of being old per se, but there are disadvantages that flow from being regarded as 'old' by society. It is these disadvantages which the law should, and does to a limited extent, address. The disadvantage is that it means that the definition of older people is less clear cut. But that does not

---

[19] H Small, *The Long Life* (Oxford University Press, 2007), at 3.

[20] For further discussion see J Herring, 'Children's Rights for Grown-Ups' in S Fredman and S Spencer, *Age as an Equality Issue* (Hart, 2003).

[21] J Fries, 'Aging, Natural Death and Compression of Morbidity' (1980) 303 *New England Journal of Medicine* 134.

[22] See the discussion in M Kapp, 'Aging and Law' in R Binstock and L George (eds), *Handbook of Aging and the Social Sciences* (Academic Press, 2006).

[23] J Vincent, *Old Age* (Routledge, 2003), ch 1.

mean that it is of no use to the law. The Employment Equality (Age) Regulations 2006 protect people from being discriminated against on the basis of their age or 'apparent age'.[24]

Law and older people

Much has been written on ageing from the point of view of science,[25] philosophy,[26] politics,[27] literature,[28] psychology,[29] and particularly sociology.[30] Gerontology has become well established as a field of study in its own right.[31] Yet lawyers appear to have been particularly (and unusually) reticent in writing on this topic.[32] In the United States, 'elder law' is a popular option at many universities and a wealth of journal articles and even books can be found on the subject, such as: *Law and Aging: The Essentials of Elder Law*;[33] *Elder Law: Cases and Materials*;[34] *Elder Law: Statutes and Regulations*;[35] and (with surely the ultimate sign that the subject has entered the academy) *Elder Law in a Nutshell*.[36] In England, by comparison, although there are a few practitioner-orientated books,[37] there is very little that is written on the law from an academic perspective and the topic appears in few, if any, law courses.

The lack of a developed 'elder law' in England may be explained by legal culture.[38] In the United States, practitioners specialize in elder law, which is, no doubt, a lucrative market to exploit. It seems that in the United Kingdom fewer lawyers seek to market themselves as specialist lawyers for older people.[39] The

----

[24] See ch 2 for further discussion.

[25] T Kirkwood, 'The Science of Ageing' (2005) 120 *Cell* 437.

[26] V Bengston, M Silverstein, N Putney, and D Gans (eds), *Handbook of Theories of Aging* (Springer, 2008).

[27] R Hudson (ed), *The New Politics of Old Age Policy* (John Hopkins University Press, 2005).

[28] H Small, *The Long Life* (Oxford University Press, 2007).

[29] R Settersten, 'Aging and the Life Course' in R Binstock and L George (eds), *Handbook of Aging and the Social Sciences* (Academic Press, 2006).

[30] R Binstock and L George (eds), *Handbook of Aging and the Social Sciences* (Academic Press, 2006); J Vincent, *Old Age* (Routledge, 2003); H-W Wahl, C Tesch-Romer, and A Hoff (eds), *New Dynamics in Old Age: Individual, Environmental and Societal Perspectives* (Baywood, 2007); and J Powell, *Social Theory and Aging* (Routledge, 2006).

[31] eg the work of the Oxford Institute of Ageing (<http://www.ageing.ox.ac.uk/>).

[32] G Zenz, 'Old Age and Family Law' [2003] *Family Law* 291.

[33] R Schwartz, *Law and Aging* (Prentice Hall, 2004).

[34] L Frolik and A Barnes, *Elder Law: Cases and Materials* (LexisNexis, 2003).

[35] T Gallanis, A Dayton, and M Wood, *Elder Law: Statutes and Regulations* (Anderson Publishing, 1999).

[36] L Frolik and R Kaplan, *Elder Law in a Nutshell* (Thompson/West, 2006).

[37] eg A McDonald and M Taylor, *Older People and the Law* (Policy Press, 2006).

[38] H Meenan and G Braodbent, 'Ageing and Policy in the United Kingdom' (2007) 2 *Journal of International Ageing, Law and Policy* 67.

[39] Although there is an organization known as Solicitors for the Elderly (<http://www.solicitorsfortheelderly.com/>).

lack of academic interest may alternatively be a wariness of 'yet another Law and...' area of study. As one experienced colleague said when I was working on this area: 'Whatever next? The law and people with blond hair?' That is, perhaps, revealing in itself. The absence of legal academic attention to issues surrounding law and older people may, however, reflect wider issues concerning the invisibility of older people within society and the sidelining of their interests.[40] Apart form the 'pensions crisis', issues relating to older people rarely surface in the media. In early 2007 the *Guardian* decided to devote a supplement to issues surrounding older people with special editors all over the age of 65 brought in especially.[41] The very fact that such a supplement was thought necessary, or appropriate, indicates the poor visibility of older people generally in the media.

Some commentators have been critical of gerontology and the more general study of older people. Stephen Katz,[42] for example, sees gerontology as part of a complex game of knowledge and power, which involves 'creating the elderly'[43] as a distinct body of people who constitute a social problem. His argument raises some important points. First, it has become natural to regard 'the elderly' as a group worthy of study in a way we would not regard 'blond haired' people as a group worthy of general sociological study. Secondly, the tendency in social science to group people together by characteristics can easily cause us to lose sight of the diversity of individuals who make up the group. What, however, I suggest Katz has insufficiently acknowledged is that it is society which has created the category of 'the elderly' rather than gerontologists. He gives academics far too much power! In chapter 2 I will look at the many ways in which ageist attitudes, with their assumptions about people based on their age, are prevalent in society. It is these which create the significance of old age. One survey on health issues affecting older people found few health issues specifically related to old age, except that older people suffered higher rates of depression and higher rates of suicide.[44] As this suggests, Katz may be right to say that age itself is of little significance, but the way society treats older people certainly is. It is the way society treats older people, rather than old age, which makes poverty, isolation, and exclusion such features of their lives.[45] As Peter Townsend explains, society creates:

the framework of institutions and rules within which the general problem of the elderly emerge or, indeed, are 'manufactured'. In the everyday management of the economy and the administration and development of social institutions the position of the elderly

[40] For an excellent history of approaches to age discrimination, see J Macnicol, *Age Discrimination* (Cambridge University Press, 2006).

[41] The *Guardian*, *Over 70s Special*, 12 January 2007.

[42] S Katz, *Disciplining Old Age: The Formation of Gerontological Knowledge* (University Press of Virginia, 1996).

[43] At p 40.

[44] P Higgs, 'Older People Health Care and Society' in G Scambler (ed), *Sociology as Applied to Medicine* (Saunders, 2003).

[45] R Lynott and P Lynott, 'Tracing the Course of Theoretical Development in the Sociology of Aging' (1996) 36 *The Gerontologist* 749, at 750.

is subtly shaped and changed. The policies which determine the conditions and welfare of the elderly are not just the reactive policies represented by the statutory social services but the much more generalised and institutionalised policies of the state which maintain or change social structure.[46]

The case against elder law

Given the lack of attention afforded to old people by lawyers it must be asked whether the law and older people is an appropriate area of study. Indeed, it is a common view that seeking to address the interaction of the law and older people is misguided and will perpetuate rather than redress ageism.[47] There should be nothing different about the law as it deals with a person aged 80 or 30. Elder lawyers with their focus on topics such as elder abuse, wills, and the regulation of nursing homes merely perpetuate the link between old age and vulnerability or incapacity.[48] Age, it is said, is an utterly arbitrary factor to use as a category of legal study.[49] It is no more than 'a number derived from a birth certificate'.[50] Indeed, it would be far more appropriate to view age as a life course: one long journey, rather than a series of shifts from one category of age to another. Mike Brogdon and Preeti Nijhar argue that: 'There are few collective characteristics that clearly mark out elderly people from younger people'.[51] Indeed, it might be thought that there are greater differences among those over 70 than any other age group.[52] It would make far more sense to consider the law and people lacking in competence, or the law and those living in institutional settings, rather than the law and older people.

The justification for elder law

The objections to elder law just mentioned, of course, have substance. However, it is argued there are very good reasons why the study of the law and older people is necessary and appropriate. I will emphasize three.

First, it is true that age is an arbitrary construct which should have no relevance to a person's legal rights, but the same can be said of sex or race. The sad

---

[46] P Townsend, 'Ageism and Social Policy' in C Phillipson and A Walker (eds), *Ageing and Social Policy* (Gower, 1986), at 2. See further C Phillipson, *Reconstructing Old Age* (Sage, 1998).

[47] M Kapp, 'Aging and the Law' in R Binstock and L George (eds), *Handbook of Aging and the Social Sciences* (Academic Press, 2005).

[48] eg R Hudson, 'Contemporary Challenges to Age-Based Public Policy' in R Hudson (ed), *The New Politics of Old Age Policy* (John Hopkins Press, 2006).

[49] B Brandl and T Meuer, 'Domestic Abuse in Later Life' (2001) 8 *Elder Law Journal* 298.

[50] J Grimely Evans, 'Age Discrimination: Implication of the Ageing Process' in S Fredman and S Spencer, *Age as an Equality Issue* (Hart, 2003), at 19.

[51] M Brogdon and P Nijhar, *Crime, Abuse and the Elderly* (Willan, 2000), at 151.

[52] R Settersten, 'Aging and the Life Course' in R Binstock and L George (eds), *Handbook of Aging and the Social Sciences* (Academic Press, 2005), at 8.

truth is that we do live in a society in which there is deeply ingrained prejudice concerning old age. Ageism leads to an extensive list of disadvantages. The law both reflects and reinforces ageist prejudices. So there is a need to ensure that the law treats older people justly, and legal intervention may be needed to ensure there is no unfair disadvantage caused by ageism.[53] To seek to ignore the vulnerabilities that affect those of old age as a group, and claim they suffer none, does nothing to advance their cause.[54] Robert Butler claims that ageism is manifested in:

stereotypes and myths, outright disdain and dislike, or simply subtle avoidance of contact; discriminatory practices in housing, employment and services of all kinds; epithets, cartoons and jokes. At times ageism becomes an expedient method by which society promotes viewpoints about the aged in order to relieve itself from the responsibility towards them, and at other times ageism serves a highly personal objective, protecting younger (usually middle-aged) individuals—often at high emotional cost—from thinking about things they fear (aging, illness and death).[55]

We will discuss further the evidence for, and manifestation of, ageism in chapter 2. But I will mention one example here, which may appear trivial, but is important. That is the provision of public toilets. Julia Neuberger writes:

Public toilets are important for everyone, but they are particularly important for older people, who may have more limited mobility and may also need to use the toilet with more frequency or with greater urgency than younger people. Those that remain open have usually also lost their traditional on-site attendant, which make them less safe—or at least they seem so—which in turn allows the remaining toilets to be ruined by poor hygiene, vandalism, drug abuse and people using them as places to have sex.[56]

Councils are willing to provide emergency toilet facilities for drunk young people leaving nightclubs, but not so that older people can visit public places with confidence.[57] This says a lot about the invisibility of older people in our society.

When considering age discrimination it is important to appreciate the intersection of old age with sex and race. The assumptions and impact of age will depend, in part, on your race and sex. It is often reported, for example, that a woman's attractiveness is judged against an extremely youthful ideal.[58] While men are commonly said to be attractive even while showing signs of ageing, a

---

[53] M Kohli, 'Aging and Justice' in R Binstock and L George (eds), *Handbook of Aging and the Social Sciences* (Academic Press, 2005), at 427.

[54] M Holstein, 'A Normative Defence of Age-Based Public Policy' in R Hudson (ed), *The New Politics of Old Age Policy* (John Hopkins Press, 2005), at 35.

[55] R Butler, 'Ageism' in G Maddox (ed), *The Encyclopaedia of Aging* (Springer, 1995).

[56] J Neuberger, *Not Dead Yet* (Harper Collins, 2008), at 106.

[57] London Borough of Lambeth press release, 'Space-Age "Pop Up" Loos to be in place in Lambeth Next Year', 29 November 2007.

[58] S Sontag, 'The Double Standard of Ageing' in V Carver and P Liddiard (eds), *An Ageing Population* (Open University Press, 1978).

woman's attractiveness requires removal of visible signs of ageing.[59] As Martha
Holstein argues:

If we older women fail to care for our bodies so that we can meet normative expectations to age 'successfully,' we may be viewed askance—at the simplest level for 'letting
ourselves go' when 'control' is putatively within our grasp—and, more problematically,
as moral failures for being complicit in our own aging. We lose our cultural relevance.
The belief in the possibility for, and moral obligation to, control and also contribute to
delegitimating old age as the foundation for policy responses. If old age can be just like
middle age—if only we had behaved differently—why should public policy single out the
old for political attention?[60]

The impact of ageing on masculinity raises interesting issues too:

The men pictured in the anti-aging advertisements drive themselves into expensive and
strenuous fun, translating the achievement orientation of the labor market into those of
recreational consumption. Banned from the competition for salaries and promotions,
they struggle for status by spending the wealth and strength they have to play as young
men do in their attempts to appear as vigorous as possible.[61]

Those, then, interested in issues of race, sex, and the law should therefore also be
interested in the issues raised by age. Among the over 50s there are 100 women
for every 85 men. Poverty and disadvantage among older people therefore especially impacts on women. Feminists should be continuing to raise issues relating
to age.

An alternative justification for elder law is to challenge the view that age is
simply an arbitrary criterion to which the law should pay no attention. The argument here, then, is that although there are prejudices about old age and unfair
assumptions that are made; that should not be used to disguise the fact that for
most people old age is different from other stages in life. These differences must
be recognized and treasured.

Richard Brooks[62] argues that it is better to see oneself not as a set of timeless desires, but a character subjected to the stages in life. The life stages form
the milestones of life. Hence people's 18th, 21st or 60th birthdays are often
celebrated as special events. They provide a structure to the story of a person's life.
That is so even if the story involves rebelling against the stage of life a person is
meant to be at. The different stages of life play an important part in the social and
personal journeys of our lives. The law should therefore properly acknowledge
their importance. Most significantly, as Brooks suggests, the law may require

---

[59]   R Binstock, J Fishman, and T Johnson, 'Anti-Aging, Medicine and Science' in R Binstock
and L George (eds), *Handbook of Aging and the Social Sciences* (Academic Press, 2006).
[60]   M Holstein, 'On Being an Aging Woman' in T Calasanti and K Slevin (eds), *Age Matters*
(Routledge, 2006), at 317.
[61]   T Calasanti and K Slevin (eds), *Age Matters* (Routledge, 2006), at 4.
[62]   R Brooks, ' "The Refurbishing": Reflections upon Law and Justice among the Stages of Life'
(2006) 54 *Buffalo Law Review* 619.

individuals to make sacrifices at one stage of their lives in order to prepare for another stage of their life. For example, it might be said, requiring children to receive education is, in part at least, done in order to benefit them later in their life. A country might opt for a system of taxation or benefits which requires an individual to pay during their years of employment in order to finance benefits paid during their retirement. Brooks argues:

the stages of life defined by the law are partly defined by the rights and duties which the stages have to each other. If the concept of stages is accepted, the role of law is not only to set the boundaries of stages, help allocate goods, and express the meanings of the stages, but also to define what the rights and duties of the stages of life are. In the process of fixing these rights and duties, the law further defines the stages themselves and the justice among them. We have seen above that there are profound questions within the law pertaining to the justice between the generations. Insofar as we envisage law as an instrument of justice, we might examine the role of law in promoting or impeding the justice of the allocation of goods among the stages of life.[63]

It is therefore submitted that a strong case can be made for studying the law and older people. While there is a danger that by regarding it as a topic worthy of analysis this may simply perpetuate the myths and assumptions surrounding old age, it need not do that. Older people suffer from prejudice in ageism and the law can quite properly seek to intervene to prevent disadvantages flowing from that. The law can be used to ensure there is recognition of the value of the work and benefits provided by older people.

Structure of the book

This book will examine a variety of issues involving the law and older people. It will draw extensively on the gerontological, philosophical, sociological, and medical literature surrounding the subject. This is because to understand how the law works it must be understood in the context within which it operates. Looking at what the law says will not necessarily tell us what it does. Further, law has a role in communicating values and educating the public.[64] This role can only be understood if the broader social meanings attached to old age are appreciated. I have attempted to avoid too much legal jargon or analysis to make the book as accessible as possible. The book does not purport to present a comprehensive guide to all legal issues relating to older people, but rather discuss the key legal issues facing older people and the theoretical issues surrounding the legal treatment of older people.

Chapter 2 will consider the legal protection offered against age discrimination. It will consider the nature and impact of ageism. Simone de Beauvoir was, no

---

[63] Ibid, at 692.　　[64] M van Hoecke, *Law as Communication* (Hart, 2002).

doubt, exaggerating when she mooted the possibility that everyone had an innate drive to cull older people to make room for the young.[65] But it will be argued that there is a pervasive and insidious ageism throughout society. The chapter will look at the current limited laws on age discrimination and consider whether they need to be extended.

Chapter 3 will consider issues surrounding mental capacity. Of course, for many older people there is no difficulty in establishing legal capacity, but old age can bring with it capacity issues. The chapter will seek to analyse the legal material defining capacity and treatment of those who lack capacity. In particular it will consider whether the interests of those lacking capacity are inadequately protected, even under the new Mental Capacity Act 2005. It will also examine the more difficult issues surrounding those who are on the borderline of lacking capacity.

Chapter 4 will look at the rights and responsibilities of those involved in caring. Many older people are carers and some are cared for, so this is an important issue for this book. The chapter will explain the ways in which the law has ignored the interests of carers and that there is inadequate legal or social recognition for care work. It will consider the range of benefits and other services available for carers and discuss how effective these are. At a broader level the chapter will consider how the law can better recognize care work and respect the values it involves.

There is increasing awareness of the issue of elder abuse. This will be considered in chapter 5. It will consider the different definitions of elder abuse and seek to estimate its extent. An analysis will be undertaken of the current legal approaches to the problem: both through the private law remedies; the response of the criminal law; and the inspection regime for care homes. The chapter will emphasize the lack of a scheme of public law protection of the kind that is available in respect of children who are suffering abuse. The chapter will look at the causes of elder abuse in institutional and private settings. It will also consider the difficult issues that can arise where the older person does not want protective legal intervention.

The financial issues surrounding old age will be examined in chapter 6. This will include how the care of older people is, and should be, funded. The current position with regard to local authorities charging for the care of older people will be examined. The distinction between health and social care, which is at the heart of the current system, will be addressed. One of the main issues in this chapter will be the 'great pension debate'. I will outline the problems with the current pensions system and consider the government's proposals for reform.

In chapter 7, the position of grandparents will be considered. An increasing amount of child care is undertaken by grandparents. Sociological data discussing the role played by grandparents will be examined. The current legal status of grandparents will be summarized and there will be an analysis of the arguments over whether there should be a more formal legal status given to them. Particular

---

[65] S de Beauvoir, *La Vieillesse* (Penguin, 1977).

attention will be paid to the position of grandparents who undertake care of children who otherwise would be taken into care or adopted.

Chapter 8 will undertake a consideration of the health care services offered to the elderly. It will analyse in particular claims that 'age-based rationing' takes place within the NHS and address the debate as to whether age should be a factor in making rationing decisions. The many other ways in which older people suffer ageism in the provision of health care services will be exposed. The chapter will also briefly discuss issues surrounding palliative care.

The ability of people to dispose of their property on their death is an important issue for many older people. Chapter 9 will consider the legal issues surrounding wills. In particular it will look at how property is distributed when an older person has not made a will and how a will may be challenged. It will also examine data on how, in fact, older people view their family obligations in relation to property and what influences their decisions in relation to wills.

Chapter 10 will bring together some of the issues which have run through the book: the difficulty the law has in dealing with older people who are both vulnerable to exploitation and yet so easily treated paternalistically. It will emphasize the importance to many older people of their relationships with their family members and carers. It will suggest that the legal tools of rights, particularly rights of dignity and non-discrimination, are important for many older people. However, for more vulnerable people who are dependent on the care of others, rights can work in too individualistic a way, and a legal system of protection that upholds just, caring relationships is necessary.

Henry Fairlie has written of the state support offered to older people:[66] 'something is wrong with a society that is willing to drain itself to foster such an unproductive section of its population, one that does not even promise (as children do) one day to be productive'.

While rarely put so bluntly, his words reflect a common perception: older people are a waste of space, no more than a drain on society. Deborah Moggach's novel *These Foolish Things*[67] provides a powerful satire of the way older people are treated. In it she imagines the care of British older people being outsourced to Bangalore. A central theme in this book is that older people contribute to society in many rich and complex ways. Be it through provision of child care, caring for those unable to look after themselves, volunteering time or donating money to charities, or simply being a source of wisdom and knowledge, their role is invaluable. We need to find ways of treasuring old age. It need not be a 'hideous inverted childhood' as Philip Larkin so memorably called it.[68] But that depends on us all changing our attitudes towards old age.

---

[66] Quoted by R Butler, 'Dispelling Ageism: The Cross Cutting Intervention' (1989) 141 *Annals of the American Academy of Political and Social Science* 503, at 503.

[67] D Moggach, *These Foolish Things* (Chatto and Windus, 2004).

[68] P Larkin, 'The Old Fools' in *High Windows* (Faber and Faber, 1974).

2

Ageism and Age Discrimination

Introduction

This chapter will consider two interrelated themes: ageism and age discrimination.[1] The terms are sometimes used interchangeably, but there are some points of difference.[2] Ageism refers to the untrue assumptions and beliefs that are held about people based on their age.[3] It has been defined in the following way:

Ageism can be seen as a process of systematic stereotyping of and discrimination against people because they are old, just as racism and sexism accomplish this for skin colour and gender. Old people are categorized as senile, rigid in thought and manner, old-fashioned in morality and skills...Ageism allows the younger generations to see older people as different from themselves, thus they subtly cease to identify with their elders as human beings.[4]

Age discrimination relates to behaviour in which a person is disadvantaged as a result of their age.[5]

This distinction, then, is between ageism, which is a feeling or belief, and age discrimination, which involves behaviour or treatment. The two concepts do not necessarily correlate. For example, a person may have ageist attitudes, but be careful to ensure they never exhibit these in the way they treat people. In such a case a person would be ageist, but not engaging in age discrimination. Of course, most commonly the two interrelate: because of a person's ageist attitudes they discriminate against an older person.

The significance of the distinction between ageism and age discrimination might be thought particularly important for lawyers. While the law cannot seek to prevent people having prejudicial attitudes; the law can prevent people

---

[1] For a history of age discrimination, see J Macnicol, *Age Discrimination* (Cambridge University Press, 2006).

[2] There are similar distinctions between sexism and sex discrimination and racism and race discrimination.

[3] See further the discussion in B Bytheway and J Johnson, 'On Defining Ageism' (1990) 10 *Critical Social Policy* 27. The term 'ageism' appears first to have been used in R Butler, 'Age-Ism: Another Form of Bigotry' (1969) 9 *The Gerentologist* 243.

[4] R Butler, *Why Survive? Being Old in America* (Harper and Row, 1975), at 35.

[5] J Feagin and K McKinney, *The Many Costs of Racism* (Rowman and Littlefield, 2003).

implementing these in a way that disadvantages others. What goes on inside a person's head cannot be controlled by the law; how they act can be. This distinction, while of some significance, should not be overemphasized. First, the distinction between the two is not watertight. The legal response to a discriminatory act may vary dependent on the motivation behind it. For example, under the criminal law an attack motivated by racism is treated as different and more serious than a similar attack not so motivated.[6] In employment law where the discriminatory act is motivated by racism or sexism, that will be relevant in the sanction imposed.[7] Secondly, if the state wishes to combat disadvantage associated with age, seeking simply to combat age discrimination may be insufficient if ageist beliefs still persist. Even if the law may have less control over a person's behaviour than their beliefs, the law through its messages and the state through education can affect societal attitudes and individual beliefs.

Age discrimination and ageism affects both the young and the old. Younger people undoubtedly suffer from assumptions made about them based on their youth and indeed middle-aged people may likewise find negative attitudes expressed towards their age group.[8] The focus of this chapter will, however, be on how ageism and age discrimination impacts on older people. That said, ageist attitudes towards older people are to some extent interconnected with such attitudes towards younger people.

Ageism

Ageism permeates society.[9] A government review accepted that there were 'deep-rooted cultural attitudes to ageing' that were hampering the government plans to improve health and social care to older people.[10] As with racism and sexism, the most deep-seated beliefs are the hardest to detect.[11] Even a person seeking to avoid having ageist attitudes will find it hard to eliminate them. Steve Scrutton writes:

Ageism surrounds us, but it passes largely unnoticed and unchallenged. Moreover, just like racism and sexism, it is so engrained within the structure of social life that it is

---

[6] See the discussion of racially motivated offences in J Herring, *Criminal Law: Text, Cases and Materials* (Oxford University Press, 2008), at 345–7.

[7] See the discussion in N Bamforth, M Malik, and C O'Cinneide, *Discrimination Law: Theory and Context* (Sweet & Maxwell, 2008), at 1247–9.

[8] I have written about younger people and discrimination in J Herring, 'Children's Rights for Grown-Ups' in S Fredman and S Spencer, *Age as an Equality Issue* (Hart, 2004).

[9] J Thornton, 'Myths of Aging or Ageist Stereotypes' (2002) 28 *Educational Gerontology* 301.

[10] Department for Communities and Local Government, *Discrimination Law Review* (The Stationery Office, 2007), para 9.12.

[11] A Cuddy, M Norton, and S Fiske, 'This Old Stereotype: The Pervasiveness and Persistence of the Elderly Stereotype' (2005) 61 *Journal of Social Issues* 267.

unlikely to be challenged effectively by rational argument or appeal to the more philan-
thropic side of human nature.[12]

A good example of unconscious ageism was the 2001 census questionnaire, which
was based on the assumptions that those over 75: did not work (whether paid or
unpaid); had no interesting or valuable educational achievements; and did not
use any kind of transport.[13] This questionnaire must have passed the desk of
countless civil servants and been subject to the most careful scrutiny and yet the
blatant ageism revealed appears to have passed unnoticed.

It is, perhaps, as often with discrimination, fear that leads to prejudice. The
fear of being old creates distaste for the status and a clear demarcation of 'them'
from 'us'.[14] As Mark Novak writes:

we fear powerlessness, weakness, dependence, ignorance, infirmity, illness, ridicule. To
the extent we identify these fears with ageing, we fear old age. But none of these fears is
of old age itself.[15]

The impact of ageism lies not just in the disadvantage suffered by older people
when they are treated in a disadvantageous way. Fear of meeting ageist attitudes
can affect the way older people behave and what they do. It also affects older
people's attitudes about themselves. It may inhibit older people from doing things
they would otherwise want to do.

A survey for Age Concern found among the general public a popular perception of an older person as doddery, but 'a dear';[16] contrasting with young people who were seen as competent, but cold.[17] The survey suggested that 28 per cent
of those older people questioned had experienced ageism in the past year, although
this tended to be 'benevolent prejudice' (for example, assuming that an older person needed help and could not understand) rather than open hostility.[18] Hence
we find 'humorous' birthday cards, referring in a derogatory way to old age, often
with sexual innuendos.[19]

Indeed, ageist attitudes can reflect a mixture of both positive and negative
assumptions about older people,[20] both of which can in some contexts have
unwanted consequences. When searching for photographs that might appear on
the cover of this book, it was easy to find images of older people as frail and

[12] S Scrutten, 'Ageism: The Foundation of Age Discrimination' in E McEwen (ed), *Age: The
Unrecognised Discrimination* (Age Concern, 1990).
[13] B Groombridge, 'Older People: Varieties of Citizenship' (2005) 5 *Age Today* 3, at 4.
[14] J Macnicol, *Age Discrimination* (Cambridge University Press, 2006), at 9.
[15] M Novak, 'Thinking about Ageing' (1979) 8 *Age and Ageing* 209. For an argument that it
is fear of death which motivates ageism, see: J Greenberg, J Schimel, and A Martens, 'Ageism:
Denying the Fact of the Future' in T Nelson (ed), *Ageism* (MIT Press, 2004).
[16] A Cuddy and S Fiske, 'Doddering but Dear: Process, Content and Function in Stereotyping
of Older Persons' in T Nelson (ed), *Ageism* (MIT Press, 2004).
[17] S Ray and E Sharp, *Ageism* (Age Concern, 2006).   [18] Ibid.
[19] J Macnicol, *Age Discrimination* (Cambridge University Press, 2006), at 13.
[20] D Bugental and J Hehman, 'Ageism: A Review of Research and Policy Implications' (2007) 1
Social Issues and Policy Review 173.

vulnerable, or as being ultra-active and healthy, engaging in activities such as surfing. There were very few images of older people engaging in normal activities.[21] The images of super-active older people, while a positive counterbalance to the frail images, can in fact reinforce ageism by implying that the best old people are like young people!

Social disadvantage among older people

It is common to illustrate ageism within our society by referring to studies revealing the plight of older people, such as:

- One in five older people in the UK lives below the poverty line.[22] Fifteen per cent of pensioners are in persistent poverty.[23]

- One in six of over-65s report feeling lonely often or all of the time[24] and 30 per cent are not happy with their quality of life.[25] One million older people spent Christmas Day alone in 2004.[26]

- In the winter of 2006/07, there were an estimated 25,393 excess winter deaths of people aged 65 and over in the UK. About 93 per cent of winter deaths are of people aged 65 and over. Every five hours an older person dies as a result of an accidental fall in the home.[27]

- Four out of ten older people admitted to hospital are malnourished; six out of ten older people in hospital remain malnourished or become more malnourished while in hospital.[28]

- Research for the Social Exclusion Unit found that 7 per cent of older people were excluded on three or more indicators and a further 13 per cent of older people are excluded on two indicators.[29] Fifty-nine per cent of older people suffer some form of social exclusion.[30]

- There is a woeful lack of provision of public toilets, an issue which particularly affects older people. Seventy-four per cent of older people in one survey complained of a shortage of public facilities.[31]

- Fashion is geared to a younger market. Seventy per cent of those questioned in one survey agreed that older people who try to dress young are seen as a

---

[21] See also J Habrison and M Morrow, 'Re-examining the Social Construction of Elder Abuse and Neglect' (1998) 18 *Ageing and Society* 691.

[22] Help the Aged, *Older People in the UK* (Help the Aged, 2008).　　　[23] Ibid.

[24] H McCarthy and G Thomas, *Home Alone* (Demos, 2004).

[25] Help the Aged, *Older People in the UK* (Help the Aged, 2008).　　　[26] Ibid.

[27] Ibid.　　　[28] Age Concern, *Hungry to be Heard* (Age Concern, 2006).

[29] Office of the Deputy Prime Minister, *A Sure Start to Later Life: Ending Inequalities for Older People* (The Stationery Office, 2006), at 19.

[30] Office of the Deputy Prime Minister, *A Sure Start to Later Life: Ending Inequalities for Older People* (The Stationery Office, 2006).

[31] Research on Age Discrimination, *Older People's Accounts of Discrimination, Exclusion and Rejection* (Help the Aged, 2007).

joke.[32] The choice of clothes and hair style which one needs to adopt if one is not to be abused as 'mutton dressed as lamb' is very limited.

- Sixty-five per cent of older people agreed that local communities neglect older people who become socially isolated.[33]
- Fifty-nine per cent of older people suffer some form of social exclusion.[34]
- Seventy-two per cent of single people and 25 per cent of couples over the age of 65 do not have a car.[35]

However, the presentation of statistics such as these, while extremely important, carries dangers. It can lead to a perception that older people are a vulnerable group who represent a 'particular problem'. Hence it is common to find expressions of anxiety at the changing age demographic.[36] Even the European Central Bank has issued statements of 'grave concern' about the increasing numbers of older people.[37] The Commission for Healthcare Audit Report stated: 'An ageing population puts pressure on health and social care services, but it also places demands on other services such as transport, leisure, and housing.'[38] True, but the same could be said about the increasing number of law professors!

So a key point to emphasize is that despite their bad press, older people play an invaluable role in our society.[39] Consider these statistics:

- The contribution of older people as carers of children is significant. One in five children under 16 are looked after by grandparents during the day-time.[40] A third of grandparents spend the equivalent of three days a week caring for their grandchildren.[41] Age Concern estimates the value of this unpaid care to be over £500 million in London alone.[42]
- Older people are great consumers. Over 50s buy 80 per cent of all top-of-the-range cars, 50 per cent of skincare products, and 80 per cent of leisure cruises. Over the last two decades, consumption by Europe's over 50s has risen three times as fast as that of the rest of the population.[43]

---

[32] Ibid.   [33] Ibid.
[34] Office of the Deputy Prime Minister, *A Sure Start to Later Life: Ending Inequalities for Older People* (The Stationery Office, 2006).   [35] Ibid.
[36] BBC News Online, 'If... The Generations Fall Out', 26 Feb 2004. See F Shaw, 'Is the Ageing Population the Problem it is Made Out to Be?' (2002) 4 *Foresight* 4.
[37] J González-Páramo, 'The Ageing Problem: The ECB's views', speech at European Central Bank (2006), availiable at <http://www.ecb.eu/press/key/date/2006/html/sp061201_1.en.html>.
[38] Commission for Healthcare Audit and Inspection, *Living Well in Later Life* (Commission for Healthcare Audit and Inspection, 2006).
[39] F Shaw, 'Is the Ageing Population the Problem it is Made Out to Be?' (2002) 4 *Foresight* 4.
[40] G Dench and J Ogg, *Grandparenting in Britain: A Baseline Study* (Institute of Community Studies, 2002).
[41] J Stogdon, 'Grandparenting: The Facts' (2005) 5 *Age Today* 18, at 18.
[42] BBC News Online, 'Ageing population: facts behind the fiction', 2 March 2004.
[43] Ibid.

- The contribution of older people as carers of adults is significant. Between one-and-a-half and two million of the 5.7 million carers in the UK are over 60 and one-fifth are 75 or over.[44]

- Older people also play an important role in community life. They provide 46 per cent of all informal volunteering, despite making up 18 per cent of the population.[45] Two-thirds of the over 50s have participated in at least one civil activity in the past year. Nearly 89 per cent of older people voted at the last election. Older people are four times as likely to vote as younger people.[46]

- Older people are more generous than any other age group in giving to charities. One-third of households headed by someone aged 70 or older gave to charity. By contrast, only 18 per cent of households headed by someone in their 20s gave to charity.[47] Not only do a greater number of older people give, they give more.

- On top of all of these points, there is the contribution of older people that cannot readily be presented in some statistical form. They provide the base of memory and the cultural fabric of so many communities.[48]

The notion that older people are simply a 'drain' on society, using up precious resources and offering little back must, therefore, be firmly rejected.[49] Tony Blair has said:

An ageing society is too often—and wrongly—seen solely in terms of increasing dependency. But the reality is that, as older people become an ever more significant proportion of the population, society will increasingly depend upon the contribution they can make.[50]

It would be wrong to see the benefits that older people can offer purely in terms of tangible gains. Queen Elizabeth II referred to some of the less concrete benefits that can be offered by older people:

As older people remain more active for longer, the opportunities to look for new ways to bring young and old together are multiplying... [T]he older generation are able to give a sense of context, as well as the wisdom of experience which can be invaluable. Such advice and comfort are probably needed more often than younger people admit or older people recognise.[51]

So, while it is important to discuss the disadvantages suffered by older people and it is right to bemoan and decry the poverty, lack of appropriate care, and

---

[44] S Fredman, 'The Age of Equality' in S Fredman and S Spencer (eds), *Age as an Equality Issue* (Hart, 2003), at 30.
[45] R White and C Williams, 'Volunteering' (2005) 5 *Age Today* 10.   [46] Ibid.
[47] Help the Aged, *Facts and Figures* (Help the Aged, 2006).
[48] Mayor of London, *Valuing Older People* (Greater London Authority, 2006).
[49] J Macnicol, *Age Discrimination* (Cambridge University Press, 2006), at 12.
[50] HM Government, *Opportunity Age* (The Stationery Office, 2005), at iv.
[51] HRH The Queen, *The Queen's Christmas Broadcast 2006*, available on BBC News Online, 25 December 2006, 'The Queen's Speech in Full'.

levels of abuse suffered by older people as a result of ageism, there is a danger in painting a picture of older people as needy, which can itself perpetuate ageist attitudes about them.

Some of the specific manifestations of ageism will now be considered.

The glorification of youth

One of the most pervasive forms of ageism is the association of beauty and good health with youth. From advertisements to film, from 'beauty products' to modelling, it is youthful beauty which is seen as the ideal and products designed to remove signs of ageing are multi-million-pound businesses.[52] A survey of the British public suggests that old age carries negative associations, particularly with its impact on health and appearance.[53] Few people greet the finding of their first wrinkle or grey hair with anything other than dismay. There is much pressure on people to 'age well' and that is understood to mean that they should maintain as youthful an appearance as possible. We are constantly encouraged to transcend our real age and avoid the appearance of the lifestyle of the old.[54] That is a costly and painful procedure for many.

Despite the popular perception, sociologists have found that old age tends to bring with it an increase in well-being.[55] Many psychologists have sought to explain this in terms of older people having better coping mechanisms than younger people, rather than seeing any positives in old age.[56] That explanation is itself revealing because it assumes that old age brings with it negatives. Interestingly, the popular perception of middle age as being the prime of life is not reflected by many studies, finding those aged around 40 as being at the bottom of a U shaped curve of assessments of well-being.[57]

Language

Researchers in the field have noted how reluctant people are to describe themselves as old.[58] It is also noticeable that although our society has developed a

---

[52] T Calasanti, 'Bodacious Berry, Potency Wood and the Aging Monster: Gender and Age Relations in Anti-Aging Ads' (2007) 86 *Social Forces* 335.

[53] J Scott and J Nolan, *Ageing Positive? Not According to the British Public* (GeNet, 2006).

[54] M Andrews, 'The Seductiveness of Agelessness' (1999) 19 *Ageing and Society* 301.

[55] C Ryff, B Singer, and G Love, 'Positive Health: Connecting Well-being with Biology' (2004) 259 *Philosophical Transactions, Royal Society* 1383.

[56] E Diener and E Suh, 'Subjective Well-Being and Age: An International Perspective' (1997) 17 *Annual Review of Gerontology and Geriatrics* 304. For positive views on old age, see P Laslett, *A Fresh Map of Life* (Macmillan, 1989). But see also S Arber and M Evandrou, *Ageing, Independence and the Life Course* (Jessica Kingsley, 1993), who emphasize how gender and ethnicity can affect the experience of age.

[57] D Blanchflower and A Oswald, 'Well-Being over time in Britain and the USA' (2004) 88 *Journal of Public Economics* 1356.

[58] C Degnen, 'Minding the Gap: The Construction of Old Age and Oldness Amongst Peers' (2007) 21 *Journal of Aging Studies* 69.

range of terms to separate categories of childhood: babies, toddlers, terrible twos, tweenagers, teenagers, etc; in the case of older people they are all lumped into the one category: the old.[59]

Other examples of ageist language abound. The use of the adjective 'old' to describe something or someone useless or feeble ('silly old me') and phrases such as 'mutton dressed as lamb' carry derogatory connotations and often reflect ageist assumptions.[60] So too does the common practice of putting failings (such as momentary forgetfulness) down to old age.[61] Jokes based on age are regarded as acceptable in a way that jokes based on race or sex would not be.[62] If you were to look up jokes on the internet, anti-old people jokes are nearly, but not quite, as common as anti-lawyer jokes; but far more prevalent than racist jokes, for example. Perhaps even more concerning than this is the way older people are talked to.[63] Studies have found that language used by shop-workers, co-workers and service personnel all reveal a form of speech which is demeaning or belittling.[64] Particularly noticeable is the language used in the context of care settings, where child-like language and even 'baby talk' is used.[65] This not only demeans their dignity, but can affect how older people perceive themselves. One survey of older people found 68 per cent agreeing that once you reach a certain age people treat you as a child.[66]

Media representation of old age

Stories in the media concerning older people nearly always portray them as frail or burdensome: a horrific attack on a helpless pensioner, the latest outcry over fuel allowances, or the 'NHS at the point of meltdown' due to the number of older people.[67] Looking at the world of advertising, rarely do older people feature. Where they do, the advertisements focus on immobility, fear of crime and vulnerability, or illness rather than the many more positive associations with old age that could be drawn.[68] Outrage greeted an advert by the betting company

---

[59] Ibid.

[60] J Nussbaum, M Pitts, F Huber, J Raup Krieger, and J Ohs, 'Ageism and Ageist Language Across the Life Span: Intimate Relationships and Non-Intimate Interactions' (2005) 61 *Journal of Social Issues* 287.

[61] J Macnicol, *Age Discrimination* (Cambridge University Press, 2006), at 11.

[62] E Palmore, 'Three Decades of Research on Ageism' (2005) 29 *Generations* 87.

[63] M Hummert and E Ryan, 'Toward Understanding Variations in Patronizing Talk Addressed to Older Adults: Psycholinguistic Features of Care and Control' (1996) 12 *International Journal of Psycholinguistics* 149.

[64] D Bugental and J Hehman, 'Ageism: A Review of Research and Policy Implications' (2007) 1 *Social Issues and Policy Review* 173.

[65] S Kemper, M Othick, J Warren, J Gubarchuk, and H Gerhing, 'Facilitating Older Adults: Performance on a Referential Communication Task through Speech Accommodations' (1996) 3 *Aging, Neuropsychology, and Cognition* 27.

[66] Research on Age Discrimination, *Older People's Accounts of Discrimination, Exclusion and Rejection* (Help the Aged, 2007).

[67] L Kotlikoff, *The Coming Generational Storm* (MIT Press, 2004).

[68] L Aitken and G Griffin, *Gender Issues in Elder Abuse* (Sage, 1996), at 55.

Paddy Power, which involved a picture of two older women crossing a road with a fast approaching car and odds printed under the women, presumably indicating the likelihood they would be hit.[69] The advert was clearly intended to be humorous, but it merely reflected the prejudices that older people are slow, unobservant, and dispensable. Another is the road sign which depicts two older people hunched and with a walking stick and is intended to warn that there are 'elderly people' about.[70]

Overt discrimination in public services

Examples of age discrimination in the provision of public services and legislation abound, often unquestioned. The Commission for Healthcare Audit and Inspection in their report, *Living Well in Later Life*, stated that there is 'evidence of ageism across all [public] services' relating to older people.[71] Even overt forms of discrimination go unchallenged, such as the fact that jurors and magistrates are not allowed to serve after the age of 70.[72] It was not until the Employment Equality (Age) Regulations 2006[73] came into force on 1 October 2006 that ageism at work has been challenged. It is remarkable that it has taken so long for this arena of discrimination to be combated, and this in part reflects the fact that so many ageist attitudes are assumed to be common sense.

Social separation and older people

There are many forces in society that separate out spaces and activities as suitable or unsuitable for a person based on age.[74] Many people can remember occasions when they entered a place and felt they were the wrong age to be there. An older person entering a night club may well be viewed with suspicion and distrust. Indeed, outside the context of families there is a sharp divide based on age.[75] Old age has been described as a separate country.[76] This metaphor is used to capture the territorial, cultural, and institutional separateness of older people.[77] Older

---

[69] Age Concern, *How Ageist is Britain?* (Age Concern, 2006), at 2.
[70] Charities Aid Foundation, *Age Concern Worried Over Road Signs* (Charities Aid Foundation, 2008).
[71] Commission for Healthcare Audit and Inspection, *Living Well in Later Life* (Commission for Healthcare Audit and Inspection, 2006).
[72] S Ray and E Sharp, *Ageism* (Age Concern, 2006).   [73] SI 2006/1031.
[74] T Nelson, 'Ageism: Prejudice Against Our Feared Future Self' (2005) 61 *Journal of Social Issues* 207.
[75] G Hagestad and P Uhlenberg, 'The Social Separation of Old and Young: A Root of Ageism' (2005) 61 *Journal of Social Issues* 343.
[76] M Pipher, *Another Country: Navigating the Emotional Terrain of our Elders* (Riverhead Books, 1999).
[77] G Hagestad and P Uhlenberg, 'The Social Separation of Old and Young: A Root of Ageism' (2005) 61 *Journal of Social Issues* 343.

people are excluded from many schools and workplaces where young and middle-aged people spend their time.

One highly active older woman, Margaret Simey, described her 90th birthday party in vivid terms:

My eyes were opened when kind but misguided well-wishers organised a surprise birthday party for me when I reached the age of ninety. Until then, I had been as active as any of them, deeply involved in voluntary work, committee meetings, consultations. Suddenly it occurred to them, that I was old. The transformation was stunning. I was no longer one of them. I was an outsider. I seemed to be in a foreign country. I didn't speak the language. I didn't know the rules. I was no longer me, Margaret, very defiantly my own person. Now I was simply one of a mass of clones, a stereotype, a number, not an individual. I was old and that was all that needed to be said.[78]

The intersection of age, race, and sex

It is crucial when discussing ageism to consider it in the context of sex and race[79] and indeed other forms of power within society,[80] such as discrimination on the basis of sexual orientation[81] or disability.[82] Ageist assumptions and practices intersect with, and build upon, racist and sexist assumptions.[83] We have already mentioned the issue of ageist attitudes towards bodies and beauty. The assumptions and impact of age will depend, in part, on your race and sex.[84] It is often reported, for example, that a woman's attractiveness is judged against an extremely youthful ideal.[85] While men are commonly said to be attractive even while showing signs of ageing, a woman's attractiveness requires removal of visible signs of ageing. Given the sales of 'anti-ageing' products this appears to be a belief that is widely held. Further, the difference in reaction when an older man dates a younger woman and when an older woman dates a younger man is remarkable.[86]

---

[78] M Simey, 'A Personal View' (2002) *Age Today* 1, at 5.
[79] A Walker and S Northmore (eds), *Growing Older in a Black and Minority Ethnic Group* (Age Concern, 2006).
[80] R Ward and B Bytheway, *Researching Age and Multiple Discrimination* (Central Books, 2008).
[81] D Kimmel, T Rose, and S David, *Lesbian, Gay, Bisexual, and Transgender Aging* (Columbia University Press, 2006); and B Heaphy, A Yip, and D Thompson, 'Ageing in a Non-Heterosexual Context' (2004) 24 *Ageing and Society* 881.
[82] M Sargenat, 'Disability and Age—Multiple Potential for Discrimination' (2005) 33 *International Journal of the Sociology of Law* 17.
[83] J Squire, 'Intersecting Inequalities: Reflecting on the Subjects and Objects of Equality' (2008) 79 *Political Quarterly* 53.
[84] H Walker, D Grant, M Meadows, and I Cook, 'Women's Experiences and Perceptions of Age Discrimination in Employment: Implications for Research and Policy' (2007) 6 *Social Policy and Society* 37.
[85] S Sontag, 'The Double Standard of Ageing' in V Carver and P Liddiard, *An Ageing Population* (Open University Press, 1978).
[86] D Fernand, 'Women Who Date Younger Men', *Sunday Times*, 18 May 2008.

Lynda Aitken and Gabriele Griffin write of attitudes towards older women:

They have outlived their status as sex objects and their usefulness as childbearers, and are to some extent freer from direct male control than younger women in whom males still have vested interests. One might argue that the patronizing attitudes frequently displayed towards older women are one means of social control of these women's behaviour, exerted because they have this greater degree of freedom.[87]

Those interested in issues of race, sex, and the law should therefore also be interested in the issues raised by age. Among the over 50s there are 100 women for every 85 men. Poverty and disadvantage among older people therefore especially impacts on women.

Thinking further about ageism

Having demonstrated some of the more obvious manifestations of ageism, it is worth pondering the concept further. Consider, for example, the assumption that older people are a burden on society because they need looking after. This assumption carries a number of prejudicial attitudes. First, already mentioned, is the assumption that simply because a person is old they will be dependent on others. As we have seen, that is a gross generalisation—indeed, plenty of older people are in good health and older people are net providers of care.[88] The second assumption is that needing care and being dependent on others is something that is undesirable and a 'burden on society'. Individualism and self-responsibility are often elevated to a high place within our society, but that should be questioned.[89] As this point shows, ageist attitudes can affect not only beliefs about older people, but also more broadly, questions about what makes a life valuable, or what are the norms of life.[90]

Another issue requiring further thought is whether there is anything to be gained from using concepts of age. There are some who see the use of age characterizations as important in a cultural way. The 18th birthday, for example, marks the entry into adulthood. Although essentially an arbitrary date, it has cultural significance and marks an acceptance into the world of adults.[91] Without it people would need to prove they deserved to be regarded as adults. Age progression also gives a shape to an individual's life as they see themselves advancing

---

[87] L Aitken and G Griffin, *Gender Issues in Elder Abuse* (Sage, 1996), at 63.

[88] J Angus and P Reeve, 'Ageism: A Threat to "Aging Well" in the 21st Century' (2006) 25 *Journal of Applied Gerontology* 137.

[89] L Tornstam, 'The Quo Vadis of Gerontology: On the Scientific Paradigm of Gerontology' (1992) 32 *The Gerontologist* 318. See further the discussion in ch 4.

[90] Of course, one can also make the case that even younger and middle-aged people are dependent on others: J Herring 'Children's Rights for Grown-Ups' in S Fredman and S Spencer, *Age as an Equality Issue* (Hart, 2004).

[91] B Bytheway, 'Ageism and Age Categorization' (2005) 61 *Journal of Social Issues* 361.

through the stages of life. Of course, the difficulty is that these stages and the social expectations that go with them can be controlling and degrading to many, even if liberating to some.[92] Richard Brooks[93] argues that it is better to see the self not as a set of timeless desires, but a character subjected to the stages in life. These life stages are commemorated and form the milestones of life. They provide a structure around which we can write our life stories and can be important to a sense of self-fulfillment. Of course it may be that our life story involves rebelling against the stage of life we are meant to be at. Nevertheless, the different stages of life play an important part in our social and personal journeys. The law should therefore properly acknowledge their importance.

This more positive picture of ageing can be contrasted with the calls of those who seek to promote 'agelessness'. A leading book by Bill Bytheway has a chapter entitled 'No more "elderly", no more old age.'[94] He argues that old age is 'a cultural concept, a construction that has a certain popular utility in sustaining ageism within societies that need scapegoats.'[95] It should, therefore, be eliminated as a conceptual category.[96] In response to such arguments, Molly Andrews[97] is concerned that agelessness would deprive older people of one of the 'hard earned resources: their age'. Betty Friedan has written:

How long, and how well, can we really live by trying to pass as young? By the fourth face-lift (or third?) we begin to look grotesque, no longer human. Obsessed with stopping age, passing as young…Seeing age only as decline from youth, we make age itself the problem and never face the real problems that keep us from evolving and leading continually useful, vital, and productive lives. Accepting that dire mystique of age for others, even as we deny it for ourselves, we ultimately create or reinforce the conditions of our own dependence, powerlessness, isolation, even senility.[98]

Molly Andrews argues that old age should be regarded as like any other stage of life. It has real challenges and difficulties which should be acknowledged. However, it carries benefits too and these would be lost if the 'agelessness' model were lost. Old age should not be regarded as the absence of youth, but rather as she sees it 'the project of a lifetime'.

---

[92] H Giles and S Reid, 'Ageism Across the Lifespan: Towards a Self-Categorization Model of Ageing' (2005) 61 *Journal of Social Issues* 389.

[93] R Brooks, 'The Refurbishing: Reflections upon Law and Justice Among the Stages of Life' (2006) 54 *Buffalo Law Review* 619.

[94] B Bytheway, *Ageism* (Open University Press, 1995).

[95] J Breda and D Schoenmaekers, 'Age: A Dubious Criterion in Legislation' (2006) 26 *Ageing and Society* 529, concluding that policy makers should consider the systematic replacement of age thresholds by other criteria.

[96] Similar arguments have been made about sex and race, with claims being made that these are merely artificial constructions. See, eg P-L Chau and J Herring, 'Defining, Assigning and Designing Sex' (2002) 16 *International Journal of Law Policy and the Family* 327.

[97] M Andrews, 'The Seductiveness of Agelessness' (1999) 19 *Ageing and Society* 301.

[98] B Friedan, *The Fountain of Age* (Jonathan Cape, 1993), at 25–6.

Toni Calasanti and Kathleen Slevin write:

Age categories have real consequences, and bodies—old bodies—matter. They have a material reality along with their social interpretation. Old people are not, in fact, just like middle-aged persons but only older. They are different. And as is the case with other forms of oppression, we must acknowledge and accept these differences, even see them as valuable.[99]

The argument is that although there are prejudices about old age and unfair assumptions are made, that should not be used to disguise the fact that for most people old age is different from other stages in life. These differences must be recognized and treasured.

There is another concern about promotion of an ageless society: that it will mean that older people will not receive the positive assistance from the state, which many of them need. As John Macnicol[100] remarked:

The controversial ideal of an 'ageless' society has as its obverse the implication that the protective walls that have hitherto shielded older people, notably via state pension systems, should be demolished. If that happens, the achievement of an 'ageless' society may not be in the best interests of older people.[101]

While moving towards an ageless society would carry benefits, it is argued that we would lose more. We would lose recognition of the benefits and importance of old age. It should be a time to be treasured and revered, not treated as being no different from any other stage of life.

Analogies between ageism and sexism or racism

It is tempting to draw analogies between ageism and racism or sexism. Indeed, I have already done so several times in this chapter. We could replicate legislation on sex or race discrimination when seeking to combat age discrimination. However, the analogy is by no means exact.[102] A full analysis of their similarities and differences would take much more space than is available. However, some distinctions are clear. First, although it is unlikely that a person will experience life in a different sex or race from that they currently live in, with old age it is extremely likely that a younger person will experience old age. This means that the 'them and us' attitude which is often a hallmark of sex and race discrimination is not present. This should mean that age discrimination law should be easier to enact and be less controversial. Self-interest can be used to generate support for the law: 'You will be glad for age discrimination laws when you are older.' Further, the fact that

---

[99] T Calasanti and K Slevin, *Age Matters* (Routledge, 2006), at 3.
[100] J Macnicol, 'The Age Discrimination Debate in Britain: From the 1930s to the Present' (2005) 4 *Social Policy and Society* 295, at 301.   [101] Ibid.
[102] R Reaves, 'One of These Things is Not Like the Other: Analogizing Ageism to Racism in Employment Discrimimination' (2007) 38 *University of Richmond Law Review* 839.

nearly everyone will be old at some point is regarded as extremely important by those who argue that as virtually everyone will experience youth, middle age, and old age, there is no reason for complaint if younger people are treated in a more or less favourable way than older people. This is because everyone will enjoy the advantages or disadvantages that go with different ages at some point. We shall be considering the strength of such a claim later, but it is not an argument that has a parallel in race or sex discrimination.

Molly Andrews has a slightly different point. She argues that ageism is promoted by an element of self-hatred or fear of what one may become; whereas racism or sexism is based on fear or hatred of the other.[103] She quotes from Simone de Beauvoir who writes on the basis of ageism:

When we look at the image of our own future provided by the old we do not believe it: an absurd inner voice whispers that *that* will never happen to us: when *that* happens it will no longer be ourselves that it happens to.

We must stop cheating: the whole meaning of our life is in question in the future that is waiting for us. If we do not know what we are going to be, we cannot know what we are: let us recognize ourselves in this old man or in that old woman. It must be done if we are to take upon ourselves the entirety of our human state.[104]

Another distinction is that the classification of groups for age discrimination is particularly difficult. There are, of course, no hard and fast boundaries between sexes[105] or racial groups. But the problems of classification are particularly acute in relation to age. Fredman states that workers as young as 35 have been classified as 'older workers'.[106] Further, the question of which age group exercises power over the others is a more complex one than it is in relation to race or sex. It has been suggested that there is not demonstrable and undoubted unfairness to older people of the kind that exists for women or racial minorities.[107]

Thirdly, the notion of age discrimination is broad. All ages can suffer prejudice as a result of their age: children are presumed to be incompetent and immature; young adults are deemed to be unreliable and unwise; middle-aged people are thought of as boring and incapable of taking on new ideas; and the old are thought of as being physical and mentally frail. It may, therefore, be more appropriate not to use the term 'age discrimination' and rather distinguish between discrimination against the young; discrimination against the older; and (maybe) discrimination against the middle aged.[108]

---

[103] M Andrews, 'The Seductiveness of Agelessness' (1999) 19 *Ageing and Society* 301.

[104] S de Beauvoir, *Old Age* (Penguin, 1970), at 11–12.

[105] P-L Chau and J Herring, 'Defining, Assigning and Designing Sex' (2002) 16 *International Journal of Law Policy and the Family* 327.

[106] S Fredman, 'The Age of Equality' in S Fredman and S Spencer (eds), *Age as an Equality Issue* (Hart, 2003), at 61.

[107] See *Massachusetts Board of Retirement v Murgia* 427 US 307 (1976).

[108] This argument will chime with debates that racism may impact on particular ethnic groups in different ways.

Fourthly, while it is now generally accepted that it is never, or hardly ever, appropriate to discriminate on the basis of sex or race, this is less well accepted in relation to age. It is still common to hear arguments that restrictions on the right to work beyond a certain age are necessary to ensure there are sufficient jobs for younger workers.[109] We shall be looking at this issue further shortly, but it is noticeable that the legislation governing age discrimination openly accepts the possibility of justifying the discrimination, to an extent not recognized in race or sex discrimination.

Age discrimination

Defining discrimination

As part of the drive of many liberal societies to produce greater levels of equality, laws prohibiting discrimination have been enacted.[110] These prohibit, in certain circumstances, the detrimental treatment of individuals on the basis of a specified characteristic such as their status, group membership, or physical characteristic. Of course, as John Gardner has pointed out, it is generally a good characteristic to be a discriminating person.[111] What discrimination law is seeking to outlaw is the *improper* use of characteristics or group membership as a factor in making public decisions. Anti-discrimination law is seeking to ensure that the reasons used in making such decisions are acceptable ones and do not lead to disadvantage on the basis of the prohibited characteristic.

At the heart of discrimination is the notion of equality. Yet despite the fact that equality is widely regarded as central to notions of human rights, it is an illusive notion. Thomas Jefferson famously declared:

We hold these truths to be sacred and undeniable, that all men are created equal and independent, that from that equal creation they derive rights inherent and inalienable, among which are the preservation of life, and liberty, and the pursuit of happiness.[112]

Yet putting such a simple concept into practice is problematic.

At its most simple, to discriminate against a person is to treat them improperly as not equal to someone else. So far so good; and that much will be agreed by most people. However, soon the disagreements appear. First, there is the issue of how we decide which cases should be treated alike. Indeed, many of the most vile regimes and discriminatory practices have been premised on the assumption that

---

[109] Even the Lord Chancellor tried to raise this argument in an unsuccessful defence against a claim of age discrimination: *Hampton v Lord Chancellor* ET/2300835/2007.

[110] H Meenan, 'The Future of Ageing and the Role of Age Discrimination in the Global Debate' [2005] *The Journal of International Aging, Law and Policy* 1.

[111] J Gardner, 'On the Ground of Her Sex(uality)' (1998) 18 *Oxford Journal of Legal Studies* 167.

[112] T Jefferson, from the 'original rough draft' of the *United States Declaration of Independence* (1776).

a class of people is not 'like' another. Hence women, black people, Jewish people, and gay people have all been regarded as different from 'normal' people and so not entitled to equal treatment.

Secondly, rules which appear to treat people equally can in fact lead to unequal treatment. Sandra Fredman gives several examples of this:

A rule which requires a high level of formal education as a precondition for employment, will, although applied equally to all, have the effect of excluding many who have suffered educational disadvantage, often a residue of racial discrimination or slavery...A rule which requires all employees or pupils to dress according to Christian traditions and take religious holidays according to the Christian calendar will perpetuate the exclusion of religious minorities.[113]

She goes on to explain the apparent paradox that equal treatment can cause people to be treated unequally. This results from the fact that equality can be conceived in at least three ways:

- *Equality of treatment.* This requires that the same set of rules applies to each person. As we have seen this can lead to unequal results, but supporters of equality of treatment would argue that the answer to any differences that result in the use of equality of treatment must be dealt with by other social changes. So if a university's admissions policies were leading to an under-representation of certain racial groups, for example, the answer would not be to change the admissions requirements, but to improve standards of education for the affected group.

- *Equality of outcome.* Here the focus is on achieving an equality of result. So, using equality of outcome, the university just discussed would have lower entry requirements for disadvantaged groups to ensure a proportionate representation for each group. That would mean unfairness in one sense (different rules were applied to candidates), but the end result, supporters would say, would be fairer.

- *Equality of opportunity.* Here the focus is on providing equal opportunities. This requires neither equality of treatment nor equality of outcome. Rather the focus is on giving everyone an equal chance to compete for particular benefits.

The arguments that may be used in favour of these different conceptions of equality are beyond the scope of this book.[114] But it will be apparent that strikingly different results will be produced depending on which approach is taken.

There is one point in the debate which is important to raise here. That is, it is easy to slip into an assumption that the way to achieve equality is to improve the position of the 'disadvantaged' group so that they are at the same place as

---

[113] S Fredman, *Discrimination Law* (Oxford University Press, 2002), at 2.
[114] Ibid, ch 1 is an excellent starting point.

the dominant group. To speak in this way is to assume that the disadvantaged group is somehow inferior and needs to be helped to improve so that they can reach the standard of the dominant group. Let us take a much discussed example, that of women's under-representation in the full-time work force due to child-care responsibilities. It may be thought that the way to remedy this inequality is to help more women to enter the work place. However, this is to assume that paid employment is better than child care. Another solution is to change the position of the dominant group, in this case to find ways of persuading more men to be involved in child care. There is another possible way of dealing with such an inequality, namely to seek to find ways of ensuring that women are not severely disadvantaged if they choose child-care work rather than employment. This may involve accepting that more women will be involved in child-care work than men, but seeking to avoid the disadvantages flowing from that. At a more general level this will involve accepting there are differences between different groups and seeking to ensure disadvantages do not emanate from that difference, rather than seeking to produce a homogenous society. So, in the context of age discrimination, it should not be thought that the aim is necessarily to enable the old to behave in the same way as the young.

Sandra Fredman has argued that 'the central aim of equality should be to facilitate equal participation of all in society, based on equal concern and respect for the dignity of each individual'.[115]

However, others will see this as placing too much on the notion of equality, and even as smuggling in a broader political agenda under the guise of equality. This might be regarded as a crafty rhetorical move because everyone agrees with the notion of equality. That argument, however, may be a red herring. The real question is what the goal of discrimination law should be. If a model based on equality of participation and equal respect is the best, it should be adopted, regardless of whether or not it is thought to be pushing the notion of equality too far.[116]

A much more limited role for discrimination law would simply be to promote rationality.[117] This view sees discrimination law as being not about equality, but about promoting more rational and therefore more effective and efficient decision-making. The objection to discrimination, according to this view, is that it is using an irrational ground to allocate a social good. This, then, is a far less expansive role for discrimination law than, say, Fredman's model.[118] It would be quite possible for social good to be allocated on a rational basis, but for there still to be a lack of equality of opportunity.

[115] S Fredman, 'The Age of Equality' in S Fredman and S Spencer (eds), *Age as an Equality Issue* (Hart, 2003), at 21.

[116] For advocacy of an approach to discrimination with social inclusion as its primary goal, see H Collins, 'Discrimination, Equality and Social Inclusion' (1993) 66 *Modern Law Review* 16.

[117] C McCrudden and H Kountouros, *Human Rights and European Equality Law*, Oxford Legal Studies Research Paper No 8/2006.

[118] Although it would cover a wider range of characteristics than those which are the usual focus of discrimination law.

As well as the meaning of discrimination itself, there are some other important issues concerning the scope of discrimination. The law does not prohibit discrimination generally. You are free to be racist and sexist in your choice of friends or where you shop; but not in 'public decisions'. This distinction between those areas of life which are 'public' and hence regulated by discrimination law and those which are 'private' is complex. A good example of a borderline case would be the few religious bed-and-breakfast operators who objected to the Sexual Orientation Regulations,[119] meaning they would have to allow same-sex couples to stay in their homes. As they are offering a service to the public, they must comply with the regulations. Had they simply been having friends to visit, they could of course decide not to invite same-sex couples. The line the law is seeking to draw is granting people a degree of liberty and privacy: it is widely thought not to be the state's or the law's job to ensure people think in the correct way and are nice people. On the other hand, individuals who are liable to be discriminated against should not lose out in relation to access to public benefits due to the prejudicial attitudes of others.[120]

Secondly, there is the question of which attitudes or characteristics should be considered prohibited grounds. Sex and race have long been accepted as grounds. More recently, disability and sexual orientation have been included. For the purposes of this book there is the issue of age and it is that which shall be considered shortly. Before doing so we need to unpack the notion of discrimination a little more.

Direct and indirect discrimination

Direct discrimination arises where one person is treated less favourably than a comparable person in a comparable situation on the basis of a forbidden criterion (for example, age). This deals with the most blatant forms of discrimination, where a worker is able to show that if he or she had been younger, he or she would not have been treated in this less favourable way. An obvious example would be a job which stated that it was only open to applicants who were under a certain age. To establish direct discrimination on the basis of age, the applicant would need to demonstrate that had they been younger, they would have been given the benefit, but because they are older they were not.

The concept of direct discrimination is, however, limited. First, it insists on there being a comparator, which may be difficult to find. It may not be possible to prove that a younger person would be treated differently. It also does not protect against more subtle forms of discrimination.

Indirect discrimination occurs where an apparently equal treatment in fact impacts more heavily on people of a particular age. An easy (and not realistic

---

[119] Equality Act (Sexual Orientation) Regulations 2007, No 1263.
[120] J Gardner, 'Liberals and Unlawful Discrimination' (1989) 9 *Oxford Journal of Legal Studies* 1.

example) would be a job which required people not to have naturally grey or white hair. Although it is not mentioned, the hair requirement is likely to be satisfied by younger people than older people and, therefore, in effect, discriminates against them. A less obvious example would be a requirement for a job that applicants have a formal qualification, which may exclude disproportionately older people because they are less likely than younger people to hold formal qualifications. Indirect discrimination is therefore less obvious, and can raise some tricky questions. For example, what if the requirement only very slightly favours younger people, for example, 15.4 per cent of younger potential applicants would have the requirement; but only 15.2 per cent of older ones? Another question is whether you compare likely would-be applicants or the population generally. So, if one of the requirements for a job as an optician was a requirement met by far more younger people than older people generally; but was found equally among older and younger opticians, would that amount to indirect discrimination? These are questions that have troubled the courts and commentators considerably.

One important point to emphasize is that indirect discrimination can be easily justified if the requirement is job related. So, if a particular job requires a particular qualification, then it would not be discriminatory for the employer to demand it, even if it were found among far more younger people than older people. The fact that age discrimination can be justified has been accepted by the European Court of Human Rights, which has held that:

a difference in treatment is discriminatory if it has no reasonable justification: that is if it does not pursue a legitimate aim, or there is not a reasonable relationship of proportionality between the means employed and the aim sought to be realised.[121]

Discrimination on the basis of age

While there has been general acceptance that discrimination on the basis of age or sex should be unlawful, the extent to which other categories should be added has been hotly debated.[122] As has already been mentioned, the categories of discrimination have changed over the years. It is noticeable that Article 14 of the European Convention on Human Rights prohibits discrimination 'on grounds such as...', indicating that the list is not a closed one and can be added to. There is now widespread acceptance that some discrimination against age should be prohibited, but seeking to legislate against age discrimination is problematic and any attempt to develop a law on age discrimination needs to address several issues:

- What ages are covered? Should the law only seek to tackle discrimination against older people or should it tackle all occasions on which age is used in

---

[121] *Belgian Linguistic Case (No 2)* Series A No 6, (1968), 1 EHRR 252, para 10.
[122] N Bamforth, M Malik, and C O'Cinneide, *Discrimination Law: Theory and Context* (Sweet & Maxwell, 2008), ch 15.

a discriminatory way, be that against an older or younger person? The case for restricting age discrimination to older people would have to be based on a claim that discrimination against older people is a particularly insidious force in society which requires government intervention, in a way that age discrimination against younger people is not. The case against would argue that younger people suffer forms of discrimination which can be just as stigmatising, but perhaps even more strongly, that as a principle of equality we should treat all people equally, regardless of their age. That principle should apply to everyone.

- In what circumstances is discrimination to be prohibited? Is the law only to prohibit discrimination in particular settings, such as the workplace, or is there to be a general prohibition on discrimination in any public sphere? As we have seen, traditionally, discrimination law does not seek to prohibit discrimination in private matters.

- Who is to be covered by the law? Is the prohibition to apply to everyone or only state bodies or state agencies?

- How is it to be assessed whether or not there is discrimination? Is the legislation to cover both direct and indirect discrimination?

- Are there any circumstances in which discrimination is justified? How will the law determine whether there is justification and how hard will it be to do so?

We shall be looking at how English law has dealt with these questions shortly. But before going further we need to consider an important argument: that there is no unfairness in age discrimination at all. The argument is that assuming there are disadvantages which are visited upon older people and advantages that younger people have, this is not unfair because virtually everyone will receive the benefits or disadvantages.[123] Everyone is treated equally in that they receive benefits when they are younger and disadvantages when they are older.[124] There is no doubt that this argument has some attraction. It is submitted, however, that it should not be regarded as persuasive, for three reasons.

First, it is argued that it does not get away from the fact that a person is being treated as disadvantaged based on a factor which should not be taken into account. A person is demeaned by being assessed on the basis of their age where that is irrelevant. It is no less demeaning if they were given an advantage at a different stage of life due to their age. Geoffrey Cupit, however, argues that the use

---

[123] N Daniels, *Am I My Parents' Keeper?* (Oxford University Press, 1988), at 41; S Issacharoff and E Worth, 'Is Age Discrimination Really Age Discrimination? The ADEA's Unnatural Solution' (1997) 72 *New York University Law Review* 780; and D McKerlie, 'Equality between Age-Groups' (1992) 21 *Philosophy and Public Affairs* 275, at 276.

[124] Of course the argument would work in the same way if you believed it was the young who were disadvantaged.

of an irrelevant characteristic is not necessarily unfair.[125] He gives the example of a local government which allows houses with odd numbers to use sprinklers on odd days of the month only and even numbered houses on even days. Although the number of a person's house is an irrelevant and arbitrary factor to decide when a person can use a sprinkler, it would not, he submits, be regarded as unfair. This, however, overlooks the point that the use of age, unlike the use of house number, carries with it a demeaning, stigmatizing quality. A person treated in a disadvantageous way due to their house number will not feel they have been demeaned or stigmatized. Where a person is disadvantaged due to their age in our society, this normally reflects assumptions about them based on their age which are derogatory.

Secondly, the 'equality over a lifetime' argument assumes that everyone chooses to spend their life, or is able to live their life, in the same way.[126] It may be, for example, that a person's circumstances mean that it is only in old age that they are able to focus on doing things they enjoy. They may before then have had their lives taken up with care for a dependent relative. For them, disadvantages in old age may work much more harshly than a person who has been able to persue their own interests and hobbies during their youth and middle age. In short, disadvantages in old age will not affect all of those who are of that age equally. A similar point is that cultural and social changes may affect the impact of the discriminatory treatment. For example, a compulsory retirement age of 60 would have affected 60 year olds very differently in the 1970s than from today, and if implemented in the future would affect 60 year olds differently again. In any event there is something rather unattractive about saying that a person must be treated unfairly because another person was treated unfairly in a similar way in the recent past, and we predict that others will be treated unfairly in the future.

Thirdly, seeking to promote equality over a lifetime is impossible. It would be far too difficult to ensure that everyone was receiving an equal amount of health or money over the course of their life. The difficulty is shown by a scenario imagined by Derek Parfit.[127] One is only able to give an anaesthetic to one of two people: A who is in great pain or B who is in lesser pain, but who has suffered more pain than A over the course of his life. To say the anaesthetic should be given to B so that over the course of his life he suffers less than A seems counter intuitive. What the Parfit example demonstrates is the dangerousness of the life-course approach: it could be used to justify terrible disadvantages imposed on older people in the name of equality over a lifetime.

Geoffrey Cupit seeks to develop an argument that age discrimination fails to take due account of profound respect or reverence due to older people. Old age should be venerable. He is not just arguing that there are good utilitarian reasons

---

[125] G Cupit, 'Justice, Age and Veneration' (1998) 108 *Ethics* 702.

[126] For a powerful critique of arguments based on a 'prefabricated life course', see B Neugarten, *Age or Need: Public Policies and Older People* (Sage, 1982).

[127] D Parfit, 'Comments' (1986) 96 *Ethics* 832, at 869–70.

for respecting older people, nor just that older people often have characteristics which entitle them to respect; but rather that respect is due and justice requires it. He admits that at first it seems unlikely that the mere passage of time would enhance a person's moral status. However, he points out that revering age is common: consider old buildings, artefacts, and trees. He suggests:

the longer we live the more extended (in time) we become, and thus the more there comes to be to us. To take this view is to conceive of ourselves as essentially historical beings. Our history—or rather the length of our history—is a constitutive feature of us. We are beings whose length of history in part makes us what we are. Our history is part of us, such that the older we get, the longer we get, the more extended we get, and the more there is of us.

This argument, it is submitted, has much attraction, although it must be seen alongside the many other reasons we have for respecting people. Certainly, it indicates that it is inappropriate to mistreat older people because they received benefits when they were young.

The Employment Equality (Age) Regulations 2006

In 2006 the Employment Equality (Age) Regulations were passed and for the first time it became unlawful to discriminate against workers based on their age. It is generally agreed that in the past there has been discrimination against older workers.[128] In the National Service Framework for Older People, March 2000, it was found that one in three people aged between 50 and state-pension age were not working in paid employment. At the age of 64, 57 per cent of men were employed in 1979, but this had fallen to 37 per cent by 2000.[129] People of Indian, Pakistani, or Bangladeshi ethnic origin aged between 50 and 65 had particularly low rates of employment.[130] From 1950 to 1995 the mean male age of retirement in the UK fell from 67.2 to 62.7[131] The loss of work at this stage of life causes genuine hardship for many people—not just at that time, but into retirement. It appears that the 50s are when many people start saving for their retirement.[132]

The costs of the ageist practices did not just fall on the individuals. They also led to a loss in skilled workers and an increase in costs to the state. Indeed, Fredman refers to evidence that between £16 and £26 billion per year have been

---

[128] For a discussion of what the future for older workers might look like, see W Loretto, S Vicerstaff, and P White, *The Future for Older Workers: New Perspectives* (Policy Press, 2007).

[129] S Fredman, 'The Age of Equality' in S Fredman and S Spencer (eds), *Age as an Equality Issue* (Hart, 2003), at 25.

[130] Ibid.

[131] G Leeson, 'The Employment Equality (Age) Regulations and Beyond' (2006) 5 *Ageing Horizons* 12.

[132] The Cabinet Office, *Winning the Generation Game* (The Stationery Office, 2000), para 3.3.

lost in GDP as a result of older workers leaving the employment market. This leads here to conclude that:

The new emphasis on combating age discrimination is not, therefore, a result of a sudden appreciation of the need for fairness, but gains its chief impetus from business and macro economic imperatives. It is the business case for combating age discrimination which is most prominent in recent policy statements.[133]

These social costs are also referred to in Recital 11 of the 2000/78/EC Directive:

Discrimination based on religion or belief, disability, age or sexual orientation may undermine the achievement of the objectives of the EC Treaty, in particular the attainment of a high level of employment and social protection, raising the standard of living and the quality of life, economic and social cohesion and solidarity, and the free movement of persons.

It appears that there has been extensive ageism in the employment arena. In a 2005 survey, one-quarter of human resources managers questioned accepted that age affected recruitment practices.[134] Another survey by the Employers Forum on Age found that one-third of people thought it not discriminatory to base pay on age, and that 39 per cent thought it appropriate that if a person's perceived age did not match a company's image they should not be employed.[135] Notably this survey was undertaken after the age discrimination legislation came into effect.

The Sex Discrimination Act 1975 prohibits discrimination on the grounds of sex, marital status, and transsexualism.[136] The Race Relations Act 1976 prohibits discrimination on the basis of colour, race, nationality, or ethnic or national origins. However, discrimination on the basis of age has not been outlawed until very recently. The pressure to outlaw age discrimination came from Equal Treatment Framework Directive 2000/78 preventing discrimination in the area of employment on the grounds of age, disability, religion, and sexual orientation.[137] However, this only covered discrimination in the areas of employment, vocational training, and members of works or employers' organisations. There is, in addition, protection from discrimination on the grounds of age under the European Convention on Human Rights. Article 14 prohibits interference in the rights protection by the convention in a way which discriminates on various grounds. Although it is not mentioned, it is generally accepted that age is included within the ambit of Article 14.[138]

---

[133] S Fredman, 'The Age of Equality' in S Fredman and S Spencer (eds), *Age as an Equality Issue* (Hart, 2003), at 62.

[134] Chartered Institute for Personnel and Development and Chartered Management Institute, *Tackling Age Discrimination in the Workplace: Creating a New Age for All* (CIPD, 2005). See also P Urwin, *Age Matters: A Review of the Survey Evidence* (DTI, 2004).

[135] Employers Forum on Age, *Defining Ageism* (EFA, 2008).

[136] Sections 1–3; as amended by Sex Discrimination (Gender Reassignment) Regulations 1999, SI 1999/1102.

[137] Council Directive 20000/78/EC [2000] OJ L303/16.

[138] *Rutherford (No 2) v Secretary of State for Trade and Industry* [2006] UKHL 19.

Extent of law

The Employment Equality (Age) Regulations 2006[139] are designed to prevent direct and indirect discrimination on the grounds of age. They apply to all employers, vocational training providers, trade unions, employee organisations, and managers of occupational pension schemes. The regulations primarily focus on employment issues covering inter alia: an employer when determining to whom employment should be offered; the terms of the employment; refusal to offer employment; and promotions and transfers.[140] They also cover contracts for work;[141] the allocation of pupilage and tenancies[142] for barristers; the allocation of certain office holders;[143] decisions concerning who to make partner in a firm;[144] memberships of trade unions;[145] qualification bodies;[146] organisations providing vocational training;[147] and institutions of higher education in offering places at higher education establishments or the provision of benefits of services to their students. The regulations do not, therefore, apply to the provision of goods and services. It is not unlawful for a restaurant to refuse to serve an older customer on the basis that their presence in the restaurant would create the wrong atmosphere. Nor would it be contrary to the law for a club to only allow those over 30 to enter.

The difficulty with this distinction is that disadvantages and discrimination in different areas of life are often interlocking and interrelated. Tackling, for example, discrimination in the workplace without examining social exclusion of older people or discrimination in health care may be unproductive. Equal access to work is only possible if there is equal access to transport, health, and education services. Fredman[148] argues that the law should prohibit all age discrimination in the exercise of public functions and the provision of goods and services. As we shall see at the end of this chapter, the government is currently considering doing exactly that. The explanation given by the government for restricting the regulations to employment is that age discrimination raises 'new, wide-ranging and complex issues'.[149] A law which prohibited age discrimination in all fields of life might create unforeseen and difficult problems. Of course, against those concerns must be weighed the fact that without the extension of the law, older people will suffer discrimination in a wide variety of arenas.

---

[139] Employment Equality (Age) Regulations 2006, SI 2006/1031 (as amended). These regulations came into force on 1 October 2006.

[140] Reg 7. There are special exceptions for a person in Crown employment, a relevant member of the House of Commons staff, and a relevant member of the House of Lords staff (regs 7(4) and 30).

[141] Reg 9.   [142] Reg 15.   [143] Reg 12.   [144] Reg 17.   [145] Reg 18.

[146] Reg 19.   [147] Reg 20.

[148] S Fredman, 'The Age of Equality' in S Fredman and S Spencer (eds), *Age as an Equality Issue* (Hart, 2003), at 53.

[149] DTI, *Equality and Diversity: The Way Ahead* (The Stationery Office, 2002), para 91.

The definition of discrimination

Regulation 3 states:

(1) For the purposes of these Regulations, a person ('A') discriminates against another person ('B') if—
   (a) on grounds of B's age, A treats B less favourably than he treats or would treat other persons, or
   (b) A applies to B a provision, criterion or practice which he applies or would apply equally to persons not of the same age group as B, but—
      (i) which puts or would put persons of the same age group as B at a particular disadvantage when compared with other persons, and
      (ii) which puts B at that disadvantage,

and A cannot show the treatment or, as the case may be, provision, criterion or practice to be a proportionate means of achieving a legitimate aim.

(2) A comparison of B's case with that of another person under paragraph (1) must be such that the relevant circumstances in the one case are the same, or not materially different, in the other.

(3) In this regulation—
   (a) 'age group' means a group of persons defined by reference to age, whether by reference to a particular age or a range of ages; and
   (b) the reference in paragraph (1)(a) to B's age includes B's apparent age.

This definition covers both direct discrimination in paragraph (1)(a) and indirect discrimination in paragraph (1)(b). As we have seen, direct discrimination requires proof that B was treated less favourably on account of his or her age. This would cover the most blatant forms of discrimination where, for example, a job advertisement stated that the job was only open to those under the age of 50. Significantly, the text includes not only age, but apparent age.[150] So, if a person is dismissed from a job because he or she looked too old (or young), this would amount to age discrimination, even if in fact in chronological years he or she was not old (or young). In *McCoy v James McGregor & Sons*,[151] a 58 year old unsuccessfully applied for a job advertised as requiring 'youthful enthusiasm'. The job was given to two less experienced but younger applicants. The Northern Ireland Employment Tribunal agreed with his claim that he was the victim of age discrimination. The regulations cover discrimination on the basis of both old age and youth.[152]

The regulations state that direct discrimination arises where the discrimination is on the ground of age, but does not extend to cases where the discrimination arises out of association on the basis of age, as other areas of discrimination do. To explain this, consider a white woman who is discriminated

[150] Employment Equality (Age) Regulations 2006, SI 2006/1031, reg 3(3)(b).
[151] 00237/07IT.
[152] *Wilkinson v Springwell Engineering*, ET/2507420/07, where it was found that a younger worker was assumed to be inexperienced.

against on the basis that her partner is black. She is not being discriminated against on the ground of *her* race, but it is from her association with a person's race that she is being discriminated against. In the area of disability discrimination, the wording 'on the ground of' was used, as it is in age discrimination. In *Corrigan v Attridge Law*,[153] the European Court of Justice held that a woman who cared for a disabled child was held to be entitled to protection under disability discrimination law, on the basis that although it was not her disability that was the cause of the discrimination, she was being disadvantaged by being associated with a disabled person. This decision may well mean that the regulations will need to be amended to make it clear that association with age can be a form of age discrimination.

A real difficulty with direct discrimination is finding a comparator. Imagine a 60-year-old worker whose contract is not renewed and she claims age discrimination. The case goes to a tribunal and the applicant shows that a similarly qualified 30-year-old worker had their contract renewed. In response, the firm shows that a similarly qualified 45-year-old worker did not, and so the 60-year-old worker was treated no differently from the 45-year-old worker. Who is to be the comparator? In sex discrimination it is easy: the comparator will be a similarly qualified male worker. Cases will become increasingly complex if each side introduces a range of possible comparators of different ages. There is evidence that this is what has happened in the United States.[154] The concern is that if this happens age discrimination will be harder and more expensive to prove. The best solution would be that age discrimination is made out if a comparator of any age would have been treated differently, even if there are other aged comparators who would have been treated in the same way. After all, it should be no defence to a charge of discrimination that other people would have been treated in just as discriminatory a way.

Also, it will be interesting to see how broadly 'on the ground of age' will be interpreted. If distinctions are drawn between employees based on years of service or experience, this would undoubtedly be indirect discrimination, but would it be direct discrimination? Bob Hepple[155] helpfully distinguishes 'age-based' criteria and age-linked criteria. Age-based criteria are criteria according to which—but for the person's age—they would be treated differently. Age-linked factors are factors separate from age, such as seniority or experience. So, using the example of experience, if a 40-year-old worker and a 60-year-old worker with the same level of experience would be treated in the same way, that suggests there is no direct age discrimination.[156]

---

[153] [2008] ICR 1128.

[154] N Bamforth, M Malik, and C O'Cinneide, *Discrimination Law: Theory and Context* (Sweet & Maxwell, 2008), at 1131.

[155] B Hepple, 'Age Discrimination in Employment' in S Spencer and S Fredman, *Age as an Equality Issue* (Hart, 2003).

[156] Although there may be indirect discrimination.

Indirect discrimination is covered in regulation 1(1)(b). It must be admitted that the concept is not always easy to apply. Mummery LJ has stated that the case law on indirect discrimination is in a 'lamentable state of complexity and obfuscation'.[157] Baroness Hale has recently explained the concept of indirect discrimination in the following way:

71. The essence of indirect discrimination is that an apparently neutral...provision, criterion or practice...in reality has a disproportionate adverse impact upon a particular group. It looks beyond the formal equality achieved by the prohibition of direct discrimination towards the more substantive equality of results. A smaller proportion of one group can comply with the requirement, condition or criterion or a larger proportion of them are adversely affected by the rule or practice.

This is meant to be a simple objective enquiry. Once disproportionate adverse impact is demonstrated by the figures, the question is whether the rule or requirement can objectively be justified.

72. It is of the nature of such apparently neutral criteria or rules that they apply to everyone, both the advantaged and the disadvantaged groups. So it is no answer to say that the rule applies equally to men and women, or to each racial or ethnic or national group, as the case may be. The question is whether it puts one group at a comparative disadvantage to the other. However, the fact that more women than men, or more whites than blacks, are affected by it is not enough. Suppose, for example, a rule requiring that trainee hairdressers be at least 25 years old. The fact that more women than men want to be hairdressers would not make such a rule discriminatory. It would have to be shown that the impact of such a rule worked to the comparative disadvantage of would be female or male hairdressers as the case might be.[158]

Baroness Hale accepts that the concept of indirect discrimination can be difficult to apply. She emphasizes later in her judgement that the rule or requirement that is said to be indirectly discriminatory should apply to a group of people who want something. So, if a greater number of younger people than older people can meet the requirement, but few older people want the benefit in question, the requirement may not be discriminatory.[159]

One difficulty with indirect discrimination in this context is that many commonly used employment criteria are indirectly discriminatory: seeking experience, knowledge, emotional maturity, or qualifications, for example. As this shows, the role played by justification will therefore be key. Bamforth, Malik, and O'Cinneide claim: 'common sense application of the objective justification test should be capable of distinguishing stereotyping use of age-linked criteria from legitimate use in making rational economic decisions.'[160]

---

[157] *Rutherford (No.2) v Secretary of State for Trade and Industry* [2004] IRLR 892.

[158] *Rutherford (No.2) v Secretary of State for Trade and Industry* [2006] UKHL 19, discussed in N Morehan 'The Ageing Model of Indirect Discrimination' (2007) 66 *Cambridge Law Journal* 37.

[159] *Rutherford (No.2) v Secretary of State for Trade and Industry* [2004] IRLR 892.

[160] N Bamforth, M Malik, and C O'Cinneide, *Discrimination Law: Theory and Context* (Sweet & Maxwell, 2008), at 1133.

Harassment on the grounds of age

Regulation 6 sets out the definition of harassment on the grounds of age. This occurs where:

(1) For the purposes of these Regulations, a person ('A') subjects another person ('B') to harassment where, on grounds of age, A engages in unwanted conduct which has the purpose or effect of—
   (a) violating B's dignity; or
   (b) creating an intimidating, hostile, degrading, humiliating or offensive environment for B.
(2) Conduct shall be regarded as having the effect specified in paragraph (1)(a) or (b) only if, having regard to all the circumstances, including in particular the perception of B, it should reasonably be considered as having that effect.

No doubt when interpreting this provision the courts will pay attention to the law on sexual harassment.[161] Notably, the regulation includes the creation of an environment which is hostile or offensive. This is important in cases where the acts of aggressive ageism are relatively minor in and of themselves, but combine to create a highly unpleasant situation.

Discrimination by victimization

This form of discrimination is found in regulation 4, which states:

Discrimination by way of victimisation
4.—(1) For the purposes of these Regulations, a person ('A') discriminates against another person ('B') if he treats B less favourably than he treats or would treat other persons in the same circumstances, and does so by reason that B has—
   (a) brought proceedings against A or any other person under or by virtue of these Regulations;
   (b) given evidence or information in connection with proceedings brought by any person against A or any other person under or by virtue of these Regulations;
   (c) otherwise done anything under or by reference to these Regulations in relation to A or any other person; or
   (d) alleged that A or any other person has committed an act which (whether or not the allegation so states) would amount to a contravention of these Regulations,

or by reason that A knows that B intends to do any of those things, or suspects that B has done or intends to do any of them.

(2) Paragraph (1) does not apply to treatment of B by reason of any allegation made by him, or evidence or information given by him, if the allegation, evidence or information was false and not made (or, as the case may be, given) in good faith.

This regulation is designed to protect those who bring proceedings under the Regulations, or are involved in them, from unfavourable treatment.

---

[161] Ibid, at ch 8.

Exemptions

There are exemptions from the Regulations. These include where A is acting in a way required by a statute[162] or where A is acting justifiably in performing an act 'done for the purpose of safeguarding national security, if the doing of the act was justified by that purpose'.[163] More significantly, there is an exemption when the discrimination is part of a programme of positive action, which will be discussed shortly. The regulation of the National minimum wage[164] is also excluded because there is a lower rate for the youngest workers to encourage employment of school leavers. There are also exemptions in relation to Crown employment, a relevant member of the House of Commons staff, and a relevant member of the House of Lords staff.[165] It is more than a little ironic that the Houses of Parliament exempted themselves from the age discrimination regulations. One cannot imagine a similar provision in relation to race or sex discrimination.

Remedies

The remedies available are set down in regulation 38:

(1) Where an employment tribunal finds that a complaint presented to it under regulation 36 is well-founded, the tribunal shall make such of the following as it considers just and equitable—
    (a) an order declaring the rights of the complainant and the respondent in relation to the act to which the complaint relates;
    (b) an order requiring the respondent to pay to the complainant compensation of an amount corresponding to any damages he could have been ordered by a county court or by a sheriff court to pay to the complainant if the complaint had fallen to be dealt with under regulation 39 (jurisdiction of county and sheriff courts);
    (c) a recommendation that the respondent take within a specified period action appearing to the tribunal to be practicable for the purpose of obviating or reducing the adverse effect on the complainant of any act of discrimination or harassment to which the complaint relates.

In a case of unlawful discrimination on the grounds of age under regulation 3(1)(b), a payment of compensation under regulation 38(1)(b) should not be ordered if the respondent provides that there was no intention to treat the complainant unfavourably on the grounds of age, unless it would be just and equitable to do so.[166]

Controversial issues

Justification for discrimination

Regulation 3, in the very definition of discrimination, states that discrimination will be justified where it is a 'proportionate means of achieving a legitimate

---

[162] Reg 27.   [163] Reg 28.   [164] Reg 31.   [165] Reg 30.   [166] Reg 38(2).

aim'.[167] Article 6(1) of the EC Directive gives examples of potentially legitimate aims: 'legitimate employment policy, labour market and vocational training'. These are very broad and not particularly helpful.

The regulations are, therefore, explicit in accepting that age discrimination can be justified.[168] This is notable because there appears to be a general consensus that it is extremely rare, if ever, that age or race discrimination is justified. However, no such consensus exists in relation to age. Jonathan Swift argues:

As such there is a conflict at the heart of the legislation not only because in the labour market conflicts of interest exist between the old and the young, but also because the characteristics of age are ones that we all possess and all use when making day to day decisions. If truthful, it is unlikely that there are many people who could honestly say that they have never allowed age to influence decisions relating to others, not merely personal decisions but also practical and professional decisions. Many occupations are dominated by notions of 'seniority' and 'experience' both of which are closely synonymous with age. Decisions are made on this basis every day.

As this quotation indicates, there is much uncertainty about when age discrimination can be justified. The first question the courts will need to address is how strong the reasons for the discrimination need to be if they are to justify it. The Department of Trade and Industry (now the Department for Business, Enterprise & Regulatory Reform) has said that the objective justification requirement is a 'tough test'.[169] It stated:

the test of objective justification will not be an easy one to satisfy. The principle remains that different treatment on grounds of age will be unlawful: treating people differently on grounds of age will be possible but only exceptionally and only for good reasons.[170]

In *Palacios de la Villa v Cortefiel Servicios*,[171] the European Court of Justice rejected an argument that age discrimination should be regarded as easier to justify than sex or race discrimination.[172] The court accepted that justification may be more common, but not that it would be easier.

In *Loxley v BAE Systems*,[173] the tribunal relied[174] on a statement in *Bilka-Kaufhas GmbH v Weber Von Hartz*[175] that the justifying reasons must 'correspond

---

[167] M Sargeant, 'The Employment Equality (Age) Regulations 2006: A Legitimisation of Age Discrimination in Employment' (2006) 35 *Industrial Law Journal* 209; and J Swift, 'Justifying Age Discrimination' (2006) 35 *Industrial Law Journal* 228.

[168] Further, under reg 32 age-related benefits do not require justification if they discriminate indirectly on age if an employee has less than five years' service.

[169] DTI, *Objective Justification* (DTI, 2006).

[170] DTI, *Coming of Age* (DTI, 2006), at para 4.1.13.

[171] Case C–411/05 [2007] OJ C277/1.

[172] In deciding this, the ECJ went against the approach taken by the House of Lords in *Rutherford (No.2) v Secretary of State for Trade and Industry* [2006] UKHL 19.

[173] [2008] UKEAT 0156_08_2907.   [174] Para 22.

[175] [1984] IRLR 317, para 36.

to a real need . . . are appropriate with a view to achieving the objectives pursued and are necessary to that end'. The tribunal also held:

The principle of proportionality requires an objective balance to be struck between the discriminatory effect of the measure and the needs of the undertaking. The more serious the disparate adverse impact, the more cogent must be the justification for it:

It is for the employment tribunal to weigh the reasonable needs of the undertaking against the discriminatory effect of the employer's measure and to make its own assessment of whether the former outweigh the latter. There is no 'range of reasonable response' test in this context.[176]

A second issue is whether it is possible to refer to the ageism of others to justify age discrimination. The DTI consultation paper on age discrimination stated that 'the legitimate aim cannot be related to age discrimination itself'. It explained what it meant by that with the following example:[177]

A retailer of trendy fashion items wants to employ young shop assistants because it believes that this will contribute to its aim of targeting young buyers. Trying to attract a young target group will not be a legitimate aim, because this has an age discriminatory aspect.

This is a rather odd way of dealing with the case. Jonathan Swift[178] says it is 'bizarre' to suggest that attracting customers is not a legitimate aim. It would be more convincing to argue that aim is insufficient to justify age discrimination. The problem with the DTI approach to the scenario is that many shops spent vast sums of money seeking to determine a target market and then addressing the look of the shop, the music played, and the design of the products to reach that particular group. Should a shop be required to ensure that their clothes and stores are attractive to all age groups? That might set an impossible aim. It seems that what is troublesome with the shop in the DTI's hypothetical example is not the aim (seeking to attract young customers), but rather their assumption that older shop assistants will not help to attract young customers. Bamforth *et al* make this comment:

When an employer is trying to sell goods to younger people, then the aim in question is to sell goods to an audience that will buy them: if this audience happens to be predominantly young people, then that aim is still nevertheless legitimate, as the aim in question is in itself no way discriminatory. There is nothing in the legitimate aims stage of the age objective justification test which has proved problematic in other jurisdictions.[179]

As this discussion demonstrates, determining when discrimination is justified is going to open a can of worms.

---

[176] Para 36.
[177] DTI, *Objective Justification* (DTI, 2006).
[178] J Swift, 'Justifying Age Discrimination' (2006) 35 *Industrial Law Journal* 228.
[179] N Bamforth, M Malik, and C O'Cinneide, *Discrimination Law: Theory and Context* (Sweet & Maxwell, 2008), at 1135.

Another issue is whether reducing expense is a legitimate aim which can justify age discrimination. The DTI has stated that business need or considerations of efficiency may be legitimate reasons, but not expense alone.[180] This is also problematic because the line between expense and efficiency may be hard to draw. The main aim of a business is to make money and that may be described as the ultimate business need. Of course, it may simply be denied that older workers cost more to business and much evidence has been produced showing the benefits to employers of a diverse workforce, with claims that older workers stay in their jobs longer and are less often absent.[181] It may, however, be that in a particular case a company can show a cost in hiring older workers. Fredman suggests that one response is to argue that, even where that is true if age discrimination remains in place, 'there is also a cost to age inequality but because this cost is borne privately by individuals and their families, it appears invisible'.[182] Seen in this way, there is a cost that will have to be borne by someone, whether or not there is age discrimination. The issue then is who should bear the costs:[183] individual older workers, companies, or the state?

The notion of proportionality is problematic too. It clearly involves weighing up the wrong in the discrimination against the legitimate aim. Yet this involves weighing up two very different things. How can you compare age discrimination with business efficiency? Swift suggests that proportionality requires an employer to show:

First, that treatment that has been afforded to the claimant is rationally related to the aim he has identified. Secondly, that he has not based the specific action taken against the claimant on uninformed assumptions about the claimant which are based on the age of the claimant. Thirdly, that he has taken reasonable steps to inform himself on all material considerations prior to taking action against the claimant. Fourthly, that the action taken represents a reasonable balance between the employer's pursuit of the aim actually pursued and the cost to the individual of that aim being pursued—i.e. that the action taken against the claimant is not an obviously excessive step having regard to the benefits that might reasonably be expected to accrue to the employer.

In *Hampton v Lord Chancellor*,[184] an employment tribunal found the Lord Chancellor guilty of age discrimination in requiring recorders[185] to retire at 65. The Lord Chancellor argued that this was justified in order to free up posts for new judges to be appointed. The tribunal found this to be a legitimate aim, but found the means used to be disproportionate. The tribunal found it unlikely that

---

[180] DTI, *Equality and Diversity: Coming of Age. Consultation on the draft Employment Equality (Age) Regulations 2006* (The Stationery Office, 2005), para 4.1.18.
[181] M Maguire, *Demographic Ageing—Consequences for Social Policy* (OECD, 1988).
[182] S Fredman, 'The Age of Equality' in S Fredman and S Spencer (eds), *Age as an Equality Issue* (Hart, 2003), at 50.
[183] J Humphries and J Rubery, *The Economics of Equal Opportunities* (EOC, 1995), at 15.
[184] ET/2300835/2007.   [185] A kind of judge.

all recorders would want to stay on beyond the age of 65 and it had not been shown that it was necessary to have a mandatory retiring age of 65 in order to create opportunities for new judges.

One important issue the court will consider is whether there were any alternatives to the discrimination. Sometimes age discrimination may be impossible to avoid. In *Bloxham v Bruckhaus*,[186] an age-related provision to deal with pension and other benefits for partners of a firm of solicitors was upheld. This was because no appropriate alternative provision which did not relate, directly or indirectly, to age had been put before the court. It was also emphasized that the provision had been chosen following a lengthy consultation involving all those affected. In *Seldon v Clarkson, Wright and Jakes*,[187] an employment tribunal considered a case of a partner of a firm of solicitors who was compulsorily retired at 65. The firm sought to justify the policy by referring to ensuring turnover of partners and that associates be given the opportunity to progress to the level of partner. This was seen as justification. The tribunal also emphasized that if the age bar was not used the only alternative would be to use performance assessments, something the court accepted would not be appropriate for partners of firms of solicitors.

Occupational requirement

There is a defence to a claim of discrimination where an age-specific characteristic is a legitimate 'occupational requirement'. This is defined in regulation 8(2):

having regard to the nature of the employment or the context in which it is carried out—
  (a) possessing a characteristic related to age is a genuine and determining occupational requirement;
  (b) it is proportionate to apply that requirement in the particular case; and
  (c) either—
    (i) the person to whom that requirement is applied does not meet it, or
    (ii) the employer is not satisfied, and in all the circumstances it is reasonable for him not to be satisfied, that that person meets it.

It will be interesting to see how the courts will interpret this provision. Is it, for example, an occupational requirement that a salesperson in a 'trendy' design company seeking to reach young people should themselves be 'young and trendy'? It has been suggested that the acting profession may be one where an occupational requirement can be relied upon.[188] So too might a job requiring the serving of alcohol.[189] The evidence suggests that there is only a very limited range of jobs where performance deteriorates with age.[190]

---

[186] ET/2205086/2006.   [187] ET/1100275/2007.
[188] M Sargeant, 'The Employment Equality (Age) Regulations 2006: A Legitimisation of Age Discrimination in Employment' (2006) 35 *Industrial Law Journal* 209.
[189] Age Positive, *Age Discrimination Legislation—Information and Help for Employers and Individuals* (DTI, 2006).
[190] P Meadows, *Retirement Age in the UK* (DTI, 2003), at 28–9:

Retirement

Alan Johnson, then Trade Secretary, said the new regulations would allow people to decide when they stopped working. He claimed: 'It's all about choice—not work till you drop but choose when you stop.'[191] But the regulations do not do this at all. Under regulation 30, if a firm has a mandatory retiring age below 65, that must be justified by the company.[192] It must be shown that the lower retirement age is appropriate and necessary. If the retirement age is 65 or above, that can provide a justification for what would otherwise be age discrimination or unlawful retirement. However, there are certain procedural requirements. Even where the retirement age is 65 an employer is required to inform an employee in writing six months before the intended retirement date.[193] The employee can request to work beyond the compulsory retirement date, and the employee must consider that request.[194] The employee can request to work on past the retirement date indefinitely or until a stated period. However, these provisions are far less important than they may appear at first sight. An employee may only *request* to work beyond the retirement age and there is no obligation on an employer to do more than *consider* the request. The employer does not need to justify the decision not to allow the employee to work beyond the retirement age.

The new regime has been described as 'an overly complex and ill-conceived New Labour experiment'[195] Critics complain that all it will produce is 'widespread uncertainty, larger employment advice bills for workers and businesses alike and increased workload and difficulties for the courts and tribunals'. Claire Kilpatrick is particularly critical of the failure to produce a joined-up approach to pension law reform. As we shall see in chapter 6, the government in responding to the so-called 'pensions crisis' is looking for ways to ease the burden of pensions on the public purse. One way of doing this is to encourage people to work longer. Indeed, the Commission strongly recommended that age discrimination law apply without any automatically justifiable retirement age.[196] Kilpatrick argues that the failure to give workers the right to work for as long as they want unless the employer can justify dismissing them works against this policy. She sees a failure of joined-up government.

There is some debate over whether or not the age of 65 is compatible with the prohibition on age discrimination in Directive 2000/78/EC.[197] Age Concern has backed litigation (which has become known as the Heyday litigation) to challenge

---

[191] Quoted in B Bytheway, 'Choose when you stop? Retirement and age discrimination' (2007) 35 *Policy & Politics* 551, at 551.
[192] C Kilpatrick 'The New UK Retirement Regime' (2008) 37 *Industrial Law Journal* 1.
[193] The details are set out in Sch 6.
[194] The request must be in writing and state that it is made under the regulations.
[195] C Kilpatrick, 'The New UK Retirement Regime' (2008) 37 *Industrial Law Journal* 1.
[196] Pensions Commission, *Second Report*, 135.　　　[197] Ibid.

the regulations in the European Court of Justice.[198] Indeed, the government has already untaken to review the exemption of retirement ages of 65 or over from the regulations.[199] So, even if not forced to by the European court, the government may nevertheless decide to change the law.

One study on the impact of the new regulations found that one-third of employers are still to introduce retirement policies and more than 40 per cent had received requests to work past retirement age.[200] Kilpatrick believes that employees probably feel short changed:

Employees using this route may legitimately feel short-changed when they discover that the introduction of age discrimination legislation has not given them a right not to be dismissed on grounds of age, nor even a right to reasons as to why an age-related dismissal is necessary, but simply a right to request not to be dismissed on grounds of age, a request which can be rejected for no reason, provided the employer goes through the steps of a meeting and an appeal.

There was evidence before the regulations came into effect that 'early retirements' were not the result of free choice by employees, but were due to discriminatory practices of employers.[201] One study found that 40 per cent of all early retirements were not freely chosen.[202] Recent research by the government has found that only a minority of people are happy on the first day of their retirement.[203] This has been used to support claims that employers should be more flexible over retirement age.[204] Nicholas Bamforth *et al* summarize well the reasons why there should not be a mandatory retiring age:

The immediate transition from employment to leisure can result in damaging financial and psychological impact, and many employees experience their mandatory retirement as humiliating, degrading and denying them liberty... by denying access to the workplace mandatory retirement can close off opportunities for individual self-realisation and constitute a paternalist intrusion in personal life that violates the principle of human dignity.[205]

---

[198] H Meenan, 'Reflecting on Age Discrimination and Rights of the Elderly in the European Union and the Council of Europe' (2007) 14 *Maastricht Journal* 39.

[199] Patricia Hewitt, Secretary of State for Trade and Industry, HC, 14 December 2004.

[200] Berwin Leighton, *New Age Discrimination Laws Begin to Kick In* (Berwin Leighton, 2007).

[201] G Leeson, 'New Horizons—New Elderly: Work and Retirement' (DaneAge, 2004); and G Leeson and S Harper, *Examples of International Case Law on Age Discrimination in Employment* (Department for Work and Pensions, 2005).

[202] R Disney, E Grundy, and P Johnson, *The Dynamics of Retirement: Analyses of the Retirement Surveys* (The Stationery Office, 1997); and S Vickerstaff, 'Entering the Retirement Zone: How Much Choice do Individuals Have?' (2006) 5 *Social Policy & Society* 507.

[203] Department of Work and Pensions, *Reinventing the Retirment Cliff Edge* (DWP, 2008).

[204] Employers Forum on Age, *Response to DWP 'Retirement Cliff' Research* (EFA, 2008).

[205] N Bamforth, M Malik, and C O'Cinneide, *Discrimination Law: Theory and Context* (Sweet & Maxwell, 2008), at 1133.

Positive action

Regulation 29 sets out the circumstances in which a company can engage in positive action in an attempt to combat the effects of ageism:

(1) Nothing in Part 2 or 3 shall render unlawful any act done in or in connection with—

    (a) affording persons of a particular age or age group access to facilities for training which would help fit them for particular work; or

    (b) encouraging persons of a particular age or age group to take advantage of opportunities for doing particular work;

where it reasonably appears to the person doing the act that it prevents or compensates for disadvantages linked to age suffered by persons of that age or age group doing that work or likely to take up that work.

(2) Nothing in Part 2 or 3 shall render unlawful any act done by a trade organisation within the meaning of regulation 18 in or in connection with—

    (a) affording only members of the organisation who are of a particular age or age group access to facilities for training which would help fit them for holding a post of any kind in the organisation; or

    (b) encouraging only members of the organisation who are of a particular age or age group to take advantage of opportunities for holding such posts in the organisation,

where it reasonably appears to the organisation that the act prevents or compensates for disadvantages linked to age suffered by those of that age or age group holding such posts or likely to hold such posts.

(3) Nothing in Part 2 or 3 shall render unlawful any act done by a trade organisation within the meaning of regulation 18 or in connection with encouraging only persons of a particular age or age group to become members of the organisation where it reasonably appears to the organisation that the act prevents or compensates for disadvantages linked to age suffered by persons of that age or age group who are, or are eligible to become, members.

It should be noted that the scope of positive action allowed under this regulation is very limited. It is restricted to affording people training and encouraging people to take up opportunities for doing particular work. Where, therefore, a company was keen to employ a greater number of older workers, it could offer training to existing or future older workers to enable them to have the skills required for jobs. It could also focus advertising on older workers. However, at the selection process regulation 29 would not authorize preferring an older candidate over a younger one purely on the basis of age. Such positive actions must reasonably appear to the person to compensate for a disadvantage. This will be a much lower hurdle than that required for justifying discrimination.

    Some commentators would like to see a more robust law allowing a company to at least take age into account in preferring an older candidate over a younger one if in all other respects they are equally well qualified. Of course, there has been fierce debate over the extent to which affirmative action is justifiable and/or effective. We cannot go into that here due to lack of space.[206]

The impact of the regulations

The new regulations certainly appear to have had some impact, but perhaps not as much as might be hoped. A study of discrimination on the basis of age in the workplace found that nine out of ten people knew it was now illegal to discriminate on the basis of age. However, more than one-half of workers questioned claimed to have witnessed ageist behaviour in the past year.[207] Another survey found that 72 per cent of establishments now had an equal opportunity policy, with 56 per cent including age.[208] Thirty-seven per cent had a compulsory retirement age, although 57 per cent had no compulsory retirement age. Revealingly, the Department for Business, Enterprise & Regulatory Reform itself has a mandatory retirement age of 65, as do 10 of 15 government departments.[209] One-quarter of companies in one survey believed they were at medium or high risk of a claim of age discrimination.[210] This reflects the uncertainty over how the regulations will be applied. Depressingly, 73 per cent of firms in one survey said that the laws would not be effective in changing age discrimination in the workplace.[211] A different report found that companies had taken steps to eliminate age discrimination, but there had been no impact in the recruitment of older people.[212]

Perhaps the most revealing statistic is that in the year after the regulations came into effect the number of those over the state pension age who were in work rose by one-sixth.[213] Whether this is due to the regulations themselves or wider changes in social and economic circumstances may be a matter for debate, but it would be surprising if the regulations had no impact on this.

There are dangers of looking at the new regulations with too rosy a coloured pair of spectacles. First, many older people lack the current skills or qualifications to take on the higher paid jobs, especially if they have been out of the employment market for some time.[214] There is, therefore, a danger that any new job market for older workers created by the regulations will be primarily in low-paid

---

[206] A McHarg and D Nicolson, 'Justifying Affirmative Action: Perception and Reality' (2006) 33 *Journal of Law and Soceity* 1.

[207] Employers Forum on Age, *Increased Awareness of Age Laws Spells Trouble for Employers* (EFA, 2007).

[208] H Metcalf and P Meadows, *Survey of Employers' Policies, Practices and Preferences Relating to Age* (DWP, 2006).

[209] C Matheson, 'Ageism—still a grey area', BBC News Online, 30 September 2007.

[210] Ibid.   [211] Eversheds, *Age Laws Don't Work Says Business* (Eversheds, 2007).

[212] H Metcalf and P Meadows, *Survey of Employers' Policies, Practices and Preferences Relating to Age* (DWP, 2006).

[213] C Matheson, 'Ageism—still a grey area', BBC News Online, 30 September 2007.

[214] K Mayhew, M Elliott, and R Rijkers, 'Upskilling Older Workers' (2008) 8 *Ageing Horizons* 13.

jobs.[215] Secondly, it should not be assumed that all older people are able to take up jobs. About three-fifths of people aged between 50 and state pension age with a health condition that affects daily activity are out of work.[216] The figure is even higher among those without qualifications, at nearly two-thirds.[217]

The new equality law

The Equality Act 2006 created the new Commission for Equality and Human Rights. Age equality is included within its remit. The Act made it an offence to discriminate in the provision of goods, facilities, and services on the ground of religion, belief, or sexual orientation.[218] Age was not included. As already mentioned, the regulations only cover employment issues. The government has published *The Discrimination Law Review* and is considering extending the reach of the law to all areas.[219]

The review recognizes that the issues raised by age discrimination can be more complex than those in other areas. Indeed, the review states that the government would want to make sure that it did not prevent justifiable discrimination. The review argues that there can be important reasons why age discrimination is appropriate. It explains:

It is part and parcel of the normal operation of our society to treat people of different ages differently, because people's capacities, needs and aspirations change as they grow up and age. Different treatment often fulfils an important function such as promoting social integration, compensating for disadvantage, or enabling services to be delivered more effectively or efficiently. It is clear that there will always be a need for age-specific facilities and services.[220]

These concerns lead the review to suggest that any age discrimination law would have to satisfy the following tests:

- it must be a proportionate response to a real problem and not create unnecessary burdens on the private, public, or voluntary sectors;
- it must not have the unintended consequence of prohibiting positive benefits for either younger or older people, such as youth clubs or clubs for older people, holidays catering for people of particular ages, or concessions and discounts which help younger or older people;
- it must pass a 'common sense' test.[221]

[215] Ibid.
[216] Office of National Statistics, *Labour Force Survey Quarter 2, 2007* (ONS, 2008).
[217] Age Concern, *The Age Agenda* (Age Concern, 2007).
[218] The Equality Act (Sexual Orientation) Regulations 2007, SI 1263/2007.
[219] Department for Communities and Local Government, *Discrimination Law Review* (The Stationery Office, 2007).
[220] Para 9.8.   [221] Ibid.

The review gives some examples of what it regards as legitimate differences in treatment based on age, which it wants to ensure will not be prevented due to any legislation:

- Age is used as a qualifying condition for many benefits, such as free TV licences for people over 75 and travel discounts for people below 25.

- Concessions such as discounted access to leisure facilities during off-peak periods are often targeted at both young and older people.

- The incidence of mortality, morbidity, criminality, and accidents varies by age and is a factor in underwriting some insurance contracts and in the calculation of annuities.

- Leisure and travel activities are aimed at and restricted to people of particular ages.

- Age limits are used widely in amateur and professional sports, for example, veterans' competitions.

- The NHS targets certain disease prevention programmes, such as cancer screening, at age groups with the greatest clinical need.[222]

This list is interesting and reveals the range of issues which the government must consider before it introduces legislation. Indeed, the review suggests that the government is not convinced that age discrimination legislation should apply to the financial services industry.

The government announced in June 2008 that it planned to extend the remit of age discrimination law.[223] The details of the proposals will doubtless generate much debate.

Conclusion

This chapter has considered the issue of ageism and age discrimination. It has been argued that ageism permeates society, often in ways which are unnoticed. Ageism is regarded as acceptable in ways racism and sexism would never be. The current law combating age discrimination is limited. The new Employment Equality (Age) Regulations 2006 seek to combat age discrimination in the workplace. Their effectiveness depends very much on how readily the courts will accept justifications for discriminatory practices. One controversial aspect of the regulations is that they still allow employers to set a mandatory retirement age of 65 or above.

The regulations are, however, a very restricted response to the issues posed by ageism. First, there is no protection from age discrimination in the provision of

---

[222] Para 9.8.   [223] BBC News Online, 'Law will ban age discrimination', 25 June 2008.

health or other social services. As argued above, tackling discrimination in the workplace without dealing with discrimination elsewhere is a rather half-hearted effort. Secondly, the response to the disadvantages suffered by old people is focused on an individualistic model. There is no attempt to challenge the wider social structures and forces which blight the lives of older people. The law could, for example, require local authorities to act in a positive way to promote the social inclusion of older people. Simply stopping individuals from doing acts of discrimination is unlikely on its own to effectively combat the impact of ageism on older people. As it is, the current law appears to be as much about ensuring that businesses are not overburdened as it is about protecting the rights of older people.[224]

It is easy to find old-age heroes who defy our fears of old age: William Gladstone (Prime Minister at 82); Michelangelo (drawing designs of St Peters at 89); Pablo Casals (performing the cello in his 90s); or Jenny Wood (running her 13th marathon at age 98).[225] In a non-ageist future one might imagine many more such characters. But, I suggest, that might be the wrong vision. The super-active old age promoted by some is not possible for all older people and there is a danger of seeing a good old age as one being where one is as much like the young as possible. We need to free older people to live their dreams for old age, but not expect these to be the same as might appeal to younger generations. What those might be no one can tell.

---

[224] L Dickens, 'The Road is Long: Thirty Years of Equality Legislation in Britain' (2007) 45 *British Journal of Industrial Relations* 463.
[225] J Macnicol, *Age Discrimination* (Cambridge University Press, 2006), at 14.

3

Capacity, Incapacity, and Old Age

Introduction

It would be quite wrong to assume that with old age comes incapacity, or that incapacity only arises in old age. In fact, 78 per cent of those aged 85 and over have *no* cognitive impairment at all.[1] Nevertheless, for a significant minority of older people issues of mental capacity do arise. The issue is particularly relevant given the rising number of older people who suffer from dementia. It has been estimated that currently 700,000 people in the UK do suffer[2] and it is estimated that by 2025 over one million will.[3] One-third of those over the age of 95 suffer dementia. Of those living in care homes, 64 per cent suffer dementia.[4] There are, of course, other conditions that affect capacity. At some point during their lives approximately 1 per cent of the UK population will suffer from schizophrenia, 1 per cent bipolar disorder, and 5 per cent will have serious or clinical depression.[5] Of course, simply because a person suffers from one of the conditions mentioned in this paragraph does not mean they lack capacity, but in some cases it will, at least for some decisions. It has been claimed that at any one time in England and Wales there are two million people unable to make decisions for themselves.[6]

The law governing incapacity has been reformed by the Mental Capacity Act 2005 which now governs the area. This needs to be read alongside the Code of Practice,[7] which provides guidance on the application of the Act. As shall be

---

[1] T Poole, *Housing Options for Older People* (King's Fund, 2005), at 2.

[2] Dementia can affect younger people too: R Harvey, M Skelton-Robinson, and M Rossor, 'The Prevalence and Causes of Dementia in People under the Age of 65' (2003) 74 *Journal of Neurology Neurosurgery and Psychiatry* 1206.

[3] Alzheimer's Society, *Dementia UK* (Alzheimer's Society, 2007), at 3.   [4] Ibid.

[5] Department of Constitutional Affairs, *Mental Capacity Bill: Full Regulatory Assessment* (The Stationery Office, 2004).

[6] M Dunn, I Clare, A Holland, and M Gunn, 'Constructing and Reconstructing "Best Interests": An Interpretative Examination of Substitute Decision-making under the Mental Capacity Act 2005' (2007) 29 *Journal of Social Welfare and Family Law* 117, at 117.

[7] Ministry of Justice, *Mental Capacity Act 2005, Code of Practice* (The Stationery Office, 2007) (hereafter, 'Code of Practice'). See also Ministry of Justice, *Deprivation of Liberty Safeguards* (Ministry of Justice, 2008).

seen, the treatment of incapacity raises some difficult legal and ethical issues. The Act opens[8] with five principles that underpin the law on this area:

1. A person must be assumed to have capacity unless it is established that he lacks capacity.

2. A person is not to be treated as unable to make a decision unless all practicable steps to help him to do so have been taken without success.

3. A person is not to be treated as unable to make a decision merely because he makes an unwise decision.

4. An act done, or decision made, under this Act for or on behalf of a person who lacks capacity must be done, or made, in his best interests.

5. Before the act is done, or the decision is made, regard must be had to whether the purpose for which it is needed can be as effectively achieved in a way that is less restrictive of the person's rights and freedom of action.

This chapter will start by outlining the basic principles of the law before examining in more detail some of its more controversial aspects.

Basic legal principles

The competent

Consent plays a crucial role in law. Generally, touching a person without their consent will amount to a criminal offence and a civil wrong.[9] Providing medical treatment without their consent will likewise be an offence. Of course there are exceptions to this: for example, 'everyday touching' (such as brushing past someone in a crowded street) can be lawful even if done without consent[10] and force can be used against someone if necessary in self-defence. But as a general principle if a person has capacity they must consent to any touching or medical treatment. In *R (on the application of Burke) v GMC*, the Court of Appeal held:

When a competent person makes it clear that he does not wish to receive treatment which is, objectively, in his medical best interests, it is unlawful for doctors to administer that treatment. Personal autonomy or the right of self determination prevails.[11]

The reasons why this principle is so important were explained by Lord Steyn in *Chester v Afshar*:

A rule requiring a doctor to abstain from performing an operation without the informed consent of a patient serves two purposes. It tends to avoid the occurrence of the particular

---

[8] Mental Capacity Act 2005 (MCA), s 1(2–6).

[9] J Herring, *Criminal Law: Text Cases and Materials* (3rd edn, Oxford University Press, 2008), ch 6.

[10] *Collins v Wilcock* [1984] 1 WLR 1172.   [11] [2005] 3 FCR 169, para 30.

physical injury the risk of which a patient is not prepared to accept. It also ensures that due respect is given to the autonomy and dignity of each patient.[12]

These principles apply equally out of the medical context. There is one important exception to the rule that a person with capacity can only be treated if they have provided consent and that is where the Mental Health Act 1983 applies. Under this legislation a person can be detained and receive treatment in respect of certain mental disorders without consent. We will briefly look at this legislation later.

As we shall see shortly, the position for those lacking capacity is very different. They can be treated without their consent as long as the treatment is in their best interests. Hence, while it would not be lawful to give a person with capacity a bath without their consent or take them for a ride in your car; it would be lawful if the person lacked capacity and doing so would be in their best interests. The distinction between having capacity and not is, therefore, extremely important.[13]

Defining capacity

There is a presumption that people are competent.[14] Therefore, in borderline cases where it is unclear whether or not a person has capacity they should be treated as having it.

The Mental Capacity Act 2005 sets out the test for capacity:[15]

a person lacks capacity in relation to a matter if at the material time he is unable to make a decision for himself in relation to the matter because of an impairment of, or a disturbance in the functioning of, the mind or brain.

Section 3(1) explains the notion of being unable to make a decision in more detail:

a person is unable to make a decision for himself if he is unable—
    (a) to understand the information relevant to the decision,
    (b) to retain that information,
    (c) to use or weigh that information as part of the process of making the decision, or
    (d) to communicate his decisions (whether by talking, using sign language or any other means).

---

[12] [2004] UKHL 41, para 18.

[13] Even if a person has capacity their consent may still be ineffective if, for example, they were insufficiently informed, or suffering from coercion or undue influence. These ideas are not discussed further in this book and are covered adequately elsewhere. See, eg J Herring, *Medical Law and Ethics* (Oxford University Press, 2007), at 143–4.

[14] MCA, s 1(2).

[15] There may be some particular contexts where the definition will not be used, eg tests for capacity to make a will or litigate: *Saulle v Nouvet* [2007] EWHC 2902 (QB). In *Re MM (An Adult)* [2007] EWHC 2003 (Fam), para 74, Mumby J thought the Act's definition of capacity had simply replicated the previous common law.

There are a number of important points to emphasize about the understanding of mental capacity in the 2005 Act:

- There is no need to prove mental illness per se; it is enough that there is an impairment in the functioning of the brain. Hence concussion or drunkenness could cause someone to lack capacity.[16] Conversely, a person may have a severe mental illness, but still retain the capacity to make decisions. One study of psychiatric patients in a hospital found that only 43.8 per cent of them lacked capacity.[17]

- Lack of capacity can arise if, even though a person is able to make a decision, they are unable to communicate it.[18]

- A person may be able to consent to some issues, but not others.[19] So, a person may be able to choose what kind of ice cream they like, but lack the mental abilities to decide whether or not to consent to heart surgery.[20] The general principle is helpfully and accurately encapsulated in the *Code of Practice*:

  An assessment of a person's capacity must be based on their ability to make a specific decision at the time it needs to be made, and not their ability to make decisions in general.[21]

  This was applied in *Re MM (an adult)*,[22] where a young woman was found to lack capacity to decide where to live, but to have capacity to decide whether to engage in sexual relations.

- A person should not be found to lack capacity unless 'all practical steps to help him' reach capacity 'have been taken without success'.[23] This may include giving someone information in simple language or using visual aids.[24]

- Capacity is not just about understanding the information, but it is also about using it to make a decision. So, a person who understands all the issues but cannot reach a decision (for example, because they are too nervous) can be treated as incompetent.[25] A person who refuses to believe a piece of information (for example, they deny they are ill) can be found to lack the understanding necessary to have capacity.[26]

---

[16] Code of Practice, para 4.12.
[17] R Cairns *et al*, 'Prevalence and Predictors of Mental Incapacity of Psychiatric In-Patients' (2005) 187 *British Journal of Psychiatry* 379–85.
[18] MCA, s 3(1).
[19] *A Local Authority v E and D* [2007] EWHC 2396 (Fam).
[20] Code of Practice, ch 4.   [21] Code of Practice, para 4.4.
[22] [2007] EWHC 2003 (Fam).   [23] Code of Practice, para 2.6.
[24] MCA, s 2(2).
[25] See, eg *Bolton Hospital NHS v O* [2003] 1 FLR 824, where a woman suffered needle phobia and could not consent to an injection required for a Caesarean section operation.
[26] *Re MM (An Adult)* [2007] EWHC 2003 (Fam), para 81.

- According to section 1(4): 'A person is not to be treated as unable to make a decision merely because he makes an unwise decision.'[27] The Code of Practice states:

  Everybody has their own values, beliefs, preferences and attitudes. A person should not be assumed to lack the capacity to make a decision just because other people think their decision is unwise. This applies even if family members, friends or healthcare or social care staff are unhappy with a decision.[28]

  This is an important point. It is all too easy to assume that a person who makes a decision you regard as foolish must lack capacity. Section 1(4) warns against making this assumption. Notice, however, the use of the word 'merely'. The fact that a person is making a bizarre decision may be used along with other information to conclude that a person lacks capacity.[29] This may be particularly relevant where the decision is seen as out of character or puts the individual at a significant risk of harm.[30]

- Section 2(3) warns against making an assessment of lack of capacity based on prejudice. It states:

  A lack of capacity cannot be established merely by reference to—
  (a) a person's age or appearance, or
  (b) a condition of his, or an aspect of his behaviour, which might lead others to make unjustified assumptions about his capacity.

  Particularly relevant for our purposes is the reference to age. All too easily assumptions of incapacity are made based on a person's age.[31] This is prohibited by section 2(3).

The law on the definition of capacity is easier to state than apply in practice. Finding a patient of uncertain competence is common. Practitioners report that even the most seasoned experts in the field can struggle to determine a person's decision-making ability.[32] As Professor Gunn has pointed out, capacity and incapacity are not 'concepts with clear a priori boundaries. They appear on a continuum... There are, therefore, degrees of capacity.'[33] It should certainly not be assumed that because a person has a severe mental illness they lack capacity.

The Mental Capacity Act 2005 applies not only to professionals making an assessment of capcity, but also family members and others caring for the person lacking capacity. This inevitably generates a concern that a relative or carer, who incorrectly decides that a person lacks capacity and treats them accordingly, could

---

[27] MCA, s 1(4).   [28] Code of Practice, para 2.10.
[29] *Re B (Consent to Treatment: Capacity)* [2002] EWHC 429.
[30] Code of Practice, para 2.11.   [31] See ch 2.
[32] R Jones and T Holden, 'A Guide to Assessing Decision-Making Capacity' (2004) 12 *Cleveland Clinical Journal of Medicine* 971.
[33] M Gunn, 'The Meaning of Incapacity' (1994) 2 *Medical Law Review* 8, at 9.

face criminal liability. This is particularly so in a case where an individual's mental capacity is fluctuating. This concern is dealt with by section 8, which states that if a person has reasonable grounds for deciding the person lacks capacity they will be protected from legal action even if in fact the person was not lacking capacity.

It should also be emphasized that the definition of incapacity and its use is not uncontroversial. Women and ethnic minorities remain particularly vulnerable to assessments that they lack mental capacity.[34] It has been argued that while notions of competence purport to be neutral, these notions in fact reflect majority interests and values.[35] Assessments of capacity may hide the subjective values of physicians, especially when an emotional end-of-life issue is involved.[36]

The assessment of incapacity is not just of legal significance. As David Wexler and Bruce Winick argue:

Incompetency labeling not only damages individuals' reputation in the eyes of the community, but profoundly affects their own self-concept in ways that can be debilitating. Branding individuals as incompetent is a trespass and an assault on their psyche in ways that can leave a lasting imprint.[37]

With this in mind, the relatively broad definition of capacity in the Act will be welcomed,[38] but with two caveats. First, much more significant than the legal definition of capacity is how it is understood and applied in practice. As just mentioned, there are concerns about that. Secondly, the law governing those who are assessed as just competent is not satisfactory and we shall consider that later.

Treatment of a person lacking capacity

As a general principle, where a person lacks capacity then decisions can be made on their behalf, based on what is in that person's best interests. Under the Mental Capacity Act 2005, the 'best interests' principle is relevant to all substitute decisions involving 'acts in connection with care and treatment'.[39] This covers anyone dealing with the incapacitated person, including medical professionals, carers, friends, donees of a lasting power of attorney,[40] deputies appointed by the Court of protection,[41] and even courts.

---

[34] S Stefan, 'Silencing the Different Voice: Competence, Feminist Theory and the Law' (1993) 47 *University of Miami Law Review* 763; and J Mosoff, 'Motherhood, Madness and Law' (1995) 45 *University of Toronto Law Journal* 107.

[35] N Knauer, 'Defining Capacity: Balancing the Competing Interests of Autonomy and Need' (2003) 12 *Temple Political and Civil Rights Law Review* 321.

[36] S Martyn and H Bourguignon, 'Physicians' Decisions About Patient Capacity: The Trojan Horse of Physician-Assisted Suicide' (2000) 6 *Psychology, Public Policy and the Law* 388.

[37] D Wexler and B Winick, *Law in a Therapeutic Key* (Carolina Academic Press, 1996), at 38–9.

[38] A Boylen, 'The Law and Incapacity Determinations: A Conflict of Governance?' (2008) 71 *Modern Law Review* 433.

[39] MCA, s 5.   [40] Ibid.   [41] MCA, s 16.

There are, however, some decisions that cannot be made on behalf of a person lacking capacity. These include consenting to marriage or civil partnership, sexual relations, or divorce.[42] There are also a few occasions on which a decision-maker is not bound by the best interests principle. First, in some circumstances approved research can be carried out on those lacking capacity, even if participation will not directly promote their welfare. Secondly, where the individual has made an advance directive setting out their wishes on the issue this can, in some circumstances, determine the question. We shall be discussing these later in this chapter.

At first sight the best interests principle appears to be a relatively unproblematic one. You simply weigh up the benefits or disadvantages of a course of action for an individual and if it is determined that more good than bad will come from it, it can be performed. The courts have promoted the drawing up of a list of the benefits and disadvantages of a proposed course of action and determining whether it is in the best interests of the individual.[43] The Code of Practice reminds decision-makers that they are meant to be making an objective assessment of what is best for the person who lacks capacity:

> When working out what is in the best interests of the person who lacks capacity to make a decision or act for themselves, decision makers must take into account all relevant factors that it would be reasonable to consider, not just those that they think are important. They must not act or make a decision based on what they would want to do if they were the person who lacked capacity.[44]

Shortly, we will discuss some of the difficulties that arise in applying this apparently straightforward test, but it is important to appreciate how flexible it is. Its focus is on the particular individual. What may be best for one patient may not be best for another. Decisions-makers are expressly told not to use generalized assumptions in determining what is in a person's best interests. This is particularly important in the case of older people. Of course, with that flexibility comes the danger of uncertainty.[45] As already mentioned, informal carers may feel unsure that they have reasonable grounds to believe they are treating the individual in accordance with their best interests. Indeed, one commentator has made the point that the statute appears to offer little guidance or control for the decision-maker.[46] This is true, but given the wide variety of circumstances in which the Act may apply it is difficult to imagine how more concrete guidance could be provided.

---

[42] For a complete list, see J Herring, *Medical Law and Ethics* (Oxford University Press, 2007), at 157.

[43] *Re A (Medical Treatment: Male Sterilization)* [2000] 1 FCR 193.

[44] Code of Practice, para 5.7.

[45] M Dunn, I Clare, A Holland, and M Gunn, 'Constructing and Reconstructing "Best Interests": An Interpretative Examination of Substitute Decision-Making under the Mental Capacity Act 2005' (2007) 29 *Journal of Social Welfare and Family Law* 117.

[46] J Miola, *Medical Ethics and Medical Law: A Symbiotic Relationship* (Hart, 2007), ch 6.

Next, some particularly problematic issues concerning the application of the best interests test will be considered.

Difficult issues in treating those lacking capacity

Use of force and best interests

In some cases, the incapacitated person will resist receiving the treatment which is in their best interests.[47] They may, for example, need a bath, but refuse to have one. In such a case, the question arises of whether force may be used to ensure that the treatment is given. It may be that if force must be used to provide the treatment in question that it will therefore cease to be in a person's best interests. The harm caused by the use of force may outweigh any benefit from the treatment. Even where that is not so, the Mental Capacity Act requires the decision-maker to use the least restrictive alternative possible in pursuing a person's best interests.[48] It will therefore be unlawful to use force if a less forceful alterative way of providing the treatment was available. Where restraint must be used the Act specifically states that the use of it must be necessary to promote the person's best interests and be proportionate to the harm or risk of harm the person may suffer otherwise.[49] It must be the minimum necessary in terms of both the amount of force used and the extent of time it is used for. It should be remembered that where a person is deprived of their liberty this will infringe Article 5 of the European Convention on Human Rights, and it may be impossible to justify it unless doing so was necessary and proportionate.[50]

To what extent are the values, character, and views while competent relevant to assessing best interests?

Imagine that someone is deciding what food to give to an older person lacking capacity. Should account be taken of their practices and beliefs prior to losing capacity? If they were a vegan before loss of capacity is that relevant in assessing their current best interests? The issue is particularly relevant if following their prior beliefs would cause them some harm (for example, if there were medical reasons against providing a vegan diet).

---

[47] The Mental Capacity (Deprivation of Liberty: Standard Authorisations, Assessments and Ordinary Residence) Regulations 2008 set out procedures that should be followed if a person is to be deprived of their liberty.

[48] MCA, s 1(6); and Code of Practice, para 2.14.

[49] MCA, ss 6(2) and 6(3)(a)–(b).

[50] Code of Practice, paras 6.44 and 6.49; and *HL v The United Kingdom* (Application No 45508/99).

Section 4(6) states that in determining a person's best interests account should be taken of:

(a) the person's past and present wishes and feelings (and, in particular, any relevant written statement made by him when he had capacity),
(b) the beliefs and values that would be likely to influence his decision if he had capacity, and
(c) the other factors that he would be likely to consider if he were able to do so.

So, sticking with our example of the person now incompetent, but who followed a vegan diet while competent, it is clear that their views while competent are to be taken into account. However, they are to be taken into account *in order to determine what is in a person's best interests*. I suggest, therefore, when deciding between two options between which on an objective measure there is nothing to choose, the decision-maker should follow that which would be in line with the prior wishes of the individual. Where, however, on an objective measure the course which would be consistent with the prior views of the individual would harm them, the statute appears to suggest that the objective assessment option should be followed. So, in our example, if following the vegan diet will cause even a little harm to the individual, it should not be provided. That is not a solution many people will feel comfortable with, but it appears to be the one based on the statute. That seems to be supported by the Code of Practice, which states:

Even if they cannot make the decision, their wishes and feelings, beliefs and values should be taken fully into account—whether expressed in the past or now. But their wishes and feelings, beliefs and values will not necessarily be the deciding factor in working out their best interests. Any such assessment must consider past and current wishes and feelings, beliefs and values alongside all other factors, but the final decision must be based entirely on what is in the person's best interests.[51]

A useful decision in this regard is *Ahsan v Universities Hospital Leicester*,[52] where in the context of tort litigation a dispute arose over the care of a Muslim woman who following an accident had lost capacity. Her family wanted her cared for in accordance with Muslim tradition, which would be more expensive than otherwise would be the case. An argument was made that as she lacked capacity and did not know what care she was receiving it could not be said to be in her best interests to receive Muslim care. Hegarty J firmly rejected this:

I do not think for one moment that a reasonable member of the public would consider that the religious beliefs of an individual and her family should simply be disregarded in deciding how she should be cared for in the unhappy event of supervening mental incapacity. On the contrary, I would have thought that most reasonable people would expect, in the event of some catastrophe of that kind, that they would be cared for, as far as practicable, in such a way as to ensure that they were treated with due regard for their personal dignity and with proper respect for their religious beliefs.[53]

[51] Code of Practice, para 5.38.   [52] [2006] EWHC 2624 (QB).   [53] Para 51.

This decision shows how where a treatment is not harmful to a patient, their previous beliefs and values may be decisive.

Some critics of the best interests test have promoted the use of substituted judgement as an alternative. This approach has found favour in some American courts, although not in English ones.[54] Its approach is to require the decision-maker to imagine what the incompetent individual would have wanted had he or she been able to make the decision. Typically, this will involve ascertaining the views and behaviour of the individual while having capacity and using these to determine the decision they would have made. Often, of course, such a decision will be in line with what would be in their best interests, but it may be that the decision-maker will decide that the individual would have made a harmful decision. Perhaps the obvious example might be where a decision-maker making a decision on behalf of a Jehovah's Witness who lacks capacity decides to refuse to consent to blood transfusion. The appeal of the substituted judgement approach is that it means we are not in a job of determining what is good or bad for people, when that is such a controversial issue. Rather, we can ask the less controversial question of what this person would have wanted had they been able to make the decision. Critics suggest that in fact it is no less certain than the best interests test. Rebecca Dresser claims the substituted judgement 'is indeterminate enough to permit almost any treatment opinion preferred by a patient's family, guardian, or physician'.[55]

Relevance of current views

It should not be thought that simply because a person lacks capacity they therefore do not have views about how they should be treated. Indeed, a person who lacks capacity should be encouraged to participate in the decision-making process.[56] Section 4(6) sets out obligations on the decision-maker:

He must consider, so far as is reasonably ascertainable—
  (a) the person's past and present wishes and feelings (and, in particular, any relevant written statement made by him when he had capacity),
  (b) the beliefs and values that would be likely to influence his decision if he had capacity, and
  (c) the other factors that he would be likely to consider if he were able to do so.

---

[54] B Rich, 'Medical Paternalism v Respect for Patient Autonomy: The More Things Change the More They Remain the Same' (2006) 10 *Michigan State University Journal of Medicine and Law* 87; and M Dunn, I Clare, A Holland, and M Gunn, 'Constructing and Reconstructing "Best Interests": An Interpretative Examination of Substitute Decision-making under the Mental Capacity Act 2005' (2007) 29 *Journal of Social Welfare and Family Law* 117.

[55] R Dresser, 'Precommitment: A Misguided Strategy for Securing Death with Dignity' (2003) 81 *Texas Law Review* 1823.

[56] MCA, s 4(5).

Notice, however, that the current views can only be taken into account in so far as they might reveal what is in the person's best interests.[57] As the Code of Practice on the Mental Capacity Act puts it:

Even if the person lacks capacity to make the decision, they may have views on matters affecting the decision, and on what outcome would be preferred. Their involvement can help work out what would be in their best interests.[58]

And:

People who cannot express their current wishes and feelings in words may express themselves through their behaviour. Expressions of pleasure or distress and emotional responses will also be relevant in working out what is in their best interests.[59]

So, the current views and feelings of an individual are relevant in ascertaining the present emotional and physical status of the patient.[60] There is the very practical point that giving treatment to a patient which they oppose may well not be clinically effective. Many treatments require the cooperation of the patient if they are to be effective. There may be difficulties in administering treatment which the person is opposing. The physical and emotional harm to the patient and those administering the treatment may counterbalance its benefits. This point is demonstrated in *A Primary Care Trust v AH*,[61] where the trust applied for an order under the Mental Capacity Act 2005 concerning an adult suffering from epilepsy (P) who was living with his mother (H). H was unhappy with the medication that was being given to P and refused to cooperate with some aspects of his treatment. The local authority wanted to have P's health and social needs assessed. H was happy to agree to this at one particular unit, although there would be a delay before that assessment could take place. The trust wanted the assessment to take place at another unit, which could make the assessment without delay. They argued that an immediate assessment was in P's best interest because of the urgency of the concerns about the situation. Sir Mark Potter emphasized that if P were removed from H without her consent, P was likely to be fearful and reluctant to cooperate. However, this needed to be balanced against the desirability for an immediate assessment. He held that H's preferred unit should be used as long as P could be seen within a week and, if not, then a reasonable degree of force could be used to remove him from his mother and assess him at another unit.[62] This case demonstrates how the views of the individual may in a practical sense affect the assessment of a person's best interests.

The Code of Practice gives this example:

Andre, a young man with severe learning disabilities who does not use any formal system of communication, cuts his leg while outdoors. There is some earth in the wound.

---

[57] MCA, s 4(6).   [58] Code of Practice, para 5.22.   [59] Code of Practice, para 5.40.
[60] N Cantor, *Making Medical Decisions for the Profoundly Mentally Disabled* (MIT Press, 2005), at 204.
[61] [2008] EWHC 1403 (Fam).   [62] MCA, s 15(1)(c) was relied upon.

A doctor wants to give him a tetanus jab, but Andre appears scared of the needle and pushes it away. Assessments have shown that he is unable to understand the risk of infection following his injury, or the consequences of rejecting the injection. The doctor decides that it is in Andre's best interests to give the vaccination. She asks a nurse to comfort Andre, and if necessary, restrain him while she gives the injection. She has objective reasons for believing she is acting in Andre's best interests, and for believing that Andre lacks capacity to make the decision for himself. So she should be protected from liability under section 5 of the Act.[63]

Despite the apparent downplaying of the significance of the incompetent person's current wishes in the Mental Capacity Act, Munby J in a recent decision has emphasized their importance. In *Re MM (An Adult)*,[64] he had this to say:

A great judge once said, 'all life is an experiment,' adding that 'every year if not every day we have to wager our salvation upon some prophecy based upon imperfect knowledge' (see Holmes J in *Abrams v United States* (1919) 250 US 616 at pages 624, 630). The fact is that all life involves risk, and the young, the elderly and the vulnerable, are exposed to additional risks and to risks they are less well equipped than others to cope with. But just as wise parents resist the temptation to keep their children metaphorically wrapped up in cotton wool, so too we must avoid the temptation always to put the physical health and safety of the elderly and the vulnerable before everything else. Often it will be appropriate to do so, but not always. Physical health and safety can sometimes be bought at too high a price in happiness and emotional welfare. The emphasis must be on sensible risk appraisal, not striving to avoid all risk, whatever the price, but instead seeking a proper balance and being willing to tolerate manageable or acceptable risks as the price appropriately to be paid in order to achieve some other good in particular to achieve the vital good of the elderly or vulnerable person's happiness. What good is it making someone safer if it merely makes them miserable?

He went on to say that 'close regard' should be paid to the current views of a person lacking capacity.[65]

Despite Munby J's comments, and they are yet to be approved at Appeal Court level, the law still appears to take the view that the views of an individual lacking capacity do not carry any weight in and of themselves outside the context of best interest. The reason for this is that their decisions are not protected by the principle of autonomy. Their decisions cannot be assumed to be an assessment of what they want for their lives, because they lack the ability to make any assessment of that kind. It has been said that dementia in particular can cause a loss of memory, an instability in desires, and an absence of connection between desires and personality which render the decision not worthy of respect under the principle of autonomy.[66]

[63] Code of Practice, para 5.38.   [64] [2007] EWHC 2003 (Fam), para 120.
[65] Para 121.
[66] See S Holm, 'Autonomy, Authenticity, or Best Interest' (2001) 4 *Medicine, Health Care and Philosophy* 153, at 154–5.

I would argue that there are good reasons for placing weight on the views of a person who lacks capacity.[67] It is true that as the person is incompetent the autonomy principle may not justify giving weight to their views. However, there are other reasons for respecting an individual's wishes. These include the right to dignity.[68] There is no getting away from the fact that the concept of dignity is unclear and that it means a variety of things to different people.[69] However, it is submitted that dignity has a broader meaning than simply respecting autonomy.[70] Norman Cantor has argued that:

It would be dehumanizing to ignore the will and feelings of a profoundly disabled person and to simply impose a surrogate's will. This would treat the prospective patient as if he or she were an inanimate object.[71]

To count the wishes and desires of an incompetent person as no more than the grunts of an animal is to show a lack of respect.[72] Forcing treatment on an objecting person (even if they lack capacity) contravenes their dignity.[73] It fails to show appropriate reverence of the person. However confused, muddled, and misled, the individual's views are those of a person and dignity requires that they be respected as the views of a person.[74] This is reflected in the common practice among health care professionals of obtaining the assent of a person to treatment, even if they clearly lack capacity to make a decision.[75] This represents an acknowledgement that the individual, whatever their mental capabilities, deserved to be treated as a fellow human being.

Other rights that might be brought into play include the right to liberty, which is protected in Article 5 of the European Convention of Human Rights. This

---

[67] J Herring, 'Losing it? Losing What? The Law and Dementia', *Child and Family Law Quarterly*, forthcoming.

[68] R Randall and R Downi, *The Philosophy of Palliative Care* (Oxford University Press, 2006); M Häyry, 'Another Look at Dignity' (2004) 13 *Cambridge Quarterly of Healthcare Ethics* 7; and L Nordenfelt, 'Dignity and the Care of the Elderly' (2003) 6 *Medicine, Health Care and Philosophy* 10.

[69] R Brownsword, 'Human rights—What Hope? Human Dignity—What Scope?' in J Gunning and S Holm (eds), *Ethics, Law and Society* (Ashgate, 2005).

[70] See the discussions in J Miola, 'The Need for Informed Consent: Lessons from the Ancient Greeks' (2006) 15 *Cambridge Quarterly of Healthcare Ethics* 152; and S Martyn, 'Substitute Judgment, Best Interests and the Need for Best Respect' (1994) 3 *Cambridge Quarterly of Healthcare Ethics* 3.

[71] N Cantor, *Making Medical Decisions for the Profoundly Mentally Disabled* (MIT Press, New York, 2005), at 206. See also E Koppelman, 'Dementia and Dignity: Towards a New Method of Surrogate Decision Making' (2002) 27 *Journal of Medicine and Philosophy* 65.

[72] L Nordenfelt, 'Dignity and the Care of the Elderly' (2003) 6 *Medicine, Health Care and Philosophy* 130.

[73] S Pleschberge, 'Dignity and the Challenge of Dying in Nursing Homes: The Residents' View' (2007) 36 *Age and Ageing* 197.

[74] See the discussion in L Örulv and N Nikku, 'Dignity Work in Dementia Care: Sketching a Microethical Analysis' (2007) 6 *Dementia* 507.

[75] V Molinaril *et al*, 'Principles and Practice of Geriatric Assent' (2006) 10 *Aging & Mental Health* 48.

right exists for the incompetent as much as the competent.[76] Requiring medical professionals to respect the wishes of an incompetent person will promote good patient-doctor relationships. It will encourage truth telling, openness, and trust, which are more likely to be fostered by listening to and attaching weight to the wishes of a patient, even where they are incompetent. Linked to this argument is the fact that a hospital is meant to be a place of cure and recovery. The sight or sound of a patient being forced to receive treatment against their will is likely to be traumatic for staff and patients. Finally, it will mean that doctors and nurses will not need to make decisions on controversial social or religious issues if they are permitted to follow the wishes of the individual.

These arguments lead me to conclude that even though the views of a person judged to lack capacity are no longer protected by the right of autonomy, this does not mean their views count for nothing. There are several other legal principles and values which can be used to give weight to their views. Valuing a person requires an acknowledgement that the person is still a sentient person who is worthy of respect and being listened to.[77] I am not suggesting that the incompetent patient's wishes should be followed regardless of the consequences. Rather, the wishes of the incompetent person should be followed unless there is a good reason for not doing so.[78]

To what extent are the views or interests of those caring for the incapacitated individual relevant?

Section 4(7) of the Mental Capacity Act states that, if practical and appropriate, when determining a person's best interests the decision-maker should take account of:

(a) anyone named by the person as someone to be consulted on the matter in question or on matters of that kind,
(b) anyone engaged in caring for the person or interested in his welfare,
(c) any donee of a lasting power of attorney granted by the person, and
(d) any deputy appointed for the person by the court, as to what would be in the patient's best interests.

This provision makes it clear that the views of carers or relatives are only to be taken into account in so far as they relate to best interests. The significance of this may be as follows. Consider a decision is being made about whether to offer P treatment to deal with incontinence. The evidence suggests that P is unaware of his incontinence and it causes him no harm. There is evidence that

---

[76] *HL v UK* Application no 45508/99, 5 October 2004.
[77] E Koppelman, 'Dementia and Dignity: Towards a New Method of Surrogate Decision Making' (2002) 27 *Journal of Medicine and Philosophy* 65.
[78] E Miller, 'Listening to the Disabled: End-of-life Medical Decision Making and the Never Competent' (2006) 74 *Fordham Law Review* 2889, at 2920.

the medication has some side effects, which may cause P very mild harm. P's carer may find dealing with P's incontinence a particular burden and the relief of it through treatment would greatly ease the burden of caring. The benefits to the carer would not carry weight as they would not relate to the best interests of the patient. That is unless the carer could say, 'if the incontinence is not dealt with I will not be able to continue caring for P, or not care as well as I am currently, and that will harm P.'

The issue of the relevance of carers' interests in making decisions is considered further in chapter 4.

End-of-life issues

As a basic principle of medical law, it is never lawful to provide medical treatment for the purpose of killing a patient. That would be murder.[79] However, there are cases where a medical team can lawfully decide not to offer life-saving treatment or to provide a treatment in order to relieve pain, but which will also hasten death. When these decisions need to be made about a person who has lost capacity the normal best interest applies. However, section 4(5) of the Act states:

Where the determination is in relation to life-sustaining treatment [the decision maker] must not, in considering whether the treatment is in the best interests of the person concerned, be motivated by a desire to bring about his death.[80]

Life-sustaining treatment is defined as 'treatment which in the view of a person providing health care for the person concerned is necessary to sustain life.'[81]

The provision, at first sight, appears to be in line with the general principles governing end of life treatment: a doctor must not intentionally kill a patient. Indeed, by using the word 'motive', the statute makes it clear that a doctor who gives pain-relieving medication in order to relieve pain, but foreseeing that it will kill the patient, will be absolved of any criminal liability.

The provision has been criticized. It has been argued that if the medical professional is providing treatment which is in the best interests of the patient, their motive should be irrelevant.[82] If a patient is suffering unbearable pain and good medical practice recommends the giving of morphine, should a doctor who gives

---

[79] J Herring, *Criminal Law: Text Cases and Materials* (3rd edn, Oxford University Press, 2008), ch 5.

[80] J Coggon, 'Ignoring the Moral and Intellectual Shape of the Law after *Bland*: The Unintended Side-Effect of a Sorry Compromise' (2007) 27 *Legal Studies* 110 for a useful discussion of this provision.

[81] MCA, s 4(10).

[82] J Coggon, 'Ignoring the Moral and Intellectual Shape of the Law after *Bland*: The Unintended Side-Effect of a Sorry Compromise' (2007) 27 *Legal Studies* 110.

that morphine incur criminal liability because his or her motive is to kill the individual? Indeed, it is interesting to note that the Code of Practice states:

Importantly, section 4(5) cannot be interpreted to mean that doctors are under an obligation to provide, or to continue to provide, life sustaining treatment where that treatment is not in the best interests of the person, even where the person's death is foreseen.[83]

This seems to imply that if a professional is following sound medical practice, their motive is not relevant. But this is not quite what the statute says.

Whether it is in a patient's interests to die is of course a controversial and complex issue. A vast amount has been written on the issue and it would not be appropriate to go into it all here.[84] There have been many cases where allowing a person to die has been found to be in their best interests, or at least not contrary to their best interests.[85]

One concern here is research indicating that when making end-of-life decisions, people tend to make very different decisions on behalf of others than they make for themselves.[86] In particular, it is noticeable that when making decisions on behalf of others, age plays an important role. The survey found that, in general, people did not think aggressive treatments were in the best interests of elderly patients.[87] This may reflect ageist assumptions and indeed our inaccurately pessimistic assessments of what it is like to suffer severe illness or disabilities.[88]

Critics of the best interests principle

The most prominent criticisms of the best interest principle will be apparent from the discussion above, namely that it leads to vagueness and unpredictability. Best interests can be made to mean pretty much whatever you want it to mean. Consider, for example, whether the best interests principle should mean that people who lack capacity should be stopped from smoking.[89] One can imagine a variety of views on that question. This has led one leading commentator to claim that the notion of best interests is 'empty rhetoric'.[90] Worse, it allows the judiciary and other decision-makers to give effect to their prejudices. While there is much truth in these concerns, supporters would argue that it is the critics who have failed to produce any more certain guidelines. Each person is so different and the circumstances in which decisions need to be taken vary so greatly that providing

---

[83] Code of Practice, para 5.33.

[84] D Wilkinson, 'Is it in the Best Interests of an Intellectually Disabled Infant to Die?' (2006) 32 *Journal of Medical Ethics* 454.

[85] *Airedale NHS Trust v Bland* [1993] 1 All ER 821 is the best known example.

[86] B Zikmund-Fisher, H Lacey, and A Fagerlin, 'The Potential Impact of Decision Role and Patient Age on End-of-Life Treatment Decision-Making' (2008) 34 *Journal of Medical Ethics* 327.

[87] Ibid.

[88] D Gilbert, *Stumbling on Happiness* (Vintage, 2005).

[89] C Ardill, *The Residents & Relatives Association Newsletter* (London, Summer 2007).

[90] J Montgomery, 'Rhetoric and Welfare' (1989) 9 *Oxford Journal of Legal Studies* 395.

any more definite guidance than that you should do what is best for the incapacitated individual is difficult, if not impossible. More rigid guidelines might create greater flexibility, but with the danger of imposing an unsuitable solution on an unusual case.

The other common criticisms have been mentioned above. We have seen that the best interests principle means that decisions are taken concerning what is in the best interests of a person, with no consideration being given to the interests of others, in particular those who care for them. In chapter 4, it will be argued that this failure to take into account the interests of those caring for the individual was inappropriate. We have also seen criticisms of the failure to attach sufficient weight to the current views of the incompetent person.

One criticism of the best interests test is that it might operate reasonably well in a hospital setting where a discrete decision has to be made, for example, what medical treatment should be given; but it is less effective in a setting such as residential care, where hundreds of decisions have to be made each day and these decisions are part of an ongoing set of relationships between the residents and staff.[91] As Dunn *et al* point out:

> making an individual discrete decision does not fit with the ongoing process of staff-resident interaction through which residents are supported in their daily lives. Instead, relational substitute decision-making was characterised by a chain of decisions extending into the past and the future.[92]

Communal living may require, for example, the setting of meal times, which may not be in the best interests of each individual. Deciding on an outing for residents, again, is unlikely to accord with the best interests of each individual there. Allowing residents to make decisions which cause them some harm may in the long term help to build up trust and independence.

There are also concerns over the application of the Mental Capacity Act to black and minority ethnic group elders. Assessment of capacity may require effective interpreters to be present, although in other contexts these services have been found lacking.[93] There may also be complicating cultural factors. It has been suggested, for example, that Jain elders are expected to disengage from economic and social responsibilities and they may therefore indicate that their eldest son should make the decisions.[94] This, however, should not be seen as evidence of incapacity. In other cases, a woman may feel that her husband should make decisions on her behalf. The Act does not clearly deal with these cases. The probable answer is that a person who has capacity is entitled to exercise their decision-making

---

[91] M Dunn, I Clare, and A Holland, 'Substitute Decision-Making for Adults with Intellectual Disabilities Living in Residential Care: Learning Through Experience' (2008) 16 *Health Care Analysis* 52.

[92] Ibid, at 56.

[93] A Shah and C Heginbotham, 'The Mental Capacity Act: Some Implications for Black and Minority Ethnic Elders' (2008) 37 *Age and Ageing* 242.

[94] Ibid.

capacity by saying 'I will do whatever X says'. After all, this is not unusual: often a patient will say 'I will agree to whatever treatment the doctor recommends'.

Advance decisions

Advance decisions are known as advance directives or 'living wills'. 'Advance decisions' is the terminology used in the Mental Capacity Act 2005. They are entered into by a competent person who wishes to make arrangements about how they will be treated if they lose capacity.

Law

The Act gives some effect to advance decisions, but only in a rather limited way. Section 24 defines an advance decision:

'Advance Decision' means a decision made by a person ('P'), after he has reached 18 and when he has capacity to do so, that if—

(a) at a later time and in such circumstances as he may specify, a specified treatment is proposed to be carried out or continued by a person providing health care for him, and

(b) at that time he lacks capacity to consent to the carrying out or continuation of the treatment,

the specified treatment is not to be carried out or continued.

If the advance decision is rejecting life-saving treatment, it must be in writing, signed by the individual, and witnessed by a third party.[95] It must also explicitly state that it is to apply even where life is at risk. If the directive is not about life-saving treatment, it need not be in writing. Indeed, there are no formality requirements at all. This could create difficulties if a relative recalls a conversation many years previously and seeks to claim it is an advance decision. *W Healthcare NHS Trust v H*,[96] a case prior to the implementation of the Act, concerned a conversation 10 years previously in which a person said 'I don't want to be kept alive by machines'. It was held that this was too vague to be an advance decision and there was no evidence that the individual had thought through the issues. That may be true of many 'off hand' comments. If an individual wants to ensure their decision is respected, putting it in writing after discussing the matter with a doctor may be the most reliable way, even though that is not required by the statute.[97] Although the Code of Practice states that formal language need not be used in an advance decision,[98] the less precise the terminology used the less likely

[95] MCA, s 25(6).   [96] [2005] 1 WLR 834.
[97] Code of Practice, para 1.14 recommends that people seek medical advice before making an advance decision.
[98] Code of Practice, para 1.12.

it is to be effective. Another benefit of obtaining medical advice is that the patient can be clear about what treatment options may be available and which they wish to receive and which they do not.[99]

The effect of an advance decision is set out in section 26:

If P has made an advance decision which is—
  (a) valid, and
  (b) applicable to the treatment,
the decision has the effect as if he had made it, and had had capacity to make it, at the time when the question arises whether the treatment should be carried out or continued.

It is important to appreciate that the enforceability of advance decisions in the Mental Capacity Act is very limited. First, the decision is only enforceable in so far as it requires treatment *not* to be provided or continued. A directive stating that certain treatment should be provided will not be binding.[100] Of course, a doctor may take an advance decision requesting a particular treatment into account when deciding what treatment to give. So, you cannot issue an effective advance directive asking that in certain circumstances you are given life-saving drugs, or even food or water.[101] The Code of Practice states this clearly:

People can only make advance decisions to *refuse* treatment. Nobody has the legal right to demand specific treatment, either at the time or in advance. So no-one can insist (either at the time or in advance) on being given treatments that healthcare professionals consider to be clinically unnecessary, futile or inappropriate. But people can make a request or state their wishes and preferences in advance.[102]

One important limitation on the ability to refuse treatment is that the Code of Practice states that an advance decision cannot be used to refuse basic elements of care, such as washing.[103] The justification for this seems to be that following such a directive would leave an individual undignified and cause distress to staff and others.

Secondly, the directive only applies in relation to medical treatment. It does not apply, therefore, to requests dealing with day-to-day issues such as where a person should live, what kind of food they should be given, or religious issues. In those cases a decision-maker should take into account an incapacitated person's earlier expressed wishes in deciding what is in the incapacitated person's best interests,[104] but is not bound by them.

A third point to notice is that even though an advance decision has been made it is not binding where it is invalid. An example would be where P made

---

[99] For evidence that many making advance decisions are ill-informed, see: E Porkensky and B Carpenter, 'Knowledge and Perceptions in Advance Care Planning' (2008) 20 *Journal of Aging and Health* 89; and R Dresser, 'Precommitment: A Misguided Strategy for Securing Death with Dignity' (2003) 81 *Texas Law Review* 1823, at 1834.
[100] *R (Burke) v General Medical Council* [2005] 3 FCR 169.   [101] Ibid.
[102] Code of Practice, para 9.5.   [103] Code of Practice, para 9.24.   [104] MCA, s 4(6).

the directive when she was under the age of 18 or lacked capacity. The Code of Practice states that the assumption should be that the maker of an advance decision had capacity unless there are reasonable grounds to doubt that.[105] An advance decision does not apply where P has withdrawn the decision or where P has done something which is 'inconsistent with the decision'.[106] This appears to give broad scope to ignore the directive. An example of the kind of case Parliament may have had in mind in making this proviso is *HE v A Hospital NHS Trust*[107] (a case decided before the Mental Capacity Act came into force). A patient, while a Jehovah's Witness, signed an advance decision indicating that she would not want to receive blood transfusions, even if without them she would die. After signing it, she ceased to be an active Jehovah's Witness and later become engaged to be married to a Muslim man. She subsequently suffered an injury which required a transfusion. The court found that the directive could no longer be considered binding given her loss of faith and other circumstances.

It is unclear how much evidence should be required before an advance directive is to be taken to have been overruled by subsequent events in an individual's life. For example, if a case like *HE v A Hospital NHS Trust*[108] arose, what kind of evidence must be provided and how strong must it be to persuade a court that an individual had lost their faith? Would hearsay evidence be sufficient? Would it be enough if a friend gave evidence that during a conversation the individual had indicated that she planned to revoke the directive, but never did?

An advance decision will also be ineffective if 'there are reasonable grounds for believing that circumstances exist which P did not anticipate at the time of the advance decision and which would have affected his decision had he anticipated them.'[109] This raises a host of possible reasons for avoiding following an advance directive: for example, that the pain suffered by P is far less than he imagined it to be. Or P did not realize when signing the advance decision that newly approved recent treatment would be available. There is ample evidence that people are very bad at imagining what it will be like to suffer a serious illness.[110] This means that it will be easy to determine that an advance decision is ineffective. The Code of Practice states:

when deciding whether an advance decision applies to the proposed treatment, healthcare professionals must consider:

- how long ago the advance decision was made, and
- whether there have been changes in the patient's personal life (for example, the person is pregnant, and this was not anticipated when they made the advance decision) that might affect the validity of the advance decision, and
- whether there have been developments in medical treatment that the person did not foresee (for example, new medications, treatment or therapies).[111]

---

[105] Code of Practice, para 9.8.   [106] MCA, s 25(2).
[107] [2003] EWHC 1017 (Fam).   [108] Ibid.   [109] MCA, s 25(4).
[110] D Gilbert, *Stumbling on Happiness* (Vintage, 2005).   [111] Code of Practice, para 9.32.

Yet another issue may arise if the current wishes of the incapacitated patient are in conflict with an applicable advance decision. For example, an incompetent patient is requesting treatment, even though there is in force an advance decision refusing consent. At first sight, it might be thought that the Act requires health care providers to comply with the advance decision. Section 24 explains that the advance decision becomes effective when the patient loses capacity. A person can revoke an advance decision,[112] but needs to have capacity to do that. However, as Peter Bartlett points out, in fact the answer to our scenario is 'not obvious'. He refers to section 25(2)(c), which states that an advance decision will be invalid if the individual 'has done anything... clearly inconsistent with the advance decision remaining his fixed decision.'[113] He argues that as the provision is not expressly limited to acts while the person has capacity, then acts during incapacity could be taken to be inconsistent with the directive and hence render it invalid.[114] Another subsection that could be used to bolster such an argument is section 25(4)(c), which states that the advance decision will not apply if 'there are reasonable grounds for believing that circumstances exist which P did not anticipate at the time of the advance decision and which would have affected his decision had he anticipated them.' I suggest that when people make an advance directive refusing any medical treatment if they suffer from dementia, they do not imagine that when they develop dementia they may actually very much want that treatment.

A fourth point is that in *HE v A Hospital NHS Trust*,[115] the court held that where there is a doubt over an advance decision concerning life-saving treatment, the court should presume in favour of preserving life. In other words, if following an advance decision will lead to death, it should be respected only if there is no doubt that it is effective. Such a presumption is not made explicit in the Act. I would not be surprised if the court took a similar line under the new legislation.

Another important provision concerning advance directives is section 26(2), which states: 'A person does not incur liability for carrying out or continuing the treatment unless, at the time, he is satisfied that an advance decision exists which is valid and applicable to the treatment.'[116] This provides a defence to a doctor who does not follow an advance decision if he or she is not 'satisfied' that the decision exists or is applicable. This appears to indicate that if the medical professional is doubtful about the validity of an advance directive, he or she is free to ignore it. However, under section 26(3), if a person withdraws treatment incorrectly believing there is a valid advance decision, no offence is committed. In effect, then, in a case where the validity of the advance decision is doubtful,

---

[112] eg MCA, s 25(2).

[113] P Bartlett, *Blackstone's Guide to The Mental Capacity Act 2005* (Oxford University Press, 2005), at para 2.115.

[114] A Maclean, 'Advance Directives and the Rocky Waters of Anticipatory Decision-Making' (2008) 16 *Medical Law Review* 2.

[115] [2003] EWHC 1017 (Fam).

[116] Also, notably, the test is subjective. If a medical professional believes the directive to be invalid, even if that is not a reasonable decision, it seems the defence is available.

no offence will be committed if the medical professional follows the advance decision, nor if he or she ignores it.

The result of these provisions means that advance directives are not as binding as might be thought. They can readily be found inapplicable if there is evidence that they no longer reflect the individual's views or if the circumstances that the person finds themselves in are not what they imagined they would be when writing the directive. Further, there is statutory protection from legal action for those who ignore a directive if there are doubts over its validity. This has led critics of the Act to claim that the law has failed to give adequate effect to directives.[117] Sabine Michalowski[118] has argued that if the law is to take seriously the right of a patient to refuse life-saving medical treatment, a physician who provides it in the face of non-consent in the form of an advance decision should be found to have committed a battery.[119] Only if the physician has made a reasonable mistake as to the validity of the absence of consent should they have a defence.

Alasdair Maclean correctly summarized the Act's approach to advance decisions:

the Government has symbolically supported individual autonomy while providing sufficient scope for interpretation to allow many advance directives to be judged invalid or inapplicable when the likely consequences are contrary to the healthcare professional's or judge's view of an appropriate outcome.[120]

Indeed, his interpretation is that:

the legal implementation of advance directives serves to facilitate the provision of healthcare, to protect the patient's welfare and to protect the healthcare professionals from liability. Any protection of autonomy is secondary to those primary goals.[121]

In support of the rather wary approach towards advance directives, it should be borne in mind how difficult it is to draft an advance directive, unless the person is facing a particular foreseeable condition. Given the variety of illnesses and circumstances a person can find themselves in, it is difficult to predict them all and then determine how one would wish to be treated. It is notable that in one postal survey of UK geriatricians,[122] 92 per cent favoured the use of living wills and only 2 per cent saw no advantages in their use. However, among those geriatricians who had dealt with patients who had made living wills, only 39 per cent changed

---

[117] C Johnston, 'Does the Statutory Regulation of Advance Decision-Making Provide Adequate Respect for Patient Autonomy?' (2005) 26 *Liverpool Law Review* 189.

[118] S Michalowski, 'Trial and Error at the End of Life—No Harm Done?' (2007) 27 *Oxford Journal of Legal Studies* 257.

[119] She argues in favour of general and special damages being available.

[120] A Maclean, 'Advance Directives and the Rocky Waters of Anticipatory Decision-Making' (2008) 16 *Medical Law Review* 2.

[121] Ibid.

[122] R Schiff, P Sacares, J Snook, C Rajkumar, and C Bulpitt, 'Living Wills and the Mental Capacity Act: A Postal Questionnaire Survey of UK Geriatricians' (2006) 35 *Age and Ageing* 116.

the treatment because of their existence. Similarly, in a recent survey on the use of advance directives in an American hospital, it was found that advance directives rarely influenced the medical treatment provided to patients.[123] Another study found that only 39 per cent of the sample wanted their advance directives to be interpreted 'strictly'. A striking 42 per cent wanted physicians to have a lot of or complete leeway to depart from the directive if they felt it was inappropriate.[124] These empirical studies lend support to the caution shown in the Mental Capacity Act towards giving effect to advance decisions.

Philosophical debates over advance directives

If it is accepted that some weight should be attached to the wishes of incompetent people, this leaves the issue of how these are to be taken account of in a case where there is an advance directive. There has been much dispute between those who emphasize the importance of the demented person's interests as they are now and those who seek to elevate the importance of the views of the person they once were. Ronald Dworkin sets out the two views:

> We may think of that person, as the putative holder of rights, in two different ways: as a demented person, in which case we emphasize his present situation and capacities, or as a person who has become demented, in which case we emphasize that his dementia has occurred in the course of a larger life whose whole length must be considered in any decision about what rights he has.[125]

Of course, in many cases there is no difficulty. The proposed treatment or course of action is in the best interests of the patient, they appear content with it, and there is nothing in an advance directive or from their earlier life which would suggest any other course of action. However, it is where there is a clash between a patient's current wishes or current best interests and their views expressed in an effective advance directive that the problems arise.[126]

Dworkin's approach

To advocates of advance directives, it is the fear of losing control which is at the heart of the issue. Few of us like being told what to do or have decisions made on our behalf without our consent. Advance directives offer the possibility of being able to make decisions about how we will be treated when we are unable to make decisions for ourselves. They enable us to make arrangements for the

---

[123] J Cohen and S Lipson, 'Which Advance Directive Matters?' (2008) 30 *Research on Aging* 74.
[124] L Francis, 'Decisionmaking at the End of Life: Patients with Alzheimer's or Other Dementias' (2001) 35 *Georgia Law Review* 539, at 572.
[125] R Dworkin, 'Autonomy and the Demented Self' (1986) 64 *The Milbank Quarterly* 4.
[126] M Newton, 'Precedent Autonomy: Life-Sustaining Intervention and the Demented Patient' (1999) 8 *Cambridge Quarterly of Healthcare Ethics* 189.

final chapter of our lives if we are unable to write it ourselves.[127] One academic has reproduced her own advance directive, which reveals the concerns of many people. It reads:

When I suffer from Alzheimer's disease and I do not recognize my children anymore, and I have to reside in a nursing home permanently, I refuse lifesaving or prolonging treatment. I would hope for euthanasia. I realize there may be a time that I myself am past caring and not unhappy. But I do not want my children to witness and to suffer from my steady decline into nothingness. I see no point at all in continuing my life when I have lost the dignity, the purposes and the emotional commitments that I consider essential to the story of my life and my person.[128]

Ronald Dworkin has written one of the persuasive cases in favour of placing weight on advance directives.[129] Only a brief outline of his views can be presented here. To him, the right of autonomy is central to our humanity. It 'encourages and protects people's general capacity to lead their lives out of a distinctive sense of their own character, a sense of what is important to and for them'.[130] At the heart of his thinking about advance directives is the distinction between critical and experiential interests.[131] He sees experiential interests as concerning the quality of enjoyment or pleasure. They might include pursuing activities such as watching television or drinking tea. Critical interests are all about doing or having in our lives the things that we consider good or valuable. Often, critical interests are pursued despite the fact that they do not provide enjoyment or pleasure. Sacrifices are made for family; projects are pursued even when they have lost some of the 'first love'. Critical interests will involve matters which go to the core of the person, such as religious beliefs and important life projects.

Dworkin argues that it is our critical interests that are most important to our autonomy. These are the things that are at the heart of our plans for our lives. For Dworkin, a person's critical beliefs survive incapacity. A person having lost capacity should be treated in a way which would be consistent with their critical interests, or at least not inconsistent with them. Dworkin can accept that some people without capacity may have experiential interests. They may be able to experience pleasure in certain activities, but respect for these experiential interests should never be at the expense of the patient's critical interests articulated during their competent life. The incompetent person's current wishes should be ignored 'because he lacks the necessary capacity for a fresh exercise of autonomy. His former decision remains in force because no new decision by a

---

[127] L Francis, 'Decision making at the End of Life: Patients with Alzheimer's or Other Dementias' (2001) 35 *Georgia Law Review* 539.

[128] I de Beaufort, 'The View from Before' (2007) 7 *American Journal of Bioethics* 57.

[129] See also, M Quant, 'Precedent Autonomy and Personal Identity' (1999) 9 *Kennedy Institute of Ethics Journal* 365.

[130] R Dworkin, *Life's Dominion* (Harper Collins, 1993), at 224.

[131] For a critical look at Dworkin's writings on this, see J Finnis, 'Euthanasia, Morality, and Law' (1998) 31 *Loyola of Los Angeles Law Review* 1123.

person capable of autonomy has annulled it'.[132] Jeff McMahan even suggests that the competent person is retrospectively harmed if an advance directive is not followed. He argues that the competent part of a person's life should be seen as dominant over the demented part, which should be 'sacrificed for the greater good of her earlier self'.[133]

Dworkin does not shy away from the implications of his approach. He refers to the much-discussed case of Margo.[134] Much discussed not because her scenario is unusual, but because it is so typical. She is described as a 54-year-old woman, suffering from dementia, but extraordinarily happy. Each day is the same. She rereads pages of a book she never finishes, eats the same food (peanut butter and jelly), and paints the same picture. Dworkin argues she has experiential interests: she is able to gain great pleasure from her activities, but she has no critical interests (in respect of her current state). She has lost the ability to develop the life goals central to one's critical interests. Dworkin asks us to imagine that when previously competent she had written an advance directive refusing life-saving treatment if she were ever to suffer dementia. She now has a chest infection and needs antibiotic treatment to cure her. Should it be provided? The scenario is well chosen because of course she is happy in her current state. Dworkin argues that her critical interests as expressed in her advance directive should trump any experiential interests. In short, she should be allowed to die.

Criticisms of Dworkin

Critics of Dworkin have attacked his argument from a number of perspectives. First, and perhaps most prominently, has been the argument that he assumes that the competent person has the right to speak for and about the incompetent person. The objection to this centres on the nature of personhood.[135] As is well known, Derek Parfit, building on the work of John Locke,[136] has argued that central to personhood is consciousness and psychological awareness. Where a person loses capacity, this can cause a loss of psychological continuity. Where the person has no recollection of who they were and loses connections with the values which governed their life, they have, in effect, become a different person. The psychological continuity of the previous person has ceased and a new person(s) has been created. Therefore, when making decisions about the person who has lost capacity, the views of the person with capacity are not the

---

[132] R Dworkin, *Life's Dominion* (Harper Collins, 1993), at 224.

[133] J McMahan, *The Ethics of Killing* (Oxford University Press, 2002), at 502–3.

[134] A Firlik, 'Margo's Logo' (1991) 9 *Journal of the American Medical Association* 201.

[135] J Hughes, 'Views of the Person with Dementia' (2001) 27 *Journal of Medical Ethics* 86; and D Degrazia, 'Advance Directives, Dementia and "the Someone Else Problem"' (1999) 13 *Bioethics* 373.

[136] J Locke, *An Essay Concerning Human Understanding* (1690; A Woozley (ed), William Collins/Fount, 1964); and D Parfit, *Reasons and Reasons* (Oxford University Press, 1984), at 205–7.

same person's views. They are no more relevant than the views of any other person.[137]

This response to Dworkin, unsurprisingly, has, in turn, its critics.[138] It appears to place a lot of weight on a Cartesian dualist split between the mind and the body. It does not recognize the part played by bodies in identity.[139] Even if there is a psychological discontinuity, there is a physical continuity. The current person is still part of the narrative of the life of the earlier person.[140] Even more significantly, these critics of Dworkin overlook the fact that to those who know them, the incompetent person is connected to and represents the competent person. No one, for example, believes that if their parent develops dementia they somehow cease to be their mother or father. When the individual is seen within a relational context they are to their family and community the same person they have always been.[141] There is an additional difficulty for lawyers in accepting Parfit's arguments in this context: that it does not fit with all kinds of legal doctrines.[142] We hardly treat a change in personality as a death of a legal identity.[143] A person facing a criminal charge has no defence based on the fact that the person who committed the crime is psychologically disconnected from them.

A second set of criticisms of Dworkin's views questions the weight he places on critical interests. It may be questioned whether it is possible to divide up a person's interests into critical and experiential ones. At what point does a person's enjoyment of a hobby become a critical interest? Further, do people really sit down and plan a great vision for their lives ruled by higher order preferences, or do they live each day as it comes, or as a life marked by contradiction and chaos, rather than a grand plan?[144] Rebecca Dresser suggests:

many people take life one day at a time. The goal of establishing a coherent narrative may be a less common life theme than the simple effort to accept and adjust to the changing natural and social circumstances that characterize a person's life.[145]

---

[137] An extreme view is that a person with severe dementia ceases to be a person at all. See the discussion in A Buchanan, 'Advance Directives and the Personal Identity Problem' (1988) 17 *Philosophy and Public Affairs* 277.

[138] E Olsen, *The Human Animal* (Oxford University Press, 1997); and M Schechtman, *The Constitution of Selves* (Cornell University Press, 1996).

[139] A Maclean, 'Advance Directives, Future Selves and Decision-Making' (2006) 14 *Medical Law Review* 291.

[140] C Taylor, *Sources of the Self: the Making of the Modern Identity* (Cambridge University Press, 1989).

[141] See the discussions in BA Rich, 'Prospective Autonomy and Critical Interests: A Narrative Defense of the Moral Authority of Advance Directives' (1997) 6 *Cambridge Quarterly of Healthcare Ethics* 138; JC Hughes, 'Views of the Person with Dementia' (2001) 27 *Journal of Medical Ethics* 86; and T Kitwood, 'The Experience of Dementia' (1997) 3 *Aging & Mental Health* 179.

[142] NK Rhoden, 'The Limits of Legal Objectivity' (1990) 68 *North Carolina Law Review* 845, at 852.

[143] BA Rich, 'Prospective Autonomy and Critical Interests: A Narrative Defense of the Moral Authority of Advance Directives' (1997) 6 *Cambridge Quarterly of Healthcare Ethics* 138, at 146.

[144] M Friedman, *Autonomy Gender Politics* (Oxford University Press, 2006), at 39.

[145] R Dresser, 'Dworkin on Dementia: Elegant Theory, Questionable Policy' in H Kuhse and P Singer (eds), *Bioethics: An Anthology* (Blackwell, 1999), at 316.

These criticisms of Dworkin's approach carry some weight. However, the difficulty in applying the distinction he seeks to draw does not necessarily mean that it is of no use. Many of the fundamental distinctions drawn by lawyers are difficult in application, but that does not mean they are not good ones to make.

A third set of criticisms highlights the difficulties in determining whether when the person made the advance directive they had sufficient information to make an informed decision about how they should be treated if they were to lose capacity. For example, they will not know what medical treatment may be available in the future for conditions they fear or even know precisely what it is like to suffer the condition they fear.[146] There is much evidence that although people are terrified of certain conditions, when in fact they suffer them they are far happier than they thought they would be.[147] At most, these arguments seem to suggest that there may be circumstances in which an advance directive is flawed by a lack of knowledge of some subsequent unforeseen development. They do not argue against their use in a situation where a fully informed decision is made about a particular condition which then materializes in exactly the circumstances foreseen by the person while they had capacity.

There is, it is argued, a more powerful objection to Dworkin's approach: the lack of weight attached to the views and welfare of the current incapacitated person. Placing all the weight on critical interests means that in the words of one learned commentator the current individual is a person 'to treat, control, restrain, or perhaps simply tolerate... To take this sort of attitude towards someone is to see him as no longer fully human'.[148] It is suggested that Dworkin's views have gained much support because they have been used in the context of life or death issues. But outside that arena the problems are immediately apparent. A patient of devout religious belief may be concerned that if they lose capacity they will no longer continue their religious devotions, and therefore create an advance directive that religious services are performed in their presence weekly. Such a directive may indeed reflect a critical interest, but should it be followed even if the incompetent person is feeling great anguish when the services take place? Should strict dietary requests expressed in an advance directive be followed if it is causing the individual serious pain? It is hard to justify the pain to the current person caused in the name of values to the previous person of which they have no recollection. While competent, we are willing to accept suffering in the name of pursuing our critical interests and the succour from knowing we are reaching for a higher goal may make those sufferings more bearable. But for the incompetent, there is no compensation, in relation to the crucial interests, for the pain.

---

[146] D Callahan, 'Terminating Life-sustaining Treatment of the Demented' (1995) 25 *Hastings Center Report* 26.

[147] D Gilbert, *Stumbling on Happiness* (Vintage, 2005).

[148] M Moody-Adams, 'On the Old Saw that Character is Destiny' in O Flanegan and A Rorty (eds), *Identity, Character, and Morality: Essays in Moral Psychology* (MIT Press, 1990), at 124.

Dresser's approach

To some commentators, the basic duty owed to those who have lost capacity is that we should protect them and promote their best interests.[149] Rebecca Dresser has been most prominent in promoting this approach.[150] She rejects an argument that the views of the competent person as expressed in an advance directive should dominate the decision as to how they should be treated, because she sees the demented person as vastly altered from the previous person:[151]

Courts have a hard time understanding the subjectivity of the incompetent patient. They sometimes speak as if a patient were still the competent person she once was; they sometimes construct a mythical, generalized competent person to inhabit the body that lies before them.[152]

Instead of focusing on what they would have wanted when competent, she proposes promoting their best interests. John Robertson takes a similar line, arguing:

The values and interests of the competent person no longer are relevant to someone who has lost the rational structure on which those values and interests rested. Unless we are to view competently held values and interests as extending even into situations in which, because of incompetency, they can no longer have meaning, it matters not that as a competent person the individual would not wish to be maintained in a debilitated or disabled state. If the person is no longer competent enough to appreciate the degree of divergence from her previous activity that produced the choice against treatment, the prior directive does not represent her current interests merely because a competent directive was issued.[153]

Dresser points out that throughout our life we change our views and perspectives on the world. Things we dread turn out to be surprisingly enjoyable; people we thought we would not like become friends. Fortunately, we are not tied to our initial experiences and views. In other words, although the person may once have had certain critical interests when they wrote the advance directive, there is no reason to assume that the current person still has them.[154] It is therefore

---

[149] R Dresser, 'Schiavo's Legacy: The Need for an Objective Standard' (2005) 35 *Hastings Center Report* 20.

[150] R Dresser, 'Missing Persons: Legal Perceptions of Incompetent Patients' (1994) 46 *Rutgers Law Review* 609.

[151] Ibid, at 611.

[152] On the difficulties of imagining what it would be like to be different, see D Dennett, *Consciousness Explained* (Little, Brown & Co, 1991), at 441–2; and T Nagel, *The View from Nowhere* (Oxford University Press, 1986), at 13.

[153] J Robertson, 'Second Thoughts on Living Wills' (1991) 21 *Hastings Center Report* 7.

[154] S Holm, 'Autonomy, Authenticity, or Best Interest: Everyday Decision-making and Persons with Dementia' (2001) 4 *Medicine, Health Care & Philosophy* 153.

inappropriate to attach weight to the views of the person before they were in an incapacitated state. Professor Jaworska[155] puts the point this way:

the moral pull of Dresser's position is undeniable: the caregiver... is faced with a person—or if not a fully constituted person, at least a conscious being capable of pleasure and pain—who, here and now, makes a claim on the caregiver to fulfil her needs and desires; why ignore these needs and desires in the name of values that are now extinct?

Considering the case of Margo, Dresser argues that following Dworkin's approach and letting her die from an infection will mean that: 'Happy and contented Margo will experience clear harm from the decision that purports to advance the critical interests she no longer cares about.'[156]

Problems with the Dresser approach

Critics of Dresser's position often criticize her argument that the two people are no longer the same. We have already discussed the 'two person' argument. There is, in fact, no need to adopt that theory to support Dresser's approach. One could readily accept that the two people are indeed the same, but argue that the claims of the now incompetent person to have their welfare promoted, trump the views of the competent person expressed in the advance directive.[157]

A second problem posed by Dresser's argument is exemplified by Dena Davis's article, which accepts Dresser's argument. She entitles her article, 'Help! My Body is being Invaded by an Alien'.[158] She expresses concern that if she develops Alzheimer's, a new form of person will take over her body. To avoid this, suicide when the first stages of Alzheimer's appear is discussed as a sensible option. This is hardly the kind of thinking Dresser would advocate, but it lends itself to it. Dresser's approach offers no hope to those who are terrified of what will happen to them if they lose capacity and want to exercise some control over it. Nor does it readily explain why in fact most carers do instinctively try and treat the incompetent person in line with the values they lived their live by. The *Ahsan* decision,[159] mentioned above, shows how a person's religious beliefs, for example, deserve respect even when they have lost capacity.

Compromise views

The debate between these two views has raged for some time and no consensus has emerged. Several commentators have sought to develop compromise views and this seems the sensible way ahead.[160] In relation to the 'one person or two'

---

[155] A Jaworska, 'Respecting the Margins of Agency: Alzheimer's Patients and the Capacity to Value' (1998) 28 *Philosophy and Public Affairs* 105.

[156] R Dresser, 'Dworkin on Dementia: Elegant Theory, Questionable Policy' (1995) 22 *Hasting Center Report* 32, at 36.

[157] A Buchanan, 'Advance Directives and the Personal Identity Problem' (1988) 17 *Philosophy & Public Affairs* 277.

[158] D Davis, 'Help! My Body is being Invaded by an Alien' (2007) 7 *American Journal of Bioethics* 60.

[159] *Ahsan v University Hospitals Leicester NHS Trust* [2006] EWHC 2624 (QB).

[160] E Boetzkes Gedge, 'Collective Moral Imagination: Making Decisions for Persons with Dementia' (2004) 29 *Journal of Medicine and Philosophy* 435.

debate, the best answer appears to be that there are senses in which the person is the same as the person they were. This is so in a bodily sense, but also in the context of their relationships with others. However, there is another sense where the psychological break is such that what is important about a person has been lost and it makes sense to talk of there being only the most tenuous link between the past and present person. So, the solution there appears to lie in acceptance of the view that the incompetent person is in some senses the same person as the competent person and in others a different person.

On the central policy to adopt, it seems that both camps are too extreme. Dresser's refusal to put any weight on advance directives or the views of the competent person appears too strong. The case of the Muslim woman mentioned earlier is compelling. Where the advance directive applies in relation to an issue which will not seriously harm the patient, it seems that a good argument can be made for respecting it. The desire people have to exercise control over what happens to them when they are no longer able to control their destiny appears to be a strong one, as is demonstrated by the use of wills. Why should it be that if a patient has requested in an advance directive that they be fed vegetarian food if they lose capacity that this wish should not be respected? Allowing some enforcement of advance directives will provide comfort to people when facing the prospect of incapacity. Indeed, Penney Lewis has suggested that a failure to allow a person to exercise some control over what happens to them when they lose capacity could infringe their human rights.[161]

On the other hand, I am not convinced by Dworkin's view that we should comply with an advance directive in relation to an experiential interest, regardless of the pain it will cause the individual. Consider the example of the person asking for a religious service to be preformed regularly in their presence, but which is now causing them anguish. While some weight can be placed on the directive, this should not be at the expense of harm to the current individual.

It is suggested that the correct approach is somewhere between that promoted by Dworkin and that promoted by Dresser. One solution comes from Alasdair Maclean.[162] He recommends following a clear advance directive unless the result would be to cause significant harm, pain, or terror to the patient. In the case of less clear directives, a balancing exercise would be required between the views expressed in the directive and the experiential interests of the person lacking capacity. He accepts that such guidelines will lead to debates over when the harm will be sufficient to mean that the directive should not be followed:

But they seem to capture what is morally important about precedent autonomy-guidance for how one's life winds down; as well as what is morally important about

---

[161] P Lewis, 'Medical Treatment of Dementia Patients at the End of Life: Can the Law Accommodate the Personal Identity and Welfare Problems?' (2006) 13 *European Journal of Health Law* 219.

[162] A Maclean, 'Advance Directives, Future Selves and Decision-Making' (2006) 14 *Medical Law Review* 291.

experiential interests: avoiding pain and continuing experiences of relative quality to the extent that clear prior autonomy is not compromised.[163]

My view would be similar to that, but with greater respect for following the views of the incompetent person. Maclean, as so many others writing in this area, has focused on autonomy to the exclusion of dignity and liberty. I would follow the current wishes of the individual unless those would cause the patient serious harm. Where the current individual does not have strong views, an advance directive can be used to determine how the patient is treated.

Lasting power of attorney

Given the difficulties just mentioned of predicting all of the medical problems one may encounter, an attractive option for some will be the use of a lasting power of attorney (LPOA).[164] This allows someone, while they have capacity, to make an LPOA, which gives authority to the person appointed (the donee) to make decisions about them when they lose capacity.[165] The donee will have no authority until the individual loses capacity. It is possible to appoint different people to oversee financial and medical issues.

The donee can only make decisions based on the best interests principle. The same principles we have just discussed apply. In the Code of Practice, an example is given of a solicitor appointed under a property and affairs LPOA for a person who was a life-long Green Party supporter. The Code recommends that the solicitor takes those values into account if any investment decisions need to be made and so ethical funds should be preferred.[166] The donee is also subject to any limitations in the document which created the LPOA. So, for example, a person may require their donee not to allow them to be moved overseas. However, the donee cannot be compelled to act in a particular way. A person cannot, for example, insist through an LPOA that if they lose capacity they be placed in a particular nursing home. It is unclear from the Mental Capacity Act what a donee is to do if their assessment of what is in the person's best interests differs from a direction in the instrument creating the LPOA.[167] A court is unlikely to interfere in a donee's decision unless it is clearly harmful to the individual.

There are some concerns over the use of lasting powers of attorney. Under the old law, evidence was given that enduring powers of attorney (as they were

---

[163] Ibid, at 310.
[164] The Lasting Powers of Attorney, Enduring Powers of Attorney and Public Guardian Regulations (SI 1253/2007).
[165] Financial LPOA can be used by both donor and donee.
[166] Code of Practice, para 7.20.
[167] P Bartlett, *Blackstone's Guide to the Mental Capacity Act 2005* (Oxford University Press, 2005), at para 2.73.

known) were misused in 10 to 15 per cent of cases.[168] The formal requirement for authorizing the donees has been tightened up in the 2005 Act. The LPOA can only be effective when it is registered. No doubt they are open to abuse as they were in the past, but a balance must be struck between having a system which is workable and efficient and one which protects against abuse.

A rather different concern has been expressed from the perspective of those managing nursing homes.[169] One manager discusses a scenario where a nurse throws away soiled underwear and chocolates found in a room. If a lasting power of attorney has made it clear that they do not want things thrown away, this could amount to the offence of theft.[170] This would be unlikely because the nurse would not be acting dishonestly, but the wider point that a troublesome LPOA may make unreasonable demands of a care home and its staff is a concern.

Deputies and the court of protection

If a person has not appointed an LPOA, the court of protection may become involved in handling their finances and welfare decisions. An application can be made to the court of protection to determine whether a person has the capacity to make a particular decision or kind of decision; or to determine whether it is lawful to treat them in a particular way.[171] So, a doctor or a carer, unsure of whether a proposed treatment was lawful, could first seek a declaration from the court. The kinds of decision that the court could make are listed in section 17 and include an order where P is to live with whom she is to have contact. The court must make the decision based on what is in P's best interests, as understood in the Mental Capacity Act. Where it is proposed to deprive a person of their liberty, an application must be made to court.[172]

If a court decides that decisions need to be made for P on an ongoing basis, it may appoint a deputy. The deputy can make decisions for personal welfare for individuals aged 18 or over. Any decision made must be based on assessment of the person's best interests. A deputy cannot make a decision if they have reasonable grounds to believe that P has capacity to make the decision in the matter.[173]

---

[168] A Martin, 'Powers of Attorney—Peace of Mind or Out of Control?' [2008] *Conveyancer and Property Lawyer* 11 discusses the many problems with the old enduring powers of attorney.

[169] C Hancock, 'Managing the Mental Capacity Act' (2006) 8 *Nursing and Residential Care* 366.

[170] Section 6 means that the protection in s 5 does not apply where the person is acting contrary to an LPOA's wishes.

[171] MCA, s 15.

[172] P Bartlett, *Blackstone's Guide to the Mental Capacity Act 2005* (Oxford University Press, 2005), at para 2.90. See there also, a discussion of other possible matters which might require a court order.

[173] MCA, s 20.

Those deemed just competent

So far, the discussion has been focused on those who lack capacity. However, there are concerns about the law in cases where a person is found to have capacity, but only just. Such cases may give rise to concerns in two main kinds of case. The first are those where a person wishes to embark on a course of action which will cause them significant harm; secondly are cases where a person seeks to engage in behaviour which is uncharacteristic and would be contrary to the values upon which their life was built.[174]

The standard legal approach is that once a person is assessed as having capacity their decisions are entitled to respect. The fact that their decision risks causing them harm is no basis for intervention. Indeed, nearly everyone chooses to engage in activities which are harmful. We all have our vices! Similarly, the fact that their lifestyles reflect different values from those they espoused in the past is no legal ground for preventing them from acting. I am sure we are all relieved we are not stuck with the views and interests of our late teens. Yet it will be argued that this standard approach is insufficiently subtle to deal with the issues at stake.

It is generally agreed that where a person wants to make a decision which appears bizarre, this provides reasons for re-examining the original assessment of capacity. What is controversial is what will be argued next, which is that even if the reassessment concludes that the individual is indeed competent, the law should in some cases allow intervention to prevent the individual from acting.

The importance of autonomy

To start, we need to consider why it is that the law generally respects people's rights to autonomy. We treasure people's autonomy and the power it gives to shape their lives according to their own values. It is seen as a fundamental aspect of our humanity that we should be free to fashion our lives and live out our version of the 'good life'.[175] Ronald Dworkin explains:

autonomy makes each of us responsible for shaping his own life according to some coherent and distinctive sense of character, conviction, and interest. It allows us to lead our own lives rather than being led along them, so that each of us can be, to the extent a scheme of rights can make this possible, what he has made himself. This view of autonomy focuses not on individual decisions one by one, but the place of each decision in a more general program or picture of life the agent is creating and constructing, a conception of character and achievement that must be allowed its own distinctive integrity.[176]

---

[174] What follows is based on material in J Herring, 'Losing it? Losing What? The Law and Dementia', *Child and Family Law Quarterly*, forthcoming.

[175] J Raz, *The Morality of Freedom* (Clarendon Press, 1986).

[176] R Dworkin, 'Autonomy and the Demented Self' (1986) 64 *The Milbank Quarterly* 4, at 5.

Does this mean that we must respect autonomous decisions, however bizarre and harmful? It is suggested not.

Autonomy and harmful decisions

Some commentators have developed the notion of 'risk-relative capacity'. Although it will be argued that this is not a completely convincing concept, discussion of it is helpful.

The 'risk-relative capacity' approach requires a higher standard of competency where an act poses a serious risk of great harm than is required where the decision involves less harm.[177] In other words, there is a sliding scale for capacity, depending on the risk carried by the decision.[178] The higher the risk of harm, the higher the bar of competence is set.[179] Note that the claim is not that riskier decisions involve more complex issues and therefore require a greater level of capacity, but rather that even if two decisions are equally complex, if one involves a higher degree of risk than the other, a greater degree of competence is required.

There are several difficulties with 'risk-relative capacity'.[180] First, it can mean that whether a patient is deemed competent to make a particular decision may depend upon the decision they reach.[181] Imagine a case where a patient is offered a life-saving treatment. If they refuse, this is a decision which will cause them a serious harm and therefore a high level test for capacity is used under the approach. If, however, they are to consent to the treatment, there is less risk of harm and therefore the test for capacity is easier to satisfy.[182] A person of borderline capacity may, therefore, have the capacity to consent to a particular treatment, but not to refuse it. The objection to this is that there is a logicality about saying a person has capacity to make a decision if they say 'yes'; but not if they say 'no'.[183]

---

[177] AE Buchanan and DW Brock, *Deciding for Others: The Ethics of Surrogate Decision Making* (Cambridge University Press, 1989); and J Drane, 'The Many Faces of Competency' (1985) 15 *Hastings Center Report* 17.

[178] M Tunzi, 'Can the Patient Decide? Evaluating Patient Capacity in Practice' (2001) 64 *American Family Physician* 299.

[179] Note that the argument is not that where there is a higher risk of harm the decision is more difficult and therefore a higher degree of capacity is required. T Buller, 'Competence and Risk-Relativity' (2001) 15 *Bioethics* 93.

[180] J DeMarco, 'Competence and Paternalism' (2002) 16 *Bioethics* 231; and G Cale, 'Continuing the Debate over Risk-Related Standards of Competence' (1999) 13 *Bioethics* 131.

[181] M Wicclair, 'The Continuing Debate over Risk-Related Standards of Competence' (1999) 13 *Bioethics* 199.

[182] I Wilks, 'The Debate over Risk-Related Standards of Competence' (1997) 11 *Bioethics* 416. cf G Cale, 'Continuing the Debate over Risk-Related Standards of Competence' (1999) 13 *Bioethics* 131.

[183] One response to this may be to say that if a possible answer to the question involves a high degree of harm, then to answer the question requires a high degree of capacity. Although this side-steps the symmetry problem, it means a wide range of questions would have the heightened degree of capacity. Even 'what would you like for breakfast?' has some possibly dangerous answers!

A second concern with the risk-relative capacity approach is that it involves a conflation of two issues: whether a person has capacity to make a decision; and whether or not a person's decision can ever be overruled on paternalistic grounds.[184] If the real reason why we wish not to respect a person's decision is that we do not agree with it, then we should be open about doing this. As Nancy Knauer[185] has argued, risk-relative capacity 'has the potential to become the ultimate self-fulfilling doctrine: those who exercise approved choices have capacity, whereas those who exercise socially undesirable choices lack capacity'.

These objections to risk-relative capacity are compelling; however, a consideration of them does indicate a more persuasive approach. The argument in favour of risk-relative capacity is that in deciding whether to comply with a person's decision we need to weigh up the importance of respecting autonomy and the value of preventing harm to others.[186] Normally, when these two values are put on the scales, autonomy will win out. However, when very serious harm is done, the scales become more evenly balanced.[187] The argument, then, is that while a decision made by a fully autonomous person will always weigh heavily, the decision of a barely competent person is lighter and can be outweighed by a serious harm. Where, therefore, a serious harm is caused, we need to ensure that the decision is fully autonomous if it is to win out the balancing exercise.[188] This is not as radical an approach as might at first appear. The law often puts in place procedural barriers where a person is about to make a decision with important consequences (eg marriage or the purchase of land), in part to ensure that the decision is a fully autonomous one. Notably, supporters of change in the law so as to permit euthanasia nearly always insist that the person requesting euthanasia must have had a period of lengthy deliberation and discussed the issue with a medical professional before their wishes are complied with.

The difficulty with using this argument in favour of risk-relative capacity is the way it is presented. To say the level of capacity that is expected changes with the degree of risk is misleading. It is not the level of capacity that changes, but rather the weight that is attached to the autonomous decision. Quite simply, not all autonomous decisions carry the same weight. To understand this point, we need to go back and consider what it is about autonomy that causes us to respect it and attach such weight.

---

[184] C Culver and B Gert, 'The Inadequacy of Incompetence' (1990) 68 *The Milbank Quarterly* 619; and T Buller, 'Competence and Risk-Relativity' (2001) 15 *Bioethics* 93.

[185] N Knauer, 'Defining Capacity: Balancing the Competing Interests of Autonomy and Need' (2003) 12 *Temple Political and Civil Rights Law Review* 321.

[186] I Wilks, 'The Debate over Risk-Related Standards of Competence' (1997) 11 *Bioethics* 416.

[187] Indeed, for most commentators there becomes a point at which your autonomy may not be respected. If you wish to remove all your limbs to make a political point, the law in many jurisdictions will prevent you. For further discussion on this, see J Herring, *Medical Law and Ethics* (Oxford University Press, 2008), at 123.

[188] S Kadish, 'Letting Patients Die: Legal and Moral Reflections' (1992) 80 *California Law Review* 857.

When a person is going to make a decision which severely restricts their options as to how they wish to live their lives, supporters of autonomy are rightly concerned. Doing so involves an exercise of autonomy *now* which will limit their autonomy *later in life*. It may be that where we are convinced that the decision is a genuine part of their life vision with a full understanding of the consequences, we can justify respecting their decision to take the risk. Where, however, we are uncertain whether the decision has been fully thought through with a full understanding of the consequences, we can decide to attach less weight to the decision. This should not necessarily be seen as disrespecting their autonomy, but rather preserving it for future use. A key issue, then, where a person is wishing to engage in a act which will cause them harm is to consider whether the act is a full exercise of autonomy, that is whether it reflects beliefs that are central to him- or herself and are an expression of identity. Where they are, they deserve respect; where they are not, they count for less.

Autonomy and decisions contrary to the individual's previous values

Can the fact that a decision appears bizarre, given the individual's values and ideals up until that point in life, itself be evidence of incapacity? The orthodox view on this is clear. It cannot. The assessment of incapacity should be independent of any assessment of whether a patient is making a wise or sensible decision.[189] Professor Ian Kennedy argues:

If the beliefs and values of the patient, though incomprehensible to others, are of long standing and have formed the basis for all the patient's decisions about his life, there is a strong argument to suggest that the doctor should respect and give effect to a patient's decision based on them...To argue otherwise would effectively be to rob the patient of his right to his own personality which may be far more serious and destructive than anything that could follow from the patient's decision as regards a particular proposed treatment.[190]

Indeed, if a person could be assessed as incompetent because she wished to make a bizarre or even mistaken decision, autonomy would be robbed of much of its value. A right of self-determination which only allowed you to make well-reasoned, careful decisions would be of limited value. Indeed, the right to be able to make mistakes is an essential part of autonomy.[191] As Jonathan Glover explains:

For many of us would not be prepared to surrender our autonomy with respect to the major decisions of our life, even if by doing so our other satisfactions were greatly

---

[189] M Parker, 'Competence by Consequence: Ambiguity and Incoherence in the Law' (2006) 25 *Medicine and Law* 1.
[190] I Kennedy, *Treat Me Right* (Clarendon, 1992), at 56.
[191] John Eekelaar writes of 'that most dangerous but most precious of rights: the right to make their own mistakes': J Eekelaar, 'The Emergence of Children's Rights' (1986) 6 *Oxford Journal of Legal Studies* 172, at 182.

increased. There are some aspects of life where a person may be delighted to hand over decisions to someone else more likely to bring about the best results. When buying a secondhand car, I would happily delegate the decision to someone more knowledgeable. But there are many other decisions which people would be reluctant to delegate even if there were the same prospect of greater long-term satisfaction. Some of these decisions are relatively minor but concern ways of expressing individuality... Even in small things, people can mind more about expressing themselves than about the standard of the result. And, in the main decisions of life, this is even more so.[192]

This is persuasive, but this explanation does not require us to follow the views of the English courts and some academics that a decision is worthy of respect even if the reasons for the decision are 'irrational, unknown or even non-existent'.[193]

Philosophers debate the extent to which in order to be autonomous a person must be able to reflect on their desires and preferences; be capable of changing their desires in response to 'higher-order values'; or be free from irrational, neurotic, or futile desires.[194] Few take the view that all decisions of those with capacity are to be respected by the principle of autonomy. Marilyn Friedman has argued that to be a decision that requires respect under the principle of autonomy requires the decision to be 'self-reflective'. This contains two requirements. First, she explains that:

what autonomy requires... is the absence of effective coercion, deception, manipulation, or anything else that interferes significantly with someone behaving in a way that reflects her wants and values as she would reflect on and reaffirm them under noninterfering conditions.[195]

Secondly, she argues that:

[Autonomous choices and behaviour] must reflect, or mirror the wants, desires, cares concerns values, and commitments that someone reaffirms when attending to them. To mirror someone's concerns is to accord with them and, especially, to promote them. Choices and actions mirror wants and values by, for example, aiming at the attainment of what is wanted or valued, promoting its well-being, or protecting it from harm.[196]

She explains further that to be autonomous, actions and choices must stem from what an agent cares deeply about. Such deep wants and desires need to be 'abiding' and 'constitute the overarching rationales that an agent regards as justifying many of her more specific choices'.[197] A rich requirement of autonomy would find sudden desires of a person losing capacity, which contradict values they have held dear during their life, not to be protected by the right of autonomy.[198] Where the

---

[192] J Glover, *Causing Death and Saving Lives* (Penguin, 1990), at 80–1.
[193] *Re T (Refusal of Treatment)* [1993] Fam 95. See also B Winick, 'Competency to Consent to Treatment: The Distinction between Assent and Objection' (1991) 28 *Houston Law Review* 15.
[194] J Savulescu and RW Momeyer, 'Should Informed Consent be based on Rational Beliefs?' (2000) 23 *Journal of Medical Ethics* 282.
[195] M Friedman, *Autonomy, Gender, Politics* (Oxford University Press, 2003), at 5–6.
[196] Ibid, at 6.   [197] Ibid, at 6.
[198] B Rössler, 'Problems with Autonomy' (2002) 17 *Hypatia* 143.

decision is impulsive or irrational in the light of their long-term goals, it ceases to deserve the same respect as those motivated by the values that underpin their life. This view takes the approach that not all decisions made by a competent individual are entitled to equal respect under the principle of autonomy. Those which are fully reasoned and based on deep-held values of the individual are entitled to the most respect, but those which are, for example, based on fleeting desires or impulses are entitled to less.

Conclusion on the just competent

It has been argued that respect for autonomy does not automatically require us to allow people who are just competent to act in a way which will cause them serious harm or which contradicts values they held dear during their life. First, it has been argued that where a decision will cause the individual serious harm, this will itself interfere with their ability to subsequently exercise autonomy, and so unless we are sure that the decision is a richly autonomous one, it need not be respected. Secondly, where the decision is one that contradicts values that underlie the individual's life, it may also be regarded as not autonomous or only weakly protected under the principle of autonomy, unless it can be shown that the individual has made a conscious decision to depart from the values that previously underpinned their life.

Mental Health Act 1983

Only a very brief discussion of the mental health legislation will be offered here.[199] The Mental Health Act 1983 was recently amended by the Mental Health Act 2007. The Act applies where a person has capacity to make decisions, but suffers from a mental disorder for which they will not consent to treatment. So, the 1983 Act is not to be used in cases where the person has capacity and consents to treatment, or in cases where the individual lacks capcity. In either of those cases the basic principles of common law or the Mental Capcity Act 2005 may allow treatment to be provided.

Under the Mental Health Act 1983 a person can be admitted to a hospital and given treatment if they suffer a mental disorder. Under section 3 a person can be admitted if criteria in section 3(2) are met:

An application for admission for treatment may be made in respect of a patient on the grounds that—
  (a) he is suffering from mental disorder of a nature and degree which makes it appropriate for him to receive medical treatment in a hospital; and

---

[199] See J Herring, *Medical Law and Ethics* (Oxford University Press, 2008), ch 10 for a more detailed discussion.

(b) it is necessary for the health and safety of the patient or for the protection of other persons that he should receive such treatment and it cannot be provided unless he is detained under this section; and

(c) appropriate medical treatment is available to him.

A mental disorder is defined as 'any disorder or disability of the mind'.[200] There are also provisions for a patient to be admitted for assessment[201] or in the case of an emergency.[202] The Act provides a raft of procedures under which detention can be challenged and to ensure a person is not being detained without receiving treatment.

The legislation is highly controversial, especially as it appears to allow the detention of a person, not for their own benefit, but because they are perceived to be a danger to the public.[203] Aisling Boylen claims that the new legislation:

marks a radical shift from therapeutic assessment to risk management, whereby psychiatric practice is guided by an evaluation of risk and dangerousness, rather than therapeutic aims.[204]

The government has openly admitted that public safety plays a central role in the legislation. In rejecting an argument that the Act should not allow involuntary treatment of those who have capacity, it stated:

The principal concern about this approach is that it introduces a notion of capacity which, in practice, may not be relevant to the final decision on whether a patient should be made subject to a compulsory order. It is the degree of risk that patients with mental disorder pose, to themselves or others, that is crucial to this decision.[205]

The boundaries between the Mental Health Act 1983 and the Mental Capacity Act 2005 are complex. It has, for example, been claimed that patients suffering from Alzheimer's disease are being given treatment against their wishes under the Mental Capacity Act 2005, whereas in fact they have capacity and should be treated under the Mental Health Act 1983, with its attendant protections.[206]

Conclusion

In the light of the discussion above, I now want to take a broader look at the issues surrounding loss of capacity.

[200] Mental Health Act 1983, s 1(2).   [201] Mental Health Act 1983, s 2.
[202] Mental Health Act 1983, s 4.
[203] See PJ Taylor and J Gunn, 'Homicides by people with mental illness: myth and reality' (1999) 174 *British Journal of Psychiatry* 9 for a challenge to the assumption that those with mental illness are particularly prone to violent criminal activity.
[204] A Boylen, 'The Law and Incapacity Determinations: A conflict of Governance?' (2008) 71 *Modern Law Review* 433.
[205] Department of Health, *Reform of the Mental Health Act 1983, Proposals for Consultation*, Cm 4480 (Department of Health, 1999), at 32.
[206] R Stewart, 'Mental Health Legislation and Decision-Making Capacity' (2006) 332 *British Medical Journal* 118.

In the UK, 700,000 peopole suffer Alzheimer's disease and this is predicted to rise to one million in the next decade or two, and to 1.7 million by 2050. It is estimated that nearly 50 per cent of people over the age of 85 will develop the condition.[207] This means that the 'them' and 'us' image that can pervade the discussion of dementia is unconvincing. Alzheimer's disease and other forms of dementia are becoming the norm for ageing, rather than a disease affecting the few.

Indeed, even the description of dementia as a disease is open to question. In Japan, for example, there is a widespread cultural belief that Alzheimer's is no more than the normal process of ageing.[208] If an older person manifests publicly signs of dementia, this is seen as indicating a failure in the care of the family, rather than an illness. I do not doubt that there are scientifically observable characteristics of dementia, but there are valid points to be made by those who are more cynical about it. First, there is an issue over the extent to which manifestations of the dementia are a result of the disease and to what extent they are a response to the social situation sufferers find themselves in, especially given the low level of care demented patients often receive.[209] Secondly, there is no getting away from the fact that prior to the discovery of Alzheimer's disease there was no separation between those with Alzheimer's and others ageing in a 'normal' way. There is a case for acknowledging that with old age comes brain ageing, which affects us all in different ways. The social narrative of Alzheimer's as an horrific terrifying disease, which is widely feared, has meant that the truth, that brain deterioration is extremely common in old age and is a natural part of ageing, has been lost.[210] We need to find a way of valuing and treasuring the natural progression of old age, just as we value the earliest stages of life. The ageing of the brain will affect nearly all of us and needs to be regarded as part of being human, rather than a humiliating disease.

A second point that emerges from the discussion in this chapter is that lawyers so easily over-emphasize the importance of autonomy.[211] Just because a person lacks capacity and is unable to make decisions, this does not mean that they lack rights or interests. Even if the view and desires of the incapacitated person are not the result of a rational decision, respect due to them as people requires us to give them weight. While rational decisions are worthy of legal respect and attention, so too should be our values, feelings, emotions, and the other aspects of our humanity. The demented person may have lost the full power of rational thought,

[207] American Alzheimer's Association, *Basics of Alzheimer's Disease* (American Alzheimer's Association, 2007), at 7.

[208] P Whitehouse, 'The End of Alzheimer Disease' (2001) 15 *Alzheimer Disease & Associated Disorders* 59.

[209] J Lynn, *Sick to Death and Not Going to Take it Anymore: Reforming Health Care for the Last Years of Life* (University of California Press, 2004).

[210] P Whitehouse, 'The Next 100 Years of Alzheimer's—Learning to Care, Not Cure' (2007) 6 *Dementia* 459.

[211] C Sargent and C Smith-Morris, 'Questioning our Principles: Anthropological Contributions to Ethical Dilemmas in Clinical Practice' (2006) 15 *Cambridge Quarterly of Healthcare Ethics* 123.

but that does not mean they have lost the ability to feel, care, or value. The emphasis on rational thought is reflected in the way in which assessments of capacity are made. These tend to be cognitivistic and rationalistic.[212] Matters such as emotion, personal identity, and narrative are not included as ways in which decisions can be reached.[213] The fact that a finding of incompetence leads us to attach no weight to the views of the incompetent in itself shows that we have elevated reasoning over other ways of interpreting and responding to the world.[214] It is only a failure to value our non-rational humanity that can lead to an assumption that the incompetent person has 'nothing to tell us'. We need much more attention to be given to the lived experiences of those with dementia and finding ways of appreciating and respecting their views, emotions, and humanity.[215]

A third point that emerges from the discussion is the individualistic nature of the legal approach. Incompetent people are assessed and treated in isolation and are not seen as relational people, in mutually inter-dependent relationships. An assessment of capacity should be of an individual located within their network of family, friends, and care-givers.[216] Instead, the assessment is made of the individual sitting alone in a doctor's office. Few of us in fact make important decisions on our own or without consultation and discussion with those around us. At least part of the assessment of capacity should be the extent to which the person within their support group of family and/or friends is able to make choices. Further, when decisions need to be made for a person of doubtful capacity, they should be made within the person's relational context.[217] George P Smith II has argued in this context for 'negotiated consent' rather than informed consent.[218] He explains:

Under the negotiated consent standard, many legitimate views must be considered involving the patient, family, and institution. The result is shared or dispersed authority for decision-making in which no single party has the exclusive power of decision and a nonalgorithmic process whereby negotiation is not governed by strict deductive rules.[219]

Further, assessment of best interests tends to view patients in isolation. Where a person lacking capacity is being cared for informally by family and friends or in an institutional setting, it is simply impossible to make every decision based on what will promote the best interests of the incapacitated person. In caring

---

[212] R Berhmans, D Dickenson, and R Ter Meulenl, 'Mental Capacity: In Search of Alternative Perspectives' (2004) 12 *Health Care Analysis* 251.

[213] Ibid, at 258.   [214] Ibid.

[215] S Post, 'Comments on Research in the Social Sciences Pertaining to Alzheimer's Disease: A More Humble Approach' (2001) 5 *Aging and Mental Health* 17.

[216] H Mun Chan, 'Sharing Death and Dying. Advance Directives, Autonomy and the Family' (2004) 18 *Bioethics* 87.

[217] S Horton-Deutsch, P Twigg, and R Evans, 'Health Care Decision-Making of Persons with Dementia' (2007) 6 *Dementia* 105.

[218] G Smith II, 'The Vagaries of Informed Consent' (2004) 1 *Indiana Health Law Review* 109.

[219] Ibid, at 121.

relationships, it becomes impossible to separate out the interests of the carer and the cared for. Indeed, it is sometimes difficult to determine who is the carer and who is the person being cared for.[220] That would put an intolerable burden on those caring for them. Inevitably within a caring relationship there is give and take. Some decisions will benefit one party more than the other, but other decisions will make up for that. This is how it is in real life in a well-working, caring relationship, and this is how it should be.[221]

A final point is to emphasize our vulnerabilities. Quite rightly there is much emphasis on the vulnerability and dependence of those lacking capacity. There are concerns that they may be taken advantage of by others or be unable to care for themselves. But it is easy to overlook the vulnerability and the dependency of the competent too. Very few patients consenting to medical treatment or people making financial decisions are in fact fully informed or acting on the basis of a rational decision. We often delegate such decisions to others.[222] Tauber has pointed out that:

Frightened and in psychological, if not also physical distress, the patient is fundamentally diseased. To think rationally and dispassionately about life-and-death choices is all too often beyond normal human ability. Indeed, fear about sickness or death is the appropriate response when we ourselves are the subject of calamity.[223]

Although those comments are made in the context of life-and-death decisions, they are true about many important decisions we take. Similarly, dependency should not be something to be afraid or ashamed of. Something has gone very wrong with our care of vulnerable older people when 'not being a burden' is reported as the main goal of their lives by patients living in nursing homes.[224] Dependency on others is an aspect of our humanity. From our earliest beginnings, we are in relationships of dependency and we remain so for much if not all of our lives. Sometimes receiving, sometimes giving, care; often doing both. We may look to puff ourselves up on our independence and boast of the rational powers we use to exercise our autonomy: the truth is a little less grand. Many decisions we take are based on little evidence and made based on irrational fears and emotions. Relationships of dependency are central to our lives. We may point to rationality and independence as marking the line between competence and incompetence, but in fact they demonstrate how blurry that line is.

---

[220] See further, J Herring, 'Where are the Carers in Healthcare Law and Ethics?' (2007) 27 *Legal Studies* 51.

[221] I have expanded upon and justified this approach in J Herring, 'The Place of Carers' in M Freeman (ed), *Law and Bioethics* (Oxford University Press, 2008).

[222] S Adler Channick, 'The Myth of Autonomy at the End-of-Life: Questioning the Paradigm of Rights' (1999) 44 *Villanova Law Review* 577.

[223] A Tauber, *Patient Autonomy and the Ethics of Responsibility* (MIT Press, Cambridge, 2005), at 143.

[224] S Pleschberge, 'Dignity and the Challenge of Dying in Nursing Homes: The Residents' View' (2007) 36 *Age and Ageing* 197.

4

Carers

Introduction

This chapter will consider the position of older people and caring.[1] Older people can be involved as the providers or recipients of care.[2] A greater number of older people are involved in the giving of care than in the receiving of it. Indeed, in many relationships it is not possible to clearly distinguish between who is the carer and who is the recipient.

The focus of this chapter will be primarily on 'informal' carers: partners, relatives, or friends providing unpaid care. The government uses the following definition of a carer:

A carer spends a significant proportion of their life providing unpaid support to family or potentially friends. This could be caring for a relative, partner or friend who is ill, frail, disabled or has mental health or substance misuse problems.[3]

Susan Dodds states that carers have been undervalued, exploited, and expected to offer unrealistic standards of care.[4] Until recently care work has gone largely unacknowledged by lawyers and politicians.[5] Care work was seen as a private matter of little public significance.

Few would say that today. The importance of the work performed by informal caregivers is receiving increasing public attention. Without it, the burden on the state of caring for those unable to care for themselves would be enormous.

---

[1] For work on carers from sociological perspectives, see J Read, *Disability, the Family and Society: Listening to Mothers* (Open University Press, 2000); J Read and L Clements, *Disabled Children and the Law: Research and Good Practice* (Jessica Kingsley, 2001); and K Stalker (ed), *Reconceptualising Work with 'Carers'* (Jessica Kingsley, 2002).

[2] J Powell, J Robison, H Roberts, and G Thomas, 'The Single Assessment Process in Primary Care: Older People's Accounts of the Process' (2007) 37 *British Journal of Social Work* 1043.

[3] HM Government, *Carers at the Heart of 21st-Century Families and Communities* (The Stationery Office, 2008), at 18. The definition interpreted literally would include parents caring for children, but that is not the government's intention. For criticism of the exclusion of professional carers from the category of carers, see L Lloyd, 'Call us Carers: Limitations and Risks in Campaigning for Recognition and Exclusivity' (2006) 26 *Critical Social Policy* 945.

[4] S Dodds, 'Depending on Care: Recognition of Vulnerability and the Social Contribution of Care Provisions' (2007) 21 *Bioethics* 500.

[5] HM Government, *Carers at the Heart of 21st-Century Families and Communities* (The Stationery Office, 2008).

Indeed, without it the NHS and social care system would rapidly collapse.[6] Yet, the support and legal rights given to carers are still limited. The exact balance of responsibilities and rights between the dependent person, carers, and the state is still very much being worked out.[7]

One study of middle-aged people[8] found considerable anxiety about care in old age. It also showed how attitudes about care in old age were changing. The authors commented:

One of the most striking and consistent findings from the focus groups was a broad agreement that one's children would be unlikely to be one's main or sole carers. Relatively few people wanted to receive a major part of their care in old age from their children or other younger members of their family. Most did not expect their children to be their main carers and, unlike them in relation their own parents, did not think that their children expected to care for them.[9]

Not surprisingly, the survey found a strong dislike of the idea of residential care, with its perceived loss of independence and concerns over the quality of care offered. How the desire for independence and informal care can be reconciled with not wanting to place the burden on one's children remains to be seen. As this survey indicates, our attitudes towards care are complex and may be undergoing change. The government acknowledges this:

family life has changed over the last 50 or so years. The move to smaller nuclear families means that it is no longer as easy to share the caring role as widely as in the past. Society is more mobile and families are more geographically dispersed. More families rely on two incomes, or longer working hours, to maintain an adequate standard of living. Many families find it difficult to balance work with the care needs of friends and relatives without significantly impacting on their own standard of living, esteem and independence—the lifestyle to which the family has become accustomed.[10]

The practice of care for older people has certainly changed. Robert Goodwin and Diane Gibson[11] have written of the 'decasualization' of care of older people. In the past, they suggest, care of older people was casual, not in the sense of being unloving or unthoughtful, but rather that it was simply integrated into normal everyday life. A person would not see themselves as specifically spending some time caring or undertaking a care task. They see the increased professionalization

---

[6] H Arksey, 'Combining Work and Care: The Reality of Policy Tensions for Carers' (2005) 15 *Benefits* 139.

[7] A Stewart, 'Home or Home: Caring about and for Elderly Family Members in a Welfare State' in R Probert (ed), *Family Life and the Law* (Ashgate, 2007).

[8] R Levenson, M Jeyasingham, and N Joule, *Looking Forward to Care in Old Age Expectations of the Next Generation* (King's Fund, 2005).

[9] At 27.

[10] HM Government, *Carers at the Heart of 21st-Century Families and Communities* (The Stationery Office, 2008), para 1.61.

[11] R Goodwin and D Gibson, 'The Decasualisation of Eldercare' in E Feder Kittay and E Feder (eds), *The Subject of Care: Feminist Perspectives on Dependency* (Rowman & Littlefield, 2003).

of care; the increased number of people requiring care; and the pressures carers face in their life as putting strain on the kind of care offered. Whether, as the study just referred to indicates, we are moving to a time when care will predominantly be carried out by professional carers remains to be seen. We certainly seem to be seeing a relocation of care from the private to the public, from collective services to commercial ones.[12]

As already mentioned, care work has largely been ignored in political and academic writings. In the political sphere it has been forcefully argued that society has gained from the unrecognized, unrewarded carework, mainly undertaken by women. The economic value of this care work is considerable. Through the notion of privacy and the venerated status of the family, women have provided considerable benefits to society for no compensation. Martha Fineman has written:

dependency is universal and inevitable—the experience of everyone in society and, for that reason, of collective concern, requiring collective response. However, the essential and society-preserving work inevitable dependency demands has been channelled by society in such a way as to make only *some* of its members bear the burdens of this work. As a result, I argue that there is a societal debate owed to caretakers... The existence of this debt must be recognized and payment accomplished, through policies and laws that provide both some economic compensation and structural accommodation to caretakers.[13]

To many feminist commentators, the failure to recognize and value care work has played an important part in disadvantaging women.

The lack of attention to carers also reflects a legal obsession with individualism. For example, medical law students are usually introduced to medical law and ethics with the principles of autonomy—*my* right to make decisions about *my* medical treatment; and of beneficence—that *I* should receive the treatment that is appropriate for *me*.[14] But this is highly individualistic. As Martha Minow points out, the question of 'who is the patient?' goes unasked.[15] The obvious answer is: 'Why, it is the person in front of the doctor'. But we cannot separate the interests of someone from those they are in interdependent relationships with. We cannot pretend there are such things as 'our' choices. What we decide about medical decisions will often impact on those we are in a relationship with. We cannot decide how much benefit a treatment provides simply by looking at the individual, but we must take into account those around them, and particularly those who care for them. In medical ethics, as in many other areas of academic and public life, the work of carers has been invisible.[16]

---

[12] S Sevenhuijsen, 'The Place of Care: The Relevance of the Feminist Ethic of Care for Social Policy' (2003) 4 *Feminist Theory* 179.

[13] M Fineman, *The Autonomy Myth* (New Press, 2004), at 263.

[14] See, eg the hugely influential T Beauchamp and J Childress, *The Principles of Biomedical Ethics* (5th edn, Oxford University Press, 2001).

[15] M Minow, 'Who's the Patient?' (1994) 53 *Maryland Law Review* 1173.

[16] M Henwood, *Ignored and Invisible* (Carers' National Association, 1998).

This lack of attention to the interests of carers is beginning to change.[17] In 2008 the government produced *Carers at the Heart of 21st-Century Families and Communities*, a major re-examination of the relationship between carers and the state. In its introduction, Gordon Brown declared:

Caring for our relatives and friends when they are in need is a challenge that the vast majority of us will rise to at some point in our lives. At any one time 1 in 10 people in Britain is a carer—the majority of them, of course, still women. It is a testimony to the importance of families that so many of us are prepared to make the personal sacrifices that caring can involve in order to help our loved ones lead fulfilling lives even in the face of incapacity or disability. Our support and appreciation for carers is therefore not just fundamental to ensuring that those of us in need of care are able to receive it, but goes right to the heart of our values as a society and our ambition to create a fairer Britain.[18]

Sadly, in the political debates it is estimates of the economic value of carers that often captures the headlines: £87 billion per year in one recent estimate.[19] Of course, the real value of care lies not in monetary terms, but the impact it has on people's lives. We will be looking later at the legal and social difficulties carers face and whether the government's reforms will improve their lot.

Before moving on, it must be emphasized that it is easy to place together 'carers' as a homogenous category, whereas, of course, they are not. The needs and interests of frail spouses looking after each other may be very different from a neighbour who gives daily help to a friend, or a child looking after a parent. Further, there may be particular issues facing carers on the grounds of their race or sexual orientation.[20]

Statistics on carers

The 2001 Census indicated that there were around six million carers,[21] while the General Household Survey estimated there are over seven million.[22] The 2001 Census found 1,247, 291 people provided more than 50 hours of care per week.[23] More than one-fifth of carers who are living with the care recipient provide care

---

[17] The Princess Royal Trust for Carers, *Eight Hours a Day and Taken for Granted* (PRTC, 1998); and P Smith, 'Elder Care, Gender, and Work: The Work-Family Issue of the 21st Century' (2004) 25 *Berkeley Journal of Employment and Labour Law* 351.

[18] HM Government, *Carers at the Heart of 21st-Century Families and Communities* (The Stationery Office, 2008), at 2. F Carmichael, G Connell, C Hulme, and S Sheppard, *Meeting the Needs of Carers; Government Policy and Social Support* (University of Salford, 2005).

[19] L Buckner and S Yeandle, *Valuing Carers—Calculating the Value of Unpaid Care* (Carers UK, 2007).

[20] J Manthorpe and E Price, 'Lesbian Carers: Personal Issues and Policy Responses' (2005) 5 *Social Policy & Society* 15.

[21] Carers UK, *Facts About Carers* (Carers UK, 2005), at 1.

[22] J Maher and H Green, *Carers 2000* (The Stationery Office, 2001).

[23] National Statistics, *2001 Census Standard Tables* (The Stationery Office, 2003).

for 100 or more hours a week.[24] These figures may be underestimates as some carers do not perceive themselves as such and rather see their care work as part of normal life.

Carers UK states that at some point in their lives three in every five people will become a carer.[25] By the age of 75, almost two-thirds of women and close to a half of men will have spent some point in their lives providing at least 20 hours of care per week.[26] Of course, these are not just carers of older people, but include other adults needing care. There is evidence that the number of older people with disabilities which may require care will increase. It has been estimated that by 2041 there will be a 50 per cent increase in the number of adults with care needs.[27] If current patterns of care continue over the next 30 years, levels of care will need to increase by nearly 60 per cent by 2031.[28]

Age is a significant factor in care-giving. In 2000, 16 per cent of those aged over 65 were providing some form of care. Twenty-eight per cent of those providing 20 hours or more of care per week were over 65.[29] Twenty-five per cent of carers in the UK are over 60[30] and over 44,000 carers are over the age of 85.[31] Ethnicity also appears to be a relevant factor, although there has been limited research on this. It appears that Bangladeshi, Pakistani, and Indian groups are more likely to care than the average for the population.[32] Given the greater incidence of inter-generational households within such communities, that is not surprising.

Gender is another highly significant factor.[33] Traditionally, women performed the bulk of caring, but an increasing number of men have been involved.[34] Still, women disproportionately bear the care burden.[35] In 2001, 11 per cent of women were main carers, compared with seven per cent of men. Five per cent of women were engaged in more than 20 hours per week in caring tasks, as opposed to three

---

[24] L Beesley, *Informal Care in England* (King's Fund, 2006).

[25] Carers UK, *Facts About Carers* (Carers UK, 2005), at 1.

[26] M Hirst, *Informal Care Over Time* (University of York, 2001).

[27] HM Government, *Carers at the Heart of 21st-Century Families and Communities* (The Stationery Office, 2008).

[28] L Pickard *et al*, 'Care by Spouses, Care by Children: Projections of Informal Care for Older People in England to 2031' (2007) 6 *Social Policy and Society* 353.

[29] L Beesley, *Informal Care in England* (King's Fund, 2006).

[30] G Hopkins, 'Duty, Love and Sacrifice' (2006) 16 *Community Care* 47.

[31] House of Commons Work and Pensions Committee, *Valuing and Supporting Carers* (The Stationery Office, 2008), para 344.

[32] L Beesley, *Informal Care in England* (King's Fund, 2006).

[33] E Watson and J Mears, *Women, Work and Care of the Elderly* (Ashgate Publishing, 1999); E Feder Kittay, *Love's Labour: Essays on Women, Equality and Dependency* (Routledge, 1999); and J Parks, *No Place Like Home? Feminist Ethics and Home Health Care* (Indiana University Press, 2003).

[34] C Ungerson, 'Thinking about the Production and Consumption of Long-term Care in Britain: Does Gender Still Matter?' (2000) 29 *Journal of Social Policy* 623.

[35] F Carmichael and S Charles, 'The Opportunity Costs of Informal Care: Does Gender Matter?' (2003) 22 *Journal of Health Economics* 781.

per cent of men.[36] In the 50 to 59 age group, 17 per cent of all men and 24 per cent of all women are carers.[37] Of the 4.3 million working-age carers in Great Britain, 1.8 million are men and 2.4 million are women, although in terms of the hours spent, women undertake a higher number of hours, supplying around 70 per cent of all care hours.[38] However, in the later stages of life there appear to be more male carers than female, with the 2001 Census indicating there were 179,000 male carers over the age of 75 and 169,000 female carers.[39] The impact of care affects women more harshly than men in economic terms. The likelihood of a male carer working is reduced by 12.9 per cent; whereas for females it is 27 per cent.[40]

Despite the joys that caring can bring, care work is associated with significant disadvantages.[41] Many carers suffer poverty due to the impact on their employment[42] and this can continue into retirement due to the impact on pension provision.[43] Carers UK have claimed that 77 per cent of carers are financially less well off as a result of their care work. One study found that carers lost an average of £11,000 per year as a result of giving up work or working fewer hours.[44] Another report suggests that one-third of carers leave work or retire early due to their caring role.[45] Older carers are particularly vulnerable, with seven out of ten said to be unable to afford adequate heating or clothing.[46] One in ten older carers were cutting back on food to make ends meet.[47]

Care work can have a negative impact on health. The 21 per cent of carers who provide more than 50 hours of care report that they are not in good health.[48] It has been claimed that four out of ten carers suffer physical effects from the work, such as back pain or other injuries.[49] These rates are likely to be higher among older carers and those combining care work and employment.[50] Nine out

---

[36] L Dahlbert, S Demack, and C Bambra, 'Age and Gender of Informal Carers: A Population-Based Study in the UK' (2007) 15 *Health and Social Care in the Community* 439.

[37] House of Commons Work and Pensions Committee, *Valuing and Supporting Carers* (The Stationery Office, 2008), para 17.

[38] Ibid, para 344.

[39] L Beesley, *Informal Care in England* (King's Fund, 2006).

[40] F Carmichael and S Charles, 'The Opportunity Costs of Informal Care: Does Gender Matter?' (2003) 22 *Journal of Health Economics* 781.

[41] M Hirst, 'Carer Distress: A Prospective, Population-Based Study' (2005) 61 *Social Science & Medicine* 697.

[42] F Carmichael and S Charles, 'The Opportunity Costs of Informal Care: Does Gender Matter?' (2003) 22 *Journal of Health Economics* 781.

[43] Carers UK, *Carers UK Welcomes White Paper* (Carers UK, 2006).

[44] House of Commons Work and Pensions Committee, *Valuing and Supporting Carers* (The Stationery Office, 2008), para 102.

[45] Carers UK, *Caring and Pensioner Poverty* (Carers UK, 2008).

[46] BBC News Online, 'Carers "missing £750m benefits"', 2 December 2005.   [47] Ibid.

[48] HM Government, *Carers at the Heart of 21st-Century Families and Communities* (The Stationery Office, 2008).

[49] M Hirst, *Hearts and Minds: The Health Effects of Caring* (Carers UK, 2004).

[50] K Glasser *et al*, 'The Health Consequences of Multiple Roles at Older Ages in the UK' (2005) 13 *Health and Social Care in the Community* 470.

of ten carers in one survey reported suffering stress, anxiety, depression, or loss of sleep.[51] In another survey, 21 per cent of carers said they found life a constant struggle.[52] A survey of female carers of patients with dementia found they suffered a 'seriously decreased quality of life' as compared with their contemporaries not undertaking such work.[53] Sociologists have written of the 'sandwich' generation, where women are having to care for both their children and their parents at the same time. It has been claimed that one-third of women are giving help to both generations.[54] Of course, it would be quite wrong to paint a picture of caring being all doom and gloom. There are many aspects of caring which people find valuable and worthwhile.[55]

State support for carers

Benefits for carers

Carer's allowance is available to a person who is providing at least 35 hours of unpaid care to a person receiving a relevant disability benefit.[56] There are 470,000 carers receiving it. Of those recipients over 65, 11,800 are women and 2,800 are men.[57]

The benefit certainly has its critics. First, there is the amount paid. The benefit is the lowest of all income-replacement benefits. As a representation of the National Autistic Society put it to the House of Commons Select Committee:

> Just to demonstrate how inadequate Carer's Allowance is, even if you did the minimum caring hours of 35 hours a week, that is equivalent to £1.44 an hour compared to a minimum wage of £5.52, which really demonstrates how we value that role. So the rate is inadequate, it sends a message to carers about how we value their role.[58]

The Committee was critical of the government's 2008 Carers' Strategy, which contained no commitment to reform benefits, at least in the short term. The government explains that the carer's allowance is not intended as a carer's

---

[51]   B Keeley and M Clarke, *Carers Speak Out Project* (Princess Royal Trust for Carers, 2002).
[52]   Ibid.
[53]   J Argimon, E Limon, J Vila, and C Cabezas, 'Health-Related Quality of Life in Carers of Patients with Dementia' (2004) 21 *Family Practice* 454.
[54]   G Emily and J Henretta, 'Between Elderly Parents and Adult Children: A New Look at the Intergenerational Care Provided by the "Sandwich Generation"' (2006) 26 *Ageing & Society* 707.
[55]   H Al-Janabi, J Coast, and T Flynn, 'What do People Value when they Provide Unpaid Care for an Older Person? A Meta-Ethnography with Interview Follow-Up' (2007) 61 *Journal of Epidemiology and Community Health* A1.
[56]   The amount paid was £50.55 in 2008.
[57]   House of Commons Work and Pensions Committee, *Valuing and Supporting Carers* (The Stationery Office, 2008), para 120.
[58]   Ibid, para 121.

wage and so any analogy with the minimum wage is unfair. Rather, it is an 'income-maintenance' benefit, similar to maternity allowance or incapacity benefit, for those unable to participate in the labour market. This overlooks two points. First, carers suffer significant losses by undertaking care work. There is the loss of income from their previous employment in many cases, and then there are the expenses involved in the care job itself. Secondly, if carers did not perform this work, the burden on the state would be enormous. They are, in effect, through their work, saving the state substantial sums. This distinguishes them from others seeking benefit payments.

Thirdly, for older carers the overlap between state pension and carer's allowance is complex. Age Concern has complained that carer's allowance is 'removed' when a person reaches state pension age. The HC Committee found the rule governing carer's allowance and overlapping benefits 'confusing and overcomplicated'.[59]

Fourthly, the benefit is only payable if the person cared for is entitled to a relevant benefit, such as incapacity benefit. The rules on these have been tightened up and there are concerns at the number of appeals being allowed against ineligibility. This means that the tests are being too strictly applied.[60]

Fifthly, Carers UK estimates £740 million a year of carers' benefits go unclaimed every year.[61] The House of Commons Select Committee was critical of the lack of access to support and information services to assist carers to navigate the complex procedures governing access to help.[62]

Sixthly, the government's keenness to encourage carers to find work has meant that claimants for carer's allowance in one area were required to attend an interview to discuss future job prospects.[63] This has been criticized by the House of Commons Select Committee as unnecessary and demeaning.[64]

Another benefit which carers can claim is a carer credit, which can be used for pensions purposes. It is available to those caring for 20 hours a week or more for a person who is severely disabled and is discussed further in chapter 6.

Availability of care services

The *National Carers Strategy*,[65] published in 1999, was a milestone in state recognition of carers in the UK. In it the government recognized the need for a coherent approach to offer support, both financial and practical, to carers. Four pieces of legislation which have sought to promote the interests of carers: the Carers (Recognition and Services) Act 1995; the Carers and Disabled Children

---

[59] Ibid.   [60] Ibid, para 123.   [61] Ibid, para 92.   [62] Ibid, para 93.
[63] H Arksey, 'Combining Work and Care: The Reality of Policy Tensions for Carers' (2005) 15 *Benefits* 139.
[64] House of Commons Work and Pensions Committee, *Valuing and Supporting Carers* (The Stationery Office, 2008), para 124.
[65] Department of Health, *National Carers Strategy* (Department of Health, 1999).

Act 2000 (the 2000 Act); the Carers (Equal Opportunities) Act 2004 (the 2004 Act); and the Work and Families Act 2006 (the 2006 Act).[66]

The 2004 Act gives a carer who provides or intends to provide a substantial amount of care on a regular basis a right to receive an assessment for services by their local authority for themselves as carers. This is separate from the assessment for the person cared for and therefore can be carried out even if the person cared for is not assessed.[67] The services to be provided can be anything that could 'help the carer care for the person cared for'. This could include support services or a direct payment to be used to buy support. An assessment should include not just an assessment of the carer's physical needs, but also of their mental health and their attitude towards care. Department of Health guidance reminds local authorities that 'some people, for example, could provide care but may feel subject to a moral obligation to do so, or may feel defeated, trapped or depressed'.[68]

The 2004 Act also contains the practically important provision that social service departments have a duty to inform carers of their right to an assessment.[69] The 2004 Act requires specific attention in such an assessment to be paid to a carer's wish for employment, learning or training opportunities, and leisure.[70] The 2004 and 2006 Acts give protection under employment law to carers, including the right to request flexible working hours.[71]

Luke Clements has written of the 2004 Act:

The new Act marks a major cultural shift in the way carers are viewed: a shift in seeing carers not so much as unpaid providers of care services for disabled people, but as people in their own right: people with the right to work, like everyone else; people who have too often been socially excluded and (like the disabled people for whom they care) often denied the life chances that are available to other people.[72]

Although there is much to welcome in this legislation, there are a number of issues of concern surrounding it.

It is important to note that these provisions are largely permissive, authorizing local authorities to provide these services if they wish, rather than dictating that they must. It is true that the existence of the statutory power may be of use in exerting pressure on local authorities to provide services, but it is unlikely to be an effective tool in pursuing legal remedies. That said, a blanket ban on providing services, or arbitrariness in the exercise of the power, could be challenged in

---

[66] Carers have limited rights to take (unpaid) time off work to care for a dependant. This right is found in the Employment Rights Act 1996, s 57A(1).

[67] Carers (Equal Opportunities) Act 2004, s 1.

[68] Department of Health, *Carers and Disabled Children Act 2000 and Carers (Equal Opportunities) Act 2004. Combined Policy Guidance* (Department of Health, 2005), para 43.

[69] L Clements, *Carers and the Law* (Carers UK, 2005), para 1.4.

[70] Carers (Equal Opportunities) Act 2004, s 2.

[71] J Lewis, 'The Changing Context for the Obligation to Care and to Earn' in M Maclean (ed), *Family Law and Family Values* (Hart, 2005).

[72] Ibid.

the courts.[73] Certainly, the Department of Health Practice Guidance encourages a radical shift in local authority practice in the provision of services to carers.[74] The reality is shown in a recent survey of the operation of the assessment, which found that budgetary constraints meant that these were often not carried out effectively by local authorities and very limited funds were available.[75] It also found significant differences between local authorities in their interpretations of 'substantial' and 'regular'. In 2007, Carers UK claimed there were only about half a million assessments a year. As they put it, 'only a tiny minority of carers go near social services'.[76] In another survey, following an assessment only 37 per cent of carers questioned saw an improvement in the services they were receiving.[77] No doubt the comments reported of one carer (Bernard) are far from atypical:[78] 'You get all these statements of intent to help, have these meetings, fill in dozens of multi-page forms, and then nothing happens. Except more talk, more forms, and endless waiting.'[79]

Even if the local authority does offer services to the carer, these can be charged for, subject to means testing.[80] This is in line with the controversial distinction between health care and social care for patients, the former being free, but the latter being liable to be charged for, subject to means testing. Carers UK opposed this move, arguing that many carers live in poverty and suffer financial hardship due to their caring role and to permit charging will only worsen their financial position.[81] Their research has shown that the extra charges were causing serious financial hardship.[82] Carers UK has also objected to inconsistency among the amounts charged by local authorities.[83] The fact that services for carers are means tested puts carers in a category similar to benefit claimants who are in need and must be provided for by the state; rather than recognizing that they provide an invaluable service to society whose work requires recognition and reward, regardless of income.

A more significant challenge to the carers' legislation is an argument that carers and the cared for cannot be assessed separately. Inevitably, their interests are intermingled. An injury to the cared-for person will affect the carer; an injury

---

[73] *R (on the application of Stephenson) v Stockton-on-Tees BC* [2005] EWCA Civ 960, [2005] 3 FCR 248.
[74] Department of Health, *Carers and Disabled Children Act 2000 and Carers (Equal Opportunities) Act 2004, Combined Policy Guidance* (The Stationery Office, 2005).
[75] D Seddon, C Robinson, C Reeves, Y Tommis, B Woods, and I Russell, 'In their Own Right: Translating the Policy of Carer Assessment into Practice' (2007) 37 *British Journal of Social Work* 1335.
[76] House of Commons Work and Pensions Committee, *Valuing and Supporting Carers* (The Stationery Office, 2008), para 39.
[77] Carers UK, *Missed Opportunities: The Impact of New Rights for Carers* (Carers UK, 2005).
[78] E Nicholas, 'An Outcomes Focus in Carer Assessment and Review: Value and Challenge' (2003) 33 *British Journal of Social Work* 31.
[79] H Marriott, *The Selfish Pig's Guide to Caring* (Polperro, 2003), at 115.
[80] Health and Social Services and Social Security Adjudications Act 1983, s 17.
[81] Carers UK, *Caring on the Breadline* (Carers UK, 2000).   [82] Ibid.   [83] Ibid.

to the carer will affect the cared-for person. The emotional well-being of the carer will affect that of the cared-for person and vice versa. Therefore, to have independent assessments of the carer and the cared-for person is problematic.

Further, it is often difficult to know who is the carer and who is the cared for. This is most obvious in the very common case of elderly couples, where it may be that both their states of health are fluctuating and at different times each will be taking care of the other. Put in another way the line between the carer and cared for is blurred. It is often only the gratitude and willingness of the 'cared for' to receive the care that enables the 'carer' to continue. The relationship is rarely all one way. Even in cases where the cared-for person is incapable of expressing anything in response to the care, care is still regarded as an aspect of the ongoing relationship between the two people.

The availability of care services is essential to many older people. They rely on them to maintain their dignity and health. A major issue about these services is the funding of the care services, which I discuss in chapter 6.[84] As explained there, these services are rarely offered for free. The Commission for Social Care Inspection (CSCI)[85] found little consistency between councils as to who was eligible for services and indeed quite a degree of inconsistency within councils.[86] One of its reports stated:

Progress in modernising social care is being hampered by financial pressures in the social care and health system, an underdeveloped care market, continuing recruitment and retention problems, and organisational turbulence.[87]

Where people have to fund services themselves, there are real problems in finding good quality care. The difficulties in obtaining these services have been summarized thus by Carers UK:

There is no quality advice and information and guidance to help people pick the right care. The care market is under stimulated. There is not enough quality and quantity out there if you want to purchase it. If we really are going to help people who wish to work return to work, we have to get the care system sorted.[88]

A report by the CSCI found that if older people and their carers did not qualify for assistance they had a poor quality of life. The Commission found that 35 per cent of carers in England said the person they were supporting did not have the benefit of any formal services. Sixty per cent of carers said there were services they would like to use, but were not able to. Of course, as a result of charges many

---

    [84] M Henwood, *NHS Continuing Care in England* (King's Fund, 2005).
    [85] Commission for Social Care Inspection, *The State of Social Care in England 2006–07* (CSCI, 2008).
    [86] Seee also King's Fund, *The Business of Caring* (King's Fund, 2005).
    [87] Commission for Social Care Inspection, *The State of Social Care in England 2006–07* (CSCI, 2008).
    [88] House of Commons Work and Pensions Committee, *Valuing and Supporting Carers* (The Stationery Office, 2008), para 222.

people decide to be without the services. One report suggests that 80 per cent of those who had stopped using care services blamed costs as a reason for doing so.[89] The Joseph Rowntree Foundation found that the social care funding was failing to meet basic needs. The lack of funding has not only meant many are denied support, but where it is paid for the staff are poorly paid, and therefore poorly trained and have a high turnover. There has been a particular problem in providing services that are accessible and appropriate for people from black and ethnic minority groups.[90]

The government's report, *Putting People First*, published in late 2007,[91] promises £520 million of ring-fenced funding for social care over the next three years, to be provided through personal care budgets. It is very much to be hoped that this improves the situation, but the amounts needed to meet the needs of carers and those they care for will be substantial. There has been an increase of 2.7 per cent in real terms in funding for personal social services between 2002/03 and 2007/08.[92] This is woefully inadequate to deal with the shortfall in funding and care.

Direct payments

A central aspect of the government's approach to carers and dependants is to encourage the use of direct payments. This system offers older people the option of receiving a cash payment in lieu of services from the local authority.[93] This money is to be used to buy in services chosen by the dependent person. The aim is that this enables individuals to manage their own social care.[94] Since 2003, local authorities have a duty to make direct payments if the individual consents and is able to manage these budgets without assistance. The services can be purchased from the local authority; private care providers; or from relatives and friends, as long as they do not live in the same household.[95] The reasoning behind this, presumably, is that the care from a co-resident is likely to be provided whether paid for or not; and so there would be no added benefit by the payment for those services. Direct payments can also be made to a carer to provide carer support, but that involves separate application.

There is much to be said in favour of the direct payments in principle. A common complaint of social service care provision is that it does not meet the needs

---

[89] Coalition on Charging, *Charging into Poverty* (NCIL, 2008).

[90] Commission for Social Care Inspection, *Putting People First: Equality and Diversity Matters* (CSCI, 2007).

[91] Department of Health, *Putting People First* (Department of Health, 2007).

[92] Age Concern, *Age Agenda 2007* (Age Concern, 2007).

[93] T Poole, *Direct Payments and Older People* (King's Fund, 2007).

[94] Department of Health, *Putting People First* (Department of Health, 2007).

[95] In exceptional cases, direct payments can be used to pay for care from a person who lives with the care recipient, but the local authority needs to agree it is the only satisfactory way of providing the care.

of the individual and is inflexible.[96] An employed carer may be reluctant to do jobs that do not fit within their formal job description.[97] One anecdotal example is the man who wanted to be taken fishing rather than taken to the local day-care centre.[98] Giving control to the individual over what services they wish to fund may ensure the services meet their particular needs. However, the take-up rate of direct payments has been limited. Less than one per cent of people over 65 receiving social care were receiving direct payments.[99]

There is relatively little evidence on what direct payments money is used for. One survey[100] found that in Hampshire it was used to pay care assistants, but that 80 per cent of the care assistants employed were known by the older person.[101] This suggests that it should not be assumed that direct payments will expand the use of the private sector. That also raises the question of whether the payments are made for services which would have been given for free otherwise. Of course, that is not necessarily a bad thing. It may be appropriate that carers receive proper recompense for their work, but it means direct payments not improving the care received.

The wider policy issues are hotly debated. Ungerson has argued:

by allowing for the payment of relatives who previously have been 'classic' unpaid and formally unrecognised informal carers, [these schemes] actually provide a means whereby the work of care-givers is recognised and recompensed, such that they become more and more like care-workers.[102]

This might create tensions between the recipient of care and the carer.[103] The relationship which was previously informal now becomes more formal with money changing hands. Quite what the impact of this might be and whether it will improve the quality of care remains to be seen.

A rather different issue is whether giving an older person choice is necessarily desirable. They may find it difficult to select or find the services they need. Indeed, they may not select the services they genuinely need, through embarrassment or lack of understanding.[104] They find the employing and supervision of care

[96] R Clough, J Manthorpe, B Green, D Fox, G Raymond, P Wilson, V Raymond, K Sumner, L Bright, and J Hay, *The Support Older People Want and the Services They Need* (Joseph Rowntree Foundation, 2007).

[97] N Raynes, J Beecham, and H Clark, *The Report of the Older People's Inquiry into 'That Bit of Help'* (Josepth Rowntree Foundation, 2007).

[98] C Ungerson 'Whose Empowerment and Independence?' (2004) 29 *Ageing and Society* 189.

[99] T Poole, *Direct Payments and Older People* (King's Fund, 2007).

[100] C Ungerson, 'Whose Empowerment and Independence?' (2004) 29 *Ageing and Society* 189.

[101] T Poole, *Direct Payments and Older People* (King's Fund, 2007).

[102] C Ungerson, 'Whose Empowerment and Independence?' (2004) 29 *Ageing and Society* 189.

[103] C Ungerson, 'Give Them the Money: Is Cash a Route to Empowerment?' (1997) 31 *Social Policy & Administration* 45.

[104] H Arksey and C Glendinning, 'Choice in the Context of Informal Care-giving' (2007) 15 *Health and Social Care in the Community* 165.

work stressful.[105] One study found that direct payments worked best where local authorities offered help and support to recipients in spending the payments.[106] Further, the extent to which the carer is, or should be, involved in how the direct payments are spent is far from clear.[107]

Government reforms

In June 2008, the government published a new 10-year vision for carers: *Carers at the Heart of 21st Century Families and Communities.* The main parts of the programme were to provide more information and advice to carers to ensure they received the benefits they were entitled to. There is to be a new information helpline and an 'expert carers' training programme'.[108] There is to be improved provision of breaks for carers and a greater level of support from the NHS. The government further seeks to provide more support so that carers are able to combine employment and care.

The government states that the strategy will mean that: 'Carers will be supported so that they are not forced into financial hardship by their caring role.' However, there must be some scepticism regarding that claim. There is nothing in the government's proposals which will compensate a well-paid person who gives up their career to undertake care responsibilities. Indeed, the report fails to increase benefits for carers, except as a long-term priority from 2011. In the light of poverty and lack of services for carers, the provision of a telephone helpline seems inadequate. The government states that its aim is to:

ensure carers experience a system which is on their side rather than enduring a constant struggle so that they are supported to have a life of their own alongside their caring responsibilities.[109]

A revealing comment is the following:

Our vision is that by 2018, carers will be universally recognised and valued as being fundamental to strong families and stable communities. Support will be tailored to meet individuals' needs, enabling carers to maintain a balance between their caring responsibilities and a life outside caring, whilst enabling the person they support to be a full and equal citizen.[110]

---

[105] C Glendinning, 'Increasing Choice and Control for Older and Disabled People' (2007) 37 *British Journal of Social Work* 1335.

[106] J Rankin, *A Mature Policy on Choice* (IPPR, 2005).

[107] K Keywood, 'Gatekeepers, Proxies, Advocates? The Evolving Role of Carers under Mental Health and Mental Incapacity Law Reforms' (2003) 25 *Journal of Social Welfare and Family Law* 355.

[108] HM Government, *Carers at the Heart of 21st-Century Families and Communities* (The Stationery Office, 2008).

[109] Ibid, at 2.   [110] Ibid.

It is noticeable that this aim is sought by 2018, perhaps a recognition of the distance that needs to be covered in respect of carers. The comment also alludes to a common theme in the report, which is to enable carers to find employment while caring. This is a convenient way of tackling poverty among carers, but whether seeking to combine employment with care work is realistic, over-burdening carers, or beneficial to the recipient of care is a matter for debate.

Housing issues

There is increasing acceptance that the current way of dealing with housing for older people is insufficiently flexible or person-centred.[111] A common misconception is that most older people end up in a nursing home. In fact, only a small minority do: over 98 per cent of those aged 85 or over can get round their home successfully, if it is on a single level.[112] Seventy-nine per cent of those over 85 are able to bathe themselves.[113] However, much housing used by older people is sub-standard and does not meet their needs. Julia Neuberger claims that a third of older people's housing is 'non-decent', with 22 per cent of homes lived in by those over 75 not having central heating or having only a badly maintained heating system.[114] Greater thought needs to be given to the layout and appliances in homes so that older people can live independently for as long as possible.[115] We need a range of forms of housing with varying levels of support to meet the needs of older people. The following are some examples of what can be available:[116]

- *Sheltered housing.* This often involves a number of self-contained flats or bungalows, each with their own entrance. There is usually an emergency alarm system which can be used to alert an onsite warden. There are also often communal areas such as a lounge or laundry.

- *Extra care housing/very sheltered housing.* These homes offer self-contained accommodation, with their own front door. They provide a higher level of support than sheltered housing. Around the clock care or nursing is offered. The service element is an integral part of what is offered. There may also be communal areas.

- *Close care housing.* These are often offered on the same site as a care home and provide an independent flat. They are often regarded as a half-way option between independent living and a care home.

---

[111] C Patmore and A McNulty, *Making Home Care for Older People More Flexible and Person-Centred* (NHS, 2005).

[112] T Poole, *Housing Options for Older People* (King's Fund, 2006).   [113] Ibid.

[114] J Neuberger, *Not Dead Yet* (Harper Collins, 2008), at 170.

[115] Department of Health, *More Older People to be given Choice to Live at Home* (Department of Health, 2006).

[116] Ibid.

- *Retirement villages.* These are estates of bungalows, flats, or houses which are intended for older people. The villages offer a range of different types of accommodation to meet various degrees of dependency.
- *'Abbeyfield society'.* These offer 'bed-sit' style accommodation, with en-suite bathrooms. Meals are taken communally.

A government survey of older people found general agreement that bungalows were the best option for older people.[117] The same survey found, unsurprisingly, that sheltered housing was seen as preferable to care homes. Those respondents in sheltered housing greatly appreciated the combination of independence and security offered.

The government has acknowledged the need to try and improve the range of housing options for older people and for more integrated housing support services.[118]

Carers and the Mental Capacity Act 2005

The issues surrounding the Mental Capacity Act 2005[119] have been discussed in chapter 3. However, the issues surrounding carers and mental capacity were not considered. As already explained, an overriding principle of the Act is that when making decisions about a person who lacks capacity, these decisions should be made on the basis of what is in the incompetent person's best interests. Can the interests of a carer be taken into account? The answer, at first sight, is a clear 'no'. Only the interests of the patient in question can be considered.

Section 4 provides some requirements for a person, or court, seeking to ascertain what is in a person's best interests. Of particular note, for the present purposes, is section 4(7):

He must take into account, if it is practical and appropriate to consult them, the views of—

...

(b) anyone engaged in caring for the person or interested in his welfare

...

as to what would be in the person's best interests.

While it is good to see a statutory acceptance of the relevance of carers' views as to what should happen to those they care for, it is important to realize the limited nature of this. Most significantly, the carer can only speak in terms of what would

---

[117] Department of Communities and Local Government, *Housing Choices and Aspirations of Older People* (The Stationery Office, 2008).

[118] Department of Communities and Local Government, *Lifetime Homes, Lifetime Neighbourhoods* (The Stationery Office, 2007).

[119] K Keywood, 'Gatekeepers, Proxies, Advocates? The Evolving Role of Carers under Mental Health and Mental Incapacity Law Reforms' (2003) 25 *Journal of Social Welfare and Family Law* 355.

be in the incapacitated person's welfare. Their views as to what would assist them as carers are not a relevant consideration, unless it can be 'dressed' up as being about the benefit of the individual. So, if the carer can say 'if my views on this issue are not listened to I will cease to care for the individual and hence it is in their interests that my views are accorded weight', then his or her views can be taken into account.[120]

Let us consider a case of a severely demented 80-year-old woman. Her primary carer is her daughter, but this is supplemented at night by paid professional carers. The daughter lives 50 miles away from the mother. The daughter proposes that her mother move to live with her. There is some evidence that this change of home will cause a little confusion and disturbance to her mother. Of course, for the daughter the task of caring will be greatly eased. If the daughter were to say that the long journey is exhausting her and the quality of care she is able to offer her mother is greatly improved by moving her, it would be possible to make an argument that the move would promote the mother's best interests. Let us say, however, that the daughter goes to the utmost length to ensure she offers her mother the best of care despite the long journey. In all honesty, she cannot say that the care will be any better in her own home, it will just greatly ease her task of caring. At first sight, we must conclude that although it is in the carer's best interests, the move is not in the patient's best interests and so should not be permitted.

I will argue, first, that such a conclusion does not necessarily follow from a reading of the Mental Capacity Act. Secondly, the law ought indeed to permit such a move, by taking into account the interests of carers when considering the best interests of a person lacking capacity.

Interpreting the Mental Capacity Act

A straightforward reading of the Act suggests that a carer's interests cannot be taken into account. The sole criterion is the interests of the individual patient. Earlier reference was made to the Mental Capacity Act 2005 and the fact that although carers' views about what would be in the best interests of the patient can be taken into account, the decision can only be made based on what is in the best interests of the patient. This narrow understanding of best interests has found its way into the Act's Code of Practice. This is most powerfully shown by its discussion of the case of Pedro:

Pedro, a young man with a severe learning disability, lives in a care home. He has dental problems which cause him a lot of pain, but refuses to open his mouth for his teeth to

---

[120] See *Re Y (Mental Patient: Bone Marrow Donation)* [1997] 2 WLR 556 (FD) for an example of a case where the courts used some rather convoluted reasoning to find a benefit to the person lacking capacity in donating bone marrow to a relative. I have discussed this case further in J Herring, 'The Welfare Principle and Parent's Rights' in A Bainham, S Day Sclater, and M Richards (eds), *What is a Parent?* (Hart, 1999).

be cleaned. The staff suggest that it would be a good idea to give Pedro an occasional general anaesthetic so that a dentist can clean his teeth and fill any cavities. His mother is worried about the effects of an anaesthetic, but she hates to see him distressed and suggests instead that he should be given strong painkillers when needed. While the views of Pedro's mother and carers are important in working out what course of action would be in his best interests, the decision must *not* be based on what would be less stressful for them. Instead, it must focus on Pedro's best interests.[121]

Despite this apparently clear statement in the guidance, I will argue that the Act should be interpreted in a way which includes the interests of carers.

First, section 4(6) requires the decision-maker, when deciding what is in the best interests of the individual, to consider:

(a) the person's past and present wishes and feelings (and, in particular, any relevant written statement made by him when he had capacity),
(b) the beliefs and values that would be likely to influence his decisions if he had capacity, and
(c) the other factors that he would be likely to consider if he were able to do so.

There are very few people indeed, I suggest, who would want decisions about them when incapacitated to be made entirely based on their own best interests and with no consideration being given to the person caring for them, especially where that is a loved one. At the very least, surely there are few people who want a decision to be made which caused enormous harm to the carer because it procured for them the most marginal of gains. And surely not where a choice is made to prefer an option which benefits them, and hugely helps the carer; over an alternative which would benefit them slightly more, but hugely harm the carer. Section 4(6) enables the decision-maker to take into account the relationship between the patient and carer when making decisions. The values of altruism, however limited, will mark most intimate relationships. The Act does not tell us what weight is to be attached to the values an individual exhibited in their life, but in earlier case law we are told that the view of a patient could be a major factor.[122] Indeed, the Code of Practice accepts this:

Section 4(6)(c) of the Act requires decision-makers to consider any other factors the person who lacks capacity would consider if they were able to do so. This might include the effect of the decision on other people, obligations to dependants or the duties of a responsible citizen.[123]

The fact that the individual will not be competent and so unable to receive the benefit of the relationships should not negate this argument. In *Ahsan v University*

---

[121] Department of Constitutional Affairs, *Mental Capacity Act 2005. Code of Practice* (The Stationery Office, 2007), para 5.7.

[122] *Re MB* [1997] 2 FLR 426, para 439.

[123] Department of Constitutional Affairs, *Mental Capacity Act 2005. Code of Practice* (The Stationery Office, 2007), para 5.47.

Hospitals Leicester NHS Trust,[124] it was confirmed that an incompetent person should be treated in accordance with their religious beliefs, even if they now lacked awareness of what was happening to them. The argument that because they did not know what was happening to them, it was of no benefit to be treated in accordance with their beliefs, was rightly rejected.

Secondly, it should be recalled that 'best interests' is not defined in the Act. It is not, however, an entirely materialistic concept. In *Re MB*,[125] it was made clear that best interests are not restricted to medical best interests. The Code of Practice states:

The Act allows actions that benefit other people, as long as they are in the best interests of the person who lacks capacity to make the decision. For example, having considered all the circumstances of the particular case, a decision might be made to take a blood sample from a person who lacks capacity to consent, to check for a genetic link to cancer within the family, because this might benefit someone else in the family. But it might still be in the best interests of the person who lacks capacity. 'Best interests' goes beyond the person's medical interests.[126]

It seems, then, that a consideration of best interests can take into account the obligations towards others that a person properly has. Would you say it would be in your best interests to be waited on hand and foot by an army of slaves, meeting your every need? Would we want our friends to be undertaking enormous sacrifices to achieve relatively minor gains for us? Would anyone find such a way of life rewarding or beneficial?[127] Should we impose that on those who are incompetent? Indeed, the Mental Capacity Act itself recognizes that people lacking capacity can be treated in a way which does not directly benefit them, when in Chapter 11 of the Act it permits an incompetent person to be involved in research.

Thirdly, an approach which fails to take account of the interests of carers is liable to infringe the European Convention rights of the incapacitated individual and carer. Those in a caring relationship must have their relationship respected as part of their private or family life under Article 8.[128] Under the Human Rights Act 1998, the concept of best interests must be interpreted and given effect to in a way which respects their rights as far as possible. It is true that any right that a carer may claim under Article 8 can be interfered with under Article 8.2 in the interests of the patient. However, it needs to be shown that the interference is necessary in the interests of the incompetent patient. If a decision will hugely interfere in the private life of the carer, but provide a tiny benefit to the

---

[124]   *Ahsan v University Hospitals Leicester NHS Trust* [2006] EWHC 2624 (QB).
[125]   [1997] 2 FLR 426.
[126]   Department of Constitutional Affairs, *Mental Capacity Act 2005. Code of Practice* (The Stationery Office, 2007), para 5.48.
[127]   J Piliavin and H-W Charng, 'Altruism: A Review of Recent Literature and Research' (1990) 16 *Annual Review of Sociology* 27 discusses recent evidence that true altruism does exist in human nature.
[128]   *Sheffield CC v S* [2002] EWHC 2278 (Fam).

person lacking capacity, I suggest it is unlikely this will be sufficient to justify the interference.[129]

So, although at first glance the Mental Capacity Act appears to make it clear that only the interests of the person lacking capacity are to be taken into account and the interests of the carers are to count for nothing, the situation is not so straightforward. The view of the patient when they had capacity must be taken into account; the term 'best interests' must be understood very broadly; and the human rights of the carer and person cared for all need to be considered. This means that in many, if not all, cases, the interests of carers can be considered. The Mental Capacity Act should not, for example, be interpreted to mean that a decision is made which hugely harms a carer, while providing only a minimal benefit to the patient.

Ethical arguments

My argument now moves onto the more theoretical level, which is assessing whether we should seek to promote the best interests of the incompetent person without taking into account the interests of their carers. It is not possible to consider the incompetent person without considering the well-being of the incompetent person's carer. The interests of the two are intertwined. No carer could possibly undertake the task of caring if every decision which has to be made was solely on the basis of what is in the interests of the cared-for person. As the US President's Council on Bioethics puts it:

As a simple rule of thumb, caregivers should do the best they can do; they are never compelled to do what they cannot do, but they are obligated to see how much they can do without deforming or destroying their entire lives. But in practice, this rule of thumb rarely leads to any fixed rules, because every person faces different demands and has different capacities. And inevitably, we cannot do our best simultaneously in every area of our life: that is to say, we cannot do our best for everyone all the time; we cannot be there for everyone all the time; we cannot devote resources to everyone equally all the time. To be a caregiver is to confront not only the limitations of the person with dementia who relies upon us entirely, but our own limitations as human beings who are more than just caregivers or who are caregivers in multiple ways for multiple people.[130]

No one would want to be cared for in a relationship in which the carer's interests counted for nothing. The relationship of caring does, and should, involve give and take. It would not be in the interests of a cared-for person to be in a relationship which was utterly oppressive of their carer. What *is* in their interests is to be

---

[129] *B BC v Mrs S, Mr S* [2006] EWHC 2584 (Fam), [2007] 1 FCR 574; *A Local Authority v Mr BS* [2003] EWHC 1909 (Fam). In *Sheffield CC v S* [2002] EWHC 2278 (Fam), Munby J said that although the best interests applied, common sense dictates that mentally incapacitated adults were normally better cared for within their family (para 48), although there was no formal legal presumption to that effect.

[130] President's Council on Bioethics, *Taking Care* (President's Council on Bioethics, 2004), at 198.

in a relationship with their carer which promotes the interests and well-being of both of them.[131] It is, therefore, argued that when considering the best interests of an incompetent person, such an assessment must consider their well-being in the context of their relationships. This might involve making decisions which in a narrow way do not explicitly promote the incompetent person's welfare or even slightly harm it, if that is a fair aspect of a caring relationship which is a necessary part of the incompetent person's well-being.

There is another important aspect of this issue, namely that emphasizing inter-dependence and mutuality means that the division between carer and cared for dissolves.[132] In truth, there is often give and take in the 'carer' and 'cared-for' relationship. Their relationship is marked by interdependency.[133] The 'cared for' provides the 'carer' with gratitude, love, acknowledgement, and emotional support. Indeed, often a 'carer' will be 'cared for' in another relationship. As Diane Gibson has argued, our society is increasingly made up of overlapping networks of dependency.[134]

So can we be more precise about how the interests of carers should be taken into account? I argue that the key is to examine the decision at issue in the context of the relationship between two people. How does this decision fit in with the giving and taking involved in this relationship? This will mean that carers will not be treated 'as objects to be manipulated as part of patient care.'[135] The relationship between carers and dependants must not be one-sided. Of course, it is extremely difficult, if not impossible, to imagine that a decision that severely harms either the carer or the dependant could be seen as justified in the context of a relationship.

It may help to add what I am not saying.[136] I am not claiming that treating a person lacking capacity in a way which is not in their best interests but promotes altruism creates a moral good. Altruism which is forced is probably not properly described as altruism. At least it does not exhibit the characteristics which we admire in altruism.[137] Nor am I saying that the procedure is justified, because making decisions which benefit the carer can be shown to create benefits for the dependent person in the long term.[138]

---

[131] For a development of this approach in relation to parents and children, see J Herring, 'The Human Rights Act and the Welfare Principle in Family Law—Conflicting or Complementary?' [1999] *Child and Family Law Quarterly* 223.

[132] M Fine and C Glendinning, 'Dependence, Independence or Inter-dependence? Revisiting the Concepts of Care and Dependency' (2005) 25 *Ageing and Society* 601, at 619.

[133] T Shakespeare, *Help* (Venture, 2000); and T Shakespeare, 'The Social Relations of Care' in G Lewis, S Gewirtz, and J Clarke (eds), *Rethinking Social Policy* (Sage, 2001).

[134] D Gibson, *Aged Care: Old Policies, New Solutions* (Cambridge University Press, 2005).

[135] M Minow, 'Who's the Patient?' (1994) 53 *Maryland Law Review* 1173.

[136] P Lewis, 'Procedures that are Against the Medical Interests of Incompetent Adults' (2002) 22 *Oxford Journal of Legal Studies* 575.

[137] J Seglow, 'Altruism and Freedom' (2002) 5 *Critical Review of International Social and Political Philosophy* 145.

[138] M Goodwin, 'My Sister's Keeper?: Law, Children, and Compelled Donation' (2007) 29 *Western New England Law Review* 357.

Rather, my claim is that the incompetent person cannot be viewed in isolation. They must be viewed in the context of the relationship which they are in. This will be a fair and just relationship which promotes the rights and interests of both parties. As with all healthy relationships, this will involve give and take. Under the orthodox analysis there will be some decisions which are in the interests of the person lacking capacity and some which are in the interests of the carer. This is how it is in real life in a well-working, caring relationship, and this is how it should be.

A common objection to the argument that it is permissible when making a decision on behalf of an incompetent person to take into account the interests of others, is that in so doing the incompetent person may simply be used to benefit others. The incompetent person ends up being used as a means to an end and is not treated as an individual in their own right.[139] However, I would argue that to view a person outside the context of their relationships—to view them as an isolated vessel of gain or loss—is even more dehumanizing. When decisions are made about an individual in the context of their relationship, this is regarding them as truly human. Secondly, it is, of course, common to impose obligations, some of them quite heavy, on people in order to benefit others. Taxation and jury service are two common examples.[140] These are not normally regarded as infringing a fundamental principle of ethics, but are rather part of the responsibilities of a good citizen.

Carers and autonomy

I have just been discussing how the interests of care-givers should be taken into account when the patient has lost capacity, but what about where the patient has capacity? For those who possess legal capacity, the cardinal principle is the right of self-determination or autonomy.[141] Subject to the constraints of the law, people remain generally free to live their lives as they wish. In the context of medical law, this is reflected in the right to bodily integrity—the right for our bodies not to be touched or interfered with without our consent. As Justice Cardozo famously declared:

Every human being of adult years and sound mind has a right to determine what shall be done with his own body; and a surgeon who performs an operation without his patient's consent, commits an assault.[142]

---

[139] L Harmon, 'Falling off the Vine: Legal Fictions and the Doctrine of Substituted Judgment' (1990) 100 *Yale Law Journal* 1.

[140] J Harris, 'In Praise of Unprincipled Ethics' (2003) 29 *Journal of Medical Ethics* 303.

[141] D Beyleveld and R Brownsword, *Consent in the Law* (Hart, 2007), at 1–35.

[142] *Schloendorff v Society of N Y Hosp*, 105 NE 92, 93 (NY 1914).

However, a consideration of caring relationships challenges the pre-eminence which is given to the principle of autonomy. As Pamela Scheininger puts it:

Because the law is conceived of in its application to the isolated individual rather than in its application to the individual's various associations and relationships, the law does not accurately reflect the reality of human existence. The legitimacy of the law is thus challenged. Individual persons do not operate as independent, separate entities, but as interdependent, connected parts of larger groups. In failing to deal with laws as they affect human relationships, lawmakers ignore a fundamental aspect of our humanity.[143]

A recognition of the significance of care-giving relationships which are central to all our lives shifts the starting point away from the autonomous individual to a person sited in inter-dependent relationships. As Susan Dobbs explains:

My emphasis is on the ways in which human vulnerability and dependency have come to be viewed as evidence of a failing to attain or retain autonomous agency, rather than as conditions for agency and autonomy among humans. I argue that the dominant social understandings of what it is to be a citizen, autonomous agent or person contribute to the exploitation and disadvantage of care workers. I argue that a better approach to the social and ethical issues raised by paid care requires a refocusing on inherent human vulnerability. In my view, it is only through this refocusing that the material, emotional and social supports that make selfhood and citizenship possible can be adequately understood…Attention to *vulnerability*, by contrast, changes citizens' ethical relations from those of independent actors carving out realms of right against each other and the state, to those of mutually-dependent and vulnerably-exposed beings whose capacities to develop as subjects are directly and indirectly mediated by the conditions around them.[144]

Once, then, we accept our inherent vulnerability and dependency on others, the image of the all-powerful rights-bearer falls away. So seen, autonomy is not so much about rational choice, but is relational. Far then from needing what Justice Brandeis identified as the 'right to be let alone',[145] we need our relationships to be recognized and protected. As Linda Barclay notes, 'our ongoing success as an autonomous agent is affected by our ability to share our ideas, our aspirations, and our beliefs in conversation with others. It is unlikely that any vision or aspiration is sustained in isolation from others'.[146]

---

[143] P. Scheininger, 'Legal Separateness, Private Connectedness: An Impediment to Gender Equality in The Family' (1998) *Columbia Journal of Law and Social Problems* 283.

[144] S Dodds, 'Depending on Care: Recognition of Vulnerability and the Social Contribution of Care Provision' (2007) 21 *Bioethics* 500, at 517.

[145] *Olmstead v United States*, 277 US 438, 478 (1928) (Brandeis J dissenting).

[146] L Barclay, 'Autonomy and the Social Self' in C Mackenzie and N Stoljar (eds), *Relational Autonomy* (Oxford University Press, 2000), at 57.

Our sense of self is a mixture of interlocking and sometimes conflicting social identities.[147] For many people, their self-definition is based on relationship, be it as a mother, a Muslim, or a Minnesota Vikings fan. We are not in reality free to 'live our lives as we choose' because we are constrained by the responsibilities, realities, and relationships which embed our lives.[148] Hence Allan Johnson[149] has called our culture's insistence that we are separate and autonomous as patriarchy's 'Great Lie'. As Eva Feder Kittay writes:

I propose that being a person means having the capacity to be in certain relationship with other persons, to sustain contact with other persons, to shape one's own world and the world of others, and to have a life that another person can conceive of as an imaginative possibility for him- or herself ... We do not become a person without the engagement of other persons—their care, as well as their recognition of the uniqueness and the connectedness of our human agency, and the distinctiveness of our particularly human relations to others and the world we fashion.[150]

Does this mean then that patients can automatically have treatment imposed on them against their wishes, because that is what those they are in relationships with think best? No. The reason why it does not is that relational autonomy recognizes the responsibilities that go with relationships. Selma Sevenhuijsen has contrasted an approach based on ethics of care with one based on traditional legal approaches: 'the ethics of care involves different moral concepts: responsibility and relationships rather than rules and rights'.[151] The responsibilities arising from a relationship are therefore central to an ethic of care. What these require and what they entail, however, cannot be set down in stone. Every relationship is different and hence the responsibilities created differ too.[152]

So understood, the responsibilities arising from the relationship affect both the patient and those they are interdependent with.[153] It would only be in an extreme case where compelling surgery would be a fair aspect of the relationships or that demanding it would be in accordance with the responsibilities the relationships create to each other. An approach based on an ethic of care would encourage a dialogue between the patient and those around them to determine what ought to be done. It would recognize that the decision needs to be made in the context of the inter-dependent relationships between all those involved.

---

[147] A Donchin, 'Understanding Autonomy Relationally' (2001) 26 *Journal of Medicine and Philosophy* 365.

[148] J Nedelsky, 'Reconceiving Autonomy: Sources, Thoughts and Possibilities' (1989) 1 *Yale Journal of Law and Feminism* 7.

[149] A Johnson, *The Gender Knot* (Temple University Press, 1997), at 30.

[150] E Feder Kittay, 'When Caring is Just and Justice is Caring: Justice and Mental Retardation' in E Kittay and E Feder (eds), *The Subject of Care: Feminist Perspectives on Dependency* (Rowman & Littlefield, 2002), at 266.

[151] S Sevenhuijsen, *Citizenship and the Ethics of Care* (Routledge, 1998), at 107.

[152] K Bartlett, 'Re-expressing Parenthood' (1988) 93 *Yale Law Journal* 293, at 299.

[153] J Bridgeman, *Parental Responsibility, Young Children and Healthcare Law* (Cambridge University Press, 2008).

Healthcare rationing and carers

The issue of healthcare rationing is discussed in chapter 8. There we consider the argument that the use of 'quality adjusted life years' (QALY) was ageist. Here I will argue that their use fails to take adequate account of the carers' interests.

QALY is normally used in a highly individualistic fashion, focusing just on the impact of the treatment on the particular patient. The improvement in the patient's quality of life alone is considered and the impact on their care-givers counts for nothing. Imagine, for example, a drug which prevents incontinence. It may be with a highly incapacitated patient receiving excellent care that the benefit of the drug will be very limited.[154] It might therefore score very low indeed on a QALY scale. The fact that that drug might have a dramatic impact on the quality of life for their care-giver would not be relevant under a traditional analysis of QALY, unless it can be shown that the impact on the care-giver is such as to affect the quality of care and thereby harm the patient.

Calculations based on QALY usually do not include an assessment of behavioural symptoms.[155] If the treatment does not impact on the health of the individual, even though it might alter their behaviour, this is not a benefit for the purposes of a QALY calculation. However, behavioural symptoms can have a huge impact on a care-giver's quality of life.

Even if the interests of care-givers are examined, they may be found to count for nothing. In 2006 NICE considered whether to approve a drug which could delay the impact of Alzheimer's disease. They considered whether to take into account the benefit of the treatment to care-givers, but concluded:

The Committee considered that although at any point in time a carer may have a higher utility if they were caring for a person responding to drug treatment than if the person were not on the drug or not responding to the drug, the effect of the drug would be to delay progression of the condition, in which case the carer would still be faced at some time in the future with the same difficulties caused by disease progression. Exceptions could be if the person did not progress to later and more difficult stages of the disease within 5 years or because of death.[156]

This argument is, with respect, unconvincing. The claim appears to be that if someone is going to have the burdens of caring for a relative suffering from Alzheimer's disease at some point in their life, then it matters not whether that

---

[154] See J Herring, 'The Place of Carers' in M Freeman (ed), *Law and Bioethics* (Oxford University Press, 2008) for a discussion of this issue as it applied to the decision of NICE to limit access to drugs to treat Alzheimer's disease.

[155] Ibid, para 4.2.6.

[156] National Institute for Health and Clinical Excellence, *Donepezil, Galantamine, Rivastigmine (Review) and Memantine for the Treatment of Alzheimer's Disease (Appraisal Consultation)* (NICE, 2006), para 4.3.10.2.

is now or at some future point in time. So, medication which simply delays the inevitable onset of Alzheimer's disease does not benefit the care-giver. However, delaying the onset of the condition provides the benefit of the care-giver having a longer time with their loved one before the condition takes its toll. Perhaps in purely financial terms the loss experienced by the care-giver is no different, but in terms of quality of life there is certainly a loss.

The failure to consider the interests of care-givers when making rationing decisions means that the costs to national health systems or insurance companies' budgets are given weight, but the costs to care-givers count for nothing. Yet the costs to the individual care-giver are costs to real people whose lives bear the blight of caring. By contrast, any cost to the state or insurance companies is spread widely. Politically, of course, the approach is understandable. Costs to the government are in the public eye and impact on the sensitive issue of levels of taxation. Costs to care-givers go unnoticed in the public arena, although they are real enough to those who suffer them, and real enough in their effect on society as a whole.

It must not be thought, however, that including the costs to care-givers when making rationing decisions is without difficulty. There are dangers that it will mean that those cared for by a large number of care-givers or a more vulnerable care-giver will be regarded as having a greater call on healthcare resources than a person who is alone, with no family or care-givers.[157] In *Rogers*,[158] the Court of Appeal approved the use of social and personal characteristics for determining which patients should be given Herceptin[159] under the NHS. The court held that it could be appropriate to 'make the difficult choice to fund treatment for a woman with, say, a disabled child and not for a woman in different personal circumstances'.[160]

Jo Bridgeman has rejected such an approach.[161] She has argued:

The needs of a child with disabilities are no different whether they are met by her mother or another. The needs of a woman with breast cancer are no different, whether she is the carer of a child with disabilities or not.[162]

In some ways, this is a surprising comment in the light of her comments in the same article which reflect many of the views expressed in this article,[163] namely

[157] Although, see D Shickle, 'Public Preference for Health Care' (1997) *Bioethics* 277 for some evidence that surveys of the general public suggest that the number of dependants should be a factor in rationing health care. Contrast P Anand and A Wailoo, 'Utility versus Rights to Publicly Provided Rights: Augments and Evidence from Health Care Rationing' (2000) 67 *Economica* 543.

[158] *R (Rogers) v Swindon Primary Care Trust* [2006] EWCA Civ 392.

[159] A drug for use in treatment of cancer. [160] At para 77.

[161] J Bridgeman, '"Exceptional" Women, Healthcare Consumers and the Inevitability of Caring' (2007) 15 *Feminist Legal Studies* 235.

[162] At 236.

[163] We would both agree that a society seeking to promote an ethic of care would ensure that such essential drugs were available.

that we should not view patients in isolation, but in the context of a network of dependencies. The problem with saying 'the needs of a woman with breast cancer are no different, whether she is the care-giver of a child with disabilities or not' is that it imagines we can assess the needs of a patient without looking at the network of relationships in which they find themselves.

However, this may be to misinterpret Bridgeman's point. Her argument is that we are all in a network of dependencies. So, all women with breast cancer have people who are dependent on them and we should not be in the job of giving greater preference to some dependent relationships over others. Indeed, there is a danger that the woman's own identity becomes subsumed within a 'caring role'. As Bridgeman notes, it is interesting that the primary care trust in *Rogers* regarded as an exceptional case for treatment for breast cancer, 'caring for a disabled child'; rather than, say, outstanding success in a career, or other criteria.[164]

There is, as Bridgeman argues, something unpleasant about seeking to compare 'the worth of the lives of women centred around their caring respon-sibilities'.[165] However, if there is to be rationing of healthcare resources, there must be some way of ranking the needs of patients. The choice is between either ignoring the network of those in caring relations or comparing them. Whilst sharing Bridgeman's distaste, if we must ration medical resources I would rather make the comparison than ignore the relationships patients are in.[166]

So, we have seen in this discussion that the primary method of allocating healthcare resources, the QALY approach, fails appropriately to take into account the interests of care-givers. In the allocation of health resources, it has been argued, the benefits to those caring for and being cared for by the patient should be taken into account, as well as the benefits to the patient themselves. Indeed, it has been argued that there is no way of separating the benefits to the patient and those they are in caring relationships with. It has, however, been acknow-ledged that this is not straightforward. There is a lack of research into the benefits on care-givers of particular medication and in particular a lack of a theoretical model of giving appropriate weight to those benefits when rationing decisions are made. Further, there are the difficulties inherent in seeking to compare different sets of caring relationships. Despite these difficulties, it is argued that ration-ing decisions should not be restricted to considering the benefit to an individual patient, without recognition being given to the network of relationships within which they live.

---

[164] J Bridgeman, '"Exceptional" Women, Healthcare Consumers and the Inevitability of Caring' (2007) 15 *Feminist Legal Studies* 235, at 236.

[165] Ibid, at 236.

[166] This discussion opens the debate over whether an alternative to the consequentialist QALY approach is preferable. See, eg J Harris, 'Justice and Equal Opportunities in Health Care' (1999) 13 *Bioethics* 392; and George P Smith II, *Distributive Justice and the New Medicine* (Edward Elgar, 2008).

Carers and other areas of the law

There are a host of other areas of the law in which the interests of carers are not adequately protected. These are discussed elsewhere, but include rights under the Human Tissue Act 2004, Mental Health Act 1983, and damages under the law of tort.[167] In all of these areas an argument can be made that the law fails to protect the interests of carers. In the light of these difficulties to date it is suggested the law's approach to carers needs to be rethought. Two possible ways of developing an approach which would seek to protect the interests of carers will now be considered: human rights and the ethic of care.

A human rights response

Carers could seek to rely on human rights to bolster their legal position. A number of different articles of the European Convention on Human Rights could be relied upon.

Let us first consider the right to protection from discrimination.[168] While discrimination on the basis of sex, race, and age is now well established, discrimination on the grounds of carer status has received little attention. Article 14 of the European Convention of Human Rights states that the rights protected by the Convention:

shall be secured without discrimination on any ground such as sex, race, colour, language, religion, political or other opinion, national or social origin, association with a national minority, property, birth or other status.

The use of the words 'such as' in that article indicate that the list of prohibited grounds of discrimination is not closed.[169] Two arguments could be made on behalf of carers. First, it might be argued that discrimination on the grounds of disability is now rightly regarded as unacceptable, and Article 14 would now cover that. It could be said that discrimination against carers of disabled people is a form of discrimination against disabled people. Anything that disadvantages the carers of disabled people will disadvantage the disabled people themselves. This argument has been considered and accepted by the European Court of Justice in the context of protection in employment law from discrimination.[170] In *Coleman v Attridge Law*,[171] it was held that discrimination in employment against a carer of a disabled person was discrimination on the grounds of disability, even though

---

[167] See J Herring, 'Where are the Carers in Healthcare Law and Ethics?' (2006) 21 *Legal Studies* 51.
[168] Art 14.　　[169] *Da Silva Mouta v Portugal* [2001] 1 FCR 653.
[170] Council Directive 2000/78/EC of 27 November 2000.
[171] Case C–303/06, [2008] IRLR 722.

the carer was not themselves disabled. That, with respect, seems right. A person who is discriminated against because their spouse is of a certain race is discriminated against on the grounds of race, even though it is not their race that has caused the issue.

Secondly, the argument could be made that carers as a group are vulnerable and disadvantaged and need protection as a group in their own right. Luke Clements writes:

Carers should have the same life chances as anyone else. The mere fact they are providing care should not disentitle them to opportunities available to people who do not have caring responsibilities. To argue otherwise would be to suggest that it is legitimate to discriminate against carers in a way that would not be acceptable for any other group.[172]

The difficulty in making this claim is that being a carer is (unlike race or sex) not an 'immutable characteristic'; rather it is a role a person has chosen to undertake.[173] Further, unlike other grounds of discrimination, carers are not a category of people with a clear group identity. In response, it can be argued that it is doubtful whether 'immutability' or 'group identity' are required for a ground of discrimination. Illegitimacy and marital status do not fall into both of these headings and yet are accepted as grounds of discrimination. As Sandra Fredman, rejecting the view that immutability is a requirement for a ground of discrimination, argues:

a person or group has been discriminated against when a legislative distinction makes them feel that they are less worthy of recognition or value as human beings, as members of society.[174]

It should be emphasized that even if either of these arguments is accepted, Article 14 can only be relied upon if one of the other rights in the Convention was engaged. The most obvious claim would be that a carer's right to respect for his or her private or family life was interfered with in a way which was discriminatory on the grounds of his or her caring status.

Secondly, let us consider the right to respect for private and family life. A carer can claim that their relationship with the cared-for person is protected by Article 8 of the Convention. If the cared-for person and carer are relatives, there will be no difficulty in arguing that their relationship falls within the category of family. However, if they are not blood relatives, there is an argument that they can still be regarded as having family life. The European Court of Human Rights has accepted that foster carers and the children they look after can have family life.[175] Even if a claim to family life fails, a strong case can be made for their relationship

---

[172] L Clements, *Carers and the Law* (Carers UK, 2005), para 4.40.
[173] *Pretty v UK* (2002) 35 EHRR 1, para 61.   [174] Ibid, para 82.
[175] *Rieme v Sweden* (1992) 16 EHRR 155; and *Cyprus v Turkey* (1976) 4 EHRR 282.

to be protected by the right to respect for private life. This part of Article 8 has been said to include the right to 'establish and develop personal relationships'.[176]

Article 8 contains both positive and negative aspects. In negative terms, the state must not interfere in an individual's private and family life unless to do so is necessary under the terms of Article 8(2)—for example, it is necessary to protect the interests of others. More significant is the positive obligation under Article 8.[177] This requires that the state, on occasion, provide services or otherwise act in a way to enable a person to maintain a family relationship. This is, of course, limited. A state is only required to take reasonable steps. A strong case can be made for there being a right to assistance where the alternative is the separation of the carer and the cared-for person.

Thirdly, the right to protection from torture or inhuman or degrading treatment is protected by Article 3 of the Convention. This article also imposes positive and negative obligations on the state. Not only must the state not torture or inflict inhuman or degrading treatment on its citizens, it must protect citizens from torture or inhuman or degrading treatment at the hands of other people, in so far as it is reasonable.[178]

Hence, if the state is aware that children are suffering abuse and fails to offer them protection, the state is said thereby to infringe the children's rights under Article 3.[179] Of course, not all carers will be able to describe their position as amounting to torture or inhuman treatment, but certainly quite a few carers may be able to claim that their standard of life has reached such a level. Further, although the obligation to protect children and other vulnerable people from inhuman or degrading treatment is established, it is not clear that the courts would be as willing to find an obligation on the state where the individual is competent.

From a broader perspective, in Martha Fineman's *The Autonomy Myth*,[180] the claim is made that as carers provide much benefit to society, there is a debt owed to them by society. She explains:

The theory of dependency I set forth develops a claim of 'right' or entitlement to support and accommodation from the state and its institutions on the part of caretakers— those who care for dependents. Their labor should be treated as equally productive even if unwaged, and should be measured by its societal value, not by economic or market indicators. The fact that dependency work has been un- or undervalued in the market is an argument *for* governmental intervention and restructuring to mandate adjustment and market accommodation, as well as more direct reparations.[181]

---

[176] A Mowbray, *The Development of Positive Obligations under the European Convention on Human Rights by the European Court of Human Rights* (Hart, 2003).
[177] Department of Health, *Carers and Disabled Children Act 2000. Practice Guidance* (The Stationery Office, 2001).
[178] *E v UK* [2002] 3 FCR 700.   [179] Ibid.
[180] M Fineman, *The Autonomy Myth* (New Press, 2004).   [181] Ibid, at 262.

She therefore argues that:

Caretaking thus creates a 'social debt', a debt that must be paid according to principles of equality that demand that those receiving social benefits also share the costs when they are able. Far from exemplifying equal responsibility for dependency, however, our market institutions are 'free-riders', appropriating the labor of the caretaker for their purposes.[182]

It is not possible here to analyse in depth the sophisticated argument which she develops. There are, however, some dangers with it. One might argue that if society is liable to 'pay' for care, it might feel a greater entitlement to police the standard of care and to consider whether there are economically more efficient ways of providing care.

As this section shows, human rights do provide some legal tools which could be used to promote the interests of carers. Indeed, we see in Fineman's writing arguments that could be developed to bolster these human rights claims. However, in the next section a rather different way ahead for the law is considered: an ethic of care.

Ethic of care

The legal and social response to caring provides a challenge to the way in which legal rights and responsibilities are understood.[183] It has been claimed that much of the law is based on the assumption that we are competent, detached, independent people who are entitled to have our rights of self-determination and autonomy fiercely protected.[184] However, the reality is that we are ignorant, vulnerable, interdependent individuals, whose strength and reality is not in our autonomy, but in our relationships with others.[185]

The law's approach should, then, be based on a norm of interlocking mutually dependent relationships, rather than an individualized vision of rights. Many of those sympathetic to such a claim have turned to ethics of care as an alternative to traditional rights-based approaches.[186] It promotes a vision of people

---

[182] Ibid.

[183] R Tong, 'The Ethics of Care: A Feminist Virtue Ethics of Care for Healthcare Practitioners' (1998) 23 *Journal of Medicine and Philosophy* 131.

[184] L Lloyd, 'Mortality and Morality: Ageing and the Ethics of Care' (2004) 24 *Ageing and Society* 235.

[185] C Meyer, 'Cruel Choices: Autonomy and Critical Care Decision-Making' (2004) 18 *Bioethics* 104; and J Tronto, *Moral Boundaries* (Routledge, 1993), at 167–70.

[186] eg C Gilligan, 'Moral Orientation and Moral Development' in E Kittay and D Meyers (eds), *Women and Moral Theory* (Rowman and Littlefield, 1987); M Friedman, *Liberating Care* (Cornell University Press, 1993); S Sevenhuijsen, *Citizenship and The Ethics of Care* (Routledge, 1998); R Groenhout, *Connected Lives: Human Nature and an Ethics of Care* (Rowman and Littlefield, 2004); V Held, *The Ethics of Care* (Oxford University Press, 2006); D Engster, *The Heart of Justice. Care Ethics and Political Theory* (Oxford University Press, 2007); and D Koehn, *An Ethic of Care* (Routledge, 1998).

with interdependent relationships as the norm around which legal and ethical responses should be built. The values that are promoted within an ethic of care are not isolated autonomy or the pursuance of individualized rights, but rather the promotion of caring, mutuality, and interdependence. This is not the place to fully flesh out what an ethic of care might mean, nor indeed the dangers associated with it. But I want to highlight five aspects relating to an ethic of care which will be relevant in the discussion which follows.

First, dependency and care are an inevitable part of being human.[187] Caring relationships are the stuff of life.[188] Although the extent of caring may vary, there is probably no point in our lives at which we are neither cared for nor are caring for another. As Jo Bridgeman has recently emphasized, it is wrong to assume that the only kinds of dependencies are those between parents and children; or in respect of those with disabilities. There is a wide range of forms of dependencies that we all have with each other, even between friends.[189] In failing to acknowledge care work properly, the law is missing an important and inevitable aspect of life. Eva Kittay writes:

My point is that this interdependence begins with dependence. It begins with the dependency of an infant, and often ends with the dependency of a very ill or frail person close to dying. The infant may develop into a person who can reciprocate, an individual upon whom another can be dependent and whose continuing needs make her interdependent with others. The frail elderly person...may herself have been involved in a series of interdependent relations. But at some point there is a dependency that is not yet, no longer an interdependency. By excluding *this* dependency from social and political concerns, we have been able to fashion the pretense that we are *independent*—that the cooperation between persons that some insist is *inter*dependence is simply the mutual (often voluntary) cooperation between essentially independent persons.[190]

Secondly, not only is care an inevitable part of life; it is a good part of life. Care should be treasured and valued. As Robin West puts it:

Caregiving labor (and its fruits) is the central adventure of a lifetime; it is what gives life its point, provides it with meaning, and returns to those who give it some measure of security and emotional sustenance. For even more of us, whether or not we like it and regardless of how we regard it, caregiving labor, for children and the aged, is the work we will do that creates the relationships, families, and communities

---

[187] M Fineman, *The Autonomy Myth* (New Press, 2004), at xvii; and T Levy, 'The Relational Self and the Right to Give Care' (2007) 28 *New Political Science* 547.

[188] F Williams, 'The Presence of Feminism in the Future of Welfare' (2002) 31 *Economy and Society* 502.

[189] J Bridgeman, 'Book Review' (2006) 14 *Feminist Legal Studies,* 407. See also, J Herring and P-L Chau, 'My Body, Your Body, Our Bodies' (2007) 15 *Medical Law Review* 34.

[190] E Feder Kittay, *Love's Labour: Essays on Women, Equality and Dependency* (Routledge, 1999), at xii (emphasis in original).

within which our lives are made pleasurable and connected to something larger than ourselves.[191]

The value of care is not, of course, simply for the individuals themselves. Without caring relationships, the burden that would fall on society would be impossible to bear.[192] Thirdly, much of medical law emphasizes the importance of rationality and intellect. The concepts of mental capacity, informed consent, and compliance with standards expected by a responsible body of opinion all prevail in legal discourse, logical thought, and sound judgement. There is nothing wrong in that, but the emotional side of health is lost. The love which goes on caring and caring; the grief, disappointment, frustration, anger, and despair, find no place. Occasionally, it peeps through (see the refusal of the medical team who had done so much work to care for the patient in *Re B (Adult: Refusal of Medical Treatment)*[193] that they felt unable to switch off her life support machine as the court ultimately ordered) and when it does it seems somehow inappropriate. The exclusion of emotion means that the voice of carers talking about how their cared-for one should be looked after finds no ready legal mouthpiece. An ethic of care seeks to acknowledge the roles that emotion and rationality play in relationships. We do not live by rational thoughts alone.

Fourthly, in relationships of caring and dependency, interests become inter-mingled.[194] We do not break down into 'me' and 'you'. To harm a carer is to harm the person cared for; to harm the person cared for is to harm the carer. There should be no talk of balancing the interests of the carer and the person cared for, the question rather should be emphasizing the responsibilities they owe to each other in the context of a mutually supporting relationship.[195]

Indeed, it is simplistic to imagine that we can identify in a caring relationship who is the carer and who the cared for. Clare Ungerson has convincingly argued that it is wrong to see the relationship between 'carer' and 'cared for' as one where the 'carer' has power over the 'cared for'.[196] The 'cared for' might have a range of powers they can exercise. The emotional well-being of the carer can depend on the attitude and response of the 'cared for' person to the carer. The 'cared for' has the power to make the life of the carer unbearable.

---

[191] R West, 'The Right to Care' in E Kittay and E Feder (eds), *The Subject of Care: Feminist Perspectives on Dependency* (Rowman & Littlefield, 2002), at 89.

[192] L McClain, 'Care as a Public Value: Linking Responsibility, Resources, and Republicanism' (2001) 76 *Chicago-Kent Law Review* 1673; and M Daly, 'Care as a Good for Social Policy' (2002) 31 *Journal of Social Policy* 251.

[193] [2002] All ER 449.

[194] T Shakespeare, *Help* (Venture, 2000); and T Shakespeare, 'The Social Relations of Care' in G Lewis, S Gewirtz, and J Clarke (eds), *Rethinking Social Policy* (Sage, 2001).

[195] G Clement, *Care, Autonomy and Justice: Feminism and the Ethic of Care* (Westview, 1996), at 11; and V Held, *The Ethics of Care* (Oxford University Press, 2005), at 1.

[196] C Ungerson, 'Social Politics and the Commodification of Care' (1997) 4 *Social Policy* 362.

Fifthly, ethics of care emphasizes the importance of responsibilities within caring relationships. Supporters of ethic of care argue that rather than the focus of the enquiry being whether it is my right to do X, the question is what is my proper obligation within the context of this relationship?[197] Virginia Held makes the point by contrasting ethics of care and an ethic of justice:

An ethic of justice focuses on questions of fairness, equality, individual rights, abstract principles, and the consistent application of them. An ethic of care focuses on attentiveness, trust, responsiveness to need, narrative nuance, and cultivating caring relations. Whereas an ethic of justice seeks a fair solution between competing individual interests and rights, an ethic of care sees the interest of carers and cared-for as importantly intertwined rather than as simply competing.[198]

It should be added that Held makes it clear that an ethic of care includes justice:

There can be care without justice. There has historically been little justice in the family, but care and life have gone on without it. There can be no justice without care, however, for without care no child would survive and there would be no persons to respect.[199]

It is easy in a discussion of an ethic of care to glamorize care. No one should overlook the sheer exhaustion and exasperation that caring brings.[200] Caring can be mucky, nasty, and frustrating.[201] Care is hard work; extremely hard work.[202] Carers can often feel trapped: their life goals come to an end and they must adopt the role of carer, while the rest of their life is put on hold.[203] Caring can become abusive for both the carer and cared for. As Robin West puts it:

Relationships of care, untempered by the demands of justice, resulting in the creation of injured, harmed, exhausted, compromised, and self-loathing 'giving selves,' rather than in genuinely compassionate and giving individuals, are ubiquitous in this society.[204]

But this is why it is so important that those sympathetic to an ethic of care emphasize the importance of upholding justice within relationships. An ethic of care which promotes mutual obligation and support within a relationship should never be used to permit abuse to fester. Indeed, a relationship-based approach can be more alert than any other to the dangers of misuse of a relationship.[205]

---

[197] V Held, *The Ethics of Care* (Oxford University Press, 2005), at 15.
[198] Ibid, at 15.   [199] Ibid, at 17.
[200] M Goldsteen, T Abma, and B Oeseburg, 'What is it to be a Daughter? Identities under Pressure in Dementia Care' (2007) 21 *Bioethics* 1.
[201] K Abrams, 'The Second Coming of Care' (2001) 76 *Chicago-Kent Law Review* 1605; and J Oliver and A Briggs, *Caring Experiences of Looking after Disabled Relatives* (Routledge, 1985).
[202] A Hubbard, 'The Myth of Independence and the Major Life Activity of Caring' (2004) 8 *Journal of Gender, Race and Justice* 327; and C Ungerson, 'Social Politics and the Commodification of Care' (1997) 4 *Social Policy* 362.
[203] Department of Health, *Caring about Carers* (Department of Health, 1999), para 69.
[204] R West, *Caring for Justice* (New York University Press, 1997), at 81.
[205] See M Chen-Wishart, 'Undue Influence: Vindicating Relationships of Influence' in J Holder and C O'Cinneide (eds), *Current Legal Problems* (Oxford University Press, 2007).

Critics of an ethic of care

Of course, the concept of an ethic of care is not without its critics. Emily Jackson has recently described the ethic of care as 'an inherently vague concept, which could be used to justify almost any plausible moral argument'.[206] She points out that in relation to euthanasia, ethics of care could be used to support or oppose euthanasia.

This is, with respect, a rather unfair criticism. Exactly the same thing could be said about the concept of human rights. Indeed, one should be highly sceptical of any broad ethical approach that provides a single answer to a complex issue such as euthanasia. An ethic of care, like the concept of rights, provides ethical tools with which to analyse a situation, but it does not provide the answer. The fact that it can be used to support and oppose euthanasia should be seen as a strength, not a weakness, of the concept.

Another common criticism of an ethic of care relates to a rather unfortunate aspect of its history.[207] Ethic of care rose to prominence with the writing of Carol Gilligan, who sought to distinguish between a 'male' approach to ethical issues, which focused on concepts of justice; and a 'female' approach to ethical issues, which focused on concepts of care. While undoubtedly the 'grandmother' of care ethics (and who would want to speak ill of their grandmother), the 'second generation' of care ethicists has tended to downplay the argument that the ethic of care is a female way of thought.[208] Further, the sharp divide between justice and care is not normally relied upon nowadays. An ethic of care wishes to promote relationships, but only those relationships which are just.

So, arguments that an ethic of care perpetuates assumptions that women are naturally drawn to caring roles, or that it overlooks the potential for abuse within relationships, are usually based on a rather old-fashioned (mis)understanding of what the ethic of care is about.

One of the most powerful criticisms of an ethic of care is that care relationships, despite their cosy sounding image, are in fact about power. John Eekelaar writes:

> to exercise care is also to exercise power. True, it is to be hoped that it is a beneficent exercise of power, but it is power nonetheless. The key element, overlooked in some communitarian accounts, is the role of force or coercion. There are many examples where the role of caregiver, even if applied with good intentions, has adverse consequences.[209]

---

[206] E Jackson, *Medical Law* (Oxford University Press, 2007), at 22.

[207] E Jackson, ibid at 22 suggests that ethics of care has nothing to say about social policy. This is simply untrue: see, eg O Hankivsky, *Social Policy and the Ethic of Care* (University of British Columbia Press, 2005).

[208] Repeats of the experiments used by Carol Gilligan in European countries have not found the differing responses to ethical issues tied to sex in the way she did: A Vikan, C Camino, and A Biaggio, 'Note on a Cross-Cultural Test of Gilligan's Ethic of Care' (2005) 34 *Journal of Moral Education* 107.

[209] J Eekelaar, *Family Law and Personal Life* (Oxford University Press, 2007), at 178–9. See also, R Wood, 'Care of Disabled People' in G Dalley (ed), *Disability and Social Policy* (Policy Studies Institute, 1991).

As mentioned earlier, it is a mistake to assume that the care-giver exercises power over the person cared for. Caring relations often involve a complex interplay of dependencies and vulnerabilities.[210] As Michael Fine and Caroline Glendinning argue:

Recent studies of care suggest that qualities of reciprocal dependence underlie much of what is termed 'care'. Rather than being a unidirectional activity in which an active care-giver does something to a passive and dependent recipient, these accounts suggest that care is best understood as the product or outcome of the relationship between two or more people.[211]

Eekelaar is right to be concerned about the power that can undoubtedly be exerted in a caring relationship. However, that is not an automatic consequence of caring, and it reminds us how important it is to emphasize the elements of justice and responsibility within an ethic of care.

Putting an ethic of care into practice

Under an ethic of care, the practice of caring would be highly valued within society. Care-givers would, far from being hidden, come to represent a norm. Social structures and attitudes would need to be set up to encourage and enable caring. This would require adequate remuneration of care-givers: not the payment of benefits of the kind paid to those 'unable to work', but payment acknowledging the key role they play.[212] Work would need to be done to ensure that the burden of caring did not fall on the few, but was shared across the community.

Susan Dodds argues that we need a legal and social system which is not premised on individualistic conceptions of autonomy, but on an acceptance of our vulnerability:[213]

A vulnerability-centered view of the self and of persons is better able to capture many of our moral motivations and intuitions than can be captured by an autonomy-focused approach. We are all vulnerable to the exigencies of our embodied, social and relational existence and, in recognizing this inherent human vulnerability, we can see the ways in which a range of social institutions and structures protect us against some vulnerabilities, while others expose us to risk. We do not have to view our obligations towards those who lack the capacity to develop or retain autonomy as having a different source from our obligations towards those whose autonomy is made vulnerable due to a degree of dependency. It may be easier to recognize the social value of provision of care if it is

---

[210] C Chorn and J Harms Cannon, '"They're Still in Control Enough to be in Control": Paradox of Power in Dementia Caregiving' (2008) 22 *Journal of Aging Studies* 45.

[211] M Fine and C Glendinning, 'Dependence, Independence or Inter-Dependence? Revisiting the Concepts of Care and Dependency' (2005) 25 *Ageing and Society* 601, at 619.

[212] The payment of carers has been said to carry dangers of causing the 'marketisation of intimacy and the commodification of care': C Ungerson, 'Cash in Care' in M Harrington Meyer (ed), *Care Work: Gender Class and the Welfare State* (Routledge, 2000), at 69.

[213] S Dodds, 'Depending on Care: Recognition of Vulnerability and the Social Contribution of Care Provision' (2007) 21 *Bioethics* 500.

viewed as something on which we all have been dependent and on which we are all likely to be dependent at different points in our lives, rather than altruistic behaviour extended to those who lack 'full personhood'.[214]

When assessing the rights of any individual or the medical needs of an individual, such a person would have to be considered in a situational context. Never should it be a matter of assessing a person in isolation. Rather, each person's needs and rights would have to be considered in the context of their relationships.

Conclusion

When thinking of older people and care it should not be forgotten that most older people care for themselves, manage their own health, and have no need for assistance.[215] Further, as mentioned at the start of this chapter, a greater number of older people provide care than need it. Therefore, the lack of social or legal recognition for carers is of great importance for older people and their carers alike.

In his book, *The Selfish Pig's Guide to Caring*, Hugh Marriott, clearly a devoted carer himself, has this to say:

We didn't apply for the job. Most of us don't have a vocation for it. We've had no training. We're certain we aren't much good at it. Plus, and this is the nub of the matter, we've got our own life to lead. Are we expected to throw that away because of somebody else's disability? We've got things to do, places to go. And now it looks as if we might not be able to.

But aren't we just as important as they are? Why are we expected to sacrifice ourselves for somebody else? And yes, I mean sacrifice. We're not talking about giving up five minutes of time once or twice a week. Or putting off a holiday from this year to next. We're talking about changing our entire way of life. The old one wasn't perfect, but it was the best we could do. This new one isn't even ours. It's somebody else's life. And it's one that doesn't suit us at all.[216]

As this reminds us, care work is often difficult, nasty, and exhausting. It can also require great skill. Peter Beresford writes:

The 'apparent ordinariness' of care is deceptive and can often hide sophisticated, highly skilled and much valued approaches to personal and social support.[217]

Yet as we have seen in this chapter, carers lack financial and social support. The Commission for Social Care Inspection had this to say about the position of carers:

Over time, the day in, day out pressures on family carers were seen to wear people down. Coping with a mix of physical and mental problems was said by carers to be particularly

214 Ibid, at 510.   215 Ibid.
216 H Marriott, *The Selfish Pig's Guide to Caring* (Polperro, 2003), at 9.
217 P Beresford, *What Future for Care?* (Joseph Rowntree Foundation, 2008).

burdensome. Despite the higher profile of carers' needs, and improvements in the number of separate assessments being done, this study found an excessive strain on some family members, especially partners who were themselves elderly and frail. In practical terms, there appeared to be still too few services available in some places specifically to respond with speed and flexibility to carers' assessed needs and professionals still tended to be relying excessively on the commitment of carers.[218]

Increasingly, people are left to fund their own care. In 2006 to 2007, people paid nearly £5.9 billion out of their own pockets for social care services for older people.[219] The report noted 'the increasingly sharp divide' between those who were supported by the state and those who were not. Those who were outside the system often had a very poor quality of life.[220]

This chapter has also considered the broader issues that are raised by a consideration of the position of carers. It has argued in favour of an ethic of care which puts relationships at the heart of a legal approach, rather than the individualistic approach based on rights. We need to value care and privilege caring relationships in legal and social policies.[221]

---

[218] Commission for Social Care Inspection, *Leaving Hospital Revisited* (CSCI, 2005).

[219] Commission for Social Care Inspection, *The State of Social Care in England* (CSCI, 2008).

[220] J-M Robine, J-P Michel, and F Herrmann, 'Who will Care for the Oldest People in our Society' (2007) 334 *British Medical Journal* 570.

[221] The Law Commission, *Tenth Programme of Law Reform* (Law Commission, 2008), para 1.14 promises a review of the law under which residential care, community care and support for carers is provided.

5

Elder Abuse

Introduction

'Abuse of older people is a hidden, and often ignored, problem in society.'[1]

So opens the House of Commons Select Committee Report on the abuse of older people, a report which has played an important role in galvanizing responses to this problem in England and Wales. Increased public awareness of the problem of elder abuse[2] and the political will to try and tackle it has meant that the government is now taking positive steps to address it. Elder abuse, it has been claimed, has reached the position domestic violence did 15 years ago.[3] There is now an acceptance of the problem and that something needs to be done, although there is much dispute over what the correct response is.

In seeking to find the correct approach to elder abuse, some have sought to draw an analogy with legal responses to domestic violence, while others have turned to the law on child abuse. Those who refer to the domestic violence model emphasize empowering victims by providing them with a range of legal remedies they can use to protect themselves, while the child protection model emphasizes the obligations on the state to protect vulnerable citizens. In fact, it will be argued in this chapter, that neither model provides a perfect match. Elder abuse requires its own unique legal response.

It is easy to portray elder abuse as an outright evil which must be combated. Consider this extract from one recent tabloid newspaper article:

Nursing home patients crying out in pain because of rotting bed sores, freezing to death by an open window and having fingernails ripped out by a heartless carer are just some of the unbelievably cruel accounts of what's happening to Britain's elderly today. Vulnerable folk being abused by the very people who are paid to make sure their later years are comfortable and dignified. Yet the plight of these victims is being ignored. And the

---

[1] House of Commons Health Committee, *Elder Abuse* (The Stationery Office, 2004), at 1.
[2] J Ogg and G Bennett, 'Elder Abuse in Britain' (1992) 305 *British Medical Journal* 998.
[3] District Judge Marilyn Mornington, *Responding to Elder Abuse* (Age Concern, 2004).

hidden scandal has reached epidemic proportions—on a scale similar to the child abuse revelations of the 80s.[4]

The vision of elderly people being tortured by those who are meant to be caring for them cries out for a response. But this is only a part of the picture. Elder abuse is not just the result of the behaviour of wicked individuals. That ignores the wider societal responsibility for the problem and ignores the more insidious, if less dramatic forms of abuse. Abuse of older people reflects wider societal attitudes towards elderly people. Further, the way in which society arranges the care of older people enables and, in some sense, causes abusive behaviour. This is not to excuse or justify the abuse, but to argue that given the way care of older people is approached in our society abuse is a predictable, maybe even inevitable, result. The 'wicked individual' image of elder abuse also overlooks the gendered nature of the abuse: that violent elder abuse is most commonly performed by men against women.

This chapter will start by discussing the definitions of elder abuse and assessing the extent of the problem. It will then look at the legal responses to the problem. It will then move to consider how more effective legal responses could be developed. Of course, the law can play only a relatively small part in combating the problem. As the Toronto Declaration on the Global Prevention of Elder Abuse puts it: 'Ultimately elder abuse will only be successfully prevented if a culture that nurtures intergenerational solidarity and rejects violence is developed.'[5]

Two final points before addressing the definition of elder abuse. It is easy when discussing elder abuse to reinforce an image of the vulnerable older person as a passive victim. It should not be forgotten that whether or not the victims of elder abuse, older people are active contributors to society. Further, we must remember that perpetrators of elder abuse can themselves be older people.[6] Secondly, it is probably misleading to deal with 'elder abuse' as a unitary concept. As will become clear under that label, there are a host of different forms of behaviour in different settings and contexts. The behaviour of nurse Colin Norris[7] who killed four elderly patients is very different from the harm done to an older man suffering dementia who is neglected by his exhausted wife. Elder abuse involves a complex amalgam of causes and requires sensitive and subtle responses.

---

[4] R Wynne-Jones and N Webster, 'Betrayed: Scandal of UK's Million Abused Pensioners', *Daily Mirror*, 25 April 2006.

[5] World Health Organization, *The Toronto Declaration on the Prevention of Elder Abuse* (WHO, 2002).

[6] M Ayres and A Woodtli, 'Concept Analysis: Abuse of Ageing Caregivers by Elderly Care Recipients' (2001) 35 *Journal of Advanced Nursing* 326.

[7] BBC News Online, 'Killer Nurse Must Serve 30 Years', 4 March 2008.

The difficulties in defining elder abuse

There is no standard definition of elder abuse.[8] The abuse of older people can take many forms. It can involve sexual abuse,[9] financial abuse, misuse of medication, physical abuse, neglect, and humiliating behaviour.[10] It can be carried out by relatives, carers, friends, or strangers.[11] As it covers such a wide range of behaviour it is not possible to set out a single concept of elder abuse.[12] Pillemer and Finkelhor have written of the 'definitional disarray'[13] surrounding elder abuse. This, however, is not necessarily a bad thing. It is better to recognize the complexity of the forms of abuse than try to simplify the issue by portraying it as a single entity. Any definition that could seek to cover all the forms of abuse is likely to be vacuous. This is not to argue against seeking definitions of elder abuse or their characteristics, but is to argue against a single definition.[14] As Phillipson and Biggs argue:

Attempts to define and map the extent of elder abuse indicate that it should not be seen as a single monolithic phenomenon, but that it takes a variety of forms in different settings and in different kinds of relationships.[15]

One way forward would be to offer definitions within different professional spheres; for example, it has been suggested[16] that we need separate legal definitions, care management definitions, and research definitions of elder abuse. The difficulty in seeking to define the concept is that the different professions are using the notion of elder abuse for different purposes. A medical professional seeking to see if there is 'elder abuse' requiring medical intervention is likely to rely on a very different definition from a police officer wanting to know if it is appropriate to investigate a possible crime. The medical professional is more likely to focus on the perspective of the abused person and the impact on their wellbeing of the conduct in question, while the police officer will be interested in the blameworthiness of any alleged perpetrator. That said, there are, of course, certain forms of conduct which would on any definition, and for any purpose, be elder abuse.

---

[8] A Brammer and S Biggs, 'Defining Elder Abuse' (1998) 20 *Journal of Social Welfare and Family Law* 385.

[9] R Hawks, 'Grandparent Molesting: Sexual Abuse of Elderly Nursing Home Residents and its Prevention' (2006) 8 *Marquette Elder's Advisor* 159.

[10] House of Commons Health Committee, *Elder Abuse* (The Stationery Office, 2004), at 1.

[11] C McCreadie, 'A Review of Research Outcomes in Elder Abuse' (2002) 4 *Journal of Adult Protection* 3.

[12] C McCreadie, *Elder Abuse: Update On Research* (1996, Age Concern).

[13] K Pillemer and D Finkelhor, 'The Prevalence of Elder Abuse: A Random Sample Survey' (1988) 28 *The Gerontologist* 51, at 52.

[14] For a discussion of the benefits of a single definition, see K O'Connor and J Rowe, 'Elder Abuse' (2005) 15 *Reviews in Clinical Gerontology* 47.

[15] C Phillipson and S Biggs, *Elder Abuse in Perspective* (Open University Press, 1995), at 202.

[16] G Bennett, P Kingston, and B Penhale, *The Dimensions of Elder Abuse* (Macmillan, 1997).

Elder abuse is, of course, not unique in not having a precise definition. Domestic violence, for example, similarly lacks a precise definition.[17] What is more useful than seeking to produce a single definition that is appropriate for all purposes is to set out the factors that need to be considered by anyone seeking to analyse the abusive nature of the conduct and the factors that would need to be taken into account in producing a definition of elder abuse in a particular context.

Elder abuse or abuse of vulnerable people

The goal of the Department of Health in this area is to provide protection for all 'vulnerable adults'.[18] No distinction is drawn between the abuse of those who are vulnerable through age, disability, or homelessness. The Department of Health defines a vulnerable person as one:

who is or may be in need of community care services by reason of mental or other disability, age or illness; and who is or may be unable to take care of him or herself, or unable to protect him or herself against significant harm or exploitation.[19]

This approach, then, does not regard elder abuse as a unique conceptual category; but sees it as merely an aspect of the broader category of abuse of vulnerable people. Indeed, it excludes from its approach the abuse of older people who are not vulnerable.[20]

There are clear benefits to doing this. The issues surrounding abuse of vulnerable adults of whatever age are similar. It might be thought that there is much more in common between a case of abuse involving an older person lacking capacity and a case of abuse of a younger person also lacking capacity, than with a case where an older victim is fully competent. Indeed, it has been claimed that older people are not abused because they are older, but because they are vulnerable.[21] Vulnerability, rather that age, is therefore the distinguishing feature. Further, providing professionals working in the area with one set of guidance dealing with all forms of abuse against vulnerable people is likely to lead to a welcome reduction of paperwork and promote a coherence of approach. It avoids what might otherwise be difficult overlaps between, for example, protocols dealing with

---

[17] See M Madden Dempsey, 'What Counts as Domestic Violence? A Conceptual Analysis' (2006) 12(2) *William and Mary Journal of Women and the Law* 301.

[18] Department of Health, *No Secrets* (Department of Health, 2002), para 2.3 suggested that all vulnerable people should be covered by an overarching approach. Previously, Department of Health, *No Longer Afraid* (Department of Health, 1993) had focused specifically on elder abuse. For discussions of the changing approach, see P Slater, 'Elder Abuse, Adult Protection and Social Care' (2005) 7 *Journal of Adult Protection* 33.

[19] Department of Health, *No Secrets* (The Stationery Office, 2002), at para 2.3.

[20] It might be argued that being the victim of abuse automatically renders a person vulnerable, but there seems no reason why this is necessarily so if the incident has no likelihood of repetition and has no lasting effects.

[21] House of Commons Health Committee, *Elder Abuse* (The Stationery Office, 2004), evidence 163.

the abuse of disabled people and those dealing with the abuse of older people. A strong case can, therefore, certainly be made for treating elder abuse as an aspect of the wider problem of abuse of vulnerable adults.

However, I think that there are greater advantages in considering elder abuse as a unique category. So, what, if anything, may be unique about elder abuse? The answer lies in the explanation for why elder abuse occurs and why it has for so long not been acknowledged as a problem. Much writing on domestic violence has highlighted the fact that domestic violence occurs and is tolerated because of attitudes towards women and violence towards women.[22] Domestic violence is seen as both a reflection, and a reinforcement, of wider social attitudes about the domination of women by men. A similar point can be said about violence against older people. Elder abuse reflects and reinforces attitudes about older people in a way which interacts with the attitudes about them. Many of the victims are women, and then we see the interaction of both ageism and sexism in creating and reinforcing the structures that enable abuse to take place.

For example, abusive behaviour in a nursing home is often normalized and comes to be regarded as 'standard treatment'. The use of force against uncooperative older people is accepted as necessary for the 'smooth running' of the home. Older people in some residential settings are seen as a waste of space, incapable of feeling. The routines and bureaucracy of the nursing home sometimes seem to count for more than the interests of the individual residents. Even where there are not such overly hostile attitudes, many older people in residential settings are seen as needing 'looking after' and infantilized in a way which perpetuates and enables the abuse itself.[23] For example, 'baby talk' or overtly insulting terms are demeaning.[24] Often, abusive behaviour is not even recognized as such and is dismissed as 'what she wants' or 'she doesn't mind because she doesn't really know what's going on'. Even very serious incidents of abuse tend to be seen as 'one offs' rather than reflecting broader attitudes towards older people.[25] At worst, it may be labelled 'bad practice'.[26] We shall be looking at the treatment of older people in care homes later. But their treatment is often but a reflection of broader ageist attitudes within society and the social structures that set the social position of care homes.

Similarly, elder abuse in the domestic context is encouraged and perpetuated as a result of ageist and sexist attitudes. As shall be seen later, a significant proportion

[22] See M Burton, *Legal Responses to Domestic Violence* (Routledge, 2008), at ch 1 for a brief summary.

[23] S Salari, 'Infantilization as Elder Mistreatment: Evidence from Five Adult Day Centers' (2006) 17 *Journal of Elder Abuse and Neglect* 53.

[24] H Giles, E Fox, and E Smith, 'Patronizing the Elderly: Intergenerational Evaluations' (1993) 26 *Research on Language and Social Interaction* 129.

[25] BBC News Online, '"Talcum Powder Abuse" Settlement', 11 July 2006 for a report of a case where a court awarded damages after a care worker had force-fed talcum powder to a care home resident.

[26] G Fitzgerald, 'The Realities of Elder Abuse' in A Wahidin and M Cain (eds), *Ageing, Crime and Society* (Willan, 2006).

of elder abuse is, in fact, domestic violence 'grown old',[27] that is, domestic violence which has been ongoing throughout the relationship between the parties. In old age the form and method of abuse can take on new forms and have further consequences. Professionals can take some convincing that long-standing violence can be particularly serious.

Hence, it is argued that the maltreatment of an older person may not be related in truth to their vulnerability, but is a reflection of the attitudes of an individual, organization, or society towards older people in general, and older women in particular. Also, to treat elder abuse as just a sub-set of abuse of the vulnerable is to ignore the fact that non-vulnerable older people can suffer elder abuse on account of ageist attitudes and practices.

At what age does abuse become elder abuse?

In the United States, where states have enacted legislation specifically to address elder abuse, they have tended to use the age of 60 or 65.[28] The World Health Organization uses 60 in its discussions.[29] Given the argument above that a central part of elder abuse is the social construction of age, it is submitted that the key issue is when a person is treated as being elderly in our society. I would argue that abuse becomes elder abuse when a person becomes subject to the social dis-advantages and prejudicial attitudes that can attach to old age. On this approach it is the social role adopted by the individual and their treatment by society which determines whether or not their abuse is elder abuse. In other words, if a per-son is regarded and treated as an older person then they are such, whatever their chronological age.

Who perpetuates elder abuse?

Should the definition of abuse include a categorization of the person who is doing the abuse? Most writing on elder abuse accepts that abuse can be at the hands of a relative or carer. This includes both professional carers and 'informal' carers. What is less clear is whether the definition includes abuse at the hands of a stranger. For example, if a 'confidence trickster' deceives an older person out of money, is this a form of elder abuse? Can the failure to provide services amount to abuse, and if so, could a social service department or even a government be guilty of elder abuse? The major study in the UK on elder abuse distinguished between cases where the abuse was perpetrated by a partner, relative, carer, or friend and other cases.[30] The government's *No Secrets*

---

[27] I Blood, *Older Women and Domestic Violence* (Help the Aged, 2004).
[28] B Brandl and T Meuer, 'Domestic Abuse In Later Life' (2001) 8 *Elder Law Journal* 298.
[29] WHO, *Views of Older Persons on Elder Abuse* (WHO, 2002).
[30] M O'Keeffe, A Hills, M Doyle, C McCreadie, S Scholes, R Constantine, A Tinker, J Manthorpe, S Biggs, and B Erens, *UK Study of Abuse and Neglect of Older People Prevalence Survey Report* (Department of Health, 2007).

guidance stressed that a vulnerable adult might be abused by a wide range of people, and cited:

relatives, family members, professional staff, paid care workers, volunteers, other service users, neighbours, friends and associates, people who deliberately exploit vulnerable people and strangers.[31]

Also debated is whether self-abuse falls within the definition of elder abuse. It may be argued that self-abuse is indicative of a lack of appropriate care by the older person's carers,[32] but not inevitably. Certainly, self-neglect may require a different kind of intervention from other forms of elder abuse.[33]

Limiting abuse to physical abuse?

There is a real difficulty in seeking to define abuse in any context. A narrow definition, for example, focusing on physical harm may be regarded as inappropriately downplaying other forms of abuse, such as emotional abuse or neglect which can be regarded as serious as physical harm. But extending the term to cover all forms of unpleasant behaviour may stretch the definition to such an extent that it loses any real meaning.

Michelle Madden Dempsey's instructive article[34] on the meaning of domestic violence can be useful in this context. She separates out three elements of domestic violence: violence, domesticity,[35] and structural inequality.[36] She argues that:

Domestic violence has two senses. In its strong sense, domestic violence reflects the intersection of violence, domesticity, and structural inequality. In its weak sense, domestic violence reflects only the intersection of violence and domesticity.

As well as distinguishing domestic violence in its strong and weak sense, she goes on to argue in favour of recognizing domestic abuse: conduct which is not violent, but perpetuates inequality. Financial abuse could fall within this category. The benefit of this analysis is that it enables us to break down more clearly the forms of abusive behaviour into significant categories. It provides a means of separating out verbal abuse from physical abuse,[37] and abuse which is part of a structure of power and abuse which is not.

---

[31] Department of Health, *No Secrets* (Department of Health, 2000), at 6.
[32] J Longres, 'Self-Neglect among the Elderly' (1995) 7 *Journal of Elder Abuse and Neglect* 69.
[33] Neglect was excluded from the concept of abuse in M O'Keeffe *et al, UK Study of Abuse and Neglect of Older People Prevalence Survey Report* (Department of Health, 2007).
[34] M Madden Dempsey, 'What Counts as Domestic Violence? A Conceptual Analysis' (2006) 12 *William and Mary Journal of Women and the Law* 301.
[35] This includes the location of the violence (the home) and the relationship between the parties (an intimate or familial one).
[36] She defines these (at 314) as 'social structures that sustain or perpetuate the uneven distribution of social power'. See also, MP Johnson, 'Patriarchal Terrorism and Common Couple Violence: Two Forms of Violence Against Women' (1995) 57 *Journal of Marriage and Family* 283.
[37] C Weerd and G Paveza, 'Verbal Mistreatment in Older Adults: A Look at Persons with Alzheimer's Disease and Their Caregivers in the State of Florida' (2005) 15 *Journal of Elder Abuse and Neglect* 11.

Must the abuse be age-related?

The issue here is whether to amount to elder abuse the conduct needs to be in some way related to age.[38] For example, if an older person's car is stolen from a car park, should this amount to elder abuse? Using Madden Dempsey's discussion, I would distinguish elder abuse in the strong sense if it was violent and reflected structural inequality relating to age; while in a weaker sense it could involve any abuse of an older person in circumstances reflecting structural inequality. In the case of theft of the car, if this is theft by a stranger it would not be elder abuse in either sense.

Legitimacy

Michelle Madden Dempsey in her discussion of domestic violence is adamant that the definition of domestic violence must include a finding that the violence is illegitimate.[39] This, then, would reject a view that any violence is automatically abusive. An older person might, for example, be pulled back from a fire that was posing a danger to them. This 'violent' act, all things considered, would not be regarded as wrongful. It is argued that this is correct. To characterize as elder abuse behaviour which is legitimate would water down the censure which properly attaches to the label.

Questions of legitimating may raise issues of cultural relativism. As already mentioned, a lack of respect can be regarded as a form of abuse. Yet what will be disrespectful will vary from culture to culture[40] and, perhaps more significantly, generation to generation.[41]

Must the abuse be intentional?

Surveys of the general public have found motive[42] and intention[43] to be significant factors in deciding whether or not there was abuse. Where the definition is to be used to define criminal liability, it is likely to require proof of some kind of blameworthy state of mind. Those more concerned about whether an older person requires protective intervention will be much less concerned about the blameworthiness of the abuser than the harm the victim has suffered. It is

---

[38] See further, S Lister and D Wall, 'Deconstructing Distraction Burglary: An Ageist Offence?' in A Wahidin and M Cain (eds), *Ageing, Crime and Society* (Willan, 2006).

[39] M Madden Dempsey, 'What Counts as Domestic Violence? A Conceptual Analysis' (2006) 12 *William and Mary Journal of Women and the Law* 301.

[40] M Hudson, C Beasley, R Benedict, J Carlson, B Craig, and S Mason, 'Elder Abuse: Some African American Views' (1999) 14 *Journal of Interpersonal Violence* 915.

[41] See, eg E-L Marcus, C Fassberg, J Namestnik, D Guedj, and Y Caine, 'Strict Vegan, Low-Calorie Diet Administered by Care-Giving Daughter to Elderly Mother—is this Elder Abuse?' (2005) 24 *Medicine and Law* 279.

[42] R Gebotys, D O'Connor, and K Mair, 'Public Perceptions of Elder Physical Mistreatment' (1992) 4 *Journal of Elder Abuse and Neglect* 151.

[43] A Moon and O Williams, 'Perceptions of Elder Abuse and Help-Seeking Patterns among African-American, Caucasian American, and Korean-American Elderly Women' (1993) 33 *The Gerontologist* 386.

suggested that intention should not be required as part of a definition of abuse, but that intentional abuse may be a further requirement in determining what legal response is appropriate.

How serious must the abuse be?

A definition of abuse should seek to define how serious the harm or wrong must be before it amounts to elder abuse. Is there, in other words, a minimum level of harm to amount to abuse? If there is, how are we to assess the degree of harm? Is that to be measured on an objective or subjective basis? It seems sensible to keep the hurdle of the definition low and then decide how serious elder abuse must be before a particular legal response is justified.[44]

Societal elder abuse

Earlier it was argued that it is crucial to appreciate the way that societal attitudes perpetuate elder abuse and enable it to continue. But there is more to it than this: social and political forces can themselves be abusive.

It is interesting to observe that the government appears to be tackling elder abuse and the inadequacy of services for older people as two separate issues.[45] Some of the leading reports seeking to improve social care of older people generally contain no, or virtually no, reference to abuse issues: *Developing Effective Services for Older People*;[46] *Independence, Well-Being and Choice*;[47] and *Living Well in Later life*.[48] The government has addressed elder abuse in separate documents. This, it is submitted, is misguided for three reasons. First, the lack of provision of services can itself be seen as a form of abuse. In 2006, the Audit Commission, the Healthcare Commission, and the Commission for Social Care produced a report[49] which highlighted the lack of dignity and respect accorded to older people while in hospital. Standards of care were said to be 'unacceptably poor'. This is but one in a long list of reports highlighting the way in which services to older people are inadequate.[50] Secondly, the lack of services can enable abuse to occur or at least not be detected. Thirdly, the attitudes which permit elder abuse are the same attitudes which are behind the lack of provision. These documents promote the importance of autonomy of older people, which is undoubtedly important, but dignity and security need to go hand in hand

---

    [44] See further, the discussion at p 190.
    [45] J Robinson and P Banks, *The Business of Caring* (Kings Fund, 2005).
    [46] National Audit Office, *Developing Effective Services for Older People* (National Audit Office, 2003).
    [47] Department of Health, *Independence, Well-Being and Choice* (Department of Health, 2005).
    [48] Healthcare Commission, *Living Well in Later Life* (Healthcare Commission, 2006).
    [49] Ibid.
    [50] D Wanlass, *Securing Good Care for Older People* (Kings Fund, 2006).

with autonomy. Without protection from abuse, offering older people a broader range of services and opportunities to participate in public life are unlikely to be effective.

A consideration of some popular definitions

The difficulty in defining elder abuse can be seen in the definition of it proposed by one of the leading pressure groups working in this area—Action Against Elder Abuse:[51] 'a single or repeated act or lack of appropriate action occurring within any relationship where there is an expectation of trust, which causes harm or distress to an older person.'

While this would capture anything we are likely to want to label elder abuse, it is far too wide. It could cover, for example, a gay man coming out to his parents. Or perhaps even an adult child failing to send a Mother's Day card. Both of these could be said to cause distress. As these examples indicate, the definition of what is a required level of injury to amount to elder abuse ('harm or distress') is set low.[52] Contrast the American National Center for Elder Abuse, an American organization, whose definition requires 'suffering'.[53] Also, it is notable that the Action Against Elder Abuse definition contains no requirement that the act or omission be intended to harm or cause distress to the older person. Indeed, it is not even necessary to show that it was caused negligently.

As an alternative, consider the definition from the American National Council on Child Abuse and Family Violence:[54] 'any unnecessary suffering, whether self-inflicted or other inflicted, which negatively affects the quality of life of the older person.'

What is interesting about the definition is that it includes within the definition of Abuse self-inflicted injuries (which are not included in the previously considered definition). Again, it sets a low hurdle of what is abuse by referring only to it 'negatively affecting the quality of life'. The use of the word 'unnecessary' is important because it recognizes that sometimes the causing of suffering may be necessary. A son informing his parents that his marriage has come to an end may cause suffering, but this is necessary.

The National Center on Elder Abuse uses the following definition:

Elder abuse is a term referring to any knowing, intentional, or negligent act by a caregiver or any other person that causes harm or a serious risk of harm to a vulnerable adult.[55]

---

[51] The definition was adopted in World Health Organization, *The Toronto Declaration on the Prevention of Elder Abuse* (WHO, 2002).

[52] There is an absence of a requirement that the behaviour be illegitimate or unjustified.

[53] National Center on Elder Abuse, *Frequently Asked Questions* (NCEA, 2005).

[54] American National Council on Child Abuse and Family Violence, *Elder Abuse Information* (American National Council on Child Abuse and Family Violence, 2006), at 1.

[55] National Center on Elder Abuse, *Frequently Asked Questions* (NCEA, 2005).

This definition excludes self-inflicted harm, but includes a requirement of at least negligence.

Although there is no 'right answer' to the definition of elder abuse, it is submitted that human rights provide a framework around which a definition could be structured. In *No Secrets*,[56] the following definition is used:

Abuse is a violation of an individual's human and civil rights by any other person or persons. Abuse may consist of a single or repeated acts. It may be physical, verbal, or psychological, it may be an act of neglect or an omission to act, or it may occur when a vulnerable person is persuaded to enter into a financial or sexual transaction to which he or she has not consented, or cannot consent. Abuse can occur in any relationship and may result in significant harm to, or exploitation of, the person subjected to it.

One benefit of this definition is that it gives it a degree of clarity, because by referring to human rights, it ties into the vast quantity of analysis on the nature of human rights. Even if that does not necessarily produce certainty, at least it means that we are clear about what the issues are. For lawyers, it also provides a form of language which is readily transmittable into legal argument.

In *Safeguarding Adults*, in 2005,[57] the government sought to shift the focus of the approach away from the language of vulnerability. The focus instead was on risks to independence. This sees independence as the norm and thereby promotes a more positive view, it is claimed, of old age. The report sees safeguarding adults as:

all work which enables an adult 'who is or may be eligible for community care services' to retain independence, wellbeing and choice and to access their human right to live a life that is free from abuse and neglect.[58]

The report explains that vulnerability:

can be misunderstood, because it seems to locate the cause of abuse with the victim, rather than in placing responsibility with the actions or omissions of others.[59]

While there are welcome aspects of this approach, there are major grounds for concern: first is the focus on independence as a goal. I shall return to this later, but I do not think that is a desirable or realistic goal for anyone, let alone older people. Secondly, the grouping together of elder abuse and anything that restricts independence is in danger of downplaying the wrongfulness of abuse. Indeed, there is a danger that the concept becomes so watered down as to become meaningless. What is welcome about the *Safeguarding Adults* approach is the awareness that what makes elder abuse particularly serious is the wider social context of the abuse.

---

[56] Department of Health, *No Secrets* (Department of Health, 2000).
[57] Association of Directors of Social Services, *Safeguarding Adults* (Association of Directors of Social Services, 2005).
[58] Ibid.   [59] Ibid.

The forms of elder abuse

As has been indicated by the disputes over definition, the forms of elder abuse are highly varied. One commentator has suggested that there are 43 different forms of abuse.[60] The Department of Health's document *No Secrets* lists the following six forms of abuse:

- physical abuse, including hitting, slapping, pushing, kicking, misuse of medication, restraint, or inappropriate sanctions;
- sexual abuse, including rape and sexual assault or sexual acts to which the vulnerable adult has not consented, could not consent to or was pressured into consenting;
- psychological abuse, including emotional abuse, threats of harm or abandonment, deprivation of contact, humiliation, blaming, controlling, intimidation, coercion, harassment, verbal abuse, isolation, or withdrawal from services or supportive networks;
- financial or material abuse, including theft, fraud, exploitation, pressure in connection with wills, property or inheritance or financial transactions, or the misuse or misappropriation of property, possessions or benefits;
- neglect and acts of omission, including ignoring medical or physical care needs, failure to provide access to appropriate health, social care or educational services, the withholding of the necessities of life, such as medication, adequate nutrition and heating; and
- discriminatory abuse, including racist, sexist, that based on a person's disability, and other forms of harassment, slurs, or similar treatment.

For others, a more useful way of analysing the abuse is not by its form, but by where it takes place. Such an approach may distinguish between:

- domestic elder abuse which takes place in the house where the older person is living or staying; commonly this abuse is carried out by the relatives or friends of the older person;
- institutional abuse, which takes place in the context of institutional care which the older person is receiving; and
- self-neglect or self-abuse, where the older person is harming or failing to look after themselves.[61]

---

[60] P Hall, 'Elder Maltreatment Items: Subgroups and Types: Policy and Practice Implications' in J Hendricks (ed), *The Ties of Later Life* (Baywood, 1995), at 97.
[61] National Clearing House on Family Violence, *Abuse and Neglect of Older Adults* (NCHFV, 1998), at para 2.1.

The advantage of such an approach is that it highlights the fact that different ways of tackling elder abuse may be appropriate in different settings. For example, formal regulatory inspections may be appropriate in an institutional setting, but not in a domestic one. Before considering that issue further, a little more needs to be said about some of the kinds of abuse.

Financial abuse

The definition of financial abuse is problematic. It can range from deliberately taking an older person's property to improperly pressurising them into making a will.

The Public Guardianship Office describes it thus:

The term 'financial abuse' describes the situation where an abuser misappropriates a vulnerable person's money and/or other assets through various means (eg theft or fraud); misuses or wrongfully spends a vulnerable person's assets while having legitimate access to these; or fails to use a vulnerable person's assets to meet that person's needs.[62]

There is a real difficulty here.[63] There is a widespread concern that older people can be taken advantage of by unscrupulous people and be persuaded to give over their money.[64] The issue comes to a head in cases where an older person has given a gift to someone or changed a will in someone's favour while there is doubt over the older person's ability to understand what they have done.[65] Such a case can create a clash between the principles of property law and those of criminal law. A criminal lawyer may focus on the dishonesty of the person receiving the money. For property lawyers, it is important that ownership of property passes with possession, so that where a transfer has been made only in the most unusual of circumstances should the ownership not pass. An example will explain why. If a rather confused person buys 10 Kit-Kats from a corner shop, we may take the view that if they were rather befuddled and had not full understood what they were doing then the transfer would be invalid. But saying that would cause a host of problems for property lawyers. It means the money handed to the shop keeper remains the property of the befuddled person and that in turn means that the shopkeeper does not have ownership. Problems will arise if the shopkeeper gives the money as change to the next customer and on the problems could go. It is not surprising then that a property lawyer would rather say that although a bit confused, the person knew they were buying something and so the confusion is insufficient to upset the transaction.

---

[62] Public Guardianship Office, *Are you Aware of Financial Abuse?* (PGO, 2008).
[63] C Dessin, 'Financial Abuse of the Elderly: Is the Solution a Problem?' (2003) 34 *McGeorge Law Review* 267.
[64] Ibid.
[65] J Langan, 'In the Best Interests of Elderly People? The Role of Local Authorities in Handling and Safeguarding the Personal Finance of Elderly People with Dementia' (1997) 19 *Journal of Social Welfare and Family Law* 463.

The case of *R v Hinks*[66] highlights the issues well. A 38-year-old woman (Karen Hinks) befriended a 53-year-old man (John Dolphin), who was described as of limited intelligence. In the period of eight months, £60,000 was given to Ms Hinks. Her conviction for theft was upheld. Although it appeared that no threats or deceptions had been used (which would have made the case an easy one), it was felt that she had behaved dishonestly in receiving the money. What is notable about the case is the House of Lords' willingness to find that there was theft, even though there was no civil wrong (in other words the gifts may have been valid under the law of property). Lord Steyn noted the possible differences between civil and criminal law as mentioned above. He saw this justifying a finding that a criminal offence had taken place, even though there may have been an effective transfer of ownership.[67]

A rather different concern arises with cases where an older person has lost capacity. In such a case someone may well need to make financial decisions on their behalf, including spending money on their needs.[68] There are concerns that in the past powers of attorney have been misused to appropriate incapacitated people's property.[69] The Mental Capacity Act 2005 has amended the law to provide closer regulation of guardianship and powers of attorney. Those provisions are discussed in greater detail in chapter 3.

Sexual abuse

The sexual abuse of older people is a disturbing issue. Sexual abuse in this context can be defined as non-consensual sexual contact with an older person.[70] This might include a violent sexual attack or the manipulation of a demented person into 'agreeing' to have sexual relations.[71] Little dispute surrounds the violent sexual assault, but less clear are cases where the individual suffers from some level of cognitive impairment. Consider, for example, a patient suffering from Alzheimer's who has virtually no short-term memory, but whose husband, her primary carer, continues to have sexual relations with her.[72] There will be some for whom the issue is straightforward: sexual touching for which there is no active consent is impermissible. If the wife in this scenario is unable to give her consent

---

[66] [2000] UKHL 53.

[67] The case has generated much debate among criminal lawyers. This is summarized in J Herring, *Criminal Law: Text, Cases and Materials* (Oxford University Press, 2008), at ch 8.

[68] Ibid.

[69] Joint Committee on the Draft Mental Incapacity Bill, *Draft Mental Incapacity Bill*, HC1083–1 (*Hansard*, 2003).

[70] J Hagerty Lingler, 'Ethical Issues in Distinguishing Sexual Activity from Sexual Maltreatment among Women with Dementia' (2003) 15 *Journal of Elder Abuse and Neglect* 85.

[71] The Sexual Offences Act 2003 creates a variety of sexual offences which could be applicable, including rape, sexual assault, and a series of offences protecting those suffering from a mental disorder. These are discussed in J Herring, *Criminal Law: Text, Cases and Materials* (Oxford University Press, 2008), at ch 8.

[72] Ibid discusses such a case.

due to her mental state, her husband may not engage in sexual contact with her. To others this is too strict an approach. Jennifer Hegerty Lingler[73] has argued that in a case like this the issue must be looked at in the context of the relationship between the parties. She argues that where there is no resistance and in the past there was no reluctance to engage in sexual relations, it may be permissible in the context of the relationship between the parties. Not to permit sexual relations causes her concern: 'The oppressive triad of ageism, sexism, and hyper-cognitivism puts women with dementia at risk of an inappropriate blanket condemnation of non-consensual sexual activity.'[74]

In *Re MM (an adult)*,[75] Munby J held that the question of capacity to consent to sex depended on the woman 'having sufficient knowledge and understanding... of the sexual nature and character—of the act of sexual intercourse, and of the reasonably foreseeable consequences of sexual intercourse'. She must also have 'the capacity to choose whether or not to engage in it'. This test he deliberately set fairly low to ensure that those suffering limited mental impairment were not prevented from enjoying sexual relations. In the case at hand he held, remarkably, that although the young woman lacked the capacity to decide where to live or with whom to have contact, she did have the capacity to consent to sexual relations.[76]

As Munby J indicated, the balance to be struck is between protecting a person from abuse and protecting their right to enjoy consensual sexual relations. To properly consider the issue would involve a detailed examination of the philosophical and legal literature on sexual contact and rape. That would take us well outside the scope of the book.[77]

The misuse of medication

The temptation to prescribe 'calming' medication in the care environment is understandable. Medication is used to sedate patients and make their management easier and lighten the burden of caring. Indeed, it is easy to imagine that if a patient is shouting out angrily and in frustration, a healthcare professional might quickly decide that it is in their 'best interests' that they be given some sedation. However, over-medication can be regarded as a form of abuse. The House of Commons Health Committee has expressed concern that in care homes medication levels and use are often overseen by unqualified staff.

There is a particular concern about the use of anti-psychotic medicine in controlling those with dementia. Between 1999 and 2002, there was a 6.2 per cent

---

[73] Ibid.
[74] However, there is no risk in this case that the woman will be subject to criminal proceedings.
[75] [2007] EWHC 2003 (Fam), para 87.
[76] See further, T Elliott, 'Capacity, Sex and the Mentally Disordered' (2008) 2 *Archbold News* 6.
[77] For my starting point, see M Madden Dempsey and J Herring, 'Why Sexual Penetration Requires Justification' (2007) 27 *Oxford Journal of Legal Studies* 467.

increase in the community prescription of anti-psychotic drugs.[78] One study of 22 South London nursing homes found that 24.5 per cent of the residents were being prescribed anti-psychotic drugs. In 82 per cent of those cases, the prescription was inappropriate.[79] A report produced by the Liberal Democrats claimed that up to 22,233 older people are kept in a state of sedation without medical justification.[80] The Commission for Social Care Inspection reported that 12 per cent of providers failed to meet the National Minimum Standards on medication.[81] The government has responded to such concerns with a report detailing the proper use of medication: *Handled with Care?*[82]

Elder abuse and gender

Elder abuse reflects and is reinforced by both ageist and sexist attitudes. Incidents of elder abuse must, therefore, be seen in the context of gender. There is a fundamental difference between a violent incident involving an older woman and a man.[83] Of course, men can be the victims of elder abuse,[84] but the social meaning and impact of abuse can only be properly appreciated once the gendered aspect of it is taken into account. We will return to this issue when we look at the causes of elder abuse.

Statistics

Given the uncertainty over the definition of what actually counts as elder abuse, it should come as no surprise that it is not possible to provide a definitive head-line-grabbing figure setting out the number of elderly people being abused.[85] Of course, the difficulty in compiling statistics in this area is not just a definitional one, but also the point that elder abuse takes place in environments (for example, individuals' houses or care homes) which are not readily amenable to external recording. Further, individuals may not recognize themselves as victims[86] or fear

[78] P Burstow, *Keep Taking the Medicine* (Liberal Democrats, 2003), at 3.
[79] C Oborne, R Hooper *et al*, 'An Indicator of Appropriate Neuroleptic Prescribing in Nursing Homes' (2002) 31 *Age and Ageing* 435.
[80] P Burstow, *Keep Taking the Medicine* (Liberal Democrats, 2003).
[81] NCSC evidence to House of Commons Health Committee, *Elder Abuse* (The Stationery Office, 2004).
[82] Commission for Social Care Inspection, *Handled with Care?* (CSCI, 2006).
[83] J Hightower, *Violence and Abuse in the Lives of Older Women* (INSTRAW, 2002).
[84] J Pritchard, *Male Victims of Elder Abuse: Their Experiences and Needs* (Jessica Kingsley, 2001).
[85] J Manthorpe, B Penhale, L Pinkney, N Perkins, and P Kingston, *A Systematic Literature Review in Response to Key Themes Identified in the Report of the House of Commons Select Committee on Elder Abuse* (Department of Health, 2004).
[86] O Matsuda, 'An Assessment of the Attitudes of Potential Caregivers Toward the Abuse of Elderly Persons With and Without Dementia' (2007) 19 *International Psychogeriatrics* 892.

retaliation; or love the person abusing them.[87] In some cases, there may be difficulties in determining who is the abuser and who is the victim of abuse. Even
in the United States, where millions of dollars have been spent seeking to discover the realities of elder abuse, one researcher concluded, having examined the
collected research, 'we know virtually nothing about elder abuse for certain'.[88]

In the UK, we now have the benefit of a major recent study of elder abuse carried
out for Comic Relief and the Department of Health.[89] It found that 2.6 per cent
of people aged 66 or over who were living in their own private household reported
mistreatment involving a family member, close friend, or care worker in the past
year. If the sample is an accurate reflection of the wider older population, it would
mean 227,000 people aged over 66 are suffering mistreatment in a given year.
The figures rise to 4 per cent or 342,400 people if we include incidents involving
neighbours or acquaintances.[90] Three-quarters of those interviewed said that the
effect of mistreatment was either serious or very serious. The researchers believed
these figures to be on the conservative side, as they did not include care home
residents in their survey and some of those most vulnerable to abuse lacked the
capacity to take part. Also, even among those interviewed there may have been
those who, for a variety of reasons, did not wish to disclose abuse.[91]

Another recent study looked at the general public's perception and understanding of elder abuse.[92] In a survey of 1,000 people, it was found that younger
people believed there was more neglect and mistreatment of older people than
older people did. Women were more likely to perceive it than men. One-quarter
of those questioned said they knew an older person who had experienced neglect
or mistreatment. The most frequent reports were of abuse in care homes (53 per
cent of those who knew of abuse or neglect) or hospitals (48 per cent) and 29
per cent in their own home. It was neglect which was the most common form
of abuse.

A recent literature review looking at evidence of elder abuse around the world
concluded that six per cent of older people had suffered significant abuse in the
last month; 5.6 per cent of older couples had experienced physical violence in

---

[87] C McCreadie, *Elder Abuse: Update on Research* (Age Concern, 1996).

[88] G Anetzbeiger, 'Moving Forward on Elder Abuse and Guardianship: Will it Take a Thesis
or a Scream?' (2005) 45 *The Gerontologst* 279; and E Wood, *The Availability and Utility of
Interdisciplinary Data on Elder Abuse* (National Center on Elder Abuse, 2005).

[89] M O'Keeffe, A Hills, M Doyle, C McCreadie, S Scholes, R Constantine, A Tinker,
J Manthorpe, S Biggs, and B Erens, *UK Study of Abuse and Neglect of Older People Prevalence
Survey Report* (Department of Health, 2008). See also, A Mowlam, R Tennant, J Dixon, and C
McCreadie, *UK Study of Abuse and Neglect of Older People: Qualitative Findings* (Department of
Health, 2008); and C Cooper, A Selwood, and G Livingston, 'The Prevalence of Elder Abuse and
Neglect: A Systematic Review' (2008) 37 *Age and Ageing* 151.

[90] M O'Keeffe *et al*, *UK Study of Abuse and Neglect of Older People Prevalence Survey Report*
(Department of Health, 2008), at 4.

[91] Ibid, para 7.4.

[92] S Hussein, J Manthorpe, and B Penhale, *Public Perceptions of the Neglect and Mistreatment of
Older People: Findings of a United Kingdom Survey* (Kings College, 2005).

their relationships; and 25 per cent of older people had suffered significant psychological abuse.[93]

Finding evidence on the levels of abuse in a residential setting is even harder. Professionals assert that, for example, 'the institutional abuse of older people is common'.[94] Although there is widespread anecdotal evidence to support this, there is little hard empirical evidence.[95] Care homes are more heavily regulated than domestic care and that may be thought to reduce the likelihood of abuse.

A rather dissident duo of voices is Joan Harbison and Marina Morrow, who emphasize that elder abuse is not a concern raised by older people themselves.[96] This, they suggest, indicates that either the problem is less serious than is generally imagined or older people feel they have sufficient resources to deal with it. Older people tend to be more vocal about issues such as poverty or transport than abuse. On the other hand, it may be that victims of abuse are less able to speak out than other older people.

Who is abusing?

Help the Aged, relying on data from those who telephone a helpline, claim that 46 per cent of those who abuse are related to the person they are abusing and that around 25 per cent of abusers are children of the victim.[97] However, care must be taken with such evidence. Those who phone a helpline are unlikely to be those in residential homes and are unlikely to be the most frail or vulnerable victims of abuse. Further, as we know from research on domestic violence, many victims of abuse do not recognize themselves as such and hence are unlikely to contact a helpline.

More reliable is the Comic Relief study.[98] This found that 51 per cent of mistreatment in the past year involved a partner/spouse, 49 per cent another family member, 13 per cent a care worker, and five per cent a close friend. Respondents were allowed to mention more than one person. There is a strong correlation between gender and interpersonal abuse (physical, psychological, or sexual abuse). Eighty per cent of interpersonal abuse was carried out by men and only 20 per cent by women. Noticeably, in relation to financial abuse there was less of a gendered split, with 56 per cent of perpetrators being men. Another distinctive

---

[93] C Cooper, A Selwood, and G Livingston, 'Prevalence of Elder Abuse and Neglect: A Systematic Review' (2008) 37 *Age and Ageing* 151.

[94] J Garner and S Evans, 'An Ethical Perspective on Institutional Abuse of Older Adults' (2002) 26 *Psychiatric Bulletin* 166.

[95] S Hussein, J Manthorpe, and B Penhale, *Public Perceptions of the Neglect and Mistreatment of Older People: Findings of a United Kingdom Survey* (Kings College, 2005).

[96] J Harbinson and M Morrow, 'Re-examining the Social Construction of Elder Abuse and Neglect' (1998) 18 *Ageing and Society* 691.

[97] Help the Aged, *Facts About Elder Abuse* (Help the Aged, 2006).

[98] M O'Keeffe *et al*, *UK Study of Abuse and Neglect of Older People Prevalence Survey Report* (Department of Health, 2008).

feature of financial abuse was that only 25 per cent of perpetrators lived with the victim, while in the case of interpersonal abuse it was 65 per cent.

Who is abused?

The typical victim is a woman living alone aged over 70.[99] The Comic Relief survey found that 3.8 per cent of female respondents had suffered maltreatment, as compared with 1.1 per cent of men. So, the rate of maltreatment for older women is over three times that for men. Those suffering from bad health, depression, or loneliness suffered abuse at an increased rate. A notable aspect of the Comic Relief study was the prevalence of abuse among women who were recently divorced or separated: 7.8 per cent reported interpersonal abuse and 15.4 per cent mistreatment. This supports the claim that a significant portion of elder abuse is a form of domestic violence, as it is well known that levels of domestic violence increase when a relationship ends.[100]

There has been much dispute over whether women are more or less likely to be the victims of elder abuse than men.[101] Some argue that, contrary to the popular assumption, men are more likely than women to be subject to mistreatment.[102] However, most studies indicate that gender plays a significant role: females are more often abused than males and a majority of abusers are male.[103] The major study by Comic Relief, referred to in the previous paragraph, would support that.

What kinds of abuse take place?

The Comic Relief study found that when focusing on mistreatment by family members, close friends, or care workers; 1.1 per cent of older people had suffered neglect; 0.7 per cent financial mistreatment; 0.4 per cent psychological mistreatment; 0.4 per cent physical mistreatment;[104] and 0.2 per cent sexual mistreatment. This demonstrates that non-violent forms of abuse are more commonly reported to researchers than violent forms.

The causes of elder abuse

Given the wide range of elder abuse, it is not surprising that there is a general consensus that there is no single cause of elder abuse. The debate surrounding

---

[99] G Fitzgerald, 'The Realities of Elder Abuse' in A Wahidin and M Cain (eds), *Ageing, Crime and Society* (Willan, 2006).

[100] J Herring, *Family Law* (Pearson, 2007), at ch 6.   [101] Ibid.

[102] E Pittaway, A Westhues, and T Peressi, 'Risk Factors for Abuse and Neglect Among Older Persons' (1995) 14 *Canadian Journal on Aging* 20.

[103] S Crichton, J Bond, C Harvey, and J Ristock, 'Elder Abuse: Feminist and Ageist Perspectives' (1999) 10 *Journal of Elder Abuse & Neglect* 115.

[104] 0.8% had suffered physical mistreatment at some point since the age of 65.

the causes of elder abuse shares similarities with that surrounding the causes of domestic violence. In that context, Joanna Miles[105] has usefully separated out 'micro causes' and 'macro causes'. 'Micro causes' refers to issues related to the individual perpetrator and victim. They may include, for example, claims that abuse is caused by character flaws of the perpetrator. 'Macro causes' are those that rely on wider social forces, for example, the position of women in society. She argues that a proper understanding of domestic violence requires an appreciation of both of these factors. It is suggested that a similar comment is true in the context of elder abuse.

Micro causes

For some, the causes of elder abuse are found in the characteristics of the victim,[106] while others have sought to identify characteristics of the abuser[107] and yet others focus on aspects of the relationship between the abuser and victim.[108] The Public Health Agency of Canada, adopting a mixture of these views, sees the causes of elder abuse as the following:[109]

(1) Victims of psychological and physical abuse usually have reasonably good physical health, but suffer from psychological problems. Their abusers have a history of psychiatric illness and/or substance abuse, live with the victim, and depend on them for financial resources ...

(2) Patients with dementia, who exhibit disruptive behaviour and who live with family caregivers, are more likely to be victims of physical abuse. Their abusive caregivers may suffer from low self-esteem and clinical depression ...

(3) There may not be a 'typical' victim of financial abuse; however, when the abused person is dependent on the abuser, the financial abuse may be more serious ...

(4) Victims of neglect tend to be very old, with cognitive and physical incapacities. Their dependency on their caregivers serves as a source of stress.

The British Geriatric Society in its evidence to the House of Commons Select Committee identified the following risk factors for elder abuse in a domestic setting:

• social isolation—those who are abused usually have fewer social contacts than those who are not abused;

---

[105] J Miles, 'Domestic Violence' in J Herring (ed), *Family Law: Issues, Debates, Policy* (Willan, 2001).

[106] R Wolf, 'Major Findings from Three Model Projects on Elder Abuse' in K Pillemer and R Wolf (eds), *Elder Abuse: Conflict in the Family* (Auburn House, 1986).

[107] E Hocking, 'Caring for Carers: Understanding the Process that Leads to Abuse' in M Eastman (ed), *Old Age Abuse: A New Perspective* (2nd edn, Chapman and Hall, 1994); and K O'Leary, 'Through a Psychological Lens: Personality Traits, Personality Disorders, and Levels of Violence' in R Gelles and D Loseke (eds), *Current Controversies on Family Violence* (Sage, 1993).

[108] A Homer and C Gilleard, 'Abuse of Elderly People by their Carers' (1990) 301 *British Medical Journal* 1359.

[109] Public Health Agency of Canada, *Abuse and Neglect of Older People: A Discussion Paper* (Public Health Agency of Canada, 2005), at 5.

- a history of a poor quality long-term relationship between the abused and the abuser;
- a pattern of family violence (the abuser may have been abused as a child);
- dependence of the person who abuses on the person they abuse (for example, for accommodation, financial, and emotional support); and
- a history of mental health problems or a personality disorder, or drug or alcohol problem in the person who abuses.[110]

As these indicate, supporters of the micro causes explanation focus on matters personal to the individuals or their relationship. Hence, there is emphasis on the personality of the abuser;[111] 'situational stresses' facing the care-giver;[112] childhood abuse of the abuser;[113] or the lack of social support provided to carers. These problems can be exacerbated if the care-giver turns to alcohol[114] or other drugs.[115] Some studies suggest that abuse is caused when the abuser feels they lack power.[116] There is some evidence to suggest that perpetrators are often heavily dependent on the person they are mistreating.[117]

Of the different micro causes that have been mentioned, it is the 'care-giver stress' for elder abuse which has been the most influential and so it will be considered further.

'Care-giver Stress'

In the public imagination, elder abuse is popularly regarded as caused by carer stress.[118] A loving carer lashes out in desperation, driven to the point of despair in physical and emotional exhaustion. This claim has been described by academic specialists in the field as a 'persistent characterization'[119] and 'widely accepted'.[120] Professors Gainey and Payne state that care-giver burden is the most

---

[110] Ibid, para 37.

[111] K Pillemer and D Finkelhor, 'Causes of Elder Abuse: Caregiver Stress versus Problem Relatives' (1989) 59 *American Journal of Orthopsychiatry* 179.

[112] M Lee and S Kolomer, 'Design of an Assessment of Caregivers' Impulsive Feelings to Commit Elder Abuse' (2007) 17 *Research on Social Work Practice* 729.

[113] E Rathbone-McCuan, 'Elderly Victims of Family Violence and Neglect' (1980) 61 *Social Casework* 296.

[114] There are consistent findings of links between alcohol and elder abuse: A Reay and K Browne, 'Risk Factor Characteristics in Carers Who Physically Abuse or Neglect Their Elderly Dependants' (2001) 5 *Aging and Mental Health* 56.

[115] G Anetzberger, J Korbin, and C Austin, 'Alcoholism and Elder Abuse' (1994) 9 *Journal of Interpersonal Violence* 184.

[116] K Pillemer and J Suitor, 'Violence and Violent Feelings: What Causes Them Among Family Caregivers?' (1992) 47 *Journal of Gerontology* 165.

[117] K Pillemer, 'Elder Abuse is Caused by the Deviance and Dependence of Abusive Caregivers' in D Loseke, R Gelles, and M Cavanaugh (eds), *Current Controversies on Family Violence* (Sage, 2004); and J Greenberg, M McKibben, and J Raymond, 'Dependent Adult Children and Elder Abuse' (1990) 2 *Journal of Elder Abuse & Neglect* 73.

[118] J Pritchard, *Working with Adult Abuse: A Training Manual* (Jessica Kingsley, 2007), at 310.

[119] National Center on Elder Abuse, *Preventing Elder Abuse by Family Caregivers* (NCEA, 2002).

[120] K Pillemer and D Finkelhor, 'Causes of Elder Abuse: Caregiver Stress versus Problem Relatives' (2006) 19 *Journal of Health and Human Services Administration* 245.

cited explanation for elder abuse.[121] Three leading English academics in one of the leading works on elder abuse describe that as a 'widespread view'.[122]

A good example of the carer stress explanation is the following statement from the National Center on Elder Abuse:

Although it is known that in 90% of all reported elder abuse cases, the abuser is a family member, it is not known how many of these abusive family members are also caregivers. Researchers have estimated that anywhere from five to twenty-three percent of all care-givers are physically abusive. Most agree that abuse is related to the stresses associated with providing care.[123]

Much work has been done in seeking to expound these claims and explain the theory in more detail.[124] It has been said that care-giver stress causes depression and mood disturbances which lead to abuse in uncharacteristic outbursts of anger.[125] Emphasis is placed on empirical evidence that carers who have to live with the dependant are particularly likely to be abusive.[126] Indeed, some research suggests that the greater the number of hours per day the carers must care, the greater the risk of abuse.[127] Further, it has been claimed that the lower the functioning of the 'victim', the higher the likelihood of abuse.[128] Carers of those suffering from dementia are particularly prone to commit abuse.[129] 'Victims' who are violent towards care-givers are more likely to suffer abuse at the hands of a care-giver.[130] Evidence has been produced which, it is said, shows that when the 'victim' engages in certain forms of behaviour, these cause the carer stress, which can lead the carer to abuse. Such behaviour includes verbal aggression, refusal to eat or take medications, calling the police, invading the care-giver's privacy, noisiness, 'vulgar habits', disruptive behaviour, embarrassing public displays, and physical aggression.[131]

---

[121] R Gainey and B Payne, 'Caregiver Burden, Elder Abuse and Alzheimer's Disease: Testing the Relationship' (2006) 2 *Journal of Health and Human Services* 245. See also, G Bennet, P Kingston, and B Penhale, *The Dimensions of Elder Abuse* (Macmillan, 1997), at 54.

[122] G Bennet, P Kingston, and B Penhale, *The Dimensions of Elder Abuse* (Macmillan, 1997), at 54.

[123] National Center on Elder Abuse, *A Fact Sheet on Carer Stress and Elder Abuse* (NCEA, 2002).

[124] L Nerenberg, *Caregiver Stress and Elder Abuse* (NCEA, 2002).

[125] J Garcia and J Kosberg, 'Understanding Anger: Implications for Formal and Informal Caregivers' (1992) 4 *Journal of Elder Abuse & Neglect* 87; and M Bendik, 'Reaching the Breaking Point: Dangers of Mistreatment in Elder Caregiving Situations' (1992) 4 *Journal of Elder Abuse & Neglect* 39.

[126] L Nerenberg, *Caregiver Stress and Elder Abuse* (NCEA, 2002).

[127] M Bendik, 'Reaching the Breaking Point: Dangers of Mistreatment in Elder Caregiving Situations' (1992) 4 *Journal of Elder Abuse & Neglect* 39.

[128] A Coyne, W Reichman, and L Berbig, 'The Relationship Between Dementia and Elder Abuse' (1993) 150 *American Journal of Psychiatry* 643.

[129] K Pillemer and J Suitor, 'Violence and Violent Feelings: What Causes Them Among Family Caregivers?' (1992) 47 *Journal of Gerontology* 165–172; C Dyer, M Connoly, and P McFeeley, 'The Clinical and Medical Forensics of Elder Abuse and Neglect' in R Bonnie and R Wallace (eds), *Elder Abuse: Abuse, Neglect, and Exploitation in an Aging America* (National Academy Press, 2002).

[130] A Coyne, W Reichman, and L Berbig, 'The Relationship Between Dementia and Elder Abuse' (1993) 150 *American Journal of Psychiatry* 643.

[131] K Pillemer and J Suitor, 'Violence and Violent Feelings: What Causes Them Among Family Caregivers?' (1992) *Journal of Gerontology* 165–72.

Others refer to the 'difficult personality' of the dependant causing carer stress and hence abuse.[132] As can be seen, there are real dangers of the arguments leading to the abused person being said to be the real cause of the abuse.

Despite its hold on the public imagination, most recent studies downplay the relevance of carer stress as a cause of elder abuse. There is now a substantial body of research suggesting that care-giver stress plays a very minor role in causing elder abuse.[133] The House of Commons Health Select Committee when looking at the issue of elder abuse received evidence from several bodies working in the field who all agreed that carer stress was rarely a factor in elder abuse.[134] Help the Aged in its evidence stated that 'few incidents of abuse are committed by loving, supportive people who have lashed out as a consequence of the burden of their caring responsibilities'.[135] This is certainly not to say that the evidence suggests that carers do not suffer stress—quite the opposite. It is clear that caring is extraordinarily hard work,[136] but there is no evidence that the stresses of caring are linked to abuse in any significant way.

The problem with seeing elder abuse as being caused by care-givers' stress is that it creates an image of a victim who is vulnerable and problematic.[137] We cannot expect them to help themselves, indeed it is their behaviour and condition which has created the stressful situation. The best response to elder abuse is, therefore, seen to be to offer support and assistance to the carer and medical support to the dependant, rather than offering protection or services to the person being abused.[138] Indeed, as Simon Biggs points out, the carer-stress model neatly fits into the logic of community care, with the support of carers in the home with a care package being the solution to the problems of the older person. The carer-stress model also clearly indicates that criminal punishments are not appropriate because the abuser is not to blame and is responding in an understandable way to an extremely difficult situation.[139]

One of the consequences of the carer-stress explanation is that it hides all the wider social factors which contribute to the practice, perpetuation, and lack of

[132] L Phillips, 'Theoretical Explanations of Elder Abuse: Competing Hypotheses and Unresolved Issues' in K Pillemer and R Wolf (eds), *Elder Abuse: Conflict in The Family* (Auburn House, 1986).

[133] K Pillemer, 'The Abused Offspring are Dependent: Abuse is Caused by the Deviance and Dependence of Abusive Caregivers' in R Gelles and D Loseke (eds), *Current Controversies on Family Violence* (Sage, 1993); B Brandl and L Cook-Daniels, 'Domestic Abuse in Later Life' (2002) 8 *The Elder Law Journal* 302; and L Bergeron, 'An Elder Abuse Case Study: Caregiver Stress or Domestic Violence? You Decide' (2001) 34 *Journal of Gerontological Social Work* 47.

[134] House of Commons Health Committee, *Elder Abuse* (The Stationery Office, 2004), at para 36.
[135] Ibid.

[136] R Gainey and B Payne, 'Caregiver Burden, Elder Abuse and Alzheimer's Disease: Testing the Relationship' (2006) 29 *Journal of Health and Human Services* 245.

[137] L McDonald and A Collins, *Abuse and Neglect of Older Adults* (NCFV, 2002).

[138] R Bergeron, 'An Elder Abuse Case Study: Caregiver Stress or Domestic Violence? You Decide' (2001) 34 *Journal of Gerontological Social Work* 47.

[139] R Pain, *Theorising Age in Criminology: The Case of Home Abuse* (British Criminology Conferences, 1999).

recognition of elder abuse, in particular the significance of ageism and patriarchy.[140] No better indication of the failure to appreciate the significance of gender in the context of elder abuse can be found than the very existence of the 'carer stress' theory itself. The fact that the vast majority of those caring are women, but the vast majority of those abusing are men, should have immediately demonstrated that the link was not as strong as had been assumed.[141]

Elder abuse and domestic violence

In many cases, elder abuse is simply the continuation of a violent relationship.[142] It is striking that elder abuse has been hived off into its own corner and so is not seen as part of the wider debates on domestic violence, violence against women, racist abuse, and anti-social behaviour.[143] It is, for example, revealing that the self-completion questionnaire on domestic violence and intimate partner abuse from the British Crime Surveys of 1996 and 2001 were not offered to women over the age of 59. Of course, the age of the victim of domestic abuse should have no effect on its categorization.[144] Domestic violence is domestic violence, whatever the age of the victim. The substantial amount of work that has been done in the area of domestic violence to demonstrate the way in which societal attitudes cause and reinforce domestic violence find no echo in much of the writing on elder abuse.[145] Just as with domestic violence, unequal gender and power relations create a context within which male violence against women can continue unacknowledged and unchallenged. In the context of elder abuse, we have the additional factor of ageism, whereby older people are stigmatized and marginalized in society in a way which enables abuse to take place and hinders an effective challenge to it.[146]

There is now ample evidence that a significant portion of elder abuse is simply the continuation of abuse that has been going on in one form or another throughout the relationship.[147] Old age, it seems, can make domestic violence

---

[140] T Whittaker, 'Violence, Gender and Elder Abuse' in B Fawcett, B Featherstone, J Hearn, and C Toft (eds), *Violence and Gender Relations: Theories and Interventions* (Sage, 1996).

[141] D Hines and K Malley-Morrison, *Family Violence in the US* (Sage, 2004), at 247.

[142] C Walsh, J Ploeg, L Lohfeld, J Horne, H MacMillan, and D Lai, 'Violence Across the Lifespan: Interconnections Among Forms of Abuse as Described by Marginalized Canadian Elders and Their Care-givers' (1999) 19 *Journal of Interpersonal Violence* 282.

[143] S Biggs, 'A Family Concern: Elder Abuse in British Social Policy' (1996) 16 *Critical Social Policy* 63, at 67.

[144] E Rathbone-McCuan, 'Elder Abuse Within the Context of Intimate Violence' (2000–2001) 69 *UMKC Law Review* 215.

[145] A Desmarais and K Reeves, 'Gray, Black, and Blue: The State of Research and Intervention for Intimate Partner Abuse Among Elders' (2007) 25 *Behavioral Sciences and the Law* 377.

[146] T Nelson, *Ageism* (MIT, 2002).

[147] B Penhale, 'Bruises on the Soul: Older Women, Domestic Violence, and Elder Abuse' (1999) 11 *Journal of Elder Abuse & Neglect* 1; C Cooney and A Mortimer, 'Elder Abuse and Dementia—A Pilot Study' (1995) 41 *International Journal of Social Psychiatry* 276; S Harris, 'For Better or for Worse: Spouse Abuse Grown Old' (1996) 8 *Journal of Elder Abuse & Neglect* 1; and M Lundy and

visible in a way which was not so apparent earlier in the relationship.[148] One leading American study found that 58 per cent of perpetrators of elder abuse were intimate partners.[149] The Comic Relief Survey found that mistreatment was performed by partners in 51 per cent of cases and interpersonal abuse carried out by them in 57 per cent.[150] Of course, it cannot be assumed that because the elder abuse is carried out by partners it is continuing domestic violence. However, the authors of the survey concluded that the implication of their data was that either these cases of interpersonal abuse by partners are 'the elderly graduates of domestic violence' or they have a condition, such as dementia, that sometimes gives rise to violent behaviour.

Linda Vinton argues:

Abuse is not primarily about old age at all but about certain damaging patterns which have continued into old age. This applies mainly to situations within the family; for example elder abuse is sometimes simple marital violence which has continued into old age.[151]

Therefore, it is not surprising that many of the factors that indicate a risk of elder abuse are the very ones that also indicate a risk of domestic violence: living situation, social isolation, cognitive impairments, physical impairments, substance abuse, and relationship dependency.[152] Women suffering elder abuse at the hands of a spouse report similar patterns of conduct as those suffering domestic violence, with constant criticism and controlling behaviour, leading then to threatening and violent actions.[153] Similarly, reasons given for not reporting elder abuse match those given by victims of domestic violence, including fear of reprisal or retaliation, misplaced loyalty or gratitude, dependency on the partner, and confusion.[154] The links between elder abuse and domestic violence can be taken further. Many of the themes of the early theoretical work on domestic violence can be seen in the treatment of elder abuse: denial of the problem; blaming the

S Grossman, 'Elder Abuse: Spouse/Intimate Partner Abuse and Family Violence Among Elders' (2004) 16 *Journal of Elder Abuse & Neglect* 85.

[148] T Koenig, S Rinfrette, and W Lutz, 'Female Caregivers' Reflections on Ethical Decision-Making' (2006) 34 *Clinical Social Work Journal* 361.

[149] K Pillemer and D Finkelhor, 'The Prevalence of Elder Abuse: A Random Sample Survey' (1988) 28 *The Gerontologist* 51.

[150] M O'Keeffe, A Hills, M Doyle, C McCreadie, S Scholes, R Constantine, A Tinker, J Manthorpe, S Biggs, and B Erens, *UK Study of Abuse and Neglect of Older People Prevalence Survey Report* (Department of Health, 2008).

[151] L Vinton, 'Battered Women's Shelters and Older Women' (1992) 7 *Journal of Family Violence* 63.

[152] C Mouton, 'Intimate Partner Violence and Health Status Among Older Women' (2003) 9 *Violence Against Women* 1465.

[153] A Mowlam, R Tennant, J Dixon, and C McCreadie, *UK Study of Abuse and Neglect of Older People: Qualitative Findings* (Department of Health, 2008), at 5.1.1.

[154] C Bitondo-Dyer, M-T Connolly, and P McFeeley, 'The Clinical and Medical Forensics of Elder Abuse and Neglect' in R Bonnie and R Wallace (eds), *Elder Mistreatment: Abuse, Neglect, and Exploitation in an Aging America* (National Academies Press, 2003).

victim; failure to provide adequate legal protection; and individualising the problem.[155] It seems indeed true to suggest that work on elder abuse is in a similar place to where work on domestic violence was 20 years ago.[156]

Macro causes

The 'macro causes' of elder abuse seek to find the causes of abuse outside the relationship between the parties. One explanation is that the way our society is arranged tends to mean that older people are outside the 'public sphere'. They live their lives in nursing homes, or in their own homes, but are not free to leave. The fact that their lives are largely spent 'behind closed doors' means that the abuse is readily undetected, and that because older people tend to be dependent on their carers for their basic needs, their options in seeking to escape from the abuse are limited. The lack of social inclusion, dependency on others, and lack of access to information and remedies can all contribute to the social circumstances that enable elder abuse to take place.[157]

A wider point is the failure of society to effectively integrate older people into mainstream society.[158] Social structure and attitudes towards the elderly marginalize them[159] and this encourages and enables the abuse to take place.[160] The Royal College of Psychiatrists suggested that dehumanization is at the root of most abuse.[161] Although notions of dehumanization and a lack of respect are vague, the benefit of emphasizing them is that they play an important role in explaining, not all the attitudes which may cause abuse, but how the abuse is perceived by the older person and society at large.

We will now focus on two particular claims: first, that elder abuse must be understood in the context of gender;[162] and secondly, that elder abuse reflects ageist attitudes.

Gender and elder abuse

Until recently, gender played a relatively small part in the analysis of elder abuse. Indeed, in a 1996 literature review, Claudine McCreadie found only one

---

[155] R Pain, *Theorising Age In Criminology: The Case Of Home Abuse* (British Criminology Conferences, 1999).

[156] District Judge Mornington, *Responding to Elder Abuse Behind Closed Doors* (Age Concern, 2004).

[157] Department of Health, *Safeguarding Adults* (Department of Health, 2005).

[158] D Schuyler and B Liang, 'Reconceptualizing Elder Abuse: Treating the Disease of Senior Community Exclusion' (2006) 15 *Annals of Health* 275.

[159] M Quinn and S Tomita, *Elder Abuse and Neglect: Causes, Diagnosis and Intervention Strategies* (Springer, 1986).

[160] Social Exclusion Unit, *Social Exclusion Among Older People* (The Stationery Office, 2005).

[161] Royal College of Psychiatrists, *Institutional Abuse of Older Adults* (RCP, 2000).

[162] B Penhale, 'Bruises on the Soul: Older Women, Domestic Violence, and Elder Abuse' (1999) 11 *Journal of Elder Abuse & Neglect* 1.

study of elder abuse that mentioned the significance of gender.[163] Since then, much more attention has been given to it.[164] There now appears to be a general acceptance that women are significantly more likely to be victims of violent elder abuse than men[165] and that most protagonists are men.[166] As already mentioned, the Comic Relief study found that 80 per cent of cases of interpersonal abuse were carried out by men; with women only responsible for 20 per cent of incidents.[167] While it is, of course, important to appreciate that elder abuse does occur to men and where it does it may have a particular significance and require a particular response,[168] this should not overlook the fact that particularly in elder abuse involving violence, men make up the substantial majority of abusers.[169]

What can we tell from the fact that the majority of physical abusers of elderly people are men and their victims are women? Action on Elder Abuse suggests not much:

The fact that more women than men are identified as suffering abuse is likely to reflect the reality that women live longer than men and are consequently more likely to be living alone. It may also be that men are also less likely to report being abused.[170]

This is not convincing, not least because there is no evidence of a change in the gender ratios among younger victims or perpetrators. Further, the links previously mentioned with domestic violence provide a powerful reason for thinking that the gendered arrangement of elder abuse is extremely significant.

There has been extensive literature on the way in which patriarchy enables, reinforces, and protects men who carry out domestic violence.[171] This indicates

---

[163] C McCreadie, *Elder Abuse: Update on Research* (Age Concern, 1996).

[164] See, eg L Aitken and G Griffin, *Gender Issues in Elder Abuse* (Sage, 1996).

[165] L Bergeron, 'Abuse of Elderly Women in Family Relationships: Another Form of Domestic Violence Against Women' in K Kendall-Tackett, *Handbook of Women, Stress, and Trauma* (Routledge, 2005).

[166] J Mears, 'Survival is not Enough: Violence Against Older Women in Australia' (2003) 9 *Violence Against Women* 1478.

[167] M O'Keeffe, A Hills, M Doyle, C McCreadie, S Scholes, R Constantine, A Tinker, J Manthorpe, S Biggs, and B Erens, *UK Study of Abuse and Neglect of Older People Prevalence Survey Report* (Department of Health, 2008).

[168] A Desmarais and K Reeves, 'Gray, Black, and Blue: The State of Research and Intervention for Intimate Partner Abuse Among Elders' (2007) 25 *Behavioral Sciences and the Law* 377.

[169] S Crichton, J Bond, C Harvey, and J Ristock, 'Elder Abuse: Feminist and Ageist Perspectives' (1999) 10 *Journal of Elder Abuse & Neglect* 115. For claims that gender plays no great role in this area, see E Pittaway, A Westhues, and T Peressi, 'Risk Factors for Abuse and Neglect Among Older Persons' (1995) 14 *Canadian Journal on Aging* 20.

[170] Action on Elder Abuse, *Hidden Voices: Older People's Experience of Abuse* (Action on Elder Abuse, 2004).

[171] L Vinton, 'Abused Older Women: Battered Women or Abused Elders?' (1991) 3 *Journal of Women and Aging* 5; L Salazar, C Baker, A Price, and K Carlin, 'Moving Beyond the Individual: Examining the Effects of Domestic Violence Policies on Social Norms' (2003) 32 *American Journal of Community Psychology* 253. But see J Pritchard, *Male Victims of Elder Abuse* (Jessica Kingsley, 2001).

that the societal structural inequalities against men are reflected in and reinforce unequal relationships at home.[172] As Michelle Madden Dempsey writes:

the patriarchal character of individual relationships cannot subsist without those relationships being situated within a broader patriarchal social structure. Patriarchy is, by its nature, a social structure—and thus any particular instance of patriarchy takes its substance and meaning from that social context. If patriarchy were entirely eliminated from society, then patriarchy would not exist in domestic arrangements and thus domestic violence in its strong sense would not exist... Moreover, if patriarchy were lessened in society generally then *ceteris paribus* patriarchy would be lessened in domestic relationships as well, thereby directly contributing to the project of ending domestic violence in its strong sense.[173]

The failure to appreciate the significance of gender in elder abuse means that approaches to combat it which focus on the vulnerability of the victim, rather than the structural inequalities within the relationship and more broadly within society, are likely to fail.[174] It may also explain the relatively little public attention received by the issue. Older women have become invisible in our society. That may be why their abuse is too.[175]

Ageism and elder abuse

The arguments made above should not lead us to conclude that elder abuse is no more than a version of domestic violence, because that would be to ignore the significance of the age of the parties and particularly the power of ageism. Ageism creates preconceptions and norms of what behaviour and attitudes are expected of older people. These are reinforced by a range of subtle means, including characterizations in the media, advertising, language, and social norms.[176] Those who transgress these norms are subject to ridicule. The power that ageism can exercise is significant and shifts over time and social context.[177]

Society portrays older people as lacking capacity or being of doubtful capacity. This can lead to services targeted at older people as primarily appropriate for those of marginal capacity or dependent on others for care.[178] This can restrict older people's access to power, public spaces, and their role in the community. These

---

[172] F Glendenning and P Decalmer, 'Looking to the Future' in P Decalmer and F Glendenning (eds), *The Mistreatment of Elderly People* (Sage, 1993).

[173] M Madden Dempsey, 'Towards a Feminist State: What does "Effective" Prosecution of Domestic Violence Mean?' (2007) 70 *Modern Law Review* 908.

[174] M Madden Dempsey 'What Counts as Domestic Violence? A Conceptual Analysis' (2006) 12 *William and Mary Journal of Women and the Law* 301.

[175] M Smith and J Hightower, *What's Age Got to Do With It?* (Yukon Society, 2000).

[176] See further ch 2.

[177] R Pain, *Theorising Age in Criminology: The Case of Home Abuse* (British Criminology Conferences, 1999).

[178] S Biggs, 'A Family Concern: Elder Abuse in British Social Policy' (1996) 16 *Critical Social Policy* 63.

have a significant impact on elder abuse. First, ageism works hard to keep older people in their homes or a few specific public places. This means that more time is spent at home and therefore the opportunity for intimate abuse is increased. Further, the lack of access to support from others or public services means that elder abuse goes undetected or unacknowledged. Society's structures can mean that older women become dependent on their partners both economically and socially, and this vulnerability can itself foster elder abuse.

Secondly, ageist attitudes create and reinforce attitudes among older people about themselves. The ageist notion that older people are a 'waste of space' and always complaining about things deter victims of elder abuse from seeking help, or indeed, even believing that the behaviour is not abusive. Such attitudes belittle and sap the confidence of those suffering abusive relationships.

Thirdly, the lack of alternative facilities for older people both in terms of housing and social support can make escaping from the abuse as terrifying as the abuse itself. Financial barriers to seeking help or leaving the relationship can be even greater among older women than younger victims of domestic violence.[179]

Fourthly, there is evidence that older people, in general, are more likely to remain with abusers than younger women.[180] Indeed, as we have seen, many have lived with the abuse for many years. Older women are likely to be influenced by the attitudes and values they were raised with.[181] These mean that, in general, older women have increased levels of religious belief;[182] a sense of powerlessness; a stronger commitment to 'privacy of the family';[183] and a belief that one should make sacrifices for 'the good of the family'.[184] It has even been suggested that some older women have come to regard abuse as normal.[185] These all deter victims of abuse from seeking help.[186] One study of services for older abused women in Scotland found shame and embarrassment as significant factors inhibiting women seeking help.[187]

Finally, there is the issue of the extent that ageist attitudes about men affect perpetrators. Is elder abuse in part an attempt by men to assert power in the home

---

[179] S Straka and L Montminy, 'Responding to the Needs of Older Women Experiencing Domestic Violence' (2006) 12 *Violence Against Women* 61.

[180] D Wilke and L Vinton, 'The Nature and Impact of Domestic Violence Across Age Cohorts' (2005) 20 *Affilia* 316.

[181] S Straka and L Montminy, 'Responding to the Needs of Older Women Experiencing Domestic Violence' (2006) 12 *Violence Against Women* 61.

[182] Ibid.

[183] P Zink, C Jacobson, S Regan, B Fisher, and S Pabst, 'Older Women's Descriptions and Understandings of Their Abusers' (2006) 12 *Violence Against Women* 851.

[184] E Buchbinder and T Winterstein, ' "Like a Wounded Bird": Older Battered Women's Life Experiences with Intimate Violence' (2003) 15 *Journal of Elder Abuse & Neglect* 23.

[185] B Brandl and L Cook-Daniels, *Domestic Abuse in Later Life* (Violence Against Women, 2002).

[186] B Dunlop, R Beaulaurier, L Seff, F Newman, N Malik, and M Fuster, *Domestic Violence Against Older Women* (US Department of Justice, 2005).

[187] L Macdonald, *Out of the Shadows: Christianity and Violence against Women in Scotland* (University of Edinburgh, 2000).

when ageism means they are losing it in other areas of their life?[188] We cannot know, but it is interesting to note the evidence that perpetrators of abuse tend to be those who are themselves highly dependent on the victim.[189]

Intersecting -isms

A proper understanding of elder abuse requires not only an appreciation of ageism and sexism, but also the way the two intersect.[190] It is not only these social forces: racism,[191] homophobia, and disability discrimination can all impact on a case of elder abuse.[192] Leah Cohen has written:

The elderly in our society are generally rejected, but we are particularly disdainful of older women. The discrimination begins in infancy and escalates as we become mature women. But it doubles as we grow older, for then we are not only women, but old women, perceived as unattractive, unneeded, and parasitical.[193]

As she indicates, in elder abuse we have structural inequalities based on age and sex within the relationship and within society which do not just operate independently, but also combine to reinforce each other and produce unique inequalities of their own. Nancy Levit writes:

On an experiential level, one person might belong to several identity groups (such as gender, race, ethnicity, socioeconomic status, and sexual orientation); moreover, individuals' experiences comprise several identity facets intersecting at once... A black woman, for instance, experiences not just racism and sexism, but the... burden of intertwined racism and sexism, which is its own unique (and perhaps particularly virulent) form of discrimination.[194]

Such attitudes about older women affect the behaviour of the perpetrator as well as the victim. It also affects the response of officials to elder abuse. A powerful example of this can be seen in research into the police practice in dealing with cases of elder abuse in Rhode Island in the United States. There it was found that the police were reluctant to arrest old men who were seen as frail and not capable of doing a serious injury, while older women tended to

---

[188] S Biggs, C Phillipson, and P Kingson, *Elder Abuse in Perspective* (Open University Press, 1995), at 21.

[189] D Hines and K Melley-Morrison, *Family Violence in the US* (Sage, 2004), at 247; and J Ogg and C Munn-Giddings, 'Researching Elder Abuse' (1993) 13 *Ageing and Society* 389.

[190] See M Madden Dempsey, *Prosecuting Domestic Violence: A Philosophical Analysis* (Oxford University Press, 2009), at ch 7 for an excellent discussion of the intersection of different forces in the context of domestic violence.

[191] L Aitken and G Griffin, *Gender Issues in Elder Abuse* (Sage, 1996), at ch 3.

[192] S Turell, 'A Descriptive Analysis of Same-Sex Relationship Violence for a Diverse Sample' (2000) 15 *Journal of Family Violence* 281.

[193] L Cohen, *Small Expectations: Society's Betrayal of Older Women* (McClelland and Stewart, 1984).

[194] N Levit, 'Theorizing the Connections Among Systems of Subordination' (2002) 71 *University of Missouri Kansas-City Law Review* 227, at 228.

be regarded as unreliable and confused, and therefore unlikely to be effective witnesses in court.[195]

Institutional abuse

There has been some debate over whether elder abuse is more prevalent in domestic settings or in institutional ones.[196] Some investigations into the problem appear to see the problem as a primarily domestic one.[197] However, a review of findings of inquiries under the 1984 Registered Homes Act found 'chilling evidence'[198] that those living in care were more at risk than those in the community.[199] Still, it should be recalled that 421,000 older people were living in care homes in 2006, which is only about four per cent of all older people.[200] In fact, the number of residents aged over 65 in registered care homes has fallen by 12 per cent between 2003 and 2006.[201]

There is increasing evidence of abuse of older people in care homes.[202] At the most extreme, it has been claimed that in nursing homes we are seeing widespread 'geronticide'.[203] A more moderate view is that the really important issue is not so much the occasional act of violence against older people in care homes as the atmosphere they have. One report into institutional care claimed that 'the predominant culture is one of warehousing older citizens'.[204] Another spoke of 'deadly institutionalisation'.[205] The Royal College of Psychiatrists has suggested that abuse 'is a common part of institutional life'.[206]

Care homes are subject to inspection by the Commission for Social Care Inspection (CSCI). In its early reports, it found that only 50 per cent of care

[195] A Klein, T Tobin, A Salomon, and J Dubois, *A Statewide Profile of Abuse of Older Women and the Criminal Justice Response* (US Department of Justice, 2004).
[196] The Care Standards Act 2000 saw the terms 'nursing homes' and 'residential homes' replaced by 'care homes' for institutions.
[197] S Biggs, 'Elder Abuse and the Policing of Community Care' (1996) 6 *Generations Review* 2.
[198] S Glendenning, 'The Mistreatment and Neglect of Elderly People in Residential Centres: Research Outcomes in the Mistreatment of Elderly People' in P Declamer and S Glendenning, *The Mistreatment of Elderly People* (2nd edn, Sage, 1993).
[199] See also, Royal College of Psychiatrists, *Institutional Abuse of Older Adults* (RCP, 2000).
[200] House of Commons Health Committee, *Elder Abuse* (The Stationery Office, 2004), at 1.
[201] The Information Centre, *Community Care Statistics 2007* (NHS, 2007). Although there was a slight increase in 2007: Laing & Buisson, *Care of Elderly People Market Survey 2007* (Laing & Buisson, 2007).
[202] B Payne and L Fletcher, 'Elder Abuse in Nursing Homes: Prevention and Resolution Strategies and Barriers' (2005) 33 *Journal of Criminal Justice* 119; and M Thobaben and R Duncan, 'Domestic Elder Abuse by Health Care Providers' (2003) 15 *Home Health Care Management Practice* 168.
[203] M Brogden, *Geronticide: Killing the Elderly* (Jessica Kingsley, 2001).
[204] Royal College of Psychiatrists, *Institutional Abuse of Older Adults* (RCP, 2000).
[205] P Terry, *Counselling the Elderly and their Carers* (Macmillan, 1997).
[206] Royal College of Psychiatrists, *Institutional Abuse of Older Adults* (RCP, 2000), at 6.

homes were meeting or exceeding the standards for complaints and protection.[207] The Commission only rarely finds cases of intentional abuse, but casual abuse is clearly common.[208] Similarly, a report by the Royal College of Psychiatrists into the institutional abuse of older adults found that most of the abuse is due to 'ignorance, unthinking and ageism',[209] rather than malicious or sadistic acts. Such attitudes may be fostered by the culture and atmosphere of many institutions, but they in fact reflect wider social attitudes towards older people. As a CSCI investigation into one institution concluded:

The Rowan ward service had many of the known risk factors for abuse: a poor and institutionalised environment, low staffing levels, high use of bank and agency staff, little staff development, poor supervision, a lack of knowledge of incident reporting, a closed inward looking culture and weak management at ward and locality level.[210]

Once abusive attitudes and behaviour develop, they can become a part of institutional culture,[211] so much so that the staff are utterly unaware of the abusive nature of their actions. Some care homes have rooms as small as 10 square metres. That is smaller than a typical student room or prison cell.[212] That such rooms are thought suitable for older people to live in says a lot about how older people are valued and how easily they are abused.

When considering the issue of abuse in care homes, it should not be forgotten that the atmosphere and conditions can be abusive for the staff too. Some reports found that staff often suffer psychological and spiritual exhaustion and it is a case of the abuse occurring despite the best efforts of the staff.[213] It should not be forgotten that caring for older people is difficult, demanding, and stressful work.[214] Professional carers can face violence from older people[215] and where that occurs evidence suggests it is more likely to be reciprocated.[216]

A major investigation into the state of care homes has been undertaken by the House of Lords Select Committee.[217] They found, predictably, evidence

---

[207] House of Commons Health Committee, *Elder Abuse* (The Stationery Office, 2004), evidence 158.

[208] Commission for Health Improvement, *Investigation into Matters Arising from Care on Rowan Ward, Manchester Mental Health & Social Care Trust* (CHI, 2003), at 2.

[209] Royal College of Psychiatrists, *Institutional Abuse of Older Adults* (RCP, 2000).

[210] Commission for Health Improvement, *Investigation into Matters Arising from Care on Rowan Ward, Manchester Mental Health & Social Care Trust* (CHI, 2003), at 2.

[211] Royal College of Psychiatrists, *Institutional Abuse of Older Adults* (RCP, 2000).

[212] J Hanson, L Kellaher, M Rowlands, J Percival, J Marcoux, and R Zako, *Profiling the Housing Stock for Older People from Domesticity to Caring* (UCL, 2003).

[213] K Pillemer and D Moore, 'Abuse of Patients in Nursing Homes: Findings from a Survey of Staff' (1989) 29 *The Gerontologist* 314.

[214] P Terry, *Counselling the Elderly and their Carers* (Macmillan, 1997).

[215] R Eastley, R MacPherson, and H Richards, 'Assaults on Professional Carers of Elderly People' (1993) 307 *British Medical Journal* 845.

[216] K Pillemer and D Moore, 'Abuse of Patients in Nursing Homes: Findings from a Survey of Staff' (1989) 29 *Gerontologist* 314.

[217] House of Lords and House of Commons Joint Committee on Human Rights, *The Human Rights of Older People in Healthcare* (Hansard, 2007).

of both excellent and appalling services in residential care. They heard 'many witnesses' expressing concern for older people and in particular relating to the following issues:

- malnutrition and dehydration;[218]
- abuse and rough treatment;
- lack of privacy in mixed-sex wards;
- lack of dignity, especially for personal care needs;
- insufficient attention paid to confidentiality;
- neglect, carelessness, and poor hygiene;
- inappropriate medication and use of physical restraint;
- inadequate assessment of a person's needs;
- too hasty discharge from hospital;
- bullying, patronizing, and infantilizing attitudes towards older people;
- discriminatory treatment of patients and care home residents on grounds of age, disability, and race;
- communication difficulties, particularly for people with dementia or people who cannot speak English;
- fear among older people of making complaints; and
- eviction from care homes.

The CSCI report has found that in 2003 only 59 per cent of residential services for older people met the National Minimum Standards, although by 2006 this had risen to 79 per cent. That still leaves just under a quarter of residential services failing to meet what are meant to be the *minimum* standards.

A particularly common complaint is that older people in residential care are neglected and not given appropriate or adequate care. The House of Lords Committee reported the following as particular examples:

- lack of hygiene, which at its most severe led to ill health and death such as the outbreak of *clostridium difficile* in Stoke Mandeville Hospital, which, according to the Healthcare Commission, resulted in the 'avoidable deaths in hospital of at least 33 patients, who were mainly elderly people';
- problems with personal care, including people being left in their own waste— this not only causes distress to individuals, but may also lead to health problems, such as the development of bedsores;
- rough handling of patients and residents by staff, for example when changing their clothes;
- older people being left with their spectacles, hearing aids, or false teeth out of reach;

[218] Department of Health, *Nutrition Action Plan Published to Address Nutrition of Older People in Care* (The Stationery Office, 2007).

- patients being repeatedly moved from one ward to another for non-clinical reasons, sometimes at night;
- hearing and visual problems not being addressed, and conditions remaining undiagnosed and untreated until they became critical; and
- patients being left for hours in hospital reception without medication, food, or water whilst awaiting transfer to another hospital or residential care.[219]

Often, the acts of neglect or abuse appear mundane, but in the environment of a nursing home even a small matter can have a dramatic effect on the well-being of a resident. The following is but one example of many of such neglect:

A woman reported that her mother, Dorothy, who is 92 and suffers from dementia, was admitted to hospital but not given the help she needed to eat. On many occasions Dorothy's food was left untouched on her bedside table and taken away at the end of mealtimes by the catering staff. Her food also needed to be pureed but often this was not done.[220]

Perhaps the most common complaint of treatment in a care home is that there is a lack of protection for the dignity and privacy of residents.[221] The arrangements are designed for the ease of the staff and the well-running of the home, rather than treating and respecting each person as an individual.[222] The following captures this concern well:

I went to visit my husband on the first day and he is a very private person, he doesn't like anything to embarrass him and when I went in he was almost in tears which is not my husband. He said 'Please, please go and get a bottle I am nearly wetting myself'. I rushed out I got a bottle and I said to him 'Well why didn't you just ring the nurse', in my innocence. 'I have for an hour and a half I've been asking for a bottle'. Well when I went out [and] told the nurse she said 'Oh don't worry we would have changed the sheets'. Now his dignity at that stage would have gone out of the window. There was no dignity.[223]

These incidents to some may be minor, but it is through a series of such dehumanizing incidents that an individual's self esteem can be lost and staff can develop demeaning attitudes towards residents.[224]

---

[219] Para 21.

[220] Age Concern, *Age of Equality? Outlawing Age Discrimination Beyond the Workplace* (Age Concern, 2007), at 23.

[221] Department of Health, *Dignity in Care. Report of the Survey* (Department of Health, 2006).

[222] A Worden, D Challis, and I Pedersen, 'The Assessment of Older People's Needs in Care Homes' (2006) 10 *Aging & Mental Health* 549.

[223] House of Commons Health Committee, *Elder Abuse* (The Stationery Office, 2004), evidence 97.

[224] M Orrell, G Hancock, and K Galboda, 'The Needs of People with Dementia in Care Homes: The Perspectives of Users, Staff and Family Caregivers' (2008) 20 *International Psychogeriatrics* 941.

This issue of infantilization appears to be a particularly prevalent concern.[225] Little acts of lack of respect, although each relatively minor, together create an atmosphere which is dehumanizing.[226] In the 'microcosm' of some care homes, negative images of old age inevitably flourish. As the Royal College of Psychiatrists suggested, unless something is done to combat that force it is likely to be prevalent.[227] The atmosphere in a ward is likely to compound the already existing attitudes of ageism. An institution so easily puts its own aims above the aims of the individuals living there. Issues such as privacy and respect for personal possessions are easily ignored. In a context where these values are some of the few things that are precious and of value to them, their loss lessens identity. In the light of this, it is not surprising, but greatly saddening, to read that depression is four times more common among those in care homes than for older people living in the community, running at 40 to 60 per cent.[228]

The voices of those in care homes

In a revealing insight into life in a care home, Help the Aged produced a report containing accounts from residents.[229] Betty Titmus[230] explained how she felt going into the home was a move away from dignified self-determination and towards the grave. She writes of the home:

routines were fairly rigid, with very definite mealtimes and distinct but unstated rules of behaviour. Behind it there was a feeling that now someone else knew best and my life would be run not by me, but for me.[231]

This loss of self-determination was a consistent theme in the report. Another resident, John Cobett, writes:

One of the things I found difficult was being treated like a child; it threatened my sense of independence. We were always told things would be nice for us. Some of the other residents felt rebellious: we didn't want things that would be 'nice' for us but things that would be a bit of a challenge sometimes. The one-size-fits-all approach to the trip to

---

[225] T Gorgen, 'As if I Just didn't Exist'—Elder Abuse and Neglect in Nursing Homes' in A Wahidin and M Cain (eds), *Ageing, Crime and Society* (Willan, 2006); and K Pillemer and D Moore, 'Abuse of Patients in Nursing Homes: Findings from a Survey of Staff' (1989) 29 *Gerontologist* 314.

[226] K Pillemer and D Moore, 'Abuse of Patients in Nursing Homes: Findings from a Survey of Staff' (1989) 29 *Gerontologist* 314.

[227] S Evans, 'Beyond the Mirror: A Group Analytic Exploration of Late Life and Depression' (1998) 2 *Aging and Mental Health* 94; and J Garner and M Ardern, 'Reflections on Old Age' (1998) 2 *Aging and Mental Health* 92.

[228] Age Concern, *Haircuts, Books and a Winter Coat* (Age Concern, 2008). Around 60 per cent of people living in private care homes receive help with fees from the local authority.

[229] Help the Aged, *My Home Life* (Help the Aged, 2008). See also, Office of Fair Trading, *Survey of Older People in Care Homes* (OFT, 2005).

[230] Some of the names in the report are pseudonyms.

[231] Help the Aged, *My Home Life* (Help the Aged, 2008), at 10.

Worthing (it was always bloomin' Worthing because it 'would be good for us') was not what several of us wanted. Why the heck couldn't we go somewhere else? We would have liked something different (and cheaper), like a trip to some woods to see the bluebells.[232]

A common theme in the report is the importance to residents of being able to maintain a sense of self-identity and self-esteem.[233] Important in doing this was finding a way of being helpful to others.[234] Many residents felt that not being able to be useful diminished their quality of life.

Another theme from the report is that apparently minor things can be hugely important to residents. Ann MacFarlane, a resident, makes this comment:

An abiding memory is of a woman who cried out each morning for her grapefruit spoon. It was her one possession from her own home and invariably it was missing from the breakfast trolley.

Another issue which is commonly raised by care home residents is money. A care home resident who is reliant on the state for meeting the cost of their care must hand over their state retirement pension, but can keep a personal expenses allowance: £19.60 in 2007. This is to be used to buy clothes, toiletries, cards, telephone calls, and birthday presents. To many this is an insufficient sum.[235]

Good care homes

There are some care homes which are happy, successful homes which create a warm and open atmosphere, while others, as we have seen, do not. The precise difference between them is hard to pinpoint. It is easy to say that a care home should 'set a tone that respects dignity, privacy, choice and control';[236] but it is harder to put that into practice. As the voices of those we have just heard indicate, it can be very little things that make the difference between a good and poor quality of life in a home. At the heart of the issue are the personalities and attitudes of the staff.

There is widespread support for person-centred care. This involves putting the interests of the resident first and seeking to provide an environment that meets their needs. The national minimal standards talk in terms of respect and dignity:

The principles on which the home's philosophy of care is based must be ones which ensure that residents are treated with respect, that their dignity is preserved at all times, and that their right to privacy is always observed.

---

[232] Ibid, at 16.
[233] K McKee, M Downs, M Gilhooly, K Gilhooly, S Tester, and F Wilson, 'Frailty, Identity and the Quality of Later life' in A Walker (ed), *Understanding Quality of Life in Older Age* (Open University Press, 2005).
[234] B Bowers, B Fibich, and N Jacobson, 'Care-as-Service, Care-as-Relating, Care-as-Comfort: Understanding Nursing Home Residents' Definitions of Quality' (2001) 41 *The Gerontologist* 539.
[235] Age Concern, *Haircuts, Books and a Winter Coat* (Age Concern, 2008).
[236] Royal College of Physicians, Royal College of Nursing, and British Geriatrics Society, *The Health and Care of Older People in Care Homes* (RCP, 2000).

Fundamentally, the test of whether these principles are put into practice or not will be a matter for the individual resident's own judgement. However, not all residents will be able to make that judgement and communicate it to their relatives or representatives, the staff or inspectors.

There is also a specific standard requiring the registered person to conduct the home in a way which maximizes service users' capacity to exercise personal autonomy and choice.[237]

The following are suggested as some of the important aspects of a regime in a good care home:[238]

- Older people want to care and be useful.[239] One study found that even giving an older person a house plant to look after had a significant impact on well-being and even death rates.[240] But there may be a host of ways of encouraging and helping older people to care for each other and feel they are being of some use.

- Listening to residents is also important.[241] As the comment above about the trip to Worthing shows, listening is crucial. This involves listening to patients' concerns and trying to act upon them, even when the issues appear trivial. The use of infantilizing and patronizing language must be avoided.

- Relationships between staff and residents are crucial. Good practice encourages assigning a staff member to each older person.

- Not insisting on rules which are unnecessary: while some rules in an institution are necessary, it is important to realize the lack of residents' freedom. The loss of self-determination is a major aspect of many older people's experience. So where there are issues where they can express themselves (for example, how they dress, personal appearance,[242] and the placing of their personal possessions), there should be flexibility.

- The offering of activities is important, but these must be optional and must not be patronising. Recognising the importance of cultural and religious practices is important.

- Perhaps the most difficult aspect is taking time to assist each individual in their particular area of need. A common complaint is that there is insufficient assistance at mealtimes[243] or when using bathroom facilities.[244]

---

[237] Standard 14.   [238] Help the Aged, *My Home Life* (Help the Aged, 2008).
[239] Ibid.   [240] D Gilbert, *Stumbling on Happiness* (Vintage, 2005).
[241] G Boyle, 'Facilitating Choice and Control for Older People in Long-Term Care' (2004) 12 *Health and Social Care in the Community* 212; S Davies, 'Creating Community: The Basis for Caring Partnerships in Nursing Homes' in M Nolan, G Grant, J Keady, and U Lundh (eds), *Partnerships in Family Care* (Open University Press, 2003), at 218; H Orchard and D Clark, 'Tending the Soul as Well as the Body: Spiritual Care in Nursing Residential Homes' (2001) 7 *International Journal of Palliative Nursing* 541; and J Ronch, 'Changing Institutional Culture: Can We Re-value the Nursing Home?' (2004) 43 *Journal of Gerontological Social Work* 61.
[242] Department of Health, *Dignity in Care. Report of the Survey* (Department of Health, 2006).
[243] Ibid.   [244] Ibid.

Links with the outside world are important too. Family members are keen to maintain a relationship and their contribution is important in improving their quality of life and engaging residents in the outside world.[245]

Restraint

One controversial and difficult issue is that surrounding the issue of restraint.[246] A CSCI report lists the following forms of restraint: physical intervention; physical restraint; denial of practical resources to manage daily living; environmental restraint (for example, locks); chemical restraint; electronic surveillance; medical restraint; or forced care. The report, surprisingly, found little evidence of actual physical restraint being used in care homes.[247] However, three-quarters of those questioned knew a person in a care home who had been restrained. The report also found that members of staff were confused as to what constituted restraint and when it was lawful to use it.[248] The report stated that using furniture to restrain people and physical confinement were completely unacceptable.[249]

The issue of restraint arises where there are concerns that the older person is going to pose a risk to themselves or another. The starting point is that in law any competent is free to go where they want and do what they want unless their act is in some way unlawful. Restraining a person will, therefore, automatically infringe their rights and be a criminal offence.[250] Where, therefore, a resident has mental capacity, it will only be lawful to restrain them if they are about to harm another person or, perhaps, commit suicide.

Where the person lacks capacity, the Mental Capacity Act 2005 will authorize conduct which promotes their best interests. If the restraint is necessary to protect the individual from harm and is proportional, it may well be justified. Section 6 of the 2005 Act specifically permits the use of restraint where the care worker reasonably believes that the use of force is necessary and is proportionate,[251] although the restraint should be stopped as soon as the danger to self or others is passed. Many question whether restraint does make a person safer in all but the most extreme of cases.[252] Indeed, it should never be forgotten that restraining a

---

[245] J Sandberg, U Lundh, and M Nolan, 'Placing a Spouse in a Care Home: The Importance of Keeping' (2001) 10 *Journal of Clinical Nursing* 406; and U Kellett, 'Bound within the Limits: Facing Constraints to Family Caring in Nursing Homes' (2000) 6 *International Journal of Nursing Practice* 317.

[246] Commission for Social Care Inspection, *Rights, Risks and Restraints* (CSCI, 2007); and Royal College of Nursing, *Restraint Revisited—Rights, Risk and Responsibility: Guidance for Nursing Staff* (RCN, 2004).

[247] Para 50. In *Bicknell v HM Coroner for Birmingham* [2007] EWHC 2547 (Admin), it was held that a coroner erred in not holding an inquest into the death of a patient who had been left in a restraining 'bucket chair'.

[248] Ibid.   [249] Para 70.

[250] At the very least battery, or more seriously, kidnapping.   [251] See p 59.

[252] J Engberg, N Castle, and D McCaffrey, 'Physical Restraint Initiation in Nursing Homes and Subsequent Resident Health' (2008) 48 *The Gerontologist* 442.

person in itself harms them and creates dangers of further harm if they struggle.[253] This means that restraint will require very strong justification.

There is also a concern over electronic tagging or video surveillance.[254, 255] The CSCI report found mixed views on this topic, although there was widespread support for the view that if it was justified it could only be used with the consent of the residents involved. These technologies are normally used where a patient is prone to wander and provide a warning to staff if the resident is leaving the building, for example. Supporters of the tags say that they can, in fact, increase the freedom of patients, who otherwise would have to be locked into their rooms.[256] Here, there is a balance between the freedom of movement offered by these devices and the invasion of privacy and dignity that occur when they are used.

Regulation

In recent years, concerted efforts have been made to improve the standards in care homes. This has primarily been through improved systems of inspection. The Registered Homes Act 1984 gave powers to local and health authorities to regulate care homes, but the legislation was vague and was applied inconsistently.[257] The Care Standards Act 2000 introduced a consistent standard of care through the National Minimum Standards.[258] The law is now governed by the Health and Social Care Act 2008. In England, the Commission for Social Care Inspection (CSCI) has the job of registering and inspecting care homes and ensuring that the national minimum standards are complied with.[259] When the 2008 Act is in force, this role will be taken over by the Care Quality Commissioner. Since 2007, the CSCI has inspected all care homes and assessed them against a set of seven outcomes: quality of life; exercising choice and control; making a positive contribution; personal dignity and respect; freedom from discrimination

---

[253] Commission for Social Care Inspection, *Rights, Risks and Restraints* (CSCI, 2007).

[254] T Kohl, 'Watching Out for Grandma: Video Cameras in Nursing Homes May Help to Eliminate Abuse' (2003) 30 *Fordham Urban Law Journal* 2083; and S Welsh, A Hassiotis, G O'Mahoney, and M Deahl, 'Big Brother is Watching You—The Ethical Implications of Electronic Surveillance Measures in the Elderly with Dementia and in Adults with Learning Difficulties' (2003) 7 *Aging and Mental Health* 372.

[255] K Eltis, 'Predicating Dignity on Autonomy? The Need for Further Inquiry into the Ethics of Tagging and Tracking Dementia Patients with GPS Technology' (2008) 3 *International Journal of Older People Nursing* 1.

[256] S Welsh, A Hassiotis, G O'Mahoney, and M Deahl, 'Big Brother is Watching You—The Ethical Implications of Electronic Surveillance Measures in the Elderly with Dementia and in Adults with Learning Difficulties' (2003) 7 *Aging and Mental Health* 372.

[257] L Nazarko, *Nursing in Care Homes* (Blackwell, 2002).

[258] Department of Health, *Care Homes for Older People: National Minimum Standards* (The Stationery Office, 2003).

[259] Care Standards Act 2000, s 23. Department of Health, *Care Standards Act 2000, Domiciliary Care, National Minimum Standards Regulations* (The Stationery Office, 2003); and CSCI, *Inspecting for Improvement* (Office of Public Sector Reform, 2003).

and harassment; improved health and emotional well-being and economic well-being; and leadership and management.[260] Homes are given a star rating and assessed as excellent, good, adequate, or poor. If a home is rated excellent, it will only be inspected every three years; if good, then every two years. Adequate homes will be inspected every year and poor homes have two inspections per year. The focus on the inspection regime is, therefore, on those homes which are regarded as struggling. The CSCI also requires care homes to provide Annual Quality Assurance Assessment reports. The Commission must also be notified of the death or serious injury of any resident or an event which adversely affects the health or safety of residents or any allegation of misconduct.[261]

The Health and Social Care Act 2008 gives the Care Quality Commissioner a number of sanctions if a care home is failing to comply with a request for action.[262] These range from an emergency closure order to a variation of condition of registration, to a fine. Inspectors are reluctant to use their power to close care homes and prefer to use threats to ensure compliance.[263] In 2007 to 2008, 19,059 adult services were inspected. There was one prosecution; 11 urgent cancellations of registration; 1,205 requirement notices issued; and 493 statutory notices issued.[264] The numbers of these have fallen over the years of inspection. Whether this is due to the inspection regime being a more effective deterrent or less rigorous inspection is a matter for debate.[265]

The effectiveness of the inspection regime is doubted by some.[266] The Commission's own report[267] accepted that too often 'box ticking' dominated the inspection process in a way which could allow unacceptable standards to continue. Of course, there are those who doubt that the CSCI's inspections are rigorous. For example, it has been complained that inspections are concerned about whether policies are in place rather than whether they are being followed or are effective.[268] In less than 10 per cent of cases are residents asked questions to discover whether the policies are being followed. Although the star ratings provide a readily accessible guide to the assessment of a care home, they have been criticized. The concern is that where a care home has an excellent rating or a good one, this reduces the number of inspections given. This provides a strong incentive on the CSCI to award these higher ratings. As the Relatives and Residents Association points out, there is something odd about the fact that the CSCI

---

[260] Commission for Social Care Inspection, *Inspecting for Better Lives* (CSCI, 2006).

[261] The Care Homes Regulations 2001 (SI 2001/3965).

[262] Health and Social Care Act 2008, ss 26–32.

[263] S Furness, 'A Hindrance or a Help? The Contribution of Inspection to the Quality of Care in Homes for Older People' (2007) *British Journal of Social Work* 1.

[264] Commission for Social Care Inspection, *Annual Report 2007–8* (CSCI, 2008).

[265] Ibid.

[266] K Sutherland and S Leatherman, *Regulation and Quality Improvement: A Review of the Evidence* (Health Foundation, 2006); and Audit Commission, *The Future of Regulation in the Public Sector* (The Stationery Office, 2006).

[267] Commission for Social Care Inspection, *Inspecting for Better Lives* (CSCI, 2006).

[268] House of Commons Health Committee, *Elder Abuse* (The Stationery Office, 2004), para 157.

claims that 40 per cent of homes failed to meet the minimum standards, yet 70 per cent were awarded a good or excellent rating.[269] Certainly, the system took a knock after it was discovered that residents in a care home for adults with mental disabilities which was given a two-star rating by the CSCI had suffered significant and extensive abuse.[270] The truth is probably that the inspection regime offers some degree of protection and does something to improve standards, but not enough.

A rather different issue concerning care homes is their ownership.[271] There has certainly been a growth in the private care home sector. Initially, this involved mainly small family run homes, but four large companies now operate a significant proportion of the market.[272] There are concerns that the substantial sums of money that are now available and the power the few companies hold makes regulation less effective.[273]

The Health and Social Care Act 2008

The 2008 Act seeks to enhance professional regulation and create a new integrated regulator, the Care Quality Commission.[274] It will take over regulation from three bodies: the Commission for Social Care Inspection, the Healthcare Commission, and the Mental Health Act Commission. Some are concerned that as the body will have the role of inspecting hospitals, inspection of care homes will be low on their agenda.[275] The Act will allow the Commission to set its own standards.[276] While on the one hand this could be regarded as a welcome piece of decentralization, it remains to be seen whether this will lead to a watering down of the protection offered.[277] In one way, the law will be tighter because the Care Quality Commission will be able to close a home if it believes 'any person will or may be exposed to the risk of harm'.[278] The Act will also increase penalties for breach of the regulations, including the introduction of custodial sentences.[279]

---

[269] Relatives and Residents Association, '*Star Ratings Don't Add Up' Says National Care Home Charity* (Relatives and Residents Association, 2008).

[270] Relatives and Residents Association, *Abuse in Care Services for People with Learning Difficulties in Cornwall—Older People Next?* (Relatives and Residents Association, 2007).

[271] M Drakeford, 'Ownership, Regulation and the Public Interest: The Case of Residential Care for Older People' (2006) 26 *Critical Social Policy* 923.

[272] Ibid.

[273] J Chapman, P Miller, and P Skidmore, *The Long Game: How Regulators and Companies Can Both Win* (Demos, 2003).

[274] Health and Social Care Act 2008, s 1.

[275] Residents and Relatives Association, *Note on The Health and Social Care Bill* (Relatives and Residents Association, 2008).

[276] S Furness, 'A Hindrance or a Help? The Contribution of Inspection to the Quality of Care in Homes for Older People' (2007) *British Journal of Social Work* 1.

[277] Residents and Relatives Association, *Dangerous, Disabling and Discriminatory* (Relatives and Residents Association, 2007).

[278] Health and Social Care Act 2008, s 31.   [279] Health and Social Care Act 2008, s 35.

A significant aspect of the Act is that it will ensure that the Human Rights Act applies to all publicly arranged care, whether that is in fact provided in the voluntary or private sector. In *YL and Others v Birmingham CC and Others (Secretary of State for Constitutional Affairs intervening)*[280] it was held that a privately owned care home was not a public authority and so was not subject to the duties in the Human Rights Act[281] to act in a way which complied with the European Convention on Human Rights. The key argument was whether a private body running a care home was performing a 'function of public nature'.[282] The significance of the decision was short lived because under the Health and Social Care Act 2008 the decision will be reversed and all care homes, whether public or private, will be covered. Section 145(1) states:

A person ('P') who provides accommodation, together with nursing or personal care, in a care home for an individual under arrangements made with P under the relevant statutory provisions is to be taken for the purposes of subsection (3)(b) of section 6 of the Human Rights Act 1998 (c. 42) (acts of public authorities) to be exercising a function of a public nature in doing so.[283]

An action can therefore be brought under section 7 of the Human Rights Act against the owners of a care home complaining that they have failed to protect the rights of a resident.[284] This could lead to a court ordering the home to act, or not act, in a particular way in order to protect the person's rights. An award of damages could also be made.[285]

The Protection of Vulnerable Adults list

It is extraordinary that before 2000 there was virtually no regulation or control of those working with older people.[286] Traditionally, care assistants have been largely untrained and badly paid. There have been difficulties in recruiting and retaining suitable staff.[287] As Julia Neuberger writes:

We have allowed our most vulnerable older people to be cared for by people to whom we show no respect. We have to do this properly, pay properly, train properly and support properly, the people who do the back-breaking work day after day, without the cost of care becoming prohibitive.[288]

---

[280] [2007] UKHL 27.   [281] s 6.   [282] s 6(3)(b).

[283] s 145 does not apply to care where the services are provided in the older person's home.

[284] Although see *R (Thomas) v Havering LBC*, 4 September 2008, QBD where a resident failed in claiming that a closure of a nursing home interfered with her right to live under Article 2.

[285] Human Rights Act 1998, s 8.

[286] There is a lack of training for care home owners: S Furness 'Recognising and Addressing Elder Abuse in Care Homes' (2006) 8 *Journal of Adult Protection* 33.

[287] Help the Aged, *My Home Life* (Help the Aged, 2008).

[288] J Neuberger, *Not Dead Yet* (Harper Collins, 2008), at 231.

There is now in place a system for the registration and regulation of professional social workers. Since 1 April 2003, such staff members have to be accredited with an NVQ level 2 within three years of being registered.[289]

One important limb of the current law protecting older people from abuse is the creation of the Protection of Vulnerable Adults list, which was introduced in July 2004 through the Care Standards Act 2000.[290] This requires employers to check whether an individual is on the list when employing workers or volunteers in regular contact with vulnerable adults. This is in addition to the need to do a Criminal Records Bureau check.

Employers must refer to the list of workers who have been guilty of misconduct that has harmed or put at risk of harm a vulnerable adult.[291] Once on the list, the individual cannot work with vulnerable adults until their name is removed. The number of referrals to the Protection of Adults scheme has run at about 180 per month, which the government has admitted is far more than they had expected.[292] In a review of the first 100 referrals,[293] it was found that 81 per cent came from residential services, even though 80 per cent of service users are receiving community-based services. This may be because it is much more likely that abuse in a residential setting will be observed by a third party than when it takes place in someone's home. Another concerning finding was that 94 per cent of referrals were from the independent sector. Almost all referrals were made by managers or senior figures within the organization. Thirty-three per cent of referrals involved neglect, 29 per cent physical abuse, 16 per cent verbal abuse, and 25 per cent financial abuse. Some referrals involved complaints of more than one kind of abuse. Of all referrals only 34 per cent involved men, but it must be remembered that there are few men in the social care workforce: one in 20 of the social care workforce are male.[294] In relation to physical abuse, 77 per cent of the allegations were made against men. In cases of sexual abuse (making up six per cent of referrals), men were 27 times more likely to be accused than women.[295] It seems that referrals are used in the most serious cases. Fifty per cent of the allegations had been preceded by a police investigation.[296] A study of referrals found that 58 per cent of referrals were not placed on the list, while only seven per cent

---

[289] There are concerns about the availability of places: House of Commons Health Committee, *Elder Abuse* (The Stationery Office, 2004).
[290] Department of Health, *Protection of Vulnerable Adults Scheme in England and Wales for Care Homes and Domiciliary Care Agencies, A Practical Guide* (DoH, 2004); and M Stevens and J Manthorpe, *POVA Referrals—the First 100* (Kings College London, 2005).
[291] Ibid.
[292] Liam Byrne MP, Speech at *Tackling Elder Abuse: Actions and Solutions*, Help the Aged event on 29 June 2005.
[293] M Stevens and J Manthorpe, *POVA Referrals—the First 100* (Kings College London, 2005).
[294] M Stevens, S Hussein, S Martineau, J Harris, J Rapaport, and J Manthorpe, *The Protection of Vulnerable Adults List* (Kings College London, 2008). It should be noted that not all of the vulnerable adults in the survey were older people.
[295] Ibid.   [296] Ibid.

were put on the list as confirmed listings. This suggests that managers are being over-cautious and referring any case where there is a suspicion of abuse. Another possible explanation is that the burden of proof before a person can be listed is high.[297]

Multi-agency work

Local authorities are required to set up multi-agency policies and practices to tackle the abuse of vulnerable people in their area.[298] In the past, a failure by different agencies to communicate their concerns about vulnerable adults left them open to abuse. Although such multi-agency approaches are now standard, there is considerable diversity in how these arrangements work and the level of resources allocated to their work.[299]

The notion of agencies involved in the care of vulnerable adults 'talking to each other' seems straightforward, but in this area, as in others, it has proved complex. Different professional approaches and even language can impede effective communication.[300] There can even be conflicts between different professions, either based on monetary concerns over who should pay for an investigation or intervention, or disputes over what kind of intervention is appropriate.[301]

Safeguarding Adults provides the government's guidance on the issue of inter-agency cooperation in cases of abuse of vulnerable adults. It requires a 'zero-tolerance' of abuse. However, the report states:

The wishes of an adult with mental capacity should normally be respected. However, statutory agencies must act to uphold the human rights of all citizens and where others are at risk this duty will take precedence.

Any action taken by an organisation to safeguard an adult should meet Human Rights standards. It should be proportionate to the perceived level of risk and seriousness. Intervention should not be arbitrary or unfair. It must have a basis in law: e.g. acting with the consent of the adult or, under duty of care, acting in the best interest of the adult; undertaken to secure a legitimate aim (i.e. to prevent a crime or protect the public) and be necessary to fulfil a pressing social need.

---

[297] For a broader discussion of the employment of social workers with criminal records, see M Cowburn and P Nelson, 'Safe Recruitment, Social Justice, and Ethical Practice' (2008) 27 *Social Work Education* 293.

[298] Department of Health, *Safeguarding Adults, A National Framework of Standards for Good Practice and Outcomes in Adult Protection Work* (DoH, 2005); and House of Commons Health Committee, *Elder Abuse* (The Stationery Office, 2004), at 1.

[299] M O'Keeffe, A Hills, M Doyle, C McCreadie, S Scholes, R Constantine, A Tinker, J Manthorpe, S Biggs, and B Erens, *UK Study of Abuse and Neglect of Older People Prevalence Survey Report* (DoH, 2007).

[300] J Manthorpe, B Penhale, L Pinkney, N Perkins, and P Kingston, *A Systematic Literature Review in Response to Key Themes Identified in the Report of the House of Commons Select Committee on Elder Abuse* (DoH, 2004).

[301] M Preston-Shoot and V Wigley, 'Closing the Circle: Social Workers Responses to Multi-Agency Procedures on Older Age Abuse' (2002) 32 *British Journal of Social Work* 299.

This indicates that normally if a vulnerable adult has mental capacity but does not want to have protection, it should not be forced upon them. However, the guidance leaves open the possibility that there may be cases where it is appropriate to intervene to protect a vulnerable adult, even without their consent. Later in this chapter I will explain when I think that is appropriate.

Not surprisingly, professionals in the area have found that the guidance offers little help in defining precisely when they should intervene. The government intends more detailed policies to be developed at a local authority level. The difficulty is that the different agencies involved have different understandings about what abuse is and how it is best to deal with it. There is much to be said for wider use of inter-agency training.[302] The bureaucratic, organizational, and historical barriers to inter-agency cooperation should not be underestimated. There has been concern expressed that risk assessments are carried out by agencies primarily to protect them from complaints or legal liability, rather than being a genuine attempt to ascertain whether or not there is a problem.[303]

Criminal law

Of course, the standard criminal law applies just as much where the victim is an older person as with anyone else.[304] So, an incident of elder abuse will often amount to one of the standard criminal offences such as assault or theft. I will here mention some of the criminal offences which are specifically related to older people.

Causing or allowing the death of a child or vulnerable adult

Section 5 of the Domestic Violence, Crime and Victims Act 2004 creates the offence of causing or allowing the death of a child or vulnerable adult.[305] The offence can only be committed against a child or a vulnerable adult.[306] It can only be committed by a person who was living in the same household as the victim or

---

[302] P Cambridge and T Parkes, 'The Management and Practice of Joint Adult Protection Investigations Between Health and Social Services: Issues Arising from a Training Intervention' (2006) 25 *Social Work Education* 824.

[303] C McCreadie, D Mathew, R Filinson, and J Askham 'Ambiguity and Cooperation in the Implementation of Adult Protection Policy' (2008) 42 *Social Policy and Administration* 228.

[304] B Payne, *Crime and Elder Abuse* (Charles C Thomas, 2005).

[305] It is discussed in detail in J Herring, 'Mum's Not the Word: An Analysis of Section 5, Domestic Violence, Crimes and Victims Act 2004' in C Clarkson and S Cunningham, *Criminal Liability for Non-Aggressive Death* (Ashgate, 2008).

[306] 'A person aged 16 or over whose ability to protect himself from violence, abuse or neglect is significantly impaired through physical or mental disability or illness, through old age or otherwise': s 5(6).

had frequent contact with him or her. The offence can be committed in two ways: first, where the defendant did an act or omission which caused the death of the victim; and secondly, where the defendant 'failed to take such steps as he could reasonably have been expected to take to protect V from the risk' of significant physical harm by the unlawful act of a person living in the same household as V and having frequent contact with V.[307] There is no need for the prosecution to prove in which of these two ways the offence was committed as long as the jury are convinced it was one or the other. The offence is particularly useful in cases where it is clear that one of two people killed the victim, but it is not clear which one did. The offence also, in effect, puts an obligation on a person living with a vulnerable adult to take steps to protect them from violence from an intimate.

Ill-treatment or neglect of a person lacking capacity

Section 44 of the Mental Capacity Act 2005 states:

(1) Subsection (2) applies if a person ('D')—
   (a) has the care of a person ('P') who lacks, or whom D reasonably believes to lack capacity,
   (b) is the donee of a lasting power of attorney, or an enduring power of attorney (within the meaning of Schedule 4), created by P, or
   (c) is a deputy appointed by the court for P.
(2) D is guilty of an offence if he ill-treats or wilfully neglects P.

This offence is centred around the concept of ill-treatment or neglect.[308] It only applies where the victim lacks capacity. However, the phrase 'lacks capacity' is unclear. Under the Act, capacity relates to a specific issue. A person may have capacity to do some things (for example, buy a cup of tea), but not others (for example, make a will). In the context of this offence, it is unclear what the victim must lack the capacity to do. One possibility is that the question turns on what D is doing to P. So, if D is taking P's property, the issue turns on whether P had capacity to make decisions in respect of his property. That could, however, become complex. If D is hitting P, what level of capacity is required? Another possibility is that *any* incapacity would be sufficient to fall within the section. Peter Bartlett[309] rejects such an interpretation. He argues: 'It is surely not the case that D is guilty of an offence for failing to provide care in a situation where D rightly believes that P retains capacity to make decisions.' A third possibility

---

[307] s 5(1)(d).
[308] Mental Health Act 1983, s 127. There is an offence to ill-treat or wilfully neglect a patient while they are receiving treatment for a mental disorder. The Care Home Regulations 2001, made under the Care Standards Act 2000, contain a number of regulations, including some criminal offences. In *Brooklyn House Ltd v CSCI* [2006] EWHC 1165 (Admin), it was held that regulations 12 and 13 concerning the administration of medicine created strict liability offences.
[309] P Bartlett, *A Guide to The Mental Capacity Act 2005* (Oxford University Press, 2006), at 67.

would be to set the hurdle high and say only where P lacks capacity to make most decisions can it be said that he generally lacks capacity and so the section becomes applicable. This issue is particularly relevant in the issue of neglect. Where D believes that although P suffers from incapacity in some areas, but believes that P is able to make decisions about what to eat, is D to be prosecuted if P becomes malnourished? It is suggested that the better interpretation is that P lacks capacity in relation to the issue about which it is alleged there was neglect or ill treatment. So, if the allegation was that D had neglected to ensure P received adequate food, the question would be whether or not P had the capacity to make decisions about how much food he himself ate.

A further ambiguity surrounds the issue of care. How is it to be determined whether or not D had care of P? If D was P's neighbour and looked in on her regularly, would that be sufficient to say that D had care of P? Care is undefined in the Act. A court is likely to look at factors such as: the length of time D has spent looking after P; their relationship; any promises or understandings between them; and the extent of the reliance between them. There is certainly no reason to think it is limited to those who are relations of each other or whether there is a legal obligation to provide services.

The key aspect of the offence is ill-treatment or wilful neglect. These are not well defined. First, there is the question of what mental element is required. In other words, does the offence require that the defendant intends to ill-treat or neglect the victim? One argument is that the use of the word wilful is placed before neglect and so presumably does not apply to ill-treatment. This might suggest that neglect must be intentional or reckless,[310] whereas ill-treatment only requires proof of negligence.[311]

As to what counts as ill-treatment or neglect, it is notable that in *R v Newington* the Court of Appeal interpreted the terms under the previous legislation as 'conduct by the appellant which could properly be described as ill-treatment irrespective of whether this ill-treatment damaged or threatened to damage the health of the victim'.[312] This indicates that even if there is not an identified 'harm', there may be ill-treatment. So, leaving an older person naked in a public place would be ill-treatment, even if a specific harm may be hard to identify. There would be little doubt that inadequate feeding or heating would be covered, again even if no harm could be specified.[313]

Failings of the current criminal law

Despite the existence of these offences, the current criminal law fails adequately to deal with crimes against older people. First, there is no acknowledgement of

---

[310] *R v Newington* (1990) 91 Cr App R 247.

[311] See the discussion in B Payne, 'An Integrated Understanding of Elder Abuse and Neglect' (2002) 30 *Journal of Criminal Justice* 535.

[312] *R v Newington* (1990) 91 Cr App R 247.

[313] M Gunn, 'Case note on R v Newington' (1990) 1 *Journal of Forensic Psychiatry* 360, at 361.

'age hate' crime. Parliament has created a range of racially or religiously aggravated offences.[314] These recognize that where an assault is aggravated by hostility to race or religion, a particular wrong is done. There is no equivalent for an assault motivated by hatred of age abuse.[315] In the Crown Prosecution Service's *Crimes Against Older People—CPS Prosecution Policy*, it is stated:

We understand that racist crime has a link to racism as a prejudicial set of ideas; just as sexual crime or domestic violence has a link to sexism and the application of power and control. Some crimes against the older person have a link to ageism as a prejudicial set of ideas. The CPS acknowledges that ageism may provide the backdrop where crimes against older people are tolerated.[316]

Crimes which are motivated by hostility to age can strike fear into older people in the community. It exacerbates existing ageist attitudes about older people.

Secondly, there is no effective offence where an older person with mental capacity has been left to suffer neglect, unless they die as a result.[317] As we have seen in this chapter and in chapter 2, older people can suffer appalling levels of neglect and suffering. They may have mental capacity and yet be unable to help themselves due to physical disabilities or social circumstances. They need the protection of a general offence of neglect or ill-treatment.

Prosecutions without the victim's consent

A separate issue concerns cases of elder abuse where the victim does not want there to be a prosecution. A similar issue arises in cases of domestic violence and these have generated considerable debate.[318] It is clear that even if the victim does not want there to be a prosecution, the state can still prosecute.[319] The views of the victims will be taken into account, but the prosecution is taken on behalf of the public at large and not the individual victim. Of course, there can be practical difficulties facing prosecutors seeking to bring a case where the victim is reluctant to give evidence, although there can be ways around these, such as relying on written statements of victims or relying on the evidence of others.[320]

At a theoretical level there has been a fierce debate among writers on domestic violence about whether the state should prosecute even if the victim has withdrawn their support for the prosecution.[321] On the one hand, there are those who

---

[314] Crime and Disorder Act 1998, ss 28–32.
[315] CPS, *Crimes Against Older People—CPS Prosecution Policy* (2008), at para 11.
[316] Para 3.2.
[317] CPS, *Crimes Against Older People—CPS Prosecution Policy* (2008), at para 88.
[318] See, eg M Madden Dempsey, *Prosecuting Domestic Violence: A Philosophical Analysis* (Oxford University Press, 2009),
[319] Ibid, para 9.5.
[320] M Madden Dempsey, *Prosecuting Domestic Violence: A Philosophical Analysis* (Oxford University Press, 2009), at ch 9.
[321] See ibid.

seek to emphasize the autonomy of the victim and argue that to prosecute despite the victim's objections is to infringe the autonomy of the victim. On the other hand, there are those who argue that a prosecution is brought by the state, not the victim, and where there has been an incident of domestic violence the state should prosecute in order to show society's opposition to domestic violence.[322] I shall be examining this issue again at the end of the chapter.

Civil law

Older people suffering violence or abuse have access to the civil remedies that are available to anyone else suffering in that way. These include seeking injunctions under the Family Law Act 1996 (FLA) or the Protection from Harassment Act 1997. Under the 1997 Act, damages are available in addition to an injunction. The law on these orders is well set out in books which describe the law on domestic violence and will not be discussed in detail here.[323] However, it is important to appreciate their limitations.

First, the remedies available under the FLA include not only a non-molestation injunction, but also an occupation order which can remove a person from their home. These latter orders are, of course, the better protection from violence. However, the legislation draws a distinction between applicants who are owners of property and those who are not; and also between those who are married to the respondent. An applicant who cannot establish a property interest in the home and is not married or civil partnered to the respondent is unable to apply for an occupation order.

Secondly, the courts have generally been reluctant to make an occupation order, describing it as a 'draconian order' and requiring 'exceptional circumstances' to justify making it.[324] So unless there is clear evidence of violence, a victim of elder abuse is unlikely to succeed in getting an occupation order.

Thirdly, the enforcement of these orders until recently has only been enforceable at the insistence of the 'victim', through an application for contempt. However, since the implementation of section 42A of the FLA, the breach of a non-molestation order will automatically be a criminal offence. In practice, this has the benefit of meaning that the victim does not need to go to the trouble and expense of enforcing the order, or face threats seeking to persuade him or her not to enforce it. The disadvantage is that the victim has no choice to decide to forgive

---

[322] S Choudhry and J Herring, 'Righting Domestic Violence' (2006) 20 *International Journal of Law, Policy and the Family* 95; and M Madden Dempsey, 'Towards a Feminist State: What does "Effective" Prosecution of Domestic Violence Mean?' (2007) 70 *Modern Law Review* 908.

[323] See J Herring, *Family Law* (Pearson, 2007), at ch 6.

[324] *Chalmers v Johns* [1999] 1 FLR 392; and *Re Y (Children) (Occupation Order)* [2000] 2 FCR 470, para 477.

the breach and not seek punishment.[325] It also means that the victim must rely on the police enforcing the order.

These civil remedies seem rarely to be used by victims of elder abuse. There may be several explanations for this. First, some victims of elder abuse may be too frail or even lack the capacity to institute proceedings on their own behalf. Secondly, in cases where the elder abuse is part of ongoing domestic violence, the victim may decide not to seek intervention for all the reasons discussed earlier in this chapter. Thirdly, the difficulty in obtaining the order and proving the facts may be a deterrent.

Civil remedies by public agencies

If a local authority is concerned by a case of suspected elder abuse and wishes to intervene to protect the victim, the most common course of action will be to assist them to leave the abuser by offering them accommodation or other services. However, where they do not want to leave, the local authority will then need to decide whether to apply for a court order to ensure that they are protected from the abuse. For example, an order could be sought requiring a person to be placed in and remain in a particular institution, such as a care home or hospital.[326] The local authority could do this by seeking an order under the Mental Capacity Act 2005[327] if the individual has lost capacity, or the inherent jurisdiction if they have not. It is still unclear whether it is appropriate to use the inherent jurisdiction if the Mental Capacity Act 2005 could be used.[328] Where the Mental Capacity Act 2005 is involved, the court will make the decision based on the best interests of the person, as discussed in chapter 3. The inherent jurisdiction must be used in cases where the individual has capacity and this is due to the absence of an effective statutory regime to protect such people.[329] This is far from being satisfactory because it means there is no formal framework governing the law in this area. Nevertheless, the case law now provides us with some guidance.

First, the jurisdiction can be used where the individual is a 'vulnerable adult'. This certainly includes those who lack capacity, but it is wider than that and includes those who have capacity but are vulnerable for some other reason.[330]

---

[325] Although a criminal prosecution where the victim refuses to participate will be difficult, but not impossible: see M Madden Dempsey, *Prosecuting Domestic Violence: A Philosophical Analysis* (Oxford University Press, 2009), at ch 9.

[326] *Re PS (An Adult)* [2007] EWHC 623 (Fam); and *Norfolk and Norwich Healthcare (NHS) Trust v W* [1996] 2 FLR 613.

[327] ss 47 and 48.

[328] M Dunn, I Clare, and J Holland, 'To Empower or to Protect? Constructing the "Vulnerable Adult" in English Law and Public Policy' (2008) *Legal Studies* 234.

[329] *Re F (Adult: Court's Jurisdiction)* [2000] 2 FLR 512 said there was a lacuna in the statutory provision.

[330] eg *Re S (An Adult)* [2003] EWHC 1909, where the inherent jurisdiction was used for a 33-year-old woman who suffered from a moderate/severe learning disability.

It may be that they have some form of disability; or are particularly pliable and open to being abused by others; or lack the ability to protect themselves from abuse.[331] The vulnerability could come from the individual's medical condition or the situation they find themselves in. The best judicial guidance on the meaning of 'vulnerable adult' is provided by Munby J in *Re SA (Vulnerable Adult with Capacity: Marriage)*:[332]

In the context of the inherent jurisdiction I would treat as a vulnerable adult someone who, whether or not mentally incapacitated, and whether or not suffering from any mental illness, or mental disorder, is or may be unable to take care of him or herself, or unable to protect him or herself against significant harm or exploitation, or who is deaf, blind, or dumb, or who is substantially handicapped by illness, injury or congenital deformity.

Secondly, there is no need to show that there is a risk of significant harm before the court can intervene.[333] There need only be a 'serious justiciable issue' which requires judicial attention.[334] The courts have been willing to make orders authorizing medical procedures,[335] preventing a marriage,[336] determining contact between the vulnerable adult and others,[337] and determining where the person shall live.[338]

Thirdly, the court will make the order which best promotes the welfare of the vulnerable person.[339] It will consider the benefits and disadvantages of the proposed order and make the order which will best promote their welfare. The courts have followed the approach suggested in Thorpe LJ in *Re A (Medical Treatment: Male Sterilisation)*:[340]

Pending the enactment of a checklist or other statutory direction it seems to me that the first instance judge with the responsibility to make an evaluation of the best interests of a claimant lacking capacity should draw up a balance sheet. The first entry should be of any factor or factors of actual benefit... Then on the other sheet the judge should write any counter-balancing disbenefits to the applicant... Then the judge should enter on each sheet the potential gains and losses in each instance making some estimate of the extent of the possibility that the gain or loss might accrue. At the end of that exercise the judge should be better placed to strike a balance between the sum of the certain and possible gains against the sum of the certain and possible losses. Obviously only if the account is in relatively significant credit will the judge conclude that the application is likely to advance the best interests of the claimant.

---

[331] M Dunn, I Clare, and J Holland, 'To Empower or to Protect? Constructing the "Vulnerable Adult" in English Law and Public Policy' (2008) *Legal Studies* 234.

[332] [2006] 1 FLR 867, para 82.

[333] *Re S (An Adult)* [2003] EWHC 1909, para 13.

[334] *Re F (No 2)* [2000] 2 FLR 512, para 210.

[335] *London Borough of Ealing v KS* [2008] EWHC 636 (Fam).

[336] *Re SA (Vulnerable Adult with Capacity: Marriage)* [2006] 1 FLR 867.

[337] *Re MM (An Adult)* [2007] EWHC 2003 (Fam).

[338] Ibid.   [339] *Re S (An Adult)* [2003] EWHC 1909, para 14.

[340] [2000] 1 FLR 549, 560F to H.

The court can consider risks of future harm, as long as these are not fanciful and are a real possibility.[341]

This all might sound straightforward, but there are difficulties.[342] The significance of relying on the best interests approach in this context is that where the court is considering the removal of a vulnerable person from their spouse, partner, or family, there is no need to show (as there is in the case of children) that the individual has suffered or is likely to suffer significant harm. Indeed, the courts have explicitly refused to restrict their use of the inherent jurisdiction by adding in conditions similar to those found in section 31 of the Children Act 1989.[343]

One striking case in this context is *B BC v S*[344] involving a 90-year-old man who lacked capacity and who had been living with his wife for nearly 70 years. The local authority took the view that she was no longer able to care for him and sought to place him in a care home. His wife opposed the move. Charles J upheld the move as being in the best interests of Mr S. He accepted that the orders amounted to a substantial interference in the couple's family life, but rejected an analogy with cases concerning the removal of a newborn child from a mother, where the courts have required there to be 'extraordinarily compelling evidence' before justifying the removal of the child.[345] It was sufficient that it was found to be in his best interests to be removed. While this approach was probably the only one open to the judge given that he was acting under the inherent jurisdiction which is rooted in the best interests principle, it is deeply concerning. That a couple can be separated after nearly 70 years of marriage without even proof of significant harm seems an inadequate safeguard of human rights.

It would not, however, be accurate to say that under the inherent jurisdiction, an unfettered approach to the best interests test should be used. First, it seems that some weight is to be attached to the view of the vulnerable adult. The court acknowledges that vulnerable people, like other competent people, are entitled to make decisions which others might regard as foolish. The problem was well put in *Re MM (An Adult)*[346] by Mumby J:

The fact is that all life involves risk, and the young, the elderly and the vulnerable, are exposed to additional risks and to risks they are less well equipped than others to cope with. But just as wise parents resist the temptation to keep their children metaphorically wrapped up in cotton wool, so too we must avoid the temptation always to put the physical health and safety of the elderly and the vulnerable before everything else. Often it will be appropriate to do so, but not always. Physical health and safety can sometimes be bought at too high a price in happiness and emotional welfare. The emphasis must be on sensible risk appraisal, not striving to avoid all risk, whatever the price, but instead

---

[341] *Re MM (An Adult)* [2007] EWHC 2003 (Fam), para 119.
[342] For an example of an unjustified removal, see *LLBC v TG* [2007] EWHC 2640 (Fam).
[343] *Re S (An Adult)* [2003] EWHC 1909, para 18.
[344] [2006] EWHC 2584 (Fam).
[345] eg *Re M (Care Proceedings: Judicial Review)* [2003] EWHC 850 (Admin).
[346] [2007] EWHC 2003 (Fam), Munby J, para 120.

seeking a proper balance and being willing to tolerate manageable or acceptable risks as the price appropriately to be paid in order to achieve some other good—in particular to achieve the vital good of the elderly or vulnerable person's happiness. What good is it making someone safer if it merely makes them miserable?

As this quote indicates, forcing a vulnerable person out of a potentially abusive situation against their wishes may remove them from abuse, but doing so will create harms of its own. Mumby J went on to say that the vulnerable adult's wishes and feelings were 'one of the most important factors' to be taken into account.[347] What he does not explain is whether the vulnerable adult's wishes are to be taken into account in ascertaining his or her best interests; or whether they operate outside of that assessment so that a judge must decide whether the proposed order is sufficiently beneficial to the individual that it justifies making an order against their wishes.[348] Munby J's comments are especially welcome given that we are dealing with people who, although vulnerable, do have capacity. The law is significantly infringing on the right to autonomy in these cases and it should only do so where there is very strong justification.[349]

The second concern about the focus on best interest is the failure to acknowledge the special bond between a vulnerable adult and their carer. As we have seen, an older person can be separated from their spouse, partner, or family, solely on the basis that the best interests test is satisfied. Such criticism, however, should be tempered by the judicial acknowledgment that where a person is well cared for by another, it is unlikely that local authority care will be more in their best interest.[350] Charles J in *A Local Authority v E,D & A*[351] summarized the current law in this way:

I start...from the position that, while there is no presumption that mentally incapacitated adults will be better off if they live with a family rather than in an institution, however benign and enlightened the institution may be, and however well integrated into the community, it is nonetheless the normal assumption that mentally incapacitated adults who have been looked after within their family will be better off if they continue to be looked after within the family rather than by the state.[352]

Wood J in *London Borough of Ealing v KS*[353] held:

we should not lightly interfere with family life. If the State—typically, as here, in the guise of a local authority—is to say that it is the more appropriate person to look after a mentally incapacitated adult than her own partner or family, it assumes, as it seems to me, the burden—not the legal burden but the practical and evidential burden—of establishing that this is indeed so.

---

[347] Para 121.   [348] See ch 3 for further discussion of this issue.
[349] M Dunn, I Clare, and J Holland, 'To Empower or to Protect? Constructing the "Vulnerable Adult" in English Law and Public Policy' (2008) *Legal Studies* 234.
[350] Although see *Re S (Adult Patient) (Inherent Jurisdiction: Family Life)* [2003] 1 FLR 292, where Munby J noted the importance of the European Convention on Human Rights.
[351] [2007] EWHC 2396 (Fam).   [352] Para 66.   [353] [2008] EWHC 636 (Fam).

Such an approach might also find support with reference to Article 8 of the European Convention on Human Rights, which protects the right to respect for private and family life. Indeed, it might be argued that a mere assumption is an adequate protection of Article 8 requirements. In respect of this, Charles J had this to say, referring to Munby J's judgement in *Re S*:[354]

Munby J also made clear that this position is in no way inconsistent with the rival considerations arising under Article 8 of the ECHR in cases of this kind which require the court to take into account not only the rights of the parents to respect for their family life (paras 18–28), but also the Article 8 rights of the incompetent adult child whose right to respect for her private life includes her rights to develop without outside interference, her personality in her relations with other human beings. In furthering and protecting this right, the court is the adult's surrogate decision maker with the responsibility to take a decision which is in her best interests.

Need for court order

If an older person is to be taken into the care of a local authority, normally a court order is required.[355] In *JE v DE*,[356] a 76-year-old man suffering from dementia was taken into the care of the county council against the wishes of his wife, with whom he had been in a relationship for many years. He now wished to return to his wife. The court determined that the key issue was whether or not his human rights under Article 5 of the European Convention on Human Rights were invaded. Article 5 protects the right not to be deprived of his liberty. If his rights were being infringed, a court order was required to authorize his detention.[357] Munby J approved the summary of the jurisprudence on Article 5 prepared by Mr Bowen, one of the barristers in the case:

77. ...the question whether a person is 'deprived of his liberty' within the meaning of Article 5(1) can be stated in the following propositions:
  (i) There are three elements relevant to the question of whether in the case of an adult there has been a 'deprivation' of liberty engaging the State's obligation under Article 5(1) (different considerations may apply in the case of a child where a parent or other person with parental authority has, in the proper exercise of that authority, authorised the child's placement and thereby given a substituted consent):
    (a) an objective element of a person's confinement in a particular restricted space for a not negligible length of time (*Storck v Germany* (2005) 43 EHRR 96 at para 74);
    (b) a subjective element, namely that the person has not validly consented to the confinement in question (*Storck v Germany* (2005) 43 EHRR 96 at para 74);

---

[354] Para 68.
[355] Ministry of Justice, *Deprivation of Liberty Safeguards* (Ministry of Justice, 2008).
[356] [2006] EWHC 3459 (Fam).
[357] *Re PS (An Adult)* [2007] EWHC 623 (Fam).

(c) the deprivation of liberty must be imputable to the State (*Storck v Germany* (2005) 43 EHRR 96 at para 89).

I need say no more about the third of these three matters for it is common ground that both the X home and the Y home are managed by SCC, a public authority.

(ii) As regards the objective element:

(a) The starting point must be the concrete situation of the individual concerned and account must be taken of a whole range of criteria such as the type, duration, effects and manner of implementation of the measure in question. The distinction between a deprivation of and a restriction upon liberty is merely one of degree or intensity and not one of nature or substance (*Guzzardi v Italy* (1980) 3 EHRR 333 at para 92, *Nielsen v Denmark* (1988) 11 EHRR 175 at para 67, *HM v Switzerland* (2002) 38 EHRR 314 at para 42, *HL v United Kingdom* (2004) 40 EHRR 761 at para 89 and *Storck v Germany* (2005) 43 EHRR 96 at para 42).

(b) In the type of case with which I am here concerned, the key factor is whether the person is, or is not, free to leave (*HL v United Kingdom* (2004) 40 EHRR 761 at para 91). This may be tested by determining whether those treating and managing the person exercise complete and effective control over the person's care and movements (*HL v United Kingdom* (2004) 40 EHRR 761 at para 91).

(c) Whether the person is in a ward which is 'locked' or 'lockable' is relevant but not determinative (*HL v United Kingdom* (2004) 40 EHRR 761 at para 92).

(iii) As regards the subjective element:

(a) A person may give a valid consent to their confinement only if they have capacity to do so (*Storck v Germany* (2005) 43 EHRR 96 at paras 76 and 77).

(b) Where a person has capacity, consent to their confinement may be inferred from the fact that the person does not object (*HL v United Kingdom* (2004) 40 EHRR 761 at para 93 and *Storck v Germany* (2005) 43 EHRR 96 at para 77 explaining *HM v Switzerland* (2002) 38 EHRR 314 at para 46).

(c) No such conclusion may be drawn in the case of a patient lacking capacity to consent (*HL v United Kingdom* (2004) 40 EHRR 761 at para 90).

(d) Express refusal of consent by a person who has capacity will be determinative of this aspect of 'deprivation of liberty' (*Storck v Germany* (2005) 43 EHRR 96 at para 77).

(e) The fact that the person may have given himself up to be taken into detention does not mean that he has consented to his detention, whether he has capacity (*Storck v Germany* (2005) 43 EHRR 96 at para [75]) or not (*HL v United Kingdom* (2004) 40 EHRR 761 at para [90]). The right to liberty is too important in a democratic society for a person to lose the benefit of the Convention protection for the single reason that he may have given himself up to be taken into detention.

Applying this to the case before him, it was held that DE was being deprived of his liberty. Even though he had freedom of movement and to contact those outside the home, Munby J thought the key point was that he was not free to leave the home as he wished.[358] As this indicates, if an older person is willing to move into a care home or is left free to leave whenever he or she wishes, then there is no deprivation of liberty and no need for a court order. If, however, he or she is not effectively free to leave, a court order is required in order to justify the detention.

Changing attitudes and responses to elder abuse

In this section I will outline some the main changes that I believe need to be made to the social and legal responses to elder abuse.

Dependency and care

Elder abuse reflects and is reinforced by wider attitudes in society. Tackling these must be at the heart of tackling elder abuse. But how is this to be done? The government sees independence as being key. The Audit Commission, in its report entitled *Older People—Independence and Well Being*, put it this way:

We need a fundamental shift in the way we think about older people, from dependency and deficit towards independence and well-being. When they are asked, older people are clear about what independence means for them and what factors help them to maintain it. Older people value having choice and control over how they live their lives.[359]

Gerry Fitzgerald argues:

by constructing older people as both dependent and a burden, it is implied that society has developed a feeling that all people over 65 years old need care. And the implication of nurturing such a dependent (and growing) population is that older people are made much more vulnerable through disempowerment, stereotyping and, ultimately, a denial of their basic human rights. Hence, the challenge is to go beyond individual prejudices and recognise that dependency is often enforced, and that we should consequently seek to work in a way which empowers people to take control over their own future and not to 'infantilize them'.[360]

To some, the dependency among older people is itself a result of government policy, societal structures,[361] and the failure to acknowledge older people's full citizenship.[362]

---

[358] *HL v United Kingdom* (2004) 40 EHRR 761.   [359] Para 5.

[360] G Fitzgerald, 'The Realities of Elder Abuse' in A Wahidin and M Cain, *Ageing, Crime and Society* (Willan, 2006), at 94.

[361] P Townsend, 'Policies for the Aged in the 21st Century: More "Structured Dependency" or the Realisation of Human Rights?' (2006) 26 *Ageing & Society* 161.

[362] Action on Elder Abuse, *Placing Elder Abuse within the Context of Citizenship* (Action on Elder Abuse, 2004).

I would argue, however, that the assumption that dependency is something to be combated is misguided.[363] Diane Gibson comments:

The problem, then, is not the problem of dependency per se. It is the problem of how dependency within social policy is constructed, at both the individual and the societal level. At the individual level, it is the lack of alternatives coupled with the discretionary control over whether the assistance is given which renders a particular exchange an undesirable one. At the societal level, it is the labelling of particular groups of people in particular circumstances, most notably those who have neither alternatives to escape the situation nor the political power to do anything about the way in which they are treated which allows the construction and application of the particular social label 'dependent'.[364]

Dependency itself is not undesirable. Dependency is often regarded as causing a loss of freedom and dignity. This is not, and should not, be so. We are all, or virtually all, dependent on others; and others are dependent on us. A recognition of the significance of relationships which are central to all our lives shifts the starting point away from the autonomous individual to a person sited in interdependent relationships. As Susan Dobbs explains:

My emphasis is on the ways in which human vulnerability and dependency have come to be viewed as evidence of a failing to attain or retain autonomous agency, rather than as conditions for agency and autonomy among humans. I argue that the dominant social understandings of what it is to be a citizen, autonomous agent or person contribute to the exploitation and disadvantage of care workers. I argue that a better approach to the social and ethical issues raised by paid care requires a refocusing on inherent human vulnerability. On my view, it is only through this refocusing that the material, emotional and social supports that make selfhood and citizenship possible can be adequately understood...Attention to *vulnerability*, by contrast, changes citizens' ethical relations from those of independent actors carving out realms of right against each other and the state, to those of mutually-dependent and vulnerably-exposed beings whose capacities to develop as subjects are directly and indirectly mediated by the conditions around them.[365]

Once, then, we accept our inherent vulnerability and dependency on others, the image of the all-powerful rights bearer falls away. As Linda Barclay notes:

our ongoing success as an autonomous agent is affected by our ability to share our ideas, our aspirations, and our beliefs in conversation with others. It is unlikely that any vision or aspiration is sustained in isolation from others.[366]

---

[363] J Harbinson and M Morrow, 'Re-examining the Social Construction of "Elder Abuse and Neglect": A Canadian Perspective' (1998) 18 *Ageing and Society* 691.

[364] D Gibson, 'Dependency: The Career of a Concept' in S Graham (ed), *Dependency, Re-examining the Social Construction of Elder Abuse and Neglect* (University of New South Wales, 1995), at 709.

[365] S Dodds, 'Depending on Care: Recognition of Vulnerability and the Social Contribution of Care Provision' (2007) 21 *Bioethics* 500, at 517.

[366] L Barclay, 'Autonomy and the Social Self' in C Mackenzie and N Stoljar (eds), *Relational Autonomy* (Oxford University Press, 2000), at 57.

This is as true for older people as it is for everyone else.

The individualistic model of independence which some of the government publications regarding old age appear to promote is undesirable and unrealistic. Older people who are dependent on others for their care should not be regarded as having failed in achieving a good old age. The problem is that too often older people in need of care are regarded as having nothing to offer. The best way ahead is to emphasize inter-dependence.[367] We need to find and emphasize the ways in which even those who need substantial levels of care can contribute to society and other people. We need to find ways of valuing them and carers generally.[368]

The notion that independence will prevent elder abuse is misguided. Indeed, it is those who are most disconnected from society and from friends who can be most at risk of abuse. Caring relationships need to be valued, acknowledged, and rewarded.[369] That involves making care work part of the wider community's responsibility. If care work was taken more seriously, many of the problems of elder abuse would diminish.

Social context

Any response to elder abuse must be put in the context of the wider social problems facing older people.[370] These include the impact that inadequate housing, and difficulties accessing social activities and transport can have on the quality of life of older people. At the moment, our society often restricts the access of older people to many public spaces. This can be through the practical difficulties of transport, but also by the attitudes of the public generally. Older people are too often excluded from sections of public life.[371] This not only enables elder abuse to take place, but is itself a form of elder abuse.[372] The government's current approach of incorporating responses to elder abuse within protection of vulnerable adults generally means that the wider consequences which play a significant role in elder abuse are overlooked.

Statutory regime for elder abuse

In a speech on 13 March 2006 Liam Byrne, the Parliamentary Under Secretary of State for Care Services, said that he was considering whether it would be appropriate to introduce an adult abuse equivalent of the protection from child

---

[367] S Biggs, 'Failed Individualism in Community Care' (1984) 8 *Journal of Social Work Practice* 137.

[368] I have developed this elsewhere: J Herring, 'Where are the Carers in Healthcare Law and Ethics?' (2007) 27 *Legal Studies* 51.

[369] Ibid.

[370] Action on Elder Abuse, *Placing Elder Abuse within the Context of Citizenship* (Action on Elder Abuse, 2004).

[371] Ibid.

[372] D Schuyler and B Liang, 'Reconceptualizing Elder Abuse: Treating the Disease of Senior Community Exclusion' (2006) 15 *Annals of Health Law* 257.

abuse.[373] Nothing further has been heard about that. However, we desperately need a specific statutory regime to deal with the issue of the abuse of older people, and vulnerable people more generally.[374]

There is a lack of power for local authorities to investigate and act against elder abuse.[375] A stark contrast can be made with the multitude of duties and powers a local authority has to investigate child abuse and then seek court orders to deal with it. There is no duty on local authorities to deal with cases of elder abuse and, as we have seen, although court orders may be available, they often have to be applied for under the inherent jurisdiction, which lacks any clear structure or guidelines.[376] The Law Commission[377] called for a law which put a duty on social services authorities to make enquiries where there is reason to believe a vulnerable adult in their area is suffering or is likely to suffer significant harm; a power to gain access to premises where it is believed a person at risk is living; the power to arrange a medical examination; the power to arrange the removal of the vulnerable person from the home; and the power to apply for temporary and long-term protection orders.[378] Currently none of these is available.

If one were to start to draft legislation along these lines, the obvious analogy is the protection of abused children. The key issue would be setting the threshold at which state intervention to protect an older person is justified. If we were to adapt the regime in Part IV of the Children Act 1989 to apply to older people, we could permit a court to make a care or supervision order in respect of an older person if the court is satisfied that making the order is in their best interests and that:

(a) the older person concerned is suffering or is likely to suffer, significant harm; and
(b) that the harm, or likelihood of harm, is attributable to—
     (i) the care given to the older person, or likely to be given to him or her if the order were not made, not being what it would be reasonable to expect a carer to give to him or her.

This is section 31 of the Children Act modified to cover older people, rather than children.[379] Looking at this proposal, a number of issues would arise.

---

[373] Speech by Liam Byrne MP, 13 March 2006, Action on Elder Abuse Conference.

[374] J Manthorpe, 'Local Responses to Elder Abuse: Building Effective Prevention Strategies' in A Wahidin and M Cain (eds), *Ageing, Crime and Society* (Willan, 2006).

[375] The National Health Service and Community Care Act 1990, s 47 gives a right to be assessed if one is in need and the Mental Health Act 1983, s 135 gives an approved social worker the right to apply to remove to a place of safety a person suffering from a mental disorder. But neither of these offer effective protection in most cases of elder abuse: J Williams, 'State Responsibility and the Abuse of Vulnerable Older People: Is there a Case for a Public Law to Protect Vulnerable Older People from Abuse?' in J Bridgeman, H Keating, and C Lind (eds), *Responsibility, Law and the Family* (Ashgate, 2008).

[376] The Care of Older and Incapacitated People (Human Rights) Bill 2006 which would have given local authorities some powers and duties was defeated in Parliament.

[377] Law Commission, *Report on Mental Incapacity* (HMSO, 1997).

[378] See also, Action on Elder Abuse, *Consultation Paper on the Potential for Adult Protection Legislation in England, Wales and Northern Ireland* (Action on Elder Abuse, 2008).

[379] s 31(2)(b)(ii) which refers to a child being beyond parental control is not relevant.

First, state intervention would only be justified if there was significant harm. Proof of lower levels of harm would be insufficient. Is this appropriate in the case of elder abuse? I suggest so for two reasons. First, we must recall that the provision of residential care for older people is far from satisfactory in many cases and inevitably impacts on rights of self-determination, as we have seen in this chapter.[380] In the absence of significant harm, it is unlikely that removal will be justified. Secondly, it should be recalled that we are dealing with cases where the older person has not chosen to be taken into care. So, there need to be extremely good reasons to justify overriding their wishes, or making up for their lack of consent.

Secondly, section 31 of the Children Act includes a reference to harm the child is suffering being attributable to the care being given to the child. Should any elder abuse statute include a similar provision? It might be argued that in the case of children this reference protects the rights of parents so that if a parent has behaved reasonably they will not have their children taken away.[381] This has no application in relation to elder abuse. However, this may overlook the interests of spouses, partners, and carers whose relationship with the older person will be seriously affected if the older person is removed. It is argued that this provision will also mean that if the real cause of the older person's harm is the lack of social support, rather than the quality of the care, then their removal into care would be unjustified.

Thirdly, and most significantly, section 31 attaches no weight to the wishes of the individual. Their wishes would, however, be relevant in assessing their best interests. However, to some that may be insufficient. Older people's rights to choose how to live their lives should be respected, whether or not they are the victims of elder abuse.[382]

It is suggested that to consider these arguments further we need to consider the issue from a human rights perspective.

The starting point is that to suffer elder abuse is a serious violation of a person's human rights.[383] At its most serious, elder abuse could constitute an infringement of the right to protection from inhuman or degrading treatment under Article 3 of the European Convention on Human Rights. The phrase 'inhuman treatment' in Article 3 includes actual bodily harm or intense physical or mental suffering.[384] 'Degrading treatment' includes conduct which humiliates or debases an individual; or shows a lack of respect for, or diminishes, human dignity. It also includes conduct which arouses feelings of fear, anguish, or inferiority capable of breaking an individual's moral and physical resistance.[385] In considering whether

---

[380] D Wanlass, *Securing Good Care for Older People* (Kings Fund, 2006).

[381] J Herring, 'The Suffering Children of Blameless Parents' (2000) *Law Quarterly Review* 550.

[382] J Pritchard, *The Needs of Older Women* (Joseph Rowntree Foundation, 2000).

[383] S Choudhry and J Herring, 'Righting Domestic Violence' (2006) 20 *International Journal of Law, Policy and the Family* 95.

[384] *Ireland v the United Kingdom*, 2 EHRR 25.

[385] See amongst recent authorities, *Price v the United Kingdom*, App No 33394/96, paras 24–30; and *Valašinas v Lithuania* [2001] ECHR 479.

treatment is 'degrading', the court will have regard to whether its object was to humiliate and debase the victim, and the effect on the victim. Clearly, serious physical assaults will fall into this category, but less serious incidents, especially when occurring over a prolonged period of time, can too. Depression, learned helplessness and alienation, post-traumatic stress disorder, guilt, and denial have been cited as resulting from elder abuse.[386]

Article 3 not only prohibits the state from inflicting torture or inhuman or degrading treatment on its citizens; it also requires the state to protect one citizen from torture or inhuman or degrading treatment at the hands of another.[387] A state will infringe an individual's right under Article 3 if it is aware that he or she is suffering the necessary degree of abuse at the hands of another and fails to take reasonable,[388] adequate,[389] or effective[390] steps to protect that individual.[391] There is a particular obligation on the state to protect the Article 3 rights of vulnerable people, such as children.[392] The obligations imposed on the state include: ensuring that there is an effective legal deterrent to protect victims from abuse; to ensure that there is proper legal investigation and prosecution of any infringement of the individual rights; and where necessary to intervene and remove a victim from a position where he or she is suffering conduct which is prohibited by Article 3. Hence, states have been found to infringe Article 3 when they have been aware that children are being abused, but have not taken steps to protect them;[393] where the law on sexual assault required proof that the victim had physically resisted the sexual assault;[394] and where the police failed to properly investigate or take steps to prosecute men alleged to have committed sexual assaults.[395]

The right under Article 3 is an absolute one. Unlike many of the other rights mentioned in the Convention, there are no circumstances in which it is permissible for the state to infringe this right. This makes it clear that the rights of another party cannot justify an infringement of someone's Article 3 rights. So, for example, it cannot be successfully argued that a family's right of privacy justifies non-intervention by the state if that non-intervention is an infringement of one family member's Article 3 rights. Indeed, and perhaps more controversially, it is suggested that other rights of the victim cannot justify an infringement of Article 3. In other words, in an elder abuse case the state cannot justify its failure to protect a victim's Article 3 rights by referring to that person's right to respect for private life.[396] It should, however, be emphasized that although Article 3 is drafted in

---

[386] R Wolf, 'Elder Abuse and Neglect: Causes and Consequences' (1997) 31 *Journal of Geriatric Psychiatry* 153.

[387] *A v UK* [1998] 3 FCR 597; *E v UK* [2002] 3 FCR 700.

[388] *Z v UK* [2001] 2 FCR 246.   [389] *A v UK* [1998] 3 FCR 597, para 24.

[390] *Z v UK* [2001] 2 FCR 246, para 73.   [391] *E v UK* [2002] 3 FCR 700.

[392] *A v UK* [1998] 3 FCR 597, para 20.   [393] *E v UK* [2002] 3 FCR 700.

[394] *MC v Bulgaria* (2005) 40 EHRR 20.   [395] Ibid.

[396] Although the state may argue that the victim's views make it unreasonable for the state to intervene.

absolute terms, the state's obligations towards its citizens in respect of Article 3 are only to take *reasonable* measures to protect an individual's Article 3 rights.[397]

Article 8 of the Convention states that:

1. Everyone has the right to respect for his private and family life, his home and his correspondence.
2. There shall be no interference by a public authority with the exercise of this right except such as in accordance with the law and is necessary in a democratic society in the interests of national security, public safety or the economic well being of the country, for the prevention of disorder or crime, for the protection of health or morals, or for the protection of the rights and freedoms of others.

Included within the right to respect for private life is the right to bodily integrity and this includes 'psychological integrity' and 'a right to personal development, and the right to establish and develop relationships with other human beings and the outside world'. Like Article 3, Article 8 has been interpreted to mean that not only must the state not infringe someone's bodily or psychological integrity, but it must ensure that one person's integrity is not interfered with at the hands of another. In other words, it is not just a 'negative right' inhibiting state intrusion into citizens' private lives, it places 'positive obligations' on the state to intervene to protect individuals.[398] However, unlike Article 3, this is a qualified right. It is permissible for the state to fail to respect an individual's right to respect for private life under Article 8(1) if paragraph 2 is satisfied. So, if the level of abuse is not sufficient to engage Article 3, but falls within Article 8, it is necessary to balance the Article 8 rights and interests of other parties. It would therefore be possible to make an argument that the rights of the abuser, or perhaps even the victim, justify the state in not intervening in an Article 8 case.

So, how can these competing rights be balanced? Rachel Taylor and I[399] have suggested that in a case of clashing rights the court should look at the values underpinning the right.[400] In the case of Article 8, the underlying value is that of autonomy: the right to pursue your vision of the 'good life'. A judge could then consider the extent to which the proposed order would constitute a blight on each of the party's opportunities to live the good life and make the order which causes the least blight. Applying that in this context, although removing the victim of elder abuse from an abusive spouse will infringe the spouse's autonomy, it will do so to a much lesser extent than leaving the victim to suffer abuse would do. But what if the victim does not want the assistance?

---

[397] *E v UK* [2002] 3 FCR 700.

[398] S Choudhry and J Herring, 'Domestic Violence and the Human Rights Act 1998: A New Means of Legal Intervention' [2007] *Public Law* 752.

[399] J Herring and R Taylor, 'Relocating Relocation' (2006) 18 *Child and Family Law Quarterly* 517.

[400] This seeks to develop a dicta of Lord in *Re S (A Child) (Identification: Restrictions on Publication)* [2005] 1 AC 593, para 17, which refers to the need to consider the values underlying the right when considering cases of clashing rights.

Here, there is a balance between protecting the current autonomous wish of the victim with the increase in autonomy they may experience if they were removed from the abuse. Many victims in these cases have conflicting wishes. They want to remain in the relationship, but they want the abuse to stop. In such a case it is not easy to determine what is promoting their autonomy. It is not possible to respect these two conflicting desires. I suggest that where the abuse is at a low level, the infringement on autonomy in remaining in the relationship will be limited. John Williams[401] discusses a hypothetical case of a son stealing £10 from his mother now and then. Here, autonomy is only infringed a little by the abuse. If, however, the relationship consisted of persistent emotional abuse, the interference in her autonomy in removing her from the relationship may be less than allowing her to remain in it.

So, where does this analysis get us? First, in cases of abuse which reach the level of Article 3, there is an obligation on the state to protect victims and ensure there are legal remedies available. This means that there needs to be an effective set of criminal offences and civil remedies available. Further, the state has a duty to take reasonable steps to protect people from this abuse. This requires a public law of protection from elder abuse of the kind we have in relation to child abuse, as discussed above.

Secondly, where the abuse is at a lower level, a set of remedies still needs to be available. Both the criminal and civil law need to provide remedies. However, where the older person does not want intervention, his or her rights of autonomy come into play. As just discussed, this can involve a delicate balancing exercise between protecting autonomy rights which are interfered with by the abuse and protecting his or her decision to remain in the relationship.

Commissioner for older people

Wales has a Commissioner for Older People.[402] Revealingly, England does not. Professor Ian Phelp is currently the National Director for Older People within the Department of Health and has colloquially become known as the Older People's Tsar. The benefit of having a commissioner would be that he or she would ensure that older people's interests were given effective recognition in the media and in government policy-making. Further, the commissioner would be able to develop an overview of the issues affecting older people and demonstrate how different forms of disadvantage compound each other. Finally, it would provide a way of investigations being undertaken in areas where it is feared older people are abused, but which have not been proved.

---

[401] J Williams, 'State Responsibility and the Abuse of Vulnerable Older People: Is there a Case for a Public Law to Protect Vulnerable Older People from Abuse' in J Bridgeman, H Keating, and C Lind (eds), *Responsibility, Law and the Family* (Ashgate, 2008).
[402] Commissioner for Older People (Wales) Act 2006.

Mandatory reporting

It is clear that there is a strong incentive not to report suspected abuse. One survey found that 60 per cent of nurses feared reporting cases of elder abuse in case they had misinterpreted what they had seen.[403] A further 26 per cent said that fear of retaliation would prevent them from reporting abuse.[404] Of course, many residents in care homes lack the capacity to make complaints themselves or are frightened of the repercussions if they do. The government is undertaking consultation to see if complaints procedures can be improved.[405]

In part of the United States, there are obligations to report cases of elder abuse.[406] In the UK, there are provisions requiring the reporting by professionals of child abuse, but there is no equivalent for elder abuse.[407] Given the human rights obligations on the state to ensure protection of people from serious cases of abuse, it is argued that imposing a mandatory reporting obligation would be desirable.

Conclusion

This chapter has discussed the complex issue of elder abuse. We have seen that while the government has now acknowledged that elder abuse is a genuine social problem, we are still a long way from tackling it in an effective and coherent way. It has been shown that elder abuse reflects ageist attitudes about older people that are prevalent in our society. A vivid example of this is that in 2006 the British Geriatric Society[408] started a campaign to keep doors of toilets closed if residents of care homes were in them. It speaks volumes about the way in which the day-to-day treatment of older people often fails to respect their humanity, that a basic element of dignity is ignored to such an extent that a leading voluntary organization sees the need to mount a campaign about it. A CSCI inspection into dementia care[409] found an astonishing 18 per cent of care homes failing to meet the *minimum* standards required to protect the privacy and dignity of older people.

We have seen too how elder abuse occurs at concerning levels in older people's own homes. In many cases, these are relationships which have been characterized

---

[403] BBC News Online, 'Nurses Fear Elder Abuse Errors', 29 August 2007.

[404] K Taylor and K Dodd, 'Knowledge and Attitudes of Staff Towards Adult Protection' (2005) 3 *Journal of Adult Protection* 26.

[405] Department of Health, *Making Experiences Count* (DoH, 2008).

[406] M Velick, 'Mandatory Reporting Statutes: A Necessary Yet Underutilized Response to Elder Abuse' (1995) 3 *Elder Law Journal* 165.

[407] Contrast the position in the US: M Rodriguez, S Wallace, N Woolf, and C Mangione, 'Mandatory Reporting of Elder Abuse: Between a Rock and a Hard Place' (2006) 4 *Annals of Family Medicine* 403.

[408] British Geriatric Society, *Dignity Behind Closed Doors* (British Geriatric Society, 2006).

[409] CSCI, *See Me, Not Just the Dementia* (CSCI, 2008).

by domestic violence for a long period of time. The current lack of an effective legal response has been criticized. I have argued for the creation of a new statute placing duties on local authorities to take steps to protect older people who are suffering significant harm. This is not just desirable, but is required by the state's obligations under the Human Rights Act 1998.

However, throughout this chapter it has been emphasized that the problems of elder abuse reflect the wider social response to older people. Their social exclusion and marginalization in our society, reinforced by private and public expressions of ageism, combine to reinforce and enable elder abuse to take place. Consider this finding of one survey: looking at older people in a care home, it found during the length of the study that 42 per cent of residents observed spent no time at all in contact with others living in the home.[410] This revelation of the utter loneliness and isolation that those older people suffered is a reflection of their position more widely in our society. Until older people are given the respect they deserve, recognized as equal citizens, and encouraged to be full members of society, abuse will continue.

---

[410] They were observed at times of the day when a higher level of interaction might be expected.

6

Older People and Financial Issues

Introduction

The country is facing a 'demographic time bomb'. At least that is a view popularly presented in the media.[1] A BBC programme in 2004 entitled 'If...the generations fell out'[2] captured some of the fears, with a portrayal of a future where the greater numbers of wealthy older people were making ever-growing demands on the smaller number of young people in work, leading to an 80 per cent increase in tax. In their imagined future, the generations regarded themselves as at war with one another, leading to violent protests. Such fears do not just lie in fiction: one commentator has declared, 'We are not going to keep quiet when a band of pampered pensioners steal the future from us'.[3] Such views tend, however, to be very much minority ones. Indeed, as we shall see shortly, even whether there is a 'demographic time bomb' is very much a matter for debate.

This chapter will consider the economic position of older people and the legal issues raised. There are several themes that emerge. One is the poverty that many older people in our society face. This inevitably leads to a discussion about what is the best way of providing for older people's economic needs. This raises some complex issues about the balance between relying on state and private funds in old age. A linked theme relates to the issues surrounding the payment of care services for older people. These issues are of great importance not only for older people, but also for society at large.

The 'demographic time bomb'

It is commonly stated that an ageing population poses a threat to the economic stability of a country, hence the talk of an 'ageing crisis'. The Center for Strategic

---

[1] F Castles, 'Population Ageing and the Public Purse' (2000) 35 *Australian Journal of Social Issues* 301.

[2] <http://news.bbc.co.uk/1/hi/programmes/if/3489560.stm>

[3] Chet Tremmel, quoted in <http://news.bbc.co.uk/1/hi/programmes/if/3489560.stm>.

and International Studies has produced a report entitled *The Global Retirement Crisis*[4] and the World Bank has published documents on 'the Old Age Crisis'.[5] It is easy to understand the cause of the concern. With an increasing number of people over the age of 65 and a decreasing number of those under that age, the fear is that there will be fewer employed people paying taxes, combined with an increase in the costs required to support older people. The sense of crisis is deepened when attention is drawn to the decreasing rates of fertility.[6] Some have put these arguments in terms of 'generational fairness': we need to ensure that each generation is treated fairly.[7] Hence, it could be claimed that providing older people with a reasonable standard of living will cost so much that the burden on younger people will be unfair.

Such a presentation of the danger makes a number of assumptions. First, it is assumed that an increased number of older people means an increase in health and other costs. As seen in chapter 8, whether increased age necessarily leads to increased health costs is much debated. While there may be increased social care costs, currently a significant portion of these are paid for by individuals themselves.

Secondly, there is an assumption that those over the age of 65 will not be financially productive. There are certainly signs that people are willing and wanting to work beyond the age of 65 and this will greatly mitigate the impact of the demographic change. Indeed, the current generation of older people are much wealthier than older cohorts in the past and so it will not follow that they will be an equal burden on the public purse.[8] A third point to make is that having an increased number of older people is not a recent phenomenon. Across the Western world in the 20th century there have been increases in the proportion of older people.[9] These have not produced clear adverse economic effects. Fourthly, reduced fertility rates are used by some to indicate a reduction in the number of taxpayers, but in fact they also show that having a large number of older people is only a short-term problem, if a problem at all. They also mean there are lower costs for the state in providing services for younger people, such as education.[10] Finally, even if the ageing population does lead to increased costs in society, the figures involved, in the grand scheme of national economics, is not large. James Schulz argues that a relatively small change in economic growth rate will

---

[4] Center for Strategic and International Studies, *The Global Retirement Crisis* (CSIS, 1996).

[5] World Bank, *Averting the Old Age Crisis* (Oxford University Press, 1994).

[6] E Schokkaert and P Van Parijs, 'Debate on Social Justice and Pension Reform: Social Justice and the Reform of Europe's Pension Systems' (2003) 13 *Journal of European Social Policy* 245.

[7] L Kotlikoff, *Intergenerational Transfer and Savings* (NBER, 1989).

[8] P Heller, *Who Will Pay? Coping with Ageing Societies, Climate Change and Other Long-Term Fiscal Challenges* (International Monetary Fund, 2003).

[9] F Castles, 'Population Ageing and the Public Purse' (2000) 35 *Australian Journal of Social Issues* 301–15.

[10] J Schulz and R Binstock, *The Economics of Ageing* (Auburn House, 2000), at 35.

substantially moderate the effects of increasing ageing.[11] And there is no reason to believe that our economy will not generally grow.

These points do not demonstrate that there is no economic cause for concern in the light of the changing age demographic. However, they do warn against an exaggeration of the economic effect that the greater number of older people will have. Certainly, talks of a crisis due to ageing seems to be exaggerated.

Poverty in old age

In 2002, Gordon Brown promised to end pensioner poverty.[12] He was setting himself an impossible task, but in doing so acknowledged that many older people do suffer severe financial disadvantage. The wealth divide in England has been increasing in recent years and this is particularly true of those in old age. While some are able to retire with generous pensions and enjoy a retirement of affluence, others struggle below the poverty line. Ascertaining the extent of poverty among older people is no easy task.[13] First, there is perennial difficulty in defining poverty.[14] Secondly, there is the difficulty in finding out what assets and income older people have. Finally, there is substantial evidence that older people spend less of their income and assets than younger people, so their paper wealth may not match the economic situation they are living with. Although the focus in this chapter will be on economic well-being, it should not be forgotten that poverty is linked with health and social problems.[15]

The government claims that the number of those over the state pension age who have a low income[16] has fallen by one-fifth in relative terms between 1996/1997 and 2003/2004, with 1.9 million people being lifted out of poverty.[17] However, the most recent figures have shown a slight increase in the number of poor pensioners. In 2006 to 2007, the number of pensioners below the poverty line was 2.5 million, an increase of 300,000 from the previous year's figures.[18] Age Concern claims that 17 per cent of all pensioners live in povety, but that poverty

---

[11] J Schulz, *Aging Nation: The Economics and Politics of Growing Older in America* (Praeger, 2006).
[12] A Shephard, *Pensioner Poverty Under the Labour Government* (Institute for Fiscal Studies, 2003).
[13] D Price, 'The Poverty Of Older People in The UK' (2006) 20 *Journal of Social Work Practice* 251.
[14] eg T Callan and B Nolan, 'Concepts of Poverty and the Poverty Line' (1991) 5 *Journal of Economic Surveys* 243.
[15] E Bardasi and S Jenkins, *Income in Later Life: Work History Matters* (Joseph Rowntree Foundation, 2002).
[16] Defined as households with an income below 60 per cent of the median household income.
[17] DWP, *Opportunity Age* (DWP, 2005). For further discussion of the statistics, see V Burholt and G Windle, *The Material Resources and Well-Being of Older People* (Joseph Rowntree Foundation, 2006).
[18] K Hopkins, 'Thousands Fall Prey to Surge in Cost of Living', *The Guardian*, 11 June 2008.

does not lie equally on gender[19] or race[20] lines. In 2004, the average wealth of those aged 80 and over was only a third of the average wealth of those aged 60 to 64.[21] Two-thirds of the poverty-stricken pensioners are women[22] and 42 per cent of pensioners from the Pakistani/Bangladeshi communities live in poverty. It has been estimated that one in ten older women are very poor, living on less than half the median household income.[23] Significantly fewer older women than men receive a private pension (35 per cent, compared with 67 per cent in one study[24]) or an occupational pension (57 per cent, compared with 71 per cent in another[25]). There is a particular problem with poverty among divorced women,[26] caused by the failure to ensure that divorce settlements provide adequately for women on retirement.[27] Not only are there an increasing number of pensioners below the poverty line, but the gap between the income of pensioners and employees has widened. One cause of this is the linking of pensions with the increase in some prices, rather than wages. The government has promised to link the pension back to earnings, but that will not take place in the near future.[28]

In 2007, 2.7 million pensioners were receiving pension credit, which is available to those pensioners on low income.[29] However, it has been claimed that a third of those entitled to it had not claimed it[30] and so the total number of pensioners on or below the minimum income acceptable under the benefits system may be closer to 4 million. A Joseph Rowntree study found that:

> The risk of poverty among older people in the UK is about three to four times higher than the typical risk of poverty in Europe. People aged 75 and over rely more on benefits as a source of income and get a smaller proportion of their income from occupational pensions and investments than younger pensioners.[31]

A more rosy picture of pensioner finances can be found in another Joseph Rowntree study which attempted to ascertain the 'minimum income standard'

---

[19] V Burholt and G Windle, *The Material Resources and Well-Being of Older People* (Joseph Rowntree Foundation, 2006).
[20] L Platt, *Poverty and Ethnicity in the UK* (Joseph Rowntree Foundation, 2007).
[21] Yet older people are likely to be in much greater need: The Equalities Review, *Fairness and Freedom—The Final Report of the Equalities Review* (The Stationery Office, 2007).
[22] Age Concern, *The Age Agenda* (Age Concern, 2008).
[23] D Price, 'The Poverty of Older People in The UK' (2006) 20 *Journal of Social Work Practice* 251.
[24] J Ginn, D Street, and S Arber, *Women, Work and Pensions: International Issues and Prospects* (Open University Press, 2001).
[25] E Bardasi and S Jenkins, *Income in Later Life: Work History Matters* (Joseph Rowntree Foundation, 2002).
[26] Ibid.
[27] The increased number of divorces is linked to poverty and old age: V Burholt and G Windle, *The Material Resources and Well-Being of Older People* (Joseph Rowntree Foundation, 2006); and J Ginn and D Price, 'Do Divorced Women Catch Up in Pension Building?' (2002) 14 *Child and Family Law Quarterly* 157.
[28] Help the Aged, *Defeating Pensioner Poverty* (Help the Aged, 2007).
[29] Age Concern, *The Age Agenda* (Age Concern, 2008).   [30] Ibid.
[31] V Burholt and G Windle, *The Material Resources and Well-Being of Older People* (Joseph Rowntree Foundation, 2006), at 1.

for pensioners.[32] This was based on interviews of the population to determine what was regarded as an essential minimal standard of living. The minimum income standard for a pensioner couple was £201.49. This is £30 lower than the minimum income guarantee/pension credit, suggesting that pensioners receiving this benefit are not in poverty. However, the report noted that the actual expenditure of pensioners was notably lower than the minimum income standard, suggesting that pensioners do go without some essential items.

As this last point indicates, one notable feature of pensioner finances is their reluctance to spend their income. The Department of Work and Pensions commissioned a report to seek to understand why some pensioners spend substantially less of their income than others.[33] As the report put it, some pensioners are 'expenditure poor' rather than 'income poor'. Those households spending less were likely to be headed by a woman and be older. The report suggested that one explanation was that older people were wanting to save money to ensure a degree of financial security.

Benefit payments for older people

A wide variety of state benefits are available to older people. The main benefits available are outlined briefly below.

Basic state pension

This is flat-rate pension which is paid depending on the number of years of contribution through national insurance contributions. The government may top up contributions to a person's national insurance record if a person has been out of work, suffered a long-term illness or been caring for someone.[34] It has been estimated that 37 per cent of UK pensioners receive mean state pensions and that this will rise to 65 per cent by 2050.[35] From April 2008, the basic state pension is £90.70 a week for a single pensioner and £145.05 for a couple. Entitlement to the pension depends on a combination of years' earnings above a certain level and years with credits for caring or other activities. As a result, among retired men 95 per cent are entitled to the full amount, but only 70 per cent of women.[36]

---

[32] J Bradshaw, S Middleton, A Davis, N Oldfield, N Smith, L Cusworth, and J Williams, *A Minimum Income Standard for Britain: What People Think* (Joseph Rowntree Foundation, 2008). See also, R Berthoud, M Blekesaune, and R Hancock, *Are 'Poor' Pensioners 'Deprived'?* (DWP, 2006).
[33] N Finch and P Kemp, *Which Pensioners Don't Spend Their Income and Why?* (DWP, 2006).
[34] These are known as National Insurance Credits.
[35] P Booth and D Cooper, *The Way Out of the Pensions Quagmire* (Institute of Economic Affairs, 2005).
[36] Ibid.

State second pension or state earnings-related pension scheme (SERPS)

This is a state pension which is paid in addition to the basic state pension. The amount paid depends on the person's earnings and national insurance record. A person who has no record of paid employment and so has not paid national insurance payments will not normally receive this benefit.

Pension credit and guarantee credit

The aim of these credits, which is part of the Minimum Income Guarantee Scheme, is to ensure that a person's income does not fall below a certain level, currently around 25 per cent of median earnings. Extra amounts of pension credit are available to a person who is a carer or is severely disabled. Around 2.7 million households receive pension credit.[37] In 2008, a person could get a credit if their weekly income was less than £124.05 for a single person or £189.35 for a couple. There are reduced levels of benefit for those whose income is just above the minimum sums, to ensure that the credits do not provide a disincentive to save.

Other benefits, discounted charges, and concessions

Other important benefits that can be obtained include housing benefit and council tax benefit. There is a free television licence for those over 75; health service prescriptions are free or at a reduced cost; and free passports are available for those over 78. Many organizations offer a discount for 'seniors'. These include, for example, senior railcards and bus passes offering concessionary travel.

Benefits and funds for special needs

Money or concessions are available for times of particular need. For example, the Independent Living Fund offers money to help people remain in their homes, rather than moving into residential care. Cold winter payments are available for those on low income for extra heating costs during cold weather. Winter fuel payments ensure that most households with people aged 60 or over will receive a lump sum for heating each winter. Over 11 million people receive it.[38] It is worth £200, but this increases to £300 for people aged 80 or over. Despite the help it provides, Age Concern has estimated that 2.25 million older households are living in fuel poverty.[39]

---

[37] Department of Work and Pensions, *Opportunity for All* (DWP, 2007).
[38] Ibid.   [39] Ibid.

Assistance with care

Attendance allowance can provide funds to pay for help with daily living care, such as help getting dressed or washed. Disability living allowance may also be available, which can include money for personal care or help with mobility.

Rather than discussing the details of these benefits, this chapter will focus on the broader issues raised.

Means-testing benefits

A central plank of the Labour Government's approach to tackling poverty in old age (and indeed poverty generally) has been through means-tested benefits. These provide benefits only to those who are assessed as being in particular need. By contrast, non-means tested benefits are paid to all those in a particular category. For example, child benefit is paid to all parents with children, whether they are millionaires or in the greatest of need. The means-tested benefits system normally requires an applicant to complete a lengthy form disclosing their savings and income. Depending on what these are, the amount of benefit (if any) will be assessed. Supporters of means-tested benefits claim that they enable payments to be targeted to those who are most in need. However, studies comparing the use of means-tested benefits across European countries have concluded that the effectiveness of means-tested benefits as a way of alleviating poverty is highly variable.[40] It should not be thought that means-tested benefits are only relevant to a few pensioners.[41] It is thought that up to 50 per cent of pensioners are entitled to the pensions credit.[42]

The disadvantages of means-tested benefits are that they are more costly to run and require complex paperwork to be completed by claimants, which can deter potential applicants.[43] The deterrent factor will be discussed shortly. A common complaint of the current system is that a large number of forms need to be completed if someone is to receive the range of benefits to which they are entitled.[44] Another complaint about means-tested benefits is that they discourage savings and encourage early retirement.[45] There is no point in saving if your savings are

---

[40] C Behrendt, 'Do Means-Tested Benefits Alleviate Poverty?: Evidence on Germany, Sweden and the United Kingdom from the Luxembourg Income Study' (2000) 10 *European Social Policy* 23; and C Mood, 'Take-Up Down Under: Hits and Misses of Means-Tested Benefits in Australia' (2006) 22 *European Sociological Review* 443.

[41] R Hancock, S Pudney, H Sutherland, G Barker, and M Hernandez, *What Should be the Role of Means-Testing in State Pensions?* (Nuffield Foundation, 2005).   [42] Ibid.

[43] O Juurikkala, 'Punishing the Poor: A Critique of Means-Tested Retirement Benefits' (2008) 28 *Economic Affairs* 11.

[44] R Hancock, S Pudney, H Sutherland, G Barker, and M Hernandez, *What Should be the Role of Means-Testing in State Pensions?* (Nuffield Foundation, 2005).

[45] O Juurikkala, 'Punishing the Poor: A Critique of Means-Tested Retirement Benefits' (2008) 28 *Economic Affairs* 11. Although for a challenge to this argument, see C Emmerson, *Taxes, Benefits and Retirement Incentives* (PPI, 2005).

going to cause you to lose an entitlement to benefits. The claim is made that a person who has saved all their life will be restricted access to benefits and will, a few years into their retirement, be in a similar financial position to a person who has made no savings during their life, but who has been able to claim benefits. Indeed, the Turner Commission recommended not using means-tested pensions, precisely because they feared they would discourage private pensions saving.[46]

Low take-up rates

A major concern about the provision of benefits to older people is that their take up is low.[47] For 2006/07, between 33 and 41 per cent of people did not claim the pension credits to which they were entitled. Between 24 and 31 per cent of the amount of money to which pensioners would have been entitled was not claimed.[48] Forty per cent of those entitled to council tax benefit had not claimed it.[49] A major study on the failure of take up of benefits by British pensioners in 2003 found 36 per cent of pensioners not taking up their benefits, although only 16 per cent were failing to do so where the benefits were worth more than 10 per cent of their income.[50] This lends some support to the claim that a significant number of those not claiming are not doing so because the sums of money they would gain would be very modest. Still, in 2005/06, between £1.6 and £2.5 billion of pension credit was unclaimed.[51] A programme introduced by Surrey County Council to encourage and assist older people taking up the benefits to which they are entitled led to £1.5 million of benefits being claimed.[52] This indicates that it is not simply the modesty of sums involved which discourages people from claiming.

The explanation for the low take-up of benefits is complex. Despite government campaigns to improve knowledge of the benefits available and offering assistance in applying for them, there has been no significant increase in their take-up rates.[53] For some, the complexity of the forms and having to deal with the bur-

---

[46] Pensions Commission, *A New Pensions Settlement for the Twenty-First Century* (Stationery Office, 2005) at 164.

[47] P Dornan, *Delivering Benefits in Old Age* (Ashgate, 2006); V Burholt and G Windle, *The Material Resources and Well-Being of Older People* (Joseph Rowntree Foundation, 2006); and D Price, 'The Poverty of Older People in The UK' (2006) 20 *Journal of Social Work Practice* 251.

[48] Department of Work and Pensions, *Income Related Benefits: Estimates of Take-Up in 2006–07* (DWP, 2008).

[49] Age Concern, *The Age Agenda* (Age Concern, 2008).

[50] R Hancock, S Pudney, G Barker, M Hernandez, and H Sutherland, *The Take-Up Of Multiple Means-Tested Benefits by British Pensioners* (University of Leicester, 2003).

[51] P Wintour, 'Ministers Trying to Save Cash on Benefits Take-Up, says Byers', *The Guardian*, 24 March 2008.

[52] There are some government initiatives to assist older people navigate the system: Department of Work and Pensions, *Helping Older People Engage with Benefits and Services: An Evaluation of the Partnership Fund* (DWP, 2008).

[53] D Price, 'The Poverty of Older People in The UK' (2006) 20 *Journal of Social Work Practice* 251; Department of Work and Pensions, *Departmental Report* (DWP, 2008), at para 87, accepts that the campaigns to increase the level of claims have largely failed.

eaucracy is off-putting. One survey found a particularly low take-up of benefits among those caring for terminally ill patients. In their case, it was suggested that the emotional and physical stresses of caring simply do not leave sufficient energy to find out what benefits may be available and complete the necessary forms.[54] For other potential applicants, the forms are seen as too difficult or inconvenient to complete,[55] or there may be a reluctance to disclose 'private information'. Further, there may be a fear that if the form is incorrectly completed, a fraud will be made unintentionally,[56] or a more vague concern that it will create some problem with 'the authorities'.[57]

Perhaps the most common explanation for the low take-up of means-tested benefits is the stigma attached to them.[58] Applying for a benefit suggests one is in special need and going 'cap in hand' to the authorities, rather than a benefit being seen as an earned entitlement.[59] To some, claiming a benefit is seen as an admission that one is not coping.[60] The application for benefits can affect a person's sense of identity. It seems that some people just do not regard themselves as the kind of people who apply for benefits.[61] This is especially so if they have not had to rely on benefits during their working life.

It has even been suggested that means-tested benefits are deliberately designed by the government to discourage the take up of benefits and thereby save money. One MP making such a claim suggests that it enables the government to save up to £9 billion per annum.[62] Others argue that this is not necessarily inappropriate. If people do not claim benefit, this indicates there is not a real need and the money can be better used elsewhere. Some economists argue that non-claimants simply decide that non-payment is preferable to the costs of applying.[63] The

---

[54] B Hanratty, A Jacoby, and M Whitehead, 'Socioeconomic Differences in Service Use, Payment and Receipt of Illness-Related Benefits in the Last Year of Life: Findings from the British Household Panel' (2008) 22 *Palliative Medicine* 248.

[55] An example of the complexity of the system is that what counts as asset qualification can vary from benefit to benefit: P Booth and D Cooper, *The Way Out of the Pensions Quagmire* (IEA, 2005).

[56] S Pudney, R Hancock, and H Sutherland, 'Simulating the Reform of Means-Tested Benefits with Endogenous Take-Up and Claim Costs' (2006) 68 *Oxford Bulletin of Economics* 135.

[57] J Stuber and M Schlesinger, 'Sources of Stigma for Means-Tested Government Programs' (2006) 63 *Social Science and Medicine* 933.

[58] C Mood, 'Take-Up Down Under: Hits and Misses of Means-Tested Benefits in Australia' (2006) 22 *European Sociological Review* 443.

[59] D Price, 'The Poverty of Older People in the UK' (2006) 20 *Journal of Social Work Practice* 251.

[60] Ibid.

[61] J Stuber and M Schlesinger, 'Sources of Stigma for Means-Tested Government Programs' (2006) 63 *Social Science and Medicine* 933.

[62] P Wintour, 'Ministers Trying to Save Cash on Benefits Take-Up, says Byers', *The Guardian*, 24 March 2008.

[63] Some have estimated that for most income support claimants the costs of application can be valued at around £3 to £4 per week: M Hernandez, S Pudney, and R Hancock, 'The Welfare Cost of Means-Testing: Pensioner Participation in Income Support' (2007) 22 *Journal of Applied Econometrics* 581.

stigma against applying for benefits is to be welcomed, as it reflects an attitude that individuals should be self-sufficient.[64] Further, we wish to encourage people to save to provide for their own retirement and if means-tested benefits act an incentive to do this, they should be welcomed. Despite these points, it is clear that there are those living below acceptable economic standards who do not receive the help they need and part of the blame for this lies with the problems associated with means-tested benefits. It is submitted that the rates of non-take up are sufficiently high to mean the current system is not adequately protecting vulnerable pensioners.

Pensions

For the majority of older people who are no longer employed, pensions provide their primary source of income. These may be pensions provided by the state or by an employer or other organization. There has been much talk in recent years of a 'pensions crisis' and many agree that the current system of pension provision is inadequate.[65] Currently, 18 million people of working age are contributing to a private pension, but it has been claimed that more than 12 million are failing to save enough.[66] One report has suggested that the costs of a retirment for a typical househould is £413,000, which includes housing, clothing, and recreation costs.[67] One international survey of views of the general public on retirement found general support for the view that governments *should* support people in their retirement, but three-quarters of all those surveyed doubted that their government would.[68] The UK government, as we shall see, has undertaken a major review of pension provision. The issue is of huge significance. The decisions taken today about pensions policy will have enormous ramifications for future generations. However, the economic consequences of pension decisions are notoriously difficult to predict.[69] While the economics tend to dominate the debate, it should not be forgotten that the form of pension provision will reflect national values and culture.[70]

---

[64] R Hancock, S Pudney, H Sutherland, G Barker, and M Hernandez, *What Should be the Role of Means-Testing in State Pensions?* (Nuffield Foundation, 2005).

[65] This is an issue troubling many western governments: S Kay and T Sinha (eds), *Lessons from Pension Reform in the Americas* (Oxford University Press, 2008).

[66] There appear to be particular issues among members of ethnic minorities: Department of Work and Pensions, *Work, Saving and Retirement among Ethnic Minorities: A Qualitative Study* (DWP, 2006).

[67] H Osborne, 'Cost of Retirement "Hits £413,000"', *The Guardian*, 3 July 2008.

[68] S Harper, *The Future of Retirement: Investing in Later Life* (HSBC, 2008).

[69] P Beynon, *Maintaining Consensus: Long-Term Goals for The UK Pensions System and Options for On-Going Policy Review* (PPI, 2008).

[70] G Clark and N Whiteside, *Pension Security in the 21st Century* (Oxford University Press, 2003); and P Saunders, 'Reviewing the Role and Structure of Pensions in National Context' (2006) 34 *Policy & Politics* 673.

Before looking at these issues in detail, more needs to be said by way of an introduction to issues surrounding pensions. Pensions raise complex economic, actuarial, and accounting issues and it is not possible to deal with all of these in this chapter. Here, an attempt will be made to introduce the reader to some of the key themes in the debate.[71]

The objectives of pension systems

The most important aim of a pensions system is to reduce poverty.[72] As we have seen, old age can be a time of great need and pensions play an important part in ensuring that individuals are not left in poverty. The World Bank recommends that the aims of a pension system should be to produce an income which is adequate, through a scheme which is affordable, sustainable, and robust.[73] In similar terms, a leading think-tank in the UK has stated that a scheme needs to be adaptable, adequate, affordable, clear,[74] fair,[75] robust, trusted, and build confidence.[76] There is widespread agreement over these aims, but it is in deciding how to implement them that the consensus breaks down. There are a number of key issues.

Balancing state and private funding

Perhaps the central issue in the pensions debate is the balance between funding pensions from private sources and the state. At one extreme, we could decide that there will be no state provision for pensioners, and everyone must rely on their own savings or family support. At the other, we could decide that the financial support of retirement should be funded generously by the state. Few people would accept either of these extremes. The former would leave too many inadequately provided for and the latter would be too expensive. Most agree that some kind of balance between state and private provision is required. Barr[77] notes that this is sometimes known as the 'cappuccino model', with the coffee part being the flat-rate pension; then a layer of cream (the occupational pensions) and finally a dusting of cocoa (the voluntary pensions). So, everyone gets the essential coffee, but whether they get all the goodies on top will depend on the payments they have made during their lifetimes. Still, Michael Hill suggests there is a crucial

---

[71] N Barr and P Diamond, 'The Economics of Pensions' (2006) 22 *Oxford Review of Economic Policy* 15.

[72] D Wanless, *Securing Good Care for Older People: Taking a Long-Term View* (King's Fund, 2006), at 11; and C Glendinning, B Davies, L Pickard, and A Comas-Herrera, *Funding Long-Term Care for Older People. Lessons from Other Countries* (Joseph Rowntree Foundation, 2004).

[73] R Holzmann and R Hinz, *Old-Age Income Support in the 21st Century* (World Bank, 2005).

[74] Ibid.

[75] D Hirsch, *Facing the Cost of Long-Term Care* (Joseph Rowntree Foundation, 2005).

[76] P Beynon, *Maintaining Consensus: Long-Term Goals for the UK Pensions System and Options for On-Going Policy Review* (PPI, 2008).

[77] N Barr, 'Pensions: Overview of the Issues' (2006) 22 *Oxford Review of Economic Policy* 1.

ideological 'fault line' running through pensions policy between two views on pensions:

On the one hand, a view of pensions as instruments of private or public economic policy, largely describable as ways of holding back returns from labour market participations; and, on the other, a view of pensions as providers of an adequate income for all in old age.[78]

The World Bank[79] has recommended a five-pillar structure. The first pillar is a mandated publicly managed system which is not dependent on contributions. The second pillar is a mandated system which is funded, privately managed, and depends on contributions. The third pillar is a voluntary system based on an individual's income. To this they have added two more pillars which must be in place to ensure poverty is avoided: access to health care and housing.

The UK Pensions Committee likewise sees the role of the state as protecting pensioners from poverty, but also encouraging people to save for their retirements:

At their heart, the Commission's recommendations accept the arguments put to us that the state should concentrate its *redistributive* power on providing a minimum platform on which people can build. But we suggest that its role does not stop there, and that it should use its *enabling* power to help people to achieve the levels of earnings replacement they generally desire.[80]

Paying now or paying later

Another key issue is the extent to which we wish to enable or encourage people to save up during their years of paid employment for their retirement. Generally, employed people are familiar with the need to set aside a portion of their income to save for a pension; indeed, this is normally done through money directly removed from pay packets so that individuals may hardly be aware that money has been taken from their pay to fund a pension. But the issue remains of how much of an individual's disposable income should be set aside for the purpose of providing for old age. If too much is retained by those in employment, less will be spent on other items and that may negatively affect the economy. Nicholas Barr and Peter Diamond talk of 'consumption smoothing':

a process which enables a person to transfer consumption from her productive middle years to her retired years, allowing her to choose her preferred time path of consumption over working and retired life.[81]

---

[78] M Hill, *Pensions* (Policy, 2007), at 16.
[79] R Holzmann and R Hinz, *Old-Age Income Support in the 21st Century* (World Bank, 2005).
[80] Pensions Commission, *A New Pensions Settlement for the Twentieth Century* (Stationery Office, 2005).
[81] N Barr and P Diamond, 'The Economics of Pensions' (2006) 22 *Oxford Review of Economic Policy* 15.

In essence, then, they suggest that a pension is a way of choosing to consume income earned not in the present, but in the future. Pension schemes provide a financially attractive way for individuals to save during employment in order to fund retirement. It would, of course, be possible for a state to decide to discourage this by putting in place taxation systems which would discourage saving in this way. However, most states in fact encourage individuals to provide for their own retirements and therefore provide attractive tax incentives to save for these purposes.

Pensions as savings or a form of insurance

One could regard pensions simply as a form of savings account. A person saves up money during their working life and spends it during retirement. Another model sees pension provision as a form of insurance. Under such a scheme, people pay insurance premiums which guarantee to provide support on retirement. Supporters of an insurance model point out that individuals cannot know how long they will live after they retire. Not knowing this makes it difficult to ensure one has sufficient savings for one's future needs. This means that under the savings model, they may well save too much or too little. A benefit of the insurance model is that one can pool resources with others and the scheme will pay out an income to all members whether they live a short time or a long time. Of course, that will mean that long-living members will get much more out of the scheme than short-living ones, but that is because it is in the nature of an insurance scheme. In England, the insurance model normally operates through the purchase of an annuity, where an individual can exchange their pension accumulation for an annuity which will pay regular payments for the rest of their life. Many annuity schemes or pensions also provide for payments to spouses or children should a worker die before retirement.[82]

Regulation of pension markets

Another issue is the extent to which the state should be involved in private pensions at all. Is the state's role limited to the provision of a minimum-level state pension, or does it also have a role in relation to private pensions? We have already noted that there is the issue of whether the state wishes to encourage or discourage such schemes through tax or other advantages. Linked to this is the question of whether the state should provide some kind of insurance should these schemes fail.[83] In recent years, a number of major employers have run into great difficulties with their pension funds, leaving members without the pensions they

---

[82] Otherwise a person who died before a pension became payable would receive no benefit.
[83] See Pensions Act 2004 which created the Pensions Protection Fund, which can offer help in some cases.

were expecting.[84] As well as the individual suffering caused, these cases have caused a loss of faith in pension products more generally. The extent to which the government is seen to guarantee such funds may affect the willingness of employees to fund them.

Secondly, there is the extent to which the state needs to regulate the market. Many pension products are complex. Some kind of regulation is required if faith is to be kept with them. As well as retaining faith in the pensions system, if individuals are not provided for by pension products they have arranged for themselves, they will become dependent on the state for financial relief.[85]

Forms of pension

There is a bewildering range of pension products available. One fundamental distinction is between fully funded schemes and 'pay as you go' schemes.[86] Under a fully funded scheme, members pay into a fund, their money is invested, and when they retire they are paid from their fund. With a 'pay as you go' pension, by contrast, income is taken from those currently employed and used to pay those who are currently in retirement. The difference, then, is whether a retired person is paid from the contributions of those members currently working or whether they are paid from the investment generated by their and other retired members' contributions. In theory, at least, fully funded schemes are more secure as the reserves to make the payments are in place. A 'pay as you go' scheme has the danger that the income from the current workers will be insufficient to pay the retired members. Due to this unreliability, 'pay as you go' schemes are normally run by the state, who can readily find money from elsewhere to pay the pensions should problems arise. The state therefore relies on current taxpayers' payments to fund the support of those who have retired. A significant aspect of the 'pay as you go' scheme is that the amounts paid out do not necessarily relate to the amount paid in: there is no sense in which you are receiving back your money. Such schemes therefore allow greater flexibility in achieving intergenerational transfers, but are subject to the danger that there will be a decrease in the funds from taxpayers, perhaps accompanied by an increase in the number of pensioners.

A second important distinction to draw is over the extent to which pension benefits are related to a worker's contributions. Peter Diamond and Nicholas Barr suggest three main approaches:

- *Defined-contribution scheme.* Under such a scheme,[87] each member pays in a fixed percentage of his or her earnings. The members' contributions are

---

[84] BBC News Online, 'Pension Fund Finances in the Red', 11 August 2008.
[85] The Financial Services Authority regulates the pensions industry.
[86] N Barr and P Diamond, 'The Economics of Pensions' (2006) 22 *Oxford Review of Economic Policy* 15.
[87] Sometimes known as a funded individual account.

invested. When the pension starts to pay out, a person receives a proportion determined by the amount they have paid in. There is, therefore, no guarantee as to how much will be paid out, because it all depends on how well the fund has been invested. In some schemes, the risk of a disastrous investment is mitigated by a guaranteed minimum payment for all members.

- *Defined-benefit scheme.* Under such a scheme, the amount paid out is guaranteed in advance. Normally it is determined by length of service and wage history. Guaranteeing the funds paid out may require finding further funds from employers, current taxpayers, or current employees if the fund is in shortfall. The risk under a defined-benefit scheme of a bad investment does not lie on the individual pensioner, as it does with a defined contribution scheme. A common form of defined-benefit scheme is a final salary scheme. These grant a pension which depends on the final salary. This provides an incentive for a person to remain with a firm until retirement and can also be an incentive to aid recruitment. More critically, it has been suggested that these schemes can work as an incentive for old workers to overwork in order to increase their final salary. It is also said that such schemes favour those who are able to greatly increase their incomes, usually those in a senior position in a company. Some therefore oppose final salary schemes and prefer a strict relationship between contributions and benefits. Such a scheme will have less impact on labour supply and encourage later retirement. It also gives individuals more scope to determine how to balance their finances during employment and in retirement.

- *Notional defined-contribution scheme.* This is a mixture of the two schemes described above. These have been generally run by governments. They require the payment of a fixed percentage of a person's earnings and credit to a notional individual account for that person. They are subject to a notional interest rate selected by the government, based on what it is thought the scheme can afford. This fund is then used to purchase an annuity on an individual's retirement, with an interest rate set by the government.

Economic issues

The economic issues raised by pensions are hugely complex. Devising appropriate products is far from straightforward given the uncertainty over any individual's life expectancy and in predicting the economic situations, sometimes decades in the future. Diamond and Barr[88] emphasize that the most important part of pensions is output: what they produce on retirement. But that, they explain, is only part of the picture, because an estimate also needs to be made of what can be bought with that money.

---

[88] N Barr and P Diamond, 'The Economics of Pensions' (2006) 22 *Oxford Review of Economic Policy* 15.

Another troublesome issue for economists is that individual consumers find it very difficult to make informed pensions decisions. They lack information about themselves (for example, how long they will live, what expenses they will face), but also the forms of risk of different products and economic conditions more generally. Therefore, relying on the market to find economically efficient products may be ineffective.[89]

What retirement age should be used?

It is important to appreciate that the term 'retirement' can be used in a variety of ways.[90] It can be used to indicate the age of expected retirement after which a person may receive a lower or higher pension. It may, in a national system, indicate the age at which a person is first entitled to receive state benefits. Setting a low eligibility age will harm some workers and benefit others. It hurts those who cannot stop working; but helps those who can afford to retire earlier. Barr and Diamond suggest there are good reasons for providing a flexible retirement age:

Some workers enjoy their work and want to continue working. Others no longer enjoy their work (if they ever did) and want to stop as soon as they can afford a decent retirement. A good pension system will not excessively discourage the first group from continuing to work at ages at which the second group will already have retired.[91]

While it is sometimes claimed that early retirement eases unemployment problems, few experts take this view.[92] International comparisons do not support the existence of a link between early retirement and low unemployment. This may appear counter-intuitive, but is in fact explicable: later retirement means a larger number of workers, which puts downward pressure on wages, making it more affordable to employ more workers or create new jobs.[93] It also seems that even though a person retires and receives a pension, they may still work in a variety of capacities. Further, other factors such as migration may have a far more significant impact on employment rates than the age of retirement.

Our understanding of retirement in 50 years time is likely to be something very different from how it is understood today.[94] The practice of people simply stopping work at 60 or 65 and then entering a time of rest does not represent the current reality and certainly will not be the picture in years to come.[95] I suggest that what retirement means and what people will intend to do during retirement

[89] Ibid.

[90] J Banks and S Smith, 'Retirement in the UK' (2006) 22 *Oxford Review of Economic Policy* 40.

[91] N Barr and P Diamond, 'The Economics of Pensions' (2006) 22 *Oxford Review of Economic Policy* 15, at 25.

[92] Ibid.   [93] Ibid.

[94] J Banks and S Smith, 'Retirement in the UK' (2006) 22 *Oxford Review of Economic Policy* 40; P Wink and J Boone James, 'Is the Third Age the Crown of Life' in J Boone James and P Wink (eds), *The Crown of Life: Dynamics of the Early Postretirement Period* (Springer, 2007).

[95] J Banks and S Smith, 'Retirement in the UK' (2006) 22 *Oxford Review of Economic Policy* 40.

is likely to undergo some profound changes.[96] We are likely to see greater levels of employment among older people, whether that be in part-time or full-time jobs. It is unlikely that people will move from full-time employment to no job at all, as often happens currently. Computer technology is full of potential for possibilities among older people.[97] More interestingly, we may see older people becoming even more active in public life and public spaces. Volunteering, mentoring, and community work may become a more significant role in old age. Work opportunities as 'consultants' in a wide variety of professions may become more common. One word of warning, however, and that is that pictures of retirement in the future often feature the active, multi-tasking, high achieving older person. That, of course, may simply not be an option for older people with serious health problems or caring responsibilities. It may also not be what some older people want.[98]

The current state of pensions

The UK public pension provision is in a rather sorry state; but as we shall see that is regarded as a good thing by some people. The UK has the lowest public pension of all 30 OECD countries.[99] For a person on average earnings working a full career, the net state pension is 41 per cent of pre-retirement earnings, while the average is 70 per cent in OECD countries. In general, the shortfall in public provision is made up by savings or private pensions, although there are gaps in coverage. An OECD report states that seven per cent of earnings would be required to be saved by a UK worker to reach the average OECD rate, while nine per cent is in fact the average saved. However, only 43 per cent of the workforce has an occupational pension, so the coverage is not extensive.[100]

Reform of pensions is a complex matter. There are a large number of interest groups and the sums involved can be substantial. Politicians are wary of entering the area because voters rarely understand it, and finding ways of increasing funding for pensions is unlikely to be a vote winner. Currently, with an increasing number of voters being of pensioner age, politicians will be particularly wary of appearing anti-pensioner.[101] Not only are there few votes in the issues, the issues are enormously complex. Booth and Cooper have argued that a proper reform of

---

[96] L Stone, *New Frontiers of Research on Retirement* (Statistics Canada, 2007); and R Weiss, *The Experience of Retirement* (Cornell University Press, 2005).

[97] J Lloyd, *Retirement Capital and Online Social Networking* (ILC, 2007).

[98] K Mann, 'Activation, Retirement Planning and Restraining the "Third Age"' (2007) 6 *Social Policy and Society* 279.

[99] OECD, *Pensions at a Glance—Public Policies across OECD Countries* (OECD, 2007).

[100] Ibid.

[101] P Booth, 'The Young Held to Ransom—A Public Choice Analysis of the UK State Pension System' (2008) 28 *Economic Affairs* 4.

the pensions issue would require a complete overhaul of the tax and social security systems.[102]

The current system

The current system of state provision for pensions is based around the Minimum Income Guarantee for pensioners. The government claims that this has raised the minimum income pensioners are entitled to from £68.80 per week in 1997 to £124.05 in 2008. However, the crucial words to note are 'entitled to'. As we have seen, for many pensioners to reach this sum, they need to successfully apply for a range of means-tested benefits and tax credits.

The government has also sought to encourage more people to take out private pensions. The Pension Act 2004 was passed specifically to improve security and confidence for occupational pension schemes. The Act creates the Pension Protection Fund, which should ensure that members of salary-related schemes covered by the Act (some 10 million people) will be compensated if their employer becomes insolvent and the pension scheme is unable to make the payments.[103]

The current pensions system is made up of the following elements:[104]

State provision

As discussed earlier, this is made up of the basic state pension, which can be supplemented by the second state pension. On top of this there is the pensions credit, which ensures that a person's income does not fall below a certain level.

Private pension systems

There are grave concerns over the current state of the private pension scheme.[105] The Pensions Commission states that private voluntary pensions are in 'serious and probably irreversible decline'.[106] It is clear from a variety of sources that confidence in the private pension sector has dropped.[107] In 2005, households were less likely to be contributing to a private pension than in 1995.[108] Only 47 per cent of men aged 18 to 59 and 38 per cent of women are currently contributing to

---

[102] P Booth and D Cooper, *The Way Out of the Pensions Quagmire* (IEA, 2005).

[103] There is also a Financial Assistance Scheme to help those close to retirement before the scheme was implemented.

[104] J Hills, 'A New Pension Settlement for the Twenty-First Century? The UK Pensions Commission's Analysis and Proposals' (2006) 22 *Oxford Review of Economic Policy* 113.

[105] R Blackburn, *Age Shock* (Verso, 2007) claims to have uncovered 'skullduggeries' used by managers in the private sector to hive off pensions for their own gain.

[106] Ibid, at 2.

[107] P Ring, 'Trust in UK Pensions Policy: A Different Approach?' (2005) 55 *Policy & Politics* 55.

[108] R Boreham and J Lloyd, *Asset Accumulation Across the Life Course* (International Longevity Centre, 2007).

a private pension. One-third of respondents to one survey had never contributed to a private pension.[109] This lack of confidence has resulted from the mis-selling of pensions[110] and widely reported cases of pension schemes collapsing through lack of funds.[111] It has been estimated that there is a total deficit in relation to final salary pension schemes of £500 billion on a buy-out basis, or £124 billion on a standard accounting basis.[112] Most companies, it has been claimed, if they ceased trading, would face an immediate liability much larger than the assets in the scheme or even the company itself. Some blame government legislation, stating that it has added to the cost of final salary pension schemes, thus making them unattractive.[113]

Non-pension assets

Many people seek to rely not on pension provision, but on other assets to provide for their retirement.[114] Most significantly, this is wealth tied up in housing.[115] Of course, reliance on house prices to meet the costs of retirement involves faith in the housing market retaining value, but then most pension schemes rely on success in equity markets.[116]

Gender and pensions

A major theme in the current debate is the interaction of gender and pensions.[117] Two fundamental assumptions have consistently worked against the interests of women in the area of pension provision. First, in the past the pensions system was premised on the assumption that women in retirement would be provided for through their husbands' pensions.[118] This assumption was always flawed. Eighty per cent of women over 80 are widows and one-half of all women over 65 are

---

[109] Age Concern, *The Age Agenda* (Age Concern, 2008).

[110] BBC News Online, 'Pensions Scandal Costs £11.8bn', 27 June 2002.

[111] eg BBC News Online, 'Staff Lose Most of Their Pensions', 3 December 2004.

[112] N Silver, *The Trouble With Final Salary Pension Schemes* (IEA, 2006).

[113] N Silver, *Private Pensions Crisis* (IEA, 2007).

[114] J Lloyd, *Asset Accumulation in Focus: The Challenges Ahead* (International Longevity Centre, 2007).

[115] J Banks, C Emmerson, Z Oldfield, and G Tetlow, *Prepared for Retirement? The Adequacy and Distribution of Retirement Resources in England* (Institute for Fiscal Studies, 2005).

[116] J Hills, 'A New Pension Settlement for the Twenty-First Century? The UK Pensions Commission's Analysis and Proposals' (2006) 22 *Oxford Review of Economic Policy* 113.

[117] P Marier, 'Affirming, Transforming, or Neglecting Gender? Conceptualizing Gender in the Pension Reform Process' (2007) 14 *International Studies in Gender, State & Society* 182; D Sainsbury, *Gender and Welfare State Regimes* (Oxford University Press, 1999); S Leitner, 'Sex and Gender Discrimination Within EU Pension Systems' (2001) 11 *Journal of European Social Policy* 99; and N Fraser, 'From Redistribution to Recognition? Dilemmas of Justice in a "Post-Socialist" Age' (1995) 212 *New Left Review* 68.

[118] Department of Work and Pensions, *Women and Pensions* (DWP, 2005).

widows.[119] Increasing rates of divorce and relationship breakdown have removed any shred of respectability that that approach may have had. Secondly, pensions are based on a link between paid employment and pension provision. This means that child care, care work, and other unpaid work is not rewarded. As women still undertake the largest portion of such work, they are severely disadvantaged in pension provision. More than 40 per cent of women aged 16 to pension age out of the labour market have caring responsibilities.[120] In the UK, 20 per cent of women who started caring stopped working, and 20 per cent significantly reduced their working hours.[121] While female employment rates increased from 55 per cent in 1983 to 70 per cent now,[122] over 40 per cent of all women in employment are part time, compared with only 10 per cent of men.[123] Overall, 38 per cent of today's working-age women are contributing to a private pension compared with around 46 per cent of working-age men. And where women do contribute, they do so with smaller sums.[124] When considering the pension poverty of women, it should not be forgotten that older women in ethnic minorities are particularly disadvantaged under the current system. There are particularly low employment rates among Pakistani and Bangladeshi women.[125]

There are 1.3 million female pensioners below the poverty line, compared with 750,000 men. Among the over 75s who are single, poor women outnumber poor men by four to one.[126] In 2004, 73 per cent of those receiving means-tested Pensions Guarantee Credit were women, indicating that women were much more likely than men to require benefits to maintain a satisfactory income. More concerning is evidence that women are much less likely than men to claim benefits they are entitled to, meaning it is particularly likely that women are below the pensioner's 'guaranteed income'. A study by the Department for Work and Pensions found that partnered men received about twice as much income in later life from the state as partnered women, and the men had far more private pension and other income.

Reform of pensions

The need for reform: 'the pensions crisis'

The view that we are currently suffering a worldwide 'pensions crisis' has received extensive support.[127] Quite simply it is claimed that the cost of pensions

---

[119] S Arber and J Ginn, 'Ageing and Gender: Diversity and Change' (2004) 34 *Social Trends* 34.
[120] Ibid, at para 8.
[121] M Evandrou and K Glaser, 'Combining Work and Family Life: The Pension Penalty of Caring' (2003) 23 *Ageing and Society* 583.
[122] Department of Work and Pensions, *Women and Pensions* (DWP, 2005), at para 16.
[123] Ibid, at para 22.   [124] Ibid, at para 58.   [125] Ibid, at para 68.
[126] D Price, 'The Pensions White Paper: Taking Account of Gender' (2006) 15 *Benefits* 45.
[127] N Barr, 'Pensions: Overview of the Issues' (2006) 22 *Oxford Review of Economic Policy* 1.

is increasing and there are higher levels of pensioner poverty. We are seeing increased life expectancy, meaning that pensions must be paid out for longer, and lower birth rates, meaning there are fewer taxpayers funding the schemes. In 2001, the average pension spending in the OECD on pensions was 7.4 per cent of the GDP. If no action is taken, this percentage is set to increase. For Greece, for example, if nothing is done, 25 per cent of the GDP will be required in 2050.[128] As mentioned at the start of the chapter, there is some reason for believing that the arguments supporting an 'old age' crisis are over egged.[129]

Surprisingly, there is widespread agreement over the difficulties facing the UK pension system.[130] Some of these have already been mentioned, but they form an important part of the backdrop to the reform process. First, people's life expectancy has increased. In 1950, a man aged 65 could expect to live another 11 years. In 2006, he could expect another 20 years and it is estimated that by 2050 another 24. For women, the figures are even higher. All of this is fantastic news. As the government has said, it ranks 'among the greatest social achievements of the last century'.[131] However, this means that our pensions have to last for a longer time than in the past and therefore more money is required.

Secondly, the ratio of working-age people and those over the state pension age has changed. There are fewer working-age people and more over-state-pension-age people. In 1950, the pensioner population was 19 per cent of the working-age population. In 2006, this was 27 per cent and by 2050 it will be 47 per cent. The concern is, therefore, that there are fewer people paying taxes to fund an ever-increasing number of people needing pensions.

Thirdly, there has been a decrease in employers offering occupational pension schemes. The increased life expectancy and rising salaries have made these schemes expensive to run. Many have claimed that in recent years government tax and regulatory changes have made them even less attractive. In 2004, there were two million fewer members of open private occupational pension schemes than there were in 2000[132] and there is no sign that many people are saving in other ways to ensure appropriate pension income. The Pensions Commission found that between 9.6 and 12 million people were saving at a rate which would not provide what the commission described as a benchmark replacement rate. The government has suggested that the reasons for this include a lack of trust in the pension system, a lack of appropriate vehicles, complexity in the system, and inertia.[133]

---

[128] P Whiteford and E Whitehouse, 'Pension Challenges and Pension Reforms in OECD Countries' (2006) 22 *Oxford Review of Economic Policy* 78.

[129] Ibid.

[130] K Ambachtsheer, *Pension Revolution: A Solution to the Pensions Crisis* (Wiley, 2007).

[131] Department of Work and Pensions, *Security in Retirement: Towards a New Pensions System* (DWP, 2006), at para 14.

[132] There has also been a marked move away from defined benefit and towards defined contribution: Department of Work and Pensions, *Security in Retirement: Towards a New Pensions System* (DWP, 2006), at para 22.

[133] Ibid, at para 24.

Fourthly, as already mentioned, there is also a concern that the pension system works against the interests of women and carers. When reaching state-pension age, around 85 per cent of men have entitlement to a full basic state pension, while only 30 per cent of women do.[134] This explains the poverty along gendered lines that is found among the older population. Now that more women are working, these figures may improve, but a system based on paid contributions during working lives is likely to mean that carers and women will suffer.[135]

The government summarized the problems facing the country concerning pensions in its White Paper as follows:[136]

In the next 50 years, the number of people over pension age will increase by more than half and there will be only two people working for every one person in retirement—compared with four today. Millions of people today are not saving enough for their futures. And our pension system suffers from structural problems. Because of the historical legacy of complexity few people understand how it fits together. It is unfair to many who are caring for others, and particularly to women. It reflects a view of family relationships that dates back to the early years of the State Pension itself. As the Pensions Commission has made clear, we face some stark choices about the path ahead. We don't want the retirees of the future to be worse off than those today. But neither should our response be simply to spend more public money on the State Pension alone. A new balance must be struck between State, employers and individuals to share the responsibility to save and provide for the future.[137]

The reforms

One option, which until fairly recently, seemed the most popular, was to ignore the problem and hope it would go away! Or, to put it more kindly, a perception that the problem of future pensions was so complex, and involved so many unknown variables, that to attempt a solution at this stage was unlikely to be effective. Better to wait and see.

The government has now determined that delay is no longer an option. It created a Pensions Commission, which produced three reports.[138] The government

---

[134] Ibid, at para 28.

[135] Department of Work and Pensions, *Women and Pensions* (DWP, 2005).

[136] PPI, *An Evaluation of the White Paper State Pension Reform Proposals* (PPI, 2006) at 113; and J Hills, 'A New Pension Settlement for the Twenty-First Century? The UK Pensions Commission's Analysis and Proposals' (2006) 22 *Oxford Review of Economic Policy* 113.

[137] Department of Work and Pensions, *Security in Retirement: Towards a New Pensions System* (DWP, 2006).

[138] Pensions Commission, *Pensions: Challenges and Choices* (The Stationery Office, 2005); Pensions Commission, *A New Pensions Settlement for the Twentieth Century* (The Stationery Office, 2005); and Pensions Commission, *Implementing an Integrated Package of Pension Reform* (The Stationery Office, 2006).

has responded with a White Paper[139] accepting many of their proposals and has started to legislate to give effect to the new scheme. The key elements of the reforms are as follows:

1. The state pension age is to be raised. This proposal has already been implemented in section 13 of the Pensions Act 2007. Following equalization of the state pension age for men and women at 65 in 2020, it will increase between 2024 and 26 from 65 to 66, between 2034 and 2036 from 66 to 67 and between 2044 and 2046 from 67 to 68.[140]

2. The state pension is to rise in line with earnings rather than inflation.[141] A common complaint about the current system is that pensions are increased in line with inflation rather than earnings. This means the gap between the wealth of pensioners and those in employment has increased. The Pension Commission had recommended that the basic state pension be linked to earnings from 2010, but the government plans to re-establish the link by 2012 'subject to affordability and the fiscal position',[142] by which point the state pension will be only 13 or 14 per cent of average earnings.

3. The state second pension is to be reformed so that it is a flat-rate weekly top up to the basic pension.[143] There will also be reforms to take account of those caring for children[144] or severely disabled adults.

4. There is to be a new 'personal account', which[145] will be a 'low-cost person account to give those without access to occupations pension schemes the opportunity to save'. The scheme is to be overseen by the Personal Accounts Delivery Authority.[146] The details of the scheme are not yet known, but two of its most important elements are outlined here. First, the scheme is to be an 'opt-out' one. Employees will be enrolled into the scheme unless they specifically elect not to be. The hope is that inertia will mean more people will have a personal pension provision than would be the case if they had to opt in to the system. Secondly, employers will be required to make a compulsory contribution of three per cent of an employee's salary; employees must contribute four per cent;[147] and the state must contribute one per cent.[148] The three per cent contribution by employers had been criticized by some employers' organizations as imposing too heavy a burden, especially on small companies.

---

[139] Department of Work and Pensions, *Security in Retirement: Towards a New Pensions System* (DWP, 2006).

[140] C Kilpatrick, 'The New UK Retirement Regime, Employment Law and Pensions'(2008) 37 *Industrial Law Journal* 1.

[141] Pensions Act 2007, s 5.   [142] Ibid.   [143] Pensions Act 2007, ss 1–2.

[144] But only up until the age of 12. The Pensions Committee had recommended that care until the age of 16 be covered.

[145] The legislative framework is Pensions Act 2007, Part 3.   [146] Ibid.

[147] This will be paid on bands of earnings between £5,000 and £33,000.

[148] This will be through a tax relief.

The success of the scheme will depend on a number of factors.[149] One important issue is whether the scheme can be run in a cheap and reliable way. The compulsory contributions aspect will have to be enforced and that could prove problematic and expensive. The scheme must also gain the confidence of the public. It will be interesting to see how many people will decide to opt out. The government hopes that most people will not bother to opt out.

The Pensions Commission[150] believed personal accounts would be more acceptable among voters than increasing taxation to provide higher levels of state pension. They argued:

People may be more willing to accept... savings into an account which is legally theirs, and the value of which is defined in clear capacity terms, than to accept taxation to support a PAYG system.[151]

It remains to be seen whether this is so and how the personal account will be regarded by members of the public. They could come to be seen as a form of 'stealth tax'. They may also lose popularity if those unable to afford them are left in unacceptable levels of poverty.

Consideration of the reforms

The government has laid down a number of key principles which must be met when reforming the pension system:

- to promote personal responsibility—tackling the problem of under-saving for retirement;
- to be fair—protecting the poorest, and being fair to women and carers, to savers, and between generations;
- to be simple—clarifying the respective roles of the state, the employer, and the individual;
- to be affordable—maintaining macroeconomic stability and striking the right balance for provision between the state, the employer, and the individual; and
- to be sustainable—setting the basis of an enduring national consensus, while being flexible to future trends.[152]

---

[149] For further discussion of these personal accounts, see PPI, *How Personal Accounts Could Impact on UK Provision* (PPI, 2007).

[150] Pensions Commission, *A New Pensions Settlement for the Twentieth Century* (The Stationery Office, 2005), at 164.

[151] Ibid, at 164.

[152] Department of Work and Pensions, *Security in Retirement: Towards a New Pensions System* (DWP, 2006), at para 33.

Of course, these aims can contradict each other and putting them into practice is a challenge. As the Pensions Commission points out, despite the difficulties, in fact there are in essence only four options available to a government:[153]

- pensioners becoming poorer relative to the rest of the population;
- later retirement;
- a greater amount of tax and/or national insurance contributions as a share of national income devoted to state pensions; and
- greater savings for retirement.

The reforms seem to involve a combination of these options.[154] The government clearly hopes that most people will use personal accounts and that these will become a key element of funding old age.[155] However, the greater the weight which is put on private provision, the greater the danger that those who do not or are not able to make private provision will end up in poverty. Certainly, there is a widespread belief that using increased elements of private pension will intensify existing inequalities in the distribution of pensions.[156] For Michael Hill, the UK pensions debate has often involved two opposing perspectives:

One of these has as its key plank the raising of the basic state pension to a level at which it (rather than a means-tested scheme deterring saving) would be the main device to prevent pension poverty. The other is the advocacy of ways to secure much higher levels of pensions saving by lower-income people.[157]

He sees the current reform programme as adopting both.

One issue which has rightly played a significant role in the debates over the reform of the law is to what extent the proposals will protect women.[158] It is notable how the government's proposals have generally been supported by lobby groups promoting interests of women.[159] Debra Price doubts the claims that the reforms will protect the interests of women. She points out that under the models trialled

---

[153] J Hills, 'From Beveridge to Turner: Demography, Distribution and the Future of Pensions in the UK' (2006) 169 *Journal of Royal Statistical Society* 663.

[154] K Howse, 'Updating the Debate on Intergenerational Fairness in Pension Reform' (2007) 41 *Social Policy and Administration* 51.

[155] T Clark and C Emmerson, 'Privatising Provision and Attacking Poverty? The Direction of UK Pension Policy Under New Labour' (2003) 2 *Journal of Pension Economics and Finance* 67.

[156] C Behrendt, 'Private Pensions: A Viable Alternative? Their Distributive Effects in a Comparative Perspective' (2003) 3 *International Social Security Review* 3.

[157] J Hill, *Pensions* (Policy Press, 2007), at 160.

[158] Equal Opportunities Commission, *Response to the Department for Work and Pensions: Pensions White Paper—Security in Retirement: Towards a New Pension System* (Equal Opportunities Commission, 2006).

[159] Age Concern, *Dignity, Security, Opportunity: A Decent Income for All Current and Future Pensioners* (Age Concern, 2006); Help the Aged, *Consultation Response: Security in Retirement: Towards a New Pension System* (Help the Aged, 2006); and The Fawcett Society, *Response to the Pensions White Paper: Security in Retirement: Towards a New Pension System* (The Fawcett Society, 2006).

by the Department for Work and Pensions, they will protect women's interests, but only in the long term and only if there is a departure from the traditional gendered patterns for work and family life. Women who follow the now traditional path of part-time work and looking after children and other relatives will depend on their partner. If they have no partner, Price is not convinced they will be better off and will have to rely on means-tested benefits. As she argues:

These inequalities are the result of gendered differences in the life course. Women are much more likely than men to undertake care work and housework within the household, are more likely to work part-time and for low pay, are more likely to have interrupted histories of paid work, and are less likely to be in the paid workforce as they approach state pension age. Pension reforms that do not account sufficiently for social, cultural and labour force differences will do little to reduce gender inequalities, even if other aims, such as fiscal sustainability, are achieved.[160]

She refers to several social trends which might mean that the government's assumptions about women undertaking more paid employment will not prove accurate: increased rates of divorce and relationship breakdown will mean that more women spending time as single mothers; age differences on second marriage or non-marital relationships mean more working age women may need to be caring for older partners in later life; and higher life expectancy may lead to older parents requiring care in a woman's mid-life years. She is also concerned by the continued weight attached to means-tested benefits, despite the evidence that women in particular are deterred from applying for these. Nevertheless, she concludes that women will benefit under the proposed schemes:

On average, compared with a married or cohabiting woman, a married or cohabiting man will get approximately twice as much in state benefit, far more in private pension, and more in other income. Widowed, divorced and separated women pensioners have more income in their own right than married women pensioners, but less than the equivalent men.[161]

A third issue is that related to risk. It is commonly argued that it would be risky for individuals to rely on the state to provide for them in retirement. Further, it would be risky for the government to promise it will continue to provide generous pension provision. As Michael Hill notes, however, it should not be thought that private pension planning is risk free:

In the doomsday scenario from the private sector side of the argument the future problem is seen to be that governments will be unable to meet their obligations, a perspective that only makes sense in the context of a related belief that there are—these days—severe limits upon government capacities to increase taxation. At the same time the advocates of private solutions disregard the potential economic problems—with similar costs very

---

[160] D Price, 'Closing the Gender Gap in Retirement Income: What Difference Will Recent UK Pension Reforms Make?' (2007) 36 *Journal of Social Policy* 561.

[161] Department of Work and Pensions, *Women and Pensions* (DWP, 2005), at para 8.

like increased taxation for workers—that will arise if the payment obligations of private schemes rise sharply.[162]

Behind all of these issues is money: how much of our GDP the state wishes to spend on pension provision. The Pensions Commission thought it reasonable to assume that in the future between 7.5 and 8 per cent of GDP would be spent on pensions. There is, in fact, wide variation among OECD members, from less than 1 per cent to over 10 per cent of GDP.

Funding care

There is widespread acceptance that there is a particular problem over the funding of care for older people.[163] As seen in chapter 8, the current position is that while health care costs are covered by the NHS, social care is not automatically free and can be charged for, following a means-tested system. Some support from social services departments to those most in need of social care may be available, but this is limited and it is increasingly difficulty to qualify for assistance.[164] Under the current system, those with eligible assets of more than £21,500 normally get no funding.[165]

In 2006 to 2007, gross current expenditure by councils in England on personal social services was £20.1 billion.[166] Forty-three per cent of this was on older people. Projecting the potential cost of care for older people into the future is not an easy task.[167] One study has predicted an increase of between 30 and 50 per cent in the volume of care that will be needed by 2050.[168] One major investigation into the future care needs of older disabled people concluded:

the supply of intense informal care to disabled older people by their adult children in England is unlikely to keep pace with demand in future years. Demand for informal care by disabled older people is projected to exceed supply by 2017, with the 'care gap' widening over the ensuing years. By 2041, the gap between the numbers of people projected to provide informal care and the numbers needed to provide care if projected demand is to be met amounts to nearly 250 thousand care-providers.[169]

---

[162] J Hill, *Pensions* (Policy Press, 2007), at 141.

[163] J Lloyd, *A National Care Fund for Long-Term Care* (ILC, 2008).

[164] Commission for Social Care Inspection, *The State of Social Care in England 2005–06* (CSCI, 2006).

[165] Caring Choices, *The Future of Care Funding* (Caring Choices, 2008).

[166] NHS, *Personal Social Services Expenditure and Unit Costs: England 2006/07* (The Information Centre, 2008).

[167] J Malley, A Comas-Herrera, R Hancock, A Juarez-Garcia, D King, and L Pickard, *Expenditure on Social Care for Older People to 2026: Projected Financial Implications of the Wanless Report* (LSE, 2006).

[168] M Karlsson *et al*, 'Future Costs for Long-Term Care: Cost Projections for Long-Term Care for Older People in the United Kingdom' in (2006) 75 *Health Policy* 187.

[169] L Pickard, *Informal Care for Older People Provided by Their Adult Children: Projections of Supply and Demand to 2041 in England* (Department of Health, 2008).

All the signs are that there will be an increasing number of older people. However, it is unclear whether or not they will be healthier than the current cohort; whether the levels of voluntary care provided by families and friends will increase or decease; or whether levels of migration in old age will increase. Sometimes, the future figures are put in dramatic terms. It has been suggested that long-term care costs will quadruple from £12.9 billion in 2000 to £53.9 billion in 2051 in real terms. However, that rise is less dramatic when put in terms of a percentage of GDP: from 1.37 to 1.83 per cent.[170]

The government has acknowledged that there is a problem. Gordon Brown, in introducing a Government Consultation on payment of care, stated:

> In a civilised society, we have a moral obligation to ensure that people in need are not left without any care or support. The existing care and support system is not sustainable, because of the impact of changing demographics and expectations in our society. We need to address these challenges now, before their effects are felt on the system and impact on people's lives.[171]

Even though the future may be somewhat uncertain, it is clear that there is a real problem with the way in which social care is funded.[172] Two major independent reviews in 2006, one published by the Joseph Rowntree Trust and the other by the King's Fund, revealed the problems inherent in the current system.[173] A survey of professionals working in the area found no support for the current system. Ninety-nine per cent believed more financial support was needed and three-quarters believed there needed to be better sharing of the financial costs of care between individuals and the government.[174] The following are issues of particular concern:

1. The system is seen as being under-funded and therefore leading to a poor quality of care. It is claimed by many that the current system encourages local authorities who are paying for a person's care to transfer them to a care home because then the local authority can recover the costs through sale of the individual's home. A King's Fund report states:

> There is evidence of significant unmet need. The proportion of all people in their own homes who have care needs and who have those needs met is low, and has been falling. Budget-limited public resources are successfully being aimed at those with the highest levels of need but, even among this group, services are only being used

---

[170] Ibid.

[171] HM Government, *The Case for Change—Why England Needs a New Care and Support System* (HM Government, 2008), at 4.

[172] C Deeming and J Keen, 'A Fair Deal for Care in Older Age? Public Attitudes Towards the Funding of Long-Term Care' (2003) 31 *Policy & Politics* 431.

[173] Joseph Rowntree Foundation, *Paying for Long-Term Care: Moving Forward* (Joseph Rowntree Foundation, 2006); and D Wanless, *Securing Good Care for Older People: Taking a Long-Term View* (King's Fund, 2006).

[174] Caring Choices, *The Future of Care Funding* (Caring Choices, 2008).

by a relatively small proportion of people with apparently similar levels of need. The Review also finds that unmet need is particularly high among moderately dependent people. Overall, the proportion of older people receiving home care in England is low by international standards.[175]

2. The current system is seen to be lacking in fairness. A person should not be blamed for needing care. Whether a particular individual needs care, the extent of the care needed, and the length of time it is needed, varies from person to person, just as is true with health generally. This means that chance determines whether or not a person has to spend large sums on personal care. Under the NHS, differences in a person's health should not cause economic disadvantage due to health costs, but the same is not true for personal care. Another aspect of unfairness is that the extent of local authority assistance can vary greatly across the country, meaning that there is a 'postcode lottery' over whether or not a person is able to gain access to services.

3. The funding process is complex and confusing. As discussed in chapter 8, the distinction between personal care and healthcare is hard to define and hard to implement.

4. In chapter 4, the role of informal carers was discussed. They are central to the issue. Although there has been much discussion of the economic costs of care of older people, the personal costs to individuals caring for relatives and friends can so easily get lost in the heat of the debate.

Summarizing these concerns, a Joseph Rowntree Foundation report concluded:

There are several areas where current evidence points to unmet need. One concerns *quality*—for example, where cost containment has resulted in poorly trained staff, low pay and high turnover. A second emerging shortfall concerns *supply*—with, for example, a recent fall in the number of 'low-level' domiciliary care packages. Third, *affordability* of domiciliary packages is an issue, with evidence that some people on modest incomes are having in some cases to pay large amounts to get adequate care in their homes.

Counsel and Care, a voluntary organization, paint a grim picture on the availability of care:

Older people are struggling to get the urgent care and support they need, and, as a result, are forced to rely on the support of families and carers, or face huge care bills at a time when their fixed incomes are becoming increasing inadequate due to the rising cost of living. Council provision for lower level care services vital to maintaining an older person's independence and dignity, and ensuring they remain an integral part of their local community, have all but disappeared across England. Instead, exhausted families and carers or over-subscribed voluntary services are bearing the brunt of this 'care gap'.[176]

---

[175] D Wanless, *Securing Good Care for Older People: Taking a Long-Term View* (King's Fund, 2006).
[176] Counsel and Care, *Care Contradictions: Putting People First?* (Counsel and Care, 2008), at 2.

It must never be forgotten that behind all these reports of inadequate services are the suffering of real people. One woman records her expereiences thus:

I feel unclean half the time. I felt deprived when social serices cut me down from two to one bath a week in 2004—deprived of feeling like a normal adult. Then they told me I had to stop having the one bath a week I have now because my care was taking longer than the one hour I was allocated. I told them I was doubly incontinent and why on earth couldn't I have a bath? Wasn't I entitled to be properly clean? They told me that time and money would not allow it. But we're talking about 15 minutes.[177]

Solutions

The following are some of the suggestions to deal with the costs of funding care:[178]

1. *Private insurance schemes.* Many people insure against relatively minor risks, such as car accidents and mobile phone theft. Oddly, few take out insurance against the more significant risks: the costs of care in old age. So, one option would be to rely on people insuring against their care costs in old age.[179] However, there would be difficulties in relying on that as the solution to the problem. First, there is the issue of whether they would be compulsory. If not, there is then the question of how to deal with those who do not take it up. Leaving them completely without care would be generally unacceptable; but if care is provided, that may act as a disincentive to take out insurance. Secondly, there is the cost of such schemes, which are likely to be high. It is notable that the market in these policies is decreasing. In 2004, there were only 18,825 care insurance policies in force, and only one company was offering them.[180] This indicates that few people can afford them, or at least see the need for them. One solution to affordability for some people would be if they were paid for on death from a person's estate.

2. *Funding from general taxation.* One argument in favour of funding care from general taxation is that the NHS has established the tradition of meeting the basic needs of citizens and this should be extended to care needs as well as health. Of course, this would create an extra burden on government expenditure and would require an increase in taxation revenue or a cut back in other services. The Royal Commission on Long Term Care for the Elderly in 1999 backed this proposal, but it was rejected by the UK Government (although in Scotland a form of funding care from general taxation was introduced). The Royal Commission divided costs into living

---

[177] Quoted in J Neuberger, *Not Dead Yet* (Harper Collins, 2008), at 197.
[178] R Wittenberg and J Malley, 'Financing Long-Term Care for Older People in England' (2007) 6 *Ageing Horizons* 28.
[179] This could be a state-run system: J Lloyd, *A National Care Fund for Long-Term Care* (ILC, 2008).
[180] T Poole, *Funding Options for Older People's Social Care* (King's Fund, 2007).

costs,[181] housing costs, and personal care costs. Only personal care costs were to be paid for by the government. These were defined as the 'additional cost of being looked after arising from frailty or disability'.[182]

The government's rejection of the recommendation for free personal care was based on the argument that the cost would be shifted from the individual to the state, without improving the quality of the care. In short, it was too expensive. One team of researchers[183] estimated that the introduction of free personal care throughout the UK would cost between £1.3 and £1.8 billion in additional public expenditure in 2002 and would take up between 2.15 and 2.40 per cent of GDP by 2051. At the end of the day, the issue is a political one. Supporters will feel that expenditure on ensuring that the basic day-to-day needs of our older people is money well spent and argue that, if necessary to provide for such needs, taxes should be increased or cutbacks in other less important areas be made. Certainly, the percentages of the GDP required do not suggest that free personal care is utterly unaffordable.

Some commentators have objected that the proposal would be, in effect, a transfer of wealth from younger to older people at a time when older people are doing significantly better, especially due to the housing market:

> trends in assets and debt have seen current older cohorts becoming the wealthiest in history, resulting from rising property wealth and reflected in increasing mortgage debt among the young who have commensurately become the most indebted cohort in modern times. This represents an unprecedented transfer of wealth from young to old that has occurred through the property market during an extended period of above-average price inflation.[184]

Another concern about making care services state funded is that state care systems can be monopolistic in effect and so there becomes little incentive to provide excellence in services. Further, there are concerns that the interface between informal care and funded care becomes difficult. Ready availability of state-funded care may mean that fewer people undertake informal care, increasing the costs to the government, and perhaps lowering the quality of care.

3. *Combined approaches.* The Wanless Report[185] proposes a partnership model with two-thirds of a person's care package being free of charge and the remaining third expected to be funded by the individual themselves,

---

[181] eg food and clothing.
[182] Royal Commission on Long Term Care for the Elderly, *With Respect to Old Age* (The Stationery Office, 1999), at 65.
[183] R Hancock, R Wittenberg, L Pickard, A Comas-Herrera, A Juarez-Garcia, D King, and J Malley, *Paying for Long-Term Care for Older People in the UK* (LSE, 2006).
[184] J Lloyd, *A National Care Fund for Long-Term Care* (ILC, 2008).
[185] D Wanless, *Securing Good Care for Older People: Taking a Long-Term View* (King's Fund, 2006).

although the state would match pound for pound any contribution. If a person was unable to fund contributions, they could apply for means-tested benefit. The Wanless report promoted a partnership approach as being more efficient, being based on need and not ability of pay, and providing individuals with a good choice.[186] Wanless estimated that this would cost some £1.7 to £4.2 billion per year.[187] Another option would be to limit the amount a person would be expected to fund themselves without state funding to a certain number of years or amount of money.[188]

Messages from Scotland

Much interest has attached to Scotland where, departing from the English approach, free care is offered.[189] Under the scheme there is non-means-tested care at home and a flat rate non-means-tested support for nursing and personal care costs in care homes, but not so as to cover the so-called 'hotel costs' of a stay in a care home. Since the introduction of free personal care, the number of people receiving free personal care at home has risen by 74 per cent.[190] The scheme has particularly assisted those suffering dementia and people of modest means.[191]

However, there are some interesting aspects of the Scottish scheme.[192] One is that it had not led to a reduction in the level of informal care. It appears that informal carers have changed the kind of care work they provide, but not the extent of it. Secondly, the scheme has proved more costly than expected and its costs are predicted to rise.[193] Thirdly, there is evidence that what is offered varies between different parts of Scotland.[194] Fourthly, although the state now contributes to costs in a care home, care homes increased their prices when the scheme came into effect and the average cost in 2004 was £427, while the state contribution was £210. Notably 40 per cent of care home residents are self-funders.[195]

Family financial obligations and older people

So far the focus on economic issues has concentrated on the responsibilities of older people to provide for themselves or on the state to provide for older people.

---

[186] Ibid, at 269–70.   [187] Ibid.
[188] T Poole, *Funding Options for Older People's Social Care* (King's Fund, 2007).
[189] D Bell and A Bowes, *Financial Care Models in Scotland and the UK* (JRF, 2006).
[190] H Dickinson and J Glasby, *Free Personal Care in Scotland* (King's Fund, 2006).
[191] A Bowes and D Bell, 'Free Personal Care for Older People in Scotland: Issues and Implications' (2007) 6 *Social Policy & Society* 435.
[192] Audit Scotland, *A Review of Free Personal and Nursing Care* (Audit Scotland, 2007).
[193] A Bowes and D Bell, 'Free Personal Care for Older People in Scotland: Issues and Implications' (2007) 6 *Social Policy & Society* 435.
[194] Caring Choices, *The Future of Care Funding* (Caring Choices, 2008).
[195] D Wanless, *Securing Good Care for Older People: Taking a Long-Term View* (King's Fund, 2006).

However, there is also the issue of to what extent older people's families should be financially responsible for the needs of older people.[196] Some countries have created statutes which require adult children to support their needy parents. Linked to this is the issue of whether parents should in any way be required to support their adult children.

There is, of course, a long history of family members helping each other out in financial or practical ways.[197] In the recent OASIS survey, 75 per cent of older people in the UK had face-to-face contact at least weekly; 61 per cent received instrumental help; and 76 per cent felt very close to their children.[198] However, social changes are putting strains on these relationships, in particular: later age at child birth, higher levels of paid work among women; increased rates of relationship breakdown; and more movement of people around the country and internationally.[199] However, the pressures are not all one way. There is the increasing number of adult children living with their parents because they are unable to enter the housing market: 23 per cent of twenty somethings in a recent survey.[200]

Although the law has much to say on the responsibilities between parents and minor children, once children reach the age of 18 there are surprisingly few rights and obligations that are owed.[201] As Mika Oldham has pointed out:

We are free to refuse to render any form of assistance to our parents or grandparents, regardless of their, or our own, circumstances. Support for the elderly is considered to fall within the realm of public rather than private intergenerational transfer.[202]

Some countries have filial support legislation under which an adult can be required to pay the costs of their parents' care.[203] In England and Wales, absent a contract the between parties, a parent would have no cause of action against an adult child seeking financial support.[204]

---

[196] J Herring, 'Together Forever? The Rights and Responsibilities of Adult Children and Their Parents' in J Bridgeman, H Keating, and C Lind, *Responsibility, Law and the Family* (Ashgate, 2008).

[197] E Grundy and M Murphy, 'Kin Availability, Contact and Support Exchange' in F Ebtehaj *et al* (eds), *Kinship Matters* (Hart, 2006).

[198] A Lowenstein and S Olav Daatland, 'Filial Norms and Family Support in a Comparative Cross-National Context: Evidence from the OASIS Study' (2006) 26 *Ageing and Society* 203.

[199] D Gans and M Silverstein, 'Norms of Filial Responsibility for Aging Parents Across Time and Generations' (2006) 68 *Journal of Marriage and Family* 961.

[200] R Wicks and J Asato, *Lifelong Parenting* (Social Market Foundation, 2003), at 3.

[201] M Oldham, 'Financial Obligations Within the Family—Aspects of Intergenerational Maintenance and Succession in England and France' (2001) 60 *Cambridge Law Journal* 128; and M Oldham, 'Maintenance of the Elderly and Legal Signalling—Kinship and State' in F Ebtehaj *et al* (eds), *Kinship Matters* (Hart, 2006).

[202] M Oldham, 'Maintenance of the Elderly and Legal Signalling—Kinship and State' in F Ebtehaj *et al* (eds), *Kinship Matters* (Hart, 2006).

[203] S Moskowitz, 'Adult Children and Indigent Parents: Intergenerational Responsibilities in International Perspective' (2002) 9 *Marquette Law Review* 401; K Wise, 'Caring for our Parents in an Aging World: Sharing Public and Private Responsibility for the Elderly' (2002) 5 *New York University Journal of Legislation and Public Policy* 563; and L Fennell, 'Relative Burdens: Family Ties and the Safety Net' (2004) 45 *William and Mary Law Review* 1453.

[204] There may be circumstances in which they would have a claim on their child's estate (*Bouette v Rose* [2000] 1 FCR 185). This is discussed in chapter 9.

Financial liabilities of parents towards adult children

The law is a little, but only a little, more willing to accept financial responsibilities owed by parents towards their adult children. Normally a parent is only required to support a child until their 18th birthday.[205] In exceptional circumstances, a parent can be required to support an adult child. Under the Children Act 1989, Schedule 1, paragraph 2, if a child is a student or trainee and if his or her parents are living apart, he or she can apply to the court for a lump sum or period payments order. This is true even beyond the age of 18. In relation to married couples who are divorcing, an application can be made under the Matrimonial Causes Act 1973. Section 29 makes it clear that financial support for a child cannot be ordered beyond a child's 18th birthday, unless he or she 'is, or will be or [if provision extending beyond 18 years of age were made] would be, receiving instruction at an educational establishment, or undergoing training for a trade, profession or vocation, whether or not he is also or will also be in gainful employment' or there are 'special circumstances which justify' the making of a different order.[206]

So, then, children beyond the age of 18 can seek orders against their parents under the Children Act 1989 or, where the parents are divorcing, a court can make an order under the Matrimonial Causes Act 1973. However, this is subject to two important restrictions. First, they must show that they are receiving full-time education or training, or are suffering a disability.[207] Secondly, and more significantly, the liability arises only where the children's parents are divorcing or, if unmarried, have separated.

These restrictions can be criticized. A child may have genuine needs even though the parents have not separated. The explanation for this restriction which is commonly given is that there would be too great an intrusion into family privacy if a claim could be brought by the child against parents who are still together. A better explanation may be that these provisions are not actually about giving an adult child a claim against a parent. Rather, what the courts are doing here is, in effect, requiring one parent to meet a financial burden which would otherwise unfairly fall on another parent. In other words, it is about ensuring that the financial burden of supporting the adult child is shared equally between the parents, rather than giving a child a claim against his or her parents. Another criticism of the law is that although disabled children and those in education have a claim against their parents, other adult children in dire need who are equally worthy are not.

---

[205] Child Support Act 1991.
[206] *B v B (Adult Student: Liability to Support)* [1998] 1 FCR 49.
[207] *T v S (Financial Provision for Children)* [1994] 1 FCR 743.

Should we enforce filial responsibility?

In many countries there has been debate over whether or not filial responsibilities should be enforced. Judge Wald, an American judge, expressed well the ambiguous feelings some people have over this issue:

On the one hand, the dependency of frail or ill elderly people is viewed as 'not their fault' and as part of the 'natural progression of life.' Younger people can picture themselves in the same unenviable spot down the road and feel strong filial responsibilities to the parents who cared for them as children. Nonetheless, negative feelings toward the elderly run strong in our society...Many Americans feel that the care of the elderly should be paid for by their families or from their own savings, rather than by the government—they resent subsidizing other people's failure to plan ahead. Conversely, younger working Americans resent the notion that in their peak years, they must bear the burden of supporting older relatives.[208]

As this quotation indicates, on the one hand, the idea of an adult child having been well raised by his or her parents living in luxury while the parent lives in dire penury appears unjust. Yet at the same time the idea of the state forcing such payments seems an intrusion into family privacy.

One way into the debate is to consider whether there is a moral obligation on an adult child to care for their parents.[209] There is general agreement that there usually is, although finding its source has generated much dispute. Perhaps the most popular theory is based on reciprocation. Given all that the parent has done for the child when the child was in need of care, the child is morally obliged to assist the parent when the parent is in need. Despite its attraction, the argument is not without problems. It might be claimed that parents choose to become parents and caused the child to be born and can therefore be said to have consented to undertake the responsibilities of parenthood. The same cannot be said of children vis-a-vis their parents.[210] Indeed, parents are entitled to cease their obligations by handing a child to the state to be adopted. Should not an adult child be entitled to do the same in relation to their parents?

An attractive form of the reciprocity argument has been put by the Lindemann Nelsons:

The parental giving and filial receiving characteristic of early childhood is a major theme of the very beginning of the child's story, and one cannot yet tell what moral significance the child will make of it. But when that child grows into full moral agency, he is able retrospectively to make that giving and receiving mean a variety of things, depending

---

[208] P Wald, 'Looking Forward to the Next Millennium: Social Previews to Legal Change' (1997) 70 *Temple Law Review* 1085, at 1091.
[209] M Collingridge and S Miller, 'Filial Responsibility and Care of the Aged' (1997) 14 *Journal of Applied Philosophy* 119.
[210] N Daniels, *Am I My Parents Keeper?: An Essay on Justice Between the Young and the Old* (Oxford University Press, 1988).

on how he treats his parents now. If his parents now come to him in need and he spurns them, he is declaring that the relationship he had with them as a child was largely instrumental: he was using them only as a means to his own ends, and they are no more to him than that. Alternatively, if he now responds to their needs, he is redeeming that childhood relationship of its instrumentality, and declares by his actions that he was not merely using his parents to provide goods and services for him.[211]

The benefit of putting the argument this way is that it is sensitive to the long-term nature of the relationship. Adult children who are legitimately unable to assist their parents due to their own financial difficulties may not be showing that they have declared their parents were being used instrumentally, especially if they are able to offer whatever assistance they can. Similarly, what is required of the adult child depends on the appropriate response given the relationship and the parties' current needs, rather than simply how much was given during childhood.

Jane English has argued that the parent-child link on its own does not generate obligations.[212] However, the quality of the current relationship might create obligations, just as the relationship between two friends might. This would mean that a child who was currently in a hostile relationship (or indeed a non-existent one) with his or her parents would owe them nothing. The difficulty with this argument is that many children do feel obligations towards parents, even where the relationship is a bad one. A parent-child relationship is not just like a relationship between two friends. There must be few people who if required at the same time to be both at the bedside of a sick parent with whom they got on well, and a friend with whom they got on equally well would not feel the obligation towards a parent to be the stronger.

By contrast with Jane English's argument, Stephen Kellet[213] has argued that the child-parent relationship is 'like nothing else'. He argues:

There are important goods that you can provide only to your parents, and that your parents can receive from no one but you. My suggestion is that the reason why you have special duties to your parents is that you are uniquely placed to provide them with these goods and find yourself in a relationship in which they have provided (and perhaps continue to provide) special goods to you. And the duties themselves are duties to provide the special goods to your parents, within the context of the reciprocal relationship that you and your parents share.

There is much to this argument. It is, however, weaker when it comes to the kind of duties which the law is most likely to enforce: duties to pay money. The payment of money is not a need which a child is in a unique position to meet.

---

[211] H Lindemann Nelson and J Lindemann Nelson, 'Frail Parents, Robust Duties' (1992) 3 *Utah Law Review* 747.

[212] J English, 'What Do Grown Children Owe Their Parents' in C Sommers and F Sommers (eds), *Vice and Virtue in Everyday Life* (Harcourt, 1993).

[213] S Kellet, 'Four Theories of Filial Duty' (2006) 56 *The Philosophical Quarterly* 233, at 254.

Having considered the question of whether the child is obliged to support the frail parent, it is important to consider the issue from the parent's point of view. It is also sometimes argued that most older people would prefer to receive care and support from their children, rather than the 'impersonal, unfeeling' care provided at an institutional or state level. This, however, is not the correct question in this context—which is whether an older person would prefer to receive care from an adult child who has been compelled to offer this care or to receive care from the state. It is far from clear that a parent would prefer enforced care from a child to state care.

Let us accept for the moment that a case is made out for there being a moral obligation that is owed by some adult children to their parents and some parents to their adult children. How should the law respond? An obvious point to make initially is that the law does not directly enforce every moral obligation. There are plenty of immoral behaviours which are not subject to legal sanctions. Indeed, it is submitted that there would be some very real disadvantages in this context of seeking to enforce filial obligations. As Mika Oldham points out:

The advantages of public provision include safeguarding the independence of elderly people, who are not made to feel they have become a burden on their families, and the redistribution of wealth, via the state, to those in greatest need. But when public provision fails or is inadequate, its tendency to isolate different generations is accompanied by other adverse consequences. Chief among these is the fact that insufficient funding means that the system depends hugely on informal carers who are unrecognised, uncompensated and inadequately supported.[214]

There is a major concern, to which Oldham alludes, that enforced support by adult children may weaken the link between children and parents. Further, there is the concern that if filial obligations are enforced, this may disadvantage those older people without children or whose children could not care for them.

Another important concern about any filial support legislation would be the practical issues surrounding enforcement. As anyone who has studied the operation of the Child Support Acts will attest, enforcement is a major issue. This appears true in those countries which have enacted filial support legislation.[215] Examples of countries which currently have filial support legislation are Canada, France, Japan, and some states in the United States. In the United States, where filial responsibility statutes exist, in a surprising number of states (around 30), they are rarely enforced. In fact, in nearly half of those which have them, they have never been used.[216]

---

[214] M Oldham, 'Financial Obligations Within the Family—Aspects of Intergenerational Maintenance and Succession in England and France' (2001) 60 *Cambridge Law Journal* 128, at 163.

[215] S Edelstone, 'Filial Responsibility: Can the Legal Duty to Support Our Parents Be Effectively Enforced?' (2002) 36 *Family Law Quarterly* 501.

[216] M Oldham, 'Maintenance of the Elderly and Legal Signalling—Kinship and State' in F Ebtehaj *et al* (eds), *Kinship Matters* (Hart, 2006).

It appears then that filial support legislation is unlikely to be effective or desirable. However, it must not be thought that where there is a moral obligation the legal response is either to enforce it or ignore it. The law is far more subtle than that. It can uphold, bolster, or reinforce the obligation in other ways, free of direct enforcement. For example, the law can leave an obligation not legally enforceable, but offer benefits or advantages to those who fulfil their obligations. The law could be used to provide encouragements for family members to undertake practical or financial aid for aged dependent members.[217] This could include tax advantages for those providing financial care for elderly relatives; employment protection for those caring for dependants; state support for children wishing to move closer to their dependant parents to care for them; and changes in inheritance law allowing a carer to make a claim on the estate for financial support.

Conclusion

For far too many pensioners, retirement is a time of poverty. Although through extending means-tested benefits it has been possible to reduce that number, many are left behind—too many for a society of our wealth. The government, in its recent pension reforms, has sought to tackle the issue of funding in retirement. It seeks to strike the correct balance between encouraging private saving for pensions and providing a state pension to ensure a minimum income level. Striking that balance is complex and depends on many factors. It remains to be seen how successful it has been. Much will depend on the popularity and success of the personal accounts.

The current state of funding old age care is unacceptable. Few would disagree with this, but the solution is harder to find. A strong case can be made for the state provision of free personal care, but the political will to find the funding for this seems to be lacking. However, without it far too many older people are going without the basic personal care which should be theirs as part of their right to dignity.

---

[217] K Wise, 'Caring for Our Parents in an Aging World: Sharing Public and Private Responsibility for the Elderly' (2002) 5 *New York University Journal of Legislation and Public Policy* 563.

7

Grandparenthood

Introduction

Grandparents. The very word conjures up the most homely of images in the popular imagination, of the kind found in old-fashioned children's books. Jane is in the kitchen baking scones with granny; while Peter is out fishing with grandpa. For a grandmother to say she was not interested in her grandchildren would be a heresy. Even if it were true it would be socially unacceptable for her to say so. To mount a campaign to persuade the public that grandchildren did not benefit from seeing their grandparents would be likely to have as much success as a campaign to ban rhubarb crumble. To many older people, grandparenting is one the most enjoyable aspects of old age. Indeed, with current levels of life expectancy it has been claimed that we can expect to spend at least half our lives as grandparents.[1]

It has been estimated that there are 13 million grandparents in the UK.[2] Twenty-nine per cent of all adults are grandparents and three-quarters of those over 66 are.[3] In recent years, the government has been keen to emphasize that grandparents play an important role in children's lives by providing stability and security.[4] In 2006, the Parliamentary Under-Secretary of State for Education and Skills stated:

The Government recognise and value the important role that grandparents play in their grandchildren's lives. Whether families are together, divorced or otherwise, grandparents play an essential part in the upbringing of any child lucky enough to have them. No one disputes that.

[M]ost children see their grandparents as important figures in their lives and enjoy the time that they spend with them . . . I want to make it clear that there is no dispute about the grandparents' importance in the lives of their grandchildren.[5]

---

[1] E Marcus, 'Over the Hills and Through the Woods to Grandparents House We Go: Or do We, Post-Troxel?' (2001) 43 *Arizona Law Review* 751.

[2] Grandparents Plus, *Statistics* (Grandparents Plus, 2008).

[3] S Harper, 'Grandparenthood' in M Johnson, V Bengston, P Coleman, and T Kirkwood, *The Cambridge Handbook of Age and Ageing* (Cambridge University Press, 2005).

[4] Home Office, *Supporting Families* (The Stationery Office, 1998).

[5] M Eagle, 'Grandparents: Access to Grandchildren', Westminster Hall Debates, 18 January 2006.

Yet, the cosy image of grandparent/grandchild relationships can disguise some harsher truths. Grandparents are being called upon to play an ever-increasing role in child care with increased rates of dual-earning households and lone parent employment. This in turn produces its own stresses for grandparents. Divorce and relationship breakdown can mean that treasured relationships between grandparents and grandchildren end or become highly strained. The abuse of grandparents by teenage grandchildren is becoming an increasingly problematic issue.[6]

All in all, the role of the grandparent in modern society is subject to conflicting tensions and this is reflected in the law. Indeed, the issue of grandparents' rights has become a politically controversial issue.[7] The government has even mooted paying grandparents to look after their grandchildren so that lone parents would be able to return to work.[8]

Sociological issues

Of course, there are grave dangers in making general statements about the roles that grandparents play in the lives of their children. They differ hugely from family to family. Further, the grandparental role should not be seen in isolation from the parent-child relationship. Parents can, in effect, restrict or enable contact between children and grandparents.[9] And, indeed, grandparents can play a role in strengthening or undermining the relationship between a parent and a child. The grandparent-grandchild relationship must therefore be seen as part of the network of interlocking family relationships. Further, the ethnic and religious backgrounds of families can play a huge role in determining how grandparents are perceived.[10] Finally, it should be noted that becoming a grandparent, in historical terms, is a relatively recent phenomenon. In 1900, around one-fifth of children could expect to be orphaned before they were 18. Nowadays, two-thirds will have both sets of grandparents alive when they are 18.[11]

---

[6] E Podnieks, J Kosberg, and A Lowenstein, *Elder Abuse* (Howarth Press, 2005).

[7] L Clarke and C Roberts, 'The Growing Interest in Fathers and Grandparents in Britain' in A Carling, S Duncan, and R Edwards, *Analysing Families* (Routledge, 2002).

[8] J Carvel, 'Grannies May Get Paid for Childcare', *The Guardian*, 21 March 2002. Although this has received little support form grandparents: S Arthur, D Snape, and G Dench, *The Moral Economy of Grandparenting* (National Centre for Social Research, 2003). For a discussion of this proposal in the broader context of paying for childcare, see A Mumford, 'Marketing Working Mothers: Contextualising Earned Income Tax Credits within Feminist Cultural Theory' (2001) 23 *Journal of Social Welfare and Family Law* 411.

[9] M Mueller and G Elder, 'Family Contingencies Across the Generations: Grandparent-Grandchild Relationships in Holistic Perspective' (2003) 65 *Journal of Marriage and Family* 404.

[10] J Jackson, E Brown, T Antonucci, and S Olav Daatland, 'Ethnic Diversity in Ageing, Multicultural Societies' in M Johnson (ed), *The Cambridge Handbook of Age and Ageing* (Cambridge University Press, 2005).

[11] Ibid.

The changing nature of families and the role of grandparents

It is not surprising that as the nature of families changes, this impacts on the role of grandparents.[12] Ever more grandparents are undertaking care of their grandchildren. Grandparent Plus (a campaign group) has claimed that 82 per cent of children receive some care from their grandparents, and nearly 5 million grandparents spend the equivalent of three days a week caring for grandchildren. Over one-half of women in paid work with a child under five leave their child with the child's grandparents.[13] One recent survey found that 45 per cent of grandparents are regularly involved in the care of their under-two-year-old grandchildren.[14] The mean level of care provided is 10 hours per week, although the fact that the mode is 2.5 hours a week demonstrates that there is wide variation in the levels of care offered.[15] Another survey found that 62 per cent of grandparents saw grandchildren at least once a week.[16] Indeed, 1 per cent of grandparents have their grandchildren living with them.[17] Age Concern estimates that each year grandparents undertake childcare worth £3,886 million.[18]

The explanation for this increasing role of care for grandparents is a result of both rising levels of marital break-up and, especially, increasing rates of employment among mothers. The expense, unreliability, and guilt that can be associated with non-familial childcare leads many mothers needing childcare support to turn to their own mothers.[19] This has led some commentators to suggest that the traditional nuclear family is being challenged by a three-generational model: child-mother-grandmother. As Dench and Ogg[20] have put it:

We can see a clear tendency at the moment for matrilineal ties (through the mother) to become the more active, while patrilineal, through the father, may often be very tenuous or even non-existent... [There is now] a growing frailty in ties between parents... an increasing marginalisation of men, and of ties traced through men, and a stronger focusing of families around women.

[12] G Ochiltree, *The Changing Role of Grandparents* (Australian Family Relationships Clearing House, 2006).

[13] Social and Community Planning Research, *Women's Attitudes to Combining Paid Work with Family Life* (SCPR, 2000).

[14] E Fergusson, B Maughan, and J Golding, 'Which Children Receive Grandparental Care and What Effect Does it Have?' (2008) 49 *Journal of Child Psychology and Psychiatry* 161.

[15] Ibid.

[16] L Clarke and C Roberts, 'The Meaning of Grandparenthood and its Contribution to the Quality of Life of Older People' in A Walker and C Hagan Hennessy (eds), *Growing Older: Quality of Life in Old Age* (Open University Press, 2004).

[17] Grandparents Plus, the Grandparents Association and Family Rights Group, *Celebrating Grandparents and the Extended Family—A Call to Action* (Grandparents Plus, 2005).

[18] Age Concern, *The Economic Contribution of Older People* (Age Concern, 2004).

[19] Although there is some evidence that especially as children get older parents prefer more formal childcare arrangements over grandparental care.

[20] G Dench and J Ogg, *Grandparenting in Britain: A Baseline Study* (Institute of Community Studies, 2002).

Other factors that may explain the increased availability of grandparents to care for children are increased longevity, improved health, and, perhaps, greater worries among older people about how they will be cared for later in life. Surely there are few grandparents who care for their grandchildren explicitly in the expectation that as a result they will be cared for when they lose capacity, but that may be a subtle influence.[21] There is also the fact that, with birth rates falling, the average number of grandchildren per grandparent has been steadily falling, enabling grandparents to spend more time on those they have.[22]

Of course, it should not be thought that all the social pressures are in the direction of increasing the involvement of grandparents in the lives of children. There is pressure on people to work beyond traditional retirement age and this means that less time may be available for grandparenting activities.[23] Indeed, several commentators have highlighted the potential contradiction between the government encouraging people to work beyond retirement and encouraging grandparents to be involved in childcare.[24] Further, as Heather Crook has pointed out, in dual-earning families time with children may be seen as more precious by the parents, and hence they are more reluctant for children to spend spare time with grandparents.[25] Another factor which can work against grandparental involvement with grandchildren is relationship breakdown between both grandparents and parents, which can have a negative impact on the extent of contact between children and grandparents, particularly for the parents of the non-resident parent and the grandchildren. It has been claimed that 1 million grandchildren are denied contact with their grandparents as a result of divorce, separation, or adoption.[26] A final point is that as the quality and affordability of childcare available improves, there is evidence that an increasing number of

[21] See the discussions in D Friedman, M Hechter, and D Kreager, 'A Theory of the Value of Grandchildren' (2008) 20 *Rationality and Society* 31; and G Douglas and N Ferguson, 'The Role of Grandparents in Divorced Families' (2003) 17 *International Journal of Law Policy and the Family* 41.

[22] A Dunning, 'Grandparents—An Intergenerational Resource for Families: A UK Perspective' (2006) 4 *Journal of Intergenerational Relationships* 127.

[23] G Dench, J Ogg, and K Thomson, 'The Role of Grandparents' in R Jowell, J Curtice, A Park, and K Thomson (eds), *British Social Attitudes Survey, 16th Report* (Ashgate, 2000) found that although two-thirds of grandmothers under 60 had paid jobs, this did not reduce contact with grandchildren. See also, A Dunning, 'Grandparents—An Intergenerational Resource for Families: A UK Perspective' (2006) 4 *Journal of Intergenerational Relationships* 127.

[24] See the calls for grandparents involved in childcare to have rights to flexible working: S Arthur, D Snape, and G Dench, *The Moral Economy of Grandparenting* (National Centre for Social Research, 2003).

[25] H Crook, 'Case Commentary: Grandparent Visitation Rights in the United States Supreme Court' (2001) 13 *Child and Family Law Quarterly* 101.

[26] Grandparents' Association, '*Stop Press!*' (Grandparents' Association, 2008). Although as I Dey and F Wasoff, 'Mixed Messages: Parental Responsibilities, Public Opinion and the Reforms of Family Law' (2006) 20 *International Journal of Law, Policy and the Family* 225, at 237–8 observe, there is little evidence for this.

parents are preferring formal childcare over grandparental care, especially in the case of children over the age of two.[27]

We are seeing a higher public profile for the role of grandparents, especially in government publications and public discussions. They are seen as providing an important source of stability for children; a reliable source of childcare provision; and perhaps most significantly as alternative carers when parents are unable to take care of their children. Cynics might argue that grandparents are being tapped into as a cheap source of foster caring or childcare; saving the government money and disguising the lack of state provision in these areas. But the public acknowledgement of their role is greater now than it ever has been. Pressure groups such as The Grandparents Association and Grandparents Action Group have been formed, which seek to create 'pro-grandparent' government policy and increase the media exposure of grandparents.

The motivation for grandparental care is not as straightforward as may be thought.[28] Anne Gauthier has argued that it is best understood as grandparents continuing to help their own children.[29] In other words, the care springs from a desire to assist the parents, as much as any obligation felt towards the grandchild. Evidence for this claim may be found in the fact that maternal grandparents do more care for the grandchild than the paternal grandparents[30] and that the level of grandparental care tends to be highest at the time when the mother is in greatest need. However, for many grandparents time with grandchildren is deeply satisfying and pleasurable. One study found 90 per cent of grandparents agreeing with the proposition that 'Grandparenting is a very rewarding aspect of my life'.[31] Psychologists have argued that it can avoid a sense of 'stagnation' for older people.[32] However, as that same statistic indicates, there is a small proportion of grandparents for whom the role is not a pleasure. Indeed, it often carries burdens. In one survey, 74 per cent of all grandparents agreed that they 'often put themselves out' in order to help with grandchildren.[33] There are particularly

[27] A Gray, 'The Changing Availability of Grandparents as Carers and its Implications for Childcare Policy in the UK' (2005) 34 *Journal of Social Policy* 557.

[28] D Friedman, M Hechter, and D Kreager, 'A Theory of the Value of Grandchildren' (2008) 20 *Rationality and Society* 31.

[29] A Gauthier, 'The Role of Grandparents' (2002) 50 *Current Sociology* 295.

[30] D Friedman, M Hechter, and D Kreager, 'A Theory of the Value of Grandchildren' (2008) 20 *Rationality and Society* 31.

[31] G Dench and J Ogg, *Grandparenting in Britain: A Baseline Study* (Institute of Community Studies, 2002).

[32] D Thiele and T Whelen, 'The Nature and Dimensions of the Grandparent Role' (2006) 40 *Marriage and Family Review* 1; and D Thiele and T Whelan, 'The Relationship between Grandparent Satisfaction, Meaning and Generativity' (2008) *International Journal of Aging and Human Development* 21.

[33] G Dench and J Ogg, *Grandparenting in Britain: A Baseline Study* (Institute of Community Studies, 2002).

heavy burdens when grandparents have taken on the role of primary carer for the child.[34]

What do grandparents do with grandchildren?

Sometimes in the media there is criticism of academic research which appears to prove the blindingly obvious. Such a criticism may be made of studies which show that children generally hold their grandparents in special affection.[35] But there is much more to such affection than granny-made scones and big presents at birthdays. As already mentioned, grandparents now play a major role in child-care arrangements. They can be a source of emotional support for children, particularly in the event of parental separation.[36] The role played by grandparents usually depends on the age of the child. With younger children, grandparents tend to be involved in outings and activities, while with older children talking and giving advice plays a bigger role.[37] Emotional help is also seen as important, with one survey finding that one-third of grandparents felt they acted as a confidant or friend to grandchildren.[38]

Not surprisingly, empirical studies demonstrate the wide range of roles that grandparents can play.[39] These depend on their personal circumstances and the social structures and support available to the family.[40] Grandparental help in childcare can cover practical, financial, and emotional assistance.[41] In one survey of grandparents in the UK, it was found that 60 per cent looked after a grand-child under the age of 15 during the daytime and 54 per cent did babysitting.[42] As to financial help, 64 per cent of grandparents gave this, again, particularly in times of especial need, such as following separation.

---

[34] J Lumpkin, 'Grandparents in a Parental or Near-Parental Role: Sources of Stress and Coping Mechanisms' (2008) 29 *Journal of Family Issues* 357.

[35] G Douglas and M Murch, *The Role of Grandparents in Divorced Families* (Family Studies Research Centre, 2002).

[36] Judy Dunn and Kirby Deater-Deckard have suggested that maternal grandparents can provide an important emotional support to grandchildren whose parents divorce, by acting as confidants (J Dunn and K Deater-Deckard, *Children's Views of Their Changing Families* (Joseph Rowntree Foundation, 2001), at ch 5).

[37] N Ross, M Hill, H Sweeting, and S Cunningham-Burley, *Grandparents and Teen Grandchildren* (ESRC, 2005).

[38] A Dunning, 'Grandparents—An Intergenerational Resource for Families: A UK Perspective' (2006) 4 *Journal of Intergenerational Relationships* 127, at 130.

[39] Grandparents provide particular help with disabled children: W Mitchell, 'The Role of Grandparents in Intergenerational Support for Families with Disabled Children: A Review of the Literature' (2007) 12 *Child and Family Social Work* 94.

[40] T Hill, 'What's a Grandparent to Do? The Legal Status of Grandparents in the Extended Family' (2001) 22 *Journal of Family Issues* 594.

[41] L Clarke and C Roberts, 'The Meaning of Grandparenthood and its Contribution to the Quality of Life of Older People' in A Walker and C Hagan Hennessy (eds), *Growing Older: Quality of Life in Old Age* (Open University Press, 2004).

[42] Ibid.

Gauthier suggests that the role played by grandparents can be divided into three main categories: educational subcontractors, where the grandparents in effect take on the role normally carried out by a parent while the child is with them; specialists, where grandparents are seen as having a specific role or skill to pass on to the grandchild; and passive grandparents, where their involvement with the child is limited to visits only once or twice a year. As she points out, which of these roles is carried out by a grandparent to a large extent depends on the parents.[43] Perhaps added to these categories should be the role of grandparents as rescuers, who enter into the family and take over primary care of a child in times of crisis.[44] Sarah Harper's study of grandmothers separated out the following roles: carer; replacement partner (for example, confidante, guide, and facilitator); replacement parent (for example, listening, teaching, and disciplining); and family anchor (for example, transferring values, attitudes, and history).[45]

Another attempt to analyse the grandparental role suggested a separation between different models. Douglas and Ferguson suggest three variables by which to consider the grandparental role. First is the extent to which grandparents assume a parental role or whether they are seen supporting the parents. This may not simply be a matter of the amount of time the grandparent has with the children. It may turn on the personality and health of the grandparent.[46] Second is the extent to which the grandparent is partisan as between the two parents. This is an issue which is particularly relevant in the case of separated parents. Thirdly, there is the question of whether the grandparent is really understanding their role as support for their own child (the grandchild's parent) or as carer for the grandchild him- or herself.[47]

Parental separation has a significant impact on the role that grandparents play. About 38 per cent of grandparents had children who were not living with both parents and one-fifth of grandparents had at least one step-child.[48] The impact of parental separation on grandparents is particularly significant for the parents of the non-resident parent. Douglas and Ferguson, however, argue that the nature of the grandparent/grandchild relationship prior to the separatation is often reflected in the relationship after separation. This suggests that separation does not normally affect the grandparent/grandchild relationship in a fundamental way.

[43] A Gauthier, 'The Role of Grandparents' (2002) 50 *Current Sociology* 295.

[44] E Marcus, 'Over the Hills and Through the Woods to Grandparents House We Go: Or do We, Post-Troxel?' (2001) 43 *Arizona Law Review* 751.

[45] S Harper, T Smith, Z Lechtman, I Ruchiva, and H Zelig, *Grandmother Care in Lone Parent Families* (OIA, 2004). See also, V Bengston, 'Diversity and Symbolism in Grandparental Roles' in V Bengston and J Robertson (eds), *Grandparenthood* (Sage, 1985).

[46] M Dolbin-Macnab, 'Just Like Raising Your Own? Grandmothers' Perceptions of Parenting a Second Time Around' (2006) 55 *Family Relations* 564.

[47] G Douglas and N Ferguson, 'The Role of Grandparents in Divorced Families' (2003) 17 *International Journal of Law Policy and the Family* 41.

[48] L Clarke and C Roberts, 'The Meaning of Grandparenthood and its Contribution to the Quality of Life of Older People' in A Walker and C Hagan Hennessy (eds), *Growing Older: Quality of Life in Old Age* (Open University Press, 2004).

Grandparent-headed homes

Around 1 per cent of grandparents have grandchildren living with them.[49] There has been relatively little research on such families.[50] The role can be complex.[51] A study for the Family Rights Group found that there were two main groups of grandparent-headed families. First, there were young, white or Afro-Caribbean, maternally related grandparents. There, the grandparents were normally undertaking care following some kind of crisis.[52] In such cases, in the absence of the grandparents having the child to live with them, the child would be taken into care. The second group were Chinese, Pakistani, Muslim, or Indian Sikh grandparents who were housing and caring for children to enable parents to work.

There are reports that caring for grandchildren at home can lead to increased levels of stress[53] and depression.[54] This is not surprising given that the circumstances in which grandparents take over care of grandchildren are associated with difficult family backgrounds. There is ample evidence of a lack of financial and practical help for grandparents who are caring for grandchildren.[55] We shall return to these issues later in this chapter.

Differences between grandparents

As already indicated, it would be misleading to treat all grandparents as a homogenous group. Gender is one important distinguishing feature. It is commonly assumed that grandmothers play a greater role in children's lives than grandfathers,[56] although there is a surprising lack of evidence to demonstrate this.[57] This is because most of the research has focused on grandmothers and there have been complaints that insufficient attention has been paid to the unique

[49] L Clarke and H Cairns, 'Grandparents and the Care of Children: The Research Evidence' in B Broad (ed), *Kinship Care: The Placement of Choice for Children and Young People* (Russell House, 2001).

[50] A Orb and M Davey, 'Grandparents Parenting Their Grandchildren' (2005) 24 *Australasian Journal on Ageing* 162. For a review of the US literature, see B Hayslip and P Kaminski, 'Grandparents Raising Their Grandchildren' (2005) 45 *The Gerontologist* 262.

[51] L Lundry-Meyer and B Newman, 'An Exploration of the Grandparent Caregiver Role' (2004) 25 *Journal of Family Issues* 1005.

[52] A Richards, 'Second Time Around for Grandparents' (2003) 33 *Family Law* 749.

[53] S Kelley, 'Caregiver Stress in Grandparents Raising Grandchildren' (2007) 25 *Journal of Nursing Scholarship* 331.

[54] J Blustein, S Chan, and F Guanais, 'Elevated Depressive Symptoms Among Caregiving Grandparents' (2004) 39 *Health Services Research* 1671.

[55] A Richards, 'Second Time Around for Grandparents' (2003) 33 *Family Law* 749.

[56] A Gray, 'The Changing Availability of Grandparents as Carers and its Implications for Childcare Policy in the UK' (2005) 34 *Journal of Social Policy* 557.

[57] N Ferguson, G Douglas, N Lowe, M Murch, and M Robinson, *Grandparenting in Divorced Families* (The Policy Press, 2004), at 13–14.

role that a grandfather can play.[58] It seems that the kinds of activities that grand-mothers and grandfathers do with their grandchildren differ.[59]

There is more evidence that maternal grandparents on average play a greater role in grandchildren's lives than paternal grandparents.[60] This is particularly so after divorce.[61] This is not surprising given that most resident parents are mothers and it will be easier for the grandparents on the resident parent's side to have contact. One leading study involving separated families found that three in four maternal grandparents said that their relationship with grandchildren was close; whereas the figure was only one in three on the paternal side.[62] However, it should not be thought that divorce only has negative consequences for grandparents. In some cases it can strengthen the bonds with grandchildren, and it may mean if repartnering follows that there is a new set of children who can be treated as grandchildren.[63]

A little researched issue is the effect of a divorce of grandparents on their relationship with grandchildren. It appears from what little research there is that where this happens it has a detrimental effect on both grandparents' relationship with their grandchildren, although it is particularly pronounced in the case of grandfathers.[64]

The law of grandparents

It is perhaps surprising that there is no special legal status that applies to grand-parents. They are recognized in section 105 of the Children Act 1989 as being relatives, along with uncles, aunts, and siblings. Not that that means much. The significance of being a relative lies in two areas. First, if a relation has lived with the child for three years they can apply for a residence or contact order without leave of the court. If the time spent is less than three years, then leave of the court is required. Secondly, when deciding whether or not to make an adoption order the child's links with the wider family should be considered. So as far as the Children Act 1989 is concerned, apart from the few grandparents who have their

---

[58] R Mann, 'Out of the Shadows?: Grandfatherhood, Age and Masculinities' (2007) 21 *Journal of Aging Studies* 271.

[59] G Douglas and N Ferguson, 'The Role of Grandparents in Divorced Families' (2003) 17 *International Journal of Law Policy and the Family* 41.

[60] Ibid; and V King, 'The Legacy of a Grandparent's Divorce: Consequences for Ties Between Grandparents and Grandchildren' (2003) 65 *Journal of Marriage and Family* 170.

[61] J Dunn and K Deater-Deckard, *Children's Views of their Changing Families* (Joseph Rowntree Foundation, 2001), at ch 5.

[62] G Douglas and N Ferguson, 'The Role of Grandparents in Divorced Families' (2003) 17 *International Journal of Law Policy and the Family* 41.

[63] C Smart, 'Changing Commitments: A Study of Close Kin After Divorce in England' in M Maclean (ed), *Family Law and Family Values* (Hart, 2005).

[64] V King, 'The Legacy of a Grandparent's Divorce: Consequences for Ties Between Grandparents and Grandchildren' (2003) 65 *Journal of Marriage and Family* 170.

grandchildren living with them and grandparents whose grandchildren are being considered for adoption, being a grandparent does not mean special legal rights or responsibilities.

So, in strict legal terms most grandparents are in the same formal legal position in relation to their grandchildren as any other adult in the country. However, as we shall see, the courts are normally willing to find that a child benefits from relationships with grandparents. Further, the benefit of grandparent-grandchild contact is widely accepted in our society as a benefit and this norm is often reflected in negotiated settlements between parents. So, even though being a grandparent does not grant one a special legal status, courts seek to promote the interests of the child and will often seek to preserve the grandparent/grandchild link.

ECHR and grandparents

Is the relationship between grandparents and children protected under Article 8 of the European Convention on Human Rights (ECHR) as being an aspect of family life?[65] The answer is not automatically. That should not be a surprise because even the relationship between a father and child does not automatically give rise to family life.[66] For grandparents, the European Court of Human Rights (ECtHR) has advocated a careful examination of the relationship between the grandparent and grandchild. In *Marckx v Belgium*,[67] the ECtHR confirmed that Article 8 rights were not restricted to parents and children and 'includes at least the ties between near relatives, for instance those between grandparents and grandchildren, since such relatives may play a considerable part in family life'. For the tie to exist, there must be a fairly close relationship between the child and grandparent.[68] So, no doubt there would be family life if the child were living with his or her grandparents[69] or had regular contact with them.[70]

Disputes over residence

Where a grandparent is seeking a residence order[71] as against the parent they will face an uphill task. The court will consider any application by a grandparent based on what will promote the child's welfare.[72] The courts have stated that in

---

[65] See the excellent discussion in F Kaganas and C Piper, 'Grandparents and Contact: *"Rights v Welfare"* Revisited' (2001) 15 *International Journal of Law Policy and the Family* 205.

[66] For an argument that there should be an acknowledgment of grandparental legal rights, see M Ognibene, 'A Constitutional Analysis of Grandparents' (2005) 72 *University of Chicago Law Review* 1473.

[67] (1979) 2 EHRR 330.

[68] *S and S v United Kingdom*, Application no 10375/83, (1984) 40 DR 196; *X, Y and Z v United Kingdom* [1997] 24 EHRR 143, para 52.

[69] *X v Switzerland*, Application no 8924/80, (1981) 24 DR 183.

[70] *Price v United Kingdom*, (1988) 55 DR 224. See also, *Boyle v United Kingdom* (1994) 19 EHRR 179.

[71] Children Act 1989, s 8. That is an order which determines with whom a child shall live.

[72] Children Act 1989, s 1.

deciding a dispute over residence it is strongly presumed that a child is better off with a 'natural parent' than anyone else. This presumption was applied in *Re D (Care: Natural Parent Presumption)*,[73] where a father of a child had a history of drug abuse and had had a number of children by different women. The child's grandparents sought a residence order. The application failed with the court preferring the natural parent (that is, the father). Only had he been shown to be clearly unsuitable would the court consider giving residence to the grandparents.

An example of a case where a grandparent did succeed in a residence dispute with a birth parent is *Re H (Residence: Grandparent)*.[74] There the child had been living with grandparents for about six years when the mother sought the return of the child. This time, the grandparents were awarded residence because the grandparents had become the 'natural parents' of the child.[75] The psychological bond between the child and grandparents had come to resemble that between children and parents. These cases suggest that grandparents are only likely to succeed in obtaining a residence order against the wishes of a parent where the parent is clearly posing a risk of harm to the child or where the child has lived with the grandparents for sufficient time so that they become the social parents of the child.

Where a grandparent does succeed in obtaining a residence order, their position may still be vulnerable. In *Re C (Children)*,[76] grandparents had been awarded residence, although the children remained in contact with their father. The grandparents were finding the contact sessions difficult and disruptive. The trial judge drew an analogy with adoption and held that as adoptive parents would be entitled to prevent contact with the birth parents, so too should the grandparents. However, this argument was rejected on appeal. There was no evidence that the children were at risk of emotional harm due to the grandparents' difficulties with contact and, therefore, despite the grandparents' objections, the order for contact should continue. Had the positions been reversed and the grandparents were seeking an order for contact with the children against the wishes of the children's parents, it is unlikely that contact would be ordered. This is the issue we shall consider next.

Disputes over contact

More common than residence disputes are cases where a grandparent seeks a contact order. This is most likely to arise where following a divorce or separation the resident parent refuses to allow the child to see the non-resident parent's parents.

---

[73] [1999] 1 FLR 134.   [74] [2000] Fam Law 715.

[75] Contrast *Re N (Residence: Appointment of Solicitor: Placement with Extended Family)* [2001] 1 FLR 1028, where the child had lived with an uncle and aunt for two years following his mother's death, but it was ordered he should return to his father. The first instance judges who had ordered that the child stay with the aunt and uncle were held on appeal to have paid insufficient attention to the fact that the child should be raised within the birth family.

[76] [2005] EWCA Civ 705.

In such a case, if the grandparents are seeking a contact order they must first obtain the leave of the court to make the application.

Seeking leave

The precise role and nature of the leave requirement is uncertain. Before the application for contact can be made, a short hearing will be required before a judge. The judge is required when considering whether to grant leave to consider the factors in section 10(9) of the Children Act 1989:

(a) the nature of the proposed application for the section 8 order;
(b) the applicant's connection with the child;
(c) any risk there might be of that proposed application disrupting the child's life to such an extent that he would be harmed by it; and
(d) where the child is being looked after by a local authority—
  (i) the authority's plan for the child's future; and
  (ii) the wishes and feelings of the child's parents.

According to the Court of Appeal in *Re A (Minors) (Residence Order: Leave to Apply)*,[77] the principle that in making a decision concerning the upbringing of a child that the child's welfare should be paramount[78] does not apply. The general view among commentators appears to be that this is of little significance. It is hard to imagine a court granting leave where the court believes that to do so would harm a child. At one time, the courts had suggested that the applicant had to have a 'good arguable case' before leave could be granted, but more recently the Court of Appeal held that that test was not part of the requirements.[79] Therefore, it should not be thought that because leave has been granted this is an indication that the application is likely to succeed.[80]

There is little doubt that a grandparent seeking contact with a child with whom they have a good relationship is likely to be granted leave.[81] Clearly, the issue could not be said to be a frivolous one. Indeed, it has been held that refusal to give leave is a serious issue and reasons must be provided for the refusal.[82] Refusing leave could be seen as potentially violating a party's rights under Articles 6 or 8 of the ECHR.[83] However, leave requirements do not automatically infringe convention

---

[77] [1992] Fam 182 CA.   [78] Children Act 1989, s 1.
[79] *Re J (Leave to Issue Application for Residence Order)* [2002] EWCA Civ 1346. *Re M (Care: Contact: Grandmother's Application for Leave)* [1995] 2 FLR 86 had suggested such a requirement.
[80] *Re A (Section 8 Order: Grandparent Application)* [1995] 2 FLR 153. For an argument that there is in effect a presumption in favour of grandparents being granted leave, see C Talbot and P Kidd, 'Special Guardianship Orders—Issues in Respect of Family Assessment' [2004] *Family Law* 273, at 274.
[81] *Re M (Care: Contact: Grandmother's Application for Leave)* [1995] 2 FLR 86, at 95; and Law Commission Report 172, *Review of Child Law* (Law Commission, 1988), at para 4.41.
[82] *T v W (Contact: Reasons for Refusing Leave)* [1996] 2 FLR 473.
[83] *Re J (Leave to Issue Application for Residence Order)* [2002] EWCA Civ 1346; discussed in G Douglas, 'Case Commentary—*Re J (Leave to Issue Application for Residence Order)*—Recognising

rights. The ECtHR has approved of leave requirements in other contexts as long as it is seen as proportionate and appropriate.[84]

The interpretation given to the leave requirement means that unless there are good reasons, leave will be granted. Perhaps the most common example of where leave is refused is where there is intense animosity between the grandparents and parents.[85] In *Re A (A Minor) (Contact: Leave to Apply)*,[86] Douglas Brown J upheld the decision of the magistrates' court not to allow leave to apply for contact, given the 'long-standing, serious disharmony between the parties'. Any order for contact against the wishes of the parents was likely to cause the child more harm than good, he concluded.[87] In *Re A (Section 8 Order: Grandparent Application)*,[88] Butler-Sloss LJ also noted that contact between a grandparent and child may not benefit the child where there was animosity between the grandparent and the parent. However, she emphasized that it should not be thought that simply because the parents oppose contact that leave should not be granted. Indeed, it has been argued that while parents may have a good reason for opposing contact, it will be rare that there will be a good reason for objecting to leave.[89] What, however, the court will be wary of is allowing an application to proceed which will significantly increase the animosity between the parties and as a result harm the child.

The substantive hearing

As with any application concerning the upbringing of children, the welfare of the child will be the paramount consideration when a court considers an application by a grandparent for a contact order.[90] In *Re A (Section 8 Order: Grandparent Application)*, the Court of Appeal said that there was no presumption in favour of ordering contact between a grandparent and child. However, if it is shown that in the circumstances of the particular case contact between the child and grandparent would be in the child's welfare, then the court will order contact.[91] Thorpe LJ has commented:

It is important that trial judges should recognise the greater appreciation that has developed of the value of what grandparents have to offer, particularly to children of disabled parents.[92]

Grandparents' Concern or Controlling Their Interference?' (2003) 15 *Child and Family Law Quarterly* 103.

[84] *Golder v United Kingdom* (1979–80) 1 EHRR 524; *H v United Kingdom* (1985) 45 DR 281; and *Re P (Section 91(14) Guidelines) (Residence and Religious Heritage)* [1999] 2 FLR 573.

[85] *Re M (Minors) (Sexual Abuse: Evidence)* [1993] 1 FLR 822, at 825.

[86] [1995] 3 FCR 543.

[87] To similar effect, see *Re A (Section 8 Order: Grandparent Application)* [1995] 2 FLR 153, p 154.

[88] [1995] 2 FLR 153, p 154.

[89] R Nugee (ed), *Relative Values… Missing Out on Contact* (Grandparents' Association, 2003), at 5.

[90] Children Act 1989, s 1(1).

[91] *Re M (Care: Contact: Grandmother's Application for Leave)* [1995] 3 FCR 550.

[92] *Re J (Leave to Issue Application for Residence Order)* [2002] EWCA 1364.

When considering the approach adopted by the courts in relation to grand-parental contact, it is worth remembering that there is not even a presumption in favour of there being contact between a father and child, although the courts will assume that contact is beneficial.[93] Seen in this light, the courts' rejection of a presumption in favour of grandparental contact is less surprising.

Even where it is found that contact will benefit the child, the court may not order contact if it involves forcing unwilling parents to allow contact, and that will be a cause of greater harm to the children than denying contact.[94] In *Re S (Contact: Grandparents)*,[95] Wall J found the mother's hostility to contact to be unreasonable and found the child would suffer significant harm without contact. However, that case appears to be exceptional. In *Re W (Contact: Application by Grandparent)*,[96] Hollis J held that where there was ongoing hostility between the mother and the maternal grandmother, it was a matter of 'common sense' that contact might harm the child. Indeed, it is now generally accepted that it will be very unlikely that a court would order contact to a grandparent against the wishes of a parent.[97]

Even if there is no presumption in favour of contact for grandparents, Felicity Kaganas has argued that it has become an extra-legal norm that grandparents should see their grandchildren, and this has become so gener-ally accepted that it exercises a powerful influence over negotiations to settle disputes within families.[98] Indeed, it may be that the establishment of such a norm is more important than any formal legal status, simply because the vast majority of disputes are settled between the parties than by means of a con-tested court case.[99]

Having summarized the law, we will now consider whether the law needs to be reformed.

---

[93] See the discussion of the law on fathers and contact in J Herring, *Family Law* (Pearson, 2008), at ch 9.

[94] *Re F and R (Section 8 Order: Grandparent's Application)* [1995] 1 FLR 524; *Re A (Section 8 Order: Grandparent Application)* [1995] 2 FLR 153; and *Re W (Contact: Application by Grandparent)* [1997] 1 FLR 793.

[95] [1996] 1 FLR 158.

[96] [1997] 1 FLR 793, p 797.

[97] F Kaganas and C Piper, 'Grandparents and Contact: "Rights v Welfare" Revisited' (2001) 15 *International Journal of Law, Policy and the Family* 250, at 254. See also, C Smart, V May, A Wade, and C Furniss, *Residence and Contact Disputes in Court* (Department of Constitutional Affairs, 2003). Those authors suggest that courts seemed unlikely to order contact in favour of a grandpar-ent against a parent's wishes. However, they found that, although the court made an order for 'no order' in one case out of the seven in their sample, the rest of the applications were withdrawn and the cases settled (at 28–9).

[98] F Kaganas, 'Grandparents' Rights and Grandparents' Campaigns' (2007) 19 *Child and Family Law Quarterly* 17.

[99] N Ferguson, G Douglas, N Lowe, M Murch, and M Robinson, *Grandparenting in Divorced Families* (The Policy Press, 2004), at ch 12.

Debate over the law

Given that the leave requirement may be regarded as 'scarcely a hurdle at all',[100] there are inevitably debates over whether it should be a requirement at all.[101] The Lord Chancellor during the debate preceding the Children Act 1989 sought to justify it in this way:

There is often a close bond...between a grandparent and a grandchild...and in such cases leave, if needed, will no doubt be granted. Indeed, in many cases it will be a formality; but we would be naïve if we did not accept that not all interest shown by a grandparent in a child's life is necessarily benign, even if well intentioned. Arguably, at least until we have some experience of wider rights of application, the law should provide some protection to children and their parents against unwarranted applications by grandparents when they occur.[102]

So, the argument is that although there are often good reasons why grandparents should be allowed to bring applications for contact, there may be some applications which are inappropriate and even pose a risk to the child. Some grandparent applications may be part of a personal dispute between the grandparents and parents rather than reflect a desire to see the children; or more likely a continuation of the battle between the parents, with the non-resident parent's parents being used as a tool in the battle between the parents.[103] Providing a filtering mechanism means that judges can prevent parents and children being disturbed by having to defend an application. It also ensures that cases involving children are not unnecessarily delayed by application by grandparents. As one American academic has put it:

One cannot lose sight of the irony in this situation; a grandparent's petition for visitation[104] is meant to enhance the child's well-being by increasing the number of loving adults in the child's life, but the petition launches the sort of conflict inherent in any court-adjudicated custody dispute; such conflict may be so disruptive to family life that it brings harm rather than benefit to a child.[105]

Opponents of the leave requirement could respond that the same thing could be said about applications from fathers and mothers. Yet, there is no leave requirement before they are entitled to have their applications heard. Further, it might be said that since Lord Mackay's comments we do now have years of experience

[100] Law Comission Report 172, *Review of Child Law* (Law Commission, 1988), at para 4.41.
[101] I Dey and F Wasoff, 'Mixed Messages: Parental Responsibilities, Public Opinion and the Reforms of Family Law' (2006) *International Journal of Law, Policy and the Family* 225.
[102] 503 HL Official Report (5th series) col 1342.
[103] G Douglas and N Ferguson, 'The Role of Grandparents in Divorced Families' (2003) 17 *International Journal of Law Policy and the Family* 41.
[104] Visitation is the American terminology for what in England is known as contact.
[105] T Stein, 'Court-Ordered Grandparent Visitation: Welcome Event or Unwarranted Intrusion into Family Life?' (2007) 18 *Social Service Review* 229, at 237.

of applications from grandparents and they do not appear to be maliciously motivated.[106] There is simply little evidence that many frivolous or harmful applications would be brought by grandparents if the leave requirement were removed.[107] Indeed, prior to the Children Act coming into force, grandparents could apply for contact orders without leave and there is little evidence of that being abused.[108] The number of undesirable applications deterred by the leave requirement may well be very small.

Another point made against the leave requirement is that although it is only a procedural loophole; in practice it operates as a deterrent. It means there is extra cost and effort involved for grandparents seeking contact with their children.[109] This means, it is claimed, that far from deterring inappropriate applications, in fact it deters justifiable ones.[110] It has been argued that leave is a paper exercise, and that it is very rare for parents to have a good reason to object to leave, even though they may have reasons to object to contact.[111]

Gillian Douglas[112] has questioned whether the leave requirement should be seen as no more than a procedural hoop. She suggests that it should be regarded as an important procedural stage before the full hearing. In *Re F and R (Section 8 Order: Procedure)*,[113] Cazalet J regarded the leave issue as a substantial matter, on which the views of the respondent should be sought. He held that magistrates should hear evidence from the main parties to clarify the issues of dispute between them so these can be clarified or resolved before the full hearing. Similarly in *Re W (Contact Application: Procedure)*,[114] Wilson J considered that the grant of leave is a 'substantial judicial decision' and one on which the respondent should normally be permitted to express their views. However, Douglas notes that in fact written procedures are normally used and leave is often granted without notice so that this aspect of the leave application is not being performed. She suggests that 'courts may have been regarding the leave application, particularly by grandparents, as a very minor hurdle to be overcome before the main action'.[115] If, however, the court uses the leave requirement as a device for assisting agreement between the parties and avoiding lengthy litigation, there appears less objection

---

[106] See *Re A (A Minor) (Contact: Leave to Apply)* [1995] 3 FCR 543, where a refusal to grant leave was upheld. The key factor in the refusal appeal was the strong opposition of the parents and the resulting very low chance of success of an application.

[107] House of Commons Constitutional Affairs Committee, *Family Justice: The Operation of the Family Courts. Fourth Report of Session 2004–5. Vol 1* (The Stationery Office, 2005), at paras 9 and 64.

[108] R Nugee (ed), *Relative Values…Missing Out on Contact* (Grandparents' Association, 2003), at 5.

[109] S Jackson, 'Grandparents: Access to Grandchildren', Westminster Hall Debates, 18 January 2006.

[110] L Drew, 'Grandparents and Divorce' (2000) 10 *Journal of the British Society of Gerontology* 3, at 7–10.

[111] R Nugee (ed), *Relative Values…Missing Out on Contact* (Grandparents' Association, 2003), at 5.

[112] G Douglas, 'Case Commentary—*Re J (Leave to Issue Application for Residence Order)*— Recognising Grandparents' Concern or Controlling Their Interference?' (2003) *Child and Family Law Quarterly* 103.

[113] [1995] 1 FLR 524.   [114] [2000] 1 FLR 263, at 265.   [115] Ibid, at 105.

to it. This is a convincing argument. If the leave requirement is to be justified, it should be regarded as a serious matter. If leave is no more than a 'rubber stamping' exercise, it becomes much harder to justify.

The government has, to date, rejected calls to abolish the leave requirement. In 2006, the Parliamentary Under-Secretary of State for Education and Skills stated:

The Government are not convinced that the safeguard of requiring leave to apply should be removed. We must do what we can to avoid involving children in unnecessary court proceedings, especially adversarial court proceedings, which can be distressing and bewildering for adults, let alone children. Such proceedings are costly, too. Removing the requirement would immediately bring in four more parties to start court proceedings.[116]

Leading academic commentators Gillian Douglas and Neil Ferguson have also argued against removal of the leave requirement or enhancing the formal legal status of grandparents.[117] They argue that in the clear majority of cases, families are able to resolve appropriately issues surrounding relationships between grandparents and grandchildren following a separation. Indeed, as mentioned earlier, their research suggests that the nature of the grandparent/grandchild relationship before the breakdown is normally reflected in what happens post-separation. They are concerned that legal intervention is normally used not as a way of asserting grandparental rights, but rather as part of the battle between the mother and father. The general norm governing grandparent/grandchild relationships is that the grandparents respect the decisions of parents concerning the raising of children, including the issue of contact with grandparents. They are concerned that giving grandparents a more formal legal status will challenge that norm. They see no case for giving grandparents as a group special legal help in the process over and above other people who may play a significant role in the child's life.

As mentioned earlier, grandparents have no special legal status in relation to grandchildren. There have been calls from some for grandparents to have a more formal legal status. This might, for example, mean that there was a presumption that following divorce of the parents, grandparents should have contact with their grandchildren. Or at the very least, that grandparents do not need leave to be able to apply for contact orders. However, there is a danger in assuming that because a relationship has benefit that it should be given legal effect or recognition. As Thompson *et al* argue:

All of these legal proposals assume, however, that adjudicated solutions to domestic disputes of this kind are desirable. Alternatively, however, it might be wise to question the assumption that family law should strive to protect all the significant relationships which a child shares with adults. Given the complexity of both children's needs and family functioning, the fact that the law is a blunt instrument for ensuring relational ties should

---

[116] M Eagle, 'Grandparents: Access to Grandchildren', Westminster Hall Debates, 18 January 2006.
[117] G Douglas and N Ferguson, 'The Role of Grandparents in Divorced Families' (2003) 17 *International Journal of Law Policy and the Family* 41.

introduce caution into efforts to extend legal protection to the relationships with non-parental figures possibly significant to children. While children doubtlessly benefit from the various adults contributing to their development, these relationships are meaningful as they occur naturally, not as they are judicially enforced. Legalizing the ties that bind may, in the end, undermine the relationships nurturing the children we seek to assist.[118]

There is another reason to doubt the wisdom of creating a special legal status for grandparents, and that is recognition of the diversity of roles played by grandparents. As Neil Ferguson *et al* comment:

the range of grandparenting styles, and the diversity in the quality of family relationships across generations, refutes the suggestion that the fact of being a grandparent is enough, per se, to justify special recognition.[119]

Perhaps the strongest way of challenging the current approach of the courts would be to turn to the ECHR. A grandparent with a good relationship with a grandchild should, as we saw above, be able to establish family life to which there is a right of respect under Article 8(1). A grandparent may well be able to establish a right to respect for family life in Article 8, although the weight attached to that right may be less than that attached to a parent and child.[120] In *L v Finland*, the ECtHR stated:

The Court recalls that the mutual enjoyment by parent and child, as well as by grandparent and child, of each other's company constitutes a fundamental element of family life.[121]

However, establishing the existence of family life will be only the first hurdle for any human rights claim. Article 8(2) justifies an interference in the rights of grandparents where that is (*inter alia*) necessary in the interests of others. Kaganas and Piper argue that if the parents object to grandparental contact the case will be seen as involving a clash between the rights of grandparents and parents. They argue in that case that the strong line of cases from the ECtHR on respecting parental authority[122] means that the rights of parents will win out. Harris *et al* agree, suggesting that in such a case the parents 'right to control the personal relationships... of their children' will win the day.[123] Douglas and Ferguson also support such a line, referring to *L v Finland*,[124] where the grandparental relationship was held not to have the same quality or significance as the parental one.

---

[118] R Thompson, M Scalora, S Limber, and L Castrianno, 'Grandparent Visitation Rights: A Psycho-Legal Analysis' (1991) 29 *Family and Conciliation Courts Review* 9.
[119] N Ferguson, G Douglas, N Lowe, M Murch, and M Robinson, *Grandparenting in Divorced Families* (The Policy Press, 2004), at 141.
[120] *L v Finland* [2000] 2 FLR 118.   [121] At para 101.
[122] eg *Neilsen v Denmark* (1989) 11 EHRR 175.
[123] D Harris, M O'Boyle, and C Warbrick, *Law of the European Convention on Human Rights* (Butterworths, 1995), at 317.
[124] [2000] 2 FLR 118.

Despite the academic support for this view, it is not beyond question. I have two reasons for suggesting that it is harder to predict how a Human Rights Act analysis would operate than the courts have suggested. First, in the analysis presented above, the cases are treated as involving a clash between the rights of parents and grandparents. However, there are the rights of the children to take into account. Indeed, the ECtHR has held that the rights of children should be regarded as crucial. It may be argued that children, especially where they have a close relationship with their grandparents, have important rights to the relationship being retained, even if that is against the wishes of their parents.

Secondly, even if the case is seen as one involving a clash between the parents and grandparents, I am not as convinced, as most commentators are, by the argument that grandparents will inevitably lose out. Although the Human Rights Act does not explicitly address the problem of clashing rights in cases between private parties, a jurisprudence on horizontal clashing rights is emerging from the House of Lords.[125]

This approach requires the court to consider the interference with each right individually, with an 'intense focus' on the specific right claimed. The discipline that flows from the decisions of the House of Lords builds on the 'parallel analysis' developed in the academic literature and requires the following exercise. First, each right should be weighed separately, by considering the values that underlie that right and the extent to which they are engaged in the particular context. Secondly, the justifications for interfering with the right should be considered and the proportionality test applied. Finally, having considered each right separately, the court should carry out the ultimate balancing exercise, by weighing the interference with each right against the other in order to find a solution that minimizes the interference with both rights.[126]

Adopting such an approach in this case it is necessary to look carefully at the values underlying the rights claimed. For the grandparent seeking contact, the value at stake is the relationship with his or her grandchildren. In a contact case, the whole relationship is at stake. For parents, there is the value of deciding with whom their child will have a relationship. It is not clear to me that comparing these values will necessarily lead to a preference for the parental wish, especially where the relationship with the grandparent is a good one and the inconvenience to the parent limited. It is argued that Kaganas's and Piper's argument that 'grandparents' rights are inferior to those of parents' is too much of a generalization. That may be true generally, but it is not correct to suggest that any parental right will always trump a grandparental right.

---

[125] *Re S (A Child) (Identification: Restrictions on Publication)* [2004] UKHL 47, [2005] 1 AC 593; and *Campbell v MGN Ltd* [2004] UKHL 22, [2004] 2 AC 457.

[126] R Taylor, '*Re S (A Child) (Identification: Restrictions on Publication)* and *Re W (Children)* Children's Privacy and Press Freedom in Criminal Cases' (2006) 17 *Child and Family Law Quarterly* 269.

Wilson J in *Re W (Contact Application: Procedure)*[127] held:

I anticipate that, when the Human Rights Act 1998 comes into force, it will be argued that a child's respect for his or her family life under Article 8 of the Convention requires the absence of such a presumption in the case of a grandparent to be revisited.

That may be putting it too strongly. First, as we have seen, grandparents do not automatically have a right to respect for their family life. It will only be where there is a strong relationship between the grandparents and child that there needs to be good reason for not ordering contact. Secondly, simply because a grandparent has a right does not mean that having that contact is in the welfare of the child. If the courts were to create such a presumption, that would need to come from the empirical data. As we shall see, that is unclear.

It may be that in considering such a rights-based claim the courts will draw assistance from the decision of the American Supreme Court in *Troxel v Granville*.[128] Tommie Granville and Brad Troxel had lived together in an unmarried relationship which produced two children. The children were in regular contact with the father's parents until the father committed suicide. Following that event, the grandparents were told by Tommie that they would only be able to see the children once per month. The grandparents sought an order to increase their visitation rights. The case reached the Supreme Court. In part, the case concerned issues of interpretation of Washington statutes, but it was also seen as raising important issues involving constitutional rights.

For the mother, the case concerned the right of liberty in the care, custody, and control of their children. In short, it concerned protection of parents' rights to make decisions concerning their children, including, in this case, the extent to which they could see their grandparents. While it was accepted that such a right could be interfered with if the parent was unfit, it was argued that otherwise the state should not interfere. In this case, there was no suggestion that the mother was unfit. For the grandparents the focus was on the best interests of the child. They argued that the state could intervene to protect children's best interests when parents were making a decision which harmed the child. In the Washington Superior Court, the starting point had been that it was in the best interests of the children to spend time with their grandparents. A court, it was held, in assessing a child's best interests, placed special weight on what the parents believed the child's best interests were, but at the end of the day the decision was for the court. On appeal, a key point was that the mother was not seeking to exclude all contact with the children, but simply to limit it.

The majority view written by Justice O'Connor found that the provision in the Washington legislation violated the due process right of the mother to make decisions concerning children. The legislation allowed any third party to subject a parental decision to state court review and no weighting to a parent's opinion.

---

[127] [2000] 1 FCR 185.   [128] 530 US 57 (2000).

The Supreme Court confirmed that where no challenge to the fitness of the parent arose then respect for a parent's fundamental rights entails a presumption that the parent knew what was in the best interests of the child. The dissenting judges disagreed that there was a 'constitutional shield', to use Justice Stevens' phrase, protecting parents. There was a presumption that parents' decisions generally serve the best interests of the child, but no more.[129] By six to three it was held that the statute which gave right to apply for visitation as applied in the case violated the 14th amendment, which provides that the state should not 'deprive any person of life, liberty or property without due process of law'.

It should not be assumed that the English or European courts will follow the approach taken by the American Supreme Court. One important point to note is that generally American law has placed less emphasis on children's rights than English law has. Further, the emphasis on parental autonomy has been subject to greater protection in American law than in European law. Nevertheless, the debates that arose in *Troxel* are likely to resurface in the ECtHR if the issue of grandparental contact right is considered.

In conclusion, an approach under the ECHR would recognize that grandparents with a close relationship with their grandchildren would be able to rely on their right to respect for their family life under Article 8. This right could be interfered with if necessary in the interests of others. Unlike other commentators, I doubt the courts will place much weight on the rights of parents to determine how their children will be raised; rather the focus will be on the harm to the children of court-ordered contact. If there was real harm, an interference in the rights of grandparents would be justified.

This brings us back to the question of how important the link between grandparents and children is. The following quote from the Grandparents' Association reflects the assumptions of many:

Where the child is young, grandparents provide an additional source of affection and entertainment for a grandchild. As the child grows older, the grandparents become an increasingly important means for the child to gain knowledge of family origins and roots, and a child may find it difficult to grasp the existence of the other side of his or her family when the other parent is absent. Grandparents can give a child a sense of his or her origins and heritage, as well as emotional and sometimes practical support that can be very important to an adolescent.[130]

There is empirical evidence that grandparents contribute significantly to the welfare of children.[131] Further, there is evidence that children with a strong

---

[129] H Crook, 'Case Commentary: Grandparent Visitation Rights in the United States Supreme Court' (2001) 13 *Child and Family Law Quarterly* 101.

[130] Grandparents' Association, *Arguments to be Used by Grandparents Seeking Contact with a Grandchild* (Grandparents' Association, 2008).

[131] V Adkins, 'Grandparents as a National Asset: A Brief Note' (1999) 24(1) *Activities, Adaption & Aging* 13. But see A Cherlin and F Furstenberg, *The New American Grandparent: A Place in the Family, A Life Apart* (Harvard University Press, 1986), at 178 and 181–3.

relationship with their grandparents are more secure;[132] especially following parental separation or death.[133] However, it is easy to over-emphasize the benefits.

First, the studies focus on either grandparents and grandchildren in intact families or cases where grandparents have contact, with parental agreement, with children following separation. There is no substantial evidence of the benefits of contact with grandparents where the contact has been ordered by a court against the wishes of the parent.

Secondly, it is clear that while some grandchildren benefit from relationships with grandparents, not all do.[134] There have been claims that the benefits of grandparental relationship have been exaggerated because the studies have focused on the adult perspective.[135] Indeed, Neil Ferguson *et al*, after a thorough review of the evidence, concluded:

it cannot be assumed that the grandparent-grandchild relationship is a valuable resource for children without taking account of the nature and quality of the particular relationships in the individual family.[136]

It may therefore be truer to say that contact where the relationship between grandparents and children are close is beneficial, rather than saying that contact is of benefit in all grandparent/grandchild cases.[137]

Thirdly, it is unclear whether the benefits provided by a grandparent are necessarily any greater or less than those provided by others involved in the child's life, such as siblings, aunts, uncles, and friends. Indeed, one major study found that whether closeness to grandparents helped a child adjust to parental separation may depend on the age of the children. While having some impact with younger children, it appears to have little, on average, for teenagers.[138] One explanation for this is that in the teenage years support from friends becomes increasingly important.

---

[132] M Purnell and B Bagby, 'Grandparents' Right: Implications for Family Specialists' (1993) 42 *Family Relations* 175. See also, A Kornhaber and K Woodward, *Grandparents and Grandchildren: The Vital Connection* (Anchor Press, 1985).

[133] G Kennedy and C Kennedy, 'Grandparents: A Special Resource for Children in Step Families' (1993) 19 *Journal of Divorce and Remarriage* 45.

[134] D Goldberg, *Grandparent-Grandchild Access: A Legal Analysis* (Department of Justice, Canada, 2003), at 16.

[135] See V Wood and J Robertson, 'The Significance of Grandparenthood' in J Gubrium (ed), *Time, Roles, and Self in Old Age* (Human Science Press, 1976), at 287.

[136] N Ferguson, G Douglas, N Lowe, M Murch, and M Robinson, *Grandparenting in Divorced Families* (The Policy Press, 2004), at 32.

[137] N Ross, M Hill, H Sweeting, and S Cunningham-Burley, *Grandparents and Teen Grandchildren: Exploring Intergenerational Relationships* (Centre for Research on Families and Relationships, 2005); and P Thompson, 'The Role of Grandparents When Parents Part or Die: Some Reflections on the Mythical Decline of the Extended Family' (1999) 19 *Ageing and Society* 471, at 499.

[138] L Bridges, A Roe, J Dunn, and T O'Connor, 'Children's Perspectives on Their Relationships with Grandparents Following Parental Separation: A Longitudinal Study' (2007) 16 *Social Development* 539; and S Ruiz and M Silverstein, 'Relationships with Grandparents and the Emotional Well-Being of Late Adolescents and Young Adult Grandchildren' (2007) 63 *Journal of Social Issues* 793.

So, to conclude this discussion, while there is good evidence that grand-parents play an important role in the lives of children, it does not follow that the law should recognize that by giving it an official status, and in particular that it should make court orders forcing parents to allow those relationships to develop. There may be cases where a close relationship between a grandparent and grandchild is protected by the ECHR, in which case the court should require good evidence that it is necessary to interfere in that relationship or not allow it to continue.

Public law

The position of grandparents in public law cases is rather different. Grandparents tend to play a more prominent role in such cases. This is unsurprising because if the primary reason for reticence in enforcing grandparents' rights in the private law setting is due to fear of disruption of the parent-child relationship, that concern is lessened in the public law sphere where the parents are unable to look after the child. Of course, where the mother is a minor living with her parents, the case becomes even more complex.[139] One study carried out before the Adoption and Children Act 2002 was in force found that in 39 per cent of all cases where a local authority placed a child with family or friends, they were placed with grandparents.[140]

Grandparents when the local authority removes the child

Where a local authority has decided to remove a child from parents, the possibility of care within the family must be considered, and grandparents are likely to figure highly in considerations at that stage. There are several different issues to consider.

Adoption of children and privacy

There have been several cases where a mother has not wanted the wider family (including her parents) to be informed about the birth of a child.[141] Generally, in such a case, the rights of the mother to anonymity have been seen to trump any rights of the grandparents to be considered as carers of the child. Alternatively, care can therefore be arranged by the local authority, without consideration being

---

[139] J Crews, 'When Mommy's a Minor: Balancing the Rights of Grandparents Raising Grandchildren Against a Minors' Parental Rights' (2004) 28 *Law and Psychology Review* 133.

[140] B Broad, 'Kinship Care: Children Placed with Extended Families or Friends' (1999) 155 *ChildRight* 16.

[141] *Re R (A Child) (Adoption: Disclosure)* [2001] 1 FCR 238.

given to the grandparents as carers, nor indeed them even knowing that the child has been born. This was explained by Holman J in *Z CC v R*:[142]

There is, in my judgment, a strong social need, if it is lawful, to continue to enable some mothers, such as this mother, to make discreet, dignified and humane arrangements for the birth and subsequent adoption of their babies, without their families knowing anything about it, if the mother, for good reason, so wishes.

However, it would be wrong to think that the privacy rights of the parents will always win out in such cases. In *Birmingham CC v S, R and A*,[143] an unmarried couple's relationship had ended before the birth of the child. There were serious concerns over the mother's ability to care for the child, especially given her previous history of parenting. It was likely that the child would be removed from the parents shortly after birth and the local authority were considering assessing both sets of grandparents as alternative carers. However, the father strongly objected, having initially agreed to the proposal. He did not want his parents to know he had fathered a child. He was living with his devout Muslim parents who did not know about his relationship with the mother or imminent birth of the child. He argued that his parents would not accept the child even if they were told abut him. In other words, telling them would only cause them grief and would carry no benefits because they would not want to be considered as carers. However, the Court of Appeal held that the father's objections could not carry weight because it could not be assumed that his parents would not be interested in caring for the child. They explained:

Adoption is a last resort for any child. It is only to be considered when neither of the parents nor the wider family and friends can reasonably be considered as potential carers for the child. To deprive a significant member of the wider family of the information that the child exists who might otherwise be adopted, is a fundamental step that can only be justified on cogent and compelling grounds.[144]

Such grounds were not found in that case. It is interesting to note that this case involved the father, rather than the mother, wishing to keep the birth secret. The court made little of this point, but it is interesting to speculate whether the courts think that a mother has a greater right to secrecy than a father.

A rather different attitude can be detected in *Re C v XYZ CC*,[145] where the Court of Appeal confirmed that there was nothing in the Adoption and Children Act 2002 which compelled a local authority to disclose the identity of a child to the extended family against the mother's wishes. The mother wanted neither the father nor either of their wider families to know of the birth. Under the Act, the question of whether the wider family should be informed was simply one of statutory interpretation and required an assessment of what was in the best interests of the child. One factor in that assessment is the child's interest in retaining her

---

[142] [2001] *Family Law* 8.   [143] [2006] EWHC 3065 (Fam).
[144] At para 75.   [145] [2007] EWCA Civ 1206.

identity within the birth family. However, that is only one factor, and indeed the Court of Appeal thought that section 1 did not privilege the birth family over adoptive parents 'simply because they are the birth family', although placing a child with a birth family will 'often be in the best interests of the child'.[146] The Court of Appeal believed that the requirement in section 1(4)(f) of the 2002 Act to consider the relationships which a child has could include relationships which have the potential to develop in the future, even if there is currently no relationship. That included, in this case, the grandparents. However, the overall conclusion of the court was that in this particular case informing the family would further delay finding an alternative home for the child. As to any Human Rights Act claims, it was held that the father had no family right with the child and so he could not claim a right to be informed of the birth. Interestingly, it was held that the grandparents did have a right to be informed of the birth under Article 8(1), but that interference in their rights was justified. Brief mention was made of the argument that the child may have a right to family life, but any interference in that could be justified if the adoption was approved under Article 8(2). It is surprising that the grandparents, but not the father, were found to have a right to be informed of the birth. This is not fully explained in the judgement, but it may have been because the father had indicated that he had no interest in the child and wanted to play no role in the child's life, while the grandparents had not had an opportunity to develop family life with the child.

The contrast between the two cases is striking and it is clear that there are a number of issues at play. First, there is the argument in *Birmingham CC v S, R and A*[147] that care within the family is less interventionist in family life than arranging care outside the family, and so that possibility should be investigated properly to ensure that extra-familial care is a proportionate response to the risks of harm facing the child. Secondly, there is the argument in *Re C v XYZ CC*[148] over whether the father or wider family had rights protected by the ECHR, with the rather surprising conclusion that the father did not, but the grandparents did.[149] Both of these arguments reflect an interesting issue about the definition of family life and whose family life we are talking about. If the focus is on the right of the child to family life and this is taken to include a right to be raised by his or her family, it could be argued that a court should be satisfied that wider family members are not appropriate as carers of a child. However, if a child's primary right to family life is to be cared for by his or her parents or at least have contact with them, it is not hard to imagine cases where contact is more likely to flourish where the child is cared for outside the family—for example, where the relationship between the child's grandparents and parents is bad.

---

[146] At para 18.   [147] [2006] EWHC 3065 (Fam).   [148] [2007] EWCA Civ 1206.
[149] For strong opposition to this decision, see A Bainham, 'Arguments about Parentage' (2008) 67 *Cambridge Law Journal* 322, at 350.

The issues discussed above raise some complex clashes between the parties' rights. There seems to be a strong public policy in favour of not discouraging parents to hand their children over to social services if they feel unable to care. If without a guarantee of privacy parents will be deterred from cooperating with social services, that would gravely endanger children's welfare. Where, however, offering such a guarantee of privacy is not a prerequisite for seeking social service help, the claims for privacy seem weaker, especially when compared with those of the child. If care by kin is preferable to care by strangers (and, as we shall see shortly, this cannot be assumed), I argue that the child's right to have the best upbringing will trump the parents' desire for privacy. So, unless a guarantee of privacy is necessary to ensure the child is protected, grandparents should be informed and involved in social service decisions involving their grandchildren. This is not in the name of grandparental rights, but in the name of children's rights.

Involving grandparents in decision-making

If there is no objection from parents, the consideration of grandparents (and other family members) as alternative carers for the child has become standard practice in care work. This means that grandparents should normally be considered as carers; and should be entitled to sufficient involvement in decision-making as is appropriate, given their right to respect for family life with the child. Further, they should normally be permitted to be parties to care proceedings. In *Mr and Mrs W v Vale of Glamorgan CC*,[150] a local authority had applied for an interim care order in respect of a child. The grandparents sought to be joined as parties. The magistrates declined to hear them and made the order. Headly J stated that the order would lead to the removal of the child and this would have a serious intervention in the child's life with the mother and grandparents. The judge should have allowed them to be joined as parties. Notably, in *Re H (Children)*,[151] the Court of Appeal was in favour of granting leave to join the grandparents as parties, even though they had never seen the child.

There are concerns in care proceedings that adding grandparents as parties will simply add to the complexities and costs of the case. These concerns will be heightened where the views of the grandparents are likely to reflect those of the parents.[152] Against these must be weighed the potential benefits that can be gained if the grandparents are able to continue to be involved in the child's life.

If the local authority has decided not to place the child with grandparents, the grandparents may still challenge the adoption order. In particular, when the court makes an adoption order the court must consider its effect on his

---

[150] [2004] EWHC 116 (Fam).   [151] [2003] EWCA Civ 369.
[152] *Re M (Minors) (Sexual Abuse: Evidence)* [1993] 1 FLR 822.

or her family.[153] The courts' focus will be on the best interests of the child. Where the adoption placement has been successful, it is unlikely that the court will wish to disrupt the current placement of the child. In such a case, the grandparents' best argument may be that a special guardianship will be more appropriate than adoption so that the grandparents can retain the link with the child.

If a child has been taken into care, a local authority is under a duty to promote contact between the child and wider family. Grandparents are likely to succeed in securing contact with children taken into care. In *Re M (Care: Contact: Grandmother's Application for Leave)*,[154] the court spoke warmly of the benefit to a child in care of seeing their grandparents regularly.

Orders where the grandparent is to be the carer

As shall be discussed shortly, many cases are resolved without formal applications being made to the court. For now, it will be supposed that the local authority has decided that care proceedings are needed. A key question when a local authority is involved with a child is whether they are best adopted by a stranger, or care by members of the child's family or friends should be relied upon. If it is concluded that the grandparents should care for the child, there is a range of options open to a court in formalizing the grandparents' position. Adoption, special guardianship, a residence order, or no order at all are all options.[155]

One key question will be what rights do the grandparents need? If the grandparents are to take over the primary role of caring for the children, they are likely to need at least parental responsibility. This can be awarded by either adoption, special guardianship, or a residence order. So, although it would be possible for the grandparents simply to take on the role of the carers for the child, without any formal court order, doing so would have the disadvantage that they would lack parental responsibility. Without formal parental responsibility, the grandparents will lack the official authority to make medical and educational decisions. So, leaving a child with grandparents without a formal legal court order is unlikely.[156] In *Re R (A Child)*,[157] it was held:

Making no order is, in our judgment, not an option. It would leave parental responsibility with M's parents who, by common consent, are not in a position to exercise it. The prospect that they may do so by placing M voluntarily with her grandparents leaves M wholly unprotected and vulnerable to parental whim. An order of some sort is plainly required.[158]

---

[153] Adoption and Children Act 2002, s 1(4)(f).   [154] [1995] 2 FLR 86.
[155] *Re R (A Child)* [2006] EWCA Civ 1748, para 84.
[156] A Richards, 'Second Time Around for Grandparents' (2003) 33 *Family Law* 749 found evidence of some grandparents pressurized into accepting some order.
[157] [2006] EWCA Civ 1748.   [158] At para 82.

As between adoption, special guardianship, and a residence order, one key difference is that adoption grants the status of parenthood, which the others do not.
The significance of having the parental role is, however, debatable. It is sometimes
said that adoption provides a formalization of their role.[159]

Special guardianship: when is it suitable?

The legal status of special guardian was created in the Adoption and Children Act
2002.[160] Commentators have debated the circumstances in which it will be used,
and indeed whether it will be used much at all. The Court of Appeal recently
heard three cases together to consider the circumstances in which a special
guardianship order should be made: *Re S (Special Guardianship Order)*;[161] *Re AJ
(Special Guardianship Order)*;[162] and *Re M-J (Special Guardianship Order)*.[163] The
cases all involved applicants who originally sought adoption, but for whom the
local authority had proposed special guardianship. The courts made the following important points about special guardianship.

First, the court explained that there were fundamental differences between
adoption and special guardianship. These are helpfully summarized in a table at
the end of the *Re AJ* judgement. The most significant is that while adoption ends
the parental status of the birth parents, special guardianship does not. The Court
of Appeal was clear that these differences should be considered carefully when
deciding between an adoption and special guardianship order.

Secondly, the court refused to accept that there were particular categories of
cases in which a special guardianship order was preferable to an adoption order or
vice versa. In every case the question was simply one of asking what order would
best promote the welfare of the child in question. In particular, there was no
presumption that where the child was to be raised within the wider family that a
special guardianship was preferable to an adoption order. In *Re AJ*, the argument
that it would be confusing for a child to be raised under an adoption order by his
uncle and aunt was rejected because the child knew the true family relationship.
There was, therefore, no danger that the family relationships would be 'distorted'
by an adoption order. In *Re R (Children)*,[164] an eight-year-old child opposed the
making of a special guardianship order over him. His opposition was seen as an
important factor justifying not making the order. However, the court added that
as a matter of principle it might be perfectly proper to make a special guardianship order against the wishes of a child.

Thirdly, the court emphasized that under the Human Rights Act 1998 the
court must ensure that the intervention in family life was necessary and proportionate. As a special guardianship order was a less fundamental intervention than

159 *Re J (A Child)* [2003] EWCA Civ 1097.   160 See s 115.
161 [2007] EWCA Civ 54.   162 [2007] EWCA Civ 55.
163 [2007] EWCA Civ 56.   164 [2007] EWCA Civ 139.

an adoption order, it should be preferred if it protects the welfare of the child to the same extent as an adoption order. In *Re S*, it was held:

In choosing between adoption and special guardianship, in most cases Article 8 is unlikely to add anything to the considerations contained in the respective welfare check-lists. Under both statutes the welfare of the child is the court's paramount consideration, and the balancing exercise required by the statutes will be no different to that required by Article 8. However, in some cases, the fact that the welfare objective can be achieved with less disruption of existing family relationships can properly be regarded as helping to tip the balance.[165]

However, one recent study indicates that rather than being used as an alternative to adoption, special guardianship is used when the alternative would have been fostering or a residence order.[166]

Fourthly, when considering whether to make a special guardianship order it should be remembered that the child's parents will still be able to apply for section 8 orders. This is not true in the case of adoption. The special guardianship does not, therefore, provide the same permanency of protection as adoption. In a case (like *Re AJ*) where the carers and child needed an assurance that the placement could not be disturbed, adoption may well be more appropriate. While it was true that where a special guardianship order was made a parent would need leave before making an application for a residence order, that did not provide the same level of security as an adoption order. A court could also make an order under section 91(14) of the Children Act 1989 to require a parent seeking any section 8 order to obtain leave of the court first. Even then the level of security for special guardians would not match that available for adoption.

Special guardianship: what is its effect?

Special guardianship was created in order to provide a status with a greater degree of security than a residence order, but without the effect of an adoption order in severing the ties with the birth family.[167] In *Adoption: A New Approach*,[168] it was explained:

The Government will legislate to create this new option, which could be called 'special guardianship'. It will only be used to provide permanence for those children for whom adoption is not appropriate, and where the court decides it is in the best interests of the child or young person. It will:-

- give the carer clear responsibility for all aspects of caring for the child or young person, and for making the decisions to do with their upbringing. The child or young person will no longer be looked after by the Council;

---

[165] At para 49.
[166] A Hall, 'Special Guardianship: A Missed Opportunity—Findings from Research' [2008] *Family Law* 148.
[167] See also the Special Guardianship Regulations 2005 (SI 2005/1109).
[168] Department of Health, *Adoption of a New Approach* (DoH, 2000), at para 5.10

- provide a firm foundation on which to build a life-long permanent relationship between the carer and the child or young person;
- preserve the legal link between the child or young person and their birth family;
- be accompanied by a proper access to a full range of support services including, where appropriate, financial support.

Special guardianship does not terminate the parental status of the birth parents and special guardians do not become the parents of the child. However, they are given parental responsibility and can make decisions about the child's upbringing without needing to consult with the parents.[169] The status can only be revoked if there is an order of the court. In *Re R (A Child)*,[170] it was held:

special guardianship is an issue of very great importance to everyone concerned with it, not least, of course, the child who is its subject. It is plainly not something to be embarked upon lightly or capriciously, not least because the status it gives the special guardian effect-ively prevents the exercise of parental responsibility on the part of the child's natural par-ents, and terminates the parental authority given to a local authority under a care order (whether interim or final). In this respect, it is substantially different from a residence order which, whilst it also brings a previously subsisting care order in relation to the same child to an end, does not confer on any person who holds the order the exclusivity in the exercise of parental responsibility which accompanies a special guardianship order.[171]

The nature of the status and the tensions that can arise in defining it are well demonstrated in a recent case. In *Re L (A Child) (Special Guardianship Order and Ancillary Orders)*,[172] the parents of child L were drug addicts in a volatile relation-ship. When L was just three months old she was placed with her grandparents, who were granted a residence order. Two years later, the grandparents sought an adoption order, but the judge made a special guardianship order. On appeal to the Court of Appeal, there were two key issues: first, whether there should be contact with the parents. The trial judge had ordered that contact take place six times a year, away from the grandparents' house, supervised by the local author-ity. Further contact could be agreed between the mother and grandparents if approved by a social worker. Secondly, there was the issue of whether the grand-parents were entitled to change the surname of the child to their own. This, they explained, would mean that they would not need to explain the family history to everyone who came into contact with the child and queried the difference in surname. The trial judge had refused to grant this request, a conclusion with which the Court of Appeal agreed.

At the heart of both of these issues was the extent to which special guardians are permitted to make decisions concerning the child. At the general level, the Court of Appeal explained that special guardianship did give guardians the right to exercise parental responsibility in the best interests of the child. However, that

---

[169] Although there are a few exceptions to this: see, eg Children Act 1989, s 14C(3), concerning changing a name.
[170] [2006] EWCA Civ 1748.   [171] At para 78.   [172] [2007] 1 FCR 804.

did not mean that there was no judicial control over the decisions of the guardians. Indeed, in the two issues under consideration, section 14B of the Children Act 1989 required the court, when making a special guardianship order, to consider whether to make a contact order and enable the court to give leave to change the surname. The response by the parents was:

What real value... does the name tag have if it does not give the guardians the autonomy to bring up the child in a normal way without 'big brother', the social workers, exercising the real control which, absent a care order, the local authority does not have.[173]

The court's response was that:

It is intended to promote and secure stability for the child cemented into this new family relationship. Links with the natural family are not severed as in adoption but the purpose undoubtedly is to give freedom to the special guardians to exercise parental responsibility in the best interests of the child. That, however, does not mean that the special guardians are free from the exercise of judicial oversight.[174]

On the surname issue, the court held that it was important that the child know of her background and live with the fact that she is being brought up by her grandparents. However, given that the child was to have regular contact with her birth parents, it is not realistic to assume that the child could be misled as to the relationship. As the court admitted: 'In the scale of things in this child's life, her surname is a fact of little real significance.'[175] With that in mind, one might have thought that allowing the special guardians who had undertaken, somewhat reluctantly, the enormous task of raising this troubled child, the liberty to change the name would be a minor concession. The court accepted 'that the care offered by the grandparents was exemplary', but the litigation and surrounding dispute had left them 'not far short from breaking point'.[176]

On the contact issue, the relationship between the grandparents and mother was volatile and so having them together at the time of the contact session was potentially harmful to the child. However, it was held that the requirement that a social worker approved of contact in excess of that ordered was unnecessary.

Payment of special guardians

There was some uncertainty in the regulations over the entitlement of special guardians to payment. In *B v London Borough of Lewisham*,[177] the local authority paid a grandmother special guardian £114.61 per week as an allowance. This was based on the sum paid to adopters. She sought to challenge the level awarded by way of judicial review, arguing that the statutory guidance indicated that the level paid to foster carers (which was much higher than that for adopters) should provide the guide. She succeeded in her claim, Black J holding that the policy

---

[173] At para 30.   [174] At para 33.   [175] At para 40.   [176] At para 22.
[177] [2008] EWHC 738 (Admin).

of the local authority paid attention to the guidance. Of more interest were the comments more generally about payments. She held:

the intention of the legislation and regulations about special guardians is that financial support should be made available to special guardians to ensure that financial obstacles do not prevent people from taking on this role. I do not go so far as to say that there must be *uniform* financial support to every type of carer. Different types of placement have different attributes, cost different amounts and require different schemes. To state the obvious, for example, by adopting a child, the adopters make the child their own which does not happen with any other form of alternative care. To give another example, children who are living with foster parents, or special guardians or with a non-parent who has a residence order are none of them living with their own parents but there is a manifest difference between special guardianship and a residence order to a non-parent on the one hand and local authority foster care on the other. However, putting it at its lowest, a local authority is not free, in my view, to devise a scheme which fails to do what is required by regulation 6 or which dictates that some types of placement for a child carry a significant financial disadvantage in comparison with others or, worse, would impose such a financial strain on a carer that they would be forced to choose another type of placement.[178]

Grandparental care

It is commonly assumed that it is preferable for children whose parents cannot look after them to be cared for by members of the broader family. Joan Hunt has summarized the main factors behind the increasing use of kin carers:

—A rising demand for out of home placements, a shortage of foster homes, particularly for minority ethnic children, and increasing numbers of hard to place children;
—Evidence of poor outcomes for children in public care, and the potential benefits of kinship care;
—Changing theories about family functioning, from dysfunction and the intergenerational transmission of abuse to ecological and strengths-based theories;
—Increased sensitivity to the needs of ethnic minority children and communities;
—Political philosophies aimed at reducing the role of the State and the costs of public services.[179]

However, as Joan Hunt, in an excellent summary of the research, argues:

It clearly cannot be said…that research has demonstrated that kinship care is *better* for children than non-related foster care. Nonetheless the evidence is broadly positive: children appear to do at least as well and possibly better and there is little to suggest that they do worse.[180]

---

[178] At para 57.
[179] J Hunt, 'Substitute Care of Children by Members of their Extended Families and Social Networks: An Overview' in F Ebtehaj, B Lindley, and M Richards, *Kinship Matters* (Hart, 2006), at 115–16.
[180] At 124.

Even though the evidence is lacking, it would be surprising if being cared for by grandparents was not less traumatic and less unsettling than being completely uprooted to a new environment.[181] Of course, there may be cases where the risk posed by the parents is ongoing, and placing the children with grandparents will simply be too risky.

Grandparents or other kin are often keen to look after a child who needs care. As one grandparent put it: 'She was our granddaughter. She belongs to us. Family should stay together.'[182] Not surprisingly, Hunt finds that it is particularly likely that grandparents will come forward as carers where there is a strong link between the child and grandparent beforehand. There may also be an element of wishing to avoid any stigma that might attach to the family of a child being taken into care.

While grandparents and other relatives caring for children may be given some financial support, unless they are made official foster parents they will not have a legal entitlement. Further, assuming the care of grandparents is adequate, they will normally not be regarded as being in need and therefore entitled to provision of services under section 17 of the Children Act 1989.[183] Joan Hunt has described the schemes for financial support for non-parents caring for children as 'arbitrary confusing and inconstant'.[184] She claims there is a lack of adequate information or advice for grandparents and others kin caring for children. The financial difficulties they face are linked to a variety of health, social, and other personal problems that looking after these vulnerable children can cause.

Many grandparents are undertaking care of their children without any formal legal status or recognition of their role.[185] One study has suggested there may be 200,000 grandparents raising grandchildren in this informal way.[186] Local authorities are happy to allow this because it means that they do not need to provide financial help. For grandparents, it means there is no formal recognition of the right to be able to make decisions about the child and they can face difficulties in dealing with education and health authorities.[187] Judith Masson and Bridget Lindley have argued that there should be universal state support for all children who do not live with their parents.[188]

One study looking at grandparents looking after grandchildren found that 85.5 per cent had made financial sacrifices and 71 per cent reporting financial

---

[181] B Broad, 'Kinship Care for Children in the UK: Messages from Research, Lessons for Policy and Practice' (2004) 7 *European Journal of Social Work* 211.

[182] J Hunt, S Waterhouse, and E Lutman, *Outcomes for Children Placed with Family or Friends After Care Proceedings* (OxFLAP, 2007).

[183] *Re C (Responsible Authority)* [2005] EWHC 2939 (Fam).

[184] At 126.

[185] J Masson and B Lindley, 'Recognising Carers for What They Do—Legal Problems and Solutions for the Kinship Care of Children' in F Ebtehaj, B Lindley, and M Richards, *Kinship Matters* (Hart, 2006).

[186] E Farmer and S Moyers, *Children Placed with Family and Friends: Placement Patterns and Outcomes* (University of Bristol, 2005).

[187] Ibid.   [188] Ibid.

hardship.[189] Twenty-one per cent reported not receiving child benefit as the benefit book was not handed over. Only 28 per cent of children cared for by grandparents following a care or residence order received financial help. It has been said to be 'exceptionally unusual' for a parent to contribute in such a case.[190] The financial difficulties can be compounded by personal problems faced by the grandparents. One study found that 69 per cent of grandparents found it hard to adapt to physical and emotional change.[191] A common comment was to mourn the loss of a normal grandparental role because the grandparents had to act as parents.[192]

As these points show, there needs to be an overhaul of the legal position of those, such as grandparents, who care for children whose parents cannot care for them. As Hunt *et al* argue:

Kinship care can be a positive option for many abused and neglected children but it is not straightforward and requires careful assessment and adequate support. Therefore, if the full potential of kinship care is to be realised, there must be clear central and local policies, appropriate infrastructures and adequate resourcing.[193]

Conclusion

In seeking to bring together the threads of this chapter, one runs throughout, and that is the significance of the grandparent/grandchild relationship. Does its value lie in the quality of the actual relationship itself, or is there something special about the status of a grandparent per se? To some, the grandparental status per se deserves protection:

Every time a child is born, a grandparent is born, too. In the natural order of things the generations emerge telescopically, one out of the other. Genetically, every child is the sum of two parents and four grandparents. The child in the womb already possesses instincts, temperament, and emotions that are not his or hers alone. Psychologically, every child develops not only in the world of its parents but within the larger world of its grandparents, of our 'father's fathers' and our 'mother's mothers'.[194]

But as we have seen in courts, both domestic and European, it is the quality of the relationship which is central. This is in line with wider pressures in family law which are emphasising more the 'doing' of relationships as opposed to their status.[195]

---

[189] Ibid.   [190] Ibid.
[191] Ibid. M Hughes, L Waite, T LaPierre, and Y Lo, 'All in the Family: The Impact of Caring for Grandchildren on Grandparents' Health' (2007) 62 *Journal of Gerontology* S108.
[192] Ibid.
[193] J Hunt, S Waterhouse, and E Lutman, *Outcomes for Children Placed with Family or Friends After Care Proceedings* (OxFLAP, 2007).
[194] E LeShan, *Grandparenting in a Changing World* (Newmarket Press, 1993), at 93 (quoting Dr Arthur Kornhaber, founder of the Foundation for Grandparenting).
[195] L Glennon, 'Displacing the "Conjugal Family" in Legal Policy: A Progressive Move?' (2005) 17 *Child and Family Law Quarterly* 141.

A second issue is that it is overly simplistic to simply consider the relationship between grandparent and grandchild on its own. So, it has been said: 'Grandparents who love their grandchildren and have strong ties with them can nurture the child, love him or her, and protect the child's self-esteem during a very trying period.'[196]

This is true, but we must remember that the grandparent/grandchild relationship is interdependent on the child/parent relationship, and indeed the other relationships within which a child is living. Where the parents are objecting to the contact with the grandparent, this has a significant impact on the role that the grandparent can play.[197]

A third point to make is that the issues become very different when a child's parents are unable to care for the child: the role played by grandparents then becomes especially important. However, they are also highly problematic. The current position as regards funding of grandparental care is inadequate. Further, finding a legal status which balances the current interests of the grandparents and the interests of the birth parents has proved difficult. That is an issue we can expect the courts will have to deal with on many occasions in the future.

Finally, it is interesting to consider the Scottish Executive's Charter for Grandchildren, which states that they expect the following:

- To be involved with, and helped to understand, decisions made about their lives.
- To be treated fairly.
- To know and maintain contact with their family (except in very exceptional circumstances) and other people who are important to them.
- To know that their grandparents still love them, even if they are not able to see them at the present time.
- To know their family history.
- The adults in their lives to put their needs first and to protect them from disputes between adults—not to use them as weapons in quarrels.
- Social workers, when making assessments about their lives, to take into account the loving and supporting role grandparents can play in their lives.
- The courts, when making decisions about their lives, to take into account the loving and supporting role grandparents can play in their lives.
- Lawyers and other advisers, to encourage relationship counselling or mediation when adults seek advice on matters affecting them and their children.

Notably, most of these are not legally enforceable. They are no more than a formal state declaration about what should happen. This may be the most desirable way ahead. These are things we should wish for all children, but making them legally enforceable may have the opposite effect.

---

[196] M Elkin, 'Grandparents are Also Forever' (1977) 15 *Family and Conciliation Courts Review* iii.
[197] Ibid.

8

Older People and Healthcare

Introduction

This chapter will consider older people and health. There is a general acceptance that in the past ageism was 'rampant' within the NHS and many believe that still to be true.[1] The Department of Health accepts that 'older people and their carers have experienced age-based discrimination in access to and availability of services.'[2] The National Service Framework for Older People requires the NHS to root out age discrimination:[3]

Denying access to services on the basis of age alone is not acceptable. Decisions about treatment and health care should be made on the basis of health needs and ability to benefit rather than a patient's age... That is not to say that everyone needs the same health or social care, nor that these needs should be met the same way. As well as health needs, the overall health status of the individual, their assessed social care needs and their own wishes and aspirations and those of their carers, should shape the package of health and social care.

A large section of this chapter will focus on the issue of rationing and in particular whether rationing decisions do, and should, take account of the age of patients concerned. There is no getting away from the fact that rationing is an everyday part of the NHS and many of the difficulties facing older people seeking to access healthcare come down to a combination of ageist attitudes and financial constraint.

It is, of course, difficult, if not impossible, to separate out health issues from other issues affecting older people. The impact of housing, income, social exclusion, and discrimination can all impact on a person's health and similarly health provision can impact on many other aspects of their life. For example, England's level of winter deaths are higher than those in other countries, but the root causes of this lie not in health provision, but in wider social and economic factors.[4] There

---

[1] R Levenson, *Auditing Age Discrimination: A Practical Approach to Promoting Age Equality in Health and Social Care* (The King's Fund, 2003).

[2] Department of Health, *National Service Framework for Older People* (Department of Health, 2001), at 6.

[3] Ibid, at para 1.7.

[4] S Fredman, 'Age of Equality' in S Fredman and S Spencer (eds), *Age as an Equality Issue* (Hart, 2003), at 32.

is also a tendency when thinking about health issues to focus on medical professionals, whereas, especially for older people, many of the health needs are met by informal carers. Indeed, on a day-to-day basis the role played by informal carers plays a more significant role in the health of older people than professionals.

A common perception that will be addressed in this chapter is that older people are a 'drain' on the NHS resources. It is true that although 16 per cent of the general population is over 65, two-thirds of acute hospital beds are occupied by that group of people and they account for 25 to 40 per cent of NHS expenditure.[5] Forty-five per cent of NHS expenditure is on older people.[6] However, we shall see that the conclusion that older people are 'endangering NHS services' does not follow. Even if it was true, as one government minister has stated:

An ageing population is not a burden—it's a benefit. Older age should be a time to enjoy the rewards flowing from years of service to the community and helping their own families to grow and develop into independence.[7]

The social care and healthcare distinction

A central aspect of government policy concerning the health of older people is the distinction drawn between social care and health care.[8] In short, health care falls under the remit of the NHS, while social care falls under the auspices of the social services department of local authorities. The significance of this distinction is far greater than merely the jurisdiction of public bodies. NHS care is provided free of charge, but local authorities are able to charge for social or personal care.[9] The reinforcement of the distinction between health and social care in recent years has meant that services previously offered free under the NHS are now classified as personal care and need to be paid for. The kinds of service in question include washing someone, general personal hygiene, and foot care. As these services are primarily used by older people, this has led to claims that the state's failure to provide free personal care is a form of age discrimination.[10]

Of course, this distinction can be criticized quite readily apart from reference to arguments of age. The point is powerfully made that those who are unable to provide their own personal care are in that position because they are suffering some kind of health problem. Their problems are therefore symptoms, at least,

---

[5] J Robinson, 'Age Equality in Health and Social Care' in S Fredman and S Spencer (eds), *Age as an Equality Issue* (Hart, 2003).

[6] Commission for Healthcare Audit and Inspection, *Caring for Dignity* (The Stationery Office, 2007).

[7] L Byrne, 'Introduction' in Department of Health, *A New Ambition for Old Age* (DoH, 2006).

[8] S Player and A Pollock, 'Long-Term Care: From Public Responsibility to Private Good' (2001) 21 *Critical Social Policy* 231.

[9] NHS and Community Care Act 1990, s 47.

[10] P Knight, 'Is the NHS Guilty of Ageism by Not Giving Free Personal Care for Some Older People in England?' (2001) 323 *British Medical Journal* 337.

of their ill-health. Indeed, without the personal care, they are likely to develop further health problems. So, whether the inability to care is seen as an aspect of health promotion or dealing with the consequence of ill-health, the distinction is hard to justify. Indeed, it is hard to avoid the perception that the division has more to do with attempts to cut costs to the state, while holding on to the claim that health services are provided free at the point of delivery, rather than being than one based on a sound policy.[11]

As mentioned earlier, the local authority can require the client to pay as much of the cost of personal services as is reasonable.[12] The distinction thus created between healthcare services, which are free at the point of delivery, and community care, which is not, is one that is hotly debated. An example of the difficulties the distinction can create is found in *R v North and East Devon HA ex p Coughlan*,[13] where it was decided to close a residential unit for those with severe disabilities. This meant that Ms Coughlan, a resident, would be transferred from the NHS to local authority services and that meant she would be liable to contribute to the cost of care. The key point before the Court of Appeal was that under the NHS Act 1977 all nursing care had to be provided and funded by the NHS. However, the Court of Appeal thought that nursing care in this context did not include all after care. The Court of Appeal identified two categories of person who should receive care at NHS expense: (i) those whose needs were so great that they should be regarded as the responsibility of the health authority, rather than the social services; and (ii) those who have additional requirements beyond the need for basic services. In response to this decision, the Health and Social Care Act 2001, section 49 was enacted, which provides that nursing care cannot be charged for by a local authority. This is defined as being care given by, or planned and supervised by, a registered nurse, unless it cannot be said to be required for a person. The section states:

(1) Nothing in the enactments relating to the provision of community care services shall authorise or require a local authority, in or in connection with the provision of any such services, to—
   (a) provide for any person, or
   (b) arrange for any person to be provided with,

nursing care by a registered nurse.

(2) In this section 'nursing care by a registered nurse' means any services provided by a registered nurse and involving—
   (a) the provision of care, or
   (b) the planning, supervision or delegation of the provision of care,

other than any services which, having regard to their nature and the circumstances in which they are provided, do not need to be provided by a registered nurse.

---

[11] Ibid.
[12] Health and Social Services and Social Security Adjudications Act 1983, s 17.
[13] [2000] 3 All ER 850.

Local authorities' criteria for payment, based partly on this section, have been described as 'confusing and unsettled'.[14] The problems were highlighted by a series of complaints heard by the Health Service Ombudsman in 2003 and 2004.[15] The investigation of those complaints made it clear that a significant number of people were wrongly denied funding. The ombudsman found evidence of delays and difficulties in interpreting eligibility criteria for full funding. Reviews were carried out improperly and even where it was found that money was due to individuals there were delays in making restitution. The ombudsman found in over half of the cases examined that assessment had not been carried out properly. Similar problems were found in the Department of Health's own study of the issue.[16] In her most recent report, the numbers of complaints on funding had decreased, which may be in part due to the Department of Health's *National Framework for NHS Continuing Care and NHS Funding Care*[17] which provides national standards. In 2007, the NHS Ombudsman heard 352 cases and upheld the complaint in 85 per cent of them. What is concerning about these figures is the high number of complaints upheld, presumably cases where the local authorities were convinced that they had made mistakes.[18] Worse still, the ombudsman found maladministration in the Department of Health's decision making and communication in cases where compensation was due for those wrongly denied continuing care funding.[19] Even after this report, the ombudsman fears the government's response has left those receiving care and their carers with inadequate compensation.[20]

The division between social and health care has led not only to difficulties in relation to payment, but also in relation to integrating the different services. As the Parliamentary Select Committee on Health stated in 1999:

If we were building a new service to provide long term care to vulnerable groups it would seem logical to have a single, integrated community care provider so that service users, their carers and families could move seamlessly between services they may require over time.[21]

In 2005, the same committee[22] reported:

In nearly every inquiry undertaken in recent years, the absence of a unified health and social care structure has been identified as a serious stumbling block to the effective

---

[14] C Newdick, *Who Should We Treat?* (Oxford University Press, 2005), at 118.
[15] Parliamentary and National Health Services Ombudsman, *NHS Funding for the Long-Term Care of Elderly and Disabled People* (The Stationery Office, 2005).
[16] Department of Health, *Continuing Care: Review, Revision and Restitution* (DoH, 2004).
[17] Department of Health, *National Framework for NHS Continuing Care and NHS Funding Care* (DoH, 2007).
[18] Parliamentary and Health Service Ombudsman, *Annual Report* (The Stationery Office, 2008).
[19] Parliamentary and Health Service Ombudsman, *Retrospective Continuing Care Funding and Redress* (The Stationery Office, 2007).
[20] Parliamentary and Health Service Ombudsman, *Annual Report* (The Stationery Office, 2008).
[21] Parliamentary Select Committee on Health, *The Relationship Between Health and Social Services* (Hansard, 1999).
[22] Select Committee on Health, *Sixth Report* (Hansard, 2005), at para 24.

provision of care. The problems relate to structure, financial accountability and, fundamentally, to the distinction between health care, which is mainly free at the point of delivery, and social care, which is means-tested and charged to the individual. The evidence we have received in this inquiry once again indicates that the artificial distinction between health and social care lies at the heart of most of the difficulties that have arisen concerning eligibility for continuing care funding.

One solution to the difficulties that the division has created is the use of a care manager from the healthcare staff who oversees all aspects of the older person's care.[23] The government has recognized the problem caused by the distinction in the provision of services and in their White Paper, *Our Health, Our Care, Our Say*,[24] accepted that 'at the moment too much primary care is commissioned without integrating with the social care being commissioned by the local authority'. The government recognized the need to develop models and guidance to encourage joint commissioning and produced a shared framework. Notably, when the government organized a meeting of members of the public to discuss issues surrounding social care in 2007, integrating health and social care was voted as the priority issue.[25]

Ageing and health

The exact link between health and age is problematic. While there appears to be a general acceptance that bodies change as they age,[26] there is dispute over the extent to which ageing amounts to ill-health.[27] Further, there is much debate over the extent to which socio-economic or environmental factors, rather than age itself, affects ill-health among older people.[28] This is reflected in the fact that there is some debate over whether geriatric medicine should be accepted as a speciality at all.[29]

---

[23] K Weiner, J Hughes, D Challis, and I Pedersen, 'Integrating Health and Social Care at the Micro Level: Health Care Professionals as Care Managers for Older People' (2003) 37 *Social Policy and Administration* 498.

[24] Department of Health, *Our Health, Our Care, Our Say* (DoH, 2006).

[25] Department of Health, *Our Health, Our Care, Our Say—One Year On* (DoH, 2007).

[26] C Stein and I Moritz, *A Life Course Perspective of Maintaining Independence in Older Age* (WHO, 1999).

[27] S Giordano, 'Respect for Equality and the Treatment of the Elderly: Declarations of Human Rights and Age-Based Rationing' (2005) 14 *Cambridge Quarterly of Healthcare Ethics* 83.

[28] C Stein and I Moritz, *A Life Course Perspective of Maintaining Independence in Older Age* (WHO, 1999).

[29] C Denaro and A Mudge, 'Should Geriatric Medicine Remain a Specialty? No' (2008) 337 *British Medical Journal* 515; and L Flicker, 'Should Geriatric Medicine Remain a Specialty? Yes' (2008) 337 *British Medical Journal* 516. The *British Medical Journal* undertook a survey of readers and found 80% saying that geriatics should remain a specialty.

Even the definition of ageing is problematic. One leading expert comments as follows:

we may define aging as the time-independent series of cumulative, progressive, intrinsic, and deleterious functional and structural changes that usually begin to manifest themselves at reproductive maturity and eventually culminate in death. A simple mnemonic for this definition is CPID (cumulative, progressive, intrinsic, deleterious) ...

Using the points emphasized above as a working definition of aging or senescence has the advantage of allowing us to be precise in categorizing a particular process as a normal age-related change. For example, we can easily distinguish deleterious changes due to aging from changes due to infectious disease (the latter is the result of a parasite and is not intrinsic), or from changes that have no obvious deleterious effect (for example, gray hair).[30]

Although it is commonly claimed that older people 'cost the NHS more' and that as life expectancy increases the burden on the NHS due to older people will only get greater, that may be a misleading claim. First, there is good evidence that what is expensive is dying rather than being older.[31] How close an individual is to death is a much better predictor as to their cost on the NHS than their age. Dying is expensive whatever age you die,[32] although, of course, dying most commonly occurs in old age. Indeed, younger people die more expensively than older people because more desperate attempts are made to prevent death.[33] It is proximity to death rather than age which is the best predictor of health costs.[34] As Dey and Fraser put it:

The problem lies not so much in an ageing population as in the changing pattern of illness and disease, with a shift in mortality from sudden and acute infections to mortality as a termination of longer term morbidity.[35]

---

[30] R Arking, *The Biology of Aging: Observations and Principles* (Oxford University Press, 2006), at 11 and 13.

[31] Z Yang, E Norton, and S Stearns, 'Longevity and Health Care Expenditures: The Real Reasons Older People Spend More' (2003) 58 *Journal of Gerontology* S2; C van Weel and J Michels, 'Dying, Not Old Age, to Blame for Costs of Health Care' (1997) 350 *Lancet* 1159; and A Werbowa, S Felder, and P Zweifel, 'Population, Ageing and Health Care Expenditure: A School of "Red Herrings"?' (2007) 16 *Health Economics* 1109.

[32] T Dixon, M Shaw, S Frankel, and S Ebrahim, 'Hospital Admissions, Age, and Death: Retrospective Cohort Study' (2004) 328 *British Medical Journal* 1288.

[33] P Zweifel, S Felder, and M Meiers, 'Ageing of Population and Health Care Expenditure: A Red Herring?' (1999) 8 *Health Care Economics* 485.

[34] F Denton, A Gafni, and B Spencer, 'Exploring the Effects of Population Change on the Costs of Physician Services' (2002) 21 *Journal of Health Economics* 731; P Zweifel, S Felder, and M Meiers, 'Ageing of Population and Health Care Expenditure: A Red Herring?' (1999) 8 *Health Care Economics* 485; and D Johnson and J Yong, 'Costly Ageing or Costly Deaths? Understanding Health Care Expenditure using Australian Medicare Payments Data' (2006) 45 *Australian Economic Papers* 57.

[35] I Dey and N Fraser, 'Age-Based Rationing in the Allocation of Health Care' (2000) 12 *Journal of Aging and Health* 511.

A study of health expenditure in Oxfordshire between 1970 and 1999 compared the costs of treating an 80-year-old person and a 65-year-old person. It was found that in the last year of their life, expenditure on their health was 30 per cent higher for women and 37 per cent higher for men. However, when the comparison was made with 95 year olds and 80 year olds, there was a 20 per cent drop for both men and women.[36] One explanation is that the 95 years olds were more frail and therefore died more quickly. Another explanation is that it reflects discriminatory attitudes, with less effort being made to keep them alive. All of this therefore suggests that there is no reason to believe that increased life expectancy will necessarily lead to increased costs for the NHS.[37]

A major survey was recently published providing a snapshot of the health of older people in England in 2005.[38] It provides an important guide to health issues affecting older people. The key findings for those aged over 65 were summarized as follows:[39]

- more than half said their health was 'good' or 'very good';
- more women than men—65 per cent compared with 48 per cent—found it difficult to walk up a flight of 12 stairs without resting;
- 23 per cent men and 29 per cent of women had fallen in the last 12 months;
- CVD[40] was the most common chronic disease reported by men (37 per cent);
- arthritis was the most common chronic disease reported by women (47 per cent);
- almost two-thirds were hypertensive;
- 22 per cent had visited their GP is the last two weeks; and
- 12 per cent of women and 9 per cent of men reported low levels of psycho-social well-being based on 12 items measuring general levels of happiness, depression and anxiety, sleep disturbance, and the ability to cope over the last few weeks.

These figures demonstrate that any assumption that ill-health is the norm in old age should be rejected. Fifty-six per cent of older people reported generally being in good or very good health, although that should be read alongside the fact that 71 per cent of over 65s reported long-standing illness. And these were not always trivial ones, with 42 per cent of men and 46 per cent of women reporting that their illnesses limited their activities in some way.

---

[36] M Seshamani, *The Impact of Ageing on Health Care Expenditures: Impending Crisis, or Misguided Concerns?* (Office of Health Economics, 2004).

[37] Although, see A Werbowa, S Felder, and P Zweifel, 'Population Ageing and Health Care Expenditure: A School of "Red Herrings"?' (2007) 16 *Health Economics* 1109, where there is an acceptance that in terms of long-term care expenses there may be an increase of costs due to an ageing population.

[38] R Craig and J Mindell, *Health Survey for England 2005* (Department of Health, 2007).

[39] Ibid, at 4.   [40] Cardio-Vascular Disease.

The popular misperception that older people cannot walk well is also challenged by the survey, with only 39 per cent of men and 47 per cent of women reporting any difficulty with walking a quarter of a mile.[41]

Another common misperception is that once a person reaches the age of 80 they become frail and lose mental capacity. In fact, 78 per cent of those aged 85 and over have *no* cognitive impairment; 79 per cent of those aged 85 and over are able to bathe themselves; and 98 per cent of those aged 85 and over can get around their home successfully if it is on a single level.[42]

Medicalization and old age

There is some dispute over whether or not ageing should be regarded as a disease.[43] The argument may sound a rather semantic one, but it can have some significance. If old age is treated as a disease, then medication and treatments which seek to delay or reverse the impact of ageing could be regarded as having as much priority as any other treatment for diseases. Indeed, there are some who see it is a proper role of medicine to seek so far as possible to restrict the bodily impacts of ageing.[44] They argue that the impact of ageing is very similar to a disease. If a younger person had the stiff joints associated with old age we would not hold back from describing that as a disease. Where aspects of ageing are impeding how a person wishes to live their life, it is correct to keep them in check so far as is possible.[45]

Those who reject the notion of old age being a disease argue that we should be celebrating the ageing process and regard older bodies as different, but not necessarily worse, than younger bodies. The language of disease would suggest the body has in some way malfunctioned or is not behaving as it should; but that is an inappropriate way of perceiving ageing bodies. Indeed, seeing ageing bodies in those ways reflects ageist assumptions.[46] There is much in common here with the debates over the nature of disability.[47]

Certainly, anti-ageing treatments have become big business.[48] Wrinkles, greying hair, baldness, and yellow teeth are all seen as susceptible to medical treatment, rather than accepted as a normal part of life. Indeed, failure to put in

[41] T Poole, *Housing Options for Older People* (King's Fund, 2005).
[42] Ibid, at 2.
[43] H Moody and A Caplan, *Is Aging a Disease?* (Sage, 2004). For a discussion of the biology of ageing, see, T Kirkwood, 'The Biological Science of Human Ageing' in M Johnson, V Bengston, P Coleman, and T Kirkwood (eds), *The Cambridge Handbook of Age and Ageing* (Cambridge University Press, 2005).
[44] C Farrelly, 'Has the Time Come to Take on Time Itself' (2008) 337 *British Medical Journal* 414.
[45] S Ebrahim, 'The Medicalisation of Old Age' (2002) 324 *British Medical Journal* 861.
[46] J Twigg, *The Body in Health and Social Care* (Palgrave Macmillan, 2006).
[47] eg T Shakespeare, 'Disability or Difference?' (2005) 11 *Nature Medicine* 917.
[48] For a discussion of the profound sense of loss some older women feel as their bodies age, see L Hurd, 'We're Not Old!: Older Women's Negotiation of Aging and Oldness' (1999) 13 *Journal of Aging Studies* 419.

check the signs of old age, for example, by dying hair, can be regarded as 'letting yourself go'. It has been suggested that the anti-ageing industry in the United States is worth up to $64 billion.[49]

In one survey of GPs, old age was listed at the top of 'non-diseases' for which people come to seek the help of their GP.[50] This is interesting. It could be read as a failure by GPs to take seriously the health problems of older people, seeing them as a natural part of ageing which a person should accept. Or it may reflect growing media representations of old age being a time of vibrant good health and activity. Visits to the doctor indicate that people are not expecting the changes which are occurring. The indications are that people are not certain what ageing is like and in part this is because ageing bodies rarely appear in the media.[51] John Vincent[52] draws a useful distinction between 'liberation from old age' and the 'liberation of old age'. The first sees the role of medicine as seeking to reverse or negate the impact of the ageing, the goal being 'eternal youth', while the second aims to find an old age which is appealing and enjoyable.

In the heated debate it is interesting to compare the amount of money poured into seeking to reverse the impact on the body of ageing and the money put into alleviating the social disadvantages of ageing.[53] As one commentator put it:

We have botulinum toxin for the treatment of wrinkles, minoxidil for male pattern baldness, tooth whitening treatments; hormone replacement therapy for women (but not men, yet). But medicalisation of the two commonest social scourges of old age—poverty and loneliness—has not occurred.[54]

As with all forms of discrimination, beliefs about the disadvantaged groups can be taken as common sense or natural. This is particularly true of old age. Older people are seen as simply dependent, costly to society, and having nothing to offer a 'Cool Britannia'. In a fascinating study on the myths of old age, Sir John Grimley Evans[55] notes that many of the assumptions about ageing are mistaken. Although he accepts that older people may have different characteristics from younger people, this has less to do with age and more to do with cultural changes and factors. He points to the common assumption that older people are slower at learning new tasks. This he puts down to educational techniques aimed at younger people. In the healthcare setting, the less appropriate healthcare that is provided to older people can explain much of the

---

[49] T Calastani, 'Bodacious Berry, Potency Wood and the Aging Monster: Gender and Age Relations in Anti-Aging Ads' (2007) 86 *Social Forces* 335.

[50] F Godlee, 'Conquering Old Age' (2008) 338 *British Medical Journal* 847.

[51] J Vincent, *Old Age* (Routledge, 2003), at ch 1.

[52] J Vincent, 'The Cultural Construction and Demolition of Old Age: Science and Anti-Ageing Technologies'; available at <http://www.people.ex.ac.uk/JVincent>.

[53] Ibid.

[54] S Ebrahim, 'The Medicalisation of Old Age' (2002) 324 *British Medical Journal* 861.

[55] J Grimley Evans, 'The Nature of Human Ageing' in S Fredman and S Spencer (eds), *Age as an Equality Issue* (Hart, 2003).

loss of functioning. He goes on to argue that while some differences between older and younger people may be due to age, other apparent differences are not. They may be due to selective survival. He explains, 'certain characteristics might be more frequent or pronounced in very old people not because they have come on with age, but because only people with such characteristics have survived to old age'.[56] He also emphasizes that any two age cohorts have lived in different periods and been subject to different cultural influences. So, to say, for example, that 'old people are bigoted' is to neglect the impact of society on shaping individuals' values. It may not be older people who are bigoted so much as that older people have lived in a society pervaded by bigoted attitudes for much of their life. Grimley Evans points out that there are some people in their 80s who are functioning well within the normal limits for those of age 30. He is adamant that we must treat people as individuals and not on the basis of the characteristics of their age.

Rationing and older people

General issues

One of the most complex issues facing medical ethics today is how healthcare resources should be rationed.[57] The controversial starting point in the debate is that we cannot afford to meet the healthcare needs of every person.[58] There therefore needs to be a method by which to determine who does and does not get healthcare services. This is what rationing involves.

It will be assumed in this book that there is a need to ration healthcare resources. Of course, a perfectly respectable view is that society should meet the healthcare needs of every citizen and no one should be denied care on the grounds of cost. If that requires greatly increased levels of taxation, so be it.[59] It shall be assumed here that for political or other reasons it is not possible to meet all the health needs and so a mechanism is needed to decide how to allocate the limited resources.

---

[56] Ibid, at 58.

[57] GP Smith II, *The Elderly and Health Care Rationing* (The Catholic University of America, 2008). See E Wicks, *Human Rights and Healthcare* (Hart, 2008), at ch 2, for a useful overview of the legal and ethical issues.

[58] See G Smith, S Frankel, and S Ebrahim, 'Rationing for Health Equity: Is it Necessary?' (2000) 9 *Health Economics* 575 for an argument that it should be possible to meet the health needs of every person, although their argument places much weight on the argument that the needs, but not demands, of all patients can be met.

[59] Such a view, of course, has many attractions, although it does depend somewhat on how one classifies 'need'. It also assumes that health needs should trump other needs citizens may have, such as to education or a clean environment.

The focus in this chapter will be on the relevance of age.[60] To what extent in making rationing decisions should the age of patients be a factor at all?[61]

It is important to get one red herring out of the way. There is relatively little dispute over the suggestion that the effectiveness of a treatment can be a legitimate factor to take into account.[62] So, if a doctor can only afford to fund one of two patients, A and B, and it is apparent from their medical condition that the treatment will have little chance of being effective for patient A, but a greater chance of being effective for patient B, the doctor can ration so that B receives the treatment. It may be that this will mean that some older people will be denied treatment on the basis that their state of health is such that the treatment is very unlikely to be effective.[63] Of course, there are those who will claim that as long as a person may benefit from a treatment they should receive it, but that comes back to an argument over whether there should be any kind of rationing at all.[64] If there are limited resources available, providing treatment to a patient for whom the treatment is very unlikely to be effective is an inefficient use of those resources and hard to justify.

Generally, the disagreement begins where there is reason to believe the treatment is more or less likely to be effective. The question is then simply whether in choosing between patients, promoting the health of younger patients should be preferred to promoting the health of older ones.[65] At its most dramatic, the question may be whether to give a donated organ to a younger or older patient both of whom are at the top of the transplant waiting list.[66] Less dramatic would be a broader policy issue of whether the NHS should seek to focus resources on a condition affecting younger people, and less on conditions affecting older people. Indeed, the rationing can take place in an almost unconscious way, where, for example, a doctor decides not to offer a treatment to an older person which they would have offered to a younger person. Concerns that the treatment may just cause distress; 'the patient hasn't got long anyway'; 'she doesn't really know what is happening to her'; 'she's going to die from something soon and it may as well be this', may all be used to justify what is in effect age-based rationing.[67] The

---

[60] See L Pickering Francis, 'Age Rationing Under Conditions of Injustice' in R Rhodes, M Battin, and A Silvers (eds), *Medicine and Social Justice* (Oxford University Press, 2002).

[61] See J Herring, *Medical Law and Ethics* (Oxford University Press, 2008), at ch 2, for a discussion of the wider issues concerning healthcare rationing.

[62] Although, see E Gampel, 'Does Professional Autonomy Protect Medical Futility Judgments?' (2006) 20 *Bioethics* 92.

[63] For a discssuion of which treatments are less effective in old age, see J Grimley Evans, 'The Nature of Human Ageing' in S Fredman and S Spencer (eds), *Age as an Equality Issue* (Hart, 2003), at 19.

[64] Contrast J Savelescu, 'Consequentialism, Reasons, Value and Jusice' (1998) 12 *Bioethics* 213; and J Harris, 'What is the Good of Health Care?' (1996) 10 *Bioethics* 269.

[65] For a discussion of the different approaches, see A Tsuchiya, 'Economic Evaluation QALYs and Ageism: Philosophical Theories and Age Weighting' (2000) 9 *Health Economics* 57.

[66] C Hackler and D Hester, 'Age and the Allocation of Organs for Transplantation' (2005) 13 *Health Care Analysis* 129.

[67] J Grimley Evans, 'The Rationing Debate: Rationing by Age: The Case Against' (1997) 314 *British Medical Journal* 822.

rationing process can take place at a variety of different levels of the healthcare system. It could occur at the governmental level, with the government deciding what should be the healthcare priorities for the NHS; or indeed that money should be spent on things other than health. It can occur at the local level when a primary care trust determines how its budget should be allocated. It can also occur at the individual level when a doctor is deciding whether or not to provide a particular patient with a treatment.

The issue of age-based rationing raises high emotions. On the one hand, there are those who argue that it is simply a matter of fairness that older people should let younger people have priority in terms of health resources. If we have a heart available for transplant and two possible recipients—a 12 year old and an 80 year old—is there any logic in giving the heart to the older person? As two commentators have put it: 'Other things being equal we ought, when distributing resources essential for survival, favour the young.'[68] Alan Williams argues that there should come a time when older people should recognize that younger people have a stronger claim on healthcare resources:

This attempt to wring the last drop of medical benefit out of the system, no matter what the human and material costs, is not the hallmark of a humane society. In each of our lives there has to come a time when we accept the inevitability of death, and when we also accept that a reasonable limit has to be set on the demands we can properly make on our fellow citizens in order to keep us going a bit longer.[69]

By contrast, opponents of age-based rationing argue that each individual should be treated on their own merits. There is no reason to treat the lives of older people as less valuable than younger people.[70] Grimley Evans argues:

Individual lives are incommensurable since each can be valued only by the person living it and there is no way in which different lives can be brought to a common measure. It is no business of the British state to determine that the lives, and desire for life, of some citizens are worth more or less then [sic] the lives, and desire for life, of others.[71]

So seen, the key point is that everyone has the right to receive the healthcare they need. To deny it to a person based on nothing more than their age would be as unacceptable as to deny healthcare to a person based on their race or sex.

In one sense, the debate over age-based discrimination comes down to a dispute between consequentialists and a deontological approach to ethics. Is rationing to be determined based on a consequentialist's assessment of which treatments produce the greatest gains to individuals or society? This is likely to benefit younger people over older ones, because they are more likely to live longer and gain from

---

[68] K Kappel and P Sandøae, 'QALYs, Age and Fairness' (1992) 6 *Bioethics* 297.

[69] A Williams, 'The Rationing Debate: Rationing by Age: The Case For' (1997) 314 *British Medical Journal* 820.

[70] J Grimley Evans, 'The Rationing Debate: Rationing by Age: The Case Against' (1997) 314 *British Medical Journal* 822.

[71] Ibid.

the benefits. Or is a deontological approach to be preferred, where the concerns of justice and rights determine the issue? In this case, the claim that everyone has the right to be treated equally may rule the day. We will be exploring these arguments later.

The debate is sometimes presented as a clash between the generations (an intergenerational conflict), with the young wanting age-based rationing and the old opposing it. That would be rather misleading. The young will in all likelihood become old and would not necessarily support a healthcare system that would leave them abandoned in old age. Further, the old are likely to have younger relatives and friends whom they care for and would not want to see denied treatment. Nevertheless, the simmering of intergenerational conflict does appear to bubble beneath the surface of the debate on some occasions.

A further point is that political naivety is apparent in some of the debate. If age-based rationing becomes accepted and older people are denied treatment based on age, there is no guarantee that the money saved will be spent on addressing the health needs of the young. Political pressures may simply mean that the money saved will be spent elsewhere.[72] This is, of course, not in itself an argument against age-based rationing, but a reminder of the broader political issues raised by it. Certainly it should never be forgotten that denying healthcare to older people will necessarily mean increased healthcare provision for younger people.

Quality adjusted life years (QALY)

Quality adjusted life years (QALY) is probably the most popular way of analysing the cost-effectiveness of treatments and is widely used in decision-making in relation to rationing. It is used by the National Institute of Health and Clinical Excellence, the body that provides guidance on what treatments should be available under the NHS.[73] There is a wide range of subtle variations on the way in which QALY are calculated and used. We shall focus on the basic version. QALY, as used in rationing decisions, requires an assessment of three factors:

• How many years' extra life will the treatment provide this patient?
• What will the quality of those extra years be?
• How expensive is the treatment?

A treatment that provides a year of perfect health scores as one; however, a year of less than perfect health will score less than one. Death is equivalent to zero. In some schemes it is possible to have a state of health worse than death and this may achieve a negative score. Under QALY, therefore, a treatment which provided

---

[72] C Andre and M Valesquez, *Aged-Based Health Care Rationing* (Markkula Center for Applied Ethics, 1990).
[73] J Fox-Rushby, *Disability Adjusted Life Years for Decision-Making?* (Office of Health Economics, 2002).

a patient with an extra year of perfect health would be preferred to a treatment which provided a patient with an extra year, but a year of pain and low-life quality. A treatment which offered a large number of QALY for a small amount of money would be highly cost effective, while one that produced a low number of QALY for a large amount of money would not be.

There are some clear benefits for decision-makers in using QALY. It provides a figure for assessing the benefits of the treatment, which enables a comparison between different treatments for the same person and between individuals. It can be used to decide which of two treatments is best value in relation to, say, back pain, but also to assess whether it is more cost efficient to fund treatment A for back pain or treatment B for migraine.

At first sight, QALY appears to be a logical way of assessing benefits. It considers not just the extra length of time provided for by a treatment, but the quality of life. It produces a ready way of assessing the actual gain of a treatment, and comparing that gain with that offered by another treatment. Nevertheless, it has been criticized. There are many criticisms which will not be discussed here, such as the difficulties in assessing quality of life;[74] the fact that it can operate against the interests of disabled people; and that it fails to take account of the benefits to carers.[75] For the purposes of this book, the focus will be the issues relating to age.

Ageism and QALY

One powerful complaint is that the use of QALY discriminates on the basis of age. Quite simply, 'if the effects of treatment are expected to last for life, patients with a short life expectancy cannot expect to come out as favourably as those with long to live'.[76] If an 80 year old and a 10 year old suffer from the same condition and QALY are used to determine whom to treat, the 80 year old is unlikely to be able to show as many years of benefit as the 10 year old will be able to. QALY will therefore usually benefit the younger patient. Indeed, given the life expectancy of the 10 year old, a treatment which offered only a low level of benefit may be preferred over another which offered a higher gain to an older person.[77] It should not be thought that this always follows. An older person taking a drug may gain fewer years from its use than a younger person with the same condition

---

[74] P Dolan, 'Developing Methods that Really do Value the "Q" in the QALY' (2008) 3 *Health Economics, Policy and Law* 69; and the response from D Hausman, 'Valuing Health Properly' (2008) 3 *Health Economics, Policy and Law* 83.

[75] J Herring, 'The Place of Carers' in M Freeman (ed), *Law and Bioethics* (Oxford University Press, 2008).

[76] J Taylor, 'NICE, Alzheimer's and the QALY' (2007) 2 *Clinical Ethics* 50.

[77] Note, however, that no distinction on age would arise if treatment is ongoing (eg the taking of medication). This is because although a younger person taking the medication would live for longer than the older person taking the medication, the costs of medicating the younger would be proportionately much higher.

taking the drug, but the older person, assuming their life expectancy is lower, will take the drug for a shorter period of time and therefore it will cost less.[78] Nevertheless, this is true only of ongoing treatments, and in the case of one-off treatments QALY will clearly benefit those with a greater life expectancy.

Supporters of QALY have denied that QALY work against the interests of older people. Any discrimination is between the life expectancy of people. Indeed, QALY draw no distinction between a 10 year old and an 80 year old who will both gain an extra two years of good quality life.[79] The discrimination, if any, is, therefore, on the basis of life expectancy rather than age.[80]

This response is, however, in danger of overlooking the distinction between direct and indirect discrimination. It is true that QALY do not directly discriminate on the grounds of age, but by relying on life expectancy they do so indirectly.[81] It is much harder for an older person to establish years of benefit than a younger one. Therefore, the fact of discrimination should be accepted and the proper question is whether or not the discrimination is justified.

This takes us back to the argument that if faced between giving a life-saving treatment to a 10 year old or to an 80 year old, we should prefer the younger person. Two reasons are commonly given for this. The first is that the benefit to the individual and to society is greater. Put simply, the 10 year old will receive many years' benefit from the treatment, while the older person will receive only a few.[82] Society will gain from all the 10 year old will have to contribute during their life, while the 80 year old is likely to contribute less. Or putting it another way, the loss to the 10 year old of a substantial part of their life will be greater than the loss of a few extra years for the 80 year old.

The second justification is based on fairness, ie that the 80 year old has already enjoyed many years of life and should step aside and let the 10 year old enjoy their life. There must be few grandparents who, faced with the awful alternative of either dying themselves or having their grandchild die, would not think it preferable that they were the ones to go.[83] If we had some food and were deciding whether to give it to a person who had just enjoyed a good meal and a person who was hungry we would prefer the latter. So it should be with health resources. It is only fair that when there are limited resources available, they should be given to the person who has enjoyed little, rather than the person who has enjoyed much.

---

[78] K Claxton and A Culyer, 'Not a NICE Fallacy: A Reply to Dr Quigley' (2008) 34 *Journal of Medical Ethics* 598.

[79] R Segev, 'Well-being and Fairness in the Distribution of Scarce Health Resources' (2005) *Journal of Medicine and Philosophy* 231.

[80] M Rawlins and A Dillon, 'NICE Discrimination' (2005) 31 *Journal of Medical Ethics* 683.

[81] Although life expectancy itself is a troublesome concept because it depends in part on what treatment a patient receives and a variety of other socio-economic factors. See R Small, 'The Ethics of Life Expectancy' (2002) 16 *Bioethics* 307.

[82] C Sunstein, 'Lives, Life-Years and Willingness to Pay' (2004) 104 *Columbia Law Review* 205.

[83] A Shaw, 'In Defense of Ageism' (1994) 20 *Journal of Medical Ethics* 188.

These defences of QALY might in fact lead to an argument that QALY are not 'ageist enough'.[84] As just mentioned, QALY would draw no distinction between providing two years of extra high quality life for an 80 or a 10 year old both suffering from a terminal illness.[85] But before considering that point further, we need to consider the argument that these justifications for QALY are inadequate.

Opponents of ageism in rationing are generally happy to accept that one can argue that there will be greater benefits in some cases in treating a younger person rather than an older person. However, they see this as overly consequentialist. We cannot compare the values of people's lives. All lives are equally precious. We cannot make assumptions about the worth of individuals based on their age or their life expectancy.[86] The attitude of 'it's not worth saving this person's life because they have not got long to live' leads to a degrading of life as something precious. Once we start comparing the value of person A's life or person B's life and deciding it is more worthwhile saving A than B, we are in extremely dangerous territory. We should, it is argued, value all life equally and give people the treatment they need, regardless of their age.[87] John Harris has argued that age should be regarded as an utterly arbitrary criterion. As he points out, if there is a fire in a lecture theatre do we really think we should try and get the 19-year-olds out before the 20-year-olds?[88] The real problem, then, with aged-based rationing is that it symbolically devalues the lives of older people and fails to accord sufficient respect for the right to life.[89]

Supporters of QALY will reply that this response misses the point. QALY is not being used to choose between lives and is not suggesting some lives are more valuable than others. It is choosing between treatments and assessing the effectiveness of treatments.[90] A use of treatment which produces more years of good quality life is preferable to one that produces less. Hence it has been claimed that using scarce resources on older people produces limited returns.[91] But this attempt to focus on the effectiveness of the treatment rather than the impact on individuals is a rhetorical device: by saying one life-saving treatment

---

[84] M Lockwood, 'Quality of Life and Resource Allocation' in J Bell and S Mendus (eds), *Philosophy and Medical Welfare* (Cambridge University Press, 1988), at 54.

[85] Some varieties of QALY give weighting to benefits depending on the age of the individuals: F Sassi, 'Calculating QALYs, Comparing QALY and DALY Calculations' (2006) 21 *Health Policy and Planning* 402.

[86] E Loewy, 'Age Discrimination at its Best: Should Chronological Age be a Prime Factour in Medical Decision Making?' (2005) 35 *Healthcare Analysis* 101.

[87] S Giordano, 'Respect for Equality and the Treatment of the Elderly: Declarations of Human Rights and Age-Based Rationing' (2005) 14 *Cambridge Quarterly of Healthcare Ethics* 83.

[88] J Harris, 'QALYfying the Value of Life' (1987) 3 *Journal of Medical Ethics* 117.

[89] E Loewy, 'Age Discrimination at its Best: Should Chronological Age be a Prime Factour in Medical Decision Making?' (2005) 35 *Healthcare Analysis* 101; and M Kapp, 'De Facto Health-Care Rationing by Age' (1998) 19 *Journal of Legal Medicine* 323.

[90] K Claxton and A Culyer, 'Not a NICE Fallacy: A Reply to Dr Quigley' (2008) 34 *Journal of Medical Ethics* 598.

[91] A Smith and J Rother, 'Older Americans and The Rationing of Health Care' (1992) 140 *University of Pennsylvania Law Review* 1847, at 1849–50.

provides more benefits than another, you are in effect looking at the value of lives. Muireann Quigley[92] argues:

If I need to decide whether to give a treatment to either patient A or patient B and I utilise the QALY, then I am effectively balancing the improvement (or deterioration) in the quality of A's life multiplied by the number of life-years he gains (or loses) against the same calculation for B. The best score will determine which person will be the most cost effective to treat from my limited resources. Unfortunately, what we are doing when we engage in this type of calculation, in particular, is making value judgments about the lives of those two patients (identifiable or not), because the result is that their lives and health are given lower priority.

In response, Claxton and Culyer state:

NICE's methodology is firmly consequentialist—interventions are recommended or not, as the case may be, according to their estimated consequences for people's future health, not according to people's 'worth', whether 'worth' be their current health, their past health, their moral deservingness, their pecuniary wealth or their economic productivity. NICE has the same basic business as the rest of the NHS of which it is a part: promoting the nation's health. Its prioritisation of technologies depends on the capacity of technologies to enable people to become healthier than they otherwise would be (ie, with e ither no treatment or with an alternative) and the relative cost of realising that gain in health (these are with-and-without comparisons; not before-and-after ones).[93]

This difference in opinion in part depends on the perspective from which you look at the issue. From the perspective of the NHS or the health professional, it is possible to rationalize this as about maximizing health, but from the individual patient's point of view it appears to be an assessment of the value of life. It is submitted that Claxton's and Culyer's reply is not really convincing. It begs the question of why we wish to maximize health. Health is not an abstract thing: it is of value because it enhances an individual's life. There is, in reality, no getting away from the fact that these rationing decisions do involve weighing up the value of different people's lives.

Fair innings

Some other commentators argue that there comes a point in time when a person has had a 'fair innings'.[94] When that happens, healthcare resources should be allocated to those who have not yet had a fair chance at a reasonably lengthy life. This notion has been described in this way:

[This theory reflects] the feeling that everyone is entitled to some 'normal' span of health (usually expressed in life years, e.g. 'three score years and ten') and anyone failing to

---

[92] M Quigley, 'A NICE Fallacy' (2007) 33 *Journal of Medical Ethics* 465, at 465.
[93] K Claxton and A Culyer, 'Not a NICE Fallacy: A Reply to Dr Quigley' (2008) 34 *Journal of Medical Ethics* 598.
[94] A Williams, 'Intergenerational Equity: An Exploration of the "Fair Innings" Argument' (1997) 6 *Health Economics* 117.

achieve this has been cheated, whilst anyone getting more than this is 'living on borrowed time'.[95]

Daniel Callahan has developed an approach based on the 'fair innings' argument. He argues that the solution to the dilemma of age-based rationing is to focus on the need to provide a fair rationing of healthcare across a person's life. So, rather than asking how we balance the interests of younger people and older people, we should ask across a person's life how we should allocate healthcare resources.[96] He believes that most people would prefer to have healthcare allocated during their early years than later ones. Hence, he advocates a point in time when healthcare resources would no longer be used to keep a person alive—this might be in a person's late 70s or early 80s.[97] Building on that starting point he suggests that our society has become obsessed with avoiding death and that we need to rediscover the notion of an acceptable death.

Callahan's proposal, and variations on it, have some attraction, although they have proved highly controversial.[98] However, we need to be aware of their limitations. It is far from clear under his proposal what will happen to those who reach the cut-off point. He refers to a decent minimum level of care being available to those who have reached the cut-off point, but what that means is unclear. Presumably they will not be denied all healthcare—for example, pain relief and time in hospital must be available. Presumably some treatments should be provided to a very older person if needed to prevent more serious or costly illnesses developing. This means that even if Callahan's approach were adopted, it is unlikely that it would solve all the funding problems facing modern healthcare systems.[99]

As well as probably not answering the problem of rationing, there are other objections to his approach.[100] One is that it appears to presuppose one particular view of life: an active youth and middle age, followed by an old age of little worth.[101] Many people may regard life like that, but many do not. Many look forward to old age as a time of rest and respect. In other words, he imposes one particular vision of how to live a life on everyone, and it is one that many people feel does not show a sufficient respect for old age. It has also been pointed out that the proposal is likely to work against the interests of women, as a far higher

---

[95] Ibid.
[96] R Veatch, 'Justice and the Economics of Terminal Illness' (1988) *Hastings Center Report* 34.
[97] D Callahan, *Setting Limits: What Kind of Life?* (Simon and Schuster, 1990).
[98] R Cohen-Almagor, 'Dutch Perspectives on Palliative Care in the Netherlands' (2002) 17 *Issues in Law and Medicine* 247.
[99] T Beauchamp and J Childress, *Principles of Biomedical Ethics* (Oxford University Press, 2001), at 262.
[100] J Harris, *The Value of Life* (Routledge, 1994), at 27; and M Rivlin, 'Why the Fair Innings Argument is Not Persuasive' (2001) 1 *BMC Medical Ethics* 12.
[101] M Kapp, 'De Facto Health-Care Rationing by Age' (1998) 19 *Journal of Legal Medicine* 323.

percentage of women than men reach the age of 80.[102] Further, as Pickering Francis points out:

To a woman who has been a caregiver for most of her life—first for children, then for elderly parents, and perhaps then for an ill husband—the thought of age rationing might seem at best a cruel loss of the only turn she might have.[103]

More generally, it should also be pointed out that a fair innings approach will favour men over women, as women are more likely than men to live longer and reach the 'cut-off point'.[104]

It would be possible to develop a slightly more sophisticated version of a fair innings argument, which would not directly relate to age. It would argue that each person is entitled to a fair innings of healthy life. A person who has a life of bad health may have a stronger claim than a person of the same age who has a life of good health. The latter have had a better innings than the first.[105]

John Harris challenges such uses of fairness in the allocation of health. He imagines the following scenario:

Peter is twenty years old, Paul is forty, they both need a kidney transplant and can each expect an extra forty years as a result. If the young get priority Paul will die at forty and Peter will overtake him and live to be sixty, gaining twenty unfair years. He will thus end up with the same unfair advantage over Paul that Paul enjoyed over him when the allocation was made and upon which its justification was based.[106]

Indeed, if one were to take the notion of a fair distribution of health seriously it would require considerable intervention by the government to combat social and economic inequalities which impact on health.[107] This would lead us into even broader arguments about the meaning of equity.[108]

Rawls/Daniels

An approach with some similarities to that just outlined has been developed by Norman Daniels, basing his approach on the writing of John Rawls.[109] This asks

[102] K Dixon, 'Oppressive Limits: Callahan's Foundation Myth' (1994) 19 *Journal of Medicine and Philosophy* 613.

[103] L Pickering Francis, 'Age Rationing Under Conditions of Injustice' in R Rhodes, M Battin, and A Silvers, *Medicine and Social Justice* (Oxford University Press, 2002), at 271.

[104] P Anand, 'Capabilities and Health' (2005) 31 *Journal of Medical Ethics* 299.

[105] A Williams, 'Intergenerational Equity: An Exploration of the "Fair Innings" Argument' (1997) 6 *Health Economics* 117.

[106] J Harris, 'Does Justice Require That We Be Ageist?' (1994) 8 *Bioethics* 74.

[107] S Anand, F Peter, and A Sen (eds), *Public Health, Ethics and Equity* (Oxford University Press, 2006); and A Culyer and A Wagstaff, 'Equity and Equality in Health and Health Care' (1993) 12 *Journal of Health Economics* 431.

[108] See, eg the debate between Harris and Savulescu: J Harris, 'What is the Good of Health Care' (1996) 10 *Bioethics* 269; J Savulescu, 'Consequentialism, Reasons, Values and Justice' (1998) 12 *Bioethics* 212; and J Harris, 'Justice and Equal Opportunities in Health Care' (1999) 13 *Bioethics* 393.

[109] M Battin, 'Age Rationing and the Just Distribution of Health Care: Is There a Duty to Die?' (1987) 97 *Ethics* 317.

us to imagine that we are yet to be born, but can decide what kind of world we would like to be born into. Crucially we do not know what our lives will be like. In this context we may be born with bad health or excellent health. Behind this 'veil of ignorance' we are asked to determine what allocation of health resources we would think appropriate. The thinking behind this approach is that it generates a fair societal and legal structure for all. Daniels sees this as a useful tool for allocating healthcare resources.

He suggests this would lead to support for a 'capabilities approach' under which we determine what are 'acceptable levels of functioning' for particular ages. We then provide healthcare resources to enable 'acceptable functioning' for a person's age.[110] Julian Savulescu argues that there is a right to a decent minimum of healthcare. Hence: 'The goal of the distribution of healthcare should be to ensure that the maximum number of people receive a decent minimum of healthcare.' He explains that the decent minimum is that necessary to promote a minimally decent life.

These approaches have the danger of seemingly promoting ageist attitudes about what one's state of health should be at different times in life. It also ignores the fact that people may deliberately adopt a lifestyle with a particular aim of health in mind. They may, for example, choose to live a 'wild youth', even though it may mean their health in later life will be poorer; or indeed to moderate their behaviour while young to increase the chance of having very good health in old age. Another difficulty with this approach is that we cannot really imagine what it is like to suffer particular illnesses, nor will be know what changes in medical knowledge or societal attitudes will alter the impact of these conditions.[111]

Harris

We have mentioned the writings of John Harris at several points in this chapter.[112] He is an eloquent and outspoken critic of the use of QALY and age-based rationing systems. He is adamant that each person should be treated as an individual.

All of us who wish to go on living have something that each of us values equally although for each it is different in character, for some a much richer prize than for others, and we none of us know its true extent. This thing is of course 'the rest of our lives'. So long as we do not know the date of our deaths then for each of us the 'rest of our lives' is of indefinite duration. Whether we are 17 or 70, in perfect health or suffering from a terminal disease we each have the rest of our lives to lead. So long as we each fervently wish to live out the rest of our lives, however long that turns out to be, then if we do not deserve to die, we

---

[110] P Anand, 'Capabilities and Health' (2005) 31 *Journal of Medical Ethics* 299.

[111] M Battin, 'Age Rationing and the Just Distribution of Health Care: Is There a Duty to Die?' (1987) 97 *Ethics* 317.

[112] J Harris, 'It's Not NICE to Discriminate' (2005) *Journal of Medical Ethics* 373. See K Claxton and A Culyer, 'Wickedness or Folly? The Ethics of NICE's Decisions' (2006) 32 *Journal of Medical Ethics* 375 for a powerful rejoinder to Harris's views.

each suffer the same injustice if our wishes are deliberately frustrated and we are cut off prematurely.

Critics have claimed that although he is keen to attack the positions of others, he has failed to produce a solution of his own. He has, however, made clear what his starting point would be: that is that as between two individuals we should meet the healthcare needs of both and if that is not possible, we should treat them impartially.

My point is now and has always been that where we have to choose between lives, we must choose in a way which shows no preference. Two people have their interest in survival satisfied to the same degree if the wish of each to survive as long as they can is satisfied.

He does not explain precisely what he means by impartiality. Clearly treating both or neither of the needy people would be treating equally. But presumably a system based on a lottery would similarly be acceptable.

He argues:

The principal objective of the NHS should be to protect the life and health of each citizen impartially and to offer beneficial health care on the basis of individual need, so that each has an equal chance of flourishing to the extent that their personal health status permits.[113]

Perhaps the most controversial aspect of his approach is his refusal to even place weight on the likelihood of success of treatment. To allocate a scarce organ to a person for whom it is likely to fail when there are others who need the organ and have a better chance of thriving with it seems hard to justify. Critics understandably argue that his approach could lead to a squandering of resources. To provide treatments to those with only a few months to live and deny the same treatment to a person with many years of life ahead of them is likely to increase social and financial costs for the state.

Public opinion and age discrimination

Some argue that there is no right answer to the question of age discrimination and healthcare rationing. The best approach is simply to follow the opinion of the general public. Surveys of the public suggest that there is some support for age discrimination in allocation of healthcare resources. For example, in determining who should receive livers for transplants, children are preferred over older adults.[114] Another study found variation between kinds of treatment. When faced with giving life-saving treatments, children were preferred over adults;

---

[113] J Harris, 'Maximising the Health of the Whole Community' (1997) 314 *British Medical Journal* 670, at 670.

[114] M Johri and P Ubel, 'Setting Organ Allocation Priorities: Should We Care What the Public Cares About?' (2003) 9 *Liver Transplantation* 878.

but in relation to treatments for depression, no age preferences were stated.[115] A survey of older people asked if they were willing to give up their place on a queue for cardiac surgery in favour of younger people. Fifty-eight per cent of those questioned would not want to give up their place and 62 per cent did not think they should.[116] A survey of those over 50 asked if there should be a policy of discrimination against those over 60, showed the majority believed that that was wrong.[117]

An ICM survey carried out on behalf of NICE was revealing.[118] When asked the extent to which age should be important in deciding which treatments should be given on the NHS, there was no clear consensus, with views expressed across the spectrum. However, if asked, 'If extra money became available for the NHS, how would you prioritise where the money should go? Young children? People of working age? People over the age of 65?', 45 per cent preferred children; 19 per cent those of 'working age'[119] and 12 per cent those over 65. Although NICE described these as conflicting results, probably the best interpretation is that the public would rather there be no age discrimination, but if there must be age discrimination it should be in favour of younger people.

NICE and age

How does NICE use QALY?[120] Professor Rawlins, chair of NICE in 2002, argued that if the QALY value was over the range £25,000 to £35,000 there needed to be special reasons for regarding the treatment as cost effective.[121] There is, however, no absolute threshold for QALY.[122] Writing in 2004, its past and current director said it was unlikely NICE would reject technology costs between £5,000 and £15,000 on the basis of cost ineffectiveness. However, there would need to be special reasons to approve a technology costing over £25,000 to £35,000 per QALY. They argue that:

a QALY gained or lost in respect of one disease is equivalent to a QALY gained or lost in respect of another. It also means that the weight given to the gain of a QALY is the same, regardless of how many QALY have already been enjoyed, how many are in

[115] M Johri, L Damschroder, B Zikmund-Fisher, and P Ubel, 'The Importance of Age in Allocating Health Care Resources: Does Intervention-Type Matter?' (2005) 14 *Health Economics* 669.

[116] A Bowling, A Mariotto, and O Evans, 'Are Older People Willing to Give Up Their Place in the Queue for Cardiac Surgery to a Younger Person' (2002) 31 *Age and Ageing* 187.

[117] Saga, *Research Shows Majority Against NHS Age Discrimination* (Saga, 2000).

[118] National Institute for Health and Clinical Excellence, *Social Value Judgements* (NICE, 2007), at 22.

[119] This was an ageist way of expressing it.

[120] M Schlander, 'The Use of Cost Effectiveness by the National Institute for Health and Clinical Excllence' (2008) 34 *Journal of Medical Ethics* 534.

[121] M Rawlins and A Culyer, 'National Institute for Clinical Excellence and its Value Judgments' (2004) 329 *British Medical Journal* 224.

[122] Ibid.

prospect, the age or sex of the beneficiaries, their deservedness, and the extent to which the recipients are deprived in other respects than health. The decision to give no differential weight is the result of a social value judgment that an additional adjusted life year is of equal importance for each person.[123]

In 2008, NICE decided not to recommend the use of bevacizumab, sorafenib, sunitinib, and temsirolimus for kidney cancer, because they were not cost effective, costing up to £71,000 per QALY.[124] These drugs were known to save lives, but it was decided that this was at too great a cost.

There is much debate over whether, or how, age should be taken into account when allocating healthcare resources. The Citizens Council decided that health should not be valued more highly in some age groups than in others and that social roles at different ages should not affect decisions about cost effectiveness. They said, though, that where age is an indicator of benefit or risk, it can be taken into account.

NICE[125] has specifically addressed the issue of age discrimination in the area of making decisions about the availability of treatments on the NHS. NICE's general principle is that patients should not be denied or have restricted access to NHS treatment simply because of their age. NICE guidance should refer to age only when one or more of the following apply:

- There is evidence that age is a good indicator for some aspect of patients' health status and/or the likelihood of adverse effects of the treatment.

- There is no practical way of identifying patients other than by their age (for example, there is no test available to measure their state of health in another way).

- There is good evidence, or good grounds for believing that, it is likely that, because of their age, patients will respond differently to the treatment in question.

Where NICE needs to refer to age in its guidance, it should explain the reasons why within the guidance.[126]

There have been objections to the first bulleted point on the basis that it allows generalizations to be made about people's state of health based on their age.[127] In other words, the guidance appears to accept that if a drug is generally not suitable for a particular age group it can be recommended not to be used for that age group, even though there may be some individuals who would benefit from it.

One defence of NICE's use of QALY is that when deciding on the QALY produced by two alternative treatments, it looks at all age groups. In other words,

---

[123] Ibid, at 224.
[124] BBC News Online, 'Row Over NHS Kidney Drug Decision', 7 August 2008.
[125] NICE, *Draft Social Value Judgments* (NICE, 2008).   [126] At 25–6.
[127] J Grimley Evans, 'The Nature of Human Ageing' in S Fredman and S Spencer (eds), *Age as an Equality Issue* (Hart, 2003).

NICE tends to be involved with deciding on the cost-effectiveness of a particular drug for all age groups. However, age will be relevant where the medication is used for a condition which affects primarily older or younger patients.[128]

In evidence to the House of Lords select committee,[129] the chief executive of NICE told the committee:

in practice, we have found that estimates of the cost per QALY can be advantageous to older people... Older people would only be potentially disadvantaged by QALYs in the event of a hugely expensive, curative procedure whose benefits were lifelong.

However, he added, 'I have no experience of QALYs acting in a way that disadvantages older people'. Despite this guidance, not recommending certain drugs for Alzheimer's and cancer has particularly affected older people.[130]

Legal challenges to rationing decisions

An older person facing the denial of treatment based on a rationing decision could seek to challenge the decision in the courts.[131] The most common way of doing so is judicial review.[132] Such attempts have rarely succeeded.[133] Most applications in this context will involve the unreasonableness ground. This is difficult to prove because it is not enough to show the decision was not the best one that could be made, but rather that no reasonable decision-maker could have made that decision. The following are some of the key points that emerge from the case law:

1. Although there is a statutory duty to provide medical treatment, that is not an absolute duty because resources are finite.[134] In *R v North and East Devon Health Authority, ex p Coughlan*,[135] the Court of Appeal said that, in exercising judgements about resource allocation, the Secretary of State for Health (and therefore all bodies which took their powers from him) had:

   to bear in mind the comprehensive service which he is under a duty to promote.... However, as long as he pays due regard to that duty, the fact that the service will not be comprehensive does not mean that he is necessarily contravening

---

[128] J Taylor, 'NICE, Alzheimer's and the QALY' (2007) 2 *Clinical Ethics* 250.

[129] Joint Committee on Human Rights, *The Human Rights of Older People in Healthcare* (Hansard, 2008), at para 196.

[130] J Taylor, 'NICE, Alzheimer's and the QALY' (2007) 2 *Clinical Ethics* 250.

[131] J Herring, *Medical Law and Ethics* (Oxford University Press, 2008), at ch 2.

[132] K Syrett, 'NICE and Judicial Review: Enforcing "Accountability for Reasonableness" Through the Courts?' (2008) 16 *Medical Law Review* 127. In *R (On the Application of Cavanagh) v Health Service Commissioner* (2005) 91 BMLR 40, it was held that the Health Service Commissioner could not hear a complaint about a rationing decision.

[133] The detail of the law generally on judicial review can be found in textbooks on administrative law.

[134] In *R v Secretary of State for Social Services and others, ex p Hincks* (1980) 1 BMLR 93.

[135] [2000] 3 All ER 850.

[his statutory duty]. The truth is that, while he has the duty to continue to provide a comprehensive free health service and he must never...disregard that duty, a comprehensive health service may never, for human, financial and other resource reasons, be achievable...In exercising his judgment the Secretary of State is entitled to take into account the resources available to him and the demands on those services.

2. A fixed policy that is unresponsive to the needs of individuals may be unlawful. This would include a policy with a fixed-age-based criterion. In *R v NW Lancashire HA, ex p A*,[136] a rigid policy against funding gender reassignment surgery was found to be unlawful, as it fettered the discretion of the authority and failed to enable it to consider the individual facts of each case. Of course, a policy which stated that generally a certain kind of treatment would not be available would be permissible, as long as each case was considered individually. However, in *R (Rogers) v Swindon NHS Primary Care Trust*,[137] it was held that a policy of funding the drug in exceptional circumstances could only be lawful if the policy maker had envisaged what kind of cases would be exceptional. If, in reality, it was not possible to imagine such exceptional circumstances and the policy was in fact one of complete refusal, this would be irrational because it failed to take into account each individual case.

3. Patients should have a chance to explain why they should be given treatment and ask why they are being denied it.[138] This does not mean that the patient should be able to directly address the decision maker, but that the patient's views must be properly considered.[139]

4. A successful judicial review challenge could be brought if in reaching its decision the NHS body had taken into account irrelevant considerations or failed to take into account relevant considerations. It is clear that the likelihood of success of the treatment[140] and NICE guidelines would be relevant factors. So, in *R v Derbyshire HA, ex p Fisher*,[141] it was found to be improper to fail to follow an NHS circular without explanation. Obviously a decision which was based on sex or race would also be unlawful. It is less clear whether age would be an impermissible factor. It is submitted that an age-based factor should be regarded as prima facie discriminatory under Article 14 of the European Convention on Human Rights, but that the discrimination could be justified if there was an objective and reasonable ground for doing so.

5. It is not yet clear how the Disability Discrimination Act 1995 will impact on rationing decisions. The Act makes it illegal for service providers to

[136] [2000] 2 FCR 525.   [137] [2006] EWCA Civ 392.
[138] *R v Ethical Committee of St Mary's Hospital, ex p Harriott* [1988] 1 FLR 512.
[139] *R v Cambridge DHA, ex p B* [1995] 2 All ER 129.
[140] *R v Sheffield HA, ex p Seale* (1994) 25 BMLR 1.   [141] [1997] 8 Med LR 327.

discriminate on the basis of a disability (that is a 'physical or mental impairment which has a substantial and long-term adverse effect on [a person's] ability to carry out normal day-to-day activities').[142] This would mean, for example, that it would be unlawful for a health authority not to allocate resources to someone to deal with a physical problem simply on the grounds that they suffered from a mental illness. As we have seen in chapter 2, there is currently no equivalent law outlawing age discrimination in the health context.

6. Financial considerations can be taken into account in deciding whether to offer treatment. The courts have tended to take the view that it is appropriate for health authorities in deciding whether or not to offer treatments to take into account their limited resources.[143] When doing so, it is for the health authorities and not the courts to make the assessment.[144] In *R (Rogers) v Swindon NHS Primary Care Trust*,[145] the court appeared to conclude that if the primary care trust had openly said that budgetary considerations would be a factor in deciding whether or not the drug could be granted, then it would be permissible to deny a patient the drug on the grounds, of cost. The trust had denied that money was an issue in deciding not to provide the drug, but that left them unable to explain how they would decide who would be entitled to get it. Interestingly, Sir Anthony Clarke[146] suggested that it might be appropriate in such a case to decide that a drug could be funded for a mother caring for a disabled son, but not a woman with no dependants.[147]

It is clear that the courts are unlikely to find a particular rationing policy unlawful on the basis of it being unreasonable. An application is more likely to succeed where the complaint is essentially procedural: the proper reasons for the decision are not given; the policy was misapplied or the applicant's individual circumstances were not taken into account. Ironically, this may mean that it is far harder to challenge the decision of a trust which boldly states: 'we cannot afford your treatment—there are other needier patients' than a trust which tries to hide behind a formula based on exceptional cases.

Therefore, while a policy openly based on age would be readily challengable, it is unlikely that one based on QALY or a policy which indirectly discriminated against older people would be subject to challenge. The courts have taken a conservative role when considering judicial review in these cases. Supporters of

---

[142] Disability Discrimination Act 1995, s 1(1).

[143] *R v Secretary of State for Social Services, ex p Hincks* (1980)1 BMLR 93; and *R v Sheffield HA, ex p Seale* (1995) 25 BMLR 1.

[144] *R v Secretary of State for Social Services, ex p Walker* (1987) 3 BMLR 32. See for further discussion J King, 'The Justicability of Resource Allocation' (2007) 70 *Modern Law Review* 197.

[145] [2006] EWCA Civ 392.   [146] At para 77.

[147] See also, *R (Gordon) v Bromley PCT* [2006] EWHC 2462, para 41, where care for young children was mentioned as a possible exceptional circumstance.

such a role for the courts will emphasize how the courts are ill equipped to make rationing decisions. Not just because, arguably, they lack the skills, but more importantly because they lack the information. They will be aware of the applicant's situation, but they will not know about the other patients needing treatment. As Christopher Newdick asks:

during litigation on behalf of an individual patient, who will speak for the large numbers of patients who are not party to the dispute but who may be affected by its outcome, and for those particular patients whose operations will have to be cancelled if someone else is treated first?[148]

Bingham MR has made the point this way in *R v Cambridge Health Authority, ex p B*:[149]

I have no doubt that in a perfect world any treatment which a patient, or a patient's family, sought would be provided if doctors were willing to give it, no matter how much it cost, particularly when a life was potentially at stake. It would however, in my view, be shutting one's eyes to the real world if the court were to proceed on the basis that we do live in such a world. It is common knowledge that health authorities of all kinds are constantly pressed to make ends meet. They cannot pay their nurses as much as they would like; they cannot provide all the treatments they would like; they cannot purchase all the extremely expensive medical equipment they would like; they cannot carry out all the research they would like; they cannot build all the hospitals and specialist units they would like. Difficult and agonising judgments have to be made as to how a limited budget is best allocated to the maximum advantage of the maximum number of patients. That is not a judgment which the court can make.

An alternative route for an applicant would be to seek to rely on his or her rights under the European Convention on Human Rights.[150] This could either be as an aspect of a claim for judicial review, or a freestanding application under the Human Rights Act 1998, sections 6 and 7.[151] There are four main articles that might be relied upon, although as we will see only rarely will they provide the basis of a right to treatment.[152] In the case of life-saving treatment, the applicant could rely on right to life under Article 2. However, this has not been interpreted to mean that a person has a right to every form of medical treatment to be kept alive.[153] Article 3 provides a right to protection from torture or inhuman or degrading treatment. However, like Article 2, Article 3 does not entitle a person

---

[148] C Newdick, *Who Should We Treat?* (Oxford University Press, 2005), at 99.

[149] [1995] 1 WLR 898, at 906C.

[150] G Sayers and T Nesbitt, 'Ageism in the NHS and the Human Rights Act 1998: An Ethical and Legal Enquiry' (2002) *European Journal of Health Law* 5.

[151] There is no right under common law to receive treatment: *Re J (A Minor) (Wardship: Medical Treatment)* [1990] 3 All ER 930.

[152] C Foster, 'Simple Rationality? The Law of Healthcare Resource Allocation in England' (2007) 33 *Journal of Medical Ethics* 404.

[153] A Maclean, 'The Human Rights Act 1998 and the Individual's Right to Treatment' (2000) 5 *Medical Law International* 205.

to all forms of treatment that might avoid degradation.[154] These two articles are only likely to be effective in a case involving a decision to deny standard life-saving treatment which is generally available to other patients. It might be argued that the right to respect for one's private life could include a right to receive treatment one wants.[155] However, in *North West Lancashire v A, D and G*, it was held that Article 8 could not be relied upon to found a right to receive treatment.[156]

The most promising claim would be to use Article 14 which protects from discrimination. It would need to be shown that the denial of treatment interfered with another right under the ECHR in a way which was discriminatory on the basis of age. Although Article 14 does not specifically mention age, the House of Lords has held that the reference to discrimination on the basis of status includes age. The key issue then would be whether or not the decision was 'objectively justifiable'. In the light of the litigation on judicial review, it is submitted that the courts will take some persuading that following NICE guidance would not provide an objective justification. Where the trust is not following NICE guidance it may face a harder task to persuade a court that there was a sufficient reason for the discrimination.

Treatment overseas

Following *R (on the application of Yvonne Watts) v Bedford Primary Care Trust and Secretary of State for Health*,[157] a patient can require the NHS to fund treatment overseas in a member of the European Union if treatment on the NHS will only become available after an unacceptable delay.[158] It is not open to the NHS to claim that the delay is acceptable given the monetary difficulties facing an NHS Trust. Trusts will now need to set up schemes to deal with applications for those seeking authorization for funding for treatment in other European countries. Such a scheme will have to be non-discriminatory and readily accessible.[159] It is likely that this decision will assist those patients with sufficient education and articulacy to make the relevant claim. Cynics might see it as providing an effective way of jumping the queue to treatment for the middle classes. Christopher Newdick complains that 'those willing and able to travel abroad will have greater access to expensive treatments than those who are too ill, old or disabled to travel'.[160]

---

[154] *R v North West Lancashire Health Authority, ex p A* [2000] 1 WLR 977, at 1000G (Buxton LJ).

[155] R Epstein, *Moral Peril. Our Inalienable Right to Health Care?* (Addison Wesley, 1997) fiercely rejects claims to a right to medical treatment.

[156] *North West Loncashire v A, D and G* [1999] Lloyds Med Rep 399.

[157] [2003] EWHC 2228 and [2004] EWCA 166 and Case C-372/04.

[158] See J McHale, 'Rights to Medical Treatment in EU Law' (2007) 15 *Medical Law Review* 99 for a useful analysis of the decision.

[159] J McHale, 'Rights to Medical Treatment in EU Law' (2007) 15 *Medical Law Review* 99.

[160] C Newdick, 'Judicial Review: Low-Priority Treatment and Exceptional Case Review' (2007) 15 *Medical Law Review* 236.

Examples of age discrimination in the health setting

The National Health Service Framework for Older People stated that NHS services will be provided 'regardless of age, on the basis of clinical need alone'.[161] However, assessing whether this requirement has been met or whether there has been age discrimination is complex. It would not be sensible, for example, to compare the health outcomes of different ages as this would be affected by the following factors:

period effects (what happened during a particular year or decade), cohort effects (the experience of that group born during a particular year or group of years), the process of ageing itself and the social as well as physiological aspects of growing older. Moreover there has been an upward trend in the reporting of sickness.[162]

The Department of Health has sought to develop benchmarking tools which are designed to mirror and measure age discrimination in health and social care provision, seeking to compare the number of procedures by age and the number of individuals of that age in the country.[163] These are used in NHS equality audits, which are designed to deal with health inequalities generally, including age discrimination.[164]

The NHS Framework contains 10 programmes: dignity in care; dignity at the end of life; stroke services; falls and bone health; mental health in old age; complex needs; urgent care; health records; healthy ageing; and independence, well-being, and choice. In an attempt to implement these programmes, the Department of Health has recommended that trusts try to develop specialist services for older people.[165] A survey into the success of implementation of this proposal found that there were variations in the way in which the framework was being interpreted, and there was confusion over precisely how the diverse needs of older people should be met.[166]

It is difficult to find examples of overt ageism in the modern-day provision of health services,[167] but there are plenty of examples of covert age discrimination. Indeed, it has been claimed that ageism is endemic in the NHS.[168] Grimley Evans argues that too often in medical practice age is lazily used as the basis

---

[161] Department of Health, *National Framework for Older People* (DoH, 2001).
[162] R Carr-Hill and P Chalmers-Dixon, *The Public Health Observatory Handbook of Health Inequalities Measurement* (NHS, 2005).
[163] Department of Health, *Priorities and Planning Framework* (DoH, 2002).
[164] Department of Health, *Health Equity Audit: A Guide for the NHS* (DoH, 2003).
[165] J Reed, M Cook, G Cook, P Inglis, and C Clarke, 'Specialist Services for Older People: Issues of Negative and Positive Ageism' (2006) 26 *Ageing and Society* 849.
[166] Ibid.
[167] Age Concern's submission to the Joint Committee on Human Rights' inquiry into the human rights of older persons in healthcare.
[168] E Roberts, J Robinson, and L Seymour, *Old Habits Die Hard* (King's Fund, 2002).

of prejudice about the needs and desires of older people.[169] He regards this as unacceptable, arguing:

Age is a number derived from a birth certificate and cannot be a cause of anything (apart from prejudice). Poorer outcomes from health care interventions, where these are not attributable to poorer treatment are due to physiological impairments that may or may not be present in a particular individual even if the probability of their presence, where nothing else is known abut the individual, rises with his or her age. If one knows enough about the physiological condition of the patient, age should drop off the end of the predictive equation for outcome.

Medical decisions which are in fact based on ageist assumptions are usually presented on the basis of a clinical assessment. Abrams complains that:

Instead of openly advising patients that economic and societal considerations are the constraint (to dialysis) they [patients] are led to believe a medical decision has been made, assumed (incorrectly) to be in the patient's best interests.[170]

One American commentator states that it is 'one of the world's best known secrets' that British physicians limit access to coronary care, hypertension medicine, and proper cancer treatment due to age.[171] One survey asking medical practitioners if there were unofficial age limits on surgery, found 34 per cent saying there were for heart bypass, 12 per cent saying there were for knee replacements, and 35 per cent saying there were for kidney dialysis.[172] Research has found evidence of ageism in provision of the following services: cancer;[173] coronary care;[174] angina;[175] prevention of vascular disease;[176] emergency treatment;[177] mental health;[178] HIV treatments and services;[179] and strokes,[180] to name but a few. It is also revealing

[169] J Grimley Evans, 'The Nature of Human Ageing' in S Fredman and S Spencer (eds), *Age as an Equality Issue* (Hart, 2003).

[170] F Abrams, 'Patient Advocate or Secret Agent?' (1986) 256 *Journal of the American Medical Association* 1784; and D Brahams, 'End-Stage Renal Failure: The Doctor's Duty and the Patient's Right' (1984) 1 *The Lancet* 386.

[171] M Kapp, 'De Facto Health-Care Rationing by Age' (1998) 19 *Journal of Legal Medicine* 323.

[172] Age Concern, *New Survey of GPs Confirms Ageism in the NHS* (Age Concern, 2000).

[173] N Turner, R Haward, G Mulley, and P Selby, 'Cancer in Older Age—Is it Adequately Investigated and Treated?' (1999) 319 *British Medical Journal* 309.

[174] N Dudley and E Burns, 'The Influence of Age on Policies for Admission and Thrombolysis in Coronary Care Units in the UK' (1992) 21 *Age and Ageing* 95.

[175] C Harries, D Forrest, N Harvey, A McClelland, and A Bowling, 'Which Doctors are Influenced by a Patient's Age? A Multi-Method Study of Angina Treatment in General Practice, Cardiology and Gerontology' (2007) 16 *Quality and Safety in Health Care* 23.

[176] S DeWilde, I Carey, S Bremner, N Richards, S Hilton, and D Cook, 'Evolution of Statin Prescribing 1994–2001: A Case of Agism But Not Sexism?' (2003) 89 *Heart* 417.

[177] O Grant *et al*, 'The Management of Elderly Blunt Trauma Victims in Scotland' (2000) 31 *Inquiry* 519.

[178] A Burns, T Dening, and R Baldwin, 'Care of Older People: Mental Health Problems' (2001) 322 *British Medical Journal* 789.

[179] C Emlet, '"You're Awfully Old to Have This Disease": Experiences of Stigma and Ageism in Adults 50 Years and Older Living With HIV/AIDS' (2006) 46 *The Gerontologist* 781.

[180] J Fairhead and P Rothwell, 'Underinvestigation and Undertreatment of Carotid Disease in Elderly Patients with Transient Ischaemic Attack and Stroke: Comparative Population Based

that doctors specializing in geriatrics are seen to be in a lowly position, the care of those suffering from dementia being seen as a 'Cinderella' service.[181] When considering all of these negatives, it should not be forgotten that there are ways in the NHS in which older people positively benefit from their age, with the over 60s being offered free prescriptions and eyesight tests.[182]

In Age Concern's submission to the Joint Committee on Human Rights' inquiry into the human rights of older persons in healthcare, the following were listed as examples where the rights of older people were ignored:

- having hospital meals taken away before older patients can eat them (Articles 2 and 8);
- being cared for in mixed-sex bays and wards (Article 8);
- being repeatedly moved from one ward to another for non-clinical reasons (Articles 2 and 8);
- deaths of residents within weeks of being moved from care homes (Article 2);
- use of covert medication (Article 8);
- carelessness about privacy in hospitals and care homes (Article 8);
- refusal by a local authority to place couples in the same nursing home (Article 8);
- being forced to go into residential care because of a local authority's unwillingness to allocate resources for services in the person's home (Articles 8 and 14);
- care home residents not being given their weekly personal expenses allowance by the home manager (Article 1, Protocol 1);
- 'do not resuscitate' notices being used in hospitals without agreement of the individual concerned (Article 2);
- unsatisfactory hospital care for older black and minority ethnic patients owing to a number of factors, including insensitivity to cultural, religious, and linguistic needs (Articles 8, 9, and 14); and
- homophobic prejudice against same-sex couples in residential accommodation (Articles 8 and 14).

Some areas of specific concern will now be discussed further.

Study' (2006) 323 *British Medical Journal* 555; National Audit Office, *Reducing Brain Damage: Faster Access to Better Stroke Care* (Department of Health, 2005); and A Rudd, A Hoffman, C Down, M Pearson, and D Lowe, 'Access to Stroke Care in England, Wales and Northern Ireland: The Effect of Age, Gender and Weekend Admission' (2007) 36 *Age and Ageing* 247.

[181] J Robinson, 'Age Equality in Health and Social Care' in S Fredman and S Spencer (eds), *Age as an Equality Issue* (Hart, 2003).

[182] J Robinson, 'Age Equality in Health and Social Care' in S Fredman and S Spencer (eds), *Age as an Equality Issue* (Hart, 2003).

Mental health

There are grave concerns over the provision of mental health services among those of old age.[183] In its report, *Securing Better Mental Health for Older Adults*,[184] the Department of Health admitted that older adults had not benefited from some of the developments in services which had assisted younger adults. Services were still failing to meet the mental health needs of older people. In a 2006 report, *Living Well in Later Life*, three inspectorates[185] found that the system of mental health had developed in an unfair way, with an organizational division between care for adults 'of working age' and older people. Providers were 'struggling' to provide a full range of good quality services to older people.[186] One major research project found a widespread perception of those involved in older people's mental health services that:

... there were fewer services for older people and that they tended to be less well-staffed. Low levels of resources for identification and early intervention work was highlighted as having led to high levels of unmet need, particularly for older people with anxiety and depression.[187]

Depression is rife among older people, but often goes unrecognized and untreated. Twenty-eight per cent of older women and 22 per cent of older men scored highly on the geriatric depression scale. For those over 85, this increased to 43 per cent and 40 per cent respectively.[188] Notably, although around 15 per cent of the population is over 65; they account for 25 to 30 per cent of all suicides.[189] Only 15 per cent of those older people with clinical depression receive treatment.[190] Much more work needs to be done to provide an equal mental health service for older people.

Breast and cervical cancer screening

Women over 70 are not invited for breast cancer screening even though the risk of cancer increases with age. Although older women are entitled to ask for screening,

---

[183] P Hurst and J Minter, 'Mental Health in Later Life: A Neglected Area of Policy and Research Allocation: Summary of the UK Inquiry into Mental Health in Later Life' (2007) 10 *Housing Care and Support* 17; S Shepherd, 'Unhappy Old Age' (2007) 117 *Health Service Journal* 26; and G Lishman, 'How Bias Starts at 65' (2007) *Community Care* 30.

[184] Department of Health, *Securing Better Mental Health for Older Adults* (DoH, 2005).

[185] Department of Health, *Living Well in Later Life* (DoH, 2006).

[186] Age Concern's submission to the Joint Committee on Human Rights' inquiry into the human rights of older persons in healthcare.

[187] J Beecham, M Knapp, J-L Fernández, P Huxley, R Mangalore, P McCrone, T Snell, W Beth, and R Wittenberg, *Age Discrimination in Mental Health Services (PSSRU, 2008).*

[188] R Craig and J Mindell, *Health Survey for England 2005* (Department of Health, 2007).

[189] C Katona and K Shankar, 'Depression in Old Age' (2004) 14 *Reviews in Clinical Gerontology* 283.

[190] Age Concern, *Depression Casts a Dark Cloud Over Older People This Summer* (Age Concern, 2008).

they are not specifically invited in the way younger women are. Women aged between 20 and 64 are called once every five years for a cervical smear test.[191] It has been suggested that 1,500 lives would be saved each year if screening was extended to all older women.[192]

Malnourishment

It is generally accepted that there are problems with the feeding of older people in hospitals and care settings.[193] In one study, nine out of ten nurses said they did not always have time to ensure that hospital patients eat properly. Malnutrition in hospitals has become a major issue.[194] Age Concern claims that six out of ten older patients are at risk of becoming malnourished in hospital.[195] This in itself increases the costs of ill-health. The issue is also important because of what it implies. If there is not time or inclination to ensure that even food is eaten then it is unlikely that the other smaller matters of comfort will be taken account of. Malnutrition is also a major issue among older people in the community.[196] One report found that it affected over 10 per cent of those over the age of 65.[197]

Palliative care

Euthanasia is, of course, a complex and controversial set of legal and ethical issues. It is not possible to do them justice here and they have been discussed at length elsewhere.[198] The focus here will be more generally on the health services offered to those who are dying.[199]

The way people die is changing. According to Joanne Lynn, there are essentially three trajectories of health and decline towards the end of life (she excludes from her discussion sudden traumatic death). First, there is a time of good health until a sudden decline a few weeks prior to death, when a severe decline occurs. Secondly, there will be years with minor debilitations, which will be exacerbated at intervals, but death will come suddenly and unexpectedly. Members of the third group, she sees as nearly half, dwindle slowly, becoming increasingly

---

[191] E Roberts, *Age Discrimination in Health and Social Care* (King's Fund, 2000).
[192] Age Concern, *Older Women Unaware of Breast Cancer Risk* (Age Concern, 2000).
[193] Age Concern England, *Hungry to be Heard: The Scandal of Malnourished Older People in Hospital* (Age Concern, 2006); and European Nutrition for Health Alliance, *Malnutrition Among Older People in the Community* (ENHA, 2006).
[194] NICE, *Guidelines on Nutritional Support for Adults* (NICE, 2006).
[195] BBC News Online, 'Nurses Too Busy to Monitor Food', 28 August 2006.
[196] European Nutrition for Health Alliance, *Malnutrition Among Older People in the Community* (ENHA, 2006).
[197] Ibid.
[198] eg J Herring, *Medical Law and Ethics* (Oxford University Press, 2008), at ch 9.
[199] Department of Health, *End of Life Care Strategy* (DoH, 2008).

incapacitated from frailty and dementia. In her book, *Sick to Death and Not Going to Take It Anymore!*,[200] she rails against the third trajectory, which she fears is becoming increasingly common. Indeed, there is a widespread perception that 'we don't do death well'. As one report put it:

It is a tragedy, and a sad reflection on our society, that for many a 'social death' occurs long before physical death, with a sense of isolation, disenfranchisement, and loss of control too often common features of the ageing process and the approach to death.[201]

A major issue is the lack of palliative care and hospice provision.[202] These emphasize the importance of dying well with a peaceful, contented death and reject attempts to induce an early death by euthanasia. Palliative care emphasizes pain relief and psychological and emotional support to assist in the last stages of life. Supporters of palliative care claim that, apart from in a very few cases, pain can be controlled to endurable levels.[203] Where pain is utterly unbearable there is always the option of sedation.

The aim of palliative care is to put the patient at the heart of care and to seek to treat the whole person: not just their physical needs, but also their emotional, spiritual, and psychological needs. The aim is to travel with the patient on the journey of the last few days of their life.[204] Palliative care focuses not just on the patient, but on her or his family as well.[205] The World Health Organization has described palliative care as:

the active, total care of patients whose disease is not responsive to curative treatment. Control of pain, other symptoms and psychological, social and spiritual problems is paramount. The goal of palliative care is the achievement of the best qualify of life for patients and families.[206]

The existence of hospice care is often emphasized by those seeking to oppose euthanasia. However, to some the provision of hospice care is all well and good, but is of little relevance to the debate over euthanasia. Similarly, Aneurin Bevan is reported to have stated that he would 'rather be kept alive in the efficient if cold altruism of a large hospital than expire in a gush of sympathy in a small one'.[207]

---

[200] J Lynn, *Sick to Death and Not Going to Take It Anymore!: Reforming Health Care for the Last Years of Life* (University of California Press, 2004).

[201] L Lloyd, 'Dying in Old Age: Promoting Well-Being at the End of Life' (2000) 5 *Mortality* 171.

[202] R Dobson, 'Age Discrimination Denies Elderly People a "Dignified Death"' (2005) 330 *British Medical Journal* 1288.

[203] Ibid.

[204] P Schotsmans, 'Palliative Care: A Relational Approach' in H ten Have and D Clarke, *The Ethics of Palliative Care* (Open University Press, 2002).

[205] J Gilley, 'Intimacy and Terminal Care' in D Dickenson, M Johnson, and J Samson Katz (eds), *Death, Dying and Bereavement* (Sage, 2000).

[206] Cited in H Biggs, *Euthanasia* (Hart, 2002).

[207] Quoted in C Saunders, 'The Evolution of Palliative Care' (2001) *Journal of the Royal Society of Medicine* 430, at 430.

In the UK, much work is being done to expand the use of palliative care. At present, it has been particularly used among cancer patients, although it is hoped to extend it to other patients soon.[208] There is also an increasing recognition that it is inappropriate to restrict palliative care work to 'hospices', but rather palliative care should be a method of caring for those who are dying, be they in a hospice, a hospital, a nursing home, or at home. Indeed, many dying people wish to be at home and therefore much effort is currently placed on providing community-based palliative care.[209] While such wishes are of course understandable, the immense strain that can thereby be placed on carers should not be forgotten.[210]

The sad truth is that where hospices are not used the standard of care offered to the dying can be poor. In one leading study of elderly people being cared for in nursing homes, the overall standard of care was described as 'inadequate' and there was persistent overuse of unnecessary drugs and underuse of beneficial drugs.[211] Even those being cared for at home can suffer if their carers do not receive appropriate training.[212] The government has recently accepted that much needs to be done to improve the standards of palliative care in the UK, even though there have been improvements in recent years.[213]

It might be thought that no one could doubt the benefits of hospices and palliative care services. However, there is in fact only a little evidence that demonstrates that palliative care and hospices have better outcomes for patients or are cost effective.[214] Indeed, some have suggested that the unique features claimed for hospice care are in fact found in ordinary hospital wards and some of the 'bad features' said to be found in hospitals can also be found in hospices.[215] One study suggested that there were only minor differences between hospital and hospice care, and that the differences that existed were only made possible by 'entrance policies' of hospices ensuring that 'difficult patients' were not admitted.[216] That said, few people are willing to suggest that hospices provide a less effective service than hospitals. A thorough survey of the literature on palliative care performed by NICE found very slight benefits for patients from palliative care as opposed to traditional methods of caring, but that palliative care was greatly appreciated by patients and their families.[217]

[208] NHS Confederation, *Improving End of Life Care* (NHS, 2005).   [209] Ibid.

[210] G Scambler, 'Death, Dying and Bereavement' in S Scambler (ed), *Sociology as Applied to Medicine* (Saunders, 2003).

[211] T Fahey, A Montgomery, J Barnes, and J Protheroe, 'Quality of Care for Elderly Residents in Nursing Homes and Elderly People Living at Home' (2003) 326 *British Medical Journal* 580.

[212] Department of Health, *The NHS Improvement Plan* (DoH, 2004).   [213] Ibid.

[214] I Higginson *et al*, 'Do Hopsital-Based Palliative Care Teams Improve Care for Patients or Families at the End of Life?' (2002) 23 *Journal of Pain and Symptom Management* 96 is critical of the paucity of the research on the effectiveness of palliative care.

[215] G Scambler, 'Death, Dying and Bereavement' in S Scambler (ed), *Sociology as Applied to Medicine* (Saunders, 2003).

[216] C Seale, 'What Happens in Hospices?' (1989) 28 *Social Science and Medicine* 551.

[217] NICE, *Improving Supportive and Palliative Care for Adults with Cancer* (NICE, 2004).

It has also been argued that the attention paid to hospices has taken attention away from the care provided to dying people not able to find a place in a hospice. Hospices, it has been suggested, provide a high-cost service for a favoured minority of patients.[218] However, that can be taken as an argument for extending the work of hospices and palliative care units. A slightly different complaint is that the hospice movement offers a false vision of death. Hope of a dignified death rarely matches reality. Lawton[219] argues that as the body disintegrates towards the end, common symptoms are delirium, urinary and faecal incontinence, sores, and discharges. To offer death with dignity may be to suggest a false picture of what death is like. Despite all these concerns, palliative care is now widely recognized as a better all-round treatment for the dying and their families and its importance is likely to increase in the years ahead.[220]

Conclusion

The health issues surrounding old age are complex and fascinating. The exact medical status of ageing is under dispute. The rather abstract question of whether or not ageing is a disease hides issues of wider significance about the role of medicine and the public perception of ageing bodies. We are currently spending a vast amount on a range of anti-ageing treatments. The movement, and the power of its rhetoric, is such that there is now ample discussion in the academic literature of the benefits and disadvantages of immortality.[221] For lawyers, one key issue flowing from this is where we draw the boundaries of a right to healthcare treatment, or indeed whether there are sufficiently strong public policy objections to certain treatments that they should be made illegal.

Another key issue discussed in this chapter has been the question of rationing healthcare treatment and particularly the role that age should play in rationing decisions. We have seen that there has been a keen debate over the relevance of QALY in rationing. To date, the courts have been reluctant to interfere in rationing decisions provided the procedure adopted has been transparent and rational. If, however, age discrimination legislation is extended to healthcare services, the courts will need to address the issue of whether QALY is inherently ageist, and, if it is, whether that is justifiable.

In 2008, the *Journal of Medical Ethics* was happy to publish an article entitled 'To What Extent Should Older Patients Be Included in Decisions Regarding Their Resuscitation Status?'[222] If we replaced 'older' here with 'female' or 'black',

---

[218] C Douglas, 'For All the Saints' (1992) 304 *British Medical Journal* 579.
[219] J Lawton, *The Dying Process* (Routledge, 2000).
[220] Department of Health, *National Framework for Continuing Care* (DoH, 2008).
[221] See, eg J Harris, 'Imitations of Immortality' (2000) 288 *Science* 59.
[222] J Wilson, 'To What Extent Should Older Patients Be Included in Decisions Regarding Their Resuscitation Status?' (2008) 34 *Journal of Medical Ethics* 353.

the preposterousness of the question becomes apparent. That such a question be asked or thought suitable for a medical ethics journal reveals much about attitudes towards old age. These can be found among professionals, but more significantly within the structures and ethos of the NHS.[223] Of course, when saying that, it must be admitted that the attitudes found within healthcare provision are no more, and may well be much less, ageist than those found within society at large. Indeed, surveys of the general public suggest that the average person would take age into account in making medical decisions, but not if they are the patient in question![224]

Any assessment of health in old age should perhaps take place in a broader context, namely overall quality of life for older people, or successful ageing as it is sometimes called.[225] Successful ageing has been said to include the avoidance of disease, maintenance of cognitive capacity, and active engagement in life.[226] But that seems a rather narrow band of issues. Surely social engagement and interactive relationships should also play an important role. What is clear is that while maintaining good health for older people is very important, that is just one part of the much larger picture if older people's quality of life is to be improved.[227]

One survey of language[228] used by consultants to describe patients found widespread use of terms such as 'acopia',[229] 'bed-blockers', 'crumblies', and GOMERs.[230] One clinical director publicly announced he was spending too much time on market gardening (ie looking after cabbages). With such attitudes, one fears that the Department of Health's hopes of ridding the NHS of ageism are in vain. However, these attitudes are but reflections of broader attitudes in society towards older people.

---

[223] Anon, 'So, You Want to Know What's Wrong With the NHS?' (2007) 335 *British Medical Journal* 994.

[224] B Zikmund-Fisher, H Lacey, and A Fagerlin, 'The Potential Impact of Decision Role and Patient Age on End of Life Treatment Decision-Making' (2008) 34 *Journal of Medial Ethics* 327.

[225] E Grundy, A Fletcher, S Smith, and D Lamping, *Successful Ageing and Social Interaction—A Policy Brief* (ILC, 2007).

[226] Ibid.   [227] Ibid.

[228] D Price, '"Acopia" and "Social Admission" are Not Diagnoses: Why Older People Deserve Better' (2008) 101 *Journal of the Royal Society of Medicine* 168.

[229] Referring to an inability to cope.

[230] This stands for 'Get Out of My Emergency Room'.

9

Inheritance

Introduction

Issues surrounding inheritance might be thought more suitable in a book on death rather than old age. However, the law on inheritance can have a significant impact on older people. There is, first of all, the worry they may feel about what will happen to their property on their death. A recent study of older people found 64 per cent expecting to be able to leave an inheritance.[1] No doubt, for many, a primary concern is that there be no family bickering over the estate and that anyone with a genuine claim be left an appropriate legacy.[2] As the events following the death of Anna Nicole Smith show all too clearly, death can bring out the worst in people.[3] The law on wills and inheritance provides a way for people to exercise some control over what happens to their property on their death, and seek to prevent legal wrangles over the estate.

Another significance for older people of inheritance issues is that the relationship between older people and their family and others may be influenced by expectations or concerns surrounding inheritance. It has been claimed, for example, that hope of an inheritance can act as an incentive for family members to care for older people, although such suggestions are hotly disputed.[4] Certainly the case law is replete with examples of older people making promises of substantial bequests to friends or employees (gardeners appear to be a particular favourite!) in return for practical care.[5]

Further, the law and taxation on inheritance may affect whether an older person retains their property until death or seeks to dispose of it beforehand.[6] That can have a notable effect on an older person's financial position in their later

---

[1] N Finch and P Kemp, *Which Pensioners Don't Spend Their Income and Why?* (Department of Work and Pensions, 2007).

[2] J McMullen, 'Keeping Peace in the Family While You are Resting in Peace: Making Sense of and Preventing Will Contests' (2006) 8 *Marquette Elder's Advisor* 61.

[3] BBC News Online, 'Bahamas Burial for Anna Nicole Upheld', 1 March 2007.

[4] M Izuhara, 'Negotiating Family Support? The "Generational Contract" between long-term Care and Inheritance' (2004) 33 *Journal of Social Policy* 649.

[5] eg *Jennings v Rice* [2002] EWCA Civ 159.

[6] Or even migrate: K Conway, 'State "Death" Taxes and Elderly Migration—The Chicken or the Egg?' (2006) 59 *National Tax Journal* 1.

years. Many wealthier older people enter into complex financial transactions in an attempt to limit the inheritance tax payable on their estate.

The law surrounding inheritance also sheds light on the responsibilities of older people towards relatives and partners during their life. Inheritance practices reflect changing social practices and attitudes. Increasing rates of divorce and remarriage have affected how property is left in wills and created difficulties for inheritance law. We are yet to see whether the greater role played by grandparents in childcare will lead to changing inheritance practices.[7] Of course, there are also many wider issues surrounding the law in this area and it raises some important issues of public policy:[8] the use of inheritance tax, house prices, and the cost of care of older people, to name but a few.[9]

Inheritance has only become a live issue for a significant number of people in the past 50 years or so.[10] It was the increase in home ownership in the second half of the 20th century, leading to two-thirds of the population owning their own homes,[11] which meant that people had assets of notable economic value to bequeath.[12] However, even today, around 30 per cent of people have no assets to leave on their death.[13] The effect of this change in the economic significance of inheritance on the relationships between family generations and wider society is still being worked out. Janet Finch wonders whether 'essentially, inheritance could become a new tie which binds generations together through a common interest in property (in all its senses)'.[14] She accepts there is no evidence of this yet, but notes that the impact of extensive property ownership will not become most apparent until the 2020s.

In the last few years inheritance and inheritance tax have become an issue of political significance. The expectation of an inheritance means that relatives sometimes feel they are being 'robbed' of their inheritance if older people's assets are used up in their care, and older people feel guilt at not being able to leave their

[7] K Knaplund, 'Grandparents Raising Grandchildren and the Implications for Inheritance' (2006) 48 *Arizona Law Review* 1.

[8] It has even been suggested that a change in inheritance tax law in Australia had a notable impact on death rates for the weeks surrounding the change: J Gans and A Leigh, 'Did the Death of Australian Inheritance Taxes Affect Deaths?' (2006) 6 *Topics in Economic Analysis and Policy* 1.

[9] J Finch, 'Inheritance and Intergenerational Relationships in English Families' in S Harper (ed), *Families in Ageing Societies* (Oxford University Press, 2004).

[10] For a fascinating comparative history of the law on intestacy, see J Beckert, 'The *Longue* Durée of Inheritance Law. Discourses and Institutional Development in France, Germany, and the United States Since 1880' (2007) 47 *European Journal of Sociology* 79.

[11] J Finch, 'Inheritance and Intergenerational Relationships in English Families' in S Harper (ed), *Families in Ageing Societies* (Oxford University Press, 2004).

[12] Houses are the largest component of estates for most people (apart from those at the top or bottom end of the range of wealth): C Hamnett, 'Housing Inheritance in Britain: Its Size, Scale and Future' in A Walker (ed), *The New Generational Contract: Intergenerational Relations, Old Age and Welfare* (UCL Press, 1996).

[13] K Rowlingson, '"Living Poor to Die Rich"? Or "Spending the Kids' Inheritance"? Attitudes to Assets and Inheritance in Later Life' (2006) 35 *Journal of Social Policy* 175.

[14] J Finch, 'Inheritance and Intergenerational Relationships in English Families' in S Harper (ed), *Families in Ageing Societies* (Oxford University Press, 2004).

relatives the inheritance they were expecting. Tabloid newspapers have run campaigns against inheritance tax,[15] and politicians have sought to reflect the apparent dislike for the tax among the general public.[16]

People's expectations surrounding inheritance

The leading recent research into attitudes surrounding inheritance in England has been undertaken by Karen Rowlingson and Stephen McKay.[17] They found that the majority of people do not expect to receive an inheritance. Indeed, only 14 per cent thought they definitely would and a further 14 per cent thought it very likely. Of those who do expect an inheritance, 90 per cent believed it would come from a parent. Where a bequest had been received, 39 per cent came from parents and 31 per cent from grandparents. Forty-six per cent of those questioned had received some kind of inheritance in the past.

It is clear that those who receive the inheritance are those who need it least. Those who are owner-occupiers or in professional classes are the most likely to have inherited. This leads Rowlingson and McKay to comment:

This study shows that people who are already affluent are most likely to inherit and bequeath substantial amounts. Those who are very poor have very little chance of inheriting and so will be left further behind. But some of those in the middle will be the first generation in their families to inherit and bequeath.[18]

Indeed, critics of inheritance claim it can be a means by which wealth inequalities are perpetuated: 'the wealthier receive even more wealth, the prosperous become rich, the rich even richer'.[19]

However, a belief that large numbers of people are receiving substantial inheritances is incorrect. Around 2.5 per cent of the population receive an inheritance in a given year.[20] Only 5 per cent of people have ever received an inheritance of over £50,000.[21] That said, inheritances cannot be valued simply in terms of their monetary value.[22] Particular pieces of property may carry enormous sentimental value for individuals[23] and small sums of money left as recognition of friendship

---

[15] B Barrow, '10 Million Families to Face Death Tax', *Daily Mail*, 23 January 2007.

[16] BBC News Online, 'Tories Would Cut Inheritance Tax', 1 October 2007.

[17] K Rowlingson and S McKay, *Attitudes to Inheritance in Britain* (Policy Press, 2005).

[18] Ibid, at xii.

[19] M Szydlik, 'Inheritance and Inequality: Theoretical Reasoning and Empirical Evidence' (2004) 20 *European Sociological Review* 31, at 42.

[20] J Lloyd, *Navigating the Age of Inheritance* (ILC, 2008).

[21] 31 per cent of those questioned had received a lifetime gift of at least £500.

[22] S Cretney, 'Succession—Discretion or Whim, Freedom of Choice or Caprice' (1986) 6 *Oxford Journal of Legal Studies* 299.

[23] J Finch and J Mason, *Passing On: Kinship and Inheritance in England* (Routledge, 2000), at 140–61; D Miller and F Parrott, 'Death, Ritual and Material Culture in South London' in

may have great emotional significance. In particular, in some families 'the family home' is regarded as carrying great psychological importance.

A particularly interesting finding of the study is that although leaving a bequest is seen as something most people would like to do, it is not seen as an obligation. Two-thirds of those questioned in the Rawlingson and McKay survey said that in old age they would carry on enjoying their lives and not worry too much if there was no money to bequest.[24] However, this attitude varied between different sections of the population. The concept of leaving an inheritance was seen as especially important in black and ethnic minority groups and amongst those in the lowest social classes.

The ambiguity surrounding the attitude towards the obligation to leave an inheritance is revealed by the media attention paid to 'SKIers': those 'spending their kids' inheritance'. References to doing this appear as bumper stickers and in media stereotypes. This label vastly oversimplifies a complex issue. Many older people who are property owners are asset rich, but income poor.[25] Research suggests that wealthier older people do feel a tension between on the one hand having a reasonable standard of life in later life, and on the other wishing to leave something to their families.[26] Others express concerns that younger people are entering into debt assuming that an inheritance will finance the payment of debt.[27] Rowlingson found a common attitude among property-owning older people that leaving an inheritance would be nice, but that given the expenses of care and good old age, that may not be possible. She explains:

Most people appear willing to use up their assets in later life if they need to do so to maintain a reasonable living standard. People from minority ethnic groups, however, do stand out against the tide, with about 1 in 5 of the public agreeing that older people should be careful with their money and 5% even suggesting that older people should worry about leaving an inheritance, even if this means that they will not enjoy their retirement.[28]

Among some older people Janet Finch and Judith Mason found the attitude that children should not be left too much by way of an inheritance because that would inhibit thrift and hard work.[29] Rowlingson's more recent study found little evidence of such an attitude, and found much more common the view

---

B Books-Gordon, F Ebtehaj, J Herring, M Johnson, and M Richards (eds), *Death Rites and Rights* (Hart, 2007).

[24] K Rowlingson and S McKay, *Attitudes to Inheritance in Britain* (Policy Press, 2005), at 35.

[25] K Rowlingson, ' "Living Poor to Die Rich"? Or "Spending the Kids' Inheritance"? Attitudes to Assets and Inheritance in Later Life' (2006) 35 *Journal of Social Policy* 175.

[26] Over half of over 75s own homes of their own.

[27] K Rowlingson and S McKay, *Attitudes to Inheritance in Britain* (Policy Press, 2005) found few people feeling certain of getting an inheritance and so did not think this was a widespread issue.

[28] At 75.

[29] J Finch and J Mason, *Passing On: Kinship and Inheritance in England* (Routledge, 2000).

that a good parent would leave a substantial inheritance for their children if possible.[30] Rowlingson and McKay argue that their research suggests that:

people like the idea of being able to leave bequests but they are not be prepared to sacrifice their enjoyment in later life or be careful with their money in order to do so.

Indeed, rather than finding much evidence of SKIers, these researchers preferred the label OWLS (Older people Withdrawing Loot Sensibly)! A report for the DWP[31] found little support to suggest that pensioners were limiting their basic expenditure in order to ensure that bequests could be given. However, there was evidence that older people were being 'careful' to ensure there was an estate to bequeath. Such an attitude was more preveleant with the over 80s than younger age groups.

The psychology of inheritance is complex. Marin Kohli's research indicates a difference between inter vivos gifts and inheritance. Inter vivos gifts are motivated, he found, primarily by altruistic motives, for example, to help a relative in need. However, inheritance was affected by different motivations. These might include a feeling that certain property belongs to the family or that fairness between family members should be acknowledged. Although need was an important factor, it played a smaller role than with inter vivos gifts. Indeed, one survey has found that in recent years there has been an increase in levels of inter vivos gifts from parents to children. Fifty-five per cent of parents questioned had given money to children or grandchildren and the average figure was £12,610. Forty-two per cent gave the money to pay off debts and 29 per cent to help buy a house.[32]

In some cultures there is a strong sense that certain items (heirlooms) belong to the family and should be kept within the family. Such items should not be sold by the current generation and should be passed down the family line. Whatever needs friends or more distant relatives may have, the testator should not leave such items to people outside the family. It is unclear to what extent that is still true in British culture today. Certainly it plays a much lesser part than that in other countries, and indeed the weight placed in English law on protecting testamentary freedom reflects this. It may be that there are certain items and cultures where the notion of family property has a stronger hold than others. For example, at one time within farming communities the concept of the 'family farm' that was handed down from father to son was important, but whether that is still so is doubtful.[33]

---

[30] K Rowlingson, '"Living Poor to Die Rich"? Or "Spending the Kids' Inheritance"? Attitudes to Assets and Inheritance in Later Life' (2006) 35 *Journal of Social Policy* 175.

[31] N Finch and P Kemp, *Which Pensioners Don't Spend Their Income and Why?* (Department of Work and Pensions, 2007).

[32] BBC News Online, 'Kids Plundering Parents' Savings', 27 February 2008.

[33] For a fascinating discussion of the changing attitudes towards family farms and particularly the role played by women, see L Price and N Evans, 'From "As Good as Gold" to "Gold Diggers": Farming Women and the Survival of British Family Farming' (2006) 46 *Sociologica Ruralis* 280.

One issue which has interested researchers is the link between care for older people by relatives and the hopes or expectations of an inheritance. Research on the motivations for people's actions is, of course, problematic. However, the research suggests that there is not a strong link between motivations for bequest and family support in old age.[34] As a general rule, a motivation to leave something to children seems to override any notion that the person offering care in old age deserves more than the other.[35]

Making a will

As is widely known most people have not made a will. Finch *et al*[36] suggested that only about one-third of those who died aged 18 or over left a will that was admitted to probate.[37] Rowlingson's more recent study found that 55 per cent of those questioned had made wills. A survey by the National Consumer Council found that 64 per cent of adults had not made a will, a figure which indicates that 27.5 million adults do not have a will.[38] Although these figures look low, it should be recalled that many people do not have an estate of value to leave. Indeed, probably the majority of property which is transferred under inheritance law passed through a will.[39] In other words, in many of the cases where there was no will there was little or no money to be passed. Finch *et al*[40] also suggest that more women than men make wills, although Rowlingson's study did not support that conclusion.[41] The National Consumer Council found particularly low rates of will-making amongst cohabitants (17 per cent), parents with dependent children (21 per cent), and those in low socio-economic groups (27 per cent in category DE compared to 70 per cent of those in AB).

Another important finding from Rowlingson's study was that of those aged over 80, 84 per cent had made wills.[42] This suggests that the common explanation

---

[34] M Izuhara, 'Negotiating Family Support? The "Generational Contract" Between Long-Term Care and Inheritance' (2004) 33 *Journal of Social Policy* 649.

[35] M Kohli, 'Intergenerational Transfers and Inheritance: A Comparative View' in M Silverstein (ed), *Intergenerational Relations Across Time and Place* (Springer, 2004). Although, see *Re Garland* [2007] EWHC 2 (Ch), where the court thought it entirely appropriate that a man left a daughter who had not seen him for 15 years nothing, while leaving another daughter who had been much involved in his care a significant bequest.

[36] J Finch, L Hayes, J Masson, and J Mason, *Wills, Inheritance and Families* (Oxford University Press, 1996), at 32.

[37] ie they had made a will and their estate was above a certain value and therefore required admission to probate.

[38] National Consumer Council, *Finding a Will* (NCC, 2008).

[39] J Finch, L Hayes, J Masson, and J Mason, *Wills, Inheritance and Families* (Oxford University Press, 1996).

[40] Ibid.

[41] K Rowlingson, 'Attitudes to Inheritance', Focus Group Report, University of Bath, Bath.

[42] Although the researchers also admit that those responding to the survey may have said they had made a will but not in fact done so.

for not making a will is that a person has not got round to it[43] is not pure prevarication, but an accurate statement that people do intend to make a will at some point, but not until old age. The National Consumer Council Report found that only 3 per cent of respondents aged 16 to 24 had a will, while 70 per cent of those aged 65 or over did.[44] Judith Masson found that the median age for making a will was 69 for men and 73 for women.[45] The increase in making wills, especially among older people, may reflect an increase in home-ownership, and therefore a recognition that people have property worth leaving. Further, increases in divorce and remarriage have meant that people have more complicated wishes concerning their estate.

One study[46] looking at what triggered the making of a will found the most common cause was illness, or the illness or death of a friend or relative. Divorces or remarriages often led to affected individuals making a will. Age is certainly linked to making a will, as already mentioned. Among those who did not make a will, 'not getting around to it' was by far the most common explanation offered to researchers. Also, non-will-makers stated that they believed the intestacy law would deal with their estate adequately, or that they had made an agreement with their family as to what would happen and there was not need to formalize that in a will.[47] Not having enough property to leave is another common reason for not making a will or, rather sadly, that there was no one to leave anything to.[48] Predictably, not wanting to think about death was also a popular excuse.[49]

The link between ethnicity and will making is revealing. In Rowlingson's and McKay's study, 17 per cent of Asian respondents and 12 per cent of black respondents had made a will, compared with 47 per cent of white respondents. The National Consumer Council Survey found that ethnic minorities are three times less likely to have a will than the rest of the population. In part, Rowlingson and McKay argue that this is due to the age and socio-economic profiles of those groups, but they might also reflect different cultural attitudes toward inheritance. The National Consumer Council report has the following explanation:

joint ownership of assets is more common among Asian families; and standard wills might not be compliant with Sharia law. Research by the Ministry of Justice on BME attitudes towards the civil justice system found participants preferred to resolve problems within the family or community and avoid outsiders 'knowing my business'. Further, it

---

[43] 58 per cent of those without wills gave this as the explanation. Twenty per cent said they were too young and 17 per cent that they had nothing to leave.
[44] National Consumer Council, *Finding a Will* (NCC, 2008).
[45] J Masson, 'Will Making, Making Clients: Part 1' (1994) *Conveyancer* 267, at 270. Although this research is now somewhat out of date, there is no reason to suppose that the age has gone down substantially in the intervening period.
[46] K Rowlingson, *Attitudes to Inheritance* (University of Bath, 2004).
[47] J Finch and J Mason, *Passing On: Kinship and Inheritance in England* (Routledge, 2000).
[48] National Consumer Council, *Finding a Will* (NCC, 2008). Thirty per cent had not even thought about making a will because they did not think they would need to.
[49] Ibid. Nine per cent not want to think about dying.

showed language barriers compound a lack of basic awareness about sources of help and advice.[50]

One final issue concerning will writing relates to concerns about the 'will writing industry'. Remarkably, one can set oneself up as a will writer without any formal qualifications and the regulation is very limited.[51] In fact, issues surrounding wills can raise complex issues of tax and property law. Given the large sums of money involved and the importance of the issue to individuals, the lack of regulation is hard to justify.

The contents of a will

Under English law, a person making a will is allowed to leave their estate to whomever they wish. This is known as the principle of testamentary freedom and shall be discussed shortly. It is striking that despite this freedom most people follow a predictable path. Relatives are predominantly the main beneficiaries. Finch and Mason[52] found that 92 per cent of testators name at least one relative. Where a testator is married, their research indicates that it is most likely they will leave everything to their spouse. Where there is no surviving spouse, property is normally left jointly to the testator's children. None of that will come as a surprise.

There is an interesting issue concerning the leaving of property to a spouse and that is that many respondents to Finch's and Mason's survey did not regard that as really being an inheritance.[53] It was just a confirmation that their property was jointly owned with their spouse. In fact, this perception reflects some legal difficulties over the classification of marital assets, which will be discussed shortly. Children too did not regard themselves as having a claim if there was a surviving spouse (at least in cases where there had been no divorce).

Finch and Mason isolate three factors that influence who inherits: genealogical closeness to the testator, generational position, and 'next of kin'. Hence, they found that the children of the testator were three times more likely to inherit than grandchildren. They also found that most testators leave equal amounts to members of the same kin. No doubt this is an attempt to avoid arguments. Where property was not left equally, the geographical closeness of the relative and particular need explained the departure from equality. Still, as Finch and Mason emphasize, generally, the desire to leave property equally, normally trumped differences in need or care-giving between relatives.

In an important study, Janet Finch looked at a randomly selected sample of 800 probated wills, from people who died in the years 1959, 1969, 1979, and 1989. As already mentioned, she found that 92 per cent of testators left money in their

---

[50] Ibid.   [51] Ibid.

[52] J Finch and J Mason, *Passing On: Kinship and Inheritance in England* (Routledge, 2000).

[53] See also, J Dekker and M Howard, *I Give, Devise and Bequeath: An Empirical Study of Testators' Choice of Beneficiaries* (Law Reform Commission, New South Wales, 2006).

will to at least one relative and 83 per cent left their estate exclusively to relatives. Interestingly, there was little difference in these percentages between the 1959 cohort and the 1989 one. The norms governing the leaving of property appear to survive significant social changes. Finch claims that the British society has developed a norm of passing inheritance to one's children, unless there is a surviving spouse. She found that only 12 per cent of wills included grandchildren, and where they did they were often left small cash gifts. In only 2 per cent of cases did grandchildren receive part or all of the residue. Fifteen per cent of wills included those who were more distant, such as nephews, nieces, and cousins. Finch concludes that it is remarkable that even though people in England, unlike other jurisdictions, have the freedom to leave their property to whomever they like, they tend in fact to leave property in ways which would match those prescribed in other jurisdictons.[54] Indeed, she suggests that the law in England has only remained so flexible because people do tend to leave their property to their closest family. If people started not doing this, Parliament might legislate to restrict choice. She does add that the benefit of the English system is that its fleixiblity means that it readily adapts to changing times. Those countries with fixed inheritance rules need to keep this constantly under review in the light of changing social practices and attitudes.

Wills and ownership

When a person dies, property can pass either through their will or under the general law of property.[55] So, if a house is in joint names, as beneficial joint tenants, of the couple and one of them dies, the property will become the other's automatically. This is not by virtue of anything that appears in the will, but rather under the law of property. The principle of surviorship means that where property is held in a joint tenancy and one of the tenants dies, the property passes automatically to the other. Indeed, this means that a beneficial joint tenant cannot leave 'their share' in the property to someone else on their death.[56] Statistics from the Land Registry suggest that 90 per cent of married couple co-owners hold as joint tenants.[57] Similarly, one study found that joint tenancy was by far the most usual form of co-ownership among cohabitants.[58]

---

[54] J Finch, 'Inheritance and Financial Transfer in Families' in A Walker (ed), *The New Generational Contract: Intergenerational Relations, Old Age and Welfare* (UCL Press, 1996).

[55] R Kerridge, 'Reform of the Law of Succession: The Need for Change, Not Piecemeal Tinkering' [2007] *Conveyancer and Property Lawyer* 47.

[56] If a joint tenant wishes to leave their share to someone other than the other co-owner, they will need to sever the joint tenancy. Making a will and leaving the share to another will not on its own sever the joint tenancy: *Carr v Isard* [2006] EWHC 2095 (Ch).

[57] N Preston, 'A Lasting Legacy' (2005) 155 *New Law Journal* 1594, at 1594.

[58] G Douglas, J Pearce, and H Woodward, *A Failure of Trust: Resolving Property Disputes on Cohabitation Breakdown* (ESRC, 2007), at para 5.2.

This distinction between transfer of ownership through a will and transfer through the law of property can be very blurry in relation to, for example, pieces of furtnitue in a house. Where a wife dies leaving her estate to the husband, it will be clear that the husband owns all the items in the house. Some of these he may have owned anyway; others may have been jointly owned and become his under property law on death; others may have belonged to his wife and pass to him under the will. These technical distinctions matter little in practice, unless the wife left the property in her will to a third party, in which case it may become critical to determine what property was the wife's. There is also the issue of inheritance tax which attaches to property that is left under the will, but not to property whose ownership passes by virtue of the operation of property law.

The law and wills

As a basic principle of property law, while you are alive you can give your property to anyone you want. Such gifts can be subject to condition. You can make a gift of property to a person that will have effect once they reach the age of 18, for example.[59] Seen in this light, a will can be understood as similar to a conditional gift: it is a gift, which will come into effect once the donor dies. However, there are some important and interesting ways in which a will is not regarded as equivalent to other conditional gifts. First is the fact that there are special formality provisions which apply to wills, but not other gifts. Secondly, the effect of a will can be overturned by a court if it fails to provide sufficient provision for family members. Thirdly, a will, unlike a gift, can be revoked.

This chapter will not seek at present the detail of the law on testamentary dispositions, which is a technically complex area of the law and on which there are some excellent discussions available.[60] Rather, it will seek to discuss four issues of particular significance which will highlight some of the issues of broader significance to the themes in this book: first is the principle of testamentary freedom; second is the law on intestacy; third is the law as set out in the Inheritance (Provision for Family and Dependants) Act 1975; and fourth is the law on taxation at death.[61]

The law and succession: testamentary freedom?

The principle of testamentary freedom is that a person is able to leave property to whomever they like under a will: you can leave it to your partner; your cat; or the

---

[59] This can also be achieved through the mechanism of a trust.

[60] eg A Borkowski, *Textbook on Succession* (Oxford University Press, 2002); and T Angus, A Clarke, P Hewitt, and P Reed, *Inheritance Act Claims* (Law Society, 2006).

[61] There are therefore many issues not discussed here, including the transfer of tenancies.

local bowls club as your fancy takes you.[62] No relative has an automatic entitlement to a share of an estate. Alec Samuels has argued that testamentary freedom is a basic principle of English law and indeed is 'an incident of property'.[63] Although this is a popular view, it must be admitted that it is hard to find clear judicial support for it.[64] Despite the emphasis that English lawyers place on the principle of testamentary freedom, it is easy to over-emphasize its significance.[65]

Indeed, in the light of the Inheritance (Provision for Family and Dependants) Act 1975, which will be discussed shortly, it is a principle that may be questioned. In brief, under that Act a relative can claim that the will failed to provide adequately for them, and the court has power to make orders requiring payments to be made to the applicant. This, therefore, poses a challenge to the principle of testamentary freedom. In one recent case, Black J described the freedom of a married testator in these terms:

a deceased spouse who leaves a widow is entitled to bequeath his estate to whomsoever he pleases: his only statutory obligation is to make reasonable financial provisions for his widow.[66]

That statement too must be treated with care. If a married testator were to leave their spouse nothing, the will can be given effect. It is only if an application is brought by the spouse that the will can be challenged. It is only in that sense that there is an 'obligation' on a testator to make reasonable provision for a spouse. No one apart from the spouse is entitled to challenge the provision in the will. It may, therefore, be more accurate to say that there is a principle of testamentary freedom, but that the significance of that freedom is less than might be thought, because its exercise can effectively be overruled by a court if an application is made.

Even if an application is made under the Inheritance (Provision for Family and Dependants) Act 1975, the court will look at all the circumstances of the case and an award will not automatically follow. As we shall see shortly, even a child of the deceased will need to show that there are good reasons why a will leaving them nothing should be interfered with. This is by contrast with most continental legal systems, where disinheriting one's children is forbidden, and there are specified proportions to which relatives are entitled. Although there is no equivalent law in England, as we have seen, in fact, people do tend to leave their property to their closest relatives. Therefore, despite the differences in the legal regulation,

[62] P Champine, 'My Will Be Done: Accommodating the Erring and the Atypical Testator' (2001) *Nebraska Law Review* 387.

[63] A Samuels, 'Inheritance (Provision for Family and Dependants) Act 1975' (1976) *Modern Law Review* 183, at 183.

[64] It is referred to in *P v G (Family Provision: Relevance of Divorce Provision)* [2004] EWHC 2944 (Fam).

[65] For a start, married women were only able to make wills freely after the Married Women's Property Act 1893.

[66] *P v G (Family Provision: Relevance of Divorce Provision)* [2004] EWHC 2944 (Fam), para 21.

the ultimate destinations of estates in England and other countries are not that different.[67]

Another potential challenge to the principle of testamentary freedom is the requirement that a testator have full capacity when making a will. This is designed to protect testators from being taken advantage of by others and persuaded to make a will in that person's favour. In the popular imagination there are 'unscrupulous nursing-home fortune hunters'[68] manipulating older people into making wills in their favour. It is difficult to know to what extent they live in reality. Nevertheless, there are concerns that the capacity requirement is used to overturn wills which are regarded as bizarre, or failing adequately to take account of relatives' claims. In other words, the issue 'is this will sensible?' and 'did the testator have capacity?' become merged and as a result capacity can be used in order to protect the interests of relatives.

The extent to which the principle of testamentary freedom has been infringed by the judicial willingness to use either testamentary incapacity or the 1975 Act is a matter for debate. One leading commentator on the law has suggested that the principle of freedom of testation is gradually being replaced by legal enforcement of family duty and an increasing acceptance of the concept of shared family assets.[69] That, it is suggested, is an exaggeration. We shall be looking at the operation of the Act shortly and address this question again, but certainly the more recent cases have shown a reluctance to use the Act to interfere with a testator's disposition, especially in the most compelling of cases.

Is the principle of testamentary freedom a good one?[70] Central to the case favouring testamentary freedom is the claim that it is a natural right of a property owner to dispose of their property as they wish. Indeed, how a person spends their money is generally regarded as a private matter.[71] You may find the fact that a person decides to give money to a charity helping sick squirrels, rather than starving children, disturbing, but it is their business. To many, this is true in life and should also be true on death. However, that may be open to debate. While a property owner may have the right, while alive, to dispose of property as they wish, it does not follow that their wishes must be respected when they have died. The argument in short is that we respect freedom to distribute property as an aspect of protecting autonomy: individuals should be free to be able to live

---

[67] J Twigg and A Grand, 'Contrasting Legal Conceptions of Family Obligation and Financial Reciprocity in the Support of Older People: France and England' (1998) 18 *Ageing and Society* 131; and B Willenbacher, 'Individualism and Traditionalism in Inheritance Law in Germany, France, England, and the United States' (2003) 28 *Journal of Family History* 208.

[68] A Samuels, 'Inheritance (Provision for Family and Dependants) Act 1975' (1976) *Modern Law Review* 183, at 183.

[69] Ibid.

[70] A Hirsch and W Wang, 'A Qualitative Theory of the Dead Hand' (1992) 68 *Indiana Law Journal* 1.

[71] K Green, 'The Englishwoman's Castle. Inheritance and Private Property Today' (1988) 51 *Modern Law Review* 187.

their lives as they choose. Where, however, a person has died, they no longer have wishes that need to be respected. Their autonomy has run out. This argument raises all kinds of complex issues about the interests of the dead, and the extent to which an individual may claim to have interests that continue after death. It is not possible to do these arguments justice here.[72] It is submitted, however, that what happens to a person and their property after death should be regarded as part of their 'life story'. It is clear that people do have strong views about what happens to their bodies, property, and reputation following death. Indeed, some people are willing to spend substantial sums by way of donation to ensure their names live on by being attached to buildings or monuments. If the right to autonomy is seen as the power to shape your life story, this should include the power to control how one is remembered on death. That said, an interference in a person's self-determination after death is not as serious as an interference in their self-determination during life. This is because preventing a person from acting in a way they wish during life will not only interfere with their right to self-determination, but also cause them to feel degraded, frustrated, or humiliated. Such feelings will not, of course, arise in the case of the dead. Therefore, it is suggested, although there are good reasons to respect the wishes of the dead, these are less strong than those in favour of respecting the wishes of the living.[73]

Another theme which appears in the writing supporting testamentary freedom is that it operates as an incentive for individuals to be productive and save money. If on our death we lost control over our assets, it might be argued that people would feel no incentive to maximize their wealth creation. The difficulty with this argument is that the extent to which an individual's productivity or savings practices are influenced by the possibility of leaving property on their death is hard to prove.

The flexibility in testamentary freedom also means that a testator is able to ensure that those who are most in need or most deserving receive the money. An inflexible set of rules is unlikely to do this. For example, it has been claimed that studies in America show that where a spouse is disinherited this is done with the spouse's consent and for good reasons. Restricting testamentary freedom could also lower the rate of testamentary charitable giving.[74]

Opponents of testamentary freedom tend to argue that even though there may be some weight to be attached to respecting the deceased's wishes these can be outweighed by the needs of relatives or even the wider community.[75] In other words, when faced with the choice between following the bizarre wishes of a

[72] See J Herring, 'Crimes Against the Dead' in B Books-Gordon, F Ebtehaj, J Herring, M Johnson, and M Richards (eds), *Death Rites and Rights* (Hart, 2007).

[73] Ibid.

[74] T Turnipseed, 'Why Shouldn't I be Allowed to Leave My Property to Whomever I Choose at My Death? (Or How I Learned to Stop Worrying and Start Loving the French)' (2006) 44 *Brandeis Law Journal* 737.

[75] See the discussion in S Cretney, 'Reform of Intestacy: The Best We Can Do?' (1995) 111 *Law Quarterly Review* 77.

person now dead who will not know what has happened to their property and the needs of a relative in dire poverty; the latter should be preferred.

In conclusion, it is submitted that the current law has struck a sensible balance between these arguments. As argued above, the wishes of an individual, even if he or she is now dead, are still entitled to some respect, albeit less than when he or she was alive. These wishes should be respected unless there are compelling claims by family members. Under the current law a will is followed, although the Inheritance (Provision for Family and Dependants) Act 1975 provides a means of amending the will in a suitable case. While, as we will see, there are some concerns about the scope and operation of the Act, it is submitted that its basic approach is correct.

This use of wills and the respect for testamentary freedom reveals a number of things about our understanding of family relationships and property. First, the law reflects a particular understanding of property: an individualistic one. Ownership of property is determined by some fairly technical rules. My property is mine to dispose of as I wish, even if it is in fact used by my family for communal use. It is not seen as family property which belongs to all the family members.[76] English law rejects the notion of 'community of property', a concept under which on marriage the property of spouses becomes jointly owned and/or under which all future property is jointly owned.[77]

Secondly, the law's approach reflects a number of things we know from anthropological studies about the nature of kinship in English society. It reflects what Janet Finch has described as the flexibility of kinship. She explains that English kinship means that those in the same genealogical relationship are not necessarily treated equally. One son may be regarded as closer than another. This leads to the acceptance and understanding that wills may leave property to relatives not necessarily in order of genealogical closeness. Janet Finch explains:

This focus on 'persons not positions' means that the English tend not to relate to each other as 'mother', 'sister', or 'son' in the sense of playing out a role whose normative characteristics are pre-defined. If I have more than one sister or son, then my relationship with each will probably be different. It is *personal*—not *positional*.

So, one relative may be preferred to another either because of what they have done in the past, or what Finch describes as the 'affective' dimension of the relationship.[78] If this is correct, it is less surprising that English law allows the testator to decide which of their kin are 'closest' and therefore entitled to a bequest, rather than setting this down in law based on blood ties.

---

[76] Of course, this is reflected too in the rejection in English law of the notion of community of property (ie that on marriage a husband and wife jointly own each other's property or, at least, the porperty generated during the marriage).

[77] In fact, the notion of community of property can be far more sophisticated than this and there can be a range of variants on it: see E Cooke, A Barlow, and T Callus, *Community of Property* (Nuffield Foundation, 2006).

[78] J Finch and J Mason, *Negotiating Family Responsibilities* (Routledge, 1993).

Testamentary capacity

The issue of testamentary capacity can be raised in two ways. First, there is a claim that the testator did not know and approve the contents of the will. This might arise in a case where the testator signed a document but was not aware that it was a will or was not aware of the contents.[79] Secondly, the issue can be raised where there is a question mark over the testator's mental capacity at the time of making the will.[80]

The burden of proving mental capacity falls on the person seeking to uphold the will. A common way of responding to allegations of lack of capcity is to produce evidence that full legal advice was taken and received when the will was prepared.[81] The starting point for the law on testamentary capacity is the much quoted dicta of Sir Alexander Cockburn CJ, in *Banks v Goodfellow*:[82]

It is essential to the exercise of such a power that a testator shall understand the nature of the act and its effects; shall understand the extent of the property of which he is disposing; shall be able to comprehend and appreciate the claims to which he ought to give effect; and, with a view to the latter object, that no disorder of the mind shall poison his affections, pervert his sense of right, or prevent the exercise of his natural faculties—that no insane delusion shall influence his will in disposing of his property and bring about a disposal of it which, if the mind had been sound, would not have been made.

In more modern language, this test has been summarized as requiring the testator to:

understand the nature of the act of making a will; know who he should consider as possible beneficiaries; be able to understand the extent of his estate; not be subject to any disorder of the mind that would prevent the exercise of his natural faculties; and have the mental capacity to make decisions that took into account the relevant property, persons and circumstances and arrive at a rational, fair and just testament.[83]

As this test indicates, where the will is a straightforward one less will be required of the testator than where it is complex.[84] It should not be thought that because a person has some mental impediment that they lack capacity. In *Scammell v Farmer*,[85] the deceased had suffered from short-term memory loss as a result of the early stages of Alzheimer's disease, but that was not enough to amount to an absence of testamental capacity. The court emphasized that the deceased had

---

[79] *Westendorp v Warwick* [2006] EWHC 915 (Ch).

[80] The later mental state of a testator is therefore irrelevant: *CIBA v Davies* [2006] EWHC 3745 (Ch), although evidence of incapacity shortly after making the will may be evidence that the testator lacked capacity when making the will: *Fuller v Fuller* [2005] All ER (D) 120 (Feb.)

[81] *Jones v Jones* [2006] WTLR 1847. [82] (1870) 5QB 549, at 565.

[83] *Abbott v Richardson* [2006] EWHC 1291 (Ch), para 187; and *Hansen v Barker-Benfield* [2006] EWHC 1119 (Ch).

[84] *Westendorp v Warwick* [2006] EWHC 915 (Ch). [85] [2008] EWHC 1100 (Ch).

been considering changing her will for several months; consulted with her solicitor on two occasions, and discussed the will with her sister.

In many ways, issues of testamentary capacity raise issues which are similar to the general issue of mental capacity, which are discussed in chapter 3. *Scammell v Farmer*[86] left open the question of whether the Mental Capacity Act 2005 altered the law on the onus of proof under the Act. Under the Act, as a general principle, there is a presumption that a person has capacity.[87] However, the common law has held that capacity to make a will must be proved.[88] Further, case law will be required to see whether indirectly the Act is found to have changed the common law approach.[89] The burden of proof is difficult because it is difficult to prove an individual's state of mind at the time of execution.[90] The courts acknowledge this and in the absence of a mental abnormality or the will containing highly unusual terms, the courts will require little, if any, evidence to find mental capacity.

The court will consider the contents of the will in determining the testator's capacity. The more 'bizarre' the contents of the will, the more heavy will be the burden of proving capacity. In *Evans v Knight and Moore*, it was held:

Where a mental aberration is proved to have shown itself in the alleged testator, the degree of evidence necessary to substantiate any testamental act depends greatly on the character of the act itself. If it purports to give effect only to probable intentions, its validity may be established by comparatively slight evidence. But evidence, very different in kind and much weightier in degree, is required to the support of an act which purports to contain dispositions contrary to the testator's probable intentions, or savouring, in any degree, folly or frenzy.[91]

In that case the will was 'precisely such a disposition as natural affection would dictate'[92] and that was an important factor in upholding the will.[93] A contrasting example was *Kostic v Chaplin and others*,[94] where the deceased had left over £8 million to the Conservative Party and nothing to his son. The court found that the gift could only be explained on the basis that he suffered from delusional beliefs. He believed there to be international forces ranged against him and that the Conservative Party offered his only hope of protection. His delusions meant he was unable to appreciate the claims that his son had on the estate. That case does throw up the broader question of what can amount to a delusion. If he had donated money to the British National Party on the basis of a mistaken belief that

---

[86] Ibid.   [87] Even if it did, the will was entered into well before the Act came into force.

[88] *Hansen v Barker-Benfield* [2006] EWHC 1119 (Ch).

[89] Department of Constitutional Affairs, *The Mental Capacity Act Code of Practice* (DCA, 2007), at paras 4.31–3, suggests that judges could adopt the Mental Capacity Act definition in areas outside the scope of the Act (such as wills) 'if they think it appropriate'.

[90] *Hoff v Atherton* [2004] EWCA Civ 1554, para 34.

[91] [1822] 1 Add 299, 237–8.   [92] Ibid, at 238.

[93] See *Ledger v Wootton* [2007] EWHC 2599 (Ch), where it was found that the will was not 'unnatural' in preferring to leave money to some children and grandchildren, but not others. However, it was found that the testator lacked capacity on other grounds.

[94] [2007] EWHC 2298 (Ch).

'millions of immigrants were flooding into the country', would that be sufficient? The line between a delusion and a minority belief is problematic. One can see that if the line is not drawn tightly, the floodgates would be opened for challenging wills. Although not expressly mentioned in *Kostic*, it may have been crucial in that case that the delusion was as a result of a mental condition, rather than being an eccentric belief held by the individual.

Mental capacity to make a will requires not only an appreciation of the gifts that are being made, but also an awareness of the claims of others. In *Re Loxston*,[95] it was found that although the testator had the capacity to consider whether or not money should be left to an individual, she lacked the capacity to consider at the same time the competing claims of the other potential beneficiaries. This meant that she lacked capcity to make the will. In *Fuller v Fuller*,[96] the failure by the testator to provide an explanation as to why two of her five children were left out of the will was found to be evidence of incapacity.

Another common way of challenging a will is that it was executed as a result of undue influence.[97] This can most obviously include threats inducing the testator to make a will, but can also include more subtle ways of influencing a testator, for example, by a series of lies poisoning the mind of a testator against a potential beneficiary.[98] There is nothing wrong in someone encouraging another to make a will, and even in urging them to name a particular individual. It is the use of improper influence such that there is no free exercise of will which is key to the concept of undue influence.[99]

In both the law on capacity and undue influence, a delicate balance has to be struck. On the one hand, the law is appropriately alert to the fact that older people in particular seem vulnerable to being manipulated or misled into creating a will which does not reflect their genuine choice. On the other hand, even if a person is somewhat confused or is under pressure from a relative, this does not necessarily mean they are unable to make a genuine decision. The current law seeks to balance these concerns, and most cases are decided in a fact-specific way rather than on the basis of grand legal principle.

Intestacy

Where a person has made no will, or the will does not deal with the whole of a person's estate, they will be intestate or partially intestate. It has been claimed that

---

[95] [2006] EWHC 1291 (Ch).   [96] *Fuller v Fuller* [2005] All ER (D) 120 (Feb).
[97] P Ridge, 'Equitable Undue Influence and Wills' (2004) 120 LQR 617. See F Burns, 'The Elderly and Undue Influence Inter Vivos' (2003) 23 *Legal Studies* 251 for a discussion of undue influence as it applies to gifts.
[98] See, eg *In the Matter of the Estate of Edwards* [2007] EWHC 1119 (Ch).
[99] *Re Loxston (Deceased)* [2006] EWHC 1291 (Ch); and *Hansen v Barker-Benfield* [2006] EWHC 1119 (Ch).

around two-thirds of people in England and Wales die intestate every year,[100] although Masson found that there had been a recorded decline of 40 per cent in the number of administered intestacies over the last 40 years.[101] The law provides rules to determine what then should happen to such a person's property.

There has been much debate over what the purpose of the law on intestacy should be. The Law Commission of England and Wales argued that the rules of intestacy:

> should be certain, clear and simple both to understand and to operate. They do not lay down absolute entitlements, because the deceased is always free to make a will leaving his property as he chooses. They operate as a safety net for those who, for one reason or another, have not done this. If the rules can conform to what most people think should happen, so much the better. If they are simple and easy to understand, the more likely it is that people who want their property to go elsewhere will make a will. It is also important to enable estates to be administered quickly and cheaply. The rules should be such that an ordinary layman can easily interpret them and consequently administer them. Also the rules should make it unnecessary for an administrator to have to determine complex or debatable questions of fact.[102]

In a similar vein, the Scottish Law Commission has said that the law on intestacy should: reflect legal tradition; mirror the presumed wishes of the deceased; be acceptable to a broad spectrum of public opinion; be consistent and free from anomalies; and be easy to understand.[103] The problem is that, as we shall see, these aims are frequently inconsistent. This has led some commentators to complain that policy-makers on intestacy rely on a mix of preferences of the deceased, the interests of survivors, and the good of society, all without a clear overarching policy objective.[104] Given the conflicting policy objectives, it is not surprising to find a degree of unhappiness with how the law works. The National Consumer Council survey found that 15 per cent of people questioned knew of someone involved in an intestacy. Thirty-three per cent of cases were said to be stressful, 14 per cent expensive, and 21 per cent involved the estate going to the wrong person, in the opinion of the person questioned.

The law on intestacy

Where a person dies without a valid will there is a detailed set of rules that applies to the distribution of the estate.[105] The rules are complex and will be

---

[100] K Shakespeare, 'Living in Limbo' (2005) 155 *New Law Journal* 1585.

[101] J Masson, 'Will Making, Making Clients: Part 1' (1994) *Conveyancer* 267, at 269.

[102] England and Wales, Law Commission, *Family Law: Distribution on Intestacy* (Law Commission, 1989), at 7.

[103] Scottish Law Commission, *Discussion Paper on Succession* (Scottish Law Commission, 2007).

[104] A Hirsch, 'Default Rules in Inheritance Law: A Problem in Search of Its Context' (2004) 73 *Fordham Law Review* 1031.

[105] Administration of Estates Act 1925; Intestate Estates Act 1952.

briefly summarized. The first call on the estate is on a surviving spouse or civil partner.[106] How much they receive depends on whether or not the deceased left an estate and how much was in the estate. The basic structure is that any spouse or civil partner will receive the first £125,000 of the estate if there are children and the first £200,000 if there are none. They will also take personal chattels.[107] This is referred to as the statutory legacy. It means, therefore, that in cases where the estate is small, the testator's spouse will receive everything there is. However, if the estate exceeds the figures in the statutory legacy, the remainder is split between the spouse and children, or in a case with no children, the spouse and parents or siblings of the deceased. If there is a spouse but no issue and no relatives of the whole blood, the spouse will take the whole estate absolutely.

Developing a law to deal with cases where the deceased has not left a will is problematic. The law faces some difficult issues. The first question is what the basis of these rules should be?[108] Should there be an attempt to match the rules to what we predict an average member of the public would want if they were asked, what would you like to happen to your property on your death?[109] Or should there be an attempt to determine what people *should* want? Let us suppose, for example (and I have no reason to believe this to be true), that a survey of the public shows that they would want their legitimate children but not children born outside marriage to inherit; is this something that should be reflected in the rules on intestacy or not? Might not public policies opposing discrimination against children born outside marriage mean that the views of the average person be ignored? The role of fairness or need may come into play here too. So, for example, if a testator has an adult child with disabilities, should the law require them to leave money?[110] These questions raise the broader issue of the extent to which wider societal interests should be relevant in the law on intestacy.[111] These might include the promotion of the nuclear family; the avoidance of dependency on state welfare; and the avoidance of litigation.

A middle path may be that the law should follow the views of the average person, unless they are contrary to some wider social good. Let us say, for example, that it is found that fathers who have not had contact with their children tend to leave them nothing. It should not necessarily follow that this

---

[106] They must survive the deceased by 28 days.

[107] Cars, furniture, etc, but not business assets.

[108] New South Wales, Law Reform Commission, *Uniform Succession Laws: Intestacy, Report 116* (2007).

[109] eg E Spitko, 'An Accrual/Multi-Factor Approach to Intestate Inheritance Rights for Unmarried Committed Partners' (2002) 81 *Oregon Law Review* 255, at 269.

[110] S Buhai, 'Parental Support of Adult Children with Disabilities' (2007) 91 *Minnesota Law Review* 710.

[111] A Hirsch, 'Default Rules in Inheritance Law: A Problem in Search of its Context' (2004) 73 *Fordham Law Review* 1031; and New South Wales, Law Reform Commission, *Uniform Succession Laws: Intestacy, Report 116* (2007).

norm be reflected in the intestacy rules, if that is seen as undesirable. Hence, it has been argued:

The law has great potential to teach and reinforce the values that ground it or appear to ground it. Those who experience the law operating upon them personally and those who observe the law operating on others are likely to learn whom the law respects, ignores, privileges, and disadvantages. In this way, intestacy law not only reflects society's familial norms but also helps to shape and maintain them.[112]

In discussions of reform of the law, weight has been attached to surveys of the public's attitudes.[113] However, these are notoriously difficult to interpret. It can be difficult for individuals to distinguish what they would want in the event of their own intestacy and what they think should be the rules of general application. In 1989, the Law Commission, in considering the law on intestacy, referred to surveys of the public indicating support for a general rule that the deceased's current spouse should inherit all their property. The Law Commission proposed reflecting this general belief in the law. Their proposal was opposed because it failed to take into account the claims of the children (especially minor children) of the deceased and earlier spouses. Notably, the Law Commission's proposals did not make their way into the statute books.[114] They were said to be not well received.[115] A common view was that the public had failed to appreciate the complexity of cases that might arise.

Another issue is the degree of flexibility that should be allowed. The law could seek to prioritize simplicity and speed over seeking to produce a result that would be ideal for the individual. The more complex the rules governing intestacy, the greater the degree of bureaucracy, slowness, and cost. However, the less complex they are, the less likely they are to be able to deal with the particularity of the individual case.[116] The compromise position reached in English law is that there is a set of firm rules which applies, but that an application can be made under the Inheritance (Provision for Family and Dependants) Act 1975 if the rules are thought to produce unfairness in a particular case. However, the reliance on the 1975 Act to solve any unfairness may be misplaced. Roger Kerridge argues that reliance on the Act is dangerous because claims are expensive and those brought by adult children are rarely successful. In particular, he notes that under the Act adult children are only entitled to maintenance, while fairness may call for a more generous award. Kerridge is right to emphasize the practical difficulties facing a

---

[112] E Spitko, 'The Expressive Function of Succession Law' (1999) 41 *Arizona Law Review* 1063, at 1100.

[113] See, eg England and Wales, Law Commission, *Family Law: Distribution on Intestacy* (Law Commission, 1989), at paras 25 and 29.

[114] The law was reformed through the Law Reform (Succession) Act 1995.

[115] R Kerridge, 'Reform of the Law of Succession: The Need for Change, Not Piecemeal Tinkering' [2007] *Conveyancer and Property Lawyer* 47.

[116] Committee on the Law of Intestate Succession, *Report* (Cmd 8310, 1951), at para 12.

claimant under the Act. His point emphasizes the need to ensure that the number of cases which require use of the Act are kept to a minimum.

Proposals for reform

There have been consistent calls for the law of intestacy to be reformed.[117] The Law Commission[118] and a review by the Department for Constitutional Affairs in 2005 likewise proposed changes to the current system.[119] However, neither reviews have resulted in changes to the law.[120] Both reviews were primarily concerned that the current law could fail to provide adequately for spouses. The Law Commission recommended that the intestate's surviving spouse should receive the whole estate in all cases. This was said to be backed up by research suggesting widespread support for a spouse inheriting all of the estate. The one exception, supported by the research, was where the marriage was a second marriage. However, as Stephen Cretney points out, the respondents to surveys of this kind may not be aware of the courts' power to award provision for the first wife on divorce. Indeed, without a full understanding of the legal powers available, relying on surveys of public opinion in cases of this kind may be questionable. Cretney said that reaction to the Law Commission report was at best lukewarm and, as indicated, it was not implemented.

Despite the lack of political support for the Law Commission's proposals, there is something to be said for them. A major point is that under the current law on intestacy of spouses, much significance attaches to whether or not property is jointly owned (and therefore ownership passes outside the will). The statutory estate on intestacy will be the same whether a spouse has received property outside the will and so vastly differing results can occur for similar spouses, all depending on whether or not the property is in joint names. Similarly, the way a deceased's pension provides for a spouse can have a significant impact on their financial position. If all of a deceased's property were automatically to pass to a spouse, then much less significance would attach to these, sometimes arbitrary, distinctions.

The Department for Constitutional Affairs' proposals listed the following as the four key principles of the law:

First, it is clear that at all times overwhelming priority has been accorded to the surviving spouse. Secondly, prominence has been given to securing the marital home for the use of the surviving spouse. Thirdly, the expectations of the children and other relatives have been acknowledged. Fourthly, it is reasonable to assume that, latterly at least, some allowance was made for future increases in value.[121]

---

[117] In S Cretney, 'Reform of Intestacy: The Best We Can Do?' (1995) 111 *Law Quarterly Review* 77.
[118] England and Wales, Law Commission, *Family Law: Distribution on Intestacy* (Law Commission, 1989).
[119] Department for Constitutional Affairs, *Administration of Estates—Review of the Statutory Legacy* (The Stationery Office, 2005).
[120] A Jack, 'Intestacy and Statutory Legacy' (2005) 155 *New Law Journal* 933.
[121] Department for Constitutional Affairs, *Administration of Estates—Review of the Statutory Legacy* (The Stationery Office, 2005), at 1.

Another major issue for the law on intestacy is the lack of provision for a partner who was not a spouse or civil partner of the deceased. They receive nothing under the rules of intestacy and must apply under the 1975 Act for an award. Surveys of the general public find considerable support for a change in the law to entitle them to an award automatically.[122] The issue is significant given the particularly low rates of will-making among cohabitants.[123] The Law Commission in its 2008 Report on cohabitants did not support a change in the law, commenting:

> We agree that the range of relationships encompassed by cohabitation is too diverse to be appropriately accommodated within the intestacy rules. Moreover, any change in favour of cohabitants would require an appreciation of the overall effect on the intestacy rules as they affect other members of the deceased's family. We consider that any such assessment should be made in the context of a comprehensive review of intestacy.[124]

As foreshadowed in that quotation, the Law Commission has indicated that it will undertake a review of the whole of the law on intestacy.[125]

Inheritance (Provision for Family and Dependants) Act 1975

The justifications for the Act

This Act is in many ways a remarkable piece of legislation. A parent while alive is entitled to leave their adult child in dire poverty, providing them with no financial help without redress. A millionaire wife can give her husband no more than a pittance for housekeeping, with no effective legal remedy for the husband. But on death an adult child in need or a spouse in poverty can claim under the Act for financial support from the deceased. Why is it that an obligation which is regarded as non-existent or unenforceable in life becomes enforceable on death? Two days before a person's death they are free to give their entire worldly goods to the local cats' home and there is nothing their relatives can do to stop the gift;[126] but if the gift is through a will the Act provides a way of challenging it.

Of course, one response is simply to conclude that the Act is unjustifiable. It may be said that the Act represents an improper infringement on the freedom to

---

[122] See, eg A Barlow, S Duncan, G James, and A Park, 'Just a Piece of Paper? Marriage and Cohabitation' in A Park, J Curtice, K Thompson, L Jarvis, and C Bromley (eds), *British Social Attitudes: Public Policy, Social Ties. The 18th Report* (Sage, 2001); and C Williams, G Potter, and G Douglas, 'Cohabitation and Intestacy: Public Opinion and Law Reform' *Child and Family Law Quarterly*, forthcoming.

[123] A Barlow, S Duncan, G James, and A Park, 'Just a Piece of Paper? Marriage and Cohabitation' in A Park, J Curtice, K Thomson, L Jarvis, and C Bromley (eds), *British Social Attitudes: Public Policy, Social Ties. The 18th Report* (Sage, 2001).

[124] Law Commission, *The Financial Consequences of Relationship Breakdown* (Law Commission, 2008), Part 6.

[125] Law Commission, *Tenth Programme of Law Reform* (2008), at para 1.15.

[126] Assuming the donor is competent.

dispose of one's property as one wishes. Once the state starts to play the role of compelling the transfer of property from one person to another in the name of fairness or moral obligation, dangerous waters are entered and the whole system of property is under threat. So, how can the Act be justified?

One justification is the argument referred to earlier, that although the decisions of a person while alive as to how they wish to dispose of their property should be respected, once a person has died there is no (or little) reason to respect the wishes of the dead. The merits of this argument have already been briefly mentioned.[127] But it can also be added that the argument seems to prove too much. If the wishes of the deceased carry little or no weight, why are wills given any effect at all? Even if it is accepted that the claims of others may outweigh the claims of the deceased, why should the claims of family members carry any more weight than the claims of others in society in dire need?

It could be argued that the law should recognize obligations between individuals in close adult relationships. The law does not enforce these obligations for reasons of public policy. For example, as we saw in chapter 6, a good case can be made against the enforcement of obligations that an adult child has to support his or her parents. However, many of the reasons for non-enforcement rest on the negative impact enforcement could have on the relationship between the parties. It may be argued that once a person is dead our concerns about the impact on family dynamics cease and the arguments in favour of enforcement are no longer outweighed by the arguments against.

Another possible argument is that a person cannot be taken to intend that his or her nearest relatives, and those to whom are owed a special obligation, are left in dire need on his or her death. In other words, the Act is in reality designed to protect the intentions of the testator. This does not appear to explain the 1975 Act, as it can apply even where there is manifest evidence that the testator intended to leave the applicant with nothing. That said, the courts do sometimes consider what the testator would have done had he known the applicants' financial situation.[128] But that seems to be just one factor among many that are to be taken into account.

As these arguments demonstrate, the current law lacks a clear theoretical basis and a rather inconsistent set of case law has developed. Underlying the Act is a balance between respecting the wishes of the testator against the claims of their living family relatives. Fiona Cownie and Anthony Bradney undertook an interesting review of the use of the Act.[129] They found differences in the interpretation of the Act between judges in the Chancery Division and the Family Division.

---

[127] See also, S McGuinness and M Brazier, 'Respecting the Living Means Respecting the Dead Too' (2008) 28 *Oxford Journal of Legal Studies* 298.

[128] eg *Re Garland* [2007] EWHC 2 (Ch), where the court felt that the testator would not necessarily have made any greater provision.

[129] F Cownie and A Bradney, 'Divided Justice, Different Voices: Inheritance and Family Provision' (2003) 23 *Legal Studies* 566.

Family Division judges were more willing to exercise a broad discretion to ensure the needs of parties were met, while Chancery Division judges were more reluctant to disturb the allocation of property through the will in the absence of concrete evidence.

Who can apply under the Act?

The following can apply under the Act:[130] the deceased's spouse or civil partner; the former spouse or civil partner;[131] a person cohabiting with the deceased for at least two years up until the death;[132] a child of the deceased;[133] any person whom the deceased treated as a child of the family in the context of a marriage or civil partnership; and any person being maintained (wholly or partly) by the deceased immediately before the death.

There is a mass of case law which considers the precise definition of these groups.[134] Here, some general observations will be made. It is notable that the category of blood relatives is narrowly defined. Only children of the deceased can claim. Notably, parents of the deceased cannot, nor can wider relatives, including siblings. Of course, wider categories of relatives may be able to claim by virtue of falling into one of the other categories (for example, that they were being maintained by the deceased). Even a child of the deceased is unlikely to succeed in a claim unless they can establish a special need or moral obligation owed by the deceased.[135]

The Act, therefore, appears to provide greater scope for relationships of financial dependency than for blood relationships. The legislation's focus is on applicants who will be worse off as a result of the death, rather than those who have lost what they might have hoped for under the will. The fact that it is financial dependency, rather than formal aspects of the relationship, can be demonstrated by the courts' interpretation of the provisions that apply to cohabitants. In *Re Watson (Deceased)*,[136] the applicant and deceased had had a relationship for over 30 years, but only moved in together in their mid-50s. While they lived together, they did not have a sexual relationship, although they had a common life. This was found to be sufficient to constitute living together as husband and wife and hence allow the applicant to make a claim. In *Gully v Dix*,[137] the court gave a broad interpretation to the requirement that the applicant needed to have lived

---

[130] See s 1(1).   [131] Provided they have not since married or entered a civil partnership.

[132] *Baker v Thomas* [2008] EWHC 937 (Ch). This category was added by the Law Reform (Succession) Act 1995, s 2. The Civil Partnership Act 2004 (Sch 4, para 15(5)) made it clear that the category applies to same-sex as well as opposite-sex couples.

[133] This includes an adult child. It also includes adopted children: Adoption and Children Act 2002, s 67.

[134] See N Lowe and G Douglas, *Bromley's Family Law* (Oxford University Press, 2007), at 1104 ff.

[135] *Re Hancock* [1998] 2 FLR 346.   [136] [1999] 1 FLR 878.

[137] [2004] EWCA Civ 139.

with the deceased *immediately* before the date of the death.[138] The fact that the applicant had lived with the deceased for 17 years was clearly significant.[139]

The courts have also been generous in finding that the applicant was being maintained by the deceased.[140] Notably, the statute only applies to applicants who have been maintained where the money has been given otherwise than for full consideration. This means that a paid housekeeper or carer could not claim under the Act.[141] There can be difficulties here in a case where, for example, a person moves in as a lodger and pays a small rent, but then starts to become a companion and carer, and ceases to pay rent. In such a case, it is not easy to determine whether the provision of accommodation is of equal value to the care. This causes one leading textbook to suggest, 'it is submitted that companionship and the like should be brought into account only insofar as they involve services which can and should be evaluated'.[142]

Clearly, one concern is that it is common in later old age for neighbours and friends to undertake small tasks for an individual. The courts do not want to interpret the legislation in a way which allows a claim by those simply offering friendship and help to the deceased, to whom the deceased may have given gifts or small payment. What the courts appear to be looking for is an element of dependency. Hence, the contributions have to be substantial and it must be said that the applicant was being maintained by the deceased.

What we see in these cases is an attempt by the courts to focus on the loss to the applicant that has occurred as a result of the relationship breaking down. The courts are less concerned with the formal status of the relationship than the economic disadvantages caused by it and the financial vulnerability of the applicant. This, it is submitted, is the correct approach for the courts to take.

What can be claimed?

There are different rules for claimants who were spouses or civil partners of the deceased and for other claimants. First, other claimants will be considered. The applicant will only be entitled to reasonable financial provision. Notably, this means that the Act is not to be used to make generous gifts or to reward good behaviour. Reasonable financial provision may well be more than 'enough to get by'; but should not be equated to being 'an entitlement to what they desired'.[143] The sum provided is to ensure that a person has reasonable provision for their

---

[138] Law Commission, *The Financial Consequences of Relationship Breakdown* (Law Commission, 2008), at 6.31 recommends that former cohabitants should be allowed to apply.

[139] See also, *Negus v Bahouse* [2007] EWHC 2628 (Ch). For a less sympathetic approach, see *Baynes v Hedger* [2008] EWHC 1587 (Ch), involving an unacknowledged same-sex relationship.

[140] See, eg *Rees v Newbery and the Institute for Cancer Research* [1998] 1 FLR 1041.

[141] See M Oldham, 'Financial Obligations Within the Family—Aspects of Intergenerational Maintenance and Succession in England and France' (2001) 60 *Cambridge Law Journal* 128.

[142] N Lowe and G Douglas, *Bromley's Family Law* (Oxford University Press, 2007), at 1108.

[143] *Negus v Bahouse* [2007] EWHC 2628 (Ch).

maintenance.[144] In one recent case, in the light of the couple's lifestyle during their unmarried relationship, the applicant was awarded the equivalent to £38,000 per year. As this shows, 'reasonable provision' covers not just bare necessities, but also what the applicant might reasonably regard as desirable for their benefit or welfare.[145] The Act in section 3 lists the factors a court should take into account. These are the size of the estate; the financial resources and needs that an applicant (or any other claimant) has or is likely to have; and the obligations and responsibilities which the deceased had towards any applicant or any beneficiary of the estate.

Notably, missing from the factors listed is the intentions of the deceased. In *Re Hancock (Deceased)*,[146] there was some recognition of the relevance of this. The case concerned some land which at the time of probate had been estimated at around £100,000, but which had dramatically risen in value to £650,000 when it became available for redevelopment. The applicant, an adult daughter in her 70s, was in precarious financial circumstances. The Court of Appeal upheld the award to her of £3,000 per annum maintenance. One fact emphasized by the court was that the father had made it clear while alive that the applicant should receive some provision in the will.[147] However, it is clear that the courts will depart from the wishes of the deceased if fairness so requires. In *Espinosa v Bourke*,[148] where the deceased had promised to his wife that he would provide for the daughter, he had decided to leave the daughter nothing, as he disapproved of her lifestyle and she had left him to be cared for by her teenage son. The court decided that the daughter's needs justified award, despite the testator's clear views.

Spouses and civil partners are treated differently. They are entitled to claim provision that is reasonable and may be in excess of what is required for their maintenance.[149] Under section 3(2) of the Act, the court had to take account of X's age, the duration of the marriage, and any contribution by X to the welfare and upbringing of the children, and the upkeep of the family and home. It is sometimes explained that it would be unfair if a spouse were left in a worse position as a result of her spouse's death than she would be in if there had been a divorce. It would not be desirable to encourage spouses of the dying to institute divorce proceedings in order to protect their financial position.[150] That said, when determining what a widow or widower can claim under the Act, the amount that would have been awarded on divorce is only one factor to be taken into account. A spouse or civil partner could expect an award that would allow them to continue at a similar standard of living to that they enjoyed during the marriage, but not

---

[144] *Re Coventry* [1980] Ch 461, at 486.   [145] Ibid, at 485.

[146] [1998] 2 FLR 346; discussed in A Borkowski, 'Re Hancock (Deceased) and Espinosa v Bourke: Moral Obligation and Family Provision' (1999) 11 *Child and Family Law Quarterly* 305.

[147] See also, *Espinosa v Bourke* [1999] 1 FLR 747.   [148] [1999] 1 FLR 747.

[149] Inheritance (Provision for Family and Dependants) 1975, s 1(2). See G Miller, 'Provision for a Surviving Spouse' [1997] 16 *Conveyancer and Property Lawyer* 442.

[150] G Miller, 'Provision for a Surviving Spouse' [1997] 16 *Conveyancer and Property Lawyer* 442.

higher.[151] It is interesting to consider *Graham v Murphy*.[152] There the applicant was an unmarried partner who had lived with the deceased for 17 years. She was awarded £35,000 out of an estate worth £240,000. No doubt if she had married the deceased she would have received a significantly larger sum.

Attempts to avoid the Act

One revealing issue concerns whether or not it is possible for a testator to avoid the potential operation of the 1975 Act. Clearly, a statement in a will which says that the Act does not apply will be ineffective.[153] Less clear is how the law will deal with a case where a will is made subject to a condition that the beneficiary does not challenge the will.[154] The effect of such a clause (if valid) is to provide a further disincentive to a beneficiary claiming under the Act. Not only are they at risk of having to pay legal costs should they lose, they are also at risk of losing the gift under the will. There is relatively little guidance on the effect of such clauses, the only significant recent case being *In the Estate of Nathan Deceased*.[155] It seems that such a clause is not automatically void for uncertainty, although it could be. More significantly, the clause was said not to be necessarily void as contrary to public policy.[156] The Law Commission when considering the position of cohabitants did not think that they should be able to agree that the Act will not apply to them.[157] The law on this issue demonstrates again that the testator's wishes are the only factor which determines how their estate is dealt with on their death.

Comments on the Act

According to the statistics on applications brought in the Chancery Division under the Act, it is clear that the Act is little used. The number of applications has noticeably decreased in the last few years. In 2002, there were 73 applications, but by 2006 the number was 10.[158] The courts appear particularly reluctant to allow applications where the estate is small on the pragmatic basis that in such cases the costs of the application are likely to eat up the entire estate.[159]

---

[151] *Fielden & Graham v Cunliffe* [2005] EWCA Civ 1508.
[152] [1997] 1 FLR 860.   [153] *Re Raven* [1915] 1 Ch 673.
[154] I Johnson, 'Conditions Not to Dispute Wills and the Inheritance (Provisions for Family and Dependants) Act 1975' (2004) 25 *Liverpool Law Review* 71.
[155] [2002] NPC 79.
[156] See also, *Evanturel v Evanturel* (1874) LR 6 PC1; *Cooke v Turner* (1846) 15 M & W 727; and *Stevenson v Abington* (1863) 9 LT 74.
[157] Law Commission, *The Financial Consequences of Relationship Breakdown* (Law Commission, 2008), at 6.49.
[158] Judicial Statistics, *Claims and Originating Proceedings Issued in London by Nature of Proceedings (2002–2006)* (National Statistics, 2007).
[159] [1997] 3 All ER 63, at 74.

We mentioned earlier some of the possible justifications for this legislation. The interpretation of the legislation does not give a clear picture as to its theoretical foundation. The Act does not appear to be an attempt to ensure a will follows the wishes of the deceased. As we have seen, the courts will make awards even though it is clear the deceased wanted the claimant to receive nothing. Further, even if the deceased makes it clear that he or she does not want the Act to apply to his or her estate, the Act can still be used. Nor does the Act seem to be based on a principle that if the claimant is in great need this outweighs any respect due to the wishes of the deceased. Claimants have succeeded even when they are not in dire poverty.[160] Kate Green suggests the basis of the claim is that leaving the applicant money was not 'wise or right'.[161] As the discussion in this chapter shows, the current law involves the courts balancing conflicting principles, with the courts refusing to be drawn on which is to have priority or how the balancing exercise is to be done. That might free judges to ensure that what they regard as a fair result in each case is reached, but it fails to provide any predictability over what the law should be.

Proprietary estoppel

Another way of seeking to challenge a will is through proprietary estoppel. Of course, technically this is not a challenge to the will per se, but a dispute over what property forms part of the estate. In essence, the claim of a proprietary estoppel is that the property in question is subject to an equitable claim, meaning that the testator is not free to dispose of it by his or her will.[162]

The law on proprietary estoppel is complex and still in a state of evolution. At its heart, the law is designed to avoid an unconscionable result.[163] A classic case will involve the owner of a piece of land making an assurance or promise that a piece of land does or will belong to the claimant and that as a result the claimant has acted to his or her detriment.[164] These requirements may, however, be treated with a degree of flexibility. However, the courts are wary of leaving proprietary estoppel too open ended. As the Privy Council recently noted:

While recourse to the doctrine of estoppel provides a welcome means of effecting justice when the facts demand it, it is equally important that the courts do not penalize those who through acts of kindness simply allow other members of their family to inhabit their property rent free.[165]

---

[160] eg *Fielden & Graham v Cunliffe* [2005] EWCA Civ 1508.
[161] K Green, 'The Englishwoman's Castle. Inheritance and Private Property Today' (1988) 51 *Modern Law Review* 187.
[162] S Nield, '"If You Look After Me, I Will Leave You My Estate": The Enforcement of Testamentary Promises in England and New Zealand' (2000) 20 *Legal Studies* 85.
[163] *Jennings v Rice* [2002] EWCA Civ 159, para 56.
[164] *Wayling v Jones* (1993) 69 P & CR 170.
[165] *Knowles v Knowles* [2008] UKPC 30, para 27.

In *Uglow, Uglow v Uglow*,[166] Mummery LJ identified[167] six general principles that apply in such cases:

(1) The overriding concern of equity to prevent unconscionable conduct permeates all the different elements of the doctrine of proprietary estoppel: assurance, reliance, detriment and satisfaction are all intertwined.

(2) The broad inquiry in a case such as this is whether, in all the circumstances, it is unconscionable for a testator to make a will giving specific property to one person, if by his conduct he has previously created the expectation in a different person that he will inherit it.

(3) The expectation may be created by (a) an assurance to the other person by the testator and intended by him to be relied upon that he will leave specific property to him; (b) consequent reliance on the assurance; and (c) real detriment (not necessarily financial) consequent on the reliance.

(4) The nature and quality of the assurance must be established in order to see what expectation it creates and whether it is unconscionable for the testator to repudiate his assurance by leaving the property to someone else.

(5) It is necessary to stand back and look at the claim in the round in order to decide whether the conduct of the testator had given rise to an estoppel and, if so, what is the minimum equity necessary to do justice to the claimant and to avoid an unconscionable or disproportionate result.

(6) The testator's assurance that he will leave specific property to a person by will may thus become irrevocable as a result of the other's detrimental reliance on the assurance, even though the testator's power of testamentary disposition to which the assurance is linked is inherently revocable.

In some cases, where there has not been an explicit promise that a property will belong to another it is very unlikely that the claimant will succeed, unless there is some substantial detrimental reliance.[168] However, in *Thorner v Major*,[169] the Court of Appeal held there must be a promise, representation, or assurance, which is clear and unequivocal and intended to be relied upon or reasonably understood as intended to be relied upon. The Court of Appeal expressed concern at the flexibility of the proprietary estoppel remedy:

However, given the potential and inevitable fluidity and flexibility of proprietary estoppel, as a doctrine of equity based on conscience, it seems to me that there are dangers unless the established requirements of proprietary estoppel are applied with a certain degree of rigour of analysis. Otherwise not only the strict requirements of the Wills Act as to how to give effect to testamentary intentions, but also the basic proposition of freedom of testamentary disposition, might be subverted, so that A could be found much too readily to be subject to an obligation to dispose of particular property in a particular way, giving B a claim which would take effect not merely to give B the

---

[166] [2004] WTLR 1183.   [167] At para 9.
[168] *Powell v Benney* [2007] EWCA Civ 1283, para 18.
[169] [2008] EWCA Civ 732, para 54.

expected legacy or devise, but also to give B a stronger right to it than if he or she had merely been made a beneficiary under a duly executed will but with no relevant promise or representation.[170]

The courts have also given guidance on the remedy that may be available if a proprietary estoppel claim succeeds. The court has a broad discretion to make what award would be appropriate in all the circumstances. This may involve a sum of money or an award of property. In *Powell v Benney*,[171] the Court of Appeal contrasted cases involving 'bargains' and 'non-bargain' cases. In the former, the claimant has been offered property in exchange for doing work. A typical case would be an older person asking a friend to move in and care for them and offering to leave them the house in return for doing so. In a non-bargain case, the owner of the land has made a promise about it and detrimental reliance has been incurred as a result (for example, by moving into the property and doing work on it); but there is no sense that the reliance was in exchange for the promise. In a bargain case, the court will consider awarding the 'expectation'; in other words, in giving the claimant what they were promised. But that will not automatically follow, especially where the monetary value of the detriment is hugely less than the value of the property in question. In a non-bargain case, the focus will be on compensating the applicant for the damages they suffered in reliance on the promise.

Occasionally, the courts will rely on the doctrine of mutual wills. These have been defined in the following terms:

> Mutual wills provided an instance of a trust arising by operation of law to give effect to the express intention of the two testators. It was a legally necessary condition of mutual wills that there was clear and satisfactory evidence of a contract between them. It was a legally sufficient condition to establish that in return for the first testator agreeing to make a will in a certain form and not to revoke it without notice to the second testator, then the second testator would make a will in a certain form and agree not to revoke it without notice to the first testator. If such facts were established then upon the death of the first testator equity would impose upon the second a form of constructive trust shaped by the exact terms of the contract that had been made. The constructive trust was imposed because the first testator had made a disposition of property on the faith of the second testator's promise to make a certain will, and with the object of preventing the first testator from being defrauded.[172]

Both the doctrines of proprietary estoppel and mutual wills seek to ensure that one person does not unconscionably take advantage of the other. Both doctrines seek to balance protecting a person who relies on another's promise to their detriment with protecting property owners from having legal liability attaching to a casual remark which was not intended to have legal effect.

---

[170] At para 69.   [171] [2007] EWCA Civ 1283.
[172] *Re Ciebrant* [2008] EWHC 1268 (Ch).

Inheritance tax

Inheritance tax is levied on estates which are worth more than the £300,000 (the threshold) for the year 2007/08,[173] subject to certain exemptions. The tax is levied at 40 per cent of the amount that the estate exceeds the threshold. So, an estate worth £350,000 would be taxed at £20,000. It is also applied to gifts made by the deceased three years before their death, and at a lower rate on gifts made between three and seven years before death. Importantly, spouses and civil partners have an exemption from inheritance tax and so however large the estate left to them there will be no inheritance tax payable. In his pre-budget report, the Chancellor of the Exchequer announced that for deaths on or after 9 October 2007 it will be possible for spouses and civil partners to transfer their unused inheritance tax nil rate bands.

In 2006/07, £3,545 million was generated from inheritance tax.[174] Notably, this compares with £1,680 million in 1997/98.[175] Compared with other taxes, the amount raised from inheritance tax is not great and amounts to less than 1 per cent of GDP.[176] The number of estates paying inheritance tax in the UK rose by 72 per cent in the five years up to 2004.[177] The government claims that only 6 per cent of estates pay tax,[178] although that figure has been disputed[179] and, even if correct, with increasing property prices it will increase. In 2002, the value of only 16 per cent of detached properties was above the threshold for inheritance tax in 2002; by 2007 that was 29 per cent, and rising.[180]

The payment of inheritance tax has become a major political issue.[181] The debates over inheritance came to a political head in 2007 when, following sustained pressure from some newspapers with campaigns to abolish the inheritance tax, the Conservative Party indicated it would be willing to abolish the tax. This was seen in some quarters to cause a substantial increase in popularity and a rise in the polls. The government responded by permitting married couples and civil partners to be able to share their personal inheritance tax allowance, meaning in effect that spouses and civil partners could claim £600,000 tax allowance. The explanation offered was that commonly when one spouse dies, they leave their estate to

---

[173] Finance Act 2006, Part IV, set these at £312,000 for 2008–09; and £325,000 for 2009–10.

[174] N Lee, 'Inheritance Tax—An Equitable Tax No Longer: Time for Abolition?' (2007) 27 *Legal Studies* 678.

[175] Ibid.

[176] B-D Nissim, 'Why Do We Ignore the Best Solution for Improving Unequal Income Distribution?' (2007) 34 *International Journal of Social Economics* 415.

[177] BBC News Online, 'More Families Pay Inheritance Tax', 4 August 2006.

[178] K Rowlingson and S McKay, *Attitudes to Inheritance in Britain* (Policy Press 2005), at xiii.

[179] C Pratten, 'Gordon Brown Counts Dead Children: The True Impact of Inheritance Tax' (2006) 26 *Economic Affairs* 74.

[180] Halifax Building Society, *Nearly One Third of Detached Properties Valued Above Inheritance Tax Threshold* (2007).

[181] R Patrick and M Jacobs, *Wealth's Fair Measure: The Reform of Inheritance Tax* (Fabian Society, 2003).

their spouse and so do not use their personal allowance.[182] It would be fair for the second spouse to die to therefore be entitled to both their spousal allowances.

There has been a fierce debate over whether inheritance tax is justifiable.[183] Campaigns have been launched in the press against the tax.[184] Opinion polls suggest that the tax is unpopular among the general public, with 73 per cent disputing that it was a 'fair way' for the government to raise money.[185] It is only possible here to highlight some of the key issues in the tax debate.[186]

Supporters of the tax argue that it has played an important role in reducing social inequality. This may be particularly so in the current housing market, where inheriting a house will be the only realistic way most people can enter the housing market. Notably, Karl Marx advocated a 100 per cent inheritance tax as a way of challenging the class struggle.[187] Against such claims it is said that the amount raised by inheritance tax is minimal and so its role in reducing inequality can be questioned. Indeed, it is commonly said that the richest people are able to afford advice to avoid the payment of inheritance tax.[188] Further, the existence of tax avoidance in this area has led some to claim that inheritance tax is a voluntary tax only paid by those who are foolish enough not to make inheritance tax avoidance plans.[189] In addition, there is some evidence to suggest that testators prefer to give to their less well-off relatives and so it should not be assumed that inheritance always increases inequalities between the rich and poor. Taxing inheritance may undermine its effectiveness as a means of meeting the needs of the poorest relatives.[190]

---

[182] The extent to which this is true may be questioned, at least in the case of wealthier couples who had taken tax advice.

[183] Some call for increased use of inheritance tax: B-D Nissim, 'Why Do We Ignore the Best Solution for Improving Unequal Income Distribution?' (2007) 34 *International Journal of Social Economics* 415; and D Duff, 'The Abolition of Wealth Transfer Taxes: Lessons from Canada, Australia, and New Zealand' (2005) 3 *Pittsburgh Tax Review* 71. The US Congress has voted to phase out federal estate tax. Canada, Australia, and New Zealand have already done this.

[184] Discussed in A Mumford, 'Inheritance in Socio-Political Context' (2007) 4 *Journal of Law and Society* 546.

[185] Populous poll conducted for the BBC, March 2006. This poll concerned only IHT. See also the Telegraph YouGov poll (*Daily Telegraph*, 23 October 2006), where 70 per cent of all voters questioned favoured the abolition of IHT and the report of a survey in September 2006 showing that 75 per cent of those surveyed thought the tax to be unfair.

[186] A Alstott, 'Equal Opportunity and Inheritance Taxation' (2007) 121 *Harvard Law Review* 161; and A Cassone and C Marchese, *Should the Death Tax Die? And Should it Leave an Inheritance* (POLIS, 2001).

[187] For a discussion of how inequalities of wealth between races and sexes can be explained, see P Menchik and N Jianakoplos, 'Black-White Wealth Inequality: Is Inheritance the Reason?' (1997) *Economic Inquiry* 35; and T Warren, 'Moving Beyond the Gender Wealth Gap: On Gender, Class, Ethnicity, and Wealth Inequalities in the United Kingdom' (2006) 12 *Feminist Economics* 195.

[188] R Patrick and M Jacobs, *Wealth's Fair Measure: The Reform of Inheritance Tax* (Fabian Society, 2003).

[189] G Cooper, *A Voluntary Tax? New Perspectives on Sophisticated Estate Tax Avoidance* (The Brookings Institution, 1979).

[190] N Tomes, 'The Family, Inheritance, and the Intergenerational Transmission of Inequality' (1981) 89 *The Journal of Political Economy* 928.

Supporters also point to the political attractions of using inheritance tax rather than other forms of taxation:

within limits no economist will question the propriety of laying taxes on bequests and inheritances. They are collected with ease and reasonable certainty. They fall upon something which the taxpayer never yet enjoyed and the diminution of which he therefore does not full miss. The goose, to follow Colbert's maxim, is plucked so as to get the most feathers with the least squealing, and almost with none. Live goose feathers, indeed, are not required. The real victim is dead.[191]

Opponents claim it acts as a disincentive to save and accumulate wealth.[192] The desire to pass on an inheritance can be seen to encourage economically productive activity. If the inheritance tax level is too high this benefit is lost or the wealthy will leave estates which impose inheritance tax. On one discussion board, the following quote summarizes a popular sentiment about the tax:

All inheritance tax is theft. Stealing from what is left from a lifetime of paying taxes. The way to close the gap between rich and poor is to give all the chance to prosper by removing the deadweight and waste of bureaucracy, not by confiscating wealth which is a disincentive to creating it.[193]

Other objections to the inheritance tax are that the administrative and compliance costs are high[194] and indeed it has even been suggested that not charging it and collecting from its expenditure may generate greater income for the Treasury.[195]

A rather different ground of complaint applies to the exemptions. Most notable is the exemption that applies between spouses and civil partners. So, the estate of a wealthy man who died and left his estate to his wife or civil partner would not be required to pay inheritance tax, but if he had left it to a cohabitant,[196] inheritance tax would be payable. A death-bed marriage or civil partnership can be a very wise tax saving measure! The existence of this measure can lead to claims that it discriminates against those couples who have not formalized their relationship. Perhaps the obvious, but too ready, response is that they have only themselves to blame for failing to regularize their relationship. But such an argument is certainly of no weight as regards couples who are not permitted to marry or enter civil partnerships. In *Burden and Burden v United Kingdom*,[197] two sisters who had lived together for many years claimed that the fact that on either of their deaths inheritance tax would be payable amounted to discrimination.

---

[191] S Baldwin, 'The Modern "Droit D'Aubaine"' (1905) 14 *Yale Law Journal* 129, at 133.
[192] B Bracewell-Milnes, *Euthanasia for Death Duties* (IEA, 2002).
[193] T Drain, at *Your View: Should We Scrap Inheritance Tax?*, Telegraph.co.uk.
[194] N Lee, 'Inheritance Tax—An Equitable Tax No Longer: Time for Abolition?' (2007) 27 *Legal Studies* 678.
[195] B Bracewell-Milnes, *Euthanasia for Death Duties* (IEA, 2002).
[196] ie someone to whom he was not married or a civil partner.
[197] Application no 13378/05.

Their concern was in particular that if tax was payable in the event of one of their deaths, the only means of paying would be to sell their home. The government justified the existence of the exemption by saying that it promoted stable heterosexual or homosexual relationships. This was regarded as a legitimate aim by the European Court of Human Rights. The court accepted that in any field of taxation broad fields of categories were used and this could create hardship in particular cases. It was best left to individual states to decide how to resolve these. It concluded:

In the present case, [the court] accepts the Government's submission that the inheritance tax exemption for married and civil partnership couples likewise pursues a legitimate aim, namely to promote stable, committed heterosexual and homosexual relationships by providing the survivor with a measure of financial security after the death of the spouse or partner. The Convention explicitly protects the right to marry in Article 12, and the Court has held on many occasions that sexual orientation is a concept covered by Article 14 and that differences based on sexual orientation require particularly serious reasons by way of justification (see, for example, *Karner v. Austria*, no. 40016/98, § 37, ECHR 2003-IX and the cases cited therein). The State cannot be criticised for pursuing, through its taxation system, policies designed to promote marriage; nor can it be criticised for making available the fiscal advantages attendant on marriage to committed homosexual couples.[198]

A common argument against inheritance tax is that it is a form of 'double taxation'. A person has paid income tax on the money they have earned and then must pay inheritance tax when they leave that property. Some see such arguments as a myth.[199] Perhaps the first point to make is that it is common to have to pay income tax and then a further tax on top of that. VAT is commonly charged on purchases, even if made with money earned and income-taxed. So, inheritance tax is no more a double tax than VAT is, for example. That is, however, not an entirely convincing argument in that the VAT is charged to the seller rather than the purchaser and so its analogy with inheritance tax is not exact.[200] A second point is that although some property left through inheritance may have been taxed as income, much wealth has not, and so even if the double taxation has some validity it only applies to a proportion of what is left.[201]

The arguments over inheritance tax raise complex issues. It is surprising that it has proved so controversial. It is payable only by the richest and even then on

---

[198] Para 59.

[199] In a similar fashion, Dominic Maxwell, who calls the double taxation argument a 'myth', shares the view that multiple taxation is common, and states that 'transactions, not bank notes, are the proper subject of taxation': *Fair Dues: Towards a More Progressive Inheritance Tax* (Institute for Public Policy Research, 2004), at 11.

[200] N Lee, 'Inheritance Tax—An Equitable Tax No Longer: Time for Abolition?' (2007) 27 *Legal Studies* 678.

[201] W Gale and J Slemrod, *Rhetoric and Economics in the Estate Tax Debate*, Paper Prepared for the National Tax Association Spring Symposium (Washington DC, 7–8 May 2001), available at <http://www.brookings.edu/views/papers/gale/20010522.pdf>.

money they have done nothing to earn. It appears to be a tax one could easily justify in political terms. The amount raised by it is comparatively modest, but were the tax to be abolished, the burden would fall on other taxpayers. It is hard to believe those others would be better off or less deserving than those who currently bear the burden of the tax.[202]

Conclusion

It will be of little surprise that research supports the belief that few people are aware of key points of inheritance law and inheritance tax.[203] Thirty-nine per cent of those questioned thought that long-term cohabitants had the same rights in inheritance as a married couple; and 15 per cent did not even guess at whether cohabitants had the same rights as married couples. This ignorance of the law is of no surprise and matches ignorance in other areas of law. However, it reminds us of the limited impact that the law can have on the inheritance practices of individuals.

The law on inheritance tells us much about the values of a society. We see in English law a largely individualistic approach, with much weight being given to the freedom of a testator to determine the allocation of their estate. It is true that in an extreme case a relative who loses out can bring a court action to claim a portion of the estate, but these are rarely successful. Where they are, it tends to be on the basis that the applicant has suffered particular hardship as a result of the death, rather than an enforcement of family obligation.

---

[202] For a discussion of the argument that on death all monies should go to the state, see W Paxton, S White, and D Maxwell, *The Citizen's Stake* (Policy Press, 2006).

[203] J Finch, L Hayes, J Masson, and J Mason, *Wills, Inheritance and Families* (Oxford University Press, 1996), at 32.

10

Conclusion

On 6 August 2008, it was reported that the body of Brian Dean, age 70, had been found in his terrace home in Huncoat. Police estimate his body had lain there for two years undiscovered. Neighbours reported that he was a private person who was rarely seen. A local councillor said that as Mr Dean had withdrawn from society it was not surprising that he had not been seen.[1]

That an older person could die and no one notice for two years reflects the invisibility of older people in our society. Whether it was, as the councillor suggested, Mr Dean who withdrew from society, or society who withdrew from Mr Dean, may be a matter for debate. Sadly, the isolation he suffered from is all too common. In a survey of 200 councils, it was reported that in an average week there are 43 funerals for people when no families or friends attend.[2] The Social Exclusion Unit's report on older people states that social exclusion cannot be regarded as a matter only for government:

Addressing social exclusion amongst the most excluded older people has to be everyone's responsibility. Individuals, families and communities therefore need to consider the extent and cause of social isolation in their areas and consider developing the most appropriate interventions. We want to see everyone—family, neighbours, pharmacists, GPs and shopkeepers and older people themselves—acting to ensure that isolation amongst older people is reduced.[3]

Of course, it would be quite wrong to suggest that all older people are lonely and isolated: many live active and fulfilling lives, contributing to their communities and families in countless ways. However, much of that work goes unnoticed in the public eye. Indeed, when people do discover that an older person is active in some field, a common reaction is surprise: 'isn't she wonderful, for her age'.

Article 23 of the European Social Charter acknowledges:

The right of elderly persons to social protection
With a view to ensuring the effective exercise of the right of elderly persons to social protection, the Parties undertake to adopt or encourage, either directly or in

---

[1] BBC News Online, 'Man Lay Dead in Bed for Two Years', 6 August 2008.
[2] J Neuberger, *Not Dead Yet* (Harper Collins, 2008), at 155.
[3] Social Exclusion Unit, *A Sure Start to Later Life* (SEU, 2006).

co-operation with public or private organisations, appropriate measures designed in particular:

- to enable elderly persons to remain full members of society for as long as possible, by means of:
  a. adequate resources enabling them to lead a decent life and play an active part in public, social and cultural life;
  b. provision of information about services and facilities available for elderly persons and their opportunities to make use of them;
- to enable elderly persons to choose their life-style freely and to lead independent lives in their familiar surroundings for as long as they wish and are able, by means of:
  a. provision of housing suited to their needs and their state of health or of adequate support for adapting their housing;
  b. the health care and the services necessitated by their state;
- to guarantee elderly persons living in institutions appropriate support, while respecting their privacy, and participation in decisions concerning living conditions in the institution.

Throughout this book, we have seen ways in which these rights are not protected in English law. Whether it be the inadequate responses to elder abuse; the failure to support those who are providing care; the prevalence of poverty among older people; the problems with the pension provision; or age discrimination in the health service, older people's rights are breached again and again.[4]

Another theme throughout this book has been the changing nature of old age, and the slowness of the law to keep up. Tom Kirkwood opened his Reith Lectures on age thus:

Never in human history has a population so wilfully and deliberately defied nature as has the present generation. How have we defied it? We have survived. Our unprecedented survival has produced a revolution in longevity which is shaking the foundations of societies around the world and profoundly altering our attitudes to life and death.[5]

However, society is yet to respond adequately to these changes. Chris Phillipson has argued that we are in a period of crisis over the identity of old age.[6] He writes:

By the 1990s, the unravelling of the system of retirement, along with changes to the welfare state, had begun to pose significant threats to elderly people. Both institutions have, it might be argued, suffered a crisis as regards their meaning and status within society. Retirement is no longer central—for increasing numbers of men and women—as a system organizing exits from the workplace...Alongside this, the welfare state is increasingly undermined or 'residualized' in respect of providing care and support in periods

---

[4] Ibid.
[5] T Kirkwood, *The Reith Lectures: The End of Age*, available at <http://www.bbc.co.uk/radio4/reith2001/>.
[6] C Phillipson, *Reconstructing Old Age* (Sage, 1998).

such as old age…At one level, these changes have resulted in a language and ideology which scapegoats the old, defining them as a burden and cost to society…At a more individual level, however, they raise important existential issues about the nature and meaning of growing old.[7]

The law's response to retirement and support of old age is still rooted in a model based on stable marriages, full-time work up until retirement, and a refusal to value properly care work. The chapters of this book are full of examples of strains showing on these outdated approaches. The funding of personal care services is woefully inadequate, leaving far too many older people without the care they need. The public and private pensions systems are failing to provide adequately for the financial needs of older people. All of this, in brief, comes down to money. Are we as a society willing to fund the services our older people need to protect their rights to a dignified old age?

Some of the problems that have been highlighted by the law's interaction with older people reveal as much about the assumptions of the law as they do about older people. First, there is the issue of autonomy. As discussed in chapters 3 and 4, the right to autonomy is fiercely protected in the law. However, that right assumes that an adult is competent, independent, and is able to make decisions for him- or herself. This presents difficulties when seeking to apply this to older people in a care home context. As George Agich writes:

> Elders in long-term care need help with activities of daily living because they have lost functional abilities, not because their choices are suppressed; long-term care represents a response to suffering and need. This response, of course, can be unsupportive of autonomy, but it would be wrong to approach long-term care with the idea that the environment is primarily politically oppressive of elders' rights. Individuals need long-term care because their ability to act autonomously in the world has been compromised by disability or frailty. Hence, they require more and prolonged supportive care from others. The importance of autonomy in democratic societies creates ambivalence toward the dependent old. Their need for care conflicts with the tendency to support the rights of adults to maintain independence. The development of efforts to secure the rights of institutionalized elders in the name of respect for autonomy helps marginally, at best, to improve their care. At worse, these efforts foment conflict and confusion without ennobling the elders or improving their residual autonomy.[8]

As argued in chapter 4, our conceptions of autonomy tend to be individualistic and fail to account for the relational lives we live in. In the care setting, the autonomy of one person impacts upon and is dependent upon the autonomy of another. In fact, this is not just true for older people in a care home, but for all of us. We are not independent in forging our own visions of the good life, rather our goals are made in coordination with others. The discussions of the concept of autonomy among older people reveal clearly the shortcomings in individualist

---

[7] Ibid, at 2–3.
[8] G Agich, *Dependence and Autonomy in Old Age* (Cambridge University Press, 2003), at 175.

presentations of autonomy and require us to rethink the notion of autonomy in more relational terms.[9]

Another consequence of the emphasis on individualistic autonomy is the lack of respect shown to the wishes of those who lack capacity to make decisions for themselves. As we have seen in chapter 3, under the Mental Capacity Act 2005 decisions are made for those who lack capacity based simply on their best interests. Their wishes are taken into account, but only in so far as they bear on a best interests assessment. This, it was argued, fails to protect the rights of dignity and liberty of the incapacitated individual. It has been argued that even if not fully autonomous or reasoned, we should still show some respect to their views— certainly not if doing so will cause them significant harm, but there should be good reasons before overruling their views. William Shakespeare famously described old age as being 'second childishness and mere oblivion, Sans teeth, sans eyes, sans taste, sans everything'.[10] Wonderful poetry, but not good ethics. Whatever physical frailties or mental disturbance a person may suffer, they are not without their basic rights to be treated as a human being with dignity and respect.[11]

Helen Small sees wider significance in the problematization of older people. She explains:

How we respond as societies to the growing numbers of people living to be old is now regularly said to be key to the future economic prosperity of developed and developing nations and their capacity to deliver social justice. Like others before me, I see this as a misplacing of the problem. Rather than isolate the old as the difficulty, we need to think in terms of (for example) the deeper causes of a gross disparity in national life expectancies around the world; rather than thinking about the 'burden of retirees', we should think more broadly about the wider nature and purpose of work.[12]

As these thoughts indicate, perceptions about the worthlessness of older people, and their invisibility, tell us much about the over-emphasis in our society on economic production, the lack of valuing of care work, and an overly materialistic conception of what is valuable in life.

In chapter 4, it was argued that our legal system is based on a misguided approach. We start with the ideal of an isolated, competent, able man, whose right to autonomy must be respected at all costs. The reality, not just for older people, but for all of us, does not match this ideal. We are vulnerable not competent; interdependent, not dependent; not isolated but in a network of relationships. In chapter 4, it was argued that an ethic of care would provide a way ahead for the law. This would put caring relationships at the heart of the law's approach.

---

[9] See for further discussion, J Herring, 'Relational Autonomy and Rape' in F Ebtehaj *et al*, *Regulating Autonomy: Sex, Reproduction and Families* (Hart, 2008).

[10] W Shakespeare, *As You Like It*, Act 2, scene 7.

[11] J Herring, 'Losing It? Losing What? The Law and Dementia' (2008) *Child and Family Law Quarterly* forthcoming.

[12] H Small, *The Long Life* (Oxford University Press, 2007), at viii.

Interdependency would be regarded as the norm, with the law seeking to promote relationships of care. This would produce a legal system better able to respond to the needs not just of older people, but all of us.

Finally, our society needs to find new ways of recognizing and valuing old age. In part this involves, as I have already suggested, valuing care work which many older people undertake, but this is largely ignored. However, there is more to it than this. Few of us like to acknowledge that we will become old. Simone de Beauvoir put it this way:

> When we look at the image of our own future provided by the old we do not believe it: an absurd inner voice whispers that *that* will never happen to us—when *that* happens it will no longer be ourselves that it happens to. We must stop cheating: the whole meaning of our life is in question in the future that is waiting for us. If we do not know what we are going to be, we cannot know what we are: let us recognize ourselves in this old man or in that old woman. It must be done if we are to take upon ourselves the entirety of our human state.[13]

We should not, however, make the mistake of believing that a good old age is mimicking youth as much as possible. That will be to reflect the ageist assumptions that youth is best. Similarly, Simon Biggs has written of the 'youthful self trapped beneath an ageing mask'.[14] But this may reflect a view based on youthfulness as the norm. If what Biggs is describing is a common experience, and there is some evidence that it is, then there is no reason why the trapped self should be youthful, rather than old. It sounds rather as a distaste for and denial of the reality of being old. Of course, it also reflects the vast cosmetic surgery industry seeking to alter the mask so it matches the inner 'reality'.

Rather than following such an approach, we need to find new ways of valuing old age. A better starting point has been suggested by Molly Andrews, who writes:

> Throughout the lifecycle, change and continuity weave an intricate web. As we meet the new challenges, both physical and psychological, with which our lives confront us, so then we are changed, even as we remain the same. Old age is no different from the other stages of life in this regard. The changes are many and real; to deny them, as some do in an attempt to counter ageism, is folly.[15]

We should not look down or ignore or trivialize the years people have lived, the experiences they have gained, or the care they have given. Ageing is often seen in terms of what is lost: be it mobility, memory, or beauty. As argued in chapter 2, old age should be entitled to respect in and of itself, in addition to the respect due to older people. For an older person has grown and developed; has loved and

---

[13] S de Beauvoir, *Old Age* (Penguin, 1970), at 11–12.
[14] S Biggs, 'Choosing Not To Be Old? Masks, Bodies and Identity Management in Later Life' (1997) 17 *Ageing and Society* 553, at 556.
[15] M Andrews, 'The Seductiveness of Agelessness' (1999) 19 *Ageing and Society* 301, at 310.

been loved; has cared and been cared for. Those things in themselves deserve acknowledgement and admiration. What will be a good old age for each person will be different because it reflects the closing chapters in their particular life story. It is often a time for reflection and looking forward to future generations. It may be a time for quiet or for noisy childcare. It can be a time for 'a growing into ourselves'.[16]

Society has much to learn and gain from welcoming older people into mainstream life: our offices, our places of entertainment, our faith communities, and so forth. We must reject the all too common view of older people being a burden on society and a strain on our welfare state.[17] Something of what may be hoped for is found in the experience of one woman in a community of older women. These communities, she writes, are:

embodied in the way that older women treat one another—with respect, affection, and attentiveness; in conversations and gestures that affirm and hence make visible older women's pride in and attention to their bodies, and that acknowledge the pain, suffering, and loss that accompanies embodiment; in discussions of caring, of work that is valuable, necessary and demanding.[18]

A community that values caring, that is respectful, affectionate, and attentive to older people: that would be a community one would want to grow old in. And a community one would want to be young in too.

---

[16] Ibid, at 312.
[17] S Harper, *Ageing Societies: Myths, Challenges and Opportunities* (Hodder Arnold, 2006).
[18] F Furman, *Facing the Mirror: Older Women and Beauty Shop Culture* (Routledge, 1997).

Index

adoption *see also* **child care**
  adoption orders 260–2
  adoption placements 261
  anonymity 257, 258
  child's best interests 259
  child's rights 259, 260
  conflicting rights 260
  extra-familial care 259
  family care 259
  human rights issues 259
  privacy 257–60
advance decisions/directives
  capacity 71, 72 *see also* **capacity**
  change in circumstances 71
  compromise views
    acceptable policy 81
    avoidance of harm/pain 81, 82
    human rights infringements 81
    individual's current wishes 81, 82
    past/present persons 80, 81
  conflicting wishes 72
  Dresser's approach
    critical interests 79, 80
    criticisms 80
    individual's best interests 79
    individual's changing views 79
    individual's current interests 79, 80
  Dworkin's approach
    critical interests 75–8, 80
    criticisms 76–8
    experiential interests 75–7
    individual's current interests 74
    individual's prior interests 74
    right of autonomy 75, 76
  effect 70
  enforceability 70, 71, 73, 81
  evidence 71
  example 75
  foreseeable medical conditions 73
  formalities 69, 70
  healthcare 69 *see also* **healthcare**
  individual's current wishes 72
  informed decisions 78
  interpretation 74
  life-saving treatment 69, 72, 73, 76
  loss of capacity 75, 76, 78–81
  loss of control 74, 80
  medical advice 69, 70
  medical practitioner's liability 72, 73
  overruling 71

  persons lacking capacity 58, 61, 69
  philosophical debates
    current best interests 74
    individual's current interests 74
    individual's prior interests 74
  physical continuity 77
  psychological discontinuity 77
  religious beliefs 78, 80
  revocation 72
  right of autonomy 75, 76 *see also* **autonomy**
  statutory definition 69
  statutory protection 72, 73
  sufficient information 78
  treatment
    developments, in 71
    medical treatment 70
    refusal of treatment 70
    specified treatment 69
    withdrawal 72
  uncertainty 72, 73
  US experience 74
  validity 70–3
age discrimination *see also* **discrimination**
  ageism distinguished 12 *see also* **ageism**
  behaviour 12
  classification issues 25
  definition
    equality issues 26–8
    improper/detrimental treatment 26
  employment
    company image 34
    recruitment practices 34
    remuneration 34
  equality over lifetime argument 31, 32
  harassment 39
  healthcare *see also* **healthcare**
    breast cancer screening 301, 302
    cervical cancer screening 301, 302
    covert discrimination 298
    human rights 300
    lack of protection 50, 51
    malnourishment 302
    NHS equality audits 298
    NHS healthcare 298, 299, 306, 343
    lack of protection 50, 51
    medical conditions 299
    medical decisions 299, 305
    medical treatments 299, 300
    mental health services 301
    mistreatment of patients 300

age discrimination (*cont.*)
  healthcare rationing 283–5, 290, 291, 305,
    306 *see also* **healthcare rationing**
  human rights protection 30, 34
  justice 33
  justification
    alternative provisions, absence of 44
    business need 43
    efficiency considerations 43
    legitimate aim 30, 36, 40–3
    legitimate occupational requirement 44
    objective justification test 38, 41
    proportionality 30, 36, 40, 42, 43
    reducing expense 43
  legal implications 12, 13
  legal protection 7, 9, 10
  legislative provisions
    direct discrimination 31
    indirect discrimination 31
    scope 30, 31
  meaning 12
  motivation 13
  prohibited grounds 30, 31
  public services 20
  quality adjusted life years (QALY) 305 *see*
    also **quality adjusted life years (QALY)**
  race-related issues 7, 13
  respect 32, 33
  retirement *see* **retirement**
  sex-related issues 7, 8, 13
  social care provisions 298
  social inclusion 51
  social services 51
  treatment
    detrimental 26
    equal 27
    mistreatment 33
    unequal 27
    unfavourable 39
  unfair assumptions 8, 9
  unfairness 31, 32
  victimization
    protection, against 39
    unfavourable treatment 39
  workplace 31
ageing
  anti-ageing treatments 277, 278, 305
  medical status 305
  population *see* **ageing population**
  successful ageing 306
ageing population
  demographic transition 1, 2, 16, 197, 198
  dependency 17
  economic implications 1
  marginalization 2
  political dimension 1
  social implications 1, 2

ageism
  assumptions
    age characterizations 22–4
    burden on society 22
    dependency 17, 22
    end-of-life issues, 67
    racist 21, 22
    sexist 21, 22
    unfair 24
    untrue 12–15, 17, 18
  changing attitudes 50
  definition 12
  demographic changes 16 *see also*
    demographic changes
  disadvantages 7
  discrimination
    age discrimination 12
    employment 34
    race discrimination 24–6
    sex discrimination 24–6
  elder abuse 136, 147, 159–61 *see also* **elder**
    abuse
  family privacy 160
  glorification of youth 18
  healthcare rationing 118, 270 *see also*
    healthcare rationing
  impact 9, 14
  lack of confidence 160
  lack of facilities 160
  language issues 18, 19
  legal implications 12, 13
  manifestation 7, 18–22
  media representation 19, 20, 159
  medical decisions 299, 300, 305, 306
  National Health Service 270, 298, 299, 306
  nature, of 9
  preconceptions 159
  prejudice 7, 14, 22
  prevalence 5, 10, 13, 14, 50, 195
  public services 20
  quality adjusted life years (QALY) *see also*
    quality adjusted life years (QALY)
  acceptable death 287
    benefit to society 284
    discrimination 283–5, 290, 305, 306
    effectiveness of treatment 285
    "fair innings" approach 286–8
    fairness 284
    healthcare rationing 118
    justifications 284, 285
    level of benefit 283, 285, 286
    quality of life 285
    short life expectancy 283, 284
    value of lives 285, 286
  self-hatred 25
  social attitudes 159, 160
  social disadvantage 15, 16

social norms 159
social separation 20, 21
statistics/studies 15, 16
stereotyping 12
unconscious ageism 14
vulnerability 16
agelessness
ageless society 24
concept 23, 24
Alzheimer's disease
ageing process 91
medication 118, 119
statistics 91
treatment 90, 118, 119
autonomy
autonomous agency 116
autonomous decisions 86, 87
autonomy principle 63–5
bodily integrity 115
care-giving relationships 116, 117
decisions contrary to previous values 87–9
dependency 116
ethic of care 117 *see also* **ethic of care**
harmful decisions 85, 86, 89
human rights 193, 194 *see also* **human rights**
importance 84, 91, 344
individualistic conceptions 344, 345
interdependent relationships 116, 117
irrational decisions 88, 89
legal capacity 115
making mistakes 87
preserving autonomy 87
relational autonomy 116, 117, 345
respect, for 86, 87, 89, 345
right to autonomy 75, 76, 84, 88, 344, 345
risk-relative capacity 85, 86 *see also* **risk-relative capacity**
self-determination 115
self-reflective decisions 88
sense of self 117
vulnerability 116

benefit payments
attendance allowance 203
basic state pension
earnings-related increases 219
entitlement 201
national insurance contributions 201
number of pensioners 201
pension age 219
second state pension 219
state earnings-related pensions scheme (SERPS) 202
concessionary benefits
bus passes 202
passports 202

railcards 202
Television Licences 202
winter fuel payment 202
Council Tax benefit 202, 204
disability living allowance 203
earned entitlement 205
guarantee credit 202
health service prescriptions 202
housing benefit 202
low take-up rates
causes 204, 205
complexity of forms 204, 205
Council Tax benefit 204
emotional stress 205
pensions credit 204
stigma 205, 206, 222
unintentional fraud 205
means-tested benefits
deterrent factor 203, 205, 206, 222
disadvantages 203, 206
disclosure of savings/income 203
effectiveness 203
pension credit 200, 202–4
personal savings 203, 204
special needs 202
best interests principle
advance decisions/directives 58, 61 *see also* **advance decisions/directives**
assent to treatment 64
autonomy principle 63–5 *see also* **autonomy**
carers
carer's interests 65, 66, 110–13
carer's views 109, 110
criticisms 67, 68
decision-making process 67–9
deprivation of liberty 59
differing environments
communal living 68
hospital setting 68
residential care 68
family member's interests 65
general application 57, 58
human rights considerations 112
individuals
beliefs/values 111
current views 61–5, 68
obligations to dependants 111
obligations to others 112
past wishes 59–61, 111
present wishes 111
religious beliefs 112
responsible citizens 111
lack of respect 64
lasting powers of attorney 82 *see also* **lasting powers of attorney**
medical best interests 112
medical treatment 54

best interests principle (*cont.*)
  mental capacity 345
  Muslim traditions 60
  personal dignity 60, 64
  proportionate harm 59
  religious beliefs 60, 61
  restraint 59, 169 *see also* **restraint**
  right to liberty 64, 65
  substituted judgement 61
  use of force 59
breast cancer screening
  age discrimination 301, 302 *see also* **age
    discrimination**

capacity
  assessment
    capacity test 54
    carers, by 56
    cultural factors 68
    decision-making capability 55
    ethnic minorities 57, 68
    family members, by 56
    legal significance 56, 57
    practitioners, by 56
    reassessment 84
    women 57, 68
  autonomy 115–7 *see also* **autonomy**
  best interests principle 57–66 *see also* **best
    interests principle**
  competent persons
    consent 53, 54
    medical treatment 53
  consent
    medical treatment 53, 54
    persons lacking capacity 54, 55
    touching a person 53
  decision-making ability 54
  definition 54
  dementia *see* **dementia**
  end-of-life issues 66, 67 *see also* **end of life**
  fluctuating capacity 57
  harmful decisions 85, 86, 89
  incapacity *see* incapacity
  Mental Capacity Act 2005 *see* **Mental
    Capacity Act 2005**
  persons just competent 84–9 *see also*
    persons just competent
  risk-relative capacity 85–7 *see also* **risk-
    relative capacity**
care-giver stress
  cause of abuse 154
  community care 154
  depression 153
  gender factors 155
  likelihood of abuse 153
  mood disturbances 153
  National Center on Elder Abuse (US) 153

  persistent characterization 152
  research findings 153
  stress-causing behaviour 153, 154
care homes
  abusive attitudes 162
  assessment criteria 170, 171
  Care Quality Commissioner 170–2
  casual abuse 163
  dignity 165, 195
  end of life issues 304 *see also* **end of life**
  "function of a public nature" 173
  good care homes
    activities 168
    cultural/religious practices 168
    outside contacts 168
    personal assistance 168
    personal autonomy/choice 168, 344
    person-centred care 167, 168
    self-determination 168, 191
    staff/residents relationship 168
  House of Lords Select Committee
    findings 163, 164
  inspection systems 10, 170–2, 195
    see also **Commission for Social Care
      Inspection (CSCI)**
  intentional abuse 163
  national minimum standards 170
  neglect 164, 165
  outings 167
  ownership 172
  personal expenses 167
  privacy 165, 166, 195
  registration 170
  regulation
    health authorities 170
    legislative provisions 170
    local authorities 170
    standard of care 170
  residential care
    lack of dignity 165
    lack of privacy 165, 166
    loss of independence 95
    quality of care 95
    residents' accounts 166, 167
  risk factors 163
  staff stress 163
Care Quality Commissioner
  function 170–2
care services
  assessment
    direct payments 102
    means testing 103
    mental attitude 102
    physical needs 102
    right to assessment 102
    separate assessments 103, 104
    support services 102

availability 104
care managers 274
coherent approach 101
commercial services 96
Commission for Social Care Inspection
    (CSCI) 104
costs 104, 105
decasualization 95
funding 104, 105, 131
healthcare rationing *see* **healthcare
    rationing**
importance 104
legislative provisions 101, 102
personal care services 344
professionalism 95, 96
provision of services 102, 103
quality of care 95, 104
residential care 95 *see also* **care homes**
social care *see* **social care**
care work
adverse health effects 99, 100
benefit to society 123
care-giver stress *see* **care-giver stress**
child care 10, 11, 16, 236–40 *see also*
    grandparenthood
dependency 96, 123
economic value 95–7
elderly couples 104
ethic of care *see* **ethic of care**
feminist perspective 96
government reforms 107, 108
healthcare rationing *see* **healthcare
    rationing**
individualism 96
lack of attention 96, 97
personal care services 344
quality of life 100
racial issues 97
sexual orientation 97
significant disadvantages 99, 100
social debt 123, 124
social values 97
standard of care 94
true nature 127, 129, 130
unpaid care 94
carers
adverse health effects 99, 100
age factors 98
autonomy *see* **autonomy**
benefit to society 123
best interests principle 109–14 *see also* **best
    interests principle**
care-giver stress *see* **care-giver stress**
care work *see* **care work**
carer's allowance
    availability 100
    income maintenance benefit 101

level of payment 100
older carers 101
overlapping benefits 101
child care 10, 11, 16, 236–40 *see also*
    grandparenthood
criminal liability 57
decasualization 95
definition 94
direct payments
    care relationship 106
    carer support 105
    cash payments 105
    individual control 106
    local authority duty 105
    local authority support 107
    payment in lieu of services 105
    purchase of services 105, 106
    take-up rate 106
economic value 95–7
employment issues
    employment protection 102
    flexible working hours 102
ethic of care *see* **ethic of care**
ethical arguments
    altruism 114
    care relationship 113–15
    carer's best interests 113, 114
    interdependency 114
    obligations 115
ethnicity 98
feminist perspective 96
financial support 130
gender factors 8, 99
government reforms 107, 108
grandparents 10, 11, 16, 236–40 *see also*
    grandparenthood
healthcare rationing *see* **healthcare
    rationing**
housing issues
    Abbeyfield Society 109
    care homes 109
    close care housing 108
    extra care housing 108
    housing needs 108
    housing support services 109
    nursing homes 108
    retirement villages 109
    sheltered housing 108, 109
    sub-standard housing 108
human rights 121–3 *see also* **human rights**
informal carers
    friends 94
    partners 94
    relatives 94, 95
    unpaid care 94
legal protection 121
legal rights 95

carers (*cont.*)
  medical ethics 96
  pension provision 99
  poverty 99, 103 *see also* **poverty**
  professionalism 95, 96
  public attention 94, 97
  quality of life 100
  recognition 101, 130
  responsibilities/rights 95
  significant disadvantages 99, 100
  social support 130
  standard of care 94
  state benefits
    access to help 101
    carer credit 101
    carer's allowance 100
    disability benefit 100, 101
    incapacity benefit 101
    reforms 100
    unclaimed benefits 101
  statistics 97–100
  support 95
caring
  care-giver stress *see* **care-giver stress**
  care services *see* **care services**
  caring relationships *see* **caring relationships**
  ethic of care *see* **ethic of care**
  importance 10
  legal recognition 10
  residential care
    loss of independence 95
    quality of care 95
  social recognition 10
caring relationships
  autonomy 116, 117 *see also* **autonomy**
  criticisms 128
  dependency 189 *see also* **dependency**
  elderly couples 104
  ethic of care 125–31, 345 *see also* **ethic of care**
  ethic of justice, contrasted 127
  ethical arguments 113–15
  female way of thought 128
  importance 125, 126, 131
  interdependency 114
  justice within relationships 127, 128
  mutually supporting relationships 126
  obligations/responsibilities 127
  power relationships 128, 129
  putting into practice 129, 130
  reciprocal dependence 129
  true nature 127, 129
  value of care 125, 126, 131
cervical cancer screening
  age discrimination 301, 302 *see also* **age discrimination**

child care
  adoption orders 260, 261, 262 *see also* **adoption**
  care proceedings 260, 261
  child's best interests 261
  decision-making 260
  educational decisions 261
  financial support 267–9
  grandparental involvement 10, 11, 16, 236–40, 260, 261, 266–9 *see also* **grandparenthood**
  kinship care 266, 267
  medical decisions 261
  parental responsibility 261
  residence orders 244, 245, 261, 262
  respect for family life 260
  special guardianship 261, 262 *see also* **special guardianship**
civil remedies
  damages 180
  injunctions 180
  occupation orders 180
  public agencies *see* **public agencies**
Commission for Equality and Human Rights
  age equality 49
  creation 49
Commission for Social Care Inspection (CSCI)
  Annual Quality Assurance Assessment Reports 171
  function 104
  inspections 162–4, 195
  institutional abuse
    casual abuse 163
    intentional abuse 163
    risk factors 163
contact disputes
  child's welfare 247, 255
  conflicting rights 252–4
  constitutional rights (US) 254, 255
  contact orders 245
  divorce/separation 245
  due process rights (US) 254, 255
  formal legal status 251, 252
  human rights law 252–5, 257
  law reform 249–57
  leave requirement 246, 247, 249, 250, 251
  parental authority 252
  presumptions 248
  proportionality test 253
  respect for family life 252, 254, 255
  substantive hearing 247, 248
Court of Protection
  applications 83
  declarations 83
  deprivation of liberty 83
  deputy

appointment 83
  decision-making 83
financial management 83
welfare decisions 83
criminal law
care issues 177, 178
causing or allowing death 176, 177
elder abuse
  criminal liability 10, 139, 176
  ill-treatment/neglect 177–9
  victims lacking capacity 177, 178
  victims with mental capacity 179
failings 178, 179

dementia
bi-polar disorder 52
characteristics 91
clinical depression 52
instability 63
memory loss 63
schizophrenia 52
sexual activity 146
social situations 91
statistics 52
demographic changes
ageism 16 *see also* **ageism**
attitudes 16
"demographic time bomb"
  ageing population 197, 198
  economic growth 199
  economic stability 197
  fertility rates 198
  generational fairness 198
  health costs 198
  social care costs 198
  working beyond retirement age 198
generational conflict 197, 198
impact 16
projections 1, 2
scale 1, 2
dependency
ageing population 17 *see also* **ageing population**
ageism 17, 22 *see also* **ageism**
autonomy 116, 188 *see also* **autonomy**
caring relationships 189 *see also* **caring relationships**
combating dependency 187, 188
effects 187
elder abuse 157 *see also* **elder abuse**
inherent vulnerability 188
interdependency 114, 116, 117, 125, 188, 189, 345, 346
mutually dependant relationships 124
network of dependencies 120
persons lacking capacity 93 *see also* **incapacity**

social attitudes 187, 188
social policy 188
societal structures 187
dignity
best interests principle 60, 64 *see also* **best interests principle**
human rights 191
incapacity 345 *see also* **incapacity**
residential care 165
discrimination
age discrimination *see* **age discrimination**
direct discrimination
  comparators 29, 37
  example 29
  forbidden criteria 29, 36
  less favourable treatment 29, 36
  disability discrimination 29, 33, 121, 122, 161
EC Treaty objectives
  employment issues 34
  free movement of persons 34
  social cohesion 34
  social protection 34
employment
  company image 34
  recruitment practices 34
  remuneration 34
equality 26–8 *see also* **equality**
human rights protection 30, 34, 121, 122
indirect discrimination
  case law 38
  comparative disadvantage 38
  disproportionate adverse impact 38
  employment criteria 38
  equality of results 38
  example 29, 30
  job-related requirements 30
  justification 30
  meaning 29, 30
  objective justification test 38
  provision/criteria/practice 38
liberty 29
private life 29
prohibited grounds
  disability discrimination 29, 37, 121, 122, 161
  race discrimination 29
  sex discrimination 29
  sexual orientation 29
public decisions 29
rationality 28
scope 29
Discrimination Law Review
justifiable discrimination 49
legitimate differences in treatment 50

domestic violence
domestic abuse 138
domesticity 138
elder abuse 155, 156 *see also* **elder abuse**
gender factors 155, 156
illegitimacy 139
prosecutions 179, 180
social attitudes 136, 155
structural inequality 138
US experience 156
violence 138
violent relationships 155

elder abuse
abusive behaviour 132, 133, 136, 139
ageist attitudes 136, 139, 147, 159–62, 195,
    196 *see also* **ageism**
care-giver stress *see* **care-giver stress**
causes (generally) 10, 133, 136
changing attitudes/responses
    dependency 187–9
    social context 189
    statutory regime 189–94
Commissioner for Older People (Wales) 194
criminal liability 10, 139, 176–9 *see also*
    criminal law
definitional problems
    absence of single definition 134, 135
    age-related abuse 139
    degree of harm 140
    forms of abuse 134, 138
    intention 139, 140
    motive 139
    perpetrators 137, 138
    physical harm 138
    professional interests 134
dependency 187–9 *see also* **dependency**
differing professional interests
    care management 134
    medical profession 134
    police officers 134
disability discrimination 161 *see also*
    discrimination
domestic context 136
domestic violence 155, 156
extent 10
forms of abuse
    definitional problems 134, 137, 138
    discriminatory abuse 143
    domestic abuse 143
    financial abuse 143–5, 150, 151
    institutional abuse 143
    medication misuse 143, 146, 147
    neglect 143
    physical abuse 138, 143, 149, 151
    psychological abuse 143, 149, 151
    restraint 143, 169, 170

self-neglect 138, 143
sexual abuse 143, 145, 146, 149
statistics 150
gender factors
    domestic violence 155, 156
    female victims 158
    gender ratios 158
    male assertion of power 160, 161
    male perpetrators 158
    older abused women 160
    patriarchy 158, 159
    research 158
    structural inequalities 159
gendered nature 133
homophobia 161
human rights 142, 191–4 *see also* **human
    rights**
inadequate response 343
institutional abuse *see* **institutional abuse**
intention 139, 140
intentional abuse 139
legal response 132, 133, 196
local authority powers 190
macro causes
    ageism 159–62
    dehumanization 157
    dependency 157
    gender issues 157–9
    social circumstances 157
    social exclusion 157, 196
mandatory reporting 195
marginalization 196
micro causes
    abuser/victim relationship 151, 152
    care-giver stress 152–5
    characteristics of abuser 151
    characteristics of victim 151
    dementia patients 151
    dependency 152
    domestic violence 155–7
    family violence 152
    financial abuse 151
    mental health 152
    neglect 151
    physical abuse 151
    psychological abuse 151
    social isolation 151, 156
motive 139
National Director for Older People 194
nursing homes 136
perpetrators
    carers 137, 138, 149
    definitional problems 137, 138
    friends 137, 138
    older people 133
    relatives 137, 138, 149
    self-abuse 138

statistics 149
strangers 137
popular definitions (sources)
  Action Against Elder Abuse 141
  American National Council on Child
    Abuse and Family Violence 141
  National Center on Elder Abuse
    (US) 141, 142
  Safeguarding Adults (2005) 142
private law remedies 10
prosecutions
  evidence 179
  state responsibility 180
  victim's support 179, 180
protection
  intervention 139
  legal remedies 132
  public law 10
  vulnerable adults 135, 136
public awareness 10, 132
racism 161
relevant age 137
restraint *see* **restraint**
scale 132, 133
sexist attitudes 136, 147, 161
social attitudes 136, 140, 141, 187, 196
social context 189
social exclusion 157, 196
societal responsibility 133
state obligations 132
statistics
  difficulties compiling 147, 148
  forms of abuse 150
  gender abuse 149
  international statistics 148, 149
  perpetrators 149
  public perceptions 148
  residential settings 149
  UK experience 148
  US experience 148
  victims 150
statutory regime
  human rights protection 191–4
  local authority powers 190, 196
  need, for 190
  protection orders 190
  removal into care 191
  respect for individual's wishes 191
  state intervention 190, 191
  state responsibility 192–4
structural inequalities 159, 161
tackling elder abuse
  coherent approach 195
  independence 187
  well-being 187
Toronto Declaration 133
US experience 137

use of force 136
victims 133, 136, 147, 150
vulnerability 135, 137, 142, 188 *see also*
  vulnerable adults
elder law
  academic interest 5
  case, against 6
  development 4
  justification
    age discrimination 7
    protection against ageism 7
    recognising life stages 8, 9
  literature 4
  study 4
  US experience 4
electronic tagging
  use, of 170
**Employment Equality (Age) Regulations
  2006**
  background
    economic factors 33, 34
    human rights issues 34
    retirement age 33
    social costs 33
  definition of discrimination 36
  discriminatory conduct
    age-based criteria 37
    age-linked criteria 37
    age-related grounds 36, 37
    comparators 36, 37
    direct discrimination 35–7
    indirect discrimination 35, 36, 38
    less favourable treatment 36
    proportionality 36, 40, 41
    provision/criteria/practice 36
  excluded areas 35
  exemptions
    Crown employment 40
    national minimum wage 40
    national security 40
    positive action 40, 47, 48
  harassment 39
  impact 48, 49
  justification
    alternative provisions, absence of 44
    business need 43
    efficiency considerations 43
    legitimate aim 36, 40, 42, 43
    legitimate occupational requirement 44
    objective justification test 41
    positive action 40, 47, 48
    proportionality 36, 40–3
    reducing expense 43
  level of experience 37
  positive action
    exemption 40, 47, 48
    justification 47, 48

Employment Equality (Age) Regulations 2006 (*cont.*)
  scope 47
  training 47
  remedies 40
  retirement *see* **retirement**
  scope 35, 36, 50
  unlawful conduct 33
  victimization 39
end of life
  acceptable death 287
  ageist assumptions 67 *see also* **ageism**
  care homes 304
  criminal liability 66, 67
  death at home 304
  death with dignity 305
  decision-making process 67
  euthanasia 302, 303
  health trajectories 302
  hospice care 303–5
  life-sustaining treatment 66
  medical law 66
  minor debilitations 302
  palliative care 66, 303–5 *see also* **palliative care**
  severe decline 302
  "social death" 303
  sudden decline 302
  unexpected death 302
  withholding medical treatment 66
equality
  disadvantaged groups 27, 28
  dominant groups 28
  equality of opportunity 27, 28
  equality of outcomes 27
  equality of participation 28
  equality of treatment 27
  importance 26
Equality Act 2006
  discriminatory conduct 49
ethic of care
  autonomy 117 *see also* **autonomy**
  caring relationships 125–31, 345 *see also* **caring relationships**
  future influence 345
  individualized vision of rights 124, 125
  interdependent relationships 125
  legal/ethical responses 125
  legal rights/responsibilities 124
  mutually dependant relationships 124
ethnic minorities
  inheritance-related issues 310, 313, 314 *see also* **inheritance**
  mental capacity assessments 57, 68
  poverty 2, 200, 216
European Convention on Human Rights (ECHR)
  age discrimination 30, 34 *see also* **age discrimination**
  anti-discrimination provisions 121, 122, 297
  competing/conflicting rights 193
  deprivation of liberty 59, 185, 186
  employment protection 30, 34
  fair trial 246
  inhuman and degrading treatment 123, 191–4, 296, 297
  objective justification 297
  positive obligations 192, 193
  respect for private and family life 122, 123, 185, 193, 244, 246, 252, 254, 255, 257, 297
  right to liberty 64, 65
  right to life 296
  state responsibility 192–4
  torture 192
European Social Charter
  social protection 342, 343
euthanasia
  ethical issues 302, 303

families
  child care, 237–9 *see also* **child care**
  falling birth rates 238
  financial obligations *see* **family financial obligations**
  increased life expectancy 238
  marital breakdown 237
  matrilineal ties 237
  parental separation 240, 241, 256
  patrilineal ties 237
  relationship breakdown 238
  work beyond retirement age 238
  working mothers 237
family financial obligations
  filial responsibility
    employment protection 234
    enforced care 233
    enforcement 231
    inheritance law 234
    moral obligation 231, 233, 234
    parent/child relationship 232
    parent's perspective 233
    quality of relationship 232
    reciprocity 231, 232
    state support 234
    tax changes 234
    US attitudes 231
  filial support legislation 229, 233, 234
  financial responsibility 229
  legal position 229
  parental responsibilities 230
  social changes 229
financial issues

benefit payment *see* **benefit payments**
family financial obligations *see* **family financial obligations**
funding care *see* **funding care**
healthcare
  allocation of resources 286–90
  costs 279
  healthcare funding 10
  financial constraints 270
  funding policy 294
pensions *see* **pensions**
poverty *see* **poverty**
social care funding 10 *see also* **social care**
funding care
  future care needs 223, 224
  government policy 224
  healthcare funding 10
  local authority spending 223
  means-testing system 223
  personal care services 344
  political will 234
  problem areas
    affordability 225
    availability of care 225
    caring costs 225
    complex processes 225
    inadequate services 226
    lack of fairness 225
    quality issues 225
    supply issues 225
    unmet need 224, 225
  sale of individual's home 224
  Scottish experience
    care home costs 228
    cost issues 228
    free care 228
    informal care 228
  social care costs 10, 223, 224
  social services support 223
  solutions
    combined approaches 227, 228
    funding from taxation 226, 227
    private insurance schemes 226
  under-funding 224

gerontology
  criticisms 5
  field of study 4
grandparenthood
  adoption orders 243, 244
  changing nature of families
    child care, 237–9
    falling birth rates 238
    increased life expectancy 238
    marital breakdown 237
    matrilineal ties 237
    parental separation 240, 241, 256

patrilineal ties 237
relationship breakdown 238
work beyond retirement age 238
working mothers 237
child care 10, 11, 16, 236–40, 260, 261
  see also **child care**
contact disputes
  child's welfare 247, 255
  conflicting rights 252–4
  constitutional rights (US) 254, 255
  contact orders 245
  divorce/separation 245
  due process rights (US) 254, 255
  formal legal status 251, 252
  human rights law 252–5, 257
  law reform 249–57
  leave requirement 246, 247, 249, 250, 251
  parental authority 252
  presumptions 248
  proportionality test 253
  respect for family life 252, 254, 255
  substantive hearing 247, 248
distinguishing features
  divorced grandparents 243
  gender 242
  maternal grandparents 243
  paternal grandparents 243
grandparenting activities
  child care 10, 11, 16, 236–40, 260, 261
  educational role 241
  emotional support 240, 244
  motivation 239
  outings 240
  parental role 241
  parental separation 240, 241, 256
  partisan role 241
  passive role 241
  practical support 255
  rescuers 241
  specialist skills 241
  talking/advice-giving 240
grandparents
  abuse, caused to 236
  alternative carers 239
  child care 10, 11, 16, 236–40, 260, 261
  divorced grandparents 243
  financial sacrifices 267, 268
  grandparent-headed homes 242
  kinship care 266, 267
  legal status 10, 243, 244, 251, 252, 267, 269
  maternal grandparents 243
  media exposure 239
  paternal grandparents 243
  popular images 235, 236
  role 235–7, 239–41

grandparenthood (*cont.*)
  source of stability 239
  work beyond retirement age 238
grandparents/grandchildren relationship
  affection 255
  emotional support 240, 255
  entertainment 255
  financial support 267–9
  importance 268, 269
  parental separation 240, 241, 256
  practical support 255
  quality of relationship 268
  security 256
  sense of origins/heritage 255
  teenage grandchildren 236, 256
law reform 249–57, 268
public law
  adoption 257–61
  removal of children 257
Scottish Executive's Charter 269
sociological issues
  ethnic/religious backgrounds 236
  family relationships 236–40
residence disputes
  natural parents 245
  residence orders 244, 245, 261, 262
respect for family life 244, 246, 252, 254,
  255, 257
special guardianship 261, 262 *see also*
  special guardianship
statistics 235
guardianship *see* **special guardianship**

Health and Social Care Act 2008
  human rights protection 173
  penalties 172
  professional regulation 172
healthcare
  age discrimination *see also* **age
    discrimination**
    breast cancer screening 301, 302
    cervical cancer screening 301, 302
    covert discrimination 298
    human rights 300
    lack of protection 50, 51
    malnourishment 302
    NHS equality audits 298
    NHS healthcare 298, 299, 306
    medical conditions 299
    medical decisions 299, 305
    medical treatments 299, 300
    mental health services 301
    mistreatment of patients 300
  ageing
    anti-ageing treatments 277, 278, 305
    assumptions 278
    cost of dying 275

    cultural influences 279
    definition 275
    geriatric medicine 274
    health costs 275, 276
    ill-health 274, 276, 277
    media representations 278
    medicalization 277–9
    mental capacity 277
    misperceptions 277
    selective survival 279
  informal carers 271
  National Health Service
    ageism 270
    healthcare services 11
    resources 271
  medical professionals 271
  medicalization
    anti-ageing treatments 277, 278, 305
    cost issues 278
    discrimination 278
    language of disease 277
    medical treatment 277, 278
  palliative care *see* **palliative care**
  rationing *see* **healthcare rationing**
  right to healthcare 281
  social care, distinguished 271 *see also* **social
    care**
healthcare rationing
  age-based rationing 11, 270, 280–7, 289,
    305
  age discrimination 283–5, 290, 291, 305,
    306 *see also* **age discrimination**
  carer's interests 118–20
  effectiveness of treatment 280, 282
  equal treatment 282
  ethical questions 279, 281, 282
  financial constraints 270
  healthcare costs 279
  healthcare resources
    acceptable functioning approach 289
    allocation 286–90
    capabilities approach 289
    impartiality 290
    individual needs approach 289, 290
    medical ethics 279
    success of treatment 290
  intergenerational conflict 282
  justifications 280
  legal challenges
    absolute duty 293
    consideration of patient's views 294
    discrimination 294, 295, 297
    financial considerations 295
    funding policy 294
    human rights challenges 296
    judicial review 293, 294, 296, 297
    objective justification 297

procedural complaints 295
    rationing policy 295
    relevant/irrelevant considerations 294
    statutory duties 293, 294
    unreasonableness 293, 294
  network of dependencies 120
  overseas treatment 297
  patient's needs 1189–20
  political issues 282
  public opinion 290, 291
  quality adjusted life years (QALY) *see*
    quality adjusted life years (QALY)
  rationing process 281
  right to healthcare 281
  taxation levels 279
hospices
  hospice care 303–5
  palliative care 303–5 *see also* **palliative care**
human rights
  age discrimination 30, 34 *see also* **age**
    discrimination
  autonomy 193, 194 *see also* **autonomy**
  best interests principle 112 *see also* **best**
    interests principle
  bodily harm 191
  bodily integrity 193
  deprivation of liberty 59, 185, 186
  discrimination *see also* **discrimination**
    anti-discrimination provisions 34, 121,
      122
    disability discrimination 121, 122
  elder abuse 142 *see also* **elder abuse**
  employment protection, 30, 34
  healthcare rationing 296, 297 *see also*
    healthcare rationing
  human dignity 191
  inhuman and degrading treatment 123,
    191–4
  mental suffering 191
  public agencies 185–7 *see also* **public**
    agencies
  respect for private and family life 122, 123,
    185, 193, 244, 246, 252, 254, 255, 257,
    297
  right of privacy 192
  state intervention 192, 194

incapacity
  assessments 87, 92
  best interests principle 57–66, 92 *see also*
    best interests principle
  capacity test 54
  Code of Practice 52, 56, 58, 60, 62, 69, 70,
    71, 110–12
  cognitive impairment 52
  decisions
    advance decisions/directives 58, 61, 68

    contrary to previous values 87–9
    irrational 88, 89
  evidence 87
  Mental Capacity Act 2005 *see* **Mental**
    Capacity Act 2005
  onset 52
  persons lacking capacity
    advance decisions/directives 58, 61, 68
    approved research, on, 58
    assessments 92
    autonomy 91
    best interests principle 57–66, 92
    care/treatment 57
    caring relationships 93
    decisions on behalf 57, 58
    dementia 91
    dependency 93
    dignity 345
    divorce-related matters 58
    doubtful capacity 92
    emotions 91, 92
    liberty 345
    marriage/civil partnership decisions 58
    negotiated consent standard 92
    non-rational humanity 92
    relational context 92
    respect 345
    sexual relations 58
    values 91, 92
    vulnerability 93
  principles 53
inheritance
  bequests
    economic value 309
    emotional significance 310
    motivation 312
    sense of obligation 310
    sentimental value 309
    spending the children's inheritance 310
    sufficient/insufficient assets 310, 311
  concerns
    control over property 307
    family disputes 307
    family expectations 307
    family relationships 307, 308
    legacies 307
  cultural attitudes 313
  ethnic minorities 310, 313, 314
  expectations
    children's expectations 327
    ethnic minorities 310
    provision of care 312
    relatives' expectations 327
    research findings 309, 310
    sense of obligation 310
  family farms 311
  heirlooms 311

inheritance (*cont.*)
  home ownership 308, 313
  inheritance tax *see* **inheritance tax**
  inter vivos gifts 311
  intestacy *see* **intestacy**
  legal issues
    divorce/remarriage 308, 313
    public awareness 341
    public policy 308
    societal values 341
  motivation 311, 312
  property law *see* **property law**
  psychology 311
  testamentary freedom 311, 314, 316–20, 341
  wealth inequalities 309
  wills *see* **wills**
**Inheritance (Provision for Family and
    Dependants) Act 1975**
  applicants
    blood relatives 330
    child of deceased 330
    civil partners 330–2
    cohabitants 330
    persons maintained by deceased 330, 331
    spouses 330–2
  applications 317, 326, 331, 333, 341
  avoidance 333
  deceased's wishes/intentions 329, 332, 334
  effect 317, 320
  enforcement of obligation 329
  entitlement 317, 326, 331, 332
  fairness 329
  financial dependency 330, 331
  inadequate family provision 317, 326
  judicial balancing 334
  judicial interpretation 329, 330, 334
  justifications 328–30, 334
  maintenance provision 331, 332
  moral obligation 329
  reasonable financial provision 331
  testamentary freedom 317, 328, 329
inheritance tax
  civil partners 337, 339, 340
  cohabitants 339
  disposal of property 307
  double taxation 340
  exemptions 337, 339, 340
  financial transactions 308
  gifts 337
  human rights issues 340
  justification 338, 341
  limits, on 308
  objections, to 308, 309, 338, 340
  political issues 337, 338, 341
  public awareness 341
  social inequality 338
  spouses 337–40

support, for 338
tax avoidance 338
tax rate 337
value of estate 337
institutional abuse
  abusive attitudes 162
  care homes 162 *see also* **care homes**
  casual abuse 163
  dehumanization 165, 166
  demeaning attitudes 165
  geronticide 162
  infantalization 166
  intentional abuse 163
  lack of dignity 165
  lack of hygiene 164
  lack of privacy 165, 166
  lack of respect 166
  neglect 164, 165
  personal care 164, 165
  research findings 162
  residents' accounts 166, 167
  restraint *see* **restraint**
  risk factors 163
  rough handling 164
  self-determination 166
  self-identity 167
  staff stress 163
intestacy
  distribution of property 11, 324, 325
  intestacy law
    Department of Constitutional Affairs 327
    distribution of estate 324
    Law Commission views 324, 326–8
    law reform 327
    purpose 324
    Scottish Law Commission's views 324
  intestacy rules
    basis, of 325, 326
    children's expectations 327
    civil partners 325
    cohabitants/partners 328
    current spouse 326
    distribution of estate 324, 325
    earlier spouses 326, 327
    fairness 325
    flexibility 326
    future increases in value 327
    individual need 325
    law reform 327
    marital home 327
    pensions 327
    personal chattels 325
    property jointly owned 327
    public attitudes 326
    relatives' expectations 327
    societal interests 325
    statutory legacy 325

surviving spouse 325, 327
meaning 323
partial intestacy 323

lasting powers of attorney
best interests principle 82 *see also* best
    interests principle
care home concerns 83 *see also* care homes
donees 82, 83
loss of capacity 82
registration 83
unreasonable demands 83
life expectancy
ageing population *see* ageing population
increasing 1, 238
pension reform 238
quality adjusted life years (QALY) 283,
    284 *see also* quality adjusted life years
    (QALY)
life stages
age characterizations 22–4
age progression 22
end of life *see* end of life
recognition, of 8, 9
social expectations 23
living wills *see* advance decisions/directives
local authorities
adoption 258 *see also* adoption
care services 10, 102, 103 *see also* care
    services
child care *see* child care
funding care
    direct payments 105, 107
    duty 105
    local authority spending 223
powers
    child abuse 190
    elder abuse 190
responsibilities
    care homes 170
    multi-agency work 175
    removal of children 257

malnourishment
age discrimination 302 *see also* age
    discrimination
means-tested benefits *see also* benefit
    payments
deterrent factor 203, 205, 206, 222
disadvantages 203, 206
disclosure of savings/income 203
effectiveness 203
pension reform 222 *see also* pension reform
personal savings 203, 204
media representation
ageing process 278
ageism 19, 20, 159 *see also* ageism

grandparents 239
medical treatment
advance decisions/directives 70 *see also*
    advance decisions/directives
best interests principle 54 *see also* best
    interests principle
developments, in 71
informed consent 53
life-sustaining treatment 66
medical practitioner's liability 72, 73
mental disorders 54
palliative care 66 *see also* palliative care
persons lacking capacity 54
withdrawal/withholding 66, 72
mental capacity
incapacity *see* incapacity
persons lacking capacity *see* persons lacking
    capacity
Mental Capacity Act 2005
advance decisions/directives 69, 70 *see also*
    advance decisions/directives
assessments, under 56, 57, 68
best interests principle 57–61, 65, 66,
    109–11, 345 *see also* best interests
    principle
capacity
    assessments 55, 56
    assumptions of incapacity 56
    capacity test 54, 55
    consent 55
    decision-making 54–6, 61
    impairment of function 55
    refusal to believe information 55
    unwise decision-making 56
carers
    carer's best interests 110–13
    carer's views 109, 110
Code of Practice 52, 56, 58, 60, 62, 69, 70,
    71, 110–12
incapacity 52 *see also* incapacity
interpretation 110–13
life-sustaining treatment 66
restraint, under 169 *see also* restraint
mental disorders
legislative provisions 89, 90
medical treatment 54
Mental Health Act 1983
decision-making capacity 89
detention 90
mental disorder 89, 90
protection of others 90
risk management 90
treatment
    admission for treatment 89
    involuntary 90
    medical treatment 89, 90
    refusal 89

multi-agency work
communication difficulties 175
human rights standards 175
inter-agency cooperation 175, 176
intervention 175, 176
legitimate aim 175
local authority responsibility 175
professional conflicts 175
resource levels 175
Safeguarding Adults (2005) 175
social need 175

National Health Service
ageism, within 270, 343 *see also* **ageism**
cost of care 272, 273
free of charge 271, 272
healthcare services 11
nursing care 272
resources 271
National Institute of Health and Clinical Excellence (NICE)
age discrimination 292 *see also* **age discrimination**
function 282, 286
methodology 286
National Health Service treatment 292
quality adjusted life years (QALY) 282, 291–3 *see also* **quality adjusted life years (QALY)**
technology costs 291
treatment
adverse effects 292
cost effective 291–3
patient's health status 292
National Service Framework for Older People
employment statistics 33

occupation orders
effect 180
enforcement 180
entitlement 180
old age
ageing
medical status 305
successful ageing 306
changing nature 343
characteristics 3
contribution of older people
carers 16, 17
charitable giving 17
community life 17
consumers 16
cultural contribution 17
general experience 17
cultural concept 23
definition 2, 3
disadvantages 3

discrimination 4 *see also* **discrimination**
health issues 5 *see also* **healthcare**
identity, of 343
interdependence 345, 346
invisibility 345
legal response 343, 344
life stages 23 *see also* **life stages**
network of relationships 345
pension age 3 *see also* **pensions**
prejudice 7
respect 345–7
retirement 343 *see also* **retirement**
significance 5
social attitudes 5, 11, 345–7
social exclusion 2, 3, 342
social separation 20, 1
vulnerability 3, 7, 345
welfare state 343

palliative care
aim 303
benefits 304
emotional support 303
end of life 66 *see also* **end of life**
expansion of care 304, 305
hospice care 303–5
importance 305
lack of care 303
pain relief 303
standard of care 304
pensions
basic state pension
entitlement 3, 201
national insurance contributions 201
number of pensioners 201
"cappuccino model" 207
carers 99 *see also* **carers**
current position
pension reform 213, 216–23
public pension provision 213
current system
minimum income guarantee 214
non-pension assets 215
occupational pension schemes 214, 217
Pension Protection Fund 214
private pensions 206, 214, 215, 216, 221, 222
state pension 214
economic issues 211, 212
forms of pension
defined-benefit schemes 211
defined-contribution schemes 210
fully funded schemes 210
notional defined-contribution schemes 211
occupational pension schemes 214, 217
pay as you go schemes 210

gender issues
  caring responsibilities 216, 222
  child care 216, 222
  divorce/relationship breakdown 216, 222
  female pensioners 2, 8, 22, 200, 216,
      218, 221, 222
  inequalities 222
  paid employment 216, 222
  part-time work 216, 222
  pension provision 215, 16
  private pensions 216
  single mothers 222
  widows 215
inadequate provision 206
insurance model 209
intestacy rules 327 *see also* **intestacy**
pension credit 200, 202–4
pension market
  failed schemes 209, 210
  state guarantees, 210
  state regulation 210
pension age 3, 219
pensioner poverty 2, 199–201, 217, 218,
    234, 343
policy 206, 208
poverty reduction 207 *see also* **poverty**
primary source of income 206
private funding 207
private pensions 206, 214, 215, 216, 221,
    222
reform 213, 216–23 *see also* **pension reform**
retirement costs 206 *see also* **retirement**
savings model 209
state earnings-related pension scheme
    (SERPS) 202
state funding 207
state responsibility 208, 209
World Bank recommendations 208
pension reform
  employers' contributions 219
  female pensioners 218
  generally 10
  government options
    increased savings 221
    increased taxation 221
    pensioners relatively poorer 221
  government review 206
  key principles
    affordability 220
    fairness 220
    personal responsibility 220
    simplicity 220
    sustainability 220
  life expectancy 217
  lower birth rates 217
  means-tested benefits 222 *see also* **means-
      tested benefits**

need, for 216–8
occupational pension schemes 217
pension costs 216, 217
pension provision/GDP ratio 213
pensioner poverty 217, 218
Pensions Commission 218, 220, 221,
    223
personal account scheme 219–21
Personal Accounts Delivery Authority
    219
private pensions 221, 222
ratio of working-age people 217, 218
risk factors 222
Security in Retirement (2006) 219
state pension
  earnings-related increases 219
  pension age 219
  second state pension 219
women's interests 221, 222
persons just competent *see also* **capacity**
decisions
  contrary to previous values 87–9
  harmful decisions 85–7, 89
  irrational decisions 88, 89
harmful activities 84
intervention 84
reassessment of capacity 84
right to autonomy 84, 85, 88 *see also*
    autonomy
uncharacteristic activity 84
persons lacking capacity
advance decisions/directives 58, 61, 68 *see*
    also **advance decisions/directives**
approved research, on, 58
assessments 92
autonomy 91 *see also* **autonomy**
best interests principle 57–66, 92 *see also*
    best interests principle
care/treatment 57
caring relationships 93 *see also* **caring
    relationships**
decisions on behalf 57, 58
dementia 91 *see also* **dementia**
dependency 93 *see also* **dependency**
dignity 345
divorce-related matters 58
doubtful capacity 92
emotions 91, 92
liberty 345
marriage/civil partnership decisions 58
negotiated consent standard 92
non-rational humanity 92
relational context 92
respect 345
sexual relations 58
values 91, 92
vulnerability 93

poverty
  carers 99, 103 *see also* **carers**
  ethnic minorities 2, 200, 216
  health problems 199
  pensioners
    "expenditure poor" 201
    female pensioners 2, 8, 22, 200, 216
    fuel poverty 202
    "income poor" 201
    minimum income standard 200,
      201
    pension credit 200, 202–4
    pensioner poverty 2, 199–201, 207, 217,
      218, 234, 343
    risk of poverty 200
    standard of living 201
  prevalence 343
  social problems 199
  wealth divide 199
powers of attorney *see* **lasting powers of
  attorney**
property law
  beneficial joint tenants 315
  cohabitants 315
  conditional gifts 316
  co-ownership 315
  gifts 316
  intestacy rules *see* **intestacy**
  survivorship principle 315
  testamentary dispositions 316
  transfer of property 315, 316
proprietary estoppel
  detrimental reliance 334–6
  equitable claims 334
  judicial awards 336
  mutual wills doctrine 336
  promise/representation/assurance 335
  property forming part of estate 334
  purpose 334
  unconscionable conduct 335, 336
public agencies
  best interests principle 181–4 *see also* **best
    interests principle**
  court orders 181, 182, 185–7
  human rights protection 185–7
  inherent jurisdiction 181–3
  intervention 181, 182
  protection from abuse 181
  risk of harm 182, 183
  serious justiciable issues 182
  vulnerable adults 181–4
public toilets
  hygiene 7
  provision 7
  safety 7
  sexual activity 7
  vandalism 7

quality adjusted life years (QALY)
  age discrimination 305 *see also* **age
    discrimination**
  ageism *see also* **ageism**
    acceptable death 287
    benefit to society 284
    discrimination 283–5, 290, 305, 306
    effectiveness of treatment 285
    "fair innings" approach 286–8
    fairness 284
    healthcare rationing 118
    justifications 284, 285
    level of benefit 283, 285, 286
    quality of life 285
    short life expectancy 283, 284
    value of lives 285, 286
  calculations 118, 282, 283
  carer's interests 118–20
  cost effectiveness 283, 291
  criticisms 283, 289
  healthcare rationing
    acceptable functioning approach 289
    ageism 118
    allocation of resources 286–90
    capabilities approach 289
    impartiality 290
    individual needs approach 289, 290
    medical ethics 279
    rationing decisions 282
    success of treatment 290
  National Institute of Health and Clinical
    Excellence (NICE) 282, 291–3 *see
    also* **National Institute of Health and
    Clinical Excellence (NICE)**
  patient's needs 118–20
  patient's quality of life 118
  quality of life 282, 283, 285
  treatment
    cost of treatment 282
    effectiveness 282, 283, 285
    impact 118
    success of treatment 290

race discrimination
  age discrimination distinguished 24–6 *see
    also* **age discrimination**
  prohibited grounds 29, 34, 36, 37
residence disputes
  natural parents 245
  residence orders 244, 245
restraint
  best interests principle 59, 169 *see also* **best
    interests principle**
  care workers 169
  criminal liability 169
  electronic tagging 170
  forms, of 169

justification 170
physical restraint 169
proportional restraint 169
risk of harm 169
video surveillance 170
retirement
caring responsibilities 213
community work 213
consultancy work 213
continuing employment 213
discriminatory practices 46
early retirement 46, 212
EC law 45
employee's rights 3
financial support 207
government support 206
health problems 213
human dignity 46
legal response 344
mandatory retirement age 45, 50
meaning 212
mentoring 213
notification 45
pension provision 45
procedural requirements 45
psychological impact 46
public life, involvement in 213
retirement age
continuing employment 212
early retirement 46, 212
employment legislation 33, 45, 46
expected retirement 212
low eligibility age 212
state benefits 212
retirement costs 206
retirement date 3
saving for retirement 208, 209, 221
unlawful retirement 45
volunteering 213
working beyond retirement age 45, 46,
198, 238
risk-relative capacity *see also* **capacity**
autonomy
autonomous decisions 86
respect for autonomy 86, 87
borderline capacity 85
capacity level 85, 86
choices
approved choices 86
socially undesirable choices 86
decision-making capacity 85, 86
overruling decisions 86
risk level 85, 86
standard of competency 85
treatment
consent 85
refusal 85

sex discrimination
age discrimination distinguished 24–6 *see
also* **age discrimination**
comparators 37
prohibited grounds 29, 34
social care
age discrimination 51, 271, 298 *see also* **age
discrimination**
care managers, 274
community care 272, 273
cost-cutting 272
differing responsibilities 271
government policy 271
healthcare, distinguished 271 *see also*
healthcare
integration of services 273, 274
nursing care 272, 273
payment for services 271–3
personal care 271, 272
social exclusion
elder abuse 157, 196 *see also* **elder abuse**
old age 2, 3, 342
prevalence 342
responsibility 342
social isolation
appropriate intervention 342
elder abuse 151, 156 *see also* **elder abuse**
prevalence 342
social services
age discrimination 51 *see also* **age
discrimination**
special guardianship
adoption, distinguished 262, 263
child's best interests 263, 264
child's surname 264, 265
child's welfare 262, 263
effect 263, 264
grandparents' involvement 261, 262
human rights considerations 262, 263
legal status 262
parental contact 264, 265
parental responsibility 264
payments 265, 266
permanency of protection 263
purpose 263, 264
revocation 264
state pension
basic state pension
entitlement 201
national insurance contributions 201
number of pensioners 201
Council Tax benefit 202, 204
earnings-related increases 219
housing benefit 202
pension age 3, 219
pension credit 202–4
reform 219 *see also* **pension reform**

state pension (*cont.*)
   second state pension 219
   state earnings-related pension scheme
      (SERPS) 202
state support
   benefit payments *see* **benefit payments**
   carers 100, 101 *see also* **carers**
   disability benefit 100, 101
   extent, 11
   filial responsibility 234 *see also* **family**
      financial obligations
   incapacity benefit 101
   income maintenance benefit 101
   overlapping benefits 101
   pensions 207–10 *see also* **pensions**
   retirement 206, 212 *see also* **retirement**
   unclaimed benefits 101
succession *see also* **wills**
   autonomy 318, 319 *see also* **autonomy**
   continental legal systems 317
   deceased's wishes 318–20, 329
   entitlement 317
   family relationships 320
   kinship 320
   legal regulation 317, 318
   property ownership 320
   spouses 317
   testamentary freedom 311, 314, 316–20,
      341

use of force
   elder abuse 136 *see also* **elder abuse**

victimization
   protection, against 39
   unfavourable treatment 39
video surveillance
   use, of 170
vulnerable adults
   ageism 16 *see also* **ageism**
   autonomy 116 *see also* **autonomy**
   definition 135
   elder abuse 135 *see also* **elder abuse**
   multi-agency work *see* **multi-agency work**
   old age 3, 7, 345 *see also* **old age**
   persons lacking capacity 93 *see also*
      incapacity
   protection
      care assistants 173
      Criminal Records Bureau check 174
      government objective 135
      social attitudes 136
      social workers 174
   Protection of Vulnerable Adults list
      creation 174
      referrals 174, 175

wills
   beneficiaries
      equality 314, 320
      fixed inheritance rules 315
      genealogical closeness 314, 320
      generational position 314
      geographical closeness 314
      grandchildren 315
      kinship 320
      next of kin 314
      relatives 314, 315, 317
      spouses 314, 315, 317
   challenges, to 11
   contents 314, 315, 322
   disposal of property 11
   intestacy 11, 323, 324 *see also* **intestacy**
   making wills
      divorce/remarriage 313
      ethnic minorities 313, 314
      failure to make 312, 313
      illness 313
      median age 313
      prevarication 313
      regulation 314
      research findings 312, 313
      tax/property issues 314
   marital assets 314
   mutual wills doctrine 336
   property law *see* **property law**
   proprietary estoppel *see* **proprietary estoppel**
   revocation 316
   Sharia law 313
   succession *see* **succession**
   testamentary capacity
      contents of will 322
      delusions 322, 323
      knowledge/approval of will 321
      lack of capacity 321
      mental capacity 321, 322, 323
      relative's interests 318
      requirement 318
      short-term memory loss 321
      understanding required 321
      undue influence 323
   testamentary freedom 311, 314, 316–20,
      341
women
   elder abuse 160 *see also* **elder abuse**
   matrilineal ties 237
   mental capacity assessments 57, 68
   pension issues 2, 8, 22, 200, 215, 216, 218,
      221, 222 *see also* **pensions**
   poverty 2, 8, 22, 200, 216 *see also* **poverty**
   single mothers 222
   widows 215
   working mothers 237